WEAPONS AND TACTICS OF THE SOVIET ARMY

WEAPONS AND TACTICS OF THE SOVIET ARMY

David C. Isby

JANE'S

LONDON · NEW YORK · SYDNEY

Copyright © 1981 Jane's Publishing Company Limited

First published in the United Kingdom in 1981 by
Jane's Publishing Company Limited,
238 City Road,
London EC1V 2PU

ISBN 0 7106 0089 5

Published in the United States of America in 1981 by
Jane's Publishing Incorporated
730 Fifth Avenue
New York
N.Y. 10019

ISBN 0 531 03732 0

Typesetting by D. P. Media Limited, Hitchin, Hertfordshire
Printed in Great Britain by
Hartnoll Print Limited,
Bodmin, Cornwall

Introduction

"Soviet military trends . . . would provide incentives, capabilities and options to the Soviet leadership for the direct use of their military force to achieve political objectives by the early 1980s."—David Jones, general, USAF, Chairman of the Joint Chiefs of Staff, *New York Times*, January 30, 1980.

"You ought to ask: Why, what is this, what's the meaning of this?"— David Jones, private, 15th battalion, Royal Welch Fusiliers, *In Parenthesis*, Part IV.

Weapons and Tactics of the Soviet Army is a reference volume on a military subject, which is what Janes's has been publishing since 1898. Since then the nature of war has changed greatly, and a reference book must reflect today's complex realities. This book details the characteristics of the weapons currently in service with the Soviet Army, the tactics with which these weapons are used, the interrelation between weapons and tactics, and how effective each weapon is, how it works, its drawbacks and how it fits into the overall scheme of the Soviet Army. To examine the weapons themselves in isolation from their context would be misleading. Thus the analysis starts at the bottom, with the individual weapon, and works upwards through all levels of tactics, including those that the Soviets would term operations. Chapters One, Two and Three provide a broad and general overview, showing the larger framework into which the weapons and tactics fit. This book is not a handbook on the Soviet Army – there are already a number of them – but it covers much of the same ground. The format is designed for the reference user, who is advised, if looking for data on a specific weapon, to check also the material at the start of each chapter and, if possible, the chapters on offence and defence. This will give him an insight into its interaction with other weapons. Entries on related weapons can also be helpful.

Accuracy in any work dealing with the Soviet Army of today is relative. A certain amount of the information in this volume will inevitably be incorrect. Other material may be misinformation, disseminated by interested parties in both the East and the West, to mislead people such as myself. I have passed on unconfirmed reports wherever I thought that to do so would be valid, accepting that a certain percentage might be wrong. The magic words

"probably", "reportedly" and "it has been stated that" must appear frequently in any work on this topic. All statements about specific weapons being in service (and the type of service) and specific numbers of weapons must all be judged as approximate and estimated, as must all statements of specific weapons effectiveness, dead spaces and their like. Just as it is misleading to compare the characteristics of the SAU-122 (a designation which is another "probably" item) with those of the M109A1 or Abbot without comparing their different roles, mission and fire-control systems, it is also misleading to compare hit probabilities (which can be computed on paper, by computer, on the Aberdeen Proving Ground Ranges, in action in Sinai, by comparison with Western systems or, I fear, "fudged" by those who should know better) without considering what goes on behind the weapon.

Limitations of space have meant that arms such as engineers, signals, motor transport, railway troops, radioelectronic combat, intelligence, and pipeline troops have not been treated in the depth they deserve. This must be considered a reflection of the realities of book publishing rather than of any lack of Soviet emphasis on these arms. I chose to concentrate upon the combat weapons. We hope to come out with revised editions of this book in which these areas will be covered more fully.

If any readers have information, source material, corrections, photographs or anything else that might be pertinent to a revised edition, please send it to me at Jane's Publishing Company Ltd, 238 City Road, London EC1V 2PU.

This book would have been but a shadow of itself without the contributions of many people to the project. My thanks go to Joseph Backofen, Joseph Balkoski, Alain

Dupouy, Chris Foss, Mark Herman, James Loop, Virginia Mulholland, Larry Williams, and Steven Zaloga, who all gave generously of their knowledge and expertise, and who provided invaluable corrections, information and encouragement. The 330+ illustrations in this volume appear by virtue of the great assistance of *AFV G-Z*, Leon Conjour, EW Communications Inc., the Egyptian Military Attaché, Washington, V. M. Martinova, Manny Milkuhn, *The Marine Corps Gazette, Soldat und Technik, Truppendienst*, Tom Woltjer, Paul Woolf and Charles Yust. Special thanks go to Michael Isby for his efforts in checking and collating technical data. I would like to thank the many agencies who provided source materials, documents, information and illustrations: US Army Public Affairs Office, New York; US Army Still Photo Library; Department of Defense Public Information Office; the 11th MI Company; *Red Thrust*; Headquarters TRADOC; Headquarters Tactical Air Command; the Defense Intelligence Agency; *Armor* magazine; The Armor, Artillery, Infantry, Aviation and Intelligence Centers and Schools at Forts Knox, Sill, Benning, Rucker and Huachuca respectively; the Command and General Staff College and Combined Arms Training Research and Development Agency, Fort Leavenworth; and especially the indefatigable Richard Hunter and the people at the Army Foreign Science and Technology Center. I would like to thank most gratefully my friends who are past and present members of the armed forces of several nations for their insights and professional expertise. The staff of Jane's in London—especially Christy Campbell and Brendan Gallagher—went far beyond the call of duty in turning a gaggle of ideas in loose formation into this book.

Finally, I trust my British readers will excuse my comparisons with US Army practice and my use of American military terms throughout. The gap between US and British military language has not closed since, in 1918, my uncle discovered that the Doughboys relieving his battalion did not understand what a Toc Emma, Emma Gee, or a Mills Bomb was.

(Every effort has been made to ensure that the information in this volume was current as of March 1981. However, the normal time lags of intelligence-gathering and publishing mean that a book of this sort can in places be one, two or more years out of date.)

David C. Isby
New York, 1980

Contents

Glossary

armour basis The equivalent thickness in rolled, homogeneous steel armour of any armour arrangement. The way to increase armour basis (apart from thickening the armour) is by increasing the slope of the armour. The slope of the armour modifies its basis against most penetrators by the following amount:

Slope	Increase in basis
10°	101%
20°	106%
30°	115%
40°	130%
45°	140%
50°	155%
55°	174%
60°	200%
70°	290%

avoidance radius A planning figure used to determine the distance an aircraft will have to stay from a particular air-defence weapon if it is to avoid effective fire.

beam width The width of a radar beam. Fire-control radars have a narrow "pencil" beam, while search radars have a broader beam. The narrower beams are difficult to get on a target unless it is first located by another type of radar, but they are harder to jam.

burst radius The distance from the impact of a weapon at which its blast or fragmentation effects are likely to cause effective casualties.

CEP Circular error probability; the mean distance a projectile will be offset from its aiming point at impact. 50% of all projectiles will impact within the radius of the CEP from the aiming point; 90% will impact within 2.5 times the CEP and 99% will impact within 4 times the CEP.

cyclic rate of fire In an automatic weapon, the number of times the mechanism goes through the load-fire-eject-load cycle in a minute, not taking into account time to aim, reload, or adjust fire. It is a theoretical rather than a practical figure.

dead track AFV track that is not under pressure from its connectors and hence is dead weight, joined together by track pins or end connectors. It is easier to maintain than live track.

effective range For tanks, effective range is the maximum range at which a trained crew under "quasi-combat conditions" will achieve a 50% first-round hit probability against a stationary 2.5m-square target. For direct-fire weapons against armour, effective range is similar. For automatic weapons it is the longest range at which substantial losses are likely to be inflicted on a small-area target.

gradient The average slope of standard ground that a vehicle can climb. It is basically a comparative figure as in practice gradient depends heavily on type of soil; the T-62's gradient ability can vary from over 60° to less than 20°. River banks – naked and slippery slopes – reduce gradient ability most.

ground pressure The pressure, in kilograms, exerted on the ground by each square centimetre of the vehicle's tracks at combat weight. The lower the ground pressure, the more types of terrain the vehicle can cover.

horsepower All horsepower figures for vehicles are given in brake horsepower, except for helicopters, where the figures are for shaft horsepower.

infantry fighting/combat vehicle A vehicle carrying a squad of infantry that primarily fights while mounted on that vehicle. Normally has gunports for firing while under armour.

intermediate cartridge A cartridge between a rifle and a pistol cartridge in size and power.

live track Track joined together with end connectors so as to be under pressure, like a spring-hinged door. Because of this, live track requires less energy from the drive train to pick it up off the ground, as the springs raise it of its own accord. It normally uses rubber bushings. Live track is obviously more complicated than dead track and so is more difficult to maintain.

maximum range The furthest a projectile will travel. For direct-fire weapons it is normally determined by the maximum sighting distance on the direct-fire sights. For indirect fire it is how far the shell will travel. Some weapons, such as tank guns, may have to be on an incline to reach their maximum indirect-fire range, as the mounts cannot achieve the elevation of comparable field guns.

minimum range The range below which a weapon cannot be guided. It is not the same as the arming distance, which is a safety factor in most missiles and rockets.

point-blank range The range at which the highest point of the projectile's flightpath does not exceed the height of the target.

PED/probable error deflection Similar to PER, but dealing with deflection. For rifled artillery it is much smaller than PER.

PER/probable error range An index of precision of an artillery piece. The smaller the PER, the more accurate the weapon. 50% of a weapon's "overs" (shells that fall beyond the target) and 50% of its "shorts" (shells that fall short of the target) will each be within one PER (for that gun and range) of the mean point of impact. This figure is usually larger in the field than on paper.

probability of hit An estimate of the chances of a shell (or series of smaller projectiles) striking a specific target at a specific range. Most of these figures are taken from field tests or estimated on their results. Crew training and battlefield conditions can modify these results greatly.

probability of kill The US Army divides kills into K-Kills (total destruction of all combat ability), F-Kills (Firepower kills; destruction of the primary weapons system capability) and M-Kills (Mobility kills; destruction of the ability to move). The probability of kill represents the average chance of achieving one of these. The exact point at which a projectile strikes a target greatly affects the probability of kill.

projectile expenditure rate Soviet term indicating the number of artillery shells to be used in a given time to achieve the desired result against a specific target.

range Where given, range is road range with full fuel and at road march speeds. These figures are for marches on metalled roads. For dirt roads range is about 75% of this figure, and less cross-country.

rate of fire The speed with which a weapon can load, fire and reload. Again it varies widely, depending on training and conditions, which is why it is usually divided into a theoretical maximum (at which the system is fired as quickly as its design allows) and an actual or combat rate of fire, which allows for such human activities as aiming.

speed Speeds are normally given as maximum speeds along metalled roads. Speed on dirt roads is about 30–40% below this figure. Cross-country speeds depend greatly on the type of terrain, but usually are about 50% of their maximum road speed for tracked vehicles (although some are as low as 25% of the maximum), and 20% for wheeled vehicles, those with special cross-country mobility features being faster.

trench The width of a trench that the vehicle can cross at a perpendicular angle of approach. Angle and ground can also affect this capability.

trim vane A folding metal plate on the front of a vehicle that gives stability when swimming.

tilt The angle at which a vehicle can "bank" to the side. Also depends heavily on type of soil.

vertical obstacle The size of vertical step that a vehicle can surmount, although this would entail exposing its belly to any enemy position to its front. The effect of vertical obstacles is much worse on slopes. A T-62 cannot surmount a 0.6m step on a 20° slope, so that just a log on a hillside can stop even this powerful tank.

Abbreviations

AFV	armoured fighting vehicle; any armoured vehicle
AP	armour-piercing (also used with other abbreviations)
APDS	armour-piercing discarding-sabot
APFSDS	armour-piercing fin-stabilised discarding-sabot
APC	armoured personnel carrier
APHE	armour-piercing high explosive
ATGM	anti-tank guided missile
C	capped (used in conjunction with other abbreviations)
cal	length of gun in calibre
ECM	electronic countermeasures
EM	enlisted men
EW	electronic warfare
Frag	fragmentation
GHz	Gigahertz
HE	high explosive
HEAT	high-explosive anti-tank
HEP	high-explosive plastic
HESH	high-explosive squash-head
HVAP	high-velocity armour-piercing
HV	high velocity (used in conjunction with other abbreviations)
I	incendiary (used in conjunction with other abbreviations)
MHz	Megahertz
m/sec	metres per second
m/v	muzzle velocity
NBC	nuclear, biological, chemical
POL	petroleum, oil and lubricants
PPS	radar pulses per second
PRF	pulse-repetition frequency
RAP	rocket-assisted projectile
RoF	rate of fire
T	tracer (used in conjunction with other abbreviations)
Trav	traverse
WP	white phosphorus

Unit, vehicle and other symbols

Airborne infantry

Air defence

Tank

Chemical

Naval infantry

Engineers

Artillery (towed or SP, weapon type shown at side)

Motorised rifle

Infantry (non-Soviet)

Medical

Anti-tank (any)

Anti-tank artillery

Reconnaissance

Special forces

Rocket or missile artillery

Service support element

Supply installation (fixed)

Signals

SVCS Service support

(–) Unit has had components detached from it

(+) Unit has been reinforced with non-organic assets

HQ Headquarters (while moving)

Headquarters (deployed)

Unit is an ad hoc or mission-specific grouping

Observation post

• Squad or individual vehicle

•• Section (US usage of term)

••• Platoon

I Company or battery

II Battalion

III Regiment

x Brigade

xx Division

xxx Corps

xxxx Army

xxxxx Front

xxxxxx Theatre

Command post

Mortars

SAM launcher (tactical)

ZSU-23-4

Main battle tank

Light tank

Heavy tank

APC or BMP

SP gun

AVLB

Engineer APC

Minefields

—II— Unit boundary (here a battalion)

Unit defensive position (here a platoon)

	Light	Medium	Heavy	
Automatic infantry weapon	↑	↑	↑	
Mortar	↑	↑	↑	
Anti-aircraft machine gun	↑	↑	↑	
Artillery gun or gun/howitzer	‖	‖	‖	
Howitzer	‖	‖	‖	
Anti-tank rocket-launcher	↑	↑	↑	
Anti-tank gun	‖	‖	‖	
Recoilless rifle	‖	‖	‖	
Rocket launcher artillery	↑	↑	↑	
Anti-aircraft gun	‖	‖	‖	
Missile	∩	∩	∩	
Air-defence missile	∩	∩	∩	
Anti-tank missile	∩	∩	∩	

Chapter One

The Soviet Way of War

"Wars are not won by big armies, but by good ones."
MARSHAL SAXE

Military doctrine

The cornerstone of the Soviet Army is military doctrine, the officially approved system for perceiving and analysing the nature of war, how it will be waged and with what weapons. Doctrine itself flows from many sources: Marxist-Leninist thought, Russian nationalism, and changing military requirements. Military doctrine is determined at the highest level of political leadership: the Politburo and the Party Chairman. Though seen as empirical and scientific, doctrine is not static and unchangeable. Changes in doctrine reflect not only changes in military strategy and technology, but political decisions as well. The Soviets have no doubt that war is a continuation of politics (which in turn is a continuation of economics). Once doctrine is decided upon, it cannot be questioned except through indirect routes or at the highest levels.

Soviet doctrine has gone through a number of phases since 1945. The 1945–53 Stalinist phase continued the primacy of World War Two-style conventional war; the 1953–58 transitional phase came to grips with the problems of nuclear weapons, leading to the primacy of nuclear warfare, centring on strategic forces, which had emerged by 1958. After 1967 the Soviets also incorporated improved conventional war capability in their doctrine, which today combines the key importance of nuclear weapons with the ability to fight conventionally if and when required.

For all the importance the Soviets place upon doctrine, they realise it cannot be translated into reality without proper armament norms (*vooruzhenie*) and combat effectiveness (*effectivnost'*). This is simply a recognition that any armed forces require weapons in number and quality sufficient to carry out their mission as imposed by doctrine, and that these weapons must be used effectively or they are so much junk. Subordinated directly to doctrine, the "accepted system of scientifically founded views on the nature of modern wars and the use of armed forces in them," the concepts of armament norms and effectiveness prevent doctrine from becoming empty words. The high-

est level of Soviet military thought aims to understand and follow doctrine and achieve the required armament norms and combat effectiveness. Once that is achieved, all else should follow.

Doctrine must be distinguished from military science and military art. To the Soviets each is a different and precise thing. While doctrine encompasses the full range and sweep of Soviet military thought, military science is "a system of knowledge concerning the nature, essence, and content of armed conflict." The term science is deliberately chosen. The Russians have long been great believers in fundamental scientific laws (as illustrated, for example, by the work of Dmitri Mendeleyev) and have transferred this to military science. Like any science, it is based on empirical data, which can be gathered either through actual use, manoeuvres, tests and other experiments, or from historical study. According to the late Marshal of the Soviet Union A.A. Grechko, "The value of military history is in the creative perception of the experience and lessons of the past, in the capability to disclose the regular laws of the development of methods for the conduct of war, in its boundless capability for the expansion of the military world outlook and military thinking of officers and generals." Finding out the nature of war through empirical study is a key part of military science.

The other elements of military science include the general theory of military science, the theory of the organisation of the armed forces, military geography and military history, theory of military training, military training, and, most important, military art.

Military art is "the theory and practice of combat," and, despite its name, is recognised as a scientific theory. Military art encompasses the theory and practice of combat from the highest to the lowest level, and is divided by its scope into strategic, operational and tactical levels. Strategy is the major element of military art. The Soviets do not have different army, air and naval strategies; there is one common strategy for all the services. The integration of the services is seen to be possible only with a single strategy. In wartime, strategy will be planned by the highest levels of Soviet command and will deal with global operations and the grouping of forces to carry out operational missions.

Operational art is the next level of military art. Each service has a different operational art (although they are held together by having the same strategy, military science and, of course, doctrine). It deals with combat by armies and fronts, which are theatre-level forces. A front (equivalent to an army group or army) is the basic operational formation. Its actions are governed by the principles of the operational art. Possible Soviet plans for the invasion of Western Europe are examples of operational planning, and they will only be undertaken in the context of a larger, strategic, plan.

Tactics govern the actions of the military units making up an operational force. Divisions and regiments are considered tactical units; battalions and smaller are tactical sub-units. Operational success is based on the correct application of tactics, much as strategic success is based on the sum of operational results. Each different unit and sub-unit, and each individual weapon system, has its own individual tactics. The Soviets spend a great deal of time in determining the optimum tactics for each and how they should be carried out. To accomplish this, there are many numerical standards, tables and algorithms, stemming from the scientific perception of the military art at all levels. It is easy to be convinced that these numbers represent reality, but all the similar calculations made before 1914, which appeared equally impressive, proved fallacious. (Examples of this Soviet approach can be seen in the "chance of victory" table in Chapter 7.) Scepticism about this sort of approach is not uncommon in Soviet Army publications. It has been criticised as not reflecting the importance of political consciousness, nor the commander's creativity and skill. If empirical research has determined the best way for a unit to act on the battlefield, then all its commander need do is to make sure that it does indeed behave in that way. However, in the words of one writer, "a victory cannot be calculated, it must be won." Despite these reservations, the Soviets retain this empirical outlook and it is a key part of their comprehensive yet highly regimented system.

Principles

The principles of the operational art govern both operational and tactical-level Soviet units on the battlefield. They can be seen as themes that run throughout Soviet operational and tactical thought. The Soviets realise that no set of operational principles can be immutable, for changes in technology and strategy will affect them all or their relative importance. While their precise application may vary, and there are even different sets of principles, Soviet military thought at operational level and, indeed, all levels is guided by:

1 Speed and shock: mobility, manoeuvre and high rates of combat operations.
2 Concentration of effort: decisive superiority at the decisive place at the decisive time.
3 Surprise and security.
4 Combat activeness.
5 Preservation of combat effectiveness.
6 Conformity of the goal.
7 Co-ordination of forces.

Only the offensive will yield victory, and speed, shock and manoeuvre is the decisive component of the offensive. On the nuclear battlefield it may be the best defence against nuclear targeting. The Soviets insist on maintaining the momentum of the offensive. Even if nuclear weapons are not used to defeat the enemy, surprise, suppressive fire, bypassing or outflanking resistance and a greater emphasis on "daring thrusts" will contribute to the speed, shock and manoeuvre. The Soviets realise that speed and shock without manoeuvre cannot prevail, even against an outnumbered enemy. The principle of manoeuvre includes both the movement of troops and the application of firepower, "manoeuvring fire" and similar tactical concepts.

Concentration of forces demands numerical superiority, reflected in the allocation of frontage as well as the massing of weapons. Armament norms must be met if the Soviets are to achieve their objectives.

"It is necessary to take the enemy by surprise" – V.I. Lenin. Surprise is becoming more important as a principle of Soviet operations. Surprise is seen as a key "force multiplier," making the Soviet forces much more effective than they would otherwise be. The Soviets would apparently be willing to forgo some of their numerical superiority and logistical preparation to ensure that lengthy mobilisation did not alert the enemy. The Soviets also realise that surprise requires great command skill and forces that can take advantage of it. The Soviets intend to both create and exploit surprise by rapid manoeuvre of their forces. The faster the tempo of an attack, the greater the chance of surprising the enemy and the less chance he will have to recover. Nuclear weapons have increased the importance of surprise, as has the introduction of accurate conventional battlefield weapons; even the most deadly ATGM is ineffective if it is surprised before it can be deployed. The Soviets will use well developed security and deception plans to attain surprise, as they have done from the Stalingrad offensive in 1942 to the invasion of Czechoslovakia in 1968. The Soviet publication *Field Regulations for Staff* requires all plans at division or higher level to include a fully developed deception scheme.

Combat activeness is the principle of the offensive, and is often rendered as such. The Soviets stress bold and decisive action in all operations, even in the defensive. Combat activeness implies the maintenance of the offensive, and the end of the offensive is annihilation, which is frequently included as an operational principle.

Preservation of combat effectiveness includes proper organisation, effective systems of command, control and communications, and maintenance of morale.

Conformity of the goal is identical with the Western principle of "the mission." Fulfil the mission, take the assigned objective – all else is nonsense. Goals usually include a terrain goal, enemy forces to be annihilated, and a time goal.

Co-ordination is seen in the emphasis on combined-arms operations throughout the Soviet Army. This principle also includes what the West terms unity of command, which is followed in the Soviet emphasis on centralised command functions throughout the army.

These principles of war are basically offensive, and, as the principles are built around the primacy of the offensive, it should come as no surprise that Soviet weapons and tactics, even defensive ones, are also offensive. Doctrine dictates that the goal is not just to beat back the enemy or buy time; it is victory. Marxist-Leninist thought holds that if a world-wide war breaks out between the forces of socialism and those of capitalism, it can have only one result: the triumph of the socialist system.

Chapter Two

Command and Organisation

High Command

The top bodies in the Soviet national command structure are the Council of Defence, the Main Military Council, the Ministry of Defence, and the General Staff.

Comrade Leonid Brezhnev, General Secretary of the Communist Party of the Soviet Union, is also chairman of the Council of Defence. Its members are probably all Politburo members, including the Minister of Defence, although other Party and military heads may be called to attend meetings. The Council of Defence deals with preparedness at its highest level, ensuring that all the elements of the Soviet Union – armed forces, industry, transport, Party – are fit for any possible conflict. The Council has broad and far-reaching powers to affect the make-up and organisation of the Soviet armed forces.

The Main Military Council is the peacetime version of the *Stavka* (Headquarters of the Supreme High Command). Marshal Sokolovskiy described its purpose: "The direct leadership of the Armed Forces during a war will obviously be accomplished, as before, by the *Stavka* of the Supreme High Command. The *Stavka* will be a collegial agency of leadership under the chairmanship of the supreme commander-in-chief." In peace, as in war, this body is concerned with strategic planning, leadership and direction. Membership includes the Party Secretary (Comrade Brezhnev), the Minister of Defence (Marshal Ustinov in 1980), his three First Deputy and ten Deputy Ministers of Defence, the Chief of the Military Political Administration, and the commanders-in-chief of the five Soviet armed services: the Strategic Rocket Forces, the Army, the Air Force, Air Defence of the Homeland, and the Navy. In addition, the chiefs of civil defence, construction and railway troops, and rear services are also presumed to be members, as is the Deputy Minister of Defence for armaments and the Inspector-General.

In any future war the General Staff will be "the main agency of the *Stavka*," according to Marshal Sokolovskiy. The five Soviet armed services are subordinated to the Minister of Defence through the General Staff, and are controlled through it. The Soviet General Staff has much

broader functions than its US equivalent. It has ten directorates, for operations, intelligence, organisation and mobilisation, military science, communications, topography, armaments, cryptography, military assistance, and the Warsaw Pact. It also has a political section, a scientific-technical committee, and an assistant for naval affairs. The General Staff is immediately subordinate to the *Stavka* in wartime, and to the Main Military Council and the Minister of Defence in peacetime. The General Staff's job is to plan strategy, oversee the execution of strategy and co-ordinate the action of all the Soviet armed forces.

The orders of the General Staff go to the operational commands: fleets, air-defence districts, and, for the Army, military districts. Although these forces remain under the administrative direction of their parent service, the General Staff has operational command. The Soviet Army units stationed in the USSR in peacetime are assigned to 16 military districts. The only exceptions are the airborne divisions, which, though located in a military district and drawing support from it, are under the direct command of the Minister of Defence. Each military district will probably become a front headquarters in wartime, and also provides the means for centralised control of all the sinews of modern war in a particular area; thus it is far more than a simple territorial command. In case of nuclear war the military districts will probably be expected to maintain a partially self-sufficient war effort, reorganising both the economy and the administration.

The Minister of Defence is assisted by 13 Deputy Ministers of Defence, eleven of whom are members of the Central Committee of the Communist Party (helping to assure proper relations between party and military). The functions of the Ministry of Defence are similar to those of its Western counterparts, though with more concentration of decision-making power in the Minister and his associates. The General Staff is the organ of the Ministry of Defence by which the forces are actually commanded.

The front is the highest operational unit. In wartime groups of fronts will probably be subject to theatre commands set up by the General Staff. Thus a war in Europe

HIGH-LEVEL ORGANISATION

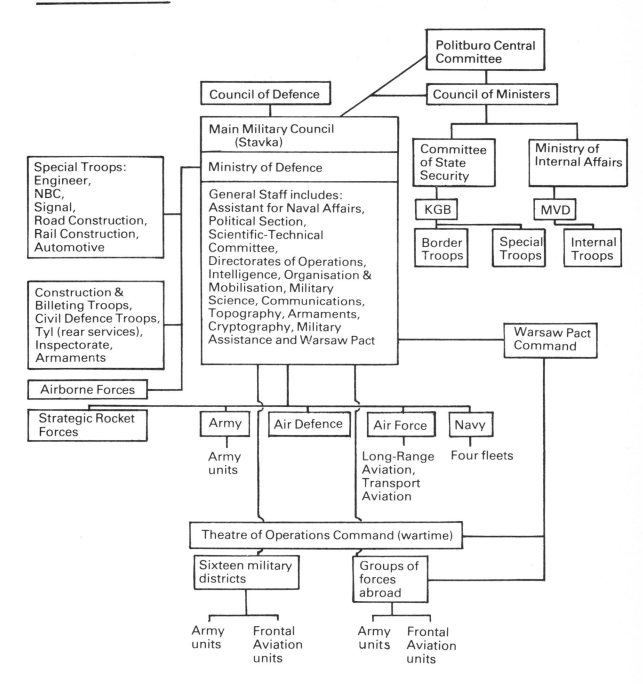

will doubtlessly involve several fronts, plus the Warsaw Pact Forces. A front itself is similar to a Western army or army group. It has one or more armies under its command, plus Air Force units, designated Frontal Aviation because they are subordinated to front command. Airborne divisions will also be attached to front command in time of war, as may naval units for a specific mission. Each front has a large and well staffed headquarters, significant logistic support, and many specialised units attached directly to it.

The army is a standard operational unit. Normally parts of fronts, they can also operate independently. Closer to Western corps than armies, Soviet armies consist of a number of divisions – usually about four – and specialised combat, combat support, and logistical units, in addition to their headquarters.

Soviet corps are used for independent operations in areas which do not require a full army. For example, the two Soviet divisions earmarked for operations against northern Norway are organised into a corps. Such corps have a headquarters and logistic and support units. *De facto* corps, without such additions, are found within an army and consist of a division in the army's first echelon and the division in the second echelon immediately behind it. These two divisions co-ordinate their actions to "leapfrog" forward and maintain the momentum of the attack.

The Communist Party of the Soviet Union maintains elements of control throughout the armed forces, from Chairman Brezhnev down to the company political officers. At the top of the Soviet leadership the Minister of Defence is a Politburo member, and most of the key military personnel, including the service chiefs, are members of the Central Committee. These groups have direct inputs to all levels of the Soviet high command. The Main Political Administration, a section of the Central Committee, operates as an independent body within the Ministry of Defence. The Main Political Administration is responsible for political education, education and deployment of political officers, and control of the ideological content of all military activities as well as supervision of military Communist and Komsomol activities. Each of the five services, and each military district or unit, has its political department or section. The political officer is usually designated *zampolit* (deputy commander for political affairs). The Main Political Administration is also represented on staffs, military councils and planning bodies, maintaining political input and control. The Committee of People's Control uses military personnel as a sort of political inspector-general's office. These organisations are another way in which the party can retain control of the military and be aware of what it is doing. The boast that "the Party and the Army are as one" is not an empty one.

The power of the Main Political Administration is tremendous, carrying the word of the Party and its *apparat* to every soldier. Howeve., in the uniquely Soviet system of checks and balances even these guardians of the Party need guarding. Thus the KGB, which is not under the Ministry of Defence, has an "00" section in every military unit down to regimenal level, acting as a counterbalance to the political officers and performing security tasks.

Other ministries also have primarily military functions. The Ministry of Medium Machinery is in charge of all nuclear weapons development and production, while the Ministry of General Purpose Machinery handles nuclear delivery systems.

Other arms

The Soviet armed forces consist of five services, compared with the West's traditional three. The Strategic Rocket Forces is the premier service, making up in prestige what it lacks in tradition. It controls all land-based missiles bigger than the Army's Scaleboard. The Air Force has the same responsibilities as its Western counterparts. Again as in Western nations, the Navy has a powerful air arm, both ship and shore-based (unlike the Army, which must rely on the Air Force for all its helicopters and aircraft). The Navy also includes the Naval Infantry and coast-defence units. The PVO, the National Air Defence, is a single service combining what were originally Army anti-aircraft and radar troops with Air Force interceptors and radar troops in a single service to counter the threat of strategic strikes against the USSR. The Army is responsible for standard equipment throughout the armed forces, and all services use the same small arms, trucks, NBC equipment and other non-role-specific equipment.

The Soviet Army itself is made up of a number of arms and branches. The Airborne Forces are the most autonomous, being almost an independent service. They have their own officers' school and publications and, in time of peace, report directly to the Ministry of Defence. In war conditions, however, the paratroopers will be integrated closely with the rest of the Army, and airborne units will be under front or theatre of operations command.

The *tyl* (rear services, equivalent to the Anglo-American administrative tail) has its own Deputy Minister of Defence. All units from strategic to tactical level in all services have a *tyl*, which includes the service support efforts of the unit. The commander of the Army *tyl* centralises and co-ordinates the service and supply activities of the Army. This includes both combat support and peacetime housekeeping. The function of centralised supervision is performed through a number of branches of the *tyl*, handling finance, medicine, military transport, food supply, clothing supply, military stores, automotive transport, quarters and veterinary medicine.

Most of these branches operate in the same way as their Western counterparts, providing centralised direction in specialised matters to units and sub-units while remaining operationally responsible to their parent unit in the same way that US Army medical personnel in a divisional field hospital are responsible to the Army Medical

Corps although under the command of the divisional commander.

Other branches of the *tyl* have a distinctly Soviet function. Military Transport and Automotive Transport are jointly responsible for planning and filling the Army's transport needs, employing air, land or sea systems as required. Automotive Transport administers the *autokolomka* system, upon which the Soviet armed forces depend for most of their trucks. Under this system, trucks used throughout the Soviet economy for civilian tasks are built to standard military designs and earmarked for military use upon mobilisation. The civilian agencies using these vehicles are responsible for maintaining them to the satisfaction of the Army, and they are inspected twice a year (although bribery of inspectors is not unknown). As civilian truck drivers are often reservists of the Automotive Troops (a branch of service equivalent to the British Royal Corps of Transport or the US Transportation Corps), truck and driver can be called up together. This was done for the 1968 invasion of Czechoslovakia, with devastating results for that year's harvest. The majority of the Army's motor transport requirements in the Soviet Union are met by the *autokolomka* system.

The Central Food and Clothing Supply administrations aim for a high degree of self-sufficiency. Not only do they procure goods from civilian sources, but they produce material themselves. Soviet military state farms, with both military and civilian workers, provide a large percentage of the Army's requirements, especially in Asia. These are supplemented by unit gardens, which are often large and well organised. The Army also has its own clothing and boot factories. This makes the Army independent of the civilian economy, with its inefficiencies and frequent failures. The Quarters Administration serves a similar function in maintaining and sustaining Army installations.

The Soviets realise the importance of the *tyl*, whether it is the central *tyl* of the Ministry of Defence, the *tyl* of the Army, providing strategic support, or a regimental *tyl*, run from the unit's rear command post and responsible for the day-to-day operations of the regiment. The Soviets believe that the organisation of this special supporting service will free the fighting soldiers to fight and give them the necessary support.

The Construction and Billeting Troops are a separate branch of the Army with a high degree of autonomy. Despite its large size – 100,000 to 400,000 men – this force is not widely known. It is basically a mobile military labour force, its prime mission being the construction of military installations and anything which might be of military value, including the 1980 Moscow Olympic site and the new Moscow International Airport. They also supplement the troops of the Railway and Road Construction branches on these projects, especially on the Baikal–Amur Railway. Men in the Construction and Billeting Troops receive only the basic 30-day conscript's course and do little military training in the remainder of their two years' service. They also receive less political education than combat troops. Large numbers of Asians serve in these units, as well as, reportedly, conscripts who are not qualified to serve in combat units. However, it has also been reported that the men of these units need building experience and share in the reimbursement the Ministry of Defence receives when they do work for other government bodies. In addition to giving the Army its autonomous construction force, insulated from the civilian economy, this force gives the Soviet Government the capability to perform quick, efficient construction work in all conditions.

The Civil Defence Troops, like the *tyl* and the Construction and Billeting Troops, is a separate force, headed by a Deputy Minister of Defence and reporting directly to the Ministry of Defence. Also like those forces, it will work in conjunction with all the Soviet armed services at a strategic level, and not just with the Army. The Civil Defence Troops were removed from the Ministry of Internal Affairs and placed under the Ministry of Defence in 1961. Some 50,000 to 100,000 troops are assigned to this force, reflecting the increasing emphasis the Soviets have placed on civil defence in recent years. These troops administer and organise civilian civil-defence efforts. Other civil-defence troops form units under the command of military districts, supplementing civilian efforts. These include fire-fighting, medical, decontamination and rescue units.

In contrast to the normal branches within the Army, such as Artillery and Tanks, certain other branches have "Special Troops" status. This means that while they are completely integrated within the Army, these branches are directly subordinate to the Ministry of Defence, and their mission includes the support of the other armed services as well as the Army. They differ from the *tyl*, Construction and Billeting Troops and Civil Defence Troops in that their commanders, though senior generals or marshals, are not Deputy Ministers of Defence. The Engineer, Chemical, Signal, and Automotive Transport branches are all in this category, and they all function in the same way as their Western counterparts. The Railway Troops and Road Construction Troops are also "Special Troops" branches, and have uniquely Soviet functions. The Railway Troops units play a key role in building and maintaining railways in the Soviet Union and lines of communication abroad. The two Soviet-gauge rail lines through Poland and East Germany were built and are run under the supervision of the Railway Troops, as are railways throughout the Soviet Union, in particular the Baikal–Amur Railway. The Railway Troops man all military trains in the Soviet Union, and have their own locomotives and rolling stock. In wartime they would be expected to keep the railways open in the face of powerful enemy air and missile attacks, and to facilitate this prefabricated bridge components are dispersed throughout Eastern Europe, especially near the vital Vistula and Oder bridges, along with Railway Troop and Engineer detachments to erect them should the bridges be knocked out. The Railway Troops will also accompany attacking Soviet forces, and will try to make captured railways usable for Soviet logistic support as quickly as possible. The Soviet Army still depends on railways for its strategic mobility and logistic support, and so the Railway Troops are a very important service.

The Road Construction Troops build and maintain roads that have a military value. Like the Railway Troops, they have done much peacetime construction work in the Soviet Union, especially in the Far North and Siberia. In wartime they will repair roads as well as build them.

There are other military ground forces outside the Army. The Naval Infantry uses purely Army equipment. This small, 18,000-man, force is intended for seaborne *desants* (q.v.) and projecting Soviet power overseas, rather than for large-unit combined-arms combat in the manner of the US Marine Corps. The Naval Infantry comprises five regiments, each similar to a motorised rifle regiment. The Baltic, Black Sea and Northern fleets each have one regiment and the Pacific Fleet has two. Additionally, the Naval Infantry provides defence for naval installations and mans 18 coastal-defence missile battalions, each with 15 to 18 SSC-1 SSMs. There are three such battalions in the Northern Fleet, six in the Baltic Fleet, five in the Black Sea Fleet and five in the Pacific Fleet.

Far more sinister than this force of sea-soldiers are the armed forces of the Ministry of Internal Affairs and the Committee for State Security (KGB). These do not come under the Ministry of Defence: under the Soviet system of checks and balances – someone must guard the guardians – these forces are directly responsible, through their parent Ministries, to the Council of Ministers. The armed forces of the MVD and the KGB are organised along military lines and equipped with standard Army weaponry, including APCs, scout cars and tanks. Conscripts serve in these forces instead of doing military service, and must be of undoubted political loyalty.

The MVD Internal Troops, organised into motorised rifle regiments and divisions, are an elite, almost praetorian, formation. The mission of its 175,000 men is the maintenance of internal security. In peacetime they operate as riot police when normal militia and police are insufficient. MVD troops mounted regiment-sized operations against Baltic and Ukrainian partisans until 1953, and were used in riots in the USSR in the early 1960s. During particularly intense rioting in Rostov province in 1963 even the MVD was not adequate to restore law and order, and the regular Army had to be called in. In addition to regular line MVD units, there are select

detachments to handle special missions and difficult situations. In wartime the MVD will restore order after strategic attacks, guard key factories, installations and transportation lines, guard POWs and political prisoners, and may even be committed to the front lines.

The KGB Border Troops, 175,000 strong, are responsible for the 67,000 kilometres of "iron curtain" surrounding the Soviet Union. Most of the border clashes with the Chinese have involved these troops. In addition to the detachments that man outposts, check passports at points of entry and patrol the borders, the Border Troops maintain tactical reserve units to respond to any large-scale border incident, calling for support from the Army if necessary. The Border Troops have a naval arm equipped with patrol boats, and use many helicopters and light aircraft in their border patrols. In wartime this formation would act as a covering and delaying force against any invasion of the USSR. They would also be responsible for internal security and anti-partisan and other rear-area protection tasks. They could also perform their rear-area protection role as security regiments or battalions while attached to armies operating outside the Soviet Union.

The Border Guards are not the only KGB military formation. In addition to its well-known espionage activities, in which it co-operates with the GRU (Military Intelligence), the KGB maintains a further special armed force. Although the Internal Troops are considered more elite than the Border Troops, this KGB force is more elite than either. It is entrusted with the most sensitive tasks in the Soviet Union, including the guarding of nuclear stockpiles and extremely important installations and personnel, and it also guards and operates the high-level strategic communications between high party, military and government officials, and between major military headquarters and their superiors. These troops, with their royal blue lapel tags, are also seen guarding Lenin's Tomb.

DOSAAF – the Voluntary Society of the Army, Aviation and Navy of the USSR – is a quasi-military organisation that fulfils an important military role. Although the DOSAAF works closely with the armed services and its chairman is an active-duty officer, it is not part of the Ministry of Defence, but is under the Central Committee of the Communist Party. DOSAAF's mission is to encourage military and civil-defence awareness amongst the whole population, but its main task is to provide pre-conscription military training for Soviet 16 and 17-year-olds. Under the 1967 Law on Universal Military Service, which reduced service time from three to two years, basic training, and even a large amount of technical training, was theoretically not to be performed by the Army but rather by DOSAAF, working with the trainees during their secondary education. This is where the Soviet soldier will supposedly learn the manual of arms, the elements of military drill and courtesies, and how to use infantry weapons. Instruction in advanced subjects is also provided. Parachuting, APC and tank driving and maintenance, and radio use and repair are all taught by the DOSAAF, using equipment phased out by the Army and retired officers as instructors. However, DOSAAF is far less effective in practice than in theory. Only 50% of Soviet conscripts have received the pre-military training that DOSAAF is supposed to provide, and which the two-year term of service is based upon. Thus Army units have to train their semi-annual intake themselves for six months before they cease to be "dead wood." Only the Strategic Rocket Forces and the Airborne units can claim to have complete pre-conscription training for their personnel. The Soviets have also criticised DOSAAF for being large, cumbersome and bureaucratic even by Soviet standards.

Objectives, echelons and reserves

The concept of deploying units in echelons is a key to Soviet offensive and defensive operations and tactics. All units, from front down to regiment and frequently to battalion, usually have two echelons and a reserve, although this can be increased to three echelons for breakthrough attacks against prepared defences or decreased to a single echelon when covering a wide front or encountering light resistance.

The first echelon of an attacking unit normally comprises two of its component units of the same type reinforced by strong attachments, advancing abreast. If a wide front must be covered, or if two component units are concentrated on a narrow sector, three such units will be put in the first echelon. The Soviets will also put fewer units in the second echelon, pushing as many forward as possible, when the enemy is surprised, outmanoeuvred or unable to defend a broad front, or when objectives are close at hand, when time is of the essence or if nuclear weapons may be used and proximity to the enemy may provide protection. In these situations, regiments or larger units may have only a first echelon and a reserve. The three-echelon formation, on the other hand, closely approximates the armoured Soviet steamroller attack of popular imagination. It is only infrequently used, but would be employed in attacks on prepared defences, especially by tank units.

The second echelon of a unit is distinct from its reserve and has no current Western equivalent (although the British Army of the First World War attacked in what the Soviets would call two echelons, and Soviet accounts of the Battle of El Alamein refer to the British armoured divisions being in the second echelon). The second echelon of a unit is intended to exploit the success of the first, and can relieve the first echelon while it rests and resupplies. These reliefs are crucial to the Soviet insistence on continuous, 24-hour combat. Keeping the pressure on the enemy by day and night is emphasised throughout Soviet offensive thought, and to do this effectively a second echelon is required to take over the offensive. The second echelon can also attack in a different sector or direction, consolidate gains and mop up bypassed strongpoints, and defeat counter-attacks. If the first echelon has been repulsed, the second echelon resumes the attack.

If a Soviet division's attack is stopped by a US Army force laterally shifting forces to the division's primary attack sector, a division from the army's second echelon, or even the division's second echelon (usually of two regiments), could be used to shift the attack away from where the US forces are concentrated, turning the first attack into a holding action. If the second attack succeeds in penetrating the US positions (weakened by the lateral shifting of forces to the first attack) by breakthrough or infiltration, it can envelop or outflank the concentrated US forces. These offensive tactics require numerical superiority and emphasise "bold and decisive manoeuvre." US defensive tactics require secure, stable flanks for their lateral shifting of forces to meet each threat in turn. Success will depend on command, control and communications, which determine who can best take advantage of a rapidly changing situation.

Command, control and communication will also determine how effective the commitment of the second echelon will be. As it passes through the first echelon it will have to contend with returning traffic, including ambulances and vehicles going in for repair, as well as logistic vehicles going forward to resupply the first echelon. Traffic jams – making excellent targets – will be unavoidable.

Soviet tactical and operational reserves are small by Western standards; a battalion deploys a platoon, a regiment deploys a company, a division deploys a battalion, an army deploys a regiment (from a division in its second echelon) and a front deploys a division. Reserves are sometimes co-located with the unit main headquarters to speed response. In addition, some battalions and most regiments, divisions and operational formations will deploy a separate anti-tank reserve to assist the reserve in defeating armoured threats in both offence and defence. Neither reserve is usually assigned a specific offensive mission, but is used by the commander to meet unanticipated situations or change the direction of the attack. On the defence the anti-tank reserve is a mobile backstop to the first echelon, while the reserve, normally positioned behind the second echelon, is the counter-attack force, supplemented by the forces of the unit behind it. These small tactical reserves, as compared with the traditional

Frontages and deployments

	Company	Battalion	Regiment	Division	Army	Front
Attack sector	1	2–3	5–10	20–40	100–200	200–500
Main frontage	0.75	1–2	4–7	10–15	40–80	80–250+
Depth (immediate objective)	–	2–4	8–15	20–30	100–150	250+
Depth (subsequent objective)	–	8–15	20–30	50–70	200–250+	300–500
Defence frontage	1–1.5	4–7	8–16	20–30	100–150	250–350
Defence depth	0.5–1	1–3	7–10	16–20	100–130	200–250
Rear boundary (from front)	–	–	10–15	30–40	75–110	150–160
Distance between echelons (attack)	–	1–3	5–15	20–30	30–35	40–80+

All figures are in kilometres. If NBC weapons are not expected to be used in the near future, front and armies have their sectors reduced by 40%, their attack frontages reduced by about 10% and their immediate objectives by about 40%. Note that units normally only operate over a portion of their attack sector for the main attack; the rest is ignored or covered by holding attacks. This will result in gaps between Soviet penetrations.

Western "two up, one back" deployment, show the Soviet emphasis on keeping the pressure on with the maximum number of troops in contact with the enemy. Even in the defence, the offensive orientation of Soviet military thought is apparent. Soviet numerical superiority allows tactical or operational units to depend on units echeloned behind them to perform functions that the larger and more self-sufficient Western units would rely on their own reserves to perform.

The Soviet system of unit frontages and objectives – the width and depth of the area to be attacked – is linked to their system of echelons and reserves.

Each Soviet unit is assigned a sector to attack or defend. In addition, each unit of division size or larger will have a main and secondary axis of advance within this sector. To achieve the required armament norms for victory, the Soviets will adjust their frontages to concentrate forces at the main sectors at the decisive moment. A superiority of three or five to one in tanks, six or eight to one in artillery and four or five to one in motorised rifle strength is normally required, although the Soviets will attack a force that outnumbers them even by two or three to one if they believe they can achieve complete surprise, or if the enemy has been neutralised by NBC or conventional fires. To achieve these levels of concentration in the main sectors, the Soviets will not only adjust unit frontages but will, if required, assault with intervals between units, relying on security parties, reserves and, primarily, the speed and shock of the attack to protect the open flanks.

In addition to the width of its sector, each attacking unit of battalion size and above is assigned a depth of attack which contains an immediate and subsequent objective or mission. Once the component units (for example, a regiment's first-echelon battalions or a division's first-echelon regiments) have achieved their immediate objective or fulfilled the immediate mission, the parent unit normally commits its second echelon, which then seizes the parent unit's subsequent objective or fulfils its subsequent mission. The immediate objective of a parent unit is usually the same as the subsequent objective of its first-echelon component units. Because each unit has two echelons, a telescoping, expanding system of exploitation is formed. The Soviets believe that this will provide the momentum, the fresh troops and high combat power that the high-speed offensive requires in mobile warfare. Thus when a regiment has seized its immediate objective, it will commit its second echelon and go on to seize *its* immediate objective, which is the same as that of the division. At this point the division commander will commit his second-echelon regiments to seize the division's subsequent objective, which is the same as the army's immediate objective. Once it is seized, the army will commit its second-echelon divisions to seize its subsequent objective, which is the front's immediate objective. Front will then commit its second-echelon armies, including the tank armies, which are designed for long-range operational exploitation. After that, everyone goes swimming from the beach at Calais. The system maintains the momentum that the Soviets believe will result in victory.

Combined arms

The Soviet Army has recognised the importance of combined-arms operations since the 1930s, but their tactical skill and weapons often did not allow them to translate their ideas into effective reality. In World War Two the Soviet Army improved its effectiveness by abandoning sophisticated combined-arms organisations and tactics and adopting simple, direct units, using them in a way that minimised its weaknesses and optimised its strength. Today the Soviets have refined their operational and tactical thought and equipped themselves with adequate weapons, so that all operations and all tactics down to company level or below are carried out by combined-arms forces. Each Soviet weapons system and each element of Soviet tactics must be perceived as an element in this overlapping, complementary, integrated system. The value of the whole is greater than the sum of its parts.

Soviet tank and motorised rifle divisions have a three-to-one mix of regiments. Each motorised rifle regiment has a similar mix of battalions, as do tank battalions, which each include a motorised rifle battalion. Until recently the tank regiment was a single-arm force, and many tank regiments still have no integral motorised rifle strength, not even the single company that appears to be an interim measure until it can be upgraded to a full battalion. This vestige of wartime organisation is probably due to the Soviet belief that the tank is supreme on the battlefield and that tanks are the best counter to anti-tank weapons. Other factors were the absence of an effective infantry combat vehicle for use with tanks until the introduction of the BMP, and the fact that tank units are not intended to make breakthrough attacks.

Artillery is organic to regiments, divisions and higher levels of organisation, and it is integrated into combined-arms forces either by direct attachment to tank or motorised rifle units or by forming artillery groups. Divisions and regiments both include a full range of organic combat support units, such as anti-tank, anti-aircraft, engineer, reconnaissance, and signal units, as do larger organisations. They are also provided with headquarters capable of preparing detailed but short-term and short-range plans. Soviet headquarters are always concerned with more immediate and less long-range objectives than their Western counterparts. The official word on the big picture tends to come down from the top, limiting even front commanders. Each unit from regiment upwards is also capable of independent operations. To facilitate this, they all incorporate a range of service support and logistic support units. While lean by Western standards, this element of the combined-arms offensive is seen as adequate for the relatively short distances and brief periods of combat that the Soviets envisage. Battalions (except independent battalions) and smaller units, being sub-units, lack headquarters capable of independent operations, combat support units or logistic support.

Combat support units and artillery are normally attached downwards to create reinforced combined-arms tactical units. Thus a division will attach many of its organic combat support sub-units, such as air defence, engineers or artillery, to its first-echelon regiments, while a regiment will similarly attach its combat support assets to its first-echelon battalions. Artillery is also allocated in a similar manner, either through direct attachment to lower headquarters or through the formation of artillery groups. The Soviets do not form combined-arms forces by cross-attaching component units in the way that Anglo-American tank and mechanised infantry battalions or companies will exchange companies or platoons. Soviet attachment works in one direction – downwards – and the Soviets will not break up the integrity of a unit by attaching its assets elsewhere. While combat support units may be attached to other units – although they are also frequently employed whole – combat units are not. Soviet units, from platoon to division, will fight as integral units, not as part of a battle group.

An exception is the tank battalion of the motorised rifle regiment. While it is capable of operating as a unit, this battalion's three companies are usually attached to each motorised rifle battalion of the regiment, which, in turn, attaches a platoon to each of its three companies, giving each motorised rifle company commander a combined-arms force of ten BMPs or APCs and four tanks. The tank company and battalion headquarters still retain control of the tanks, and they can be redistributed within the regiment as the situation requires. While little is known of the way motorised rifle battalions or companies organic to tank regiments operate, it is believed that they are attached down in the same way.

The second exception to the use of combat units as integral wholes in battle are the battalions of the tank regiment of a motorised rifle division or, more often, the motorised rifle regiment of a tank division. These battalions may be removed from their parent regiment (which is usually in the divisional second echelon) and attached to regiments in the divisional first echelon. Each battalion can either be used as an integral battalion within the regiment or broken down and attached to individual battalions and companies, as are tank battalions organic to motorised rifle regiments. These attached battalions will however revert to control by their parent regiment once that regiment, in the second echelon, is committed. This is similar to the way artillery groups have their control transferred from centralised to decentralised command during the artillery offensive. Artillery groups, being *ad hoc* groupings of artillery battalions rather than organic regimental formations, are the third exception to normal Soviet combined-arms practice. However, with the possible exception of some heavy guns, Soviet artillery battalions are never broken up, although batteries are often attached to sub-units. Engineer units are also formed into mission-orientated task forces for specific purposes.

Tactical air operations

Tactical air operations are the responsibility of the Soviet Air Force. The main elements of Soviet tactical air power are the tactical air armies of Frontal Aviation, one of which is usually under the command of each Soviet front. The Soviets realise the importance of tactical air power and attempt to integrate it into the overall mission as closely as possible.

Fighter units provide air cover for ground units and tactical aircraft. When operating on the defensive, they normally remain at medium and high altitude, leaving low-altitude air defence to air-defence units. Fighter units will also aim to achieve air superiority by defeating enemy aircraft.

Air strikes will also be used to gain air superiority by attacking enemy airfields, using the element of surprise whenever practical. They will be supplemented by long-range rockets. Soviet tactical air strikes are normally pre-planned at front or army level, although divisions have their inputs through the air liaison team and can request air strikes. Air strikes are not usually made on targets in contact with Soviet forces, or in the course of what Western forces would consider close air support. Exceptions are the support of airborne operations by fixed-wing aircraft and helicopters, hasty river crossings, mountain operations, and units which have outrun their artillery support. Close air support missions, performed by attack helicopters, have become increasingly important in recent years. The priority targets of tactical air strikes will include nuclear weapons and their means of delivery (including enemy airfields), headquarters, communications centres and enemy reserve and artillery units. They will also be used for interdiction, which will be planned over a wide front with a centralised command.

Air reconnaissance is an important role of Frontal Aviation.

Soviet tactical aircraft have high sortie rates because of their technical simplicity. However, these will probably decay significantly over extended periods as a result of the centralisation of maintenance and support functions away from the squadrons. Although four or five sorties a day are possible in a surge, a capability of two to three sorties a day for the first three days of operation, followed by a decreasing rate of one to two sorties a day, is more realistic.

Operational unit organisation

Front

HQ and HQ elements
A number of armies (a typical front might have 3–4 combined-arms armies and one or two tank armies)
One or more airborne divisions may be attached
One or more special operations forces
One tactical air army (Frontal Aviation)
One artillery division
One artillery brigade (possibly)
Two Scud SSM brigades
One to three Scaleboard SSM brigades
Two to four SAM regiments/brigades (formerly SA-2)
One signal brigade
One NBC defence brigade
One radar regiment
One AAA regiment
One long-range reconnaissance battalion
One psychological operations battalion
Two pontoon bridge regiments
One to three engineer brigades
One to three assault river crossing battalions
One radioelectronic combat battalion
One early-warning radar battalion
One intelligence regiment
One motor transport brigade (18+ battalions, 6+ of them for POL)
One pipeline brigade
One tank transport battalion (335 transporters)
Three construction regiments
One maintenance brigade
Service support elements

There is no fixed front organisation, and all unit attachments are variable.

Typical tactical air army (Frontal Aviation)

HQ
HQ light transport squadron (11 aircraft)
One fighter division comprising three 48-aircraft air regiments
One fighter-bomber division comprising three 48-aircraft air regiments
One independent light bomber regiment (36 aircraft)
One or two independent reconnaissance regiments (32 aircraft each)
One to three helicopter regiments, usually including at least one assault helicopter regiment (86 assault helicopters in an assault helicopter regiment, 44 medium and 12 heavy transport helicopters in each transport helicopter regiment)
Service support elements

Typical army

HQ and service elements
Four to five divisions (a combined-arms army will typically have two to three motorised rifle divisions and one or two tank divisions. A typical tank army has three or four tank divisions and one motorised rifle division)
One artillery brigade/regiment (independent)
One Scud missile brigade
One SA-2 SAM regiment (now usually SA-4)
One SA-4 SAM brigade
One SA-6 SAM brigade (now usually SA-4)
One signal regiment
One pontoon bridge regiment
One assault river crossing battalion
One AAA regiment
One tank transporter regiment (335 transporters)
One air-defence radar battalion
One long-range reconnaissance battalion
One traffic control battalion
One medical regiment
One engineer brigade
One NBC defence battalion
One signal intercept battalion
One radioelectronic combat battalion
One combat intelligence battalion
One motor transport regiment (1,000+ trucks)
Service support elements

Naval Infantry regiment (1,900–2,363 officers and men)

HQ company
Three infantry battalions (as motorised rifle battalions with BTR-60PBs and 82mm mortars)
One signal company
One NBC defence platoon
One tank battalion (31 PT-76 in three companies, 10 T-55 in one company)
One reconnaissance battalion (including BRDM-2s and BTR-60s)
One engineer battalion (including 20 PTS-M)
One 120mm mortar battery
One air-defence company (ZSU-23-4s)
One BM-21 battery
One anti-tank company (Saggers and SPG-9s)
One signal company
One medical company
One service company
One maintenance company
One rigging platoon
The regiment can be broken down into three independent battalion landing teams. Each fleet also has a Naval Infantry commando platoon that can be attached to the regiment. Many Naval Infantry troops are airborne-trained.

Armoured trains

The Soviets still use armoured trains. Current armoured trains are armed with ZSU-23-4 turrets, and flatcars forward and rear mount T-44 or early T-54 tank turrets.

Chapter Three

Order of Battle

Soviet Army order of battle

Unit types: G = Guards (honour title), MRD = motorised rifle division, TD = tank division, ABND = airborne division, ARTD-A = artillery division with 252 artillery pieces and 18 anti-tank guns, ARTD-B = artillery division with 72 artillery pieces and 18 anti-tank guns, Cat = readiness category. Question marks show designations or locations unknown or uncertain. Where more than one designation appears, it has not been possible to ascertain the exact designation and alternative designations may be given. "Tactical aircraft" signifies operational fixed-wing Frontal Aviation units.

Group Soviet Forces Germany
Headquarters, with staff 16 Air Army (975 tactical aircraft): Zossen-Wunstorf.
HQ 2G Tank Army: Furstenberg; 9G TD: Neustrelitz; 32G(21?) MRD: Perleberg/Prignitz; 94G MRD: Schwerin; 25 TD: Templin/Ubungsplatz-Vogelsgang (may be part of 3 Shock Army).
HQ 3 Shock (Tank) Army: Magdeburg; 12G TD: Neuruppin; 10G TD: Krampnitz, Potsdam; 47G TD: Hillersleben, Altmark; 207 MRD: Stendal, Altmark.
HQ 1G Tank Army: Dresden; 6G TD: Wittenberg/Lutherstadt; 7G TD: Dessau/Rosslau; 9 TD: Riesa/Sachsen-Zeithain; 11G TD: Dresden; 27G MRD: Halle.
HQ 8G Army: Nohra, Weimar; 20G (79?) TD: Jena; 20G MRD: Grimma; 39G MRD: Ohrdruf, Thuringia; 57G MRD: Naumburg/Saale.
HQ 20G Army: Ebersvald; 6G MRD: Bernau; 14G MRD: Juterborg; 19 MRD: Doberitz, Potsdam; 34G ARTD-A: Dazu, Potsdam.

All divisions in GSFG are Category I and in a high state of readiness within the category. 34G ARTD is three times the size of a normal artillery division; each of its regiments is actually a division in all but name. Elements of 6G TD, and possibly the HQ, were redeployed to the Soviet Union and Czechoslovakia in 1979–80.

The numerous Soviet non-divisional units in GSFG include six reinforced bridging regiments (including the 4th, 5th, 36th and 40th), six amphibious river crossing battalions, eight battalion-size commando units, one airborne regiment at Neuruppin, a GRU "diversionary unit" (size uncertain), at least two 36-helicopter Hind regiments (at Parchim and Stendal), and two assault engineer regiments for urban combat at Zossen, Berlin. There are also the usual army and front-level units.

Central Group of Forces
Headquarters: Milovice, Prague (100 tactical aircraft).
HQ Army Boleslav: Mlada-Boleslav; 18G MRD: Mlada-Boleslav; 31 (?) TD: Milovice.
HQ Army Olomouc: Olomouc; 51 (?) TD: Bruntal; 55G (48G?) MRD: Vysoke Myto; 66G (30G?) GMRD: Zvolen.
All units are Category I and stationed in Czechoslovakia.

Southern Group of Forces
Headquarters: Budapest-Matyasfold (275 tactical aircraft). 2 TD: Esztergom; 5 TD: Veszprem; 35G (93G?) MRD: Kecskemet; 102G MRD: Szekesfehervar.
All units are Category I and stationed in Hungary.

Northern Group of Forces
Headquarters, with staff 37 Air Army (350 tactical aircraft): Leignica (Liegnitz).
20 TD: Borne (Grossborn, Pomerania); 38TD: Swietoszow (Neuhammer, Schleisen).
All units are Category I and stationed in Poland. The two divisions may have exchanged places. German names in parenthesis.

Leningrad Military District (committed to Northern Europe)
Headquarters, with staff 13 Air Army (150 tactical aircraft): Pedrozavdonsk.
HQ 6 Army: Pedrozavdonsk; Corps HQ: Vyborg; Corps HQ; Archangel; 2G TD (Cat II): Leningrad; 45G MRD (Cat III): Vyborg; 37G MRD (Cat I): Pargolova, possibly near Leningrad; 64G MRD (Cat III): Priozorsk and/or Sapermaye; 111G (376? 107?) MRD (Cat III): Sortavala; 77G MRD (Cat III): Iskagorka and/or Archangel; 45 MRD (Cat III): Murmansk and/or Pechenga; 34 (54? 341?) MRD (Cat II): Kandalaksha; 69 MRD (Cat III): Vologda; 76G ABND: Pskov; ? ARTD-A: Pushkin; ? ARTD-B: Pushkin.
The 45 MRD and 34 MRD are equipped with MT-LB APCs.

Baltic Military District (committed to Central Europe)

Headquarters, with staff 30 Air Army (300 tactical aircraft): Kaliningrad (Königsberg).

HQ 11G Army: Kaliningrad; 1 TD (Cat II): Kaliningrad; 1G MRD (Cat II): Kaliningrad; 149 (129?) ARTD-A: Kaliningrad; 344 (?) ARTD-A: Kaliningrad (existence unconfirmed); 3G (23G?) MRD (Cat III): Klaipeda; 40G (28G?) TD (Cat II): Sovetsk; 24G TD (Cat II): Dobele; 88 (56G? 36?) MRD (Cat III): Tallinn; 7G (31G?) ABND (Cat I): Kaunas; 107 (16?) MRD (Cat III): Vilnus; 26G MRD (Cat III): Gusev (Gumbinnen); 44G (30? 5?) MRD (Cat III): Jonava.

Byelorussia Military District (committed to Central Europe)

Headquarters, with staff 1 Air Army (300 tactical aircraft): Minsk.

HQ 5G Tank Army: Bobriusk; **HQ 7G Tank Army:** Borisov; **HQ 28 Army:** Grodno.

120G MRD (Cat I): Minsk; 50G MRD (Cat III): Brest; 3G ARTD-A: Osipovici; 8 (46?) TD (Cat II): Slonim; 29 TD (Cat II): Slutsk; 3G TD (Cat II): Lepel; 27G (37G?) TD (Cat II): Poltosk; 8G TD (Cat I): Maryina-Gorka; ? MRD (Cat II): Borisov; 22 TD (Cat II): Bobriusk; 103G ABND (Cat I): Vitebsk; 34 TD (Cat II): Borisov (existence unconfirmed); 47 TD (Cat II): Borisov (existence unconfirmed); ? ARTD-B: Brest.

The 120 GMRD is the "Rogachev Guards Division." The 103G ABND is the Soviet "fire brigade" alert unit, normally first to be used in a crisis.

Kiev Military District (committed to Central Europe)

Headquarters, with staff 17 Air Army (100 tactical aircraft): Kiev.

HQ 1G Tank Army: Chernigov; **HQ ? Tank Army:** Dnepropetrovsk.

? TD (Cat II): Artemovsk; 72G MRD (Cat III): Belaya Tserkov; 29G (25?) MRD (Cat III): Lubny; 4 MRD (Cat III): Lugansk and/or Vorishilovgrad; 7 MRD (Cat III): Konotop; 18G TD (Cat II): Cherkassy; 20G TD (Cat II): Krivoy Rog; 75G TD (Cat II): Chuguyev; 42G TD (Cat II): Volnoye, near Dnepropetrovsk; ? TD (Cat II): Volnoye, near Dnepropetrovsk; 14 (?) TD (Cat II): Vypolozov; ? MRD: Chernigov (existence uncertain); ? ARTD-A: Novomoskovsk; ? ARTD-A: Fastov.

Six of the Category II tank divisions were Category III as recently as the late 1970s and their readiness may be low.

Carpathian Military District (committed to Central Europe)

Headquarters, with staff 57 Air Army (350 tactical aircraft): Lvov.

HQ 8G Tank Army: Zhitomir; **HQ 13 Army:** Rovno; **HQ 38 Army:** Ivano-Frankovsk.

70G MRD (Cat II): Ivano-Frankovsk; 15G MRD (Cat I): Vladimir-Volinski; 66G MRD (Cat III): Chernovtsy; 17 MRD (Cat III): Khmeinitskiy; 128G MRD (Cat II): Mukachevo; 318G (161?) MRD (Cat II): Uzhgorod and/or Izyaslav; 97G (17G?) MRD (Cat III): Slavuta; 24 MRD (Cat II): Lvov; 13 TD (Cat II): Novograd-Volinski; 117G TD (Cat II): Berdichev; 23 TD (Cat I): Ovruch; 26 ARTD-A: Kamenskaya-Bugskaya; 81 ARTD-A: Vinogradov; ? ARTD-B: Kovel; ? ARTD-B: Turka.

15G MRD is believed to be the "Iron Division." Two TD were Category III until the late 1970s at least.

Moscow Military District (committed to Central Europe)

Headquarters, with staff ? Air Army (200 tactical aircraft): Moscow.

? G MRD (Cat I): Tambov; 13 (3?) MRD (Cat III): Kovrov and/or Kursk; 32G MRD (Cat III): Kalinin; 2G (?) MRD (Cat I): Alabino, near Moscow; 4G TD (Cat II): Naro-Fominsk; 15 TD (Cat II): Gorkiy and/or Kovrov; 106G ABND (Cat I?): Tula; ? ARTD-B: Kalinin; ? ARTD-B: Skopin.

The division at Alabino is the Taman Guards division. 106G ABND has a training role in the Tula-Ryazan airborne complex and so its readiness is probably lower than that of other Soviet airborne divisions.

Odessa Military District (committed to Southern Europe)

Headquarters, with staff 5 Air Army (250 tactical aircraft): Odessa.

HQ 19 Army: Kishinev; Corps HQ: Simferopol (Crimea). 33G MRD (Cat II): Beltsy; 59G MRD (Cat II): Tiraspol; 98G (118G ?) MRD (Cat III): Bolgrad; ? MRD (Cat III): Belogorod-Dnestrovskiy; 126 MRD (Cat III): Simferopol; 28 (286?) MRD (Cat III): Odessa; 128 MRD (Cat II): Feodosiya; 92 MRD (may be 34 TD) (Cat II): Nikolayev; 102G ABND (Cat I): Kishinev; 2G ARTD-A: Zaporozh'ye; ? ARTD-A: Ungeny.

North Caucasus Military District (committed to southern front)

Headquarters: Rostov (no tactical aircraft); Corps HQ: Krasnodar; Corps HQ: Volgograd.

9 MRD (Cat III): Maykop; 73 MRD (Cat III): Novorossiysk; 266 MRD (Cat III): Volgograd; ? TD (Cat II): Novocherkassk and/or Uryupinsk; 19 MRD (Cat III): Orzhonikidzye; 24G MRD (Cat III): Grozny; 4 ARTD-A: Buynaksk and/or Mikhachkala.

Transcaucasus Military District (committed to southern front)

Headquarters, with staff 34 Air Army (300 tactical aircraft): Tbilisi.

HQ 76G Army: Yerevan; **HQ 4 Army:** Baku; **HQ 45 Army:** Kutaisi.

414 (145?) MRD: Batumi; 11 (147G?) MRD: Akhalkalaki; 10 MRD: Akhalkalaki; 31G MRD: Kriovabad; 26 MRD: Kirovakan; 164 (?) MRD: Yerevan; 261 MRD: Leninakan; 75 MRD: Nakhichevan and/or Dzul'fa; 6 MRD: Lenkoran; 216 MRD: Baku; 104G ABND (Cat I): Kirovabad; ? ARTD-A: Kutaisi; ? ARTD-B: Leninakan; 1G TD (Cat II): Tbilisi.

Three of the MRDs are Category II, remainder Category III. 1G TD may actually be a Category III MRD.

Volga Military District (strategic reserve)

Headquarters: Kubishev (no tactical aircraft).

43 MRD (Cat III): Kubishev; 96 MRD (Cat III): Kazan; 21 MRD (Cat III): Totskoye; ? ARTD-A: Totskoye.

Volga Military District headquarters may, in time of war, become an alternative supreme command post for the entire Soviet Army rather than a front headquarters.

Ural Military District (strategic reserve)

Headquarters: Sverdlosk (no tactical aircraft).

77 MRD (Cat III): Sverdlosk; ? MRD (Cat III): Chebarku; ? TD (Cat II): Kamyshlov.

Turkestan Military District (committed to the southern front)

Headquarters: Tashkent (150 tactical aircraft).

84G (54?) MRD: Kizyl-Arvat; ? MRD: Kushba; ? MRD: Ashkabad; ? ARTD-A: Bikrava and/or Ashkabad; 360 MRD: Termez; ? MRD: Samarkand; 105G ABND (Cat I): Fergona.

One of the MRDs is Category II, remainder are Category III.

Central Asia Military District (committed against China)

Headquarters: Alma Ata.

HQ 1 Army: Semipalatinsk. ? MRD: Os' and/or Karaganda; 201 MRD: Frunze and/or Dushanbe; 8 MRD: Pereval Kurdai; 80 (?) MRD: Alma Ata and/or Otar; ? MRD: Sary Ozek; 165 MRD: Semipalatinsk and/or Ust-Kamenogorsk; ? ARTD-B: Semipalatinsk; ? ARTD-B: Aktubinsk; 15 TD (Cat I): Ayaguz.

MRDs are one Category I, two Category II, three Category III. Many units from the Turkestan and Central Asia MDs have been identified in Afghanistan.

Siberia Military District (committed against China)

Headquarters: Novosibirsk.

? MRD: Abakan; ? MRD: Tumen and/or Itatka; ? MRD: Novosibirsk; 23 MRD: Biysk; ? TD (possibly MRD): Omsk; ? ARTD-B: Isham.

One MRD is Category II, remainder Category III; TD may be Category II.

Transbaikal Military District (committed against China)

Headquarters: Chita.

? MRD: Nizhneupinsk; ? MRD: Ulan Ude; 34 MRD: Sretensk; ? MRD: Dauriya; ? MRD: Borzia; 49 TD: Chita; 6 TD: Kyakhta; ? ARTD-B: Tsugol; ? ARTD-B: Naushka.

Three additional MRDs are deployed in all or some of Irkutsk, Bezrechnaya, Baklashi, Gusmooresk and Mirnaya. MRDs include three Category I, one Category II, four Category III; one TD is Category I, other is Category II (possibly III).

Soviet Forces Mongolia (committed against China)

Headquarters: Ulan Bator.

HQ 39 Army: Ulan Bator. ? TD: Barun Urt and/or Buigan (possibly MRD); ? MRD (Cat I): Sayn-Shand and/or Sumber Soma; ? TD: Choybalsan (Urf Durfal). TD are one Category I, one Category II (formerly Category III).

Far East Military District (committed against China)

Headquarters: Chabarsovil (1,225 tactical aircraft, including those in Siberia, Transbaikal and Central Asia MDs).

HQ ? Army: Belogorsk; **HQ 5 Army:** Ussuriyask; **HQ 15 Army,** Corps HQ: Yuzhno-Sakhalinsk.

31 MRD: Belogorsk and/or Svobodnye; ? MRD: Svobodnye; 265 MRD: Vozhayevka; ? MRD: Raychikhimski and/or Zavitinsk; ? MRD: Blagovershensk; 194 MRD: Khabarovsk and/or Babstovo; 73 MRD: Komsomol'ska-Amur; ? MRD: Dzeingy and/or Khabarovsk; ? MRD: Birobidzhan; ? MRD: Lermontovka; ? MRD: Sebuchar; ? MRD: Lesozavodsk; 29 MRD: Kamen-Rybolov; ? MRD: Sergeyevka and/or Programcynye; 79 MRD: Leonipovo-Sakhalinsk; 342 MRD: Yushno-Sakhalinsk; 17G MRD: Barabash and/or Kraskino; ? MRD: Ussuriyask; ? MRD: Smolyaninovo; ? TD: Sebuchar; ? TD: Programcynye; 6G ABND (Cat I): Belogorsk; ARTD: Toinichi, Birobizan, Ussuriyask, Yushno-Sakhalinsk, Pokrovka, Slavyanka (one "A," five "B" divisions); ? MR brigade: Provedennya, near Bering Strait; ? MR brigade: Anadya, on Bering Sea.

The divisions at Svobodnye and Sebuchar may not be there. One may be at Petropavlosk, Kamchatka. The two MR brigades and some divisions have artillery tractors or MT-LBs in place of APCs.

The Soviet Army reportedly has three MRDs fully cross-trained in mountain operations and several others – perhaps as many as five – that have alternative equipment appropriate for use in mountains or foothills. Other divisions are reported to have an amphibious mission, those on Sakhalin and some in the Leningrad Military District

Summary of Soviet Army deployment by readiness category

District or country	MR divisions I	II	III	Tank divisions I	II	ABN	Total line divisions	Artillery divisions A	B
E. Germany	10	–	–	10	–	–	20	1	–
Czechoslovakia	3	–	–	2	–	–	5	–	–
Hungary	2	–	–	2	–	–	4	–	–
Poland	–	–	–	2	–	–	2	–	–
Carpathian MD	1	4	3	1	2	–	11	2	2
Leningrad MD	1	1	6	–	1	1	10	1	1
Baltic MD	–	1	5	–	3	1	10	2–1	–
Byelorussia MD	1	1	1	1	5–7	1	12–10	1	1
Kiev MD	–	–	5–4	–	7	–	12–11	2	–
Moscow MD	2	–	2	–	2	1	7	–	2
Odessa MD	–	3–4	4	–	1–0	1	9	2	–
N. Caucasus MD	–	–	4	–	1	–	5	1	–
Transcaucasus MD	–	3	7–8	–	1–0	1	12	1	1
Volga MD	–	–	3	–	–	–	3	1	–
Ural MD	–	–	2	–	1	–	3	–	–
Turkestan MD	–	1	4	–	–	1	6	1	–
Central Asia MD	3	2	1	1	–	–	7	–	2
Siberia MD	–	1	3	–	1	–	5	–	1
Transbaikal MD	3	1	4	1	1	–	10	–	2
Mongolia	1–2	–	–	1	1	–	3	–	–
Far East MD	5–6	7	6	1	1	1	21–22	1	5
Totals	32	25	60	22	30	8	177+	16	17

Where figures are uncertain, italic figures are counted.

(especially the divisions at Archangel and Vyborg) being mentioned as examples.

In wartime conditions Soviet organisation will be different from that existing during peace. The Soviets will refer to units by a code name rather than a numerical designation, and may even change the numerical designation of a unit when it is committed to action to make it more difficult to keep an accurate order of battle; this practice creates much uncertainty about Soviet unit designations. In peacetime Soviet divisions in the USSR are not assigned to army or corps commands, but they are in wartime. A number of theatre of operations commands will also be set up in wartime. Northern Theatre of Operations will be in Riga, Southern Theatre of Operations in Odessa, and there will be several others, one of which will probably come from Group of Soviet Forces Germany headquarters. All will be under Warsaw Pact HQ in Lvov. There will probably be four fronts in the central European battle: Northern, Central, Southwest and Danube, commanding a total of nine Soviet, two East German, three Polish, one Hungarian and two Czech armies. Most Soviet military districts will also become front headquarters in wartime.

Soviet forces abroad

Cuba: A "brigade" of one tank, two or three motorised rifle and one artillery (or MRL) battalions is stationed on the island. Many Soviet specialists are in Cuba and some Cuban units, notably the "armoured division," are heavily Soviet.

Afghanistan: The invasion of Afghanistan marked the first Soviet military move outside their defensive perimeter since the withdrawal from North Iran in 1946. The initial Soviet presence, starting in 1978, included specialists, advisers and at least two, possibly more, helicopter regiments, including units armed with Hind-As. The invasion force that entered Afghanistan in the last days of 1979 was composed of divisions from the Turkestan and Central Asia Military Districts. The identified units include: 54 MRD at Herat and points north, 5 MRD at Farah, and 201 MRD, 360 MRD, 346 MRD and 66 MRD elsewhere in the country. The 105 Guards Airborne Division HQ is definitely in Kabul, but it is uncertain how much of the force with it is from that division. The Soviet airborne force in Afghanistan includes at least two (possibly three) reinforced regiments detached from the 103

Guards, and one or two other European-based airborne divisions. These units were lifted in along with most of the BMDs of their parent divisions, making the Soviet airborne force a mechanised force of at least a division. An army headquarters has reportedly been established in Kabul. The reservists used in the units which carried out the invasion were replaced by serving conscripts. *Raydoviki* units were reportedly sent to Afghanistan in spring 1980.

Other Soviet force levels abroad include: Ethopia, 1,200; Iraq, 1,000; Libya, 1,000; Mali, 1,800; Mauritania, 200; Vietnam, 4,000; Syria, 2,500; South Yemen, 1,500.

Readiness categories

Category I: Unit at 75–110% (assault) strength in both men and equipment. Units outside the Soviet Union are usually stronger than Category I formations inside the Soviet Union, which can use reservists and mobilised civilian equipment. Equipment strength is usually higher than manpower strength.

Category II: Units are manned at 50–70% strength, the average being slightly more than 50%. Equipment strength is close to full strength, but less than Category I divisions and most is in storage. These divisions are deployable within 30 days of mobilisation.

Category III: Units are manned at 10–33% personnel strength, and usually have only 33–50% of their required equipment, most of this being in storage. Most of the major combat items are present, although they are usually older models. Some divisions are however missing entire regiments. Normally considered not deployable until between 90 and 120 days after mobilisation; some of the Soviet divisions that invaded Afghanistan in 1979 may have been Category III units mobilised in 60 days. The additional resources available when only a few divisions are mobilised at a time may have allowed a quicker mobilisation. It has been estimated that composite divisions could be put into the field 60 days after mobilisation by merging two Category III divisions into one. The additional personnel are reservists mobilised from the area in which the division is stationed, although this is not possible for units stationed in isolated areas, especially in the Far East and Siberia.

Mobilisation only: The Soviets are known to maintain a number of formations which have no peacetime existence except for a designated cadre, mainly reservists or retirees. Their use is probably not envisaged in a short, victorious war. There may be up to 50 mobilisation-only formations, 20+ of these having larger (200–300-man) cadres. Equipment will come from national strategic reserve stocks, and civilian trucks or BTR-152s will probably be issued to motorised rifle units. Tanks will be T-54s (or maybe even T-34s), and artillery will be wartime vintage as well. Most, if not all, of these formations will be motorised rifle divisions. Mobilisation-only divisions are unlikely to be deployable even for second-line duties before 180 days after mobilisation.

Artillery divisions do not fall into standard readiness categories. The "B" type artillery divisions are relatively shadowy formations and are probably simply the administrative grouping of army-level independent artillery rather than a full artillery division. All Army units in the USSR rely heavily on impressed civilian motor transport. The Soviets have no reserve units that meet for regular peacetime training, as does the US National Guard, except for some small specialist units.

One of the great flaws of Western analysis of the Soviet Army is the ever-present tendency to "mirror image," to assume that the Soviets do or perceive things in the same way as Western armies. This applies especially to Soviet weapons strength and policy.

Because of the size of the Soviet Army it is very rare that, except in wartime, one item of equipment ever totally replaces another, as, for example, the Chieftain replaced the Centurion in the British Army. Thus the M-30 122mm howitzer is still used in some units almost 20 years after the D-30 was introduced to replace it. T-54/55s served in Category I units in Germany in 1978–79, and are still used throughout the USSR; a late-1979 photograph showed a T-54 unit operating with a BMP unit. It is often correct, but still an oversimplification, to assume that new equipment is first introduced in Category I units in Eastern Europe and the European USSR and then works its way down the readiness chain. The deployment of the T-64/72 series seems to have fitted this pattern, but others do not. The 1970s saw Category I divisions using T-54/55s while brand-new T-62s were delivered to Category III divisions. The first SA-8 and SA-11 units were deployed not into Europe, but into the central USSR, where they could be used for training and tactical evolution before larger numbers were issued.

Similarly, differences in unit organisation do not always seem to be linked to a readiness state or operational mission. Some tank battalions do have four tank companies, but they cannot be definitely linked with any particular mission or readiness category. Similarly, Soviet motorised rifle squads vary between eight and twelve men, with one or two machine guns, in a way that often belies the generalisations that Western sources wish the Soviets would fit themselves into. It is therefore incorrect simply to perceive Soviet equipment policy as a mirror of a Western model.

The use of training weapons makes it difficult to determine which weapons are front-line equipment. Thus photographs of M-30 howitzers being towed by MT-LBs in the Leningrad Military District do not provide any clue as to whether they are front-line equipment or simply

Estimated Soviet force inventories (early 1978)

	Groups of forces		Western MDs		Central MDs		Eastern MDs		Totals	
	Units	Store	Units	Store	Units	Store	Units	Store	Units	Store
Tanks										
T-54/55	2,666	–	4,025	–	9,379	–	7,252	–	23,322	–
T-62	5,932	–	4,145	–	1,596	33	2,379	–	14,052	33
T-64/72	1,747	–	757	–	1,367	–	–	–	3,871	–
Heavy (?)	252	–	31	–	1,303	423	755	–	2,341	423
Unidentified	–	–	–	418	1,655	407	111	1,770	1,766	2,596
Totals	10,597	–	8,958	418	15,300	863	10,497	1,770	45,352	3,051
APCs & IFVs										
BMPs	2,934	–	1,551	237	1,580	–	2,602	194	8,668	431
BTR-60PB	3,410	–	2,703	40	2,105	43	2,597	177	10,815	260
Others	456	–	1,170	165	6,151	153	4,587	255	12,364	573
Totals	6,800	–	5,424	442	9,838	196	9,787	626	31,847	1,264
Artillery										
122mm towed	1,902	–	1,894	745	3,765	533	3,144	205	10,705	1,483
122mm SP	384	–	126	–	14	–	–	–	–	–
130mm towed	276	–	402	23	720	400	485	45	1,883	468
152mm towed	138	–	708	160	1,546	345	1,178	93	3,570	598
152mm SP	324	–	54	–	21	–	9	–	408	–
180mm towed	?	–	48	–	105	–	72	–	225	–
Unidentified	–	–	–	839	–	2,863	–	1,336	–	5,038
Totals	3,024+	–	3,232	1,767	6,171	4,141	4,888	1,679	17,315	7,587
MRLs	630	–	646	–	1,040	–	1,052	–	3,368	–
AT weapons										
85mm+ guns	306	–	1,124	–	2,654	–	2,383	–	6,467	–
SPG-9	366	–	759	–	1,599	–	811	–	3,535	–
RPG-7	7,173	–	7,562	–	18,064	–	13,488	–	46,287	–
ATGM BRDMs	549	–	522	–	1,542	–	1,198	–	3,811	–
Suitcase ATGM	366	–	369	–	1,008	–	814	–	2,557	–
Totals	8,760	–	10,336	–	24,867	–	18,694	–	62,677	–
SSMs										
FROG	124	–	120	–	240	–	180	–	664	–
Scud	132	–	72	–	177	–	89	–	470	–
Scaleboard	?	–	36	–	52	–	48	–	136	–
Totals	256+	–	228	–	469	–	317	–	1,270	–
AAA										
S-60	582	–	576	706	1,528	3,018	879	590	3,565	4,314
ZSU-57-2	–	–	128	–	277	34	31	–	436	34
ZSU-23-4	500	–	276	–	420	49	594	286	1,790	335
ZPU-4/ZU-23	280	–	400	280	1,153	58	512	244	2,345	582
Unidentified	–	–	–	849	–	2,765	–	1,222	–	4,736
Totals	1,362	–	1,380	1,835	3,378	5,924	2,016	2,242	8,136	10,001
SAMs										
SA-4	270	–	297	–	297	–	213	–	1,077	–
SA-6	300	–	140	–	80	–	140	–	660	–
SA-7	4,125	–	3,864	–	8,618	–	6,693	–	23,306	–
SA-8	–	–	–	–	–	–	60	–	60	–
SA-9	496	–	84	–	40	–	170	–	790	–
Totals	5,191	–	4,385	–	9,035	–	7,282	–	25,893	–
Mortars										
82mm	–	–	162	–	270	–	–	–	432	–
120mm	1,079	–	1,224	190	3,012	22	2,184	120	7,499	332
240mm	–	–	48	–	48	–	61	–	157	–
Totals	1,079	–	1,434	190	3,330	22	2,245	120	8,088	332

being used to train the MT-LB drivers to tow guns cross-country. While the simplicity of most Soviet equipment and the similarity of the basic, one-task performance required of most soldiers makes the use of training weapons possible, this does not, for example, explain the continued use of the FROG-3, which is very different from the FROG-7 and so of limited training use. The only really open source for the type of weaponry still in service with the Soviet Army is often photographs in Soviet publications, and these will sometimes show weapons that should have been retired long ago.

While the estimates upon which the above table is based appear to be basically correct, certain points remain questionable: the complete absence of reserve stocks for anti-tank weapons, for example. The number of heavy tanks in service appears very high, as these vehicles were supposedly phased out by the early 1970s, and those listed may be other tanks. Many other figures also remain questionable but, despite the age of these estimates, they do provide a valid outline of Soviet strength.

The groups of forces mentioned in the table include all units in Europe outside the USSR. Western MDs are the Baltic, Byelorussian and Carpathian MDs. Central MDs are the Leningrad, Moscow, Kiev, Odessa, North Caucasus, Transcaucasus, Turkestan, Volga and Ural MDs. Eastern MDs include the Central Asia, Siberia, Transbaikal and Far East MDs, plus Soviet Forces, Mongolia.

The table figures are similar to those estimated in 1978, but even though T-72/T-64 production is reportedly 2,600 units annually, it would be difficult to attain the

Estimated Soviet tank inventory (mid-1979)

Group Soviet Forces Germany: 4,025 T-64/72, 2,030 T-62, 2,040 T-54/55
Northern Group of Forces: 650 T-62
Central Group of Forces: some T-64/72, 1,150 T-62, 180 T-54/55
Southern Group of Forces: some T-64/72, 1,140 T-62, 170 T-54/55
Total Groups of Forces: 11,380 tanks – 4,020+ T-64/72, 4,920 T-62, 2,440 T-54/55
Western Military Districts: 3,610 T-64/72, 2,400 T-62, 3,800 T-54/55
Rest of USSR: 2,110 T-64/72, 8,750 T-62, 11,785 T-54/55
Tanks stored and in war reserve throughout USSR: 12,000 all types
Total tanks: 43,835 with units, 12,000 reserve.

levels indicated. The disparity between reserve and stored figures should also be noted. These figures may be considered less accurate than the 1978 totals, and illustrate the pitfalls in tank-counting.

Annual Soviet tactical weapon systems production is estimated at 2,000–2,600 tanks, 5,000 combat vehicles (including up to 2,000 BMPs) and 500 helicopters (including 180 Hinds). Estimated total strength of the Soviet Army is 1,830,000 men, 52,600 tanks, 56,000 APCs and BMPs, 21,000 artillery pieces, 8,000 mortars, 11,000 anti-tank weapons and 9,000 AA guns.

Chapter Four

The Offensive

"The offensive is the basic form of combat action. Only by a resolute offensive conducted at a high tempo and to a great depth is total destruction of the enemy achieved."

GENERAL V.G. REZNICHKO

The Soviet offensive has its origins in the offensive thought of the Czarist Army, in the fast-moving cavalry forces of the Russian Civil War and Russo-Polish War, and it was highly developed in the decade 1926–36. Much of this was wiped away by the purges, and the Army that met the *Wehrmacht* in 1941 was inadequate both in weapons and tactics. However, the hastily improvised mass army soon rectified these failings and provided today's Soviet Army with the basis of its offensive thinking, which has been constantly refined and updated since 1945.

That victory comes only from the attack is recognised by all armies, and since the 1920s the Soviet Union has evolved its strategy, operations, tactics and technology towards the offensive. Surrounded as they are by what they perceive as hostile capitalist states and potentially unreliable allies, the nightmare of a world in arms against them has been a "worst case" for military planning from the founding of the Soviet Union. The impression the Second World War made on Soviet society as a whole – which cannot be underestimated – was compounded by the Cold War. The Soviets *will not* lose a war, for defeat must mean massacre and enslavement or, at very least, the overthrow of everything painstakingly built since 1917. The Soviets intend to win, and they intend to win quickly in a war fought off the soil of the Soviet Union. The way to do that is to attack quickly and relentlessly, using mechanised combined-arms forces with the emphasis on tanks. The end of war is victory. All else is nonsense.

Current Soviet offensive thought reflects two realities: the importance of nuclear, biological and chemical (NBC) weapons and the increased lethality of modern weaponry brought about by technological innovation, including the use of anti-tank guided missiles (ATGMs) and precision-guided munitions (PGMs).

Soviet tactics are optimised for a battlefield where NBC weapons are in use or liable to be used at any time. The Soviets apparently believe that a future war will probably begin with a conventional phase. While the war could

continue without the use of NBC weapons, they believe it likely that the "forces of aggressive capitalism," if losing, will resort to NBC weapons. If the Soviets believe such a strike is likely, they will pre-empt it by using their own NBC weapons. Similarly, if the Soviets are not winning a conventional conflict, they may initiate the use of NBC weapons to restore what they consider favourable conditions for their offensive. But the Soviets keep their options open. Before 1967 a war against NATO in which no NBC weapons were used was impossible. Today it is conceivable. But the view expressed in US Army tactical and operational-level manuals, that the conventional mode of operations will prevail and that NBC conditions can be seen as a special case, may well be wishful thinking. Soviet military thought and weapons design have addressed the problems of fighting under NBC conditions in a much more realistic manner than those of any other army.

The increased lethality of modern conventional weapons has threatened the armoured offensive that is at the heart of the Soviet operational art. The 1973 Middle East war, underlining the results of a long series of studies, tests and manoeuvres, showed that new weapons, especially ATGMs, could destroy tanks, BMPs and APCs at greater ranges and quicker than ever before. Technological innovations such as laser rangefinders for tanks and computerised fire-control systems for artillery have made these existing weapons systems more effective than in the past. Throughout modern warfare the development of new weapons technology, whether the Minié rifle, the machine gun or the ATGM, has given the concealed and camouflaged defenders more of an advantage than the moving and exposed attackers. This is the lesson learned by Grant's Army of the Potomac at Cold Harbor, by Haig's British Expeditionary Force on the Somme, and Mandler's tanks in Sinai. It is a lesson that the Soviets, who place more emphasis on the study of military history than any Western army, know very well. The Soviets have met the challenge posed by the new weapons, and have evolved their tactics to retain their validity in the face of

MARCH FORMATION OF ADVANCING MOTORISED RIFLE DIVISION

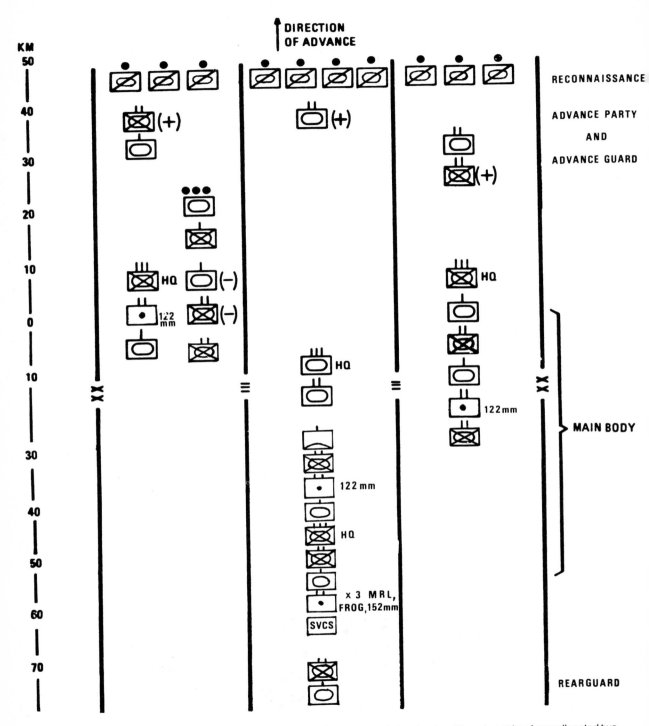

DIRECTION OF ADVANCE

RECONNAISSANCE

ADVANCE PARTY

AND

ADVANCE GUARD

MAIN BODY

REARGUARD

Notes: 1 The division is marching on four routes with three regiments up. The left-hand motor rifle regiment has been allocated two routes. 2 Flank patrols and local security detachments are not shown. 3 Engineer route-opening detachments (OODs) will accompany march security elements on each route. 4 Forward detachments, *reydy* and long-range reconnaissance patrols are not shown.

such weapons. In addition to developing new tactics for existing weapons, technological innovations – such as compound armour – are being introduced to maintain the combined-arms offensive.

It is however uncertain whether a future war in Europe would be mobile at all. The Soviets would probably initiate the use of NBC weapons to keep the offensive moving, but this will not of itself guarantee a mobile, decisive situation. The large number of nuclear warheads available to either side will make it difficult to concentrate the forces needed to achieve or, more important, to exploit a breakthrough and then keep it supplied in the face of nuclear interdiction of the supply routes. There is no guarantee that even nuclear warfare will be decisive. Modern conventional weapons, especially in the terrain of West Germany, allow overlapping fields of fire across any potential avenues of advance. In the 1973 Middle East war the Syrian front's terrain and force densities did not allow breakthroughs and mobile combat, even during the first days, when the Syrians had a large numerical superiority. The Israeli counter-offensive, though successful, had much more limited objectives, and thus a slower rate of advance, than one in Europe. Even in Sinai there were long periods when the fighting could not be described as mobile. Force densities in West Germany will be greater than those in the Middle East, and sophisticated sensors and reconnaissance will reduce the chances of surprise and infiltration. If the Soviet offensive does not achieve success in the first week of fighting, logistic problems, spurred by high ammunition expenditure, may help to bring the offensive to a halt in static warfare, the very war of attrition the Soviets reject so emphatically. Despite these limitations the Soviets are also prepared for a long war. Given either numerical superiority or surprise, the Soviet Army should be victorious in Europe. The offensive's strengths outweigh its drawbacks.

The Soviets have always planned to sustain the high rates of advance they demand by continuous offensive operations, attacking by day and night. This is very different from simply a night operations capability. There has never been an example in history of an army that carried out continuous offensive combat, but the Soviets envisage fighting at such intensity for up to 30 days, possibly longer. Whether they could actually perform as claimed is uncertain, but the fact remains that the Soviet Army is oriented towards continuous combat operations. The US Army (and many of its NATO allies) is not.

The Soviets recognise three basic forms of offensive action: the meeting engagement, the breakthrough attack, and the pursuit. The meeting engagement involves attacking the enemy while both sides are on the move; the breakthrough attack is directed against an enemy defending in place; pursuit is an attack against an enemy attempting to move away. Attacks in any situation can be made directly from the march, or with hasty or deliberate preparations. All three forms of offensive action incorporate the basic Soviet operational principles throughout.

From the march to the assault

The Soviet offensive depends on the transition from the march to the attack. Units manoeuvre in march order and fight in combat order. Soviet march formations and dispositions are standardised to allow units to attack from the march while maintaining momentum.

Although capable of cross-country movement, each Soviet unit will advance along a road whenever possible. Battalions always stay on one route, regiments one or two, and a division has up to four parallel routes in its sector, which ranges from 20–40km when not in contact with the enemy to 10km when delivering divisional attacks. This type of march formation is needed to meet the Soviet demand for rapid advance: 70–100km a day in nuclear conditions, 25–35km a day in conventional warfare, maintaining this rate through action in the enemy rear, an emphasis on hasty attacks, and the good cross-country mobility, amphibious capability and obstacle-crossing ability of Soviet vehicles. The average speed of a combined-arms unit on the march is 30–40km/hr, and two-thirds of that at night or in bad weather. Vehicle spacing is 15–50m on roads, 50–100m cross-country.

In front of the parallel advancing columns are the reconnaissance screens; patrols from the divisional reconnaissance battalion are a full day's march, up to 50–100km, ahead of the division's main body. Patrols from the regimental reconnaissance company are half a day's march – up to 20–50km – ahead of their regiments, spread over the 10–15km regimental sector. Beyond these are the *desants*, forward detachments, *reydy*, and long-range reconnaissance patrols (q.v.).

Leading the main body on each route of advance is the advance guard, a combined-arms force normally equal to a third of the total force, which precedes the main body by five to ten kilometres in a battalion column and 15–30km in a regimental column. A division may, in some situations, send out a full regiment as its advance guard. The main body follows the advance guard, protected by flank and rearguard detachments, platoons in a regimental column, squads in a battalion column. A regimental column can stretch 28–50km, making traffic control and command direction vital. Battalion commanders usually travel in their BRDM or tank-mounted forward headquarters with the battalion's advance guard company; regimental commanders will move up to their advance guard battalion if they believe that action will develop. Any battalion is supposed to be able to operate independently for 5–15h 20–30km from the rest of the regiment.

BATTALIONS ADVANCING

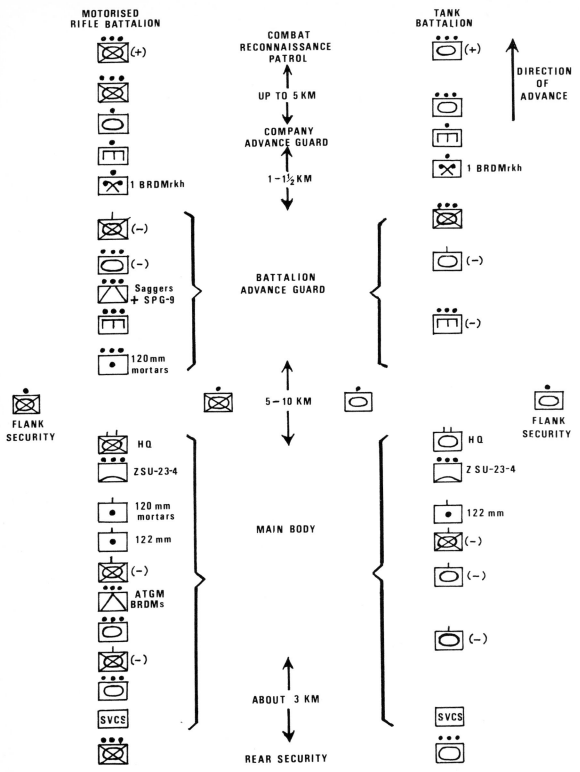

MOTORISED RIFLE BATTALION

(+)

1 BRDMrkh

(−)

(−)

Saggers + SPG-9

120mm mortars

FLANK SECURITY

HQ

ZSU-23-4

120 mm mortars

122 mm

(−)

ATGM BRDMs

(−)

SVCS

COMBAT RECONNAISSANCE PATROL

UP TO 5 KM

COMPANY ADVANCE GUARD

1 – 1½ KM

BATTALION ADVANCE GUARD

5 – 10 KM

MAIN BODY

ABOUT 3 KM

REAR SECURITY

TANK BATTALION

(+)

1 BRDMrkh

(−)

(−)

DIRECTION OF ADVANCE

FLANK SECURITY

HQ

ZSU-23-4

122 mm

(−)

(−)

(−)

SVCS

Notes: 1 The artillery battery may be increased to a battalion in some situations. 2 The rear security platoon is often only a single vehicle. 3 This diagram shows battalions advancing either as a regimental advance guard or on an independent route of advance.

The advance guard

The advance guard itself is divided into a number of parts. Its forward "point" element is the combat reconnaissance patrol. A motorised rifle unit, whether a battalion or regiment, will have a combat reconnaissance patrol consisting of a motorised rifle platoon, half a platoon of tanks, and a squad of engineers or an NBC-reconnaissance BRDM.

In a motorised rifle battalion column this patrol will be followed by the rest of the advance guard, 5–10km behind it. This force will probably consist of the other two platoons and headquarters of the motorised rifle company, the remainder of the tank and engineer platoons, half of the battalion 120mm mortars, and attachments from regimental heavy weapons, especially SAU-122 or D-30 regimental howitzers and ZSU-23-4s and SA-9 launchers for air defence, as well as additional engineer support. From this force the company commander will usually form a second combat reconnaissance patrol, identical in composition to the first, which will precede the rest of the company by 1,500–1,000m.

In a regimental column the combat reconnaissance patrol is supported by the advance party, which can provide additional firepower or extricate it from a difficult situation. The advance party is actually the advance guard of the battalion that is, in turn, serving as the main body of its regiment's advance guard. Regiments send out reinforced battalions as advance guards and these battalions, in turn, send out reinforced companies which are simultaneously the battalion's advance guard and the regiment's advance party. The rest of the battalion, regardless of whether it is being employed as a regimental advance guard or is in its own column, follows 5–10km behind this company, except for one platoon, which is dispersed for march security and deploys one squad on each flank as flank guards and another squad or platoon 3,000m behind the battalion as a rearguard. A regimental column will use platoons instead of squads for flank security parties. Tank units advance in the same way as motorised rifle units, although the proportions of tank and motorised rifle units are, of course, reversed.

The advance guard, with all its component elements, has the task of either eliminating opposition that might impede the advance of the main body or of fighting independently until the main body arrives if the enemy is too strong to be defeated by the advance guard alone. The reinforcement of advance guard units with additional weapons is intended to allow them to fight independently, clearing opposition away so that the main body is not forced to deploy and thus avoiding slowing down the advance. The advance guard clears away enemy patrols, screens and security detachments. In a regimental column the advance party can possibly defeat light opposition without the need for the rest of the advance guard to deploy or fight.

The meeting engagement

The meeting engagement is the most important form of offensive action in the Soviet view. The advance guard of a Soviet unit will attack upon encountering the enemy, seize the initiative, penetrate the enemy covering forces, and pin down the enemy main body while simultaneously covering the deployment of the Soviet main body, which will attempt to envelop or outflank the enemy. The Soviets will fully exploit the cross-country mobility of their vehicles and their willingness to take advantage of any path or track to carry out their outflanking or enveloping manoeuvres. Failing that, advance guard and main body will assault together. It is a tall order, but the Soviets claim that their meeting engagement tactics give them the capability to "with bold decisive action, fix and destroy any force we come in contact with on the battlefield."

Theoretically, a Soviet unit should not blunder into enemy units, as it will have been preceded in its advance by reconnaissance patrols. The first element of the advance guard to encounter the enemy will probably be the combat reconnaissance patrol, which will report the contact to the advance guard commander with as much information on the tactical situation and enemy dispositions as possible. The combat reconnaissance patrol may engage the enemy, attempting to get them to reveal their positions, but its main task is to look for routes with which to envelop or outflank the enemy force, and to observe.

In 10–30min, depending on spacing and road conditions, the combat reconnaissance patrol will be reinforced by the remainder of its company, functioning as battalion advance guard. This force will advance at maximum speed to develop the situation and seize and hold positions until the arrival of the rest of the advance guard. However, if the advance guard commander, on the basis of information which he is receiving, decides that the enemy is weak enough to be defeated by the company or that more information is required, he may order a probing attack. One platoon and the artillery and mortars will go into overwatch positions while the remainder of the force advances on a 400m frontage with a formation depth of about 200m, making maximum use of cover. The tanks lead, moving singly 100m apart and 100m ahead of the APCs or BMPs, which will move in pairs. If engaged, they will either keep going, trying to infiltrate or find a way around the enemy, or will attempt a hasty company assault. Alternatively, they may retire under the cover of fire from the overwatching platoons and up to 60 rounds of HE from the howitzers or mortars.

If no probing attack is ordered, if the probing attack was unsuccessful, or if the attack was forced to retire, the company will hold its positions in a hasty defence until the battalion comes up, 20–30min after the company arrived on the scene. The battalion, and possibly artillery battalion and even regimental commanders, will all pull up in their BRDMs and issue orders to the battalion. It will normally attempt to outflank or envelop the enemy, but if this is not possible it may be launched into a full-scale hasty attack from the march or an attack from the march. The difference between the two is that in the hasty attack directly from the march, companies are fed directly into battle as they arrive, whereas in the attack from the march they are first deployed along the line of departure before attacking. There is much less time to plan, bring up units and co-ordinate fire support in the hasty attack from the march. Whatever type of attack is used, co-ordination of forces and artillery support will, if necessary, be sacrificed to achieve surprise, speed or shock. The Soviets realise that any time to deploy and co-ordinate their forces before the attack, however brief, can reduce losses and increase results. However, speed of reaction is seen as vital in the meeting engagement. The side which first gains the initiative through rapid and aggressive action will probably win, despite limited knowledge of enemy strengths and dispositions. Soviet attack plans are prepared in great detail. Planning time is usually 60–180min for a divisional attack, 30–150min for a regimental attack, and 20–45min

for a battalion attack. Total time for mounting an attack when already in contact, from receipt of orders to H-Hour, is 2–4h for a division, 1–3h for a regiment, and 25–60min for a battalion. In the hasty attack directly from the march, fire support will be limited to whatever overwatching tanks or artillery can be positioned to give direct fire, although mortars are sometimes used in the indirect-fire role in such attacks. A hastily prepared attack may be co-ordinated with an artillery offensive of 10–20min, and the guns will normally not be allowed to expend more than 80% of a Unit of Fire of ammunition. The advance guard will then deliver a combined-arms assault against the enemy.

If the attack by the advance guard is successful, the main body does not deploy but continues its advance. If the advance guard is unable to defeat the enemy, it will still continue to probe and hold the enemy until the main body comes up and deploys. If required, the advance guard may have to assume a hasty defensive posture and, if the enemy attacks, the main body may be forced to join the defence and call upon the second echelon to resume the offensive.

If the main body attacks, it will normally attempt an envelopment or flank attack while the advance guard holds the enemy in position, although frontal assaults will be made when there is no alternative, or the advance guard alone may deliver a frontal holding attack. Envelopments and flank attacks (envelopments go wider

THE MEETING ENGAGEMENT

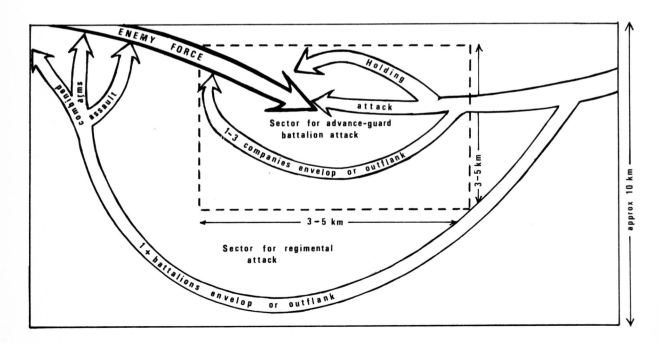

TYPES OF MANOEUVRE

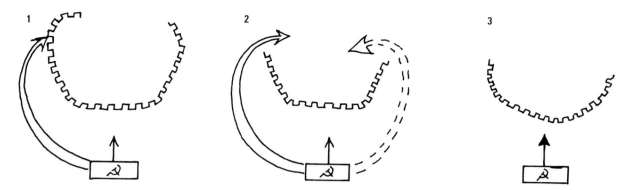

1 *Okhrat*. Flanking manoeuvre, may be performed alone or together with a frontal attack or an envelopment. **2** *Obkhod*. Envelopment, can be single or double. Can be carried out in conjunction with a frontal or flank attack. **3** *Frontal attack*. The least favoured type of Soviet offensive action. Normally carried out in conjunction with other manoeuvres or when there is no alternative.

around the enemy) depend heavily on effective route reconnaissance, knowledge of enemy dispositions and command initiative. It will take 60–90min for the main body of a regiment to come up, and the Soviets will use this time to position artillery. Both direct and indirect artillery fire will support a regimental attack with an artillery offensive lasting from 10–20min to 30–40min. The time also gives the artillery an opportunity to perform target acquisition, and allows Soviet commanders (whose use of forward command posts means they will be on the scene when decisions must be made) time to obtain and analyse reconnaissance information and co-ordinate the attack with other forces. Parallel columns may be directed to join in an envelopment or flank attack. The attack will then be launched as a combined-arms assault. Once the enemy has been defeated the pursuit will begin. If the enemy has not been defeated, the second echelon will come up to keep the pressure on, for the high tempo upon which the Soviets insist means that there will be no breathing space for their opponents between the different phases of the meeting engagement. However, it is through manoeuvre, rather than the combined-arms assault, that the Soviets hope to achieve success in the meeting engagement.

The Soviets believe meeting engagements to be crucial in both nuclear and conventional situations, and devote a large proportion of their unit tactical training to them. In NBC conditions these weapons will often create a gap that both sides will attempt to fill simultaneously. The Soviets believe that modern mechanised warfare will result in mobile warfare, and that meeting engagements, rather than breakthrough attacks, will predominate.

The strengths and weaknesses of all Soviet offensive tactics apply to the meeting engagement, their emphasis

on speed and manoeuvre and the tendency towards stereotyped manoeuvres and drill-type actions, especially when small units are forced to act independently. The enemy may outmanoeuvre them in the very way the Soviets hope to outmanoeuvre their enemy. Similarly, "bold manoeuvre" against unascertained opposition is, in the face of modern anti-tank weapons, liable to result in rapid and heavy losses. Soviet meeting engagement tactics also leave them vulnerable to the same flank attacks or envelopment that they hope to execute, although their well drilled attack from the march and the great depths of their march columns give the Soviets a capability to deal with such attacks. In such situations it will be command, control and communications that determine how quickly and effectively a unit will be able to respond to a threat.

The first battles of the next war in Europe will probably not be massive breakthrough attacks of deeply echeloned forces, but meeting engagements with Soviet advance guards, forward detachments, *desants* or *reydy*. The US Army, impressed with the power of the breakthrough attack, often does not realise that the Soviets attach more importance to the meeting engagement.

The breakthrough attack

The breakthrough attack is made whenever the enemy is already in defensive positions, even if they are makeshift defences. Such positions will be bypassed or neutralised whenever possible, but when the breakthrough attack has to be made, its aim will be the defeat of the enemy and the penetration of his positions. This will lead to mobile battles, characterised by meeting engagements, through

BREAKTHROUGH ATTACK DEPLOYMENTS (TANK UNITS)

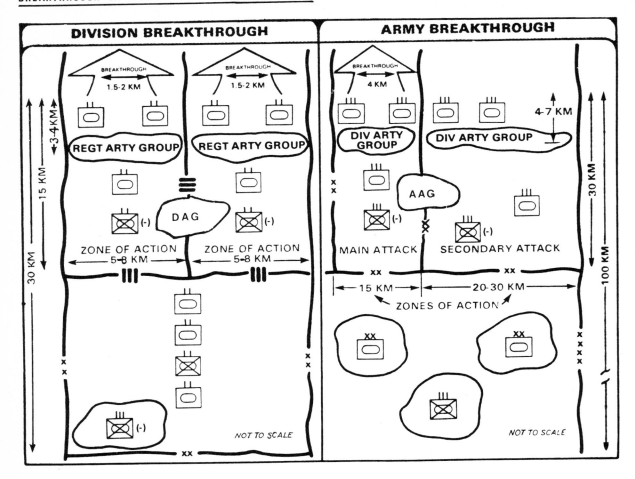

the depths of the enemy defences and rear areas, a phase that will end (theoretically) in the encirclement or destruction of the enemy and the pursuit of any survivors.

Breakthrough attacks can include hasty attacks and deliberate attacks, and are made either from the march or from contact. The difference between the types of attack lies in the time available to plan, co-ordinate and bring up supplies, mainly artillery ammunition. The greater the time spent preparing the attack, however, the greater the time the enemy has to prepare his defences.

The preparation time for an attack varies according to the size of the Soviet forces, the strength of the enemy, and the overall situation. A full divisional attack can be mounted in as little as 2–4h, and a regimental breakthrough attack can be planned in the standard 60–90 min it takes to come up and deploy. However, a breakthrough attack from contact against prepared defences might take several days of planning and stockpiling.

The breakthrough attack from the march takes place whenever advancing Soviet columns encounter a defending enemy force that cannot be bypassed or neutralised. First, enemy outposts and screening forces must be cleared away by the advance guard or forward detachments. Soviet forces will also attempt to determine enemy dispositions and strengths. This may include a reconnaissance in force or a probing attack. Sometimes the entire advance guard will make a probing or holding attack, or even a full-scale assault, before the main body moves up. If the advance guard can break through, the main body will not deploy, but will move directly to exploit the breakthrough. If reconnaissance shows that an assault by the advance guard alone is unlikely to succeed, it will engage the enemy at longer range, halt out of contact or assume a hasty defensive posture until the main body arrives. The advance guard will then join in a combined-arms assault, remain in overwatch positions or deliver a holding attack while the main body attempts to envelop or outflank the enemy position. The Soviets will not attempt to attack directly off the line of march against any but the weakest defences. In the breakthrough attack the advancing Soviet units will move from their assembly areas to the line of departure and attack from there. Artillery support has a much higher value in the breakthrough attack than in the meeting engagement, and such attacks will be co-ordinated with an artillery offensive of from ten to forty minutes' duration.

The breakthrough attack from contact occurs when the Soviet offensive has been halted for a considerable period of time – normally several days – and is being resumed opposite established enemy defences. The standard Soviet offensive of World War Two, with its precisely drafted plans and hub-to-hub deployment of artillery, was the breakthrough attack from contact, which is now seen as the exception in modern warfare. The distances between the assembly areas and the line of departure are much shorter in the breakthrough attack from contact than in any other offensive manoeuvre. Units will often jump off from front-line positions. Surprise is therefore harder to achieve, and the large troop concentrations make inviting targets. Consequently elaborate ruses, night deployment of troops, and intense security measures are as much the hallmarks of the breakthrough attack from contact as the thorough reconnaissance and detailed plans, usually drafted at army level or above, that the Soviets consider necessary for victory in these attacks. Breakthrough attacks from contact are co-ordinated with the most intense artillery offensives, lasting from 25 to 40min and using large quantities of ammunition brought forward during the preparation period. Air strikes will also be used in conjunction with the breakthrough attack from contact, as will tactical parachute drops and helicopter troop insertions behind the enemy position. The Soviets also believe that breakthrough attacks from contact will often involve a river crossing, a difficult but not impossible combat task.

The pursuit

Pursuits can be frontal, parallel or, preferably, a combination of both. Basically, a frontal pursuit is an attempt to engage from the front and break through the enemy rearguard. A parallel pursuit uses a parallel route to cut the enemy off. If these types of pursuit can be combined, with one Soviet force as the hammer and the other as the anvil, the retreat route will be cut and the trapped enemy forces annihilated. Any breakout attempts will be halted by the blocking force.

Soviet units will pursue after a successful attack, or when an enemy is seen to be withdrawing. The Soviets

realise that command control is vital but difficult in a fast-moving pursuit. They must co-ordinate separate forces, including forward detachments and heliborne units, to block retreat routes and take advantage of a quickly changing situation. Whenever possible the Soviets will plan for a pursuit even before making an attack, and these plans may include prearranged air or artillery strikes on defiles or choke points which may turn a retreat into a rout.

The frontal pursuing units will generally be the units which dislodged the enemy, and they will attempt to maintain uninterrupted contact with him, using combat reconnaissance patrols. Second-echelon units will be committed to the parallel pursuit. Artillery support is normally decentralised, with artillery battalions attached down to the leading pursuing battalions.

The daring thrust: operations in depth

Starting in the late 1960s and increasingly throughout the 1970s, the Soviets have been putting greater emphasis on operations that use surprise and manoeuvre to fight deep in the enemy positions, ahead of the march columns of the first-echelon divisions in both nuclear and conventional operations. These operations include *reydy*, *desants*, forward detachments, long-range reconnaissance patrols and the whole range of operations in depth. These are not new and revolutionary tactics. *Glubokoi boi* ("operations in depth") were stressed by Marshal Tukhachevskii in the 1930s, and similar tactics were used in Eastern Europe and Manchuria in 1944–45. These operations are not seen as substitutes for the decisive actions to be fought along the main axes of attack.

Termed "daring thrusts," or *redovaya taktika*, in addition to the historical *glubokoi boi*, they depend upon mobile warfare for their success. In a static situation they would not be able to penetrate the enemy front lines except by helicopter or parachute. Nor could they use the surprise, manoeuvre and infiltration upon which these operations depend for success. (The terms operations in depth, daring thrusts, and *redovaya taktika* have a dated ring to them in Russian. Just as the *Wehrmacht* never used the word *blitzkrieg*, today's Soviet Army may not have a specific term encompassing these operations.)

These different missions all have the same ends, acting as the keys that unlock the stability of the enemy defence by attacking vital installations, especially headquarters and nuclear weapons, providing reconnaissance and target-acquisition data, lowering enemy morale, spreading confusion and disrupting enemy rear areas. Each of the different types of operation approaches these ends in a different way. Long-range reconnaissance patrols provide information and will attack critical targets once located. Forward detachments, ranging from companies to reinforced regiments in size, are assigned a specific task in the depths of the enemy's position, usually seizing and holding a terrain feature or objective to prevent the enemy from defending it and to help secure the passage of the main force. Once the forward detachment secures its objective, it holds this until relieved. *Reydy*, similar in size and scope to forward detachments, have a general reconnaissance-and-destroy mission, rather than one of taking and holding a specific objective, although they may be called upon to do this as well. *Reydy* missions are of indefinite length. *Desants*, normally airborne, heliborne or amphibious, are inserted behind the enemy rear to perform their missions, which are similar to those of either the *reydy* or the forward detachments. As the concept of *redovaya taktika* apparently includes all operations outside the line of march of Soviet units and their advance guards, they will also include the actions of outflanking and enveloping detachments. Together, these operations will destroy the cohesion of the enemy defence and speed the Soviet advance. The emphasis the Soviets place on striking headquarters and communications centres is seen throughout their operational and tactical thought, but never more strongly than in the operations of these units. As priority targets they are second only to nuclear weapons; destroying the nerve centres of the enemy brings victory that much closer.

Forward detachments range far ahead of the march columns, immediately behind the reconnaissance patrols. Of company, battalion or, rarely, regimental size, they are usually taken from units in the second echelon to avoid weakening forces in contact with the enemy, and will seize and hold important objectives, road junctions, defiles and bridgeheads until the main body arrives. They will also attack high-priority targets, especially headquarters and nuclear weapons. On the defence, forward detachments conduct delaying actions in the security zone. Forward detachments co-operate and often link up with *desants* and may themselves be inserted by helicopter. Forward detachments would often be the first units to exploit the effects of nuclear weapons, moving to their objectives through gaps blown in enemy positions.

Reydy, of the same size and composition as forward detachments, also link up with *desants* and will operate immediately behind the reconnaissance patrols. They have no specific terrain objectives, but provide recce and attack targets of opportunity, and will avoid being engaged by superior enemy forces. The *reydy*, like the forward detachment, moves forward by using surprise, manoeuvre and infiltration. Also like forward detachments, *reydy* will mislead the enemy as to the position and direction of the overall Soviet advance. *Reydy* is different

from the Western concept of hit-and-run raids, which operate from a base. The Soviets will also perform raids, but usually on a small scale and to collect intelligence data.

Long-range reconnaissance patrols and *desants* are normally performed by specialist reconnaissance or airborne units. The role of these tactics within the Soviet concept of operations in depth is considered in those sections of this book.

Forward detachments and *reydy* are normally carried out by combined-arms forces. Any tank or motorised rifle unit can serve as a basis for these operations. One company in each regiment, usually the first, is specially trained to act as a forward detachment or *reydy*. BMP-equipped motorised rifle regiments and the independent tank battalions of motorised rifle divisions will frequently provide sub-units for these missions. The long Soviet debate on the proper use of the BMP in battle has established that the BMP, with its powerful armament and excellent cross-country mobility, is well suited to this role. BMP units, usually of company and battalion size, will be reinforced by tanks. An entire BMP-equipped motorised rifle regiment could be reinforced with the divisional independent tank battalion and attachments from divisional artillery, engineer and air-defence units. These "mini-divisions" with 91 tanks, 95 BMPs and strong support elements may be extremely powerful but are apparently unlikely to be used in action, except possibly to carry out special army-level missions. Official Soviet thinking appears to stress the use of units no larger than battalion for these missions. The BMP-equipped motorised rifle regiment and the independent tank battalion are normally in the second echelon of motorised rifle divisions, so the act of detaching units from them will not weaken the troops in contact with the enemy.

Using BMPs on these missions exploits their advantages – mobility and firepower – while minimising their vulnerability to conventional weapons, which they share with the standard, cheaper, BTR-60PB APC. The BMPs will avoid breakthrough attacks, and most combat will be in meeting engagements, possibly with enemy reserves moving forward. BMP units are also well suited, with tank support, for holding key objectives. Their Saggers and the tanks could not only repel attacks, but could weaken the enemy sufficiently to aid the main attack.

The increased emphasis on *desants* and the other tactics embraced in the concept of *redovaya taktika* may be due to the increased Soviet interest in wars other than a Warsaw Pact–NATO confrontation in central Europe or a Sino–Soviet war. The tactics used in these operations could be useful in conflicts anywhere in the world where the Soviets are likely to fight in regiments rather than fronts. The *desants*, representing the long reach of the airborne and Naval Infantry forces, allow the Soviets a capability to project their power overseas.

The combined-arms assault

The basic elements of tactics are fire and movement. Fire is how the enemy is defeated. Manoeuvre gains position to use fire. Fire without movement is indecisive. Movement without fire is likely to be disastrous.

On the modern battlefield artillery can fire much more metal than any tank or infantry unit, but artillery fire itself cannot win a battle. For artillery to fight without tanks or infantry is indecisive, but in the Soviet view tanks or motorised rifle units may be called upon to fight without the full benefit of artillery, and should be made as self-sufficient as possible, with the ability to combine fire and movement. The means chosen by the Soviets to use these two elements of tactics in the attack is the combined-arms assault. It is an attempt to reconcile fire and movement with Soviet operational principles and the strengths and limitations peculiar to the Soviet Army and the weapons with which it fights.

The combined-arms assault is basically the same under all conditions, although there will be differences in each type of attack.

In the hasty attack made directly from the march there are no assembly areas; sub-units are fed in as they come up. In the breakthrough attack from contact, attacking units may jump off directly from the line of contact and will probably be deployed there under cover of darkness.

TYPICAL DEPLOYMENT OF MOTORISED RIFLE DIVISION ON THE OFFENSIVE

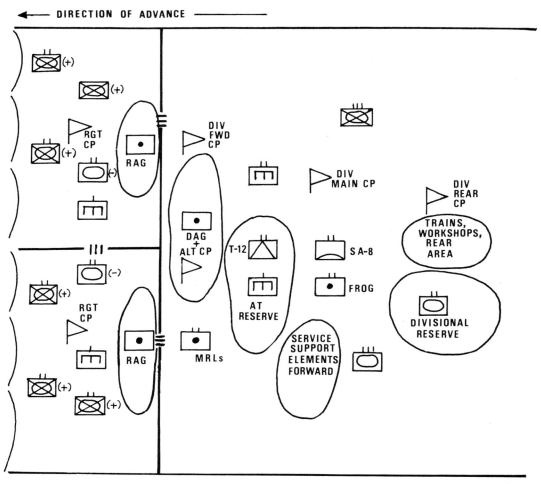

◄ — DIRECTION OF ADVANCE —————

FIRST-ECHELON REGIMENTS
(EACH IN TWO ECHELONS)

SECOND-ECHELON REGIMENTS

MOTORISED RIFLE REGIMENT ATTACKING FROM ASSEMBLY AREA

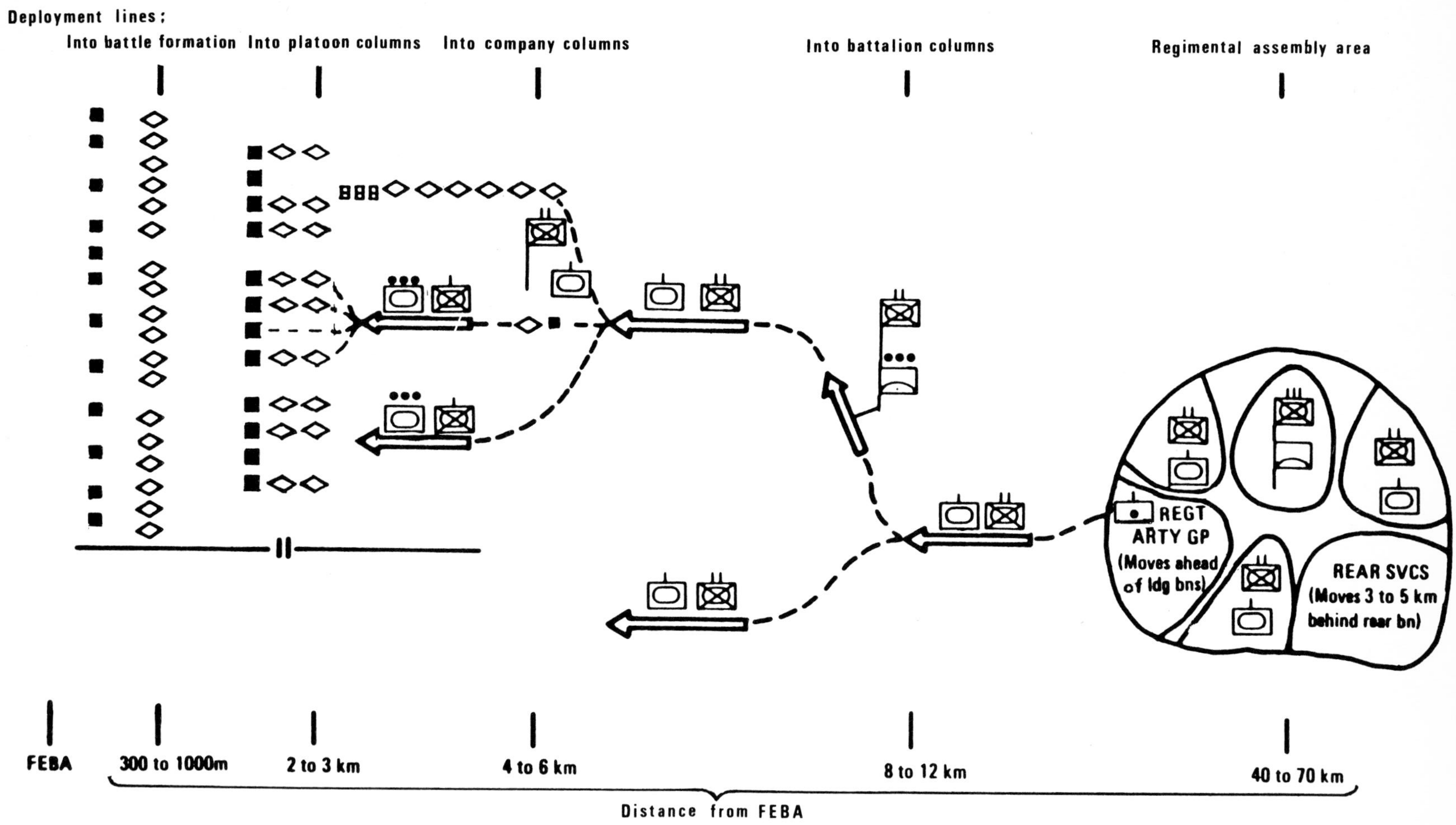

Deployment lines:

Into battle formation   Into platoon columns   Into company columns   Into battalion columns   Regimental assembly area

REAR SVCS
(Moves 3 to 5 km
behind rear bn)

REGT
ARTY GP
(Moves ahead
of ldg bns)

FEBA   300 to 1000m   2 to 3 km   4 to 6 km   8 to 12 km   40 to 70 km

Distance from FEBA

BATTALION APPROACH MARCH FORMATIONS

LINE

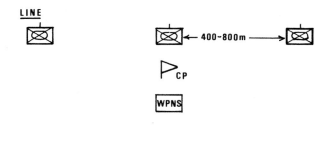

WEDGE

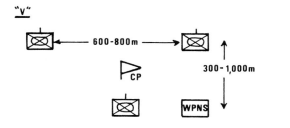

"V"

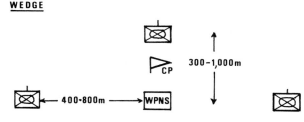

ECHELON

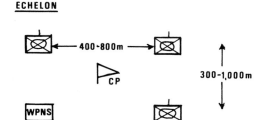

These formations are alternatives to battalion march column and are all intended to allow quick deployment. The companies themselves may have their component platoons in column or in line, wedge, "V" or echelon. Company depth is usually 300–600m.

Otherwise, assembly areas for a regimental attack may be 6–12 km or more from the line of contact. Each regiment – sometimes each battalion – has its own assembly area.

The attacking units leave the assembly areas either in a regimental column or battalion columns. But when they are 8–12km from the enemy the attacking forces will be in battalion columns, their spacing and arrangement organ-

ised so that they will have space to deploy, and all the battalions will attack together.

4–6km from the enemy, the Soviet battalion columns deploy into company columns. If one of the companies is to make up the battalion second echelon, it takes up the proper spacing behind the first echelon. Throughout the advance the Soviet artillery offensive will be hitting enemy defences, but if counterbattery fire has not silenced the enemy batteries the advancing Soviet units will probably be receiving indirect artillery fire.

Advancing at 15km/h, the company columns will deploy into platoon columns 1,500–4,000m from the enemy positions, depending upon the intensity of the fire. The heavier the resistance, the further away the Soviets will deploy. In a motorised rifle company the tank platoon column will lead the three motorised rifle platoon columns by 200m. If a motorised rifle platoon is attached to a tank company, it will follow the three tank platoon columns. Platoon columns are normally parallel but can form echelon, "V" or wedge.

Attacking units will normally traverse gaps in obstacles or minefields in platoon columns. Artillery fire may be used to clear gaps, and one tank per platoon will use KMT-4 or -5 mine ploughs and rollers. BTR-50PK combat engineer vehicles can use rocket-propelled explosive line charges to destroy mines and obstacles. If required, engineers will dismount and use bangalore torpedoes. The Soviets believe that they will normally encounter substantial minefields only when attacking deliberate defensive positions (although the introduction of the FASCAM artillery-delivered minelet system will doubtless change their thinking).

The platoon columns change formation into combat line about 1,500m from the enemy, although weak opposition may be overrun in platoon or even company columns to maintain momentum. The tank platoon leading each motorised rifle company will normally form its own combat line 150–200m ahead of the company combat line of APCs or BMPs. In rough, close or built-up terrain, when attacking at night or across a water obstacle, however, the APCs or BMPs will lead the tanks. Companies attack in a single echelon, usually line-abreast. Tank company combat lines are followed by any attached motorised infantry units. Air-defence elements will cover the assault from overwatch positions and the accompanying artillery, usually SAU-122s but sometimes D-30s, will be 500–1,000m behind the combat line, using direct fire to shoot through the gaps between companies. The tanks will normally fire from the short halt, although they will fire on the move when suppression and speed are more important than accuracy or when they are close to the enemy position. The overall rate of advance while the motorised riflemen are still mounted is about 12km/h, about 200m/min. If the tanks fire from the move rather than from the short halt, the speed of the advance is increased to 15km/h.

MOTORISED RIFLE REGIMENT IN THE ATTACK

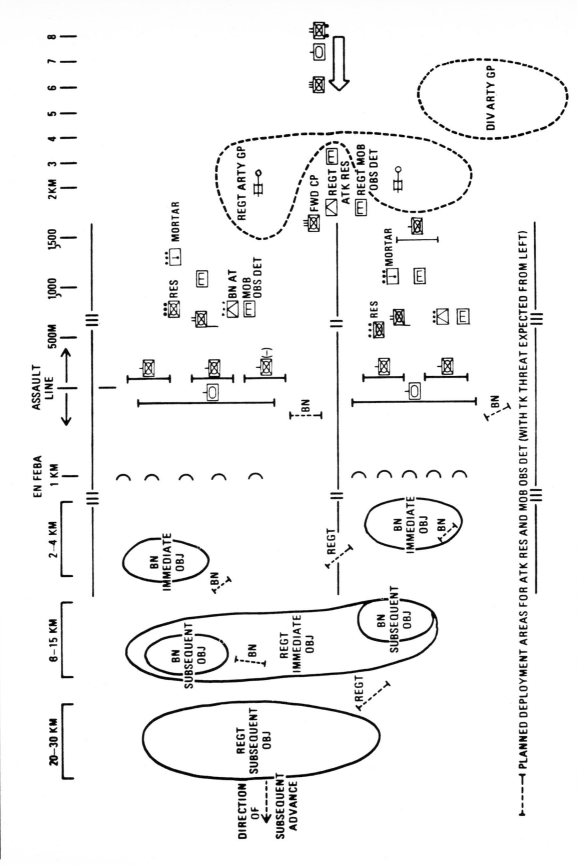

ATK RES = anti-tank reserve; TK = tank; MOB OBS DET = engineer obstacle detachment.

MOTORISED RIFLE BATTALION IN THE ATTACK (MOUNTED)

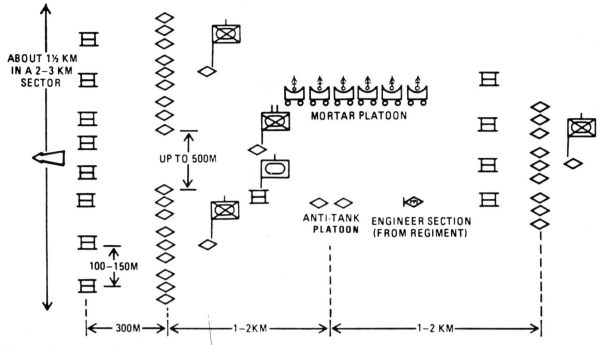

ABOUT 1½ KM
IN A 2–3 KM
SECTOR

UP TO 500M

100–150M

MORTAR PLATOON

ANTI-TANK
PLATOON

ENGINEER SECTION
(FROM REGIMENT)

←— 300M —→ ←———— 1–2KM ————→ ←———— 1–2 KM ————→

If the battalion were attacking in a single echelon, the second-echelon company would be in line with the other two. If a reserve was formed, a platoon would be detached from a company. Often the second-echelon company leads the assault. The mortar platoon may deploy in the position shown, parallel to the enemy. BMP-equipped battalions have no anti-tank platoon. BMPs or APCs are 50–100m apart.

Motorised rifle units remain mounted throughout the combined-arms assault only if the defenders have been effectively neutralised by NBC or conventional fire. In such a case the APCs or BMPs will overrun the enemy position and keep going, leaving the enemy to be mopped up by the second echelon, or the motorised riflemen will dismount behind the enemy position. The Soviets originally intended this as standard tactics in the combined-arms assault before they realised that modern weaponry would inflict heavy losses against such an attack. Today it is uncertain when the Soviets will attack mounted and when they will attack dismounted. The prevailing view seems to be close to that of Lt Cols V. Pishakov and L. Kirpach, who wrote: "A battalion normally breaks through the enemy's defences on foot, as modern defences can field many anti-tank weapons and engineer obstacles, which are greatly resistant to suppressive fire of all types. It is hardly reasonable to assume that all these will be suppressed. Those left undamaged will be able to inflict heavy losses on the BMPs." However, Col L. Raminsky qualified this: "At times in exercises, commanders try to dismount troops even when there is no necessity. This does not answer a requirement of the Ministry of Defence." The apparent official line, as expounded by Col Gen V. Merimskii, Deputy Chief of Combat Training, is

that the decision on how to attack should be made by the regimental or higher unit commander on the spot, as only he can judge battlefield conditions.

When the enemy defence is unsuppressed, strong in armour-killing weapons or in well prepared positions, or if the terrain is dense, built-up, close or otherwise unsuitable to rapid vehicle movement, the motorised riflemen will dismount, in defilade if possible, 500–1,000m or farther from their objectives and advance with the tanks from there. In this situation, the motorised riflemen will often ride in on the backs of tanks, in traditional Soviet fashion. If the terrain is completely unsuitable, the tanks will stay back to provide supporting fire with the APCs or BMPs and the motorised riflemen will deliver the attack on foot alone.

Normally, the motorised riflemen will dismount when the combat line of BMPs or APCs is 300–400m away from the enemy. While the tanks press on regardless towards the enemy, the motorised riflemen form up into dismounted skirmish lines and advance with the APCs or BMPs following 300–400m behind them, firing from the short halt through the gaps between motorised rifle squads in the skirmish line. The accompanying artillery will join in this fire. When the tanks are 100–200m from the enemy positions, the Soviet artillery offensive, which

REINFORCED TANK BATTALION IN THE ATTACK

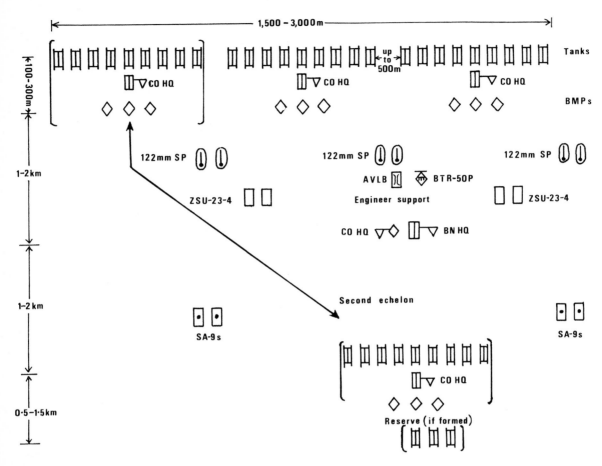

Alternative positions for the third company are shown, depending on whether the battalion is attacking in one or two echelons. If a reserve is formed, a platoon will be detached from one of the companies. The battalion has been reinforced by a motorised rifle company, an artillery battery, and engineer and air-defence weapons. Even if allocated a larger sector, the battalion will attack on a 1,000–1,500m frontage where possible. Tanks are 50–100m apart.

had shifted to enemy front-line positions when the tanks entered direct-fire range, lifts. Direct-fire artillery and supporting fire from overwatching units will continue until they too endanger the attacking tanks. The Soviets realise that the defenders will be able to start using their weapons two or three minutes after the artillery fire lifts, and therefore insist that the tanks must enter the enemy position within this time, with the supporting motorised riflemen not more than 200m behind, giving suppressive fire with their infantry weapons and followed by the APCs or BMPs and the accompanying artillery.

Each dismounted platoon or company will attack in a single skirmish line, each component squad in an identical formation. Such an attack will suffer heavy losses unless the defenders are suppressed by fire from the tanks, BMPs or APCs, and the foot soldiers' own marching fire. If the skirmish lines are forced to ground, platoons will alternately fire and advance by short rushes until the assault line is reached. The Soviets will try to keep the skirmish lines moving if at all possible, however, not only to maintain the speed of the assault, but to prevent the tanks from being left unsupported. The tanks, already attacking at close range, should theoretically suppress the defences long enough for the motorised riflemen to gain the assault line, 25–30m from the enemy foxholes. At this point the motorised riflemen raise the traditional Russian battlecry, "Urra!," and charge with grenades and automatic fire.

If the attack is successful the Soviets will try to keep moving through the depths of the defences, remounting the motorised riflemen. The second echelon will reduce

MOTORISED RIFLE COMPANY MAKING COMBINED-ARMS ASSAULT

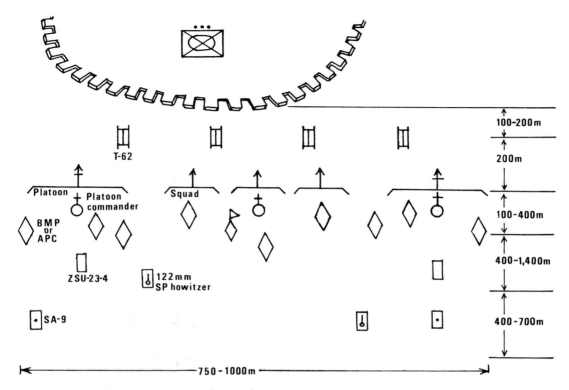

This diagram represents the moment at which Soviet artillery fire against a defending US platoon strongpoint is lifted, and shows the spacing between different elements of the attacking force.

any pockets of resistance and mop up bypassed positions. Enemy counter-attacks at this stage of the assault will probably take the form of meeting engagements, and a mobile battle will result, widening the penetration for exploitation by successive echelons. Forward detachments will be sent into the gap, moving deep into the enemy position. If the attack is halted or repulsed the surviving units will take up the hasty defence to secure the line they are holding as the new line of assault for the second echelon to move through and resume the attack.

While the combined-arms assault can be highly effective, it also has the potential to fail spectacularly. It requires a high level of co-ordination of forces. By reducing the complexities of tactics to battle drill and through intense and repetitive peacetime field training, the Soviets hope to make all the elements of the assault work together as parts of a well oiled machine. Inevitably, however, the reality of Soviet offensive tactics does not always correspond with the textbook ideal. For example, Soviet writings have observed that, under fire, there is a tendency for

the spacings between different combat lines – the tanks, the dismounted motorised riflemen, the APCs or BMPs and the accompanying artillery – to spread out, losing mutual support. Similarly, if the timing between the lifting of the artillery fire on the enemy forward positions and the moment the attacking tanks hit the position is not precise, the enemy will have time to emerge from shelter and defeat the tanks after the shellfire stops. Conversely, if the tanks have advanced too quickly they may have to attack through friendly fire.

As the timing must be prearranged before the attacking units jump off, any delays owing to enemy resistance or terrain will not be reflected in the artillery offensive, although radio or flare signals could be used to control the fire under some conditions. The increased need for the motorised riflemen to assault dismounted has made co-ordination even harder. It is easier to control and manoeuvre infantry when they are in vehicles than it is when they are on foot. Dismounted attacks also make it harder for the Soviets to achieve the high rates of advance they demand. A single unsuppressed machine gun delivering

BMP-MOUNTED MOTORISED RIFLE SQUAD
ATTACKING DISMOUNTED

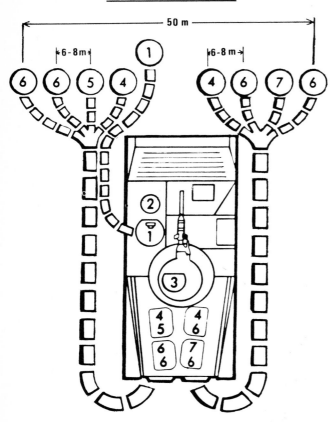

After the squad has dismounted the BMP follows 100–400m behind. Squad members are 6–8m apart laterally. **1** Squad (platoon) commander, AKMS-armed. **2** Driver. **3** Gunner. **4** PKM gunner. **5** RPG-7 (when mounted, this soldier is armed with an AKMS). **6** AKMS-armed rifleman. **7** SA-7 gunner, sniper (both also use AKMS) or rifleman.

enfilading fire can destroy an entire battalion advancing in a long, straight, Soviet-style skirmish line. If the motorised riflemen are pinned down, the tanks must either slow down – hardly a valid choice when confronted with anti-tank weapons and without the suppressive fire of the motorised riflemen – or they can drive, unsupported, into the enemy position, where they cannot do much harm to well dug-in defenders and are at the mercy of anyone who pops out of a foxhole with a LAW or similar hand-held anti-tank weapon.

The Soviets have largely reduced company and platoon-level offensive tactics to a series of geometrical formations. All the battalion commander need do is indicate when these formations are to change and the company and platoon commanders supervise the changes. Plans are made at regiment, and the sub-unit commanders have been replaced wherever possible as the dominant element in tactics by the tactical system of well rehearsed formation changes. This is perhaps necessitated by the relatively low level of technical and tactical skill that still prevails amongst Soviet junior officers, NCOs and enlisted men. It is unrealistic to expect the personnel of a mass conscript army to have the expertise of those in long-serving professional forces, and the differences between the Soviet and the Anglo-American tactical systems reflect this.

Though the officers may be inadequate and inflexible by Western standards (and sometimes even by their own), their skills are adequate for much of the Soviet way of war. Soviet companies are used in a similar way to Anglo-American platoons. Although capable of being divided, a company, like a platoon, will normally fight as a unit. An entire company will normally move or fire, rather than combining the two. Similarly, the platoons of a Soviet company will usually all be in the same formation. Soviet battalions have less flexibility than Anglo-American company combat teams, but are similar to some other Western companies. All of a Soviet battalion will usually fight within visual contact of the battalion commander in his forward post. While he may command a powerful combined-arms force, the Soviet battalion commander's task is to execute orders prepared at regiment or higher level. While Soviet sub-unit commanders will usually not be called upon to act independently in the combined-arms assault, they will have to do so when their sub-unit is used as a combat reconnaissance patrol, a forward detachment or an enveloping force. It is in such actions, rather than the combined-arms offensive, that any weakness and inflexibility in the Soviet tactical structure will be most evident.

One of the key causes of inflexibility in the combined-arms assault is the fact that Soviet commanders tend to be concerned only with their own frontages. Unit boundaries and attachments are seen as inviolable. Speed of advance rather than co-operation with flanking units is relied upon for flank protection, and no Soviet commander should delay his advance to present a united front. The Soviets do however occasionally criticise a tendency to do precisely that in manoeuvres, especially in night combat. These tactics will undoubtedly lead to many exposed flanks and the possibility of counter-attacks against them.

The Soviet emphasis on momentum in the advance makes their actions more predictable and thus easier to counter. While they stress creativity and the use of original manoeuvre, this will probably require a compromise with the rates of advance they demand. Just how great a compromise the Soviets will be willing to make is uncertain.

"Mirror imaging" is common to all armies, including the Soviet. On manoeuvres the enemy "blue" force fights

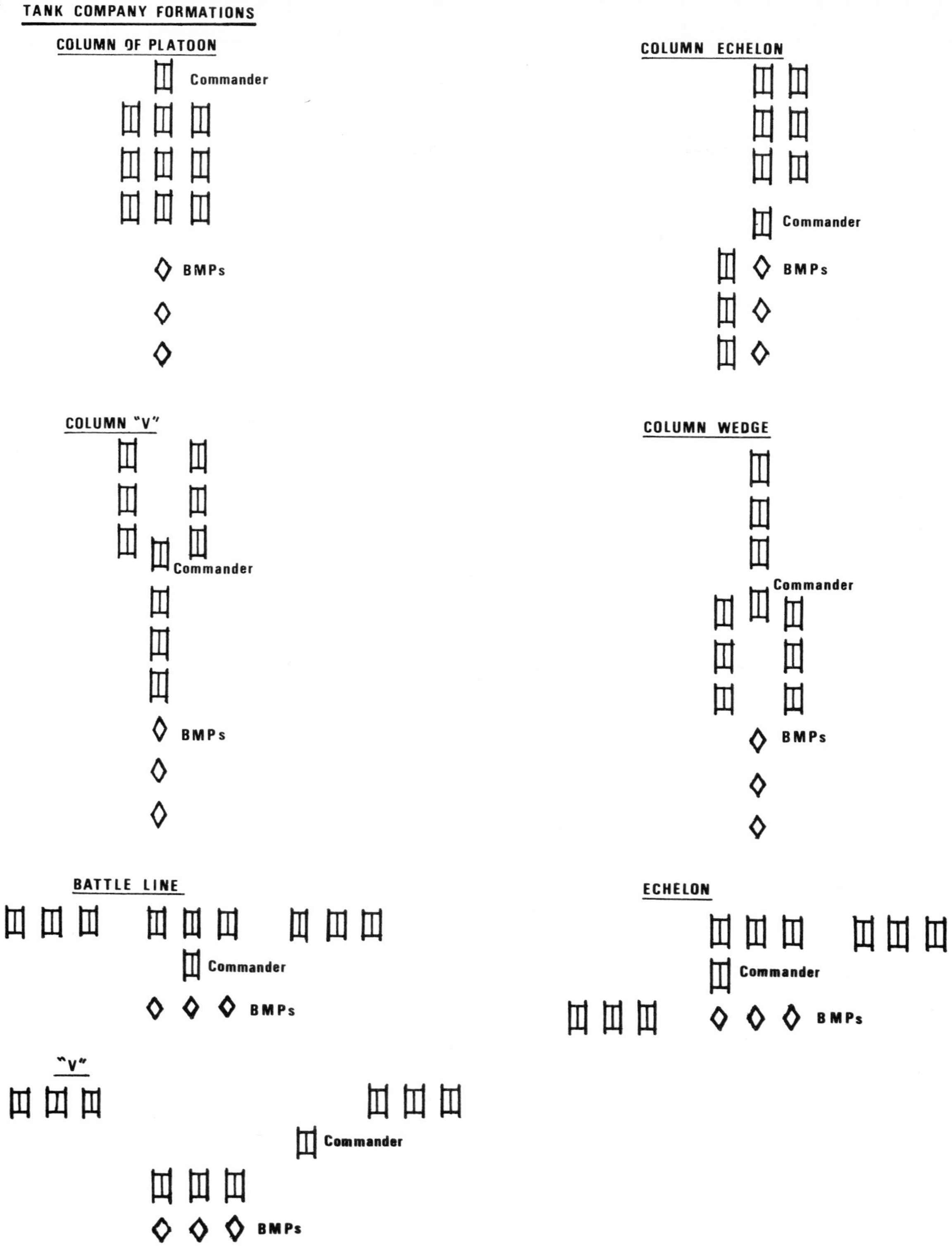

TANK COMPANY FORMATIONS

COLUMN OF PLATOON

Commander

BMPs

COLUMN ECHELON

Commander

BMPs

COLUMN "V"

Commander

BMPs

COLUMN WEDGE

Commander

BMPs

BATTLE LINE

Commander

BMPs

ECHELON

Commander

BMPs

"V"

Commander

BMPs

Notes: 1 BMPs are normally 250m behind the platoon in front. 2 In Battle Line the command tank often joins the line. (Not to scale. Frontage 0.6–1km, depth between platoons 0.25–0.6km.)

and manoeuvres in the same way as standard Soviet units, rather than using the tactics of potential enemy forces. Thus Soviet forces in Asia train to fight armoured, highly mobile formations, while their potential enemy relies on infantry, fortifications and guerrilla warfare. This is just one of many problems in Soviet exercises, and one of the more frequent complaints in Soviet publications is that their exercises are run as rehearsed, artificial setpieces – another complaint seemingly endemic to armies world-wide.

Soviet writings tend to be self-critical regarding these limitations. The quality and the speed of staff work at regiment level and higher have been criticised, as has the tendency to place more reliance on prepared and rehearsed solutions to meet the complexities of modern warfare. The Soviet answer is better and more thorough training, including specialised training for junior staff officers who have not yet had the advantage of the lengthy and deep professional education of senior officers. But it remains possible that Soviet command, control and communication may defeat the combined-arms assault as much as modern weaponry. The tendency towards inflexibility, the reliance on detailed plans from above and the battle-drill formation, more suited to the Western Desert in 1940 than West Germany in the 1980s, may all undercut the combined-arms assault despite the Soviet attempts to correct and improve.

In the final analysis, it is probable that the combined-arms offensive will carry the day, although at the cost of heavy losses. This has been the US Army experience with units trained to fight in the Soviet style as part of the OPFOR (Opposing Forces) training system. Manoeuvre evidence shows that in the initial battles the "Soviet" forces (actually whole US battalions trained in Soviet tactics) usually take their objectives by combined-arms assault, although they do suffer heavy losses. In subsequent battles, when the defenders have studied the Soviet tactics and learned from their mistakes (and in wartime, there may not be either the time or the survivors to do that), the defenders may be able to prevent the combined-arms assault from taking its objective, but in doing so they can suffer losses that would weaken them enough for the second echelon to take the position. The Soviet system will quite probably be a successful one.

The offensive in special conditions

The Soviets realise that any high-speed offensive in Europe must have an effective river-crossing capability. The Soviets have achieved this by building swimming or snorkelling capability into most of their AFVs, which possess a higher level of amphibious capability than those used by any other army. Sizeable amounts of high-quality engineer equipment for river crossings are held at regiment, division and higher levels and will be deployed well forward for river crossings.

The Soviets recognise three types of river crossing: opportunity, hasty and deliberate. Opportunity river crossings are likely to be unopposed, and will usually be carried out by an advance guard, reconnaissance patrol or forward detachment. These units will also attempt to take bridges by a surprise *coup de main*. The hasty crossing is similar to the Soviet hasty attack, while the deliberate crossing is similar to the breakthrough attack and may be a part of it.

On the march the leading APCs or BMPs will swim across and keep moving. The tanks will have to wait until their snorkels are fitted and a suitable snorkel crossing found or, more often, they will wait for the engineers to set up a bridge or ferry.

In an opposed hasty river crossing the tanks will overwatch and deliver direct fire from cover on the banks while the BMPs or APCs swim the river. Direct and indirect artillery fire will also support, as in the combined-arms assault. Once the BMPs or APCs emerge they will attack normally, except that they will probably lack tank support. If the bank is too steep or soft for the APCs or BMPs to climb out, the motorised riflemen will dismount at the water's edge and attack on foot. Once the far bank is secured the tanks will cross, preferably by ford, bridge or ferry. It normally takes 2–3h to get heavy equipment across and 8h for an entire division to cross and continue its advance. Rivers are obstacles, not objectives.

Deliberate river crossings, like the breakthrough attack, were often performed in World War Two. They require great numerical superiority, and intense artillery offensives and heavy engineer support are required. Airborne and heliborne troops will be inserted behind the enemy position for tactical missions in conjunction with such attacks.

The Soviet emphasis on continuous combat makes night operations important. Forty per cent of all field training is supposed to take place at night and Soviet weapons are well provided with night-fighting optics, including gunsights, searchlights, driving lights, and active and passive viewing equipment. While this has not yet reached the technical sophistication of US night vision devices, whose development was spurred by the Vietnam War, the Soviets have provided themselves with a wide range of effective equipment. In both 1967 and 1973 the Israelis found that Soviet equipment gave the Arabs the advantage in night combat.

Reconnaissance of terrain and approach routes and planning of attacks is more important at night. The combined-arms assault is much the same at night, except that battalions are usually in one echelon and the motorised rifle units lead the tanks. Artillery will provide illumination and mark objectives as well as performing its usual duties. Tactical formations are often modified to make command control easier at night. Vehicles stay in column as long as possible, and dismounted squad skirmish lines adopt a wedge formation, the squad leader leading.

Night attacks are a matter of course, but will be launched two or three hours before first light whenever possible to allow daylight exploitation. Night attacks will also predominate when attacking prepared positions or through minefields or dense terrain, or when surprise is particularly valuable.

Despite the importance of night combat, Soviet capability may lag behind their theory. Soviet writings criticise a lack of "bold and decisive manoeuvre" and expertise during night operations. The Soviets may also need night to replenish and rest their troops, rather than maintaining a continuous offensive.

The Soviets will attempt to avoid combat in urban areas as much as possible. City fighting can slow down the offensive and cause heavy losses. However, the increased urbanisation of Europe and the need to secure routes for supply columns will make urban fighting inevitable. Whenever possible, the Soviets hope to seize urban areas by a surprise attack from the line of march. If this is not feasible the first echelon will bypass the area, leaving it for the second echelon. Only if bypassing is impossible will the first echelon attack. Again, they will try to take advantage of surprise, but if this is not possible they will subject the city to heavy air and artillery bombardment and then assault, heavily reinforced motorised rifle battalions being assigned small sectors and limited objectives in the slow, costly house-to-house fighting in which the Soviets excelled during World War Two.

The Soviets believe that any motorised rifle division should be able to operate in mountainous terrain, although they hold specialised equipment for a number of formations whose wartime missions may take them into such country. The high-speed offensive is obviously less important in mountains, and attacks are normally made from direct contact. Communications will frequently have to rely on liaison helicopters and high-powered radios to surmount the mountains. The Soviets will aim to secure truck routes through the mountains and hold crucial peaks and crests. Dismounted operations will be emphasised. The significance of bridges and defiles will make the use of forward detachments more important, and the use of heliborne detachments will also increase.

Soviet anti-partisan operations, like their mountain operations, have increased in importance since the invasion of Afghanistan. The Soviets place great emphasis on "stability of the rear," and it appears in some statements of operational principles. Soviet Army formations were used alongside KGB and MVD units to fight partisans in the USSR and Eastern Europe up until the early 1950s.

In any anti-partisan operations the Army will work closely with the KGB, which will collect information on partisan activities by means of agents and other intelligence methods. To help guard against partisan attack, headquarters and support units will be consolidated and fortified; local defence forces will be raised from politically reliable segments of the local populations; motor transport will be run in escorted convoys (often covered by helicopter) and by daylight in threatened areas; railways, bridges and trains will be heavily guarded, usually by railway or MVD troops.

Soviet units committed to anti-partisan warfare will maintain extensive and vigorous patrols, using helicopters whenever possible. This will prevent the partisans from moving or concentrating easily. Base camps, supply routes and partisan bands will all be sought in these "search and destroy" missions. When the Soviets launch a major anti-partisan operation based on reconnaissance information, security will be kept extremely tight. The troops will then move quickly, by helicopter or aeroplane whenever possible, to surround the partisans and prevent them from retreating. The Soviets will attempt an encirclement of partisan units and then advance on them slowly by daylight, going over the country very carefully at a rate of advance not exceeding two or three kilometres per day. Breakout attempts are expected at night, and the troops will assume defensive positions. Secure communications are stressed, and liaison aircraft are frequently used to prevent intercepted radio messages or couriers from alerting the partisans. These operations will be carried out in winter whenever possible, and during periods of bright moonlight. The Soviets do not envisage a large role for artillery other than mortars in anti-partisan warfare, although its effect on morale is considerable and it will be used in assaults on partisan base camps. However, air strikes will be used throughout. Anti-partisan warfare is an unpleasant business at the best of times, and it is unlikely to be any better with the Soviets carrying it out. Meanwhile, the Soviets will attempt to set up a political structure to consolidate the work of the anti-partisan operations.

Chapter Five

The Defence

*"The Russian Army is a wall which, however far it may retreat,
you will always find in front of you."*
MARSHAL HENRI JOMINI, 1854

Offensively oriented, the Soviets perceive defence as a temporary measure, used only to gain time or consolidate an objective, or as an economy-of-force measure. All defensive operations and tactics are aimed at seizing the initiative and resuming the offensive as soon as possible. Soviet defensive thought is the result of a process of evolution starting in the 1920s, when the lessons of the First World War – especially the excellent German defensive tactics – were first adapted to Soviet conditions. But by 1941 the emphasis on the offensive was so strong that Soviet defensive concepts were unsound and the commanders, staffs and troops untrained in them, which contributed greatly to the defeats of the early war years. However, the Soviets started to improve their defensive operations and tactics, culminating in the great victory of Kursk in 1943. The well entrenched, camouflaged combined-arms defence in depth, with anti-tank weapons emphasised throughout and tank reserves deployed to counterattack, was victorious at Kursk and pointed the way to current practice.

Today the Soviet defence is less static and based more around lines of strongpoints and strong mobile reserves than the Second World War's continuous belts of defence positions with most of their strength in the front line. Modern Soviet units defend with more than half their strength in the second echelon and in reserve. But the defence is still eclipsed by Soviet belief in the primacy of the armoured offensive, and defensive training for Soviet units occupies only one fifth of the training time devoted to offensive tasks. Whether this lack of training will undercut the theoretical strength of the defence remains to be seen.

A defence can be either hasty or deliberate. The hasty defence occurs whenever a unit halts its advance to regroup, resupply, guard against counterattack, consolidate gains, secure a line of departure for second-echelon units, and to be in position to resume the advance at short notice. The Soviets view the hasty defence as the most prevalent type in modern conditions. The deliberate defence has the same goals as the hasty defence, but differs in the amount of time available for preparation.

Soviet defence is defence in depth, and the greater the time available to prepare, the greater the depth and the higher the level of command that will direct it. If time allows, front will designate the line to be defended, while army headquarters designates the defence positions and co-ordinates counterattack and artillery planning. Army also co-ordinates the preparation of divisional withdrawal plans, not so much for use in case of defeat, but if the Soviets intend to use NBC weapons on enemy troops at close range. Divisional HQs organise the strongpoints and defensive belts in their sectors, with regiments positioning sub-units. Of course, in mobile conditions, such as an advance guard unit forced to halt and await the arrival of the main body, the deployment of the hasty defence will be in the hands of the sub-unit commanders on the scene.

A complete deliberate defence will mirror an offensive formation. As in the offensive, divisional and regimental reconnaissance patrols are positioned up to 30–50km forward of the front lines. They report the advance of enemy forces, but do not engage. The security zone, behind the reconnaissance screen, is up to 16km deep. The units in the security zone are usually from the second echelon of the defending force, similar to forward detachments in the offensive. Their mission is to channel the enemy advance, call in artillery fire, and force the enemy to deploy and attack their positions, slowing the advance. These units hold a frontage four times its normal defensive length, and make much use of ambush tactics. Tank units are positioned in the security zone to support them, prevent them from being encircled, and help them disengage when they are ordered to withdraw.

Behind the security zone, and in place of it in most hasty defences, are the forward positions. Made up of companies and platoons from first-echelon defending units, they are roughly analogous to advance guards in the offensive, but are considerably weaker. Positioned 3–5km forward of the first defence belt, forward positions guard against surprise attack, engage enemy patrols and probes, and disguise the location of the defence line so that attacks

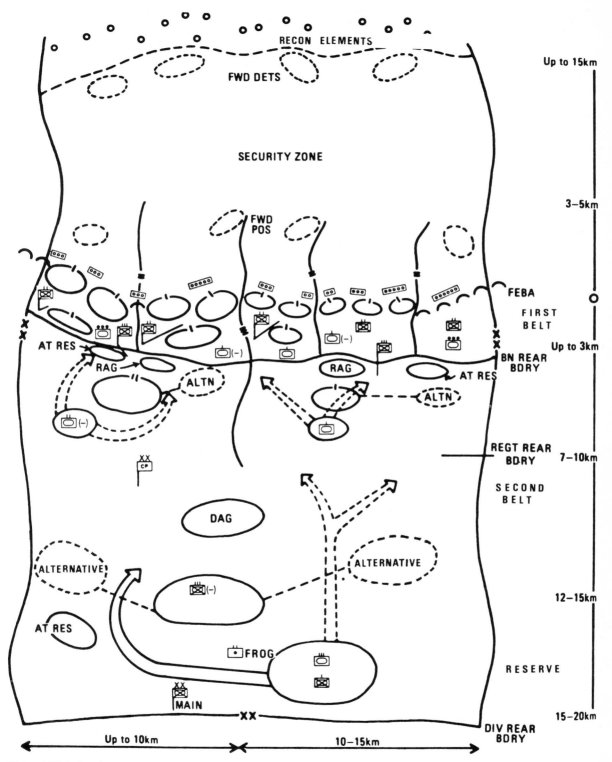

Notes: 1 Right-hand sector is a subsidiary sector. 2 RAG = regimental artillery group, DAG = divisional artillery group. 3 Planned deployment areas for the anti-tank reserve are not shown. 4 Second-belt strongpoints, when fully deployed, are similar to those in the first belt. 5 Platoon outposts are not shown.

MOTORISED RIFLE REGIMENT ON THE DEFENSIVE

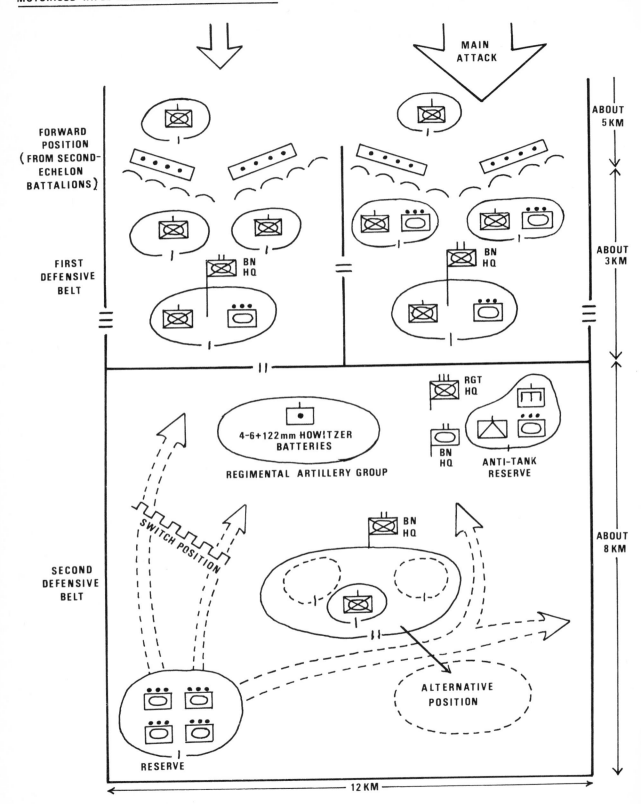

Note: Up to four alternative positions may be prepared for the anti-tank reserve.

and artillery fire aimed at the main defence line will be directed against the forward positions instead.

The observation posts, patrols and battle outposts of the first defence belt are 1–2km forward of the front lines. Sometimes, especially when forward positions are not established, each first-echelon battalion will establish a platoon-sized battle outpost 1–2km to its front, in addition to the standard observation and listening posts.

Each unit's first echelon is its first defence belt; its main line of resistance. A division's first defence belt can be 15km deep, positioned to take advantage of terrain and cover – especially water obstacles and heights – while maintaining concealment, dispersion and depth for its weapons. The purpose of the first defence belt is to engage and defeat the enemy attack.

The division of forces between the first echelon, second echelon, anti-tank reserve and reserve of each unit are the same as on the offensive, from front down to platoon. The second echelon forms the second defensive belt, 8–10km back from the first belt in an army-level defence, five kilometres in a division and three kilometres in a regiment. It contains any enemy units that break through, infiltrate past or outflank the first echelon and serves as a backstop, along with the anti-tank reserve, if NBC weapons breach the first-echelon positions. Spoiling attacks against enemy assembly areas may be launched by tank forces from the second echelon or the rear of the first echelon, which pass through the defences.

Unit anti-tank reserves are deployed in direct support behind the first defence belt as part of the overlapping fields of fire of the defence. Their long-range anti-tank weapons can supplement the fire of the first defensive echelon. They also act as a mobile force to block any threatened penetration, and each sub-unit of the anti-tank reserve may be assigned up to four alternative positions. In addition to ATGMs, anti-tank guns and sometimes tank units, anti-tank reserves often include mobile obstacle detachments of engineers using their specialised vehicles to lay minefields to channel the advance of any enemy penetration, block advance routes and prepare hasty emplacements for the anti-tank reserve.

The two forward defending echelons and the anti-tank reserve create overlapping fields of fire both in front of the position and through the depths of the defence. Obstacles and minefields will be used to channel the enemy into "fire pockets," concentrations of fields of fire along the most

MOTORISED RIFLE BATTALION : DELIBERATE DEFENCE IN TWO ECHELONS

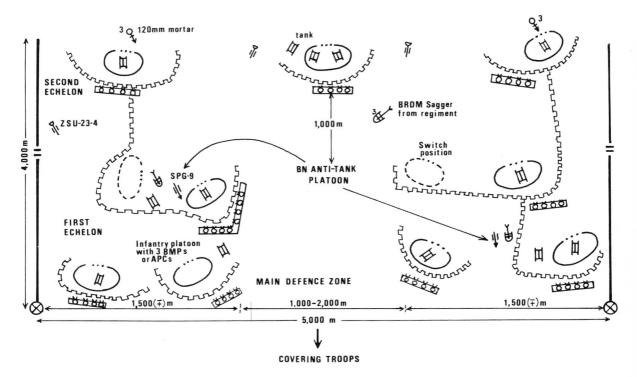

Notes: 1 Pre-arranged final protective artillery fire is ranged in on points in front of the main line of resistance and throughout the depths of the defence. 2 Each rifle platoon has 3 BMPs or APCs.

BATTALION DEFENDING IN LINE (ONE ECHELON)

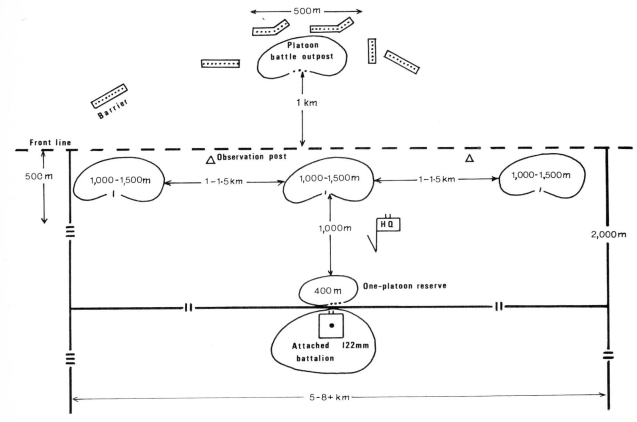

probable axes of advance. The complementary system of Soviet weaponry, especially armour-killing systems, makes this possible at all ranges. The weapons are positioned so that, if the attacker turns to engage one strongpoint he exposes his flank to another, as at Kursk. The weapons will also be concentrated on a number of predesignated points, with the ability to shift from one to another on a prearranged signal. This "manoeuvring fire" provides massed firepower that can be rapidly redirected. Ambushes are also used in conjunction with the main defence, especially when the Soviet force is covering a wide front, as in the security zone, when covering a withdrawal, or when the terrain and tactical situation favour them. Ambush forces in well camouflaged positions are often located forward of the Soviet front lines.

Behind the defensive belts of the first and second echelons is that of the reserve, the third defensive belt. This is the unit's counterattack force, deploying and attacking with the support of the first and second belts and the anti-tank reserve to repulse the enemy, seize the initiative

and resume the offensive. If the reserve (small, like all Soviet tactical and operational reserves) fails to do this, then the unit behind it will have to, as in the offensive. The task of halting the enemy and resuming the offensive may fall to the defending division's second-echelon regiment or to the defending front's second-echelon army. The Soviet telescoping system of overlapping echelons and forces works in the defence as well as the attack. Each commander has his counterattack force, in the form of the reserve, to deal with the enemy in his sector, and not only is there a second echelon behind him, but the higher commander has his own reserve, which can be committed to the critical area of his sector. The combination of interlocking defences and counterattack forces not only gives the Soviet defence great depth, but also gives it flexibility. The Israelis found the Egyptian version of this defence difficult to overcome in the first days of the 1967 war, and with better leadership and greater tactical competence might have held the Israelis to a long "break-in" battle, had the Israelis not had air superiority and worked out the counter to these tactics in advance.

MOTORISED RIFLE COMPANY IN DELIBERATE DEFENCE ("V" FORMATION)

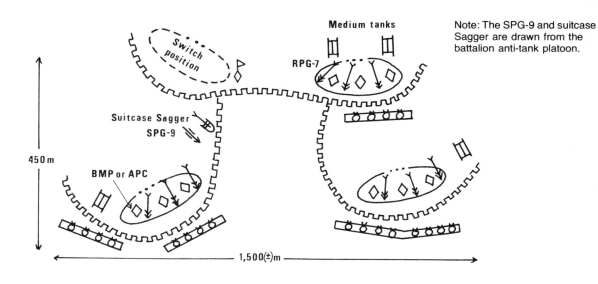

Note: The SPG-9 and suitcase Sagger are drawn from the battalion anti-tank platoon.

COMPANY DEFENSIVE STRONGPOINTS

Note: One to three tanks (if a tank company) or motorised rifle squads (if a motorised rifle company) may be deployed as outposts 200m to the front or on exposed flanks.

(Not to scale)

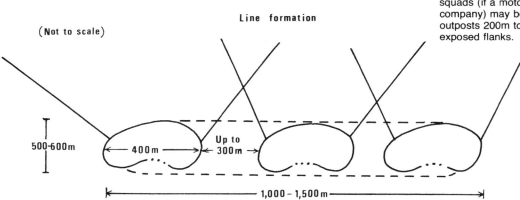

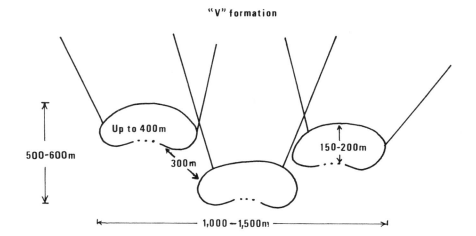

MOTORISED RIFLE PLATOON IN DELIBERATE DEFENCE (LINE FORMATION)

The Soviets see the counterattack basically as a meeting engagement, both sides being on the move. The counterattack will be aided by the fire of the strongpoints in the first and second defensive belts. These units will hold their ground to the last round unless ordered to do otherwise. They may only counterattack themselves or move on specific orders from the next highest level of command.

When the defence is to be in even greater depth than usual, the third defensive belt can be turned into the equal of the first two belts. In other situations regiments and divisions will dispense with the third defensive belt, positioning the reserve in the rear of the second.

The Soviets maintain their tripartite division of command posts for all battalions and larger units while on the defensive. The forward CP is often in the first defence belt, or in the forward part of the second defence belt. The main CP is in the rear of the second defence belt, and the rear CP is with the service support elements, behind the reserve.

Soviet sub-unit defensive tactics are based on a series of strongpoints. Each battalion, company and platoon defends in a strongpoint made up of the three strongpoints of its component units. These strongpoints are deployed in any of the normal sub-unit formations – line, "V," wedge, or with one or two echeloned to the flank – modified to take advantage of terrain and cover. Battalions often defend in a single echelon, keeping at least one company 500m back in place of the second echelon, and the reserve platoon to the rear of that position. As in the attack, companies and platoons always form single echelons. The rearmost or second-echelon companies of a battalion or battalions of a regiment may have their attached sub-units – especially tanks – removed and re-attached to the forward units. All Soviet strongpoints are deployed for all-around defence, which allows the defending forces to guard against being outflanked and to concentrate their fire on any forces behind them. Strongpoints will be sited in mutually supporting crest and

reverse-slope positions whenever possible, but the limited depression of tank and BMP guns will preclude the use of many good positions.

If a battalion is assigned a mission in the security zone, companies and platoons will occupy their usual strongpoints but the gap between companies will be doubled.

In a defensive position each motorised rifle squad digs connecting crawlways for itself and a pit for its APC or BMP, all well camouflaged. If time permits, engineer equipment and tanks with dozer blades will aid in constructing tank pits and fighting positions. Squad and platoon positions are linked to each other by communications trenches. If a squad is positioned in front of a platoon or company strongpoint as a battle outpost, a crawlway may be dug for communication. Alternative positions are also prepared, first priority going to anti-tank weapons. The Soviets will dig as deep as time permits. Camouflage is emphasised, not only against visual detection, but also against electronic reconnaissance, using dummy radar reflectors, expendable emitters and chaff from aircraft and artillery. However, camouflage training is often lacking, and camouflage discipline is often faulty in combat units.

BMP and APC-equipped motorised rifle units and their attached tanks defend in much the same way, despite the BMP's greater combat power. Some Soviet officers have however suggested that BMP-equipped squads should have their frontages increased from 50–60m to 100–150m, 200m deep, to allow the BMP to give supporting fire from the flank and rear. This has met with disagreement because of the command control problem. However, BMPs in a platoon strongpoint are often positioned 100–150m behind the squads to give depth to the defence.

Unlike tank-unit practice, there is no "wandering" BMP or APC to engage probes, which will be fired at by one vehicle per platoon. Infantry weapons will usually hold fire until the enemy is 400m away.

Soviet defensive organisation is impressive. The enemy is located by the reconnaissance patrols and forced to slow

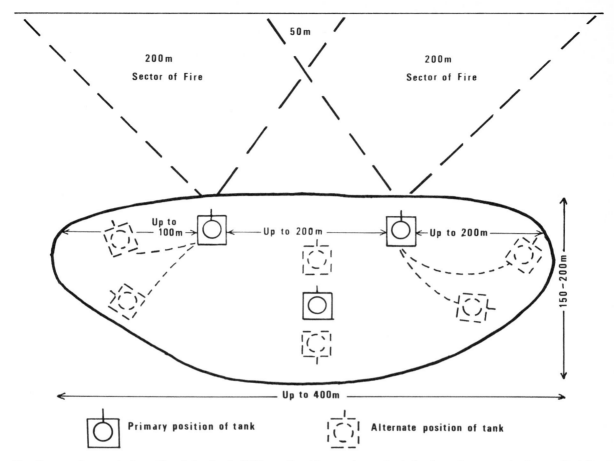

The diagram shows a tank position defending in "V" formation. Line, wedge and echelon formations can also be used to take advantage of terrain and to suit tactical requirements.

his advance in the security zone, while long-range artillery fire starts to disorganise his attacking units. The forward positions will delay, weaken and hopefully mislead the enemy. When he prepares to attack the main defensive echelon, the enemy's assembly areas will be hit by artillery, air strikes and NBC weapons. A spoiling attack may be launched to disrupt preparations, and an enemy preparatory bombardment will be met by Soviet counter-preparation, including extensive counter-battery shoots. The enemy attack itself will encounter mines, obstacles, ambushes and battle outposts between the line of departure and the Soviet front lines. Meanwhile, the Soviet artillery will lay down pre-arranged final protection fires in front of Soviet positions. The weapons in the first defensive echelon and the anti-tank reserve will then open fire, ATGMs at 3,000m, tanks and AT guns at 1,500m. The powerful overlapping fields of fire are intended to be capable of halting an attack even if the enemy preparation, which may include NBC weapons, has inflicted

heavy losses on the defenders. If the enemy succeeds in getting past the first echelon despite the minefields, fire pockets, manoeuvring fire and overlapping fields of fire, the surviving strongpoints will hold their ground when the enemy advances towards the anti-tank reserve and the second defensive echelon. If the enemy penetrates deep enough the artillery will fight with direct fire, otherwise it will continue to put down prearranged fires throughout the depths of the defence. When, in the defending commander's view, the time is correct for a counterattack, the reserve will strike out from its positions, usually in the third defensive echelon, and force the enemy to retreat in a meeting engagement. Although the reserve is small, it will be supported by artillery fire, which will probably have to be direct or prearranged, and by fire or counterattacks from the strongpoints in the first and second defensive belts. If the counterattack by the reserve is not sufficient, then the next echelon behind the defending unit will take over.

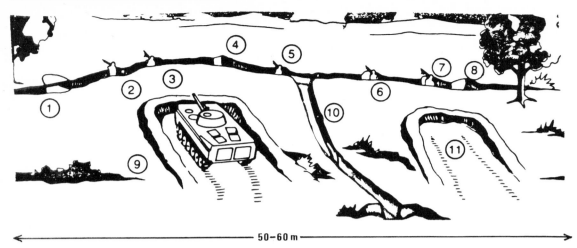

← 50–60 m →

1 Covered firing position. **2** Rifleman position (AKMS). **3** Machine-gun firing position (PKM). **4** Alternative machine-gun position. **5** Rifleman position (AKMS). **6** RPG-7 position. **7** Machine-gun firing position (PKM). **8** Alternative machine-gun firing position. **9** Firing position for squad BMP. **10** Connecting trench. **11** Alternative firing position for squad BMP.

Retrograde operations include the delaying action, the withdrawal, and the retirement. While the Soviets consider them a part of defensive operations and tactics, they seldom discuss them except as required to reduce vulnerability to NBC weapons. They are also used prior to regrouping as well as when leaving a hazardous situation.

A unit's first echelon will normally fight a delaying action when a withdrawal is ordered, using ambushes, minefields, demolitions and long-range artillery fire. If threatened with being engaged in a decisive combat, the rearguard will disengage, aided by the second echelon and reserve units kept back for that purpose. The withdrawal is planned and co-ordinated at the highest possible level, and it is covered by strong rearguards, demolitions and strong flank security detachments on parallel routes, which also occupy key terrain features until the rearguard passes through. The retirement, following a successful disengagement and withdrawal, is a road march away from the enemy, but with a third of the force acting as rearguard. A force will retire to an assembly area before re-engaging the enemy.

The Soviets' defensive concepts share many similarities with their offensive concepts, and thus many of the same weaknesses. The insistence on defending in place – units leave their strongpoints to withdraw or counterattack only on order from higher command – undercuts the ability to fight a mobile battle, although in the Soviet view mobility in the defence is obtained through depth. The Soviets must be prepared to accept that these units may often be outflanked or surrounded, and they believe that by holding their ground these units will weaken the enemy enough for the counterattacks to succeed. But the approval for a counterattack, required at all levels, may not be possible to obtain in battle, especially if there is communications jamming or the units are cut off.

The Soviets do not recognise the US distinction between active defence and a more static, strongpoint defence. The size and composition of the defending force, the time available for preparation and the terrain all determine the nature of the defence. The larger the unit, the greater the flexibility to conduct active, mobile battles. Battalions, with their limited reserves, have little flexibility; companies, without reserves and with less experienced commanders, have virtually none. The Soviets will certainly use built-up areas as part of their defensive positions – they could hardly avoid doing so considering the degree of urbanisation in Western Europe. But although they are capable of turning villages and cities into new Stalingrads, the Soviets will not make them the cornerstone of their defence.

The US concept of shifting forces laterally as part of the active defence is not part of Soviet operations. As when attacking, units assigned key sectors hold less frontage than those in secondary sectors. The Soviet concept of defence in depth is achieved by deep echeloning and counterattacks, rather than the US-style battle of alternating concentration, withdrawal and counterattack that makes up the American concept of the active defence. The depth of the Soviet defence not only gives them mobility, it makes them difficult to outflank or envelop except by the longest and most powerful operations, even if an adjacent unit has been defeated. The Soviets remember the wide German encirclements all too well. Their defences are intended to prevent a recurrence.

As with Soviet offensive tactics, many of these strengths can also become weaknesses. Units smaller than regiments lack the depth and flexibility required in modern warfare. If the series of counterattacks fails to regain the initiative, the first-echelon Soviet forces may well find themselves "in the bag."

Chapter Six

Behind the Weapons

"The general must know how to get his men their rations and every other kind of stores needed in war. He must have the imagination to originate plans, practical sense and energy to carry them through."
SOCRATES

Logistics

The effectiveness of Soviet weapons is directly dependent upon the effectiveness of the logistic system that supports them. Soviet logistic capabilities have been significantly improved since the 1968 invasion of Czechoslovakia, which revealed many shortcomings in the system. Today, while there are still weaknesses in both the means of logistic support and the way they are used, it is no longer possible to regard logistics as the pervasive Achilles heel of the Soviet Army.

There is an average of 3.285 logistics, service, communications and support soldiers behind each US fighting soldier. The comparable Soviet figure is one fifth of that: 0.68 of a soldier in support for every fighting man. The difference in the "teeth to tail" ratio is determined by the differing missions of the two armies. While the Soviets intend to be ready to fight a lengthy war, their main emphasis is on preparing for a short, intense conflict. The Soviets also lack a large, dedicated training base and overseas commitments, both of which dramatically increase the US Army's support requirements.

The aim of Soviet logistics has been to provide what they consider an acceptable level of logistic self-sufficiency, creating operational flexibility. A division, possibly with some army-level augmentation, can carry a five or six-day supply of ammunition, POL, rations and other requirements. Another one or two days' stocks are held at army level. The use of alternating first and second-echelon formations should in theory allow one echelon to resupply while the other maintains the offensive. Army-level headquarters and service support units act as a conduit for supplies coming forward from front level, which can expect to receive them by rail from the Soviet Union. The war envisaged by the Soviets should last 10–12 days in its decisive phase, perhaps 21 days in all. Soviet stockpiles in East Germany, exclusive of those with their units, contain 37 days' supply of ammunition and 16 days' supply of petroleum products, oil and lubric-

ants. The various categories of state reserves in the Soviet Union are large enough for them to fight on even if strategic strikes destroy much of their production, refining and fabrication plant. The difficulty lies in getting this matériel to the front.

The principles of Soviet logistic support include centralised planning at the highest possible level of command, forward delivery (each level of command is responsible for deliveries to the next lowest level), maximum use of bulk transport systems (especially railways and pipelines), positioning service support units as far forward as possible, setting up and adhering to a strict system of priorities, and minimising overall requirements and frequency of resupply. The demands of these principles have been built into Soviet weapons and tactics.

All Soviet service support elements are under the command of the *tyl*. The *tyl* refers to both a separate, autonomous branch of the Army which provides for strategic-level support for all armed services in the Soviet Union and is charged with getting supplies of all types to the theatres of operations, and to the service support elements found at each level of command from front down to battalion; each unit has its own "chief of the rear," the deputy commander for service support functions, who controls all service support activities from the unit's rear command post. This system allows for high-level centralisation of authority and priority decisions, while retaining the ability to adjust these directions in accordance with local conditions. Each chief of the rear is responsible for the day-to-day administration of his unit's logistics. He is assisted by a staff of officers from combat and technical arms as well as those from service support forces. Thus the tank directorate of a division's *tyl* (which, like the Tank Directorate of the central *tyl* in Moscow, is manned by men of the Tank branch) is responsible for the supply and maintenance of all AFVs, although the Artillery Directorate is responsible for all guns, including those on tanks. Similar directorates embrace each of the varied tasks of the *tyl*, including those for the Military Transport Service

(VOSO), engineers, signals, NBC troops and many others.

The forward distribution system starts at the front-level supply base, 150–200km behind the front lines. Whenever possible, supplies will be moved there by rail. The front support base will include extensive depots and workshops. In a mobile situation detachments of the front supply base will be pushed forward behind the advancing troops. The army supply base, about 100km behind the front, is similar to that found at front level but is smaller and has less workshop capability. The Soviets will try to provide rail links to army level, but realise that they may have to rely on truck convoys moving forward from front base. The army support base will also establish forward detachments when its troops are advancing rapidly. At division level all depots will be kept on trucks whenever possible, although dumps will be established when breakthrough attacks are planned. The division supply base will be positioned 25–40km behind the front lines. Combat vehicles will usually be loaded with fuel and ammunition from trucks at the regimental supply point, 10–30km behind the front. The regimental chief of the rear (the lowest level considered capable of supporting independent operations) has a small staff, without branch chiefs to aid him. Supplies are also brought from regiment to battalion support elements, and the battalion chief of the rear will resupply the individual companies, often just out of contact with the enemy.

This supply flow is subject to a strict priority system. Ammunition, POL, spares, rations and medical supplies are normally supplied in that order, with lower-priority items being dispensed with if the flow is impeded. The priorities can be changed in some situations: in a fast-moving pursuit, for instance, fuel may have priority over ammunition. Similarly, those units making the main attack get first priority for supplies, while divisions and regiments in secondary sectors may even have to send their own transport back to get whatever they have been allocated if all the forward delivery is going to the crucial sector.

POL supply is expressed in tonnes but planned in terms of "fills": the number of times a unit can refuel all its elements. Armies usually hold two fills in their POL depots, which may be increased to three or four if time permits extensive dumping. Divisions hold one or two fills, and regiments hold 0.70–0.75 of a fill, formerly 0.5 of a fill. Each vehicle holds a fill in its internal tanks and often another 0.5 fill in external tanks.

Normal POL distribution is:

Tank army/dv/rgt/bn:
    4,000–11,000/800–1,700/120–240/25–40
MR army/dv/rgt/bn:
    5,000–17,500/700–1,450/90–160/9–11

All numbers are in tonnes, the first figure showing the fuel carried in organic vehicles and the second figure the fuel carried in unit trains, depots and dumps.

Whenever possible, front and army supply bases will receive their POL through pipelines. The Pipeline Troops are a separate branch of the *tyl* of the Soviet Union and the Soviets put great emphasis on them. They include both standard pipeline construction units and mobile pipeline-laying units. A pipeline construction brigade of several battalions is attached at front level, and builds forward to reach the army supply base. A brigade can lay 70km of pipeline a day, and a completed pipeline can transport 2,000 tonnes of fuel a day.

POL is distributed to units in special tank trucks and bowsers and in tank trailers. When the demand for fuel is heavy, or if specialised trucks are not available, standard cargo trucks will carry POL in drums and, increasingly, flexible blivets (plastic storage tanks).

Ammunition is supplied in terms of units of fire, the number of rounds in a unit of fire differing for each weapon. It is purely a logistical and planning factor rather than a tactical one, although ammunition expenditure limitations are also expressed in the same terms. Each artillery-type weapon has a mixture of ammunition types in each unit of fire. There are also special chemical units of fire, normally held at division or higher levels. Tanks and AFVs carry one unit of fire on board. Another 0.5 unit per tank or AFV is divided between battalion and regimental transport, and another 0.5 unit is held at division. Artillery has one unit of fire with the gun, one at battalion/regimental level, and 0.5 unit at division. Assault rifles, light machine guns, RPGs and other infantry weapons have half a unit carried by the user or his fellow squad members, 0.5 unit is held at battalion/regiment, and 0.5 at division.

In World War Two 40% of the time taken to get a shell from the factory to the gun was spent loading and unloading in transportation. Even today, the Soviet system of successive levels of forward supply means that a shell may first be taken by rail to a front-level supply base, unloaded, then reloaded and trucked to army level, unloaded, reloaded on to a truck belonging to the army headquarters' transport assets, trucked to division, where it is unloaded and reloaded on to a divisional truck, and taken to regiment, where, if required, it could even be reloaded again. The trucks used throughout this transhipment are all standard Soviet cargo types – URAL-375, ZIL-157, ZIL-151 or ZIL-131 – but they are tied to their parent unit and will not go beyond their forward boundaries to deliver supplies directly to the user. The Soviets have realised the inefficiency of this system, and may take steps to change it in the future. Static dumps will not be possible in many mobile situations, and keeping the supplies on wheels at each level below army will strain their relatively thin transportation assets; the

Soviets still have many fewer trucks per fighting man than Western armies. The traffic jams of trucks bringing supplies forward and those acting as mobile supply columns will be extensive, especially if roads have been cratered, bridges blown or choke points blocked, or if the columns are subject to air interdiction. While the Soviet Army's tank and motorised rifle units have a high degree of cross-country mobility, the supply trucks on which they depend are still tied to the road network.

The Soviet concepts of operational military art and service support have attempted to minimise the logistic requirement. This is even reflected in Soviet tactics. The increased use of direct fire will reduce logistic requirements if, as the Soviets claim, it allows one accurately placed shell to do the damage of ten fired in standard indirect fire. Similarly, the amount of ammunition which can be expended in certain situations is strictly limited, and each unit or vehicle has an emergency reserve, usually 10–15% of a fill or unit of fire, which cannot be expended without orders from the next highest level of command.

The Soviet system of forward distribution requires that all units from front down to battalion have their own motor transport. As well as service support elements, each front has a tank transporter regiment with 300 ten-tonne MAZ-537 heavy tank transporters, which can also be used to haul bulk cargoes and large palletised shipments. The Soviets did not emphasise tank transporters for many years, preferring to rely on rail transport. The increased emphasis on troop manoeuvre after 1967 and, possibly, the lessons of the 1967 Middle East War (when the transporterless Egyptian Army was decimated in the course of its disastrous motor march into Sinai and the Israelis used transporters for tactical and strategic mobility) led to the introduction of the MAZ-537. A tank transporter regiment can carry most of the tracked vehicles of a division 500–600km per day without wear.

Maintenance

Soviet weapons, simple and rugged, have traditionally had a lower maintenance requirement than their Western counterparts. In World War Two, despite their shortage of trained personnel, the Soviets were able to repair 75–80% of their disabled vehicles, 80–90% of these within two days, a performance similar to that achieved by the Israeli Army. Today the sophistication of Soviet weaponry is increasing, and with it the maintenance requirement. A laser rangefinder cannot be built like the Dnepr Dam, big, coarse and rugged. The rise of modern technology, with its attendant high costs, may even call into question the whole validity of a mass Soviet Army, a cornerstone of doctrine ever since the Revolution. Not only may it be difficult to procure the weapons, but to train two-year conscripts to use and maintain such weapons may not be possible. The Soviets are already encountering difficulty with the technology currently in service, according to some reports. While the education of the Soviet soldier has increased arithmetically, the complexity of many of his weapons has increased geometrically. Throughout the twentieth century, the pool of skilled individuals in all fields has never been equal to the growing demands of Soviet society, and even though the military has always had first claim on many of these people, they have never had enough. It may be that today's training methods of reducing tasks to single-skill jobs learned through drills and memorisation will prove inadequate to the demands of tomorrow's weapons.

Each level of unit, from company to front, has a technical officer. He is responsible for the administration and supervision of maintenance and recovery in his unit, and at regiment and higher level is assisted by a staff responsible for different types of weapons.

The maintenance of each vehicle is the primary responsibility of its driver-mechanic, while the gunner maintains each crew-served weapon, both of them being assisted by the remainder of the crew. They perform their tasks under the direct supervision of the company or battery technical officer. The "mechanic" part of the job description is largely honorary, as their training does not give them the capability to do more than routine maintenance. As well as suffering the low skill levels of many personnel, Soviet companies and battalions cannot undertake medium repairs, and even some routine repairs have to be performed at regimental level. Centralisation is a feature of the Soviet maintenance and recovery system.

Each battalion supply and maintenance platoon includes specialised shop trucks and trained mechanics and is capable of routine repairs and recovery tasks. Regimental maintenance and repair companies can perform all routine and some medium repairs – those involving major overhaul of at least two basic assemblies – and form recovery and evacuation groups in action. Divisional maintenance battalions are more specialised, with different workshops and more technicians. Major overhauls and complete disassembly of weapons or vehicles are only possible at army and front level, although regiments and divisions can overhaul transmissions and engines.

The recovery and evacuation of vehicles and weapons during battle is the responsibility of battalion, regimental and divisional repair and evacuation groups (REG), directed by the technical observation post (TOP) of each battalion. In combat each battalion splits its maintenance and supply platoon into a TOP and a REG. The battalion TOP is commanded by the battalion technical officer (deputy commander for technical affairs, to use his full title), and includes the three company technical officers, one NBC sensor reader, and two mechanics. The remainder is organised into the REG, and is supplemented by regimental and divisional assets. REGs make heavy use of specialised recovery vehicles, such as the T-55-T and T-62-T (M-1977), as well as all the vehicles normally found in the maintenance and supply platoon.

In action the TOP is established where it can overwatch the battalion, while the REG remains further back until ordered forward when the TOP spots a vehicle or weapon that has been hit. In combat the crew will first inspect the damage. If they cannot repair it in 10–15min they will wait for elements of a REG to help them repair or evacuate the vehicle. If the vehicle or weapon cannot be repaired in 30–60min in action or in five hours while on the march, it is neither repaired on the spot nor evacuated to a rear position. Instead it is left for a higher-level unit to collect and tow to a damaged equipment collection point. Many of the Arab tanks captured in 1973 had been damaged or had broken down and had been left for rear-echelon REGs to recover or repair. Unfortunately the Israelis arrived first.

The shortcomings of the Soviet maintenance system lie in its centralisation, lack of skilled personnel and orientation towards mobile combat. Even divisions have only a limited maintenance capability, and it would be difficult to send weapons back to army or front-level workshops for repair and then return them to their units. Thus anything that cannot be repaired quickly and easily is simply left and collected later. When the division has lost enough vehicles and weapons for it to lose combat effectiveness, the whole division is replaced. This maintenance system is one of the reasons that Soviet divisions will use themselves up in combat faster than comparable Western formations. They may well do so within the five or six days of combat upon which the Soviets plan. The number of repairable vehicles is likely to overwhelm the TOPs and REGs rather easily, and even quickly repairable vehicles or weapons may have to be abandoned. However, the Soviets realise that under mobile conditions it will often not be practical to bring vehicles or weapons back for repair or maintenance, and so the repair or maintenance facilities must go forward. The concept of forward repair and Soviet numerical superiority should, theoretically, provide the impetus for the offensive to succeed.

Medical support

Soviet medical support is similar to that in Western armies. It is under control of the Medical Service, similar to the US or British Medical Corps.

Individual companies do not have specialised aid men, except for the AKMS-armed company first-aid instructor, who supervises the efforts of the soldiers and administers aid when required. The first medical treatment is the battalion post, which includes a *feldsherr*, literally a barber-surgeon but actually a *praporshchik* (warrant officer) with skills between those of a nurse and a doctor. Wounded are evacuated there in battalion vehicles. The regimental medical post, 6–10km behind the front, performs emergency surgery and classifies casualties for subsequent evacuation. It includes three doctors and supporting personnel. Major surgery is performed at divisional field hospitals, while army field hospitals provide specialised surgical facilities and convalescent units for those expected to return to duty in 15–30 days. Front medical facilities are similar, and include convalescents out of action for six weeks to eight months.

Manpower and training

Wars are fought by men, using weapons that are only as effective as the way they are used. The effectiveness of Soviet weapons and tactics is directly dependent on the effectiveness of the Soviet officers and soldiers and the way they command and are commanded. We can easily measure the effectiveness of Soviet weapons, but the men behind them are the "X" in the equation of victory.

Soviet enlisted men are conscripted for two years, with the exception of naval personnel, who serve for three. There are two annual call-ups, May Day and November 7. After processing at local level, the conscript is transported to his unit, where he spends a 30-day training period before he takes the soldier's oath. He may then go on for specialist training in his unit or take his place in the ranks. The time-expired men leave the unit when their replacements in the new crop of conscripts have reached this stage, although the Soviets may retain them if required. One of the indications of impending Soviet action in Europe would be the retention of one of the six-monthly groups of time-expired men, who would not return home but would remain with their units in East Germany. Once discharged from active service, enlisted men remain in the reserves until the age of 50 (the conscript is normally inducted at 18 and discharged at 20).

Reservists are subject to periodic refresher training. The effectiveness of this training is uncertain, and varies from area to area. However, the Soviet troops that invaded Afghanistan in 1979 were largely reservists from the Turkestan Military District, which is not a high-readiness area, and they seem to have performed well. Although the Soviets maintain few purely reserve units like the US National Guard or the British Territorial Army, reserves are important to fill out Category II and III divisions and mobilisation-only divisions, as well as to replace losses.

Despite there being every incentive to stay in the service – security, promotion, prestige – the re-enlistment rate amongst soldiers completing their two years is 1–2%, a total of 5% of the Soviet Army being long-service non-commissioned men. Most NCOs are conscripts with little more training than the men they must lead. The increasing complexity of modern weapons and warfare obviously requires greater continuity and experience in the non-commissioned ranks, and to this end the Soviets introduced the rank of *praporshchik* (equivalent to Anglo-American warrant officers) in 1971. Originally it was thought that all extended-service enlisted men would become *praporshchiki*, but this proved impractical, and many extended-service men without the qualifications remain as NCOs. *Praporshchiki* are trained in one-year courses and enjoy many of the privileges of officers. It appears that their introduction has been a success. They have freed officers from many administrative and training tasks, fill many officers' billets, and supervise and direct the NCOs in training the men. Even though they have only recently been introduced, the *praporshchiki* have developed much of the aura of respect and competence of the Anglo-American warrant officer: the wise old soldier, capable of using any weapon or performing any task. Many helicopter pilots are *praporshchiki*.

Soviet officers enter service by various means. More than a hundred specialised military schools grant a bachelor's degree and a lieutenant's commission after a four-year course. Military training offered through colleges is another source, especially for the reserves. Enlisted men with the required educational background are encouraged to extend their service and try for a commission from the ranks. Officers serve a minimum of three years. The time spent in the reserve is dependent on rank at time of discharge, ranging from the age of 55 for lieutenants to life in the case of marshals.

The rank structure into which these men fit is similar to those of most Western armies, progressing through private, private first class, junior sergeant, sergeant, senior sergeant, master sergeant and warrant officer (ensign). Commissioned ranks include junior lieutenant, lieutenant, senior lieutenant, captain, major, lieutenant-colonel, colonel, major-general, lieutenant-general, colonel-general, army general or marshal, Marshal of the Soviet Union or chief marshal.

The level of command responsibility is also similar to those of Western armies, although the Soviets retain their wartime practice of using officers to command formations that their rank would not normally entitle them to command. In the Soviet Army responsibility frequently comes before what Westerners would consider adequate rank. Lieutenants, *praporshchiki* and NCOs often command platoons; senior lieutenants and captains both command companies. Battalion commanders range from captain to lieutenant-colonel, with majors being most common. Regiments are usually commanded by colonels, sometimes by lieutenant-colonels and occasionally by majors. Major-generals and some colonels command divisions.

Training and professional military education

The Soviet Army emphasises training with a zeal that approaches mania. Improving training and its effectiveness is one of the Army's primary peacetime aims.

The six-month cycle, in which each unit loses its most experienced men and has them replaced with raw recruits who are not considered effective soldiers for at least six months, has led to many complaints from Soviet officers that they are constantly "re-inventing the wheel." As soon as a unit has worked itself up to some degree of tactical proficiency, both independently and as part of its parent unit, the cycle must begin again, with time and effort being devoted to teaching the recruits basic soldiering rather than polishing tactical skills. The six-month training cycle starts with individual training and works up in a successively larger series of manoeuvres, culminating in twice-yearly large-scale manoeuvres, when whole divisions take to the field.

Despite the introduction of pre-conscription military training when the term of service was reduced from three to two years in 1967, only the Airborne Forces and the Strategic Rocket Forces are entirely composed of soldiers who have received complete pre-conscription military training. The problems of training such a large army by using second-year conscripts to instruct first-year conscripts are vast. Even though today's Soviet soldier is not the often illiterate peasant of World War Two (most soldiers are urban, and literacy and years of education are higher than in the US Army), the demands of a mass conscript army mean that he requires simple weapons and tactics, much as his father and grandfather did.

Unlike the US or British armies, the Soviet Army maintains only a small dedicated training base. Almost all training is conducted by the unit in which each man serves his two years. Because of the increasing complexity of modern weaponry, more than half of all conscripts receive three to six months' specialist training. An extensive network of technical schools provides centralised training for many specialists, while all the Army's airborne training is undertaken at the Tula-Ryazan complex.

Soviet training is based on drill and memory. Each man has his task and is taught to perform it. The number of men available makes such narrow tasks possible, and the limited time for training precludes formal cross-training, although it is encouraged whenever it does not prejudice other training goals. The widespread use of simulators and older weapons for training in the Soviet Army is possible because of the simplicity of most of the tasks the soldier must perform and of the weapons he uses.

Nonetheless, while training may be drilled into the recruit, it is done under realistic conditions. The Soviet soldier spends much time in the field. NBC training is especially stressed, the troops using full NBC gear and actual chemicals and isotopes being used in exercises. Of course this is dangerous – there are numerous deaths each year and 3% casualties are considered acceptable on exercise – but it can hardly be bettered as a training aid. Physical conditioning is also stressed; the Soviet soldier of today could certainly match the legendary toughness shown by his predecessors in World War Two. Soviet Army service is tough, even in a society where life itself is often spartan and rough by Western standards, and this accounts in part for the low re-enlistment rate. For example, one air-defence unit near Murmansk had outdoor toilets and no hot water in their "permanent" installation. Motorised rifle units led an even more primitive existence. The Soviet soldier eats a relentlessly monotonous diet: one unit ate unpalatable fried fish every night for two years. He is not likely to see fresh fruit unless his unit grows it in its gardens (which are frequently thriving establishments) or he buys it in the canteen with his tiny salary. Sores, skin ulcers and vitamin deficiencies often result from this diet when the unit is unable to grow its own food to supplement its rations. A conscript normally receives no home leave during his two years, and seldom leaves the base except on duty or on organised "cultural" visits, usually chaperoned by the political officer. His free time is devoted to "voluntary" tasks and activities as well as organised sports. It is a rigorous team of service, but the emphasis on service to the state throughout Soviet society and the patriotic pride of the average Russian make it a burden that is accepted by the vast majority of the population. Most Soviet men serve in one form or another, except for those unfit or deferred. Conscientious objection is unknown to Soviet law, and will probably result only in a trip to the *Gulag*. Service is not easy, even for extended-service men. Alcoholism is prevalent, especially amongst "NCOs who lack the brains to make *praporshchik*" (conscripts are deliberately kept far away from drink and lack the money to buy it, but they apply tremendous ingenuity to obtaining and consuming it). The children of long-service NCOs, coming from an environment that is both privileged and brutal, are among the worst of what the Soviets call "hooligans."

Discipline is tough. The Soviets still use the firing squad, even in peacetime. A dishonourable discharge can blight an entire life. The officers, NCOs, political officers and the KGB all keep an eye on the soldier. Anyone falling out of line is dealt with very quickly. Despite this, AWOLs and desertions are relatively frequent. The naval mutinies of the mid-1970s may have been just the tip of the iceberg. The suicide rate in the Soviet Army is over twice that of the general population. Prejudice is common, especially against Asians, Moslems and Jews. Again, the long-service NCOs have been singled out as the worst offenders. Moslems are particularly badly off in those units that substitute pork for fish as the diet staple. Some Soviet

units apparently have a rather brutal, prison-like caste system in the barracks, though others are co-operative and tolerant.

The Soviet junior officer is exempted from none of the rigours of peacetime training, when, as in combat, he must lead from the front. Thus each platoon commander leads his men in morning callisthenics and shows them all the other tasks they are supposed to master. He must also supervise the training of the unit, and conducts some of it himself along with his NCOs and second-year conscripts. In addition, he must see that all equipment is combat-ready while simultaneously improving his own professional military education. For the attentive and reliable promotion can be fast: three years each as a lieutenant and a captain, with a majority and a battalion command before the age of 30 not unknown. Most officers take a three to five-year course at an advanced military academy, a necessity for any officer intending to make the army his career. Entrance is by competitive examination (after suitable checks on political reliability by the KGB), normally after three or six years' service in the field. For the rest of his career the Soviet officer will alternate between field commands, staff positions and increasingly higher levels of professional schooling. The Soviet officer may spend up to 40% of his years in uniform at various schools; in this way the Soviets hope to promote the effectiveness upon which military success depends.

Headquarters

All Soviet units of battalion and larger size have their headquarters divided into three parts: a forward command post, a main post, and a rear post.

The commanding officer is normally in the forward command post, as close to the front as possible. On the march the forward command post is near the head of the main body, often moving up to the tail of the advance guard when action is expected. It is mounted in a light mobile vehicle, usually a BRDM-2U command scout car, but command versions of tanks, APCs, BMPs, BMDs and jeeps are also used. This allows the commander to take personal control of a developing situation or make decisions on troop movement, which the Soviets consider especially important in the mobile conditions they expect in modern warfare.

The main command post handles most command functions. It is commanded by the unit chief of staff and at battalion or regiment level is also mounted in a special vehicle, usually a command version of a tank, BMP, BMD or APC. At division and higher level the main command post is divided into a main and an alternative main position, separated by a nuclear safe distance. Frequently the alternative command post is only a skeleton, owing to the shortage of staff officers, technicians and communications equipment. Alternative command posts are often co-located with division artillery group headquarters. In the main command post the chief of staff remains in contact with the forward and rear command posts, handles co-ordination of forces, and generally takes all actions poss-ible to leave the commander in the forward command post free to fight the battle.

The rear command post handles all logistics and service support functions, and is commanded by the unit's chief of the rear, the deputy commander for rear services.

Soviet battalion and regimental headquarters are small by Western standards. Division is the lowest level at which there is a full, dedicated general staff, with directo-rates for each arm of service (at regiment, sub-unit com-manders act as chief of staff for their particular speciality) and a full political directorate. Division headquarters, however, like those below them, are concerned with day-to-day action rather than the development of the battle. Army headquarters will plan four or five days in advance, and only at front and higher headquarters is there any long-range operational planning.

C-cubed

C-cubed – command, control, communications – is likely to be the decisive element of a future war in Europe. If the Soviets can maintain adequate levels of C-cubed, their system of operations and tactics and numerical superior-ity should give them victory. Conversely, NATO relies on its C-cubed to make it possible for the active defence to defeat Soviet thrusts. All the effectiveness of weapons and tactics are futile without C-cubed and another "c," cohe-sion, which distinguishes a military unit from an armed mob.

The men responsible for command and control – Soviet officers – are respected members of society, and those of major rank and above are an elite, with the special shops and other privileges that are accorded by Soviet society to those whose services it values most highly. A Soviet lieutenant receives about 20 times the pay of a private, compared with about four times the pay for the same rank in the US Army. Officers receive at least 33% more pay than they would receive in civilian life for similar skills and qualifications. With his background of intense class-room study (heavily based on military history), realistic field training and private study the Soviet officer is a skilled professional. But there are drawbacks that even the Soviets will acknowledge in order to combat them. These include a lack of technical expertise, lack of experience and professionalism (especially in the lower commis-sioned ranks), and a lack of initiative.

Until the Soviet Army entered Afghanistan in 1979, few of its members had had any combat experience since 1945, and those still in the service were now generals. While the

US experience in Vietnam has limited application in a future conflict, it did weed out a fair deal of dead wood amongst the officer corps and gave others (though not always the right ones) the chance for advancement. The Soviets have made thorough attempts to compensate for this lack of experience through realistic training and exer-cises, intense professional military education, the study of military history – emphasising the lessons of World War Two – and keeping a watchful eye on worldwide develop-ments. Critiques and evaluations can be rigorous. In war-time Soviet officers who blundered were frequently shot; today their careers just wither away.

Despite all his advantages, however, there are frequent reports that the Soviet officer, especially at lower levels of command, does not know his business. Of course this is not limited to the Soviet Army – the most dangerous thing on earth is a US second lieutenant with a map – but the size of the Soviet Army, and its limited (by Western standards) pool of skilled individuals available as officers, makes the problems worse than elsewhere. The evidence for this ranges from comradely criticism of officers forced to do jobs for inexperienced NCOs at the expense of their own command function, to the sight of two columns of Soviet tanks, lost while on manoeuvres in East Germany, appealing to a nearby US Army observer to read their maps and direct them, which he did. In action the US Army may not be so accommodating. The Soviet system does little to prevent such things. The inadequacy of much technical training is apparent, especially in units using complex equipment, and it is inevitable that the officer is personally required to do much of the work, often because he is the only one who understands it. Maps are secret, and issued to officers only on signed receipt, so familiarity with them is hardly assured.

In the Second World War the Germans considered the Soviet front and army-level commanders to be flexible, energetic and full of initiative, in contrast to the inflexible, indecisive commanders at division and lower level, who, though often technically and tactically competent, grasped the letter of their mission but not the spirit, and thus tended to rely on stereotyped action rather than "bold and decisive manoeuvre." Today the divisional and regimental commanders are far better trained than their wartime counterparts, who were survivors of the purges and who had to learn their task in battle rather than in the classrooms and manoeuvres of today. It is also doubtful whether the front or army commanders are any less skilful than the men who gained victory in 1944–45. Whatever criticism the Soviets have against men at this level, it does not often appear in available literature, adding to the existing sense of competence. But even at these levels the centralised nature of the Soviet Army means that all these commanders are implementers rather than planners.

The Soviet system of C-cubed is designed to minimise the effect of individual officers. Sub-units are expected simply to carry out orders, and the system by which these orders are to be carried out is as straightforward as possible. Problems will arise when the situation does not admit of straightforward solutions, such as when a unit is performing as an advance guard, forward detachment or outflanking force, or whenever independent action is required from a sub-unit commander. The Soviets appear to realise this, and the sub-units designated for these missions have the most experienced and highly skilled commanders. The lower they are in the chain of command, the less experienced are the commanders. The squad leaders have no more experience than their men, and have no other NCOs to assist them. This is despite the greater loads placed upon sub-unit commanders by the greater emphasis on manoeuvre, surprise and exploitation. The Soviet way of life, the simple, drilled tactics, the repetitive single-task training and the de-emphasis on communications have all contributed to what probably amounts to a weakness in sub-unit command. Whether this weakness is enough to cancel out the advantages elsewhere in the Soviet system is uncertain. It has also been suggested that bureaucratisation, buck-passing and careerism – stressing self-advancement at any cost and avoiding blame for whatever goes wrong – have a deep hold on Soviet officers. While these elements are present in any army, the Soviets may well rely on them more than others to keep at least the illusion of cohesion.

The Soviet emphasis on prearranged planning in place of radio communications reduces both tactical flexibility and dependence on the radio. Jamming and nuclear blasts may turn the airwaves into masses of static; radio direction-finders will call artillery on to active emitters. The US Army has found what can happen when its units, which depend heavily on radios for their C-cubed, are suddenly deprived of them: things suddenly revert to 1916-style chaos. The Soviets believe that an army should train the way it will fight, and they try to minimise the use of radios, although the links between artillery COPs and batteries and each unit's three-part headquarters are especially important and vulnerable. However, they minimise this vulnerability by using couriers and land-lines whenever possible and enforcing strict radio discipline. Soviet society teaches you to keep your mouth shut, if nothing else.

These limitations apply not only to sub-unit commanders, but also to junior officers on unit staffs. The Soviet press has criticised the "level of staff culture," especially at regimental and divisional level, where the plans for the sub-units are drafted. There have been complaints that the staff officers at these levels do not know their business, and this is especially important as these are the levels of command that must make the hour-to-hour decisions in mobile combat. Soviet centralisation of command normally results in over-supervision, but compounding it by weakness in the centralised authority cancels out many of the advantages that might otherwise compensate for it.

Initiative is a key factor in the effectiveness of the Soviet Army. Western sources constantly debate the quality of initiative among Soviet commanders. The Soviets have their own debates as well. The demands for initiative as a component of leadership come down from above as often as lamentations over its absence. When he was Minister of Defence the late Andrei Grechko said: "Without initiative, it is impossible to achieve victory," regardless of the soundness of doctrine and armament norms. Similarly, the late Marshal of the Soviet Union V.D. Sokolovskiy exhorted: "Generals and officers of the Soviet armed forces are not mechanical executors of the plans of their seniors."

It is wrong to picture a Soviet officer at any grade, and especially at regimental level and higher, as an automaton, the product of centuries of traditional subservience to the group and burdened by the centralisation of command and other baggage of Marxist-Leninist doctrine. Yet he is still less independent than his Anglo-American counterpart. The emphasis on complete obedience to orders and the tendency to centralise decision-making and to look to the word from above are inherent in Soviet society.

This is especially evident in the conduct of enlisted men and junior NCOs, where the low pay, poor conditions of service and minimal motivation lead to a tendency to "hide behind their comrades" and do the minimum possible while serving their time – hardly an unusual attitude for conscript soldiers anywhere in the world. The disparity between Eastern and Western personnel is greatest at NCO level – long-service professionals as opposed to short-service conscripts – and in sub-unit command. In any army the amount of permissible and even desired initiative decreases at lower levels of command. Originality is much more valuable amongst generals than second lieutenants. The Soviet company commander, for all the power he commands, is there simply to carry out evolutions as part of a battalion which fights as part of a regiment. This is a far cry from the role of the commander of a US Army company team, who is expected to perform independent operations under "mission" type orders, as opposed to the detailed instructions prepared at regiment or division for Soviet company commanders. The same is true of battalion commanders. But the higher the level, the more the Soviet commanders will be limited only by their own knowledge and imagination. The Soviets will have to pay a price if they ever fight with their current command system. They will pay it in opportunities missed, in units defeated, in heavy losses. Yet if doctrine is effective, armament norms are met, combat efficiency is achieved, and the system does not collapse or falter in the pressure of combat so intense as to make the worst days of World War Two seem easy, it may be that the price, though high, is reasonable if it brings victory.

A unit's performance in battle is probably determined

more by its cohesion than any other factor. When studying hardware and tactics it is easy to forget that a unit is not just a collection of "human resources" and weapons. It is an entity, a living thing, with its own rituals, shared values, purposes and sense of belonging, the same as any tribe, gang or other primary group. It is the strength of the primary group bond that creates cohesion, whether in the palaeolithic hunting party or an ATGM crew.

Effective leadership is probably the single most important element in creating a cohesive military unit. The shared hardship, risk and suffering produce a bond of loyalty between the led and the leader, who must use this loyalty to lead his group to accomplish its mission as a military unit. The leader must prevent his group from dissolving into a collection of scared individuals, using direct personal leadership to reinforce the group's sense of unity, while simultaneously providing a direct personal example of action under fire as he leads the unit through its mission. Without such leadership, all the weaponry and training in the world cannot yield combat effectiveness.

The Soviets have attempted to build cohesion into their tactical system, minimising the need to provide it directly; this is much as they have attempted to do with sub-unit leadership. They also rely on ideology as a motivating force. Supposedly, the "new socialist man" has no need of group attachment or loyalty to a commander to fight his best. The Soviet Union is a total state. The state is the only institution that is capable of receiving loyalty; not the family, not the church, not even the military unit. While the Soviets try hard to instil pride in units and sub-units through "socialist competition" and teaching history and tradition, Marxism-Leninism perceives a cohesive military unit as "a microcollective without socially significant values." Personal attachment to the group, not ideology, is the key to cohesion. Experience and studies have shown that, except in rare instances, ideology is of little concern to men in foxholes.

Though the Soviet soldier may be surprisingly aware of prevailing conditions inside his country, no one need doubt his patriotism. But it remains that men fight so as not to disgrace themselves in front of the group. Leadership is more than a matter of applying scientific principles in a planned manner, as a first glance at doctrine might lead one to think it is. The Soviets know the leader is important, and stress his role. But despite the tremendous Soviet concern with training, they are little concerned with cohesion, which is a very different thing. The US soldier of the Vietnam War was well trained, yet his cohesion was often poor. It would be an exaggeration to say that the primary group bond is unknown in the Soviet Army, but the systems of leadership and command do not use its full potential.

Examples abound of how Soviet tactics have been optimised to be effective despite C-cubed deficiencies.

Riflemen will not fire in combat unless they are part of a group that is firing or under the eye of their officers and NCOs. Only 15% of the US Army's riflemen of World War Two used their weapons in combat, even though they were amongst the best trained in the world. The Soviets cannot help but be aware of this problem. In an APC or BMP the riflemen are in close contact and under the eye of their commander, although he also has to command the APC. The assault rifle-armed soldiers are more inclined to spray their ammunition instead of not firing, hoping to suppress rather than to hit. Soviet dismounted skirmish lines, combined with the oft-repeated need to keep the attack moving, are basically 1916-style attack formations: simple, maintaining direction, but relying on suppressive fire from supporting tanks, APCs or BMPs to prevent enemy weapons from decimating them. This approach is dictated by the limited Soviet C-cubed capability.

The whole concept of the Soviet high-speed armoured offensive is as much a solution to a C-cubed problem as to a tactical one. Dismounted infantry can be pinned down by machine guns and artillery and separated from their tanks, making both vulnerable. In World War Two the Soviet answer was to mount infantry on the backs of tanks, thereby ensuring that the infantry would be able to stay with the tanks, would not lose its direction, and that the lack of trained NCOs and officers would not show. They only had to hang on until the dismount point was reached. It also prevented the infantry from being pinned down, and it is difficult, physically and psychologically, to abandon a moving vehicle. The widespread use of the APC and BMP – there is no Soviet foot infantry – allows the most effective use of a large force of short-service conscripts with a severe lack of skilled NCOs and junior officers. The men have only to stay in their vehicle and fire, and thus C-cubed is much easier in a mounted infantry force than a dismounted one.

Other threats to Soviet unit cohesion are language and nationality differences. Unlike the practice in World War Two, units have no regional or ethnic affiliation, and an effort seems to be made to achieve a distribution of ethnic groups in each unit. However, technical jobs attract a preponderance of Slavs, while Asians seem to be heavily represented in construction units. Category II and III divisions will however take on an ethnic character on mobilisation, as whenever possible they will draw reservists from the area in which they are stationed to bring them up to strength. The first Soviet units to invade Afghanistan had large numbers of Asian troops because the divisions were low-readiness formations brought up to strength with reservists from military districts on the Afghan border.

Up to 25% of the Soviet Army's soldiers do not speak fluent Russian, the language of all commands and instruction. Nor is there a formal training programme to help them learn, apart from comrades in the barracks helping out, for the Soviet Army abandoned its educational task along with three-year conscription. A language barrier can disrupt unit cohesion, as shown by the Austro-Hungarian Army of World War One and the US Army of the Korean War, when up to a third of the riflemen in many units were Korean recruits. This is also another reason for the Soviet insistence on memorised, lockstep drills for training and on the battlefield. It is hard to be innovative about C-cubed when a quarter of your force cannot understand your language.

The dysfunctional elements of Soviet society cannot help but be present in an Army drawn from the broad base of the population. Everything that gives daily life its own inimitable surrealistic quality persists, despite the constant striving for military efficiency. Shortages, low-quality material (with the exception of most weapons) and a reliance on centralised authority reduce motivation and give a soldier little reason to act except to follow orders, meet quotas and do whatever he has to do without rocking the boat. For example, the effectiveness of ammunition handlers is measured by the number of trucks they can load in an hour. It is easy to load the trucks so that they appear full but have only 70% of the ammunition they are supposed to be carrying. While it is unlikely that this would occur in wartime, it means that the ammunition would not be moved as quickly as the Soviets believe.

For all the improvements of recent years, the degree of technical expertise in the Soviet population is still below that of the US and Western Europe. In those countries people grow up from the cradle surrounded by machines which are alien to the Soviet Union, where consumer goods are perennially in short supply.

Throughout Soviet society, anyone who wants anything knows that there are friends to be asked, palms to be greased, favours to be exchanged. It is only to be expected that vehicle inspectors are bribed, or that soldiers on manoeuvres gladly swap their rubberised NBC suits with fishermen in exchange for fresh fish. Soldiers used to help with the harvest are tremendously inefficient. Without incentive or motivation huge quantities of food are eaten, bartered or just lost through sheer negligence. Trotsky said that "old vagabond Russia" was the weakness of the Red Army. That is probably still true today.

The political officer

Every Soviet unit has its deputy commander for political affairs, responsible to the Main Political Administration of the Armed Forces, an agency of the Central Committee of the Communist Party of the Soviet Union. The provision of political officers at every level down to company provides political control and tries to make good the slogan that "the Army and the Party are one." They are party functionaries first, rather than military officers. Their duties include creating proper support for the Party, which includes moral and political training (a big part of the Soviet soldier's service) and organising Komsomol and Communist groups in each unit. The political officer's presence, plus the near-universality of military service, makes the Army a superb instrument of indoctrination.

For all his totalitarian implications, the political officer of today is a far cry from the bungling commissar of 1941. Although he no longer has command responsibilities, the political officer still plays an important role, especially in sub-units, where he contributes greatly to cohesion, efficiency and training. He still continues his political and moral training classes, even though today's Soviet soldier is often much more knowledgeable about conditions at home than he is about world events. The main reaction to the political officer's hyperbole is boredom (except when films, usually inspirational wartime efforts, are shown) rather than disrespect. The company political officer is one of the most well respected men in the Soviet Army. Even amongst recent emigrants, who hold no love for the Soviet system, very few would say anything bad about their sub-unit political officer. His duties are not limited to political instruction. As this includes maintaining morale, the political officer also performs other classroom training and is primarily responsible for sports and whatever recreation the Soviet soldier receives. It is usually the political officer who organises and conducts off-post tours, even giving up his free time to do so. He also functions as a combined personnel officer and chaplain, and while his efforts on behalf of the soldiers are not always spectacular – obtaining home leave for someone with family trouble, for example – he is always appreciated by the unit.

The political officer also has military functions. In addition to his political training, he is also a qualified officer in the branch of service to which he is assigned. Thus an artillery battery political officer is capable of performing the duties of an artillery officer. He often acts as a direct assistant to the sub-unit commander, taking on some of his paperwork or, in action, bringing forward supplies or reorganising a battered company. In World War Two the political officer often provided an example of personal courage to the troops. He is usually a bright, aggressive young man, often on his way upwards. Most of the members of the inner circles of Soviet power were political officers in World War Two. The political officer is a powerful force for C-cubed and cohesion in the Soviet Army. In actuality, if not on paper, he wields great power and can influence the actions taken by his commander in war and peace. He brings the word (and eye) of the Party down to company level. Despite all his other duties, the political officer remains primarily that – political.

Chapter Seven

Tanks

"Only armour can assure the rapid and total destruction of the enemy. It alone can achieve swift and decisive victory under modern conditions. Armour is the basic manoeuvre element of the Soviet Army — it plays the decisive role in the attack."

MARSHAL OF TANK FORCES P.A. ROTMISTROV

Soviet tactics are tank tactics. The tank is an integral part of the Soviet way of war, and it cannot be divorced from it or considered in isolation. The Soviet Army is an offensive force, and the tank is the weapon with which high-speed offensive war is waged. The 52,600 front-line tanks in 1980 (49,000 with units, 3,000 in war reserve stocks) are to the Soviet Army what the ship of the line was to Nelson's navy: the most important weapon, the key variable in the equation of victory. But the Soviets realise that tanks can only achieve victory as part of a combined-arms force, and that tanks need the other arms as much as they need tanks.

The tank is the ideal weapon for the high-speed offensive, because the increased lethality of modern weaponry has put a greater emphasis on manoeuvre. Tank armies, divisions and regiments are intended to attack an enemy on the move or a defending enemy neutralised by conventional or NBC weapons, or to exploit success. Their mission is to outflank, envelop and pursue, defeating the enemy through manoeuvre rather than by frontal attack.

The largest Soviet tank unit is the tank army. A mobile, powerful exploitation force, it penetrates gaps in the enemy defences, plunging deep into his rear areas. The tank army is the front's strategic, offensive, exploitation force. Any commitment is expected to yield decisive results. Normally positioned in the front's second echelon, the tank army is not committed until there is a gap at least 20km wide and 40km deep. Once committed, the tank army keeps pressing on towards the front's objective, bypassing resistance, encircling and pursuing enemy units but leaving their containment or destruction to follow-up forces. The Soviets believe that the speed and shock of the advance is the best defence against enemy counter-attacks, although a typical tank army with three or four tank divisions will have a motorised rifle division in its second echelon to help secure objectives. The tank army is logistically capable of advancing 320–520km after commitment, depending upon terrain and resistance, an advance that the Soviets believe should bring victory.

Although it is not a breakthrough "steamroller" force, the tank army will be used in the first echelon of a front attack in good tank country if the enemy is weak, off balance or can be encircled or defeated by quick offensive action, or if the attack is to be preceded by NBC or conventional strikes powerful enough to destroy most of the enemy's defensive power. These criteria hold for first-echelon commitment of tank units down to regimental level. The motorised rifle units will make the breakthrough, if required, and the tanks will then exploit and pursue.

The tank army is not a defensive force. If the front is forced on the defensive, the tank army will usually not be given a sector to hold and it will be used as the main striking power of the front's counter-offensive. Any enemy thrust that penetrates the Soviet defences will be counter-attacked in a mobile, meeting-engagement battle by the tank army. If the defenders halt the enemy, the tank army will immediately pass through them and use the enemy's temporary imbalance to resume the offensive.

The tank division is the primary offensive manoeuvre force of the Soviet Army. Used as an exploitation force and normally in the second echelon of combined-arms armies, it is also the primary component of the tank army. Like the tank army, the tank division creates and maintains shock action in the enemy rear, defeating any counter-attacks in a series of meeting engagements. Again like the tank army, it can also be used in the first attacking echelon if conditions are right.

In the march to contact, the tank division will normally have the two tank regiments of its first echelon advancing abreast, each in one or two columns, following the divisional and regimental reconnaissance patrols. Their march order is intended to allow a rapid attack from the march in regimental strength. The tank division follows standard Soviet tactics, with strong pockets of resistance being left to motorised rifle units. Pursuit is envisaged as an important role of the tank division.

Tank divisions on the defensive will not usually hold a sector if they can be replaced by motorised rifle divisions, allowing the tank division to be used as a counter-attack force. However, tank divisions may be positioned in the army first defensive echelon in good tank country or where a strong enemy armoured thrust is expected. Defending tank divisions form the standard Soviet pattern, with security elements, two echelons and a reserve.

The tank division has a large logistic requirement. A day's approach march can use up each tank's fuel. A few hours of sustained action can expend its 40 rounds. Despite important and substantial improvements in Soviet logistic capability, it is still a weakness and may become especially evident in the type of fast-moving, intense continuous combat in which the tank division is intended to engage. The Soviet concept of continuous combat may impose demands far above anything ever seen in previous conflicts, even the 1973 War. The tank division already has a high maintenance requirement, and these operations will lead to their burning out and having to be replaced with other units. However, the Soviets believe that a tank division should be capable, logistically and in combat power, of five to six days of sustained operations.

The tank regiment is employed in much the same way as the larger tank units. In motorised rifle divisions it is normally deployed as an integral unit in the divisional second echelon, along with the BMP regiment. Direct support of motorised rifle sub-units is left to the tank battalions of motorised rifle regiments. Along with the independent tank battalion, the tank regiment is also used in the exploitation role, and its component units make up forward detachments and *reydy*. On the defensive, in addition to the counter-attack role, the tank regiment may detach units to hold the security zone. Tank divisions usually have two tank regiments as their first echelon.

Tank regiments had no organic regimental artillery until recently. Although tank units practise indirect fire, divisional guns are usually attached for artillery support. A motorised rifle company is organic to each tank regiment in a tank division. According to reliable but unconfirmed reports, it is probable that each Soviet tank regiment will eventually include a full, organic, BMP-equipped motorised rifle battalion. In early 1980 the organic motorised rifle component of Soviet tank regiments appeared to vary from full battalions to companies to none at all, the battalions being in the minority. If tank regiments in a tank division require additional motorised rifle support, the two first-echelon regiments will each have a battalion from the division's motorised rifle regiment attached.

There are three types of Soviet tank battalion: the 31-tank battalions of tank regiments, the 40-tank battalions organic to each motorised rifle regiment, and the 51-tank independent tank battalion in Category I motorised rifle divisions. There are also specialised tank battalions, such as those in naval infantry regiments. The 31-tank independent heavy tank battalions, with their JS-series and T-10 tanks, were phased out in the 1970s. Each type of battalion has a different mission. The tank regiment's battalions are the weapon of decision in manoeuvre and exploitation. The motorised rifle regiment's battalion provides direct support, and the independent tank battalion exploits and forms forward detachments or *reydy*, often working in conjunction with BMP-equipped sub-units.

The tactics of the tank battalions of tank regiments follow the basic pattern of larger tank units. Two battalions usually comprise the regimental first echelon in the attack, and one reinforced battalion serves as the advance guard in the march to contact. Battalions, unlike regiments, will often attack with all three sub-units abreast, the attached BMP platoon following each company. A tank platoon, frequently co-located with the battalion commander, is often positioned in reserve behind the attacking echelons to meet unforeseen circumstances or to shift the thrust of the operation. A tank attack against a strong position may be delivered in three company-sized echelons, the first echelon having the heaviest motorised rifle support.

Defending tank battalions will adopt a standard interlocking strongpoint defence, or can be used to form anti-tank strongpoints or anti-tank ambushes to strengthen other units. A division will usually keep a reinforced tank battalion (positioned behind the second echelon) as its reserve and counterattack force.

Motorised rifle regiment tank battalions are used for direct support of the motorised rifle sub-units, and rarely fight as whole battalions. A 13-tank company is normally attached to each of the regiment's three motorised rifle battalions, and a four-tank platoon is in turn attached to each of the battalion's three companies, giving combined-arms integration down to company level. The tank battalion and company HQs are normally co-located with the motorised rifle regiment and battalion HQs respectively. The tank units are under command of the motorised rifle sub-unit commanders, but the tank battalion commander can use the battalion radio network to redistribute or mass his tanks. If a regiment is attacking in two echelons, tanks will sometimes be stripped away from the second-echelon units to help lead the assault. Occasionally, the battalion will be massed and will fight in the second echelon. In the defence, one tank platoon is positioned in each motorised rifle company strongpoint. The five Naval Infantry tank battalions have basically the same mission as motorised rifle regiment tank battalions.

Tank companies normally operate as part of the tank battalion, except for tactical missions such as forming the battalion advance guard, acting as an enveloping or outflanking force, or acting as a forward detachment or *reydy*. Tank companies themselves fight as complete units, with all the tanks and any attached AFVs within sight of the company commander's tank. Companies acting independently, however, may detach platoons to serve as combat reconnaissance patrols and to act as a base of fire or an outflanking force in action.

The company commander's task is basically to supervise the company's evolution through its three basic formations in the course of combat action: from company column to platoon columns to all tanks in battle line, although platoons can be positioned to form echelon, "V" or wedge-type formations. The company commander also directs the firing of each platoon. The company tactics remain largely geometric and somewhat stylised, however. Tank companies, as an integral unit, do not have a second echelon or reserves in the attack. If operating as an advance guard, they frequently have a BMP-equipped motorised rifle platoon attached, plus a pair or more of SAU-122s or ZSU-23-4s. Defending tank companies form three platoon strongpoints.

Soviet tank platoon tactics are extremely simple. The platoon leader's main duty is to supervise his platoon's execution of formation changes ordered by the battalion or company commander, and to direct and co-ordinate long-range fire with hand or radio signals. Soviet platoons, whether of three or four tanks, have two basic formations, column and line, although they can also form wedge, "V" and echelon.

Soviet tank platoon tactics consist basically of changing from column to line and, if required, back again. A company is almost always used as a single unit: either a whole company moves or a whole company overwatches. Platoons are always used as a single unit, and the tanks always act together. Even on combat reconnaissance patrol the platoon will stay together, even though only one vehicle will go turret-down on skylines to allow the commander to observe. Because the platoon level of command does so little, the company is really the lowest-level Soviet tank unit that is capable of operating with any independence.

Offensive tank tactics

Tank units attack as part of combined-arms forces and follow the principles of the Soviet high-speed offensive. The attack will be preceded by reconnaissance, planning at regimental or higher level whenever possible, and obstacle clearing. The artillery offensive will provide fire support, the preparatory fire being timed to hit enemy front-line defensive strongpoints from the moment the first tanks enter direct-fire range to when they are 150–200m away from the enemy position. Other artillery support will be provided by accompanying artillery. Overwatching tanks will support the attack, especially when strong resistance is expected. In this case a battalion will normally overwatch the attack of another battalion of the same regiment and provide fire support. Battalions or companies operating

independently will use one or two of their sub-units as a base of fire to support an attack by the rest of the unit, enveloping or outflanking whenever possible.

Attacking tanks fire either from the halt, the short halt or on the move. Firing from the halt is usually only done by tanks on the defensive, when providing fire support, or when engaging enemy counterattacks. The halt lasts 60–90sec, enough time for a T-62 to fire four or five rounds and a T-54/55 three or four rounds. After firing, the tank will move to avoid return fire unless it is in a camouflaged or dug-in position.

During an assault tanks will usually fire from the short halt, starting when they are 2,000–1,500m from the enemy position. The gun is aimed during the advance, and the tank halts only long enough, about eight to ten seconds, for the gunner to make the final adjustments and fire. The driver starts up as soon as he hears the sound of the gun. Tanks fire on the move (10–15km/h) while advancing on enemy positions less than 800–1,000m away, or in any situation in which it is too dangerous to stop or when weight of suppressive fire is more important than accuracy.

The attack itself includes three formation changes, from battalion column to company column, each company followed by a motorised rifle platoon if one is attached. They then deploy into platoon columns and finally into line, although weak enemy positions may be attacked in platoon or even company column to keep up momentum.

Tank offensive tactics increasingly include acting as forward detachments and *reydy*. The first company of each tank regiment is specifically trained to act in these roles, as is the independent tank battalion in motorised rifle divisions, which can do so either as an integral unit or broken down into detachments.

Defensive tank tactics

Whenever possible, large tank units will avoid being forced on to the defensive. If counterattacked, the Soviets will attempt to defeat the enemy in a meeting engagement rather than put a tank unit on the defensive and wait for the attack. If an area must be secured or defended, the Soviets will attempt to replace the tank units with motorised rifle units whenever possible. BMP-equipped units have even greater armour-killing firepower than tank units.

Soviet tank units defend in the basic Soviet pattern of defence in depth, although a regiment or battalion will frequently not have a third defensive echelon and the reserves will counterattack from positions in the second echelon. If a defending battalion is in a single echelon, the reserves will be in the rear of the position.

Each defensive echelon is composed of the usual lines of strongpoints with overlapping fields of fire. Whenever possible, motorised rifle units will be integrated into these strongpoints, down to company level. Similarly, the four-tank platoons attached to motorised rifle companies are positioned as a single unit within the company strongpoint. If time permits, alternative firing positions will be prepared for each vehicle and, if there is engineer support, firing pits will be dug and camouflaged. Each battalion may deploy a tank platoon as an outpost 500m in front of the main defensive belt, while another platoon is often held in battalion reserve. Other tanks may be positioned as anti-tank ambushes, especially when the unit is covering a wide front or fighting a delaying action. Approach routes, gaps in the defences and exposed flanks are all good positions for anti-tank ambushes. Tanks are positioned in the defence to provide overlapping fields of fire in conjunction with ATGMs and other tank-killing weapons, their fire being concentrated on likely approach routes and in "fire pockets," where concentrated fire can defeat any potential breakthrough. Key terrain points are designated for massed platoon volleys. The spacing of 150m between defending tanks is intended to give overlapping fields of fire and vision when under armour.

An enemy attack will probably be preceded by probes which will be met by fire from the outposts in an attempt to conceal the strength and position of the main defences. If needed, each defending tank company will use a "wandering tank," manned by the best gunner in the company, to engage probes and patrols while the rest of the company remains concealed. Wandering tanks will displace within the company strongpoint after firing, one of the few occasions when Soviet tanks will fire independently at ranges over 1,500m.

Defending tank units may be subject to NBC or conventional preparatory fire. Tank units are considered to be capable of defending their assigned sectors even if they have suffered 30–40% losses. The overlapping fields of fire make it difficult for a large gap to be blown in the defences, and commanders will redeploy their forces until reserves or second-echelon forces can plug the gap.

Long-range fire against an attack will be conducted by the wandering tanks and any supporting ATGMs. The remainder of the Soviet tanks will open fire when the enemy is 1,500m away, or 1,000m if the tanks are in ambush positions or close terrain. Supporting motorised rifle units will simultaneously open fire to separate the enemy infantry from their tanks. A Soviet tank unit will only engage targets outside its own sector if it has first repulsed the attack in that sector. Soviet tanks rely more heavily on cover and camouflage than on displacement to avoid return fire. When alternative positions are available, they will displace every 60–90sec if the enemy fire is intense. If the enemy breaks into the position, the defending tanks may move to alternative locations within their strongpoints for flank defence, but a unit cannot do this, nor can it mount a counterattack, without approval from the next highest level of command, which may be difficult to obtain

in the heat of action. The counterattack will usually be launched by the reserve or part of the second-echelon forces.

If forced to withdraw, a tank unit will use most of its first echelon as a rearguard, which disengages in turn when covered by supporting weapons and artillery fire.

Soviet tank development

Soviet tank development since 1941 has been basically evolutionary, updating different elements of the T-34 design to meet modern conditions. Effective weapons do not have to be high-technology, multi-function, and technologically innovative, and Soviet tanks have maintained their effectiveness by remaining uncomplicated. Commonality of systems, standardisation of parts, and simplicity and ease of production are demanded by the very number of tanks the Soviet Army needs and the skill levels of the soldiers who will use them. Tank evolution has been based upon the improvement of existing types, with new systems and other innovations usually being introduced one element at a time. Parallel and independent development of improved-technology items continues in the meantime. (Only in the T-64/72 series was a premium put on innovation, and the "T-80" may signify a return to a more gradual process of development.) All these elements are brought together and tested in experimental vehicles, minimising the risk of expensive and time-consuming technical failures.

Soviet tank development has succeeded throughout the years despite the inefficiencies created by the Soviet political and economic system. While the weapons development process itself is relatively flexible and autonomous at the levels at which design, research and development are actually performed, higher policy-making levels often appear rigid and constrained in their methods. There is little motivation for risk-taking, and fulfilling the plan goals with the minimum effort possible could just as easily become the objective in weapons research and development, as it has in other aspects of the Soviet economy. That it has not happened is due to the efforts of the design bureaux and the importance that Soviet government, industry and society attach to weapons procurement and production. But they cannot escape entirely: lead times are long and development forecasts run seven to ten years in advance. Rigid, centralised planning gives little flexibility in reallocating or substituting materials, and the unreliability of supply from the civilian sector creates a reluctance to specify new components or suppliers. Political influence also appears in weapons development. The Soviet insistence on a low tank silhouette can be traced back to Stalin's intervention in the design of the T-34.

There are high-level government administrative organisations to speed production, while military production ministries and plants attempt to be self-sufficient, so that failures in other sectors of the Soviet economy will not affect weapons production. The chief designer of each weapons system design bureau is important in this system. He supplies co-ordination, leadership and innovation, and possesses a degree of autonomy and command of resources that is rare in the USSR. He and his staff are closely identified with the success or failure of their designs. If things work well they receive material benefits – shoes, homes, cars – but failure can lead to disbandment, forcing them to take lower positions in the economy.

Technical advances in Soviet tank design are gradually introduced and, if successful, tend to remain in service for a long time. The transmission, drive train and suspension of the T-62 are basically those introduced on the T-44 in 1944–45. The other features of the T-62 (tracks, stabilisation, snorkel, optics, night vision equipment, provision for mounting mine rollers, NBC protection, a turret basket, and many other elements) were introduced a few at a time in the different versions of the T-54/55. Of course, the T-62 features many of these innovations in a refined state of development and has also introduced new systems, most notably the 115mm smooth-bore gun. But even "new" items are often adapted from existing equipment. The 100mm D-10 tank gun was developed as a naval gun, and was used in the SU-100 assault gun before being fitted to tanks. The classic V-12 water-cooled diesel tank engine, with its lightweight block, is the same basic design authorised in 1932 and first produced at the Kharkov locomotive works in 1938. An original Soviet design, the V-12 has appeared in many sub-types, but its output has not increased as fast as the size of the tanks it must power, rising only from 500 to 580HP in 20 years. However, as the T-64/72 series demonstrates, even the most carefully evolved element will be replaced when it is no longer adequate and a replacement has been developed. These tanks represent a much bigger step towards innovation than ever before in Soviet tank development, introducing many new elements. But it is still possible that the T-80 will display the old evolution rather than radical redesign.

Mothballs and training tanks

At any given moment most of the Soviet Army's tanks are in storage, effectively preserved against wear and environmental conditions. It takes 24 hours to remove a tank from storage and perform all the required checks before it is ready for action. Each tank is taken out of storage every six months, thoroughly tested and given any required maintenance, although the tanks are often damaged by poor maintenance. Tanks are removed from storage for large-scale manoeuvres (at least once a year), and also when they are rotated in their role as training tanks.

Because most of their tanks are stored, the Soviet Army uses designated training tanks to maintain crew proficiency. One tank per platoon or, in lower readiness categories, one tank per company is removed from storage in rotation and used for training. Crews not using the training tanks are taught in classrooms, walked through tactical drills, or use wooden tank mock-ups with operating controls. Some units, especially those in higher readiness categories, have all or most of their standard tanks in storage and use a separate set of training tanks. In 1979–80 most of the T-64/72-equipped units in Germany kept most of these tanks in storage except for manoeuvres and retained their T-62s for training purposes. In wartime the T-64/72s would come out of storage and the T-62s could serve as pre-positioned equipment for personnel airlifted from the USSR or as war reserve stocks. However, it appears that most of the 1,200 tanks that the Soviet Union undertook to withdraw from East Germany in 1979 are training T-62s. In addition to tanks with their units, training and manoeuvre areas also hold numbers of training vehicles borrowed from unit storage or from stocks of withdrawn weapons.

This system prevents wear on first-line equipment and, given 24 hours' notice, almost every tank will be ready to go. Reportedly, whole regiments of Soviet-built tanks stay in their motor pools for weeks, receiving periodic maintenance – a "work on the treads" day, an engine oil system day, and so on – but when the regiments go on exercises, they do not leave a single tank behind. However, much valuable training time is wasted by not always having tanks available for each crew. It also prevents a crew from gaining intimate familiarity with their vehicle. This problem is more serious when the training tanks are different from the stored vehicle.

If the mass removal of Soviet tanks from storage is detected, it would provide warning of Soviet mobilisation. Thus East German troops in the 1968 invasion of Czechoslovakia used T-34 training tanks rather than their stored T-54/55 first-line equipment when they went straight from manoeuvres to the invasion. The troops were probably more familiar with the T-34, and it prevented any possible security leaks.

The Soviet Army had only 3,000 tanks in war reserve in 1979. This is much lower than comparable Western reserves, but the Soviets do not intend to replace individual tank losses. If a division is burned out, then it is pulled out and replaced by another. However, this reserve tank strength figure does not include the vast number of replaced tanks the Soviets keep in mothballs. The Soviets do not like to scrap weapons, and they keep them stored for many years. Even T-34/85s still remain in mothballs, as was shown by the fresh examples exported to Angola, Somalia and other nations during the 1970s and to the PLO in 1980. In addition to providing tanks for export, the Soviets can raise the tank requirements of an estimated 50 war-only motorised rifle divisions from their mothballed tanks. They also take the place of first-line war reserves, so in a protracted war burnt-out Soviet divisions could be reformed with outdated tanks until Soviet industry could increase production to wartime levels.

In late 1976 Group Soviet Forces Germany had 5,500 tanks, as many as 2,000 being T-64/72s. In mid-1978 there were 4,950 T-62s and 3,300 T-72/64s. In late 1979 the Soviets announced their intention of withdrawing 1,200 T-62s, some of which, it has been speculated, went to upgrade the equipment of the divisions that invaded Afghanistan (all figures are estimates).

The men behind the tanks

In tank combat the quality of the crew is often more important than the quality of the tank, a lesson of World War Two since proven repeatedly in the Middle East. Effective training is the best single way of increasing crew quality, but despite the increased education and technical competence of the Soviet conscript in the last decade, it is difficult to both train them effectively and to mould them into cohesive combat units in their two-year service. It is still possible that the limitations of Soviet tank crews may prevent the tanks from being used to full effectiveness.

Tank commanders receive six months' training before commanding their own vehicles, plus an additional course if they are platoon commanders. Gunners and driver-mechanics receive four months' specialist training, but the loaders receive only the standard 30-day basic training course before reporting to their units. In addition to his command function, the tank commander is the only crew member trained and authorised to use the radio. The driver-mechanic is responsible for automotive mainten-ance under the supervision of the company technical officer. The gunner is responsible for all weapons. The loader stores ammunition, aids the driver-mechanic and gunner and mans the anti-aircraft machine gun. There is no formal cross-training, but it is often done at unit level. Most cross-training is intended to allow the commander to take over the role of any other crew member. Other cross-training is also attempted, but only as training time, fuel and ammunition (all strictly limited) allow. In many units there are loaders only in company and platoon leader's tanks, owing to personnel shortages. This greatly reduces combat effectiveness as the loss of a crew member halves a tank's efficiency and the loss of two makes it almost useless.

In one Soviet tank unit gunners reportedly fire three full-size rounds a year to keep current, while their US counterparts fire 90–120 annual rounds, the Soviets emphasising sub-calibre firing instead. Training is largely dry runs and drills, backed up by rote memorisation of a limited number of tasks with specific steps. While many tasks are not adequately taught through these methods, others are. One Soviet tankman was surprised to learn that 47% of US ATGM gunners could not tell one type of tank from another, for his company had drilled with flash cards, models and photographs until they all qualified in tank recognition.

All Soviet tankmen must be under 1.65m tall, although T-64/72 units appear to comprise men only 1.5–1.6m tall. Like all Soviet combat troops, they must not wear glasses. Even these small and strong men find the tanks cramped and fatiguing, especially when they are required to perform demanding tasks, such as the loader's having to pick up and seat rounds with his left hand or the driver's strenuous double-clutching. The average height of the Soviet popula-tion is less than that in the West, which makes recruiting such small tankmen easier.

Soviet tanks and their opponents

For all their simplicity, Soviet tanks have often been superior to those used by the US and its allies, as the T-34 series was superior to the Sherman and the T-54 superior to the M-47. The Soviets do not undergun their tanks, and their main guns are normally ten millimetres or more bigger than their Western opposite numbers: 85mm as opposed to 75mm in the 1940s, 100mm against 90mm or 84mm in the 1950s, 115mm against 105mm in the 1960s, and 125mm against 105mm in the 1970s. However, other factors undercut the Soviet armament advantage, includ-ing less ammunition storage, much more primitive optics, lower rates of fire and inferior ammunition.

Until the advent of T-64/72 the Western superiority in optics and fire-control systems gave NATO an advantage in tank combat. Not only was the Soviet equipment less sophisticated, but the quality and workmanship were often poor. Polish and Czech-built tank optics, though of the same basic design, were generally superior. Coupled with the often inadequate crew training, it meant that Western tanks would hit their opponents more often, a situation that will change when fighting the T-64/72, however. More important, perhaps, not only will Western tanks hit more often, they will hit first, which is the most critical factor at the ranges at which most tank combat takes place. This is because Soviet tank gun sights take longer to use accu-rately, their turrets take longer to traverse and their rate of fire is lower than that of Western tanks. Crew quality is also vital in "quick draw" situations.

The influence of fire-control systems and optics can be seen in these comparisons of a Belgian M48 tank using different types of rangefinger with its 90mm gun:

Rangefinder	Range		
	500m	1,000m	2,000m
Laser	98%	86%	34%
Stereo coincidence	97%	70%	14%
Stadia reticle	98%	34.5%	4%

The figures show the probability of hit by a stationary tank against a stationary 2.3m-sq target. Notice that at close range, where armour will not stop most penetrations, there is little difference between the systems, and the best crew – the one that fires first – will win. At longer ranges the differences become more marked, which is why NATO armour attempts to engage at long range and Soviet armour attempts to close with and engage the enemy as quickly as possible.

Because of their small size, Soviet tanks carry less ammunition than their Western counterparts. However, because of the mass in which Soviet armour is intended to be employed, the second echelon will move into any battle where the difference between carrying 28 rounds (as in the T-64/72) or 40 rounds (as in the T-62) and 63 rounds (as does the M60A1) becomes critical, or so the theory goes. The Syrians were apparently running short of tank ammunition in the first days of the 1973 War, and the Soviets may do so in any future war, especially if their advances have strained their resupply capability. Soviet tanks also lack the HEP/HESH, smoke, white phosophorus, canister and beehive rounds carried by Western tanks.

The turrets of Western tanks normally rotate faster than those of Soviet tanks. An M60A1 turret rotates 24° per second and an M60A2 turret rotates 40° per second, compared with 17° per second for a T-55 or T-62.

The lightness of Soviet tanks allows them to use bridges impassable to Western tanks.

Soviet tanks have more effective NBC defence systems than Western tanks.

Soviet tank engines also take much longer to remove and change than comparable US-built engines.

Compared with Western tanks, Soviet tanks have better cross-country mobility. Until the introduction of the T-64/72 series, their armour protection was normally less than that of Western tanks, but not to a significant degree. Now it may be superior. The human engineering of Soviet tanks is acknowledged to be inferior, as is their mechanical reliability: T-62s reportedly average one breakdown every 160–200km, as opposed to one every 240–320km for the M60A1. In the 1967 Middle East war 80% of Egypt's Soviet-built tanks were broken down when the Israelis attacked.

The small dimensions of Soviet tanks appear to be both a means of reducing vulnerability by presenting a smaller target and of obtaining greater strategic mobility by allowing the use of railway rolling stock and tunnels that bigger tanks could not use. A smaller tank also allows the use of positions that bigger tanks could not use; in World War Two the German Panther was unable to find many hull-down positions in the Ukraine because of its size, and wartime experience undoubtedly influenced Soviet tank design. But the Soviets pay for this advantage with a cramped and vulnerable interior and, more important, the low silhouette limits gun depression to four degrees, as

TANK GUN DEPRESSION

US

USSR

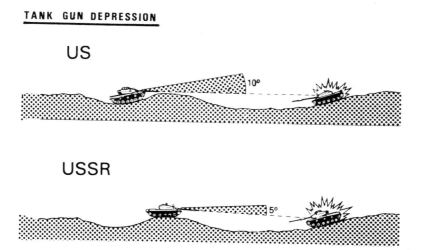

To hit the same target from identical defensive positions, the Soviet tank, with its limited tank gun depression, must come to the top of the height and expose itself.

opposed to ten or more degrees in Western tanks. This forces Soviet tanks to expose much more hull than Western tanks when firing from defilade "hull down" positions. This means that Soviet tanks will not be able to use many advantageous positions and, by increasing their exposure, the low silhouette may have actually increased vulnerability instead of decreasing it. Of course, Soviet armour is an offensive weapon and is not intended to be used on the defensive or in defilade except temporarily, and the tanks themselves seem to be designed more for the plains of the Ukraine or Manchuria, the scenes of wartime experience, rather than the hills and heath of Western Germany. In many positions, any tank will have to fight on the top of a height or on the side towards the enemy, regardless of the available depression. In addition to these drawbacks, the small height of Soviet tanks, coupled with their small tank commanders, limits the distance a Soviet tank commander can see while standing up in the turret to at least 1,000 m less than what an M60A1 commander can see. The lower mounting of Soviet tank guns also means that firing throws up a bigger dust cloud, which often blocks the gunner's vision, as he is also closer to the ground.

The characteristics of some US tank-killing systems in comparison with Soviet tanks and other AFVs are given in the following tables:

M60A1

Combat weight 48,987kg **Ground pressure** 0.79km/cm² **Power/weight ratio** 15.3HP/ton **Height** 3.26m **Max road speed** 48km/h **Max cross-country speed** 12–15km/h **Road range** 500km **Armour basis** (glacis) 225mm, (turret front) 250mm, (turret side) 138mm, (hull side) 53–48mm, (turret rear) 58mm, (turret top) 23mm

M113

Combat weight 11,156kg **Ground pressure** 0.55kg/cm² **Power/weight ratio** 19.27HP/ton **Height** 2.5m **Max road speed** 67km/h **Road range** 483km **Armour** (hull front) 38mm, thinning to 12mm elsewhere. All armour of aluminium, equal to approximately 38% its thickness of steel.

Armour penetration (approximate):

	Range (metres)					
	500	**1,000**	**1,500**	**2,000**	**2,500**	**3,000**
105mm APDS	300	275	200	225	200	175
105mm HEAT	425mm, any range					
TOW	500mm, any range					
Dragon	500mm, any range					
LAW	325mm, any range					

Probability of a hit killing a Soviet tank:

105mm APDS	54%
105mm HEAT	75%
TOW	90%
Dragon	80%
LAW	33%

Probability of hit by US tank-killing weapons (approximate) against Soviet tanks (stationary firing at stationary targets):

Weapon	Ammunition	Range (metres)								
		50	**250**	**500**	**1,000**	**1,500**	**2,000**	**2,500**	**3,000**	**3,750**
105mm	APDS	97%	94%	94%	86%	61%	44%	25%	8%	1+%
105mm gun	HEAT	97%	92%	89%	69%	50%	28%	17%	3%	nil
105mm gun	HEP	97%	92%	89%	56%	47%	28%	17%	3%	nil
TOW	ATGM	nil	75%	90%	90%	90%	90%	90%	90%	90%
Dragon	ATGM	nil	75%	90%	90%	nil	nil	nil	nil	nil
M72A2	LAW	97%	17%	nil	nil	nil	nil	nil	nil	nil

The future

The Soviets still believe that the tank is the weapon of decision, even in the face of the ATGM and the precision-guided munitions that have appeared in the last decade.

One Soviet view postulates that the chance of victory is dependent on how many tanks can attack per kilometre of frontage, and how many anti-tank weapons per kilometre oppose them.

Tanks attacking per kilometre of front	Anti-tank weapons per kilometre of front					
	5	10	15	20	25	30
15	50%	2%	nil	nil	nil	nil
20	75%	10%	1%	nil	nil	nil
25	92%	30%	5%	1%	nil	nil
30	98%	50%	10%	2%	nil	nil
40	100%	75%	65%	10%	3%	1%

This table – from Soviet sources – shows that the chance of victory, here expressed as a percentage, can no longer be improved by mass alone. The Soviets seldom attack with more than 20 tanks per kilometre, and most NATO mechanised infantry battalions can field 15 tank-killing systems per kilometre. Massing more tanks will simply make a better target for NBC and conventional weapons. It is also obvious why the Soviets have emphasised outflanking and enveloping defensive positions rather than attacking them frontally. But if the Soviets must attack, they intend to reduce the number of anti-tank systems through artillery suppression. They will also stress surprise: anti-tank systems will be of little use if they are not prepared. Technical innovations, especially compound armour, may also make each tank as effective as, perhaps, two earlier tanks in the equation of victory. The fact that the Soviets have followed all these courses shows that they are aware of the dynamics of the modern battlefield and have continuously altered their thinking to suit it.

Soviet armour is not without its limitations. Its stereotyped company and platoon tactics make the tanks excellent targets, fail to make the best use of terrain, lack flexibility and, in the words of the US Army, "should be relegated to history". Against even an outnumbered defender, predictable, textbook tactics will be disastrous. The Soviets realise this – hence their emphasis on surprise, manoeuvre and suppression – but they cannot, or will not, change their tactics. Tank crew skill superiority totally undermined numerical advantages in World War Two and the Middle East. While Soviet tank crews are much better trained and far more technically proficient than their World War Two predecessors or those of Arab armies, they are still not equal to those in some Western armies.

Logistics and mobility will also have to be improved. The increasing use of tank transporters means that the Soviet Army is less dependent on rail lines for strategic and operational mobility. Recent manoeuvres have featured long-distance motor marches. One T-62-equipped regiment moved 320km on its tracks in 24 hours and only two tanks – one with a burnt-out engine, the other with a blown transmission – failed to complete the move. The terrain of West Germany, with its valleys, defiles and many choke points, is hardly the ideal location for mobile warfare, especially in the US sector. Tanks may be able to move cross-country, but the trucks carrying their POL and ammunition cannot. The increased emphasis on helicopters is only a partial answer.

Combined-arms integration will undoubtedly be strengthened in the future. Until all tank regiments receive a motorised rifle battalion they can only receive adequate infantry support by detaching motorised rifle battalions from second-echelon regiments.

While the next generation of Soviet main battle tanks will be protected by compound armour, so will those of their NATO opponents. To penetrate this armour may require new weapons and capabilities, but it is likely to be other tanks that will carry these weapons. The tank will probably remain the best anti-tank weapon and the keystone of the armoured offensive for the rest of this century. Yet to achieve and maintain this capability in an increasingly complex battlefield may require tanks so sophisticated and expensive as to call into question the continuing validity of the Soviet concept of the mass armoured army.

Unit organisation

Tank platoon

Total strength: one officer, 11 enlisted men, three tanks; except in the tank battalions of motorised rifle regiments: one officer, 15 enlisted men, four tanks. Warrant officers or sergeants are often substituted for junior lieutenants as platoon leaders. The remaining tanks are normally commanded by sergeants. Some of the drivers and gunners will be PFCs. Each crewman has an AKMS and five grenades stowed inside the tank. The tank commander often carries a pistol. T-64/72/80s have three-man crews.

Tank company

One company HQ

Three tank platoons

Company HQ consists of: one tank, commanded by the company commander (Snr Lt or Capt) and driven by a

PFC (gunner is also often a PFC); one deputy commander (Snr Lt or Lt, political officer); one technical officer (Snr Lt or Lt); one administrative warrant officer; one clerk and one truck driver (privates). The last five men ride in the company's URAL-375 or ZIL-157 truck, and do not accompany the command tank in action. The company commander sometimes also has a GAZ-69, driven by his tank driver, for non-combat duties. While there have been reports that each Soviet tank company has three SA-7 launchers, this has not been confirmed and the storage problems would be considerable.

Tank battalion

One battalion HQ (5–7 officers, 17/18 enlisted men)
Three tank companies (five in independent tank battalion; may be increased to four in some Category I units)
One supply and maintenance platoon
One medical section
Battalion HQ, like all Soviet unit HQs, is divided into forward, main and rear CPs in combat:
    Forward CP: battalion commander, plus three enlisted men, in a special "K" command tank. Commander is usually a major, sometimes a captain or lieutenant-colonel. One GAZ-69 is provided.
    Main CP: one special "command" tracked APC (usually BMP, BTR-50 may still be used) or BRDM (less likely) containing chief of staff (Snr Lt or Capt), operations officer, signals officer, political officer, NBC officer (all Lts) and one enlisted driver. A second APC/BRDM and driver may be provided as well.
    Rear CP: technical deputy commander (Snr Lt or Capt)
Supply and maintenance platoon (3 officers, 31–33 enlisted men, 1 ARV-T, 6+ URAL-375 or ZIL-157 trucks, 1 or 2 POL tank trucks, 1 maintenance truck, 1 BRDM or APC for rear CP)
Medical section (1 warrant officer [*feldsherr*], 8 enlisted orderlies and drivers, 1 ambulance)
    At least some divisional independent tank battalions use the 40-tank organisation.

Tank regiment

Total strength: 124–133 officers, 793–1,082 enlisted men, not counting MR sub-units, 95 MBTs, 14+ light trucks, 119+ standard and specialised trucks
One regimental HQ (28 officers, 32 enlisted men, 2 "K" command tanks, 4 BRDMs, 2 tracked CP APCs or BMPs [may replace BRDMs], 8 GAZ-69, 3 URAL-375 or ZIL-157)
Three tank battalions
One motorised rifle company (reportedly being upgraded to a battalion, absent in some regiments, especially those in motorised rifle divisions and low readiness states)
Combat support units
One anti-aircraft battery

One reconnaissance company
One engineer company (with 27 mine roller-plough combinations and 9 dozer blades, issued to tank companies and battalions as required)
One signal company (4 officers, 53 enlisted men, 2 APC or BRDMs, 4 motorcycles, 3+ GAZ-69, 6+ larger trucks)
One NBC defence company
Service support units:
    One transport company (5 officers, 69 enlisted men, 1+ GAZ-69, 44+ trucks, including POL tank trucks and 1+ semi-trailers)
    One medical company (4 officers, 33 enlisted men, 6 trucks and ambulances)
    One maintenance company (4 officers, 62 enlisted men, 3 ARV-Ts, 1+ GAZ-69, 14+ maintenance vehicles and jeeps)
    One traffic control platoon (1 officer, 19 enlisted men, with APCs or trucks)
    One supply and service platoon (1 officer, 11 enlisted men, 7+ trucks)
Regiments always use a single type of main battle tank. However, training tanks may be of a different type from the standard equipment. It may be that the fourth tank company in battalions deploying such a company could be made up of training tanks, which would result in some cases in battalions using two different types of tank.
    It has been reported that Soviet tank regiments are being reinforced with a regimental 122mm SP howitzer battalion. Such battalions were present in a number of regiments in tank divisions in East Germany in 1979–80.

Tank division

Total strength: 962–1,062 officers, 7,653–8,394 enlisted men, 325 tanks (310 in Category II units), 155+ light trucks, 1,285+ standard and specialised trucks.
One divisional HQ (85 officers, 183 enlisted men, 9+ BRDMs and command APCs, 10+ light trucks, 20+ standard and specialised trucks, no command tanks)
Three tank regiments
One motorised rifle regiment
One artillery regiment
One FROG battalion
One MRL battalion
One anti-aircraft regiment
One reconnaissance battalion
Combat support units
One engineer battalion
One signal battalion
One NBC defence battalion
Service support units:
    One transport battalion (22 officers, 195 enlisted men, 5+ light trucks, 200+ other trucks)
    One medical battalion (35 officers, 123 enlisted men, 1+ light truck, 19+ trucks and ambulances)
    One maintenance battalion (19 officers, 275 enlisted

men, 3+ light trucks, 70+ other vehicles, including ARVs and heavy cranes)
One traffic control company (3 officers, 57 men with trucks and APCs)
One field bakery (2 officers, 38 enlisted men, 6 trucks)
One medical battalion (35 officers, 123 enlisted men, 31 trucks)
One divisional band
Divisional depots
Divisional service support elements

T-54/55 main battle tank

Combat weight 36 tons **Length (gun forward)** 9.0m **Length (gun rear)** 8.485m **Height (without AAMG)** 2.4m **Width** 3.27m **Track** 2.64m **Clearance** 0.425m **Track width** 0.58m **Ground contact** 3.84m **Ground pressure** 0.81kg/cm² **Max road speed** 48km/h **Fuel capacity (internal)** 580 litres **Fuel capacity (external)** 320 litres (less on early T-54) **Fuel capacity (jettisonable rear drums)** 400 litres **Fuel consumption (paved roads)** 1.9+ litres/km **Fuel consumption (unpaved roads)** 2.8+ litres/km **Fording** 1.4m **Snorkelling** 5.5m (4.6m with earlier equipment) **Gradient** 30° **Turning circle (at 10–15km/h)** 8.02m **Vertical obstacle** 0.8m **Trench** 2.7m **Horsepower/weight** 16.11HP/ton (14.44) **Engine** V-55 (V-54) V-12 diesel, water-cooled, 580 (520) HP @ 2,000rpm, 38,600cm³ **Range (paved road)** 420km (with-

out extra tanks), 615km (with extra tanks) **Range (unpaved road)** 325km (without extra tanks), 660km (with extra tanks) **Transmission** Mechanical synchromesh, 5 forward, 1 reverse gears **Steering** 2-stage planetary clutch and brake **Gun** 100mm D-10T2S (T-54 had earlier versions) **Calibre length** 56cal **Max rate of fire (theoretical)** 7rpm **Max rate of fire (actual)** 3–4rpm **Max range (direct fire)** 2,800m (APDS), 2,200m (HEAT), 2,200m (APHE), 2,200m (Frag-HE) **Effective range** 1,080m (APHE), 900m (HEAT), 1,200–1,300m (APDS) **Max range (indirect fire)** 21,031m (Frag-HE) **Ammunition types** BM-6 HVAPDS, BR-412D/B APHE, BR-412P HVAP, BK-5M/4M HEAT, OF-412 Frag-HE, D-412 smoke **Muzzle velocity** 1,415m/sec (HVAPDS-T), 916m/sec (APHE), 900m/sec (HEAT), 900m/sec (Frag-HE) **Shell weight (projectile/round)** 5.7/21.1kg (HVAPDS-T), 15.9/29.9kg (APHE-T), 10.23/?kg (HVAP), 12.4/25.5kg (HEAT, BK-5M), 15.9/28.0kg (Frag-HE) **Ammunition load** 43 (34) rounds = 23 APHE or HVAPDS, 3 HEAT, 17 Frag-HE (approx 11 APHE, 3 HEAT, 20 Frag-HE) **Co-axial MG** 7.62mm PKT (SGMT) **AA MG** 12.7mm DShKM **Bow MG** None (7.62mm SGMT) **7.62mm ammunition** 3,500 rounds (5,000) **12.7mm ammunition** 500 rounds **Small-arms ammunition** 300 rounds **Hand grenades** 20 **Main gun elevation** −4°/+17° **Traverse** 360° **Turret mechanism** Electro-hydraulic (manual in early T-54) **Armour** 100mm @ 60° (hull front), 205mm rounded (turret front), 80mm @ 0° (hull side), 20mm @ 0° (lower hull side), 130mm

Basic T-54 of the US Army. (*US Army*)

A basic T-54 of the Syrian Army passes in review. The small hull machine-gun mount is visible below the fording splashplate.

rounded (turret side), 60mm @ 0° (hull rear), 60mm rounded (turret rear), 30mm (hull top), 30mm (turret top), 20mm (hull floor) **Crew** 4 **Radio** R-123, plus R-112 in company command tanks.

All figures for T-55A, retrofitted with AAMG. Where T-54 figures differ, they are in parentheses. There are variations between models and sub-types.

The T-54/55 series of main battle tanks has been in Soviet service for over 30 years, and it will doubtless soldier on into the 1980s. These tanks have been produced in large numbers – possibly over 100,000 of all versions – and have seen more combat than any other post-war tank series. Today, despite its simplicity, ruggedness and mobility, the T-54/55 series is at a disadvantage compared to more recent designs. They are cramped, often "brew up" if hit, have a springy suspension that creates crew fatigue, are tiring to drive, shed tracks and are prone to engine overheating. They lack air conditioning and are much less effective in desert conditions. The 100mm D-10-series gun

lacks long-range accuracy and armour penetration. Its rate of fire is low and its optics are inadequate except at close range. Many foreign users of the T-54/55 series are seeking to correct these deficiencies. The Soviets have also modified and retrofitted equipment to their T-54/55s so that, for all their limitations, they are still important and viable weapons systems.

Hull and turret

The T-54/55's hull is made of welded rolled steel plates and is divided by bulkheads into three compartments: driver, turret and engine/power train. The design minimises ballistic vulnerability. This is evident in the effective interlocking joint between the glacis and the nose plates and the "half-egg" turret, which replaced an unsatisfactory enlarged version of the T-44 turret that appeared on prototype and early production T-54s. All T-54/55 turrets have standard Soviet external rails for hand grips and storage.

While the turret design provides a low silhouette and good protection despite its relatively thin armour, it is cramped and reduces crew effectiveness. The T-54 has no turret basket, which means that the floor of the fighting

Above T-54 of the US Army. (*US Army*) *Below* T-55A tanks.

Identical to the standard T-54, this Chinese-made T-59 with a DShKM machine gun was captured by the South Vietnamese Army in 1972. (*US Air Force*)

compartment does not revolve with the turret. Ammunition stored in the hull may be inaccessible when the turret is rotated. Crewmen not in the leather seats suspended from the turret roof run the risk of being crushed by the rotating gun breech. Unlike Western practice, the gunner and commander sit on the left-hand side of the turret, almost in each other's laps. The loader sits on the right of the gun, which means he must not only seat and ram home 25kg shells with his left hand, but, once the three ready ammunition rounds stowed inside the turret wall have been expended, he must leave his seat, risking being crushed by the breech, to haul shells out of the storage racks in the hull, thus reducing the rate of fire. Spent shell brass is not ejected from the turret, and will be underfoot, making the loader's footing uncertain. The introduction of the turret basket and standard seats in the T-55 made loading the 100mm gun easier, but the gun still has to be elevated after each shot to give the loader room to extract the spent brass and reload, a time-consuming process, especially in early models which lacked power elevation.

The turret also contains the ready ammunition rounds and the radio, further reducing space. The T-54A and later versions also feature a fire-extinguisher system in all compartments similar to that on the T-62.

Engine and transmission

The transversely mounted engine is the V-54 in T-54s and the V-55 in T-55s. Both engines are water-cooled, 4-stroke, 12-cylinder 60° vee diesels with a capacity of 38.88 litres. The V-54 develops 520HP at 2,000rpm, while the V-55 produces 580HP at the same revolutions. Both engines are constructed largely of light metal. The block is of magnesium-aluminium alloy, which is light but vulnerable to fire. Soviet tank engines, especially those on the T-54/55s and earlier tanks, suffered from crude workmanship and finish, which caused stress cracks and resulted in high oil consumption, especially at high speeds. The Czech Army found that Soviet-built engines had a life of only 100 hours (instead of the 500 hours claimed) unless they were rebuilt upon delivery. Eight to ten ounces of metal filings have been removed from these engines after only 25 hours' running time. The interior oil lines are so rough that the flow is often blocked. This overstresses the pump, which often breaks down, causing the engine to overheat or seize from lack of oil, and, because of its magnesium alloy construction, many engine fires result. These consume the engine block, totally destroying the engine. Other less

A T-55A(M) of the US Army with 12.7mm machine gun and two searchlights but with the fording splashplate deleted. (*US Army*)

spectacular breakdowns are also common. The Czech Army attempted to overhaul these engines by replacing all bearings, smoothing and polishing all parts and replacing the failure-prone crankshaft. The intense engine vibration, which causes crew fatigue and stabilisation problems, was partially caused by the use of a transverse engine block with an integral gearbox, as this prevented the use of flexible mountings. The engine's exhaust is fitted with the same smoke generators as on the T-62, replacing two drum-like BDSh smoke dispensers mounted on the rear of early vehicles. The engine is normally started electrically, but a compressed-air system can be used in winter. The gearbox consists of five synchronised forward gears and one reverse. Steering is by a cross-drive system with a conventional clutch and brake. The transmission is relatively effective and simple, although clutch failure is a problem. The heavy manual gear shift requires fatiguing double clutching. Newer Czech and Polish-built T-55s reportedly have hydraulic or pneumatic control boost.

Suspension and tracks

T-54/55s have a Christie-type torsion-bar suspension with no support rollers and five dual road wheels per side, with a space between and first and second road wheels, an idler at the front and a drive sprocket at the rear. The first and fifth road wheels have hydraulic shock-absorbers. The tracks are wide (58cm), thick manganese steel dead track which, because they are not under tension, hang loosely and sag at the top. The track plates are held together with a single pin, although early T-54s embodied a primitive pinless system. The single-pin design has a short tread life and is quite noisy, but is 10–15% lighter than double-pin systems. All T-54/55s have a tendency to shed tracks.

Main armament

Developed from a naval gun during World War Two, the D-10 series of tank guns is identical to the BS-3 anti-tank and KS-19 anti-aircraft guns, and all fire the same fixed ammunition. All lack a muzzle brake and have horizontal sliding-wedge breech blocks, hydraulic recoil buffers, and hydropneumatic recuperators. The D-10T on the early T-54 has no stabilisation or bore evacuator and is used with the TSh 2-22 sight. The T-54A's D-10TG was stabilised in the vertical plane and had the TSh 2A-22 sight. The

D-10T2S on all subsequent versions is stabilised in two planes and is used with the TSh 2B-22 and TSh 2-32 sights.

The basic World War Two-vintage 100mm round was the BR-412 APHE (considered an AP-T round by some sources because of its small HE charge and tracer shoe). In the mid-1950s it was replaced by the BR-412B and BR-412D APHE/AP-T rounds with the DBR-2 base detonating fuze. While adequate in comparison with their foreign contemporaries, these rounds lacked penetration against more recent tanks. In 1968 the HVAPDS-T round was introduced, and became the main anti-tank ammunition. HEAT rounds were introduced in the 1950s. Soft targets are engaged with the OF-412 Frag-HE round. The Chinese and the Czechs have developed their own 100mm ammunition, and the Czech shells are reportedly superior to the equivalent Soviet rounds.

Optics

The T-54/55's optics are earlier versions of those used on the T-62. The commander's cupola-mounted TPK-1 binocular functions in the same way as the TKN-3 on the T-62. The gunner's telescope is similar in design and use to that on the T-62. As on the T-62, there is no mechanical rangefinder or ballistic computer. The searchlights are the same L-2G and OU-3GK used on the T-62, and they are stabilised on the T-55A and possibly on modernised earlier versions. Night vision ranges are 400m for the commander's TPK-1, 800m for the gunner and 40m for the driver, using their night vision devices.

Development

There are many different T-54/55 versions. Tanks are frequently modified from one configuration to another and retrofitted with new equipment, and it is often difficult to distinguish variants.

The original T-54 appeared in 1947. Developed from the T-44 by the Morozov design bureau, the T-54 combined heavy armament with high mobility. Series production began in 1949. These early production models had the same bulbous, undercut turret as the prototype and pre-production models. Few were built, but some remained in Soviet service in the early 1970s, while others supplied to the Syrian Army were used with little success against Jordan in 1970.

The basic T-54 features the half-egg turret with two cupolas and a plain gun tube. Like all T-54s (except the T-54[X]), it has a 12.7mm DShK machine gun on the right-hand cupola. When retrofitted with infra-red equipment this model is known as the T-54(M).

The T-54A first appeared in 1955 and introduced the bore evacuator on the gun tube, which appeared on all subsequent models. The gun was stabilised, though in the vertical plane only. The T-54A also introduced improved oil filters, an electrical oil pump, bilge pumps, automatic fire extinguishers, power elevation for the main gun, and provision for external fuel tanks. Tanks retrofitted with infra-red equipment are designated T-54A(M).

The T-54B, which appeared in 1957, was similar to the T-54A and introduced infra-red equipment, two-plane stabilisation for the D-10TS gun, and improved snorkels.

T-54-T armoured recovery vehicle extracting a T-62 from soft ground.

older 7.62mm SGMT co-axial machine gun was replaced by the newer PKT. The T-55A was produced in greater numbers than any other version in the series. The new machine guns and an NBC defence system, similar to that of the T-62, were retrofitted to many earlier tanks.

In addition to these versions, there is a plethora of minor variants and sub-types, a variety made almost limitless by equipment modification and retrofitting. This includes differences in lights, night optics, the fitting or absence of a bow splashplate, design of hatches, absence or presence of the 12.7mm gun, fuel tank arrangement, and many other items, none of which seriously affect the tank's performance.

The most important piece of new equipment fitted to the T-54/55 appears to be a combination laser rangefinder and target designator. First seen in 1977–78, these large, box-like structures mounted above the gun tube increase gun accuracy and allow the tank to guide laser-homing ATGMs.

Specialised versions include the T-54-T, the standard Soviet armoured recovery vehicle. It mounts a 1,000kg-capacity jib crane, a loading platform (but no winch), and a rear spade for heavy lifting on a T-54 chassis, and weighs 32,000kg. The MTU-54/55, M-1967 and MT-55 (Czech-built) bridgelayers are all based on the T-54/55 chassis. KMT-4 and -5 mine rollers, the BTU dozer blade and the STU snowplough are easily mounted on the T-54/55. The T-55 chassis was used for a number of AFVs, including the ZSU-57-2 and the SU-130, an assault gun armed with an M-46 130mm field gun. Only a handful of these vehicles, which looked like enlarged SU-100s and had large stereo-scopic rangefinders, saw service in the 1960s. There have been reports that some T-54/55s built for export have had thinner armour, but this has never been confirmed.

Foreign production

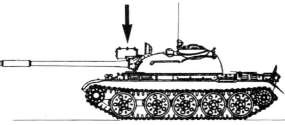

T-55 fitted with what is believed to be a laser rangefinder over the gun tube. *(Soldat & Technik)*

The T-54(X) or T-54C was the transition tank between the T-54 and T-55, its only external difference from the T-54B being that the right-hand cupola and machine gun were replaced with a simple hatch.

The T-55 was introduced in 1961 and can be distinguished from the T-54 by its lack of the bell-shaped turret dome ventilator and the right-hand cupola with its machine gun, although many tanks later received the 12.7mm machine gun. A more powerful engine, an improved transmission, a turret basket, and nine extra 100mm rounds increased the T-55's capabilities. The T-54's bow machine gun, fired by the driver, was dropped during T-55 production and was subsequently removed from many T-54s.

Introduced in 1963, the T-55A's raised hatch covers, different covering of the commander's cupola, and lack of bow machine gun indicated an internal anti-radiation lining. A PAZ NBC defence system was also fitted. The

Czech and Polish production started in the late 1950s. At first they duplicated the Soviet originals, but the rear deck design and storage box arrangements were soon modified. Czech-built machines have three curved plates mounted on each side of the hull to reduce the number of thrown tracks, and the Soviets and other nations are reportedly adopting this modification. All Polish T-55s mount a 12.7mm machine gun in the same way as on T-54s. Polish and Czech tanks exhibit a standard of workmanship superior to that of Soviet-built examples. Polish-built tanks are used by East Germany and Czech-built versions have been widely exported.

The T-59 is a simplified Chinese copy of the basic T-54. It retains all the outdated elements of that tank: no gun stabilisation, no snorkelling capability, no automatic fire extinguisher, no APDS round, and the commander cannot traverse the turret. Reliability and workmanship are reportedly even worse than on Soviet tanks. The T-62 and T-63

A flamethrower-armed T-55A at night. *(Soldat & Technik)*

Chinese light tanks are based on scaled-down versions of the T-59.

Many foreign users of T-54/55s have considered updating them with Western technology. Romania has approached several West German firms with plans to rebuild its tanks with a new Vickers-type suspension, a new track, diesel engine, and other components, although financial and political considerations seem to have halted the project. Romanian T-55s were seen in 1979 with armoured side skirts, a new 12.7mm anti-aircraft machine gun, and two additional rear cooling flaps for the engine. Bulgarian T-55s also have been fitted with the side skirts. Cost also postponed the Egyptian plan to refit their T-54/55s with the Vickers L7A1 105mm gun, a Yugoslav optical system and a Swedish laser rangefinder. Many Egyptian T-54/55s in 1973 had AEG-Telefunken infra-red searchlights. There have been reports that some Indian T-54/55s have received L7A1s as well. T-1967s or T1-67s are T-54/55s captured by Israel in 1967 and modified with a US-built Continental diesel engine, an L7A1 gun and Israeli machine guns. New radios, rangefinders, fire-control equipment, optics, electrical system, night-fighting equipment and air-conditioning were also fitted. The suspension was improved and the turret was internally rearranged to reduce vulnerability and increase crew efficiency. Despite these modifications the Israelis still do not consider the tank as effective as the M48/60 or Centurion, since many of the design's original flaws, including its

cramped interior, remain. A brigade of T-1967s under Col Gonen fought in Sinai in the 1973 war.

Weapons effectiveness and combat usage

Although the 100mm gun has been in service for over 35 years and the US Army has had test examples for years, accuracy data on the D-10 remain sparse and general, and hit probability estimates must be treated as being even more approximate than usual.

Ammunition	Range (metres)				
	500	1,000	1,500	2,000	2,500
BR-412 APC-T	90%	50%	33%	8%	4%
BK-5M HEAT	84%	43%	25%	2%	—

Soviet "textbook" estimates of the 100mm gun's accuracy are much higher. Theoretically, a gun using a BR-412B APHE round against a halted enemy tank 2.7m high and 3.6m long should have a 77% chance of hitting its target at 1,800m range. Actual accuracy would doubtless be much less in combat conditions. Maximum indirect-fire range requires a 28° slope.

Armour penetration data (mm at 0° obliquity) are better known:

Ammunition	Range (metres)			
	500	1,000	1,500	2,000
BR-412 APC-T	155	135	117	100
BM-6 HVAPDS	—	264	—	237
BK-5M HEAT	380mm at any range			
BR-412B APC-T	—	171	—	146
BR-412D APC-T	—	175	—	156

The probability of killing an M60A1 with a 100mm shell is about 50%, although this depends heavily on where the target tank is hit.

The T-54/55 has probably seen more combat than any other post-war tank. Soviet T-54/55s invaded Hungary in 1956, and were involved in at least one tank battle against Hungarian Czech-built T-34/85s. The Soviet T-54/55s that rolled into Czechoslovakia in 1968 were marked with white crosses for recognition in case the Czechs resisted. A few were lost to Molotov cocktails. Soviet T-54/55s have also clashed with Chinese forces.

The T-54/55 was the standard Arab main battle tank in both the 1967 and 1973 wars. In 1970 Syrian T-54s were

Soviet armour tactics stress all-weather operations. These T-55s are carrying ski troops.

trounced by Jordanian Centurions. In the Sudan T-54s were used in the long and bloody civil war. T-54/55s fought each other along the Trig Capuzzo and Hellfire Pass in the 1977 Egyptian-Libyan fighting. The Israelis used T-1967s in the 1973 war. The T-54/55 was a standard Indian tank in the 1971 war, and they were largely opposed by Pakistani T-59s. North Vietnamese T-54/55s were introduced into combat in 1972. Although defeated at the siege of An Loc, due largely to the failure of their supporting infantry, they were heavily engaged in the I and II Corps area. Although they suffered heavy losses to air strikes and could not always defeat South Vietnamese armour, they were extremely effective. Rumours of these big tanks panicked South Vietnamese troops throughout II Corps area in the 1972 offensive, and many of the North Vietnamese drives in I Corps area were spearheaded by T-54/55s, which served alongside T-59s. Using the lessons in armoured combat learned in the Laos invasion, the North Vietnamese emphasised tanks in their successful 1975 offensive, and later in their drive into Cambodia. Doubtless Vietnamese T-54/55s met Chinese T-59s in the 1979 fighting.

In Africa T-54/55s were standard Cuban and Angolan equipment in the Angola fighting. In the Ogaden war both sides were equipped with them. Tanzanian T-59s spearheaded the 1979 drive into Uganda, possibly opposed by Ugandan T-54s.

While their mobility and low silhouette are praised, the mechanical problems and poor crew accommodation and fighting ability are frequently criticised by all nations using these tanks. The armour and the gun seem to have elicited neither praise nor blame. The T-59 is not popular, especially amongst the Pakistanis, as it has all the drawbacks of the T-54/55. Its crude workmanship and lack of sophistication make it even more deficient, especially after in 1968 the Soviets introduced and exported the BM-6 HVADPS round, which was used by the Arabs in 1973 and the Indians in 1971. In that war, however, T-59s used APHE rounds.

Tactical employment

The T-54 and T-55 are still standard Soviet main battle tanks. They are still found in many Soviet units, especially the tank units in Category II and III motorised rifle units, and in at least some Category II (or I) tank divisions. They are also used as training tanks by many units which have later tanks in storage. T-54/55s are still used by the Naval Infantry, and are in front-line service throughout the world in forces including Warsaw Pact armies and North Korea.

Engagement sequence and Vulnerabilities and countermeasures

See T-62.

T-62As of the US Army. The tank in the foreground has its
12.7mm machine gun dismounted to protect it from dust when
travelling, a common Soviet practice. (US Army)

T-62 main battle tank

Combat weight 36.5 tons **Length (gun forward)** 9.335m
Length (gun rear) 9.068m **Height (without AAMG)**
2.395m **Width (overall)** 3.3m **Track** 2.64m **Clearance**
0.425m **Track width** 0.58m **Ground contact** 4.5m
Ground pressure 0.72kg/cm² **Max road speed** 50km/h
Fuel capacity (internal) 675 litres **Fuel capacity (external)** 285 litres **Fuel capacity (jettisonable rear drums)**
400 litres **Oil capacity (max)** 167 litres **Fuel consumption (paved roads)** 1.9–2.1 litres/km **Fuel consumption
(unpaved roads)** 3.0–3.3 litres/km **Oil consumption**
1.5–3.0 litres/h **Range (paved road)** 450km (without
extra tanks), 650km (with extra tanks) **Range (unpaved
road)** 320km (without extra tanks), 450km (with extra
tanks) **Travel speeds (1,800 rpm)** 14.5km/h (1st gear),
20km/h (2nd gear), 29km/h (3rd gear), 45.5km/h (4th
gear), 7km/h (5th gear) **Fording** 1.4m **Snorkelling** 5.5m
Gradient 38° **Generator/alternator** 1.5kW **Turning
circle (at 10–15km/h)** 8.8m **Vertical obstacle** 0.8m
Trench 2.85m **Horsepower/weight** 19.17HP/ton
Engine V-2-62, V-12 diesel, water-cooled, 580HP @
2,000rpm, 38,800cm³ **Transmission** Mechanical synchromesh, 5 forward, 1 reverse gears **Steering** 2-stage
planetary clutch and brake **Gun** 115mm U-5TS **Calibre
length** 55cal **Rate of fire (theoretical)** 7rpm **Rate of fire
(actual)** 4rpm **Max range** 4,000m (HVAPFSDS), 3,700m
(HEAT), 4,800m (Frag-HE 18), 3,600m (Frag-HE 11)
Effective range 1,500m (HVAPFSDS), 1,200m
(HEAT), 1,500–2,000m (HE) **Ammunition types** BR-5
HVAPFSDS, BK-4M HEAT, OF-18 Frag-HE, OF-11
Frag-HE **Muzzle velocity** 1,615+m/sec (HVAPFSDS),
1,000m/sec (HEAT), 780m/sec (OF-11 Frag-HE),
750m/sec (OF-18 Frag-HE) **Shell weights (projectile/
round)** 6.8/22.5kg (HVAPFSDS), 11.8/26.2kg (HEAT),
14.9/28.1kg (OF-11 Frag-HE), 17.7/30.6kg (OF-18
Frag-HE) **Ammunition load** 40 rounds = 14
HVAPFSDS, 7 HEAT, 19 Frag-HE **Co-axial MG**
7.62mm PKT **AA MG** 12.7mm DShKM (when fitted)
7.62mm ammunition 2,500 rounds **12.7mm ammunition** 500 rounds **Main gun elevation** −4°/+17° **Traverse**
360° **Turret mechanism** electro-hydraulic **Armour**
100mm @ 60° (200mm basis) (hull front), 170mm rounded

Above T-62 of the US Army advancing, showing external fuel tanks. *(US Army)*

Below A platoon of Soviet T-62s.

(200mm basis) (turret front), 80mm @ 0° (80mm basis) (hull side), 20mm @ 0° (20mm basis) (lower hull sides), 80mm rounded (120mm basis) (turret side), 60mm @ 0° (60mm basis) (hull rear), 40mm rounded (60mm basis) (turret rear), 20–30mm rounded (30mm basis) (turret top), 30mm horizontal (30mm basis) (hull top), 20mm horizontal (20mm basis) (hull floor) **Crew** 4 **Radio** R-123, plus R-112 in company command tanks

The T-62 is the standard main battle tank. Entering production in 1961–62, it predominated in Soviet armoured units throughout the 1970s and saw action in the 1973 Middle East war. Although it is being gradually supplanted by the T-64, T-72 and eventually the T-80, the T-62 will remain in front-line service throughout the 1980s.

The T-62 is basically an improved, upgunned T-55. Its hull is longer and wider, the turret is lower and more rounded, the road wheels are evenly spaced, and the commander's cupola is on the left, an integral part of the turret and not bolted on as it is on the T-55. The T-62 has no loader's cupola, just a hinged hatch. The tube of the 115mm U-5TS with its bore evacuator is longer and thicker than that of the 100mm D-10. Dust "rooster tails" behind advancing T-62s, caused by their engine blower, are another recognition feature.

The Israelis faced T-62s in the 1973 war and now use all the captured machines they did not sell to the US Army. They criticised its poor human engineering, the inaccuracy of the U-5TS at long range, and the lack of gun depression. They approved of its light weight and considered its protection, coupled with a low silhouette, adequate. The U-5TS is considered to be highly accurate, especially at 1,500m or less range. General "Bren" Adan, the Israeli tank commander, considers it better than the standard NATO L7A1 105mm tank gun.

Hull and turret

The T-62's hull is of all-welded, rolled steel construction, and the turret is a one-piece casting. Most Soviet tank armour is standard homogeneous steel. For thicknesses less than 50mm, the Soviets use chrome-manganese-silicon steels. Heat-treated to high hardness levels, they tend to exhibit brittle failure after impact. The hull is divided by bulkheads into driver's, turret, engine and power-train compartments. There is an escape hatch in the hull floor behind the driver's seat. The driver's compartment in the left front of the hull contains the driving controls and instruments, including steering laterals, a clutch pedal, brake/accelerator, manual throttle handle, fuel tank selector switch, master switch, and many gauges and indicators. The V-2-62 engine is basically an improved version of the V-55, and shares its characteristics. The power-train compartment contains the master clutch, the five forward, one reverse-speed manual transmission, steering clutch, and final drive. Clutch operation is air-assisted,

T-62 tank commander's OU-3GK searchlight, with cover fitted.

L-2G searchlight with a protective lens cover, mounted on a T-62.

reducing the effort in shifting gears and clutch wear, though both are considerable. Clutch failure causes 40% of all T-62 breakdowns that are not repairable on the spot. The clutch is basically the conventional steel-to-steel multidisc design used in earlier tanks. Before the air-assist feature was added in late-production T-55s, driver abuse created even more failures. In addition, the T-62 does not handle well at speeds of 20–25mph (32–40km/h); it is described as being "sloppy" at these speeds.

There is little ventilation in the driver's compartment, and driving the T-62 (or T-54/55) is very fatiguing, using the two laterals for steering and double clutching for the five forward and one reverse gears. US Army tests have found that in a moderately warm climate, heat build-up and fatigue cause driver performance to deteriorate after 30–45min. The effect of desert conditions can best be imagined. If the driver's hatch is left open, a safety switch prevents the turret from rotating. The cramped conditions, the high level of vibration and the springy ride caused by the suspension soon degrade the performance of even the small and hardy Soviet tankmen. The human engineering of the T-62, like that of the T-54/55, is very bad, being exemplified by the loader having to use his left hand in loading the gun and by the driver's lack of ventilation. Throughout Soviet tanks, all the many switches and projections are placed so that the crew cannot avoid hitting against them, especially when the tank is moving at high speed, adding cuts and bruises to their problems. Spinal and kidney damage is also frequent. In the 1973 War numbers of Arab tankmen were affected by these conditions, and some were asphyxiated or went into shock.

A fire-extinguisher system can be triggered manually or automatically by one of eight heat sensors. However, the fire extinguisher's ethylene bromide gas is highly poisonous; if the extinguisher discharges, the crew must bail out at once. Any weapon that can trigger the extinguisher system by creating heat – such as a Molotov cocktail on the engine decking – can knock out a T-62.

Suspension and tracks

The T-62 has a torsion-bar Christie-type suspension with shock-absorbers on the first and last of the five dual-rubber-tyre road wheels on each side, along with a com-pensating idler and a rear drive sprocket. The dead track is wide, thick, and made of relatively wear-resistant cast manganese steel. The track pins are not secured at their outer ends, and are free to travel towards the hull. The pin hammer, a raised metal projection on the hull forward of the sprocket, drives the pin back in each time it passes. The centre guides of the tracks ride between the dual road wheels. Despite all these safeguards, the T-62 still frequently throws tracks. Vibration at high speeds, quick turns, and going into reverse all cause track throws, and mud caking around components compounds the problem. Although the T-62 has been widely reported to be prone to throwing tracks during high-speed turns, tests on US Army T-62s, which included hundreds of such manoeuvres on hard and soft surfaces with varying track tensions, show that these reports were not valid. It has been reported that T-62s may receive track-retaining plates as used on Czech T-55s. Track pitch is 175mm, and there are 74 shoes per track.

Soviet dead tank track is simple (the track blocks pivot around a single metal pin) and inexpensive, but loud and easily worn out due to the metal-to-metal contact of track blocks without the rubber bushing of US-style live tank track. Track life on paved roads is estimated at approxi-

A T-62-T (M-1977) armoured recovery vehicle in Moscow in 1977. The marks on its glacis plate suggest that it was converted from a self-propelled 125mm or 130mm assault gun mount. *(US Army)*

mately 2,500km, after which it may be overhauled and used for another 2,500km. This applies to all Soviet tracked vehicles, not just to T-62s.

Development

The T-62A appeared around 1970 and differed from the standard T-62 only in having the loader's hatch assembly redesigned to accommodate a 12.7mm DShKM machine gun. T-62s were retrofitted with this weapon at the same time. The T-62M, which appeared in the late 1970s, is a T-62A with the drive sprocket and track of the T-72. The T-62K is a command tank version, used by battalion and higher-level tank commanders. It has reduced (32 round) ammunition storage, an auxiliary generator, additional radios and a TNA-3 land navigation system. The T-62-T is an armoured recovery vehicle version. A few assault guns with 130mm or larger guns were constructed on the T-62 chassis. These did not prove a success and were converted into T-62-Ts.

According to unconfirmed reports, however, the Soviets have not abandoned the idea of a self-propelled assault gun on a T-62 chassis. Reports from British sources have assigned the codenames "Rapier-2" and "Rapier-3" to assault gun versions mounting the same 125mm gun as on the T-64/72/80. None of these weapons has yet been seen, nor has their existence been confirmed.

Armament

The T-62's 115mm smooth-bore U-5TS (2A20) gun fires the BR-5 HVAPFSDS, BK-4M HEAT, and OF-18 and OF-11 Frag-HE rounds. The BR-5's steel penetrator uses fins, as the sabot falls away, to give it stability in the absence of the spin stabilisation of projectiles from rifled guns. The BR-6 has a muzzle velocity of 1,615m/sec, more than four times the speed of sound, giving it a flat trajectory but also making it too fast for the eye to follow in flight; this makes it difficult to correct aim. The penetrator's fins have a tendency to "weather-vane" in a crosswind at long range. The smooth-bore gun, in addition to having high muzzle velocity, weighs less and has a longer barrel life and less recoil than rifled weapons. The West is now moving to adopt smooth-bores almost 20 years after the Soviets did so as an answer to the M60A1, Leopard I and Chieftain.

The U-5TS is optimised for short-range accuracy, as most tank actions take place at short range and Soviet gunners would probably not be proficient enough to take advantage of long-range accuracy. Defending tanks normally hold their fire until 1,500m range, and long-range targets are engaged by selected gunners or, more often, platoon volleys. A basic stadia reticle is therefore adequate for rangefinding, while aiming is through a graduated telescope. The provision of the same combination laser rangefinder and target designator used on T-54/55s and its

associated ballistic computer is now increasing the U-5TS's accuracy, especially at long range. The T-62's improved stabilisation also increases armament efficiency, but the Soviets still fire from the short halt rather than on the move. Despite its two types of Frag-HE round, the U-5TS is intended to destroy tanks, and unarmoured targets (such as ATGM teams) will be left to accompanying SAU-122s whenever possible.

Despite its technical excellence, the U-5TS has a number of drawbacks. The turret tends to fill with carbon monoxide in action, despite the provision of a bore evacuator to remove fumes. Another problem, apparently not infrequent, occurs when the automatic cartridge ejector does not align properly with the ejection port, which often happens after high-speed vibration has disturbed the mounting. The spent brass then rebounds off the turret wall and ricochets at high speed around the cramped turret interior. The tank commander has been provided with a shield against being struck; the other crew members are not so fortunate. Although the official rate of fire of the U-5TS is seven rounds a minute, US Army tests show that the actual maximum rate of fire, aiming from a standstill, is four rounds per minute. Ammunition accessibility also affects rate of fire. Owing to safety and space constraints, only two rounds are stored in the turret ready rack. Single additional rounds are located near the gunner's and loader's feet, and the remaining 36 rounds are stored in the hull.

Optics

The commander has five, the driver two, and the loader and gunner one each of the standard 1×-power TNP-165 vision block, replaceable from the inside in case of damage.

The commander uses a TKN-3 binocular vision device, as fitted on the BMP. Mounted in the cupola, it rotates for all-around search, rangefinding (using the range stadia) and gunlaying, using turret traverse controls. It cannot be used for rangefinding at night – the gunner must perform that function – but it can be used with the OU-3GK commander's searchlight, which is mounted co-axially with it and can give white or infra-red light at a range of up to 400m. The TKN-3's night range is 800m at 4.2× and an 8° field of view, compared to 5× and a 10° field of view by day.

The gunner's TSh2B-41u has a large wrap-round headrest for use when the tank is moving. It includes a stadiametric rangefinder and five elevation reticles. Daytime magnification is 7× with a 9° field of vision, while at night it has 3.5× magnification and an 18° field of vision. A 5.5× TPN-1-41-11 infra-red monocular periscope with a 6° field of vision is used with the main searchlight for night gunnery, and allows firing up to 800m. It is being replaced with the 900m-range IPN-22MI. These optical systems, like many Soviet night optics, can detect enemy infra-red emissions.

The main 200-watt L-2G searchlight, mounted to the right of the main gun, can emit either white or infra-red light by means of filters, and has an infra-red range of 800m. It is currently being replaced with a newer model.

The loader's MK-4S periscope, fixed in the turret roof, has a 25° field of vision ahead and 16° to the rear. The driver has a TVN-2 or -3 active infra-red driving periscope with a range of 40–60m.

Snorkelling

All Soviet main battle tanks can use either the thin OPVT combat snorkel with attached periscope that is stowed on the tank, or a thick training snorkel that doubles as an escape trunk. Complete preparation for snorkelling can take from 90min to eight hours, and includes packing the turret ring with grease to ensure watertightness. Final preparation, including erecting the snorkel, is performed 2,000–5,000m from the river and takes 15–30min. The second echelon of an attacking tank unit will be prepared for snorkelling when a river crossing is anticipated, and will pass through the first echelon in order to cross. Tanks cannot fight when prepared for snorkelling, as the barrel is sealed and the turret locked. On emerging, the gun may

A T-62 with a narrow "combat" snorkel. (V.M. Martinova)

T-62s snorkelling. (Chris Foss)

be fired and the snorkel jettisoned, but the turret cannot traverse until the grease is removed. The Soviets will ferry tanks or use bridges whenever possible. It is often difficult to find a suitable snorkel site, as the technique requires a solid, flat bottom no deeper than 5.5m and a current of less than 3m/sec. A bilge pump with a capacity of 100litres/min is fitted, and a prominent splashboard in front of the glacis prevents water rushing up the hull. Tanks snorkel in single file at 2km/h, so snorkelling attacks are hardly practical. Tanks can snorkel for a maximum of 1,000m.

NBC protection

The T-62's PAZ NBC defence system is activated either manually or automatically when the RBZ-1m gamma sensor detects the initial pulse of radiation that precedes a nuclear blast, and automatically shuts all openings to the tank and cuts off the engine to alert the crew. The T-62 has a protective anti-radiation lining; hermetic sealing of the combat and driver's compartments protects the crew from shock waves, and air purification and slight overpressure protect against radioactive dust by passing incoming air through a centrifugal blower and dust separator. External rubber parts are protected with asbestos against the heat of a nuclear blast. However, the T-62 is not completely airtight unless it receives the full eight-hour waterproofing treatment, and using the gun would break the seal. The

filter has no protection against airborne chemical or biological contaminants, so individual NBC suits will have to be worn. Despite this, the Soviets believe that the NBC protection of their tanks will allow them to cross radioactive areas and exploit the use of NBC weapons. Exported T-62s have the active elements of the PAZ system removed, but they retain the internal plastic and lead anti-radiation lining.

Smoke

The T-62 is fitted with standard Soviet thermal smoke-generating equipment. A switch on the driver's panel injects raw diesel fuel into the hot engine exhausts. This creates a dense, white, opaque smoke screen 250–400m long that lasts for two to four minutes, consuming ten litres of fuel per minute for up to ten minutes non-stop; any longer would flood the engine. Tanks moving at up to 30km/h can use this to screen following troops, or a stationary tank can use it to fake its destruction. The commander of the Israeli 188th Armoured Brigade was killed in 1973 by a T-62 that apparently used this stratagem.

Cold-weather operations

Soviet tank heaters are efficient, and reportedly can be used while buttoned up. Soviet tank engines must be warmed up for at least ten minutes in cold weather. If cold

A US Army T-62 demonstrates the ability to make a smokescreen from its exhausts. This capability is common on many Soviet AFVs. *(US Army)*

inhibits a battery start, a compressed-air system can be used, so Soviet tanks operating in cold weather do not have to break noise discipline by warming up their engines in the middle of the night, unlike US tanks. A pre-heater is provided to prevent the diesel fuel from solidifying at low temperatures. Soviet tanks can move over ice 0.72m or more thick, and operate normally in snow 0.5m or less deep.

Land navigation systems

The T-62K's TNA-3 system, introduced in 1973, includes a gyrocompass, one or two compass indicators, a latitude correction device, an odometer, a power converter and a calculator.

The gyrocompass and indicators (one each for the driver and commander) give the tank's azimuth corrected for latitude. The odometer gives distance travelled in metres and the calculator displays the grid co-ordinates, calculated from those entered as the starting point, thus allowing continuous en route readout of the tank's location. It can also give distance and azimuth to a predetermined objective. Yielding 90% accuracy and giving locations to the nearest ten metres, the TNA-3 must be reset every 90min, although a correction setting can adjust for terrain. Warm-up time is 15min, and moving the vehicle during that time will damage the system. The TNA-3 is a simple, rugged system that requires little attention. Standard T-62s use the GPK-59 gyrocompass, chiefly for snorkelling, in place of the earlier GPK-58 also mounted in T-55s. The GPK-48 was accurate for only 15min at a time, while the GPK-59 is accurate for 90min. Both have a warm-up time, but the only datum they require is initial heading.

Weapons effectiveness and combat usage

The US Army obtained many T-62s from Israel after the 1973 war and so has been able to test its effectiveness, both theoretically and in the field. According to these tests and studies, the probability of a stationary T-62 hitting an M60A1-size target is:

Moving targets are assumed to be at 24km/h at a 30° angle to the T-62. Second rounds on target assume a first-round hit. If an M60A1 is hit, a BR-5 round has a 71% kill probability and a BK-4M has a 75% kill probability. Figures using a laser rangefinder are unofficial estimates based on Western equipment.

Armour penetration (BR-5 HVAPFSDS, 0° obliquity):

Range (m)	500	1,000	1,500	2,000	2,500	3,000
Armour (mm)	350	300	285	270	245	215

Armour penetration (BK-4M HEAT): 432mm regardless of range.
All figures assume steel armour at 0° incidence.

U-5TS accuracy reportedly deteriorates in sustained combat due either to the effects of a hot barrel on the shells or fouling due to incomplete combustion in the chamber.

The T-62 cannot fire as quickly as many comparable Western tanks. This is not compensated for by its accuracy or armour penetration. Even in the 1973 War, fought in vast open spaces, the average engagement range was between 300 and 800m. The mean range of engagement varies from 500m in Southern Germany to 700m in North-west Europe and 1,100m in North African-type desert. At these ranges any modern battle tank can hit and knock out any other modern main battle tank. The advantage belongs to the tank which fires first, much as it did throughout World War Two. Many tank battles, like Western gunfights, are basically "quick draw" situations. Despite this, the Israelis are reportedly satisfied with the U-5TS and consider it capable of first-round kills at up to 4,000m range. There are reports that the Israelis have decided not to replace the U-5TS with the L7A1 in the 150 T-62 tanks added to the Israeli Army.

Both Egypt and Syria used T-62s in 1973, and they constituted a higher percentage of Syrian tank strength than Egyptian. Syrian T-62s fared little better than T-54/55s. Although they inflicted heavy losses on the

Ammunition	Shot at target	Range-finder	Target	Range (metres)					
				500	1,000	1,500	2,000	2,500	3,000
BR-5 HVAPFSDS	1st	stadia	static	98%	79%	50%	27%	14%	8%
BR-5 HVAPFSDS	2nd	stadia	static	98%	84%	66%	51%	40%	32%
BR-5 HVAPFSDS	1st	laser	static	98%	86%	60%	43%	20%	10%
BR-5 HVAPFSDS	1st	stadia	moving	94%	75%	33%	19%	8%	nil
BK-4M HEAT	1st	stadia	static	89%	69%	33%	11%	3%	3%
BK-4M HEAT	1st	stadia	moving	75%	30%	5%	nil	nil	nil

Israeli 188th Armoured Brigade, they shared the fate of the rest of the Syrian armour in the "Valley of Tears." The Israelis obtained most of the T-62s used by themselves and by the US from tanks knocked out or abandoned at this stage of the fighting. Later in the campaign, Syrian T-62s were prominent in the defence of Ssassa against Israeli armour. The Egyptians used their T-62s in independent armoured brigades, although some served in armoured divisions. The T-62-equipped 25th Armoured Brigade, hurrying north to the Battle of the Chinese Farm, was annihilated in an Israeli ambush. Other Arab units also failed to use the tank to its full potential. Soviet T-62s went into Czechoslovakia in 1968 and have been in border clashes with the Chinese, who have captured at least two knocked-out T-62s.

Tactical employment

The T-62 equips most of the tank units in the Soviet Army. Each tank division in Group of Soviet Forces Germany still has one or two T-62-equipped regiments, and T-62s serve as training tanks in T-64/72-equipped units. Although T-54/55s remain, especially in lower-readiness units, many T-62s will doubtlessly replace them there as they, in turn, are replaced in Category I units by T-64/72s.

Engagement sequence

The engagement sequence for the T-62 is similar to that used on all gun-armed Soviet AFVs without laser rangefinders. The commander searches for targets with his TKN-3 target designator sight, rotating the cupola, while the gunner uses his rotating MK-4 periscope to search from the other side of the tank. The driver and loader watch to the front. Anyone spotting a target gives its bearing over the intercom, and the commander or gunner can then traverse the turret in that direction, although there must be a round in the tube and the safety must be depressed to the "fire" position for the turret power traverse to be used. If the tank commander is going to traverse the turret, he announces "override, right" (or left) over the intercom and depresses the override button on the TKN-3's left handgrip until the gunner announces "identified", when the traverse brings the target into his TSh2B-41u sight picture. Although the tank commander can traverse the gun, he cannot fire or elevate it.

The tank commander normally determines the range. If the target is approximately 2.7m high (about the height of an M60A1 tank), he can use the rangefinding stadia on the TKN-3, simply seeing which of the graticules – numbered with the range in hundreds of metres – and the baseline bracket the target. If the target's height is sub-

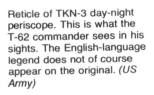

Reticle of TKN-3 day-night periscope. This is what the T-62 commander sees in his sights. The English-language legend does not of course appear on the original. *(US Army)*

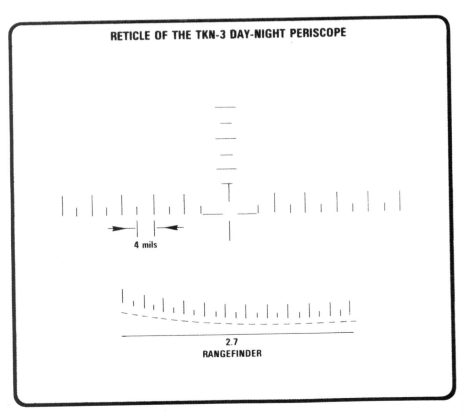

RETICLE OF THE TKN-3 DAY-NIGHT PERISCOPE

4 mils

2.7
RANGEFINDER

stantially different from 2.7m (such as a hull-down tank), the commander must use the 4-mil azimuth scale and a simple formula to determine range. If the tank commander cannot determine the range, the gunner will use the TSh2B-41u telescope's stadia rangefinder or the lateral lead and azimuth lines and the rangefinding formula.

Once the range has been determined the commander gives the firing command, including ammunition to be fired, target type, range, and direction. The gunner then elevates the gun. A black horizontal range line on the TSh2B-41u indicates the elevation, and this is adjusted to coincide with the correct range line – also numbered in hundreds of metres – on one of the five range scales for five different ammunition types. This automatically gives the gun the correct elevation. Because of the flat trajectory of the BR-5 HVAPFSDS round, he will not have to set elevation for this shell at ranges of under 1,500m. If the gun is not yet loaded, the loader is then ordered to load the proper round and depress the safety to the "fire" position. The gunner will then track the target using his power controls, either centring the aiming point on a stationary target or using the sight's lead lines to lead a moving target. He then selects the main gun switch, which also turns on the automatic shell extraction, and announces "ready."

The tank commander orders "fire." The gunner presses the electrical trigger on the right handgrip of his controls or, alternatively, the manual triggers on the elevation handcrank or the gun itself. The gun fires and, upon recoil, the breech opens and ejects the spent shell casing into the automatic ejection tray, where it is seized by grippers. The ejection tray elevates, the ejection port hatch in the rear of the turret opens, and the ejector propels the casing at great speed through the open port, which then closes. Meanwhile, the gun has automatically gone to between two and five degrees elevation to facilitate reloading. The loader then reaches his left hand behind him for a shell in the ready ammunition rack, guides it halfway into the breech and then seats it with a vigorous shove, snatching his hand away from the rapidly closing horizontal sliding breech. Throughout the loading process the gun is elevated and all power operation is automatically cut off until the loader has chambered the round and depressed the safety to "fire." This means that the gunner cannot traverse the gun to follow a moving target while reloading. After the gunner depresses the safety, the gun will, if the stabilisers are engaged, automatically return to its previous firing position.

Reticle of the TSh2B-41u telescope. This is the scope picture the T-62's gunner sees. The English-language legends do not of course appear on the originals, but the Russian-language legends and the numerals all do. *(US Army)*

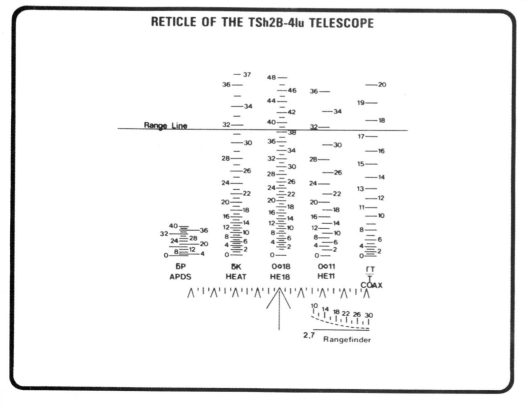

RETICLE OF THE TSh2B-4lu TELESCOPE

Visual and weapons deadspace
from Soviet tanks. (US Army)

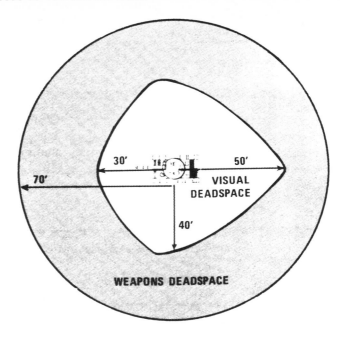

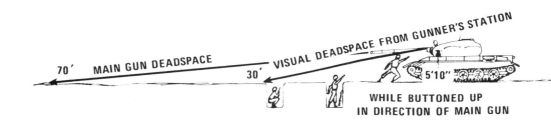

Vulnerabilities and countermeasures

T-62s and T-54/55s have driver, commander and gunner all lined up on the left side of the tank, and a single penetration can hit them all. Internal arrangement of shells and fuel and the absence of protection for either leads to many brew-ups even after non-penetrating hits. The main internal fuel tank is forward of the engine, while other fuel tanks – one in the T-54/55 and two in the T-62 – are in the right front of the hull, with ammunition storage in sleeves going into the fuel tank (i.e., ammunition surrounded by fuel!). Two large, jettisonable 200-litre fuel tanks, feeding directly into the fuel system, are mounted on all Soviet tanks after the T-54A. Fuel panniers are also mounted externally on the fenders. The T-62 mounts three 95-litre panniers on the right fender, along with a small oil tank. This fuel tank arrangement is not however as disastrous as it might seem. Soviet diesel fuel – the equivalent of US diesel No 2 – has a high flashpoint.

US Army tests show that white phosphorus shells will not detonate externally stored Soviet diesel fuel.

Nevertheless, photos from all over the world of burnt-out hulks of Soviet tanks testify to their vulnerability. The internal finish and component arrangement of Soviet tanks both promote spalling and make them vulnerable to its effects.

T-64 and T-72 main battle tanks

Combat weight 38 (41) tons **Length (gun forward)** 9.02m (9.24) **Length (hull only)** 6.35m (6.95) **Height** 2.265m (2.37) **Width** 3.375m **Track** 2.7m **Clearance** 0.37m (0.42) **Track width** 0.58m **Ground contact** 4.15m (4.26m) **Ground pressure** 0.72kg/cm² (0.79kg/cm²) **Max road speed** 60–70km/hr (60–80) **Range (paved road)** 500km (without extra tanks), 720km (with extra tanks) **Fording** 1.4m **Vertical obstacle** 0.8m **Gradient** 30° **Transmission** Synchromesh hydraulically assisted, 7 forward, 1 reverse gears **Steering** Clutch and brake **Snorkelling** 5.5m **Trench** 2.8m **Engine** Water-cooled diesel, probably V-12; T-64 engine probably approx 700–750HP, T-72 engine probably approx 780HP,

T-72 of a Guards unit in Moscow, November 1977. The gun barrel is locked in travelling position and the insulated thermal sleeve is apparent on the gun tube. *(US Army)*

though as much as 1,000HP has been suggested **Gun** 125mm **Rate of fire (theoretical)** 6–8rpm **Rate of fire (actual)** 4rpm (est) **Rate of fire (manual)** 2+rpm (est) **Effective range** c 2,000m (HVAPCFSDS), c 1,500m (HEAT) **Ammunition types** HVAPFSDS (possibly HVAPCFSDS), HEAT, Frag-HE-FS **Ammunition load** 40 rounds = 12 HVAPCFSDS, 6 HEAT, 22 Frag-HE-FS, 28 of which in auto-loader **Co-axial MG** 7.62mm PKT **AA MG** 12.7mm **Gun traverse** 360° **Armour** 200–210mm (220–240) basis (combined armour used on the front of at least some late-production versions) **Crew** 3

Figures in brackets are for T-72 where they differ from T-64 data.

"The T-72 ends, at least temporarily, our qualitative advantage in tanks. The Soviets now have technical as well as numerical superiority in main battle tanks." – Brigadier General Richard D. Lawrence, US Army.

The T-64/72 series is the result of 30 years of Soviet tank development combined with the latest weapons technology. For all their simplicity, Soviet tanks have always been amongst the finest in the world, but the T-64/72 series has introduced a new level of technical sophistication: laser rangefinders and autoloaders are still only in limited service even in NATO. The Western edge in tank optics, fire control and long-range accuracy, so long counted upon to redress Soviet numerical superiority, has been undercut, if it still exists at all.

The evolutionary link between the T-62 and the T-64/72 was the T-67, which abandoned the Christie-type suspension for a system with return rollers but retained the T-62's gun and turret, increasing long-range firepower by mounting a Sagger ATGM over the gun tube. The T-67 never entered production, possibly because it represented too limited an advance over the T-62.

The T-67 led to the M-1970 with an enlarged turret and 125mm gun, improved suspension and, apparently, a new engine. Some reportedly mounted a Sagger over the gun tube. The M-1970 was the prototype for the T-64 and

French officers inspecting a T-72. The integral bulldozer blade is lowered and the sprung skirt plates are apparent. Different ammunition types are displayed on the glacis.

T-72. Reportedly, one Soviet division had to leave one of its regiments behind during the 1968 invasion of Czechoslovakia because it was evaluating new tanks, probably M-1970s. The T-64 entered service with two regiments in Russia in 1973–74, arriving in East Germany in 1975, and was variously known to Western sources as the T-64, T-70 and T-72. The T-72, once called the T-72B in the West (the T-64 was thought to be the T-72A), was introduced by 1975, possibly earlier, and was first paraded in 1977. While the two tanks are technically similar and operationally identical, they are two distinct vehicles. The Soviets have normally avoided using two types of tank where one will suffice, so this change of policy is significant. The two tanks were probably developed in parallel by two separate design bureaux. One may eventually eclipse the other in production and service. The production and service pattern suggests that one of the tanks may have experienced some technical problems and the other was emphasised as a result until the problems could be resolved. Annual production of T-64/72-series tanks in 1979 was estimated at 2,600 units.

Hull and turret

The T-64/72's one-piece cast turret and all-welded steel hull with a rectangular cross-section are similar to those of earlier tanks. It appears to retain the three compartments of the T-62, although the driver has been moved to the centre of the glacis from the left-hand side, and his hatch is protected from rushing water by fording plates.

The turret is smaller and the silhouette lower than on the T-62, because the turret contains only two men, the commander and the gunner, the loader being replaced by the autoloader. The commander sits on the right and the gunner on the left, allowing the gunner to load rounds with his right hand if manual operation is required. Soviet tankmen cannot exceed 5ft 6in, but the small turret of the T-64/72 has led to their crews being no more than 5ft to 5ft 4in tall.

T-64/72s have better protection than the T-62. Glacis slope has increased, and the armour on the T-72 is reportedly up to 20% thicker in places than that of the T-62. Armour weight increased by 500–1,000kg over the T-62. But the armour is even more effective than these numbers can suggest. It has now been conceded that the US-built TOW and Dragon ATGMs, the mainstay of NATO's anti-tank defence, cannot penetrate the frontal armour of T-64/72s. Dmitri Ustinov, the Soviet Minister of Defence, has confirmed this, telling the Austrian Defence Minister: "Our tanks are invulnerable to ATGMs." Dr Perry Pierre, Assistant Secretary of the US Army, stated in 1979 that the T-64/72 has "at least first-generation advanced armour," including spaced armour and new metallurgical techniques. Called "combined armour" by the Soviets, it is apparently different from the British-designed Chobham armour, for the tanks lack the slab sides associated with Chobham armour. The Soviets have been working on "combined armour" since 1961, and it has apparently borne fruit in these tanks. NBC protection is reportedly also increased, to the point where the tanks are considered "mobile reactor shields". They are reportedly lined with 2–3cm of lead-based foam which limits the effects of neutron radiation and electromagnetic pulse. Both the T-64 and the T-72 can mount four 6mm-thick armoured skirting plates attached to the side to protect the suspension against small HEAT warheads and fragments. They are hinged to brush past obstacles and to give a greater degree of stand-off against rounds impacting from the front.

Suspension, tracks and engine

New suspension, tracks and engine have increased mobility. The suspension is of Vickers type, with smaller road wheels and return rollers. The engine is apparently a new design and a break with the standard Soviet tank engine dating back to the 1930s, although it is also a lightweight, water-cooled diesel. The T-64 and T-72 use different, transversely mounted models of this engine. Estimates of its output usually range from 750 to over 940 brake horsepower (although some sources think these figures are much too low, and that up to 1,200BHP, yielding a 100km/h road speed, might be attainable), and it is possible that the T-64 engine has an output at the lower end of this range and the T-72 at the higher end. The track is live, articulated in a double axis with rubber track shoes and single track pins. Controls are power-assisted, and unconfirmed reports have suggested that the tanks have automatic transmission, though this seems unlikely. The new mobility systems have not only increased both road and cross-country speed, but have apparently also reduced the vibration and track-shedding that plagued earlier tanks. Unlike the underpowered T-62, T-64/72s can keep up with BMPs moving cross-country.

Armament

The 125mm tank gun is an enlarged and improved version of the U-5TS, retaining its characteristics of high velocity and flat trajectory. A bore evacuator is positioned a third of the way down the barrel.

The ammunition consists of HVAPFSDS, HEAT and Frag-HE rounds. The HVAPFSDS round reportedly uses a "secondary cartridge" which functions as an in-barrel

T-72 with machine gun removed, showing the snorkel storage and the various attachments for mine ploughs and rollers on the glacis. *(US Army)*

booster rocket. Photographs of this round show what may be provision for a Makarov ballistic cap, making it an HVAPCFSDS round. The tungsten carbide penetrator appears to have a length–diameter ratio of about 12:1 and a diameter of about 40% of the calibre. It has been suggested that the greater size gives an increase in performance above that attributable to size alone. The cartridges appear to be of the semi-combustible type, leaving

T-64, showing snorkel and equipment storage. The machine gun, which is covered in canvas, is reported to be the new NSVT 12.7mm, or possibly a 14.5mm weapon. *(US Army)*

Right Differences between the T-64 and T-72. *(US Army)*

a large brass stub cartridge which possibly avoids the problems of carbon monoxide exhaust, case disintegration and the risk of a secondary explosion that the US found when using such cartridges.

The autoloader, based on that of the BMP, consists of two circular clips at the base of the turret basket, each clip probably containing different ammunition types. Totals of 12 HVAPCFSDS, 6 HEAT and 22 Frag-HE rounds are carried, although only four rounds are in the ready position by the breech.

The gun automatically elevates to load, as on the BMP, and the autoloader aligns a shell and a charge with the breech by using grippers. A power rammer then loads them into the automatically operating horizontal sliding breech. According to several reports, however, this does not always work as it should. Allegedly the loading system even has a tendency to grab the gunner and attempt to load *him* into the breech. In the words of one US Army

officer: "We believe this is how the Soviet Army chorus gets its soprano section". (As the gun elevates to load, like that on the BMP, ill-fitting tank suit trousers would be likely to get caught in the mechanism as well, with predictable results.) If this is the case, then modifications to the protective gun cage may prevent such accidents, although the cramped turret space and the problems of the BMP loader (which will load the gunner's arm if given the opportunity) may make this difficult. Whatever the veracity of this report, it is known that T-64/72 tanks in Group Soviet Forces Germany were not, as of 1979, using the autoloader and that it did "eat" crewmen. The gunner had to load both shell and cartridge by hand, greatly reducing the rate of fire. Poor human engineering may have seriously undercut the combat power of these tanks.

These tanks have a further improvement on the T-62 in that the commander can elevate and fire all weapons from his position.

T-64

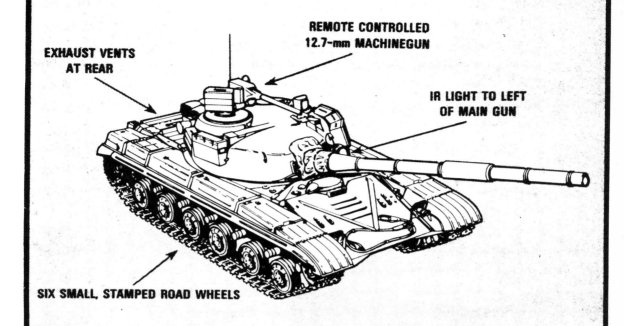

EXHAUST VENTS AT REAR

REMOTE CONTROLLED 12.7-mm MACHINEGUN

IR LIGHT TO LEFT OF MAIN GUN

SIX SMALL, STAMPED ROAD WHEELS

T-72

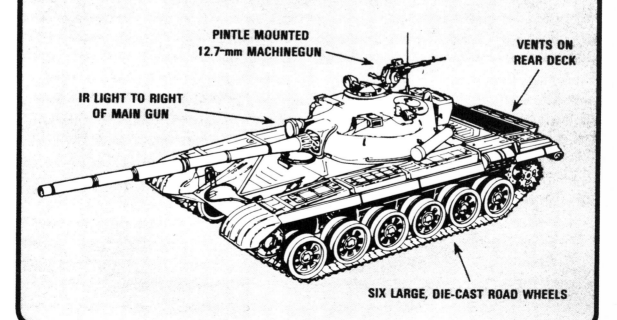

PINTLE MOUNTED 12.7-mm MACHINEGUN

VENTS ON REAR DECK

IR LIGHT TO RIGHT OF MAIN GUN

SIX LARGE, DIE-CAST ROAD WHEELS

Optics

The fire-control system on the T-64/72 is probably based around a laser rangefinder, with a coincidence rangefinder to check on laser measurements as required, as on the Leopard 2. The laser rangefinder can detect enemy laser designators, and finds their approximate bearing by rotating the turret. A stadiametric rangefinder, similar to that on earlier tanks, may serve as a back-up. An analogue ballistic computer linked to the gun converts the rangefinder inputs, plus other entered data, into range and elevation. This is the most complex system ever to appear on Soviet tanks, and it is not known whether it has proven successful. There were apparently some development problems with the laser, as early T-64s were delivered without it; the system was later retrofitted.

Other optics include passive night vision devices, improvements of those mounted on the T-62, and the usual white light or infra-red searchlights.

Model differences

Apart from what appears to be a different engine on the T-72, few of the changes from the T-64 to the T-72 appear to be operationally significant. The searchlight was moved from the left to the right of the main gun to avoid blocking the gunner's vision, and the T-64's cupola 12.7mm machine gun mount was replaced by a pintle mount in the T-72; this is apparently simpler, smaller and with better elevation. The salient recognition features of the T-72 are listed below, with data in parentheses showing how the T-64 differs:

Rubber coated (uncoated) road wheels.
Three (four) support rollers.
14 (12)-tooth drive sprocket.
Single (double)-pin track, rubber-bushed track pins.
Turret round at front, egg-shaped at back (entirely round).
Infra-red searchlight on right (left) of gun.
A few small (more, larger) storage boxes on the turret.
12.7mm MG on pintle (cupola) mount.
Single short snorkel on left side of turret (a longer snorkel, with a second snorkel for the engine inside it, on the rear edge of the turret).
Large (small) engine compartment, radiator grill near rear (turret), integral fuel cells on entire right track cover and rear half (all) of left track cover.

Other systems

Optics include a laser rangefinder with telescopic optical back-up. Passive night vision devices, improvements of those used on the T-62, are mounted, as are two white light or infra-red searchlights, the main one mounted along the gun tube and the commander's light mounted on his cupola.

An integral, retractable dozer blade is fitted to the hull front, and T-64/72s can dig themselves in in 15–30min. The dozer blade can also be used to push belly mines out of the way of the tank.

The snorkelling system appears similar to that of the T-62, although the T-64 has a second snorkel for the engine. Their NBC defence systems are at least the equal of that on the T-62, and it has been suggested that they have an air filtration system like the BMP.

Development

T-64K and T-72K command versions, with navigation and radio systems similar to those of the T-62K, are in service. They cannot move with the 10m mast antenna erected.

Weapons effectiveness and combat usage

T-72s have been seen in Afghanistan, and although some have reportedly been lost in action, Western sources have not had the opportunity to study them at any length. All estimates of effectiveness must therefore be highly approximate. However, it has been reported that at least two damaged T-64s or T-72s have been trucked out of Afghanistan and have arrived in the West for analysis and evaluation.

	Range (metres)					
Ammunition	500	1,000	1,500	2,000	2,500	3,000
HVAPCFSDS	98%	94%	70–80%	50–60%	40+%	35+%

The figures represent the probability of hitting with the first shot on target at a stationary tank, assuming the laser rangefinder and computer to be as effective as those in Western tanks. The laser's main advantage is that it allows moving targets to be engaged with minimal degradation of accuracy, even at long range. Its main disadvantages, assuming earlier Western efforts to be similar, are a lack of reliability and a tendency to be fooled by certain environmental conditions or inadvertent laser reflections.
Armour penetration (HVAPCFSDS) is also highly approximate (see table at top of page 107).
Armour penetration (HEAT): 475mm, regardless of range.

The Soviets have noted the Western development of stabiloy (depleted uranium) shells, and there have been reports that they have been working on such a projectile.

Range						
	500	1,000	1,500	2,000	2,500	3,000
Armour (mm)	450–420	425–350	400–335	375–325	350–280	325–245

Tactical employment

In 1979 each Soviet tank division in East Germany had one T-64/72-equipped regiment, as did a number of the Category I tank divisions in the European USSR. A second and third regiment will probably be added to each division, replacing T-62s. T-64/72s are also found in high-readiness motorised rifle divisions, including the "Taman" Guards at Alabino, near Moscow.

"T-80" main battle tank

Combat weight 45 tons **Length (without gun)** 7.0m **Width** 3.5m **Height** 2.2–2.3m **Track width** 0.5m **Max road speed** 70km/h **Range** 450km (with internal fuel), 650km (with external tanks) **Engine** 746BHP rear-mounted, liquid-cooled diesel **Transmission** Mechanical/hydraulic assist **Armament** 125mm gun (as T-64/72) **Main gun ammunition** 40 rounds **Fording** 1.4m **Snorkelling** 5.5m **Crew** 3

The T-80 (its temporary, Western-assigned designation) is still a creature of unconfirmed reports. Expected to enter service in 1980–81, with regiments being equipped by 1983–84, the T-80 is expected to feature the 125mm gun used on the T-64/72, possibly with improved ammunition, a laser rangefinder and a digital fire-control computer, and perhaps an improved engine and transmission. A hydropneumatic suspension, similar to that on the Swedish "S" tank, will allow the T-80 to shift up and down, varying its ground clearance. This may be an improvement of the system used on the SAU-122. Other features reported, but less likely, include an automatic transmission, Spiral ATGMs mounted along the turret sides, an automatic target designator system and an ECM device. The only thing certain about the T-80 is that it will use an improved, compound armour system, either a Soviet copy of the British-developed Chobham armour or, more likely, indigenous Soviet "combined armour," as used on T-64/T-72s. Compound armour can defeat all but the most powerful HEAT warheads, turning the West's current ATGMs from excellent to rather indifferent tank-killing systems. While it also degrades the performance of kinetic-energy penetrators, these can, given enough force, still penetrate. Although at least one T-80 has been reportedly tested with a gas-turbine engine, the development of the T-80 from the T-64/72 will probably be evolutionary rather than revolutionary, the main inno-

vation being the armour system. Those who have seen photographs of the T-80 describe it as resembling a T-72 with a more angular turret.

According to US Congressional testimony, a new, even more advanced main battle tank, designated the "T-80 Follow-on", is currently under development.

Obsolescent tanks

T-34/85 Considered by many to be the finest tank of World War Two. The Soviets still take the trouble to maintain stocks of T-34/85s for export and to produce 85mm ammunition. Those overhauled for export feature new T-55-style road wheels, infra-red driving lights and, in many cases, uprated engines. It is possible that they may be used in Soviet mobilisation-only formations and for training, or in DOSAAF. T-34/85s are also used as range targets.

Weight 32,000kg **Length** 8.1m **Width** 3.05m **Height** 2.7m **Track** 2.45m **Clearance** 0.4m **Ground contact** 3.85m **Engine** V-2-34M 500HP water-cooled V-12 diesel **Speed** 55km/h **Range** 300km **Ground pressure** 0.83kg/cm^2 **Trench** 2.5m **Vertical obstacle** 0.73m **Slope** 30° **Ford** 1.3m **Armour** 45mm @ 60° (glacis), 45mm @ 20° (upper hull side), 75mm curved (mantlet) **Gun** 85mm ZIS-S53 M-1944 **Elevation/depression** +25°/−5° **Ammunition** 50–60 rounds, other data as D-44 AT gun **Secondary armament** Box and coaxial 7.62mm DTM machine guns **Crew** 4 (5 in company command tanks)

T-10M heavy tank The later version of the T-10, first introduced in 1957, has a multi-baffle muzzle brake, night driving equipment, infra-red optics, two-plane gun stabilisation and snorkelling capability, which the T-10 lacked, and a 14.5mm anti-aircraft machine gun instead of a 12.7mm. T-10Ms spent most of their career in independent army-level tank battalions. According to most sources they were withdrawn in the early 1970s, but US Army estimates showed them soldiering on as late as early 1978. If this is the case, some may still be in use.

Weight 52,000kg **Length** 10.6m **Width** 7.04m **Height** 3.566m **Track** 2.43m **Clearance** 2.6m **Track width** 0.43m **Engine** 700HP water-cooled V-12 diesel **Speed**

42km/h **Range** 250km **Ground pressure** 0.78kg/cm² **Trench** 3m **Vertical obstacle** 0.9m **Slope** 32° **Ford** 1.2m **Armour** 120mm @ 60° (glacis), 80mm @ 45° (upper hull side), 250mm armour basis (mantlet) **Gun** 122mm tank gun **Elevation/depression** +17°/−3° **Ammunition** 30 rounds **Secondary armament** one 14.5mm co-axial, one 14.5mm anti-aircraft machine gun

---

All vehicles of the JSU, JS and SU series have definitely left Soviet service, the last leaving in the 1970s. Some of these vehicles were scrapped – and the Soviets rarely scrap weapons.

Foreign usage

T-54/55s are the standard main battle tanks in the Warsaw Pact nations, Yugoslavia, Egypt, Syria, Libya, Iraq, North Korea and China (as the T-59). Other operators are Algeria (300), Libya (1,000), Morocco (50 T-54s), Sudan (130, including T-59s), Angola (50), Yemen (North and South), Ethiopia, Mozambique, Somalia (100), Tanzania (15 T-59s), Uganda (15), Afghanistan (about 450), Bangladesh (30), India (about 600), Indonesia (a number received but none now in service),

Mongolia (100), Pakistan (50 T-55, 700 T-59), Vietnam (form the major part of the 900-tank force), Peru (250), Cuba (over 400), Israel (up to 450 rebuilt versions). Estimated Warsaw Pact T-54/55 strength is: East Germany 2,500 (plus 1,000 stored in war reserve), Poland 3,430, Czechoslovakia 3,600, Hungary 1,490, Romania 1,670, Bulgaria 670.

T-62s were received and evaluated by most Warsaw Pact armies, but, with the possible exception of Bulgaria (100 tanks), they never entered large-scale service with any of these armies. The Israelis have about 150, and they are also used by Egypt, Syria, India (300 estimated), Cuba, possibly North Korea, possibly Ethiopia, Afghanistan (about 50), and possibly others in the near future.

T-64s are used only by the Soviet Union, but T-72s serve in the East German, Polish and Czech armies and are apparently being produced in Czechoslovakia and Poland. An export version, apparently without the laser rangefinder, is in service in Syria, Iraq, India and Algeria. In mid-1979 it was estimated that East Germany had 200 T-72s, Poland 100, Czechoslovakia 300, Romania 30 and Bulgaria a few.

The US Army has had a large number of T-54/55s and T-62s, and one or two T-59s, the latter obtained in Vietnam.

Chapter Eight

Armoured personnel carriers and infantry combat vehicles

"Infantry is the nerve of an army."
FRANCIS BACON, VISCOUNT ST ALBANS

Motorised rifle units are the most numerically important type of Soviet combat unit. Functioning as part of a combined-arms force, they destroy enemy resistance in the main battle area, creating the opportunity for exploitation by tank units and other motorised rifle units, especially those equipped with BMPs. In addition, motorised rifle units, especially BMP-equipped battalions and smaller sub-units, are seen as being an ideal force to carry out the "daring thrusts" of forward detachments and *reydy* that the Soviets believe will unlock the enemy defence. Like all Soviet units, motorised rifle units now place a higher value on manoeuvre and surprise. They are also committed to the high-speed offensive in both nuclear and conventional operations, and have been ever since the motorised rifle troops replaced the infantry in 1954–63.

The motorised rifle division is the main striking power of the combined-arms army, and at least one normally forms part of each tank army. A front will normally have two or more combined-arms armies in its first echelon, and each army's first echelon, will usually consist of two motorised rifle divisions advancing abreast over a 20–80km frontage. At least one other motorised rifle division is usually kept in the second echelon of the combined-arms army, as is the motorised rifle division in the tank army. In the defence, motorised rifle divisions are used to hold ground whenever possible, releasing tank units to counter-attack and resume the offensive. In addition to operating as part of an army or an independent corps, motorised rifle divisions will operate independently when opposing weak or isolated enemy units or acting as the front reserve. Though more suited to the breakthrough attack and sustained combat than the tank division, the motorised rifle division will still burn itself out faster than Western formations. The divisional logistical base is supposedly adequate for six days of combat, although this may be an optimistic figure in the intense fighting of any future war in Europe.

A motorised rifle division marches in the standard formation, with its two BTR-60PB-equipped regiments as the first echelon. If required, the BMP-equipped regiment will also be placed in the first echelon. Normally, the BMP regiment remains in the second echelon, and the division can draw its forward detachments and *reydy* from it, and from the independent tank battalion, without weakening the power of the first echelon. The independent tank battalion often serves as the division's reserve. The anti-tank battalion is the anti-tank reserve, both in the attack and the defence.

Motorised rifle units and sub-units represent the norm of Soviet operations and tactics, and standard offensive and defensive concepts all apply.

APC development

Soviet APC development has been less evolutionary than that of tanks, possibly because it lacks the pre-war origins of tank development. The initial BTR-40 and BTR-152 designs were armoured trucks, and their replacement, the BTR-60, made up for their lack of cross-country mobility with a completely new chassis, although the powerplant was an old petrol-fuelled type, albeit not the same as used on the earlier APCs. The BTR-50 was directly taken from the PT-76 chassis and, although the BMP used many components also seen on the PT-76, notably the engine, it does not seem to have evolved directly from the BTR-50 – unless there is a prototype "missing link" unknown in the West. The MT-LB is a new design family.

Unit organisation

Motorised rifle squad (BMP-equipped)
One sergeant with an AKMS, two PKM machine gunners, one RPG-7 gunner, four riflemen with AKMSs. Two

riflemen serve as assistant machine gunners and one as assistant RPG-7 gunner. The squad is mounted in a BMP with a two-man crew (driver and gunner).

Motorised rifle squad (BTR and early BMP-equipped)

As above, with the two PKM gunners replaced by one RPK light machine gunner and one AKMS-armed rifleman. There is also only one assistant machine gunner. A PKM machine gun was added to each BTR-60PB-mounted squad starting in 1979–80. 5.45mm AKS-74 and RPK-74 weapons have replaced 7.62mm weapons in most Category I units. A BTR-60PB-mounted squad now consists of driver and gunner (with AKS), one PKM gunner, one RPK (7.62mm or 5.45mm) gunner, one RPG-7 or RPG-16 gunner, and five riflemen, including the squad leader and assistant gunners for the two machine guns and RPG.

These squad organisations are the norm, but variations with eight to twelve men and one or two machine guns have been observed. All motorised riflemen must be 1.7m or less in height and must not wear glasses.

Motorised rifle platoon

Comprises three squads and a platoon commander, normally a second lieutenant, although a *praporshchik* or sergeant is often substituted. In addition, one rifleman uses an SVD sniper's rifle rather than an AKMS.

Motorised rifle company

Comprises three platoons and a company headquarters of company commander (usually a senior lieutenant), political officer (*zampolit*, usually a second lieutenant) and technical officer (usually a second lieutenant, often a *praporshchik*), a section of three SA-7 gunners (one sergeant, two privates, also armed with AKMSs), a first sergeant with an AKMS, a messenger/clerk and a rifleman/aidman, both armed with PKMs. In addition, there is the two-man crew of the company headquarters' BMP or APC, to make a total company strength of six officers and 96 enlisted men. In combat all of a motorised rifle company fights; it has no support elements. The company headquarters is turned into a combat squad. The three SA-7 gunners, political officer, technical officer and first sergeant are each attached down to platoons, one SA-7 and one of the command personnel to each platoon. In return, each platoon sends two riflemen to the company HQ under the command of the company commander, making it an effective fighting unit. Each platoon and company commander has one R-126 radio set, which he carries himself. The SA-7s are organic to battalion and attached to company level. Each BTR-60PB-equipped motorised rifle company also has two AGS-17 grenade launchers which can be fired from tripod or vehicle mounts.

Motorised rifle battalion

Total strength: 29 officers, 401 enlisted men (30 and 414 in BTR- equipped units)

One battalion HQ (six officers: one battalion commander [usually a major, sometimes a captain or lieutenant-colonel], one battalion chief of staff [usually a captain], deputy battalion commander for political affairs [captain or lieutenant], deputy battalion commanders for technical affairs [captain or lieutenant]. Eight enlisted men: one battalion sergeant-major, who is usually with the rear CP, one GAZ-66 driver, one NBC detection technician, two company clerks, one gunner and driver for commander's BMP or APC, one driver for chief of staff's vehicle [all with AKMs]. One GAZ-66 truck, one APC or BMP, one BRDM-2, BRDM-1, ACRV-2, BTR-60, BTR-50, BMP-ShU or other "U" or command version, one UAZ-69 or 469 [for battalion commander], one R-126 radio)

Three motorised rifle companies

One mortar battery (5 officers, 56 enlisted men, 14 pistols, 37 AKMs, 6 RPG-7s, 6 120mm mortars, 7 GAZ-66 trucks or MT-LB APCs, 1 GAZ-69 jeep)

> One headquarters and headquarters platoon (one GAZ-69, one GAZ-66 or MT-LB, one battery headquarters [1 officer, 2 enlisted men], one platoon HQ and FO/reconnaissance section [1 officer, 5 enlisted men, 1 rangefinder], one communications section [5 enlisted men, 5 field phones], one transport section [8 enlisted men])

> Three mortar platoons (each of one commander and two mortar squads of two mortars towed by GAZ-66s or MT-LBs each)

One communications platoon (1 officer, 13 enlisted men, 1 command vehicle, 1 motorcycle, 1 GAZ-66, 1 GAZ-69, 1 R-104M, 2 R-105/R-147, 2 R-113/R-123, 1 R-114, 1 R-126 radio, 1 switchboard, 10 field phones)

> One platoon HQ (1 officer, 1 enlisted man)
> One radio section (6 enlisted men)
> One wire section (6 enlisted men)

One air-defence sub-unit (3 SA-7 sections)

One supply platoon (1 officer, 19 enlisted men, 4 GAZ-66, 4 URAL-375 or ZIL-157, 2 4,000 or 5,000-litre POL trucks, 1 field kitchen, 1 POL trailer, 1 water trailer, 3 kitchen trailers)

> One platoon HQ (1 officer, 1 enlisted man)
> One mess section (8 enlisted men)
> One transport section (6 enlisted men)
> One supply and service section (4 enlisted men)

One medical aid section (1 *feldsherr*, a *praporshchik* barber-surgeon, between a doctor and a nurse in skill; 3 enlisted men, 1 UAZ-450/452 ambulance with trailer. All armed with AKMs)

One repair workshop (7 enlisted men, 1 ZIL maintenance van)

One anti-tank platoon (not in BMP-equipped battalion) (1 officer, 13 enlisted men, 2 Suitcase Saggers, 2 SPG-9, 2–4 RPG-7, 2 APCs)

The old half-platoon APC organisation was known to be in use in some units in the early 1970s, and is still in use with most Warsaw Pact armies except the East Germans. Squads and platoons were organised as in a BTR-60-equipped unit, but all APCs were held by an APC platoon and attached two to each platoon and one for each company HQ. There was no battalion command APC, jeeps or scout cars being used instead, although current Warsaw Pact armies do have command APCs and anti-tank platoons of Saggers and SPG-9s or recoilless rifles. The old Soviet organisation used 82mm recoilless rifles or 57mm anti-tank guns towed by trucks.

MT-LB-equipped units are organised similarly to BTR-60PB-equipped units, but probably also use MT-LBs to tow mortars. Those units in Siberia and the Far North that use GT-T artillery tractors for APCs have six per company, with the men organised as in a BTR-60PB unit.

MT-LBs are used to tow the 120mm mortars in BMP battalions, while trucks are used in BTR-60PB battalions and some BMP-equipped battalions.

Motorised rifle regiment

Total strength: 168–198 officers, 1,695–2,168 enlisted men, 17+ jeeps, 162+ trucks

One regimental headquarters (28 officers, 32 enlisted men, 4 BRDM-2/U, 1 APC or BMP, 1 command APC or BMP, 4 motorcycles, 8+ jeeps, 3+ trucks)

Three motorised rifle battalions

One tank battalion

One artillery battalion (battery formerly, still in some units)

One anti-tank battery

One anti-aircraft battery

One reconnaissance company

One engineer company

One signal company

One transport company (5 officers, 69 enlisted men, 1+ jeeps, 44+ trucks)

One maintenance company (4 officers, 62 enlisted men, 2 tank recovery vehicles, 1 truck-mounted crane, 14+ trucks)

One NBC defence company (2 officers, 25 enlisted men, 2 NBC reconnaissance BRDMs, 4+ trucks)

One traffic control platoon (1 officer, 19 enlisted men, 2+ APCs)

One supply and service platoon (1 officer, 26 enlisted men, 7 trucks)

One band (1 officer, 16 enlisted men, 1 truck)

Motorised rifle division

Total strength: 1,163–1,217 officers, 11,608–11,921 enlisted men

One divisional HQ (93 officers, 208 enlisted men, 9+ BRDMs, 10+ jeeps, 20+ trucks)

Three motorised rifle regiments (in many Category 1 divisions: one BMP-equipped with SAU-122s in the howitzer battalion, one BTR-60-equipped with SAU-122s in the howitzer battalion, one BTR-60-equipped with D-30s in the howitzer battalion)

One tank regiment

One independent tank battalion (at least in Category I divisions)

One artillery regiment

One MRL battalion

One FROG battalion

One anti-tank battalion

One anti-aircraft battalion

One reconnaissance battalion

Combat support units

One engineer battalion

One signal battalion

One NBC defence battalion (12 officers, 138 enlisted men, 4 NBC reconnaissance BRDMs, specialist equipment)

Service support

One transport battalion (22 officers, 195 enlisted men, 5+ jeeps, 198+ trucks of all types)

One maintenance battalion (19 officers, 275 enlisted men, 8+ cranes and tank recovery vehicles, 3+ jeeps, 61+ trucks and vans)

One medical battalion (35 officers, 123 enlisted men, 1+ jeep, 19+ trucks and ambulances)

One traffic control company (3 officers, 57 enlisted men, APCs)

Field bakery

Divisional band

Divisional depots

In the late 1970s few divisions in readiness categories II and III had a BMP-equipped regiment, regimental artillery was in battery strength, and none had an independent tank battalion. All three motorised rifle regiments were equipped with BTR-60PBs. It is uncertain how much these units have been upgraded, but the continued high level of Soviet weapons production makes it inevitable that they *are* being upgraded and will continue to be so. Thus, currently, Category II and III motorised rifle divisions probably vary from being almost as well equipped as Category I units to lacking in all the new weapons. Not all Soviet new equipment or organisation goes to Category I units first, so it is hard to generalise. Unconfirmed reports suggest that some motorised rifle divisions, especially those that are part of tank armies, have two or more of their motorised rifle regiments equipped with BMPs.

BTR-152V2s, shown here armed with 12.7mm DShK heavy
machine guns, parade through Red Square. (*US Army*)

BTR-152 armoured personnel carrier

Combat weight 8.95 (9.6) tons **Length** 6.83m **Height**
2.05m (2.8) **Width** 2.32m **Track** 1.742m (front), 1.720m
(rear) **Clearance** 0.295m **Tyre size** 12.00 × 18 **Wheelbase** 3.3 × 1.13m **Max road speed** 65km/h **Fuel capacity** 300 litres **Max road range** 650km **Fuel consumption**
0.46 litres/km **Fording** 0.8m **Gradient** 30° **Vertical obstacle** 0.6m **Horsepower/weight** 12.2HP/ton (11.4)
Engine ZIL-123, 6-cylinder in-line petrol water-cooled,
110HP @ 2,800rpm **Transmission** 5 forward (with over-
drive), 1 reverse 2-speed transfer box **Steering** Wheel-
standard **Gun** 7.62mm SGMB or 12.7mm DShK
(14.5mm twin ZPU-2) **Ammunition load** 1,250 7.62mm
or 500 12.7mm (1,250 14.5mm) **Main gun elevation**
−6°/+23.5° (−10°/+90°) **Traverse** 90° (360°) **Armour**
14mm @ 35° (hull front), 9mm @ 7° (hull sides), 9mm @
0° (hull rear), 4-6mm (nil) (top), 4mm (belly)

All figures apply to the BTR-152V3 except those in parentheses,
which apply to the BTR-152A where it differs from the standard
vehicle.

The Soviets produced small numbers of halftracks during
World War Two, and these, along with US and German
vehicles, influenced the design of the BTR-152, which
appeared about 1950. The basic BTR-152 is a large vehicle without overhead cover, intended to carry or tow
heavy weapons or to mount half a platoon of infantry, who
dismount over the sides or through rear exit doors, and
who fire over the sides of the troop compartments or
through three side firing ports, which are present in most
models.

The engine and chassis were originally those of the
ZIL-151 truck, but were replaced during production by
those of the ZIL-157, featuring more power and large
single tyres. The simple, all-welded steel box body has
truck-type windshields for driver and commander which
can be covered by steel screens containing a vision block,
as can the glassless side door windows. The gearbox has
the standard one reverse and five forward gears. Suspension is by leaf springs and hydraulic shock-absorbers. A
single 7.62mm SGMB – later replaced by a 12.7mm or
14.5mm gun – is pintle-mounted on the cab roof. Another
machine gun is sometimes mounted on the hull sides.
Basically an armoured truck, the BTR-152 lacks
amphibious capability.

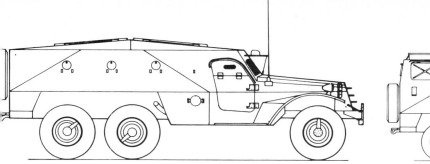

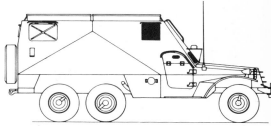

BTR-152K with overhead armour (not to scale). *(US Army)*

BTR-152U command vehicle (not to scale). *(US Army)*

The basic BTR-152 (Model A) had no tyre pressure regulation device or rear winch, while the BTR-152V1 (Model B) had both. BTR-152V2s were BTR-152s with internal air lines for a tyre pressure regulation system added. The BTR-152V3 (Model C) had internal air lines, a winch and infra-red driving lights. The BTR-152K, which appeared in 1961, was a BTR-152V3 with an armoured roof. The forward exit hatch had one firing port and the rear one had two. The BTR-152U command version had a high, enclosed raised superstructure with multiple radios and a catwalk on top, and was built on a BTR-152V1 or V3 chassis. Power was usually provided by a generator trailer. The BTR-152A was an early self-propelled anti-aircraft gun, mounting a twin 14.5mm ZPU-2. The Egyptians mounted four 12.7mm AAMGs on a BTR-152.

Weapons effectiveness and combat usage

The BTR-152, primarily in the open-top version, was used by the Arabs in the 1967 War. The Israelis upgunned large numbers of captured BTR-152s with 12.7mm and 7.62mm machine guns and they were used by the Border Police. Arab BTR-152s also saw action in various incidents between 1967 and 1973 and in the 1973 War. Other nations which received the BTR-152 include China (where they were produced under licence as the Type 56 APC), North Yemen, Somalia, Cuba, the Congo, Cyprus, India, Indonesia, Cambodia, Sudan, Tanzania (Type

BTR-152A self-propelled anti-aircraft mount, reportedly designated BTR-ZPU in the Soviet Union. *(US Army)*

BTR-152V2 captured by Israeli forces in 1973, next to similar Egyptian Walid vehicle. *(Tom Woltjer)*

56s) and Uganda. The BTR-152 has thus undoubtedly seen much combat in recent years. BTR-152As, apparently fresh from Soviet reserve stocks, were in action in the Ogaden War in 1978.

BTR-152s built on the ZIL-151 chassis shared that truck's maintenance problems and poor cross-country mobility. These shortcomings were reduced, but by no means eliminated, in those with the ZIL-157 chassis, which is still crude and underpowered even by 1950s standards. Serviceability and reliability are low, especially in hot or desert conditions.

Tactical employment

The BTR-152, as a half-platoon APC, was used differently from current squad APCs. Half-platoon APCs were designed to follow the tanks behind nuclear strikes or artillery offensives. Mounted attacks were considered possible in some situations, but the infantry would normally have to dismount and form up away from the enemy, and the tanks would then either have to attack at a walking pace or have the infantry ride on their backs, with resultant heavy losses.

The BTR-152 was still in Soviet service in the late 1970s, primarily towing mine planters in regimental engineer companies. Some traffic regulation troops of the commandant's service use BTR-152s, as do DOSAAF and other paramilitary groups.

BTR-50 armoured personnel carrier

Combat weight 14 tons (14.5) **Length** 6.9m **Height** 1.97m **Width** 3.18m **Clearance** 0.37m **Track** 2.74m **Track width** 0.35m **Ground pressure** 0.52kg/cm² **Max road speed** 44km/h **Max swimming speed** 10km/h **Fuel capacity** 250 litres **Fuel consumption** 0.96 litres/km **Range** 260km **Vertical obstacle** 1.1m **Trench** 2.8m **Gradient** 38° **Horsepower/weight** 16.9HP/ton **Engine** V-6, 6-cylinder in-line diesel, water-cooled, 240HP @ 1,800rpm **Transmission** Mechanical synchromesh, manual, 5 forward, 1 reverse gears **Gun** 1 12.7mm or 7.62mm SGMB or none **Rounds carried** 500 12.7mm, 2,500 7.62mm **7.62mm elevation** −6°/+23.5° **7.62mm traverse** 90° **Armour** 11mm @ 60° (hull front), 10mm @ 0° (upper hull side), 7mm @ 0° (hull rear), 10mm (hull roof), 6mm (hull floor) **Crew** 2 **Passengers** 12 (18–20 in open-top versions)

All figures are for BTR-50PK except where noted.

The BTR-50 was the first full-tracked Soviet APC. First seen in 1957, the BTR-50 uses the PT-76's chassis, suspension, engine, power train and water propulsion, with a variety of troop compartments welded to the hull. The driver, seated in the centre of the hull front, has a one-piece hatch cover incorporating a vision block and three periscopes, one of which can be elevated for better vision

Above BTR-50PK of the Egyptian Army armed with a 7.62mm SGMT machine gun. *(Egyptian Army)*

Below Egyptian BTR-50PU command APCs lead a parade. They are recognisable by their additional antennae, generators and power pack on the rear deck, extra cupola, altered hatch arrangement, and ventilators. *(Egyptian Army)*

OT-62 TOPAS-2 of the Egyptian Army, showing the Czech 82mm recoilless anti-tank gun and co-axial machine gun mounted on the right-hand cupola and the large side doors that distinguish it from Soviet-built versions. *(Egyptian Army)*

BTR-50PK captured by the Israelis. Its trim vane is extended and the white-light searchlight normally mounted is missing. The two early-model gunports (without NBC protection) are apparent in the troop-compartment sides. *(Tom Woltjer)*

while swimming. The commander's cupola, on the left, has three vision blocks. An infra-red driving light and searchlight are often mounted.

The initial BTR-50P version was an unarmed, open-top, half-platoon APC, although a pintle-mounted 7.62mm SGMB was later fitted. Anti-tank guns and recoilless rifles could be mounted in the troop compartment by means of the rear loading ramps and could be fired on the move. The BTR-50PA lacked the loading ramps but had a ring-mounted 14.5mm KPV HMG on the commander's cupola. The BTR-50PK was a squad APC with an armoured roof and an NBC defence system, displaying a dome-shaped ventilator. No armament is fitted, although the squad's weapons can be fired through the two roof hatches that serve as the only exit from the

Open-topped BTR-50P APC. *(US Army)*

troop compartment, or from the one or two firing ports on each side provided on some late-production vehicles. The BTR-50's low freeboard of 0.15–0.20m and its lack of a snorkel in most versions limit its use in all but the calmest water.

The BTR-50 was produced in far smaller quantities than the BTR-152 or BTR-60.

The Czechs have further developed the BTR-50 design as the OT-62 TOPAS series, adding a more powerful engine, an improved NBC system, and doors on either side of the troop compartments. It has two small front cupolas and is normally unarmed, although the Czech Army's improved OT-62B has a small turret on top of the right-hand cupola. The most advanced BTR-50 version is the OT-62C TOPAS-ZAP, which equips the Polish 7th Amphibious Assault Division. It has a Czech-designed turret with a 14.5mm KPV and 7.62mm PKT capable of 78° elevation. The Poles have experimented with mounting Saggers on these vehicles. The WPT-TOPAS is a Polish recovery version with a one-ton-capacity crane. The old Czech 82mm recoilless rifle was often fitted to OT-62s. Command versions of the OT-62 are in service.

MTP maintenance vehicle. *(Soldat & Technik)*

BTR-50Ps captured by the Israeli Army. *(Tom Woltjer)*

The BTR-50PU, recognisable by its multiple radio aerials and two front commander's cupolas, is the Soviet command version. In addition to the radios, it is fitted with a land navigation system similar to that used in the T-62K. These vehicles are still used in many armoured units, although they are being replaced by modified BMPs and ACRV-2s.

A combat engineer version of the BTR-50, firing rocket-propelled line charges to clear gaps in obstacles and minefields, is used by engineer units.

A modified BTR-50PK with four commander's cupolas is used to train tank commanders.

The MTP maintenance and recovery version of the BTR-50PK is an attempt to give Soviet units maintenance capability that can move up to the battle area with the troops. The MTP's cross-country mobility allows it to keep up with tanks, and its NBC protection system means it can cross contaminated areas. The raised roof over the passenger compartment contains a workshop in which technicians can repair components. A recovery hook and anchor with a maximum capacity of 15,000kg is installed. Two firing ports and a PK machine gun are provided for self-defence. There is no lifting crane or large roof hatch, so it would not be possible to bring entire engines into the workshop, though components and modularised systems could be. The MTP also carries a pump for fuelling vehicles and oxy-acetylene welding equipment. The MTP is important because it brings maintenance specialists to the fighting units, rather than the other way round, and helps to achieve on-the-spot repair and reduce the maintenance problems that the Soviet rates of advance will create.

Weapons effectiveness and combat usage

The BTR-50PK saw action in the 1967 Middle East war, when it equipped the mechanised units of Egyptian armoured divisions along with a number of OT-62s. The Israelis armed their captured vehicles with three 7.62mm machine guns, fired from the troop compartment, and used them in a number of raids into Egypt in the War of Attrition period. BTR-50s and OT-62s were used in Egyptian armoured divisions in 1973. They also equipped the 130th Mechanised Infantry Brigade, which swam across the Great Bitter Lake on October 6 and advanced into Sinai, where it was defeated by Israeli reserves. The Indian Army used several different types of Soviet and Czech-built BTR-50s during the 1971 War. BTR-50s were used in Vietnam.

Tactical employment

The half-platoon versions of the BTR-50 were used in the same way as the wheeled half-platoon vehicles. The BTR-50PK still equipped the motorised rifle regiment of some Category II tank divisions in the late 1970s.

BTR-60PB of the US Army, showing the armoured windshield covers and folded trim vane. The machine guns have been removed from this particular vehicle. *(US Army)*

BTR-60 armoured personnel carrier

Combat weight 10.3 tons (10 tons PK, 9.98 tons P) **Length** 7.56m (7.2m PK) **Height** 2.31m (2.27m PK, 2.055m P) **Width** 2.825m (2.8m PK) **Track** 2.37m (2.34m PK) **Clearance** 0.475m (0.4m PK) **Tyre size** 13.00 (12) × 18 **Max road speed** 80km/h **Max water speed** 9–10km/h **Fuel capacity** 290 litres (two 145-litre tanks) **Fuel consumption** 0.58litres/km **Road range** 500km (110km water) **Gradient** 30° **Vertical obstacle** 0.4m **Trench** 2.0m **Turning radius** 12m **Engines** Two GAZ-49B 6-cylinder in-line, water-cooled petrol, 90HP @ 3,400rpm **Transmission** Manual, 4 forward, 1 reverse, 2-speed transfer case **Steering** Power, through front four wheels **Main gun** 14.5mm KPV (12.7mm DShKM or nil) **Secondary gun** 7.62mm PKT co-axial (7.62mm PKT, SGMB, or nil) **Ammunition load** 500 14.5mm, 2,000 7.62mm (500 12.7mm, 2,000 7.62mm) **Elevation** −5°/+30° (−6°/+23.5° P) **Traverse** 360° (90°) **Armour** 7mm @ 86° (upper hull front), 9mm @ 47° (lower hull front), 7mm @ 0° (hull side), 5mm @ 65° (hull rear), 7mm @ 40° (nil) (turret, all around), 6mm (nil) (turret top), 7mm (nil) (hull top), 5mm (belly) **Crew** 2 **Passengers** 14 (16 P) **Radio** R-123, plus R-107 in company command vehicles **Night vision devices** TVN-2B (60m range) (driver), TKN-1 (250–300m range) (commander)

Figures apply to BTR-60PB; those in parentheses are earlier versions where they differ.

The BTR-60 (BTR = *Bronetransportr*, armoured personnel carrier) is numerically the most important APC in the Soviet Army. Each motorised rifle division has two regiments equipped with BTR-60s and one equipped with BMPs, while motorised rifle divisions in lower readiness categories often have no BMP regiment and are completely BTR-60-equipped. BTR-60-equipped regiments are normally in the division's first echelon, and the BMP and tank regiment make up the second echelon. Units equipped with the BTR-60 will fight the mobile battles of encounter, or make the breakthrough attacks, before the exploitation forces are committed. While it is an old design, technically unsophisticated and unrevolutionary even when introduced, the BTR-60 is still an important weapons system.

All versions of the BTR-60 feature a long, boat-shaped welded steel hull. All eight wheels are powered by two six-cylinder, rear-mounted petrol engines, their design dating back to the 1930s. The front four wheels are used for steering. Suspension is by torsion bar, and the steering wheels have two hydraulic shock-absorbers each; the other wheels have one each. All versions have the standard Soviet central tyre pressure regulation system and foam-filled tyres. The manual transmission has one reverse and four forward speeds and a two-speed transfer case.

The BTR-60PB is the standard APC of motorised rifle

Above BTR-60PB of the US Army, showing the propeller housing (marked with star). *(Leon Conjour)*

Below BTR-60PB of the US Army, showing the many hand and footholds provided to allow troops to climb over the top. The open hatch and gun tube in the background are from a PT-76. *(Leon Conjour)*

BTR-60Ps of the Naval Infantry swim ashore through a calm sea, with their trim vanes extended and SGMT machine guns manned. *(Chris Foss)*

divisions, easily identifiable by its small, conical turret with a 14.5mm KPV and co-axial 7.62mm PKT. The troop-compartment roof hatches are rearranged compared with earlier versions, but are still the only, inadequate, exits. The driver and commander each has his own side door and roof hatch, with tank-type periscopes rather than vision blocks. Later-production vehicles have three firing ports and a large vision block in each side of the troop compartment. The BTR-60PB has improved NBC protection, although not as complete a system as that used on the BMP.

The BTR-60PU command vehicle is a modification of the BTR-60P with an R-311, R-107, R-112 and two R-123 radios. Beneath a large, tent-like canvas top are a generator and map tables. It is used by the chiefs of staff of BTR-60PB-equipped battalions and as a COP by larger artillery units, although it is being replaced by the ACRV-2. The forward air control version is found at division level (one per division), or is attached to units that will need air support. It is a modified BTR-60PB with a Plexiglas window replacing the machine guns. A generator is mounted on the rear decking. It apparently carries an R-122 and other ground and aircraft-type radios, but has no radar beacon or blind bombing aid. A long-range communications BTR-60PK version has a 10m aerial and a large railing-style aerial running along three sides of the vehicle's top, which has a large external

generator and transmitting gear. This version is also used by the East German Army.

Compared with tracked APCs, wheeled APCs have 45–60% less production cost, 60–80% better fuel consumption, three times the lifespan, three to five times the interval between repairs and overhauls, and greatly reduced maintenance requirements. Wheeled APCs can operate on flat tyres, while a broken track will immobilise a tracked APC. They do not damage the roads upon which they operate and they create less damage during peacetime manoeuvres, although the Soviet Army never pays for damage it causes on manoeuvres (the local government does that). Wheeled APCs are lighter than tracked APCs and can use bridges which the latter cannot take. They have higher maximum road speeds than tracked APCs and, while their cross-country mobility is inevitably less, the use of all-wheel drive means that only 10% of the terrain in Europe that is accessible to tracked APCs is inaccessible to wheeled APCs. Considering the number of BTR-60s the Soviets require, the use of wheels is a good idea.

The BTR-60 has good amphibious characteristics, and the BTR-60PB is the standard APC and landing craft of the Naval Infantry. In the water the BTR-60 is powered by a single hydrojet at speeds of up to 10km/h; a bilge pump is fitted and a trim vane under the nose gives stability while swimming. While the BTR-60 is suitable for river crossings as long as the bank exit gradient does not exceed six to ten degrees, it is inadequate for amphibious assaults. Given a launch 3,000m offshore, their 20min

BTR-60PAs swim ashore through "enemy" fire with their trim vanes extended. *(V.M. Martinova)*

run-in to the beach would be suicidal in the face of any opposition. The BTR-60 can only land through two feet of surf, while the US LTVP-7 assault amphibian can surmount 12 feet of surf.

The original, 1961, BTR-60P has no overhead cover except a tarpaulin. It has three firing ports, a half-door and a vision block on each side of the troop compartment. Armament varies, most mounting a single 12.7mm DShKM; others have a 7.62mm SGMB in addition to or in place of this weapon. Two more 7.62mm weapons are sometimes placed on outrigger mounts and fired from the troop compartment. This version was replaced by the BTR-60PK (also called BTR-60PA) with an armoured roof and an NBC defence system. The only exit from the troop compartment is through two roof hatches. The driver and commander both have the usual periscopes and hatches. The pedestal-mounted 12.7mm or 7.62mm has no gunshield and cannot be fired from under armour. One or two 7.62mm weapons are also often mounted at the forward roof hatch. Driver and commander have 8mm-thick armoured Plexiglas windscreens fitted with hinged steel covers, each containing a vision block for use when under fire; these greatly reduce visibility, however. All models have infra-red driving lights and many have infra-red searchlights.

A number of experimental armament installations have been tried on BTR-60s. Turrets with 76mm and automatic 37mm cannon were tried in the early 1960s, perhaps as forerunners of the BMP. A mortar-carrying version of the BTR-60P reached prototype stage, but this vehicle, which allowed the mortar to be fired while mounted, apparently never entered large-scale service.

The BTR-60PB is now the standard version in Soviet service, although older types are known to be in use in first-line roles, some being used by Guards units in late 1978.

The Romanian TAB-72 version of the BTR-60PB has a turret with improved elevation; a TAB SP 82mm mortar version lacks the turret.

BTR-60PA, showing small exit hatches and gunports. Main armament is a 12.7mm DShK. *(US Army)*

BTR-60P with 12.7mm DShK main armament and 7.62mm
SGMTs on outrigger mounts. *(US Army)*

The BTR-60 is, like the rest of today's APCs, heading towards replacement, but its vulnerability to conventional weapons is no greater than that of any other APC, or even the BMP. The BTR-60PB's NBC protection is superior to that on US APCs. Its cross-country mobility is excellent for a wheeled vehicle, and US Army-owned BTR-60s regularly outdistance M60 tanks at Fort Hood, Texas. In the words of one US Army officer: "The BTR-60 is great fun to drive – it's the ultimate RV [recreational vehicle]."

Weapons effectiveness and combat usage

The BTR-60 was used in relatively small numbers in the 1967 Middle East war, and the BTR-60PB was the standard Arab APC in the 1973 War. The Israelis do not appear to have adopted captured vehicles. North Vietnamese BTR-60s were first encountered in the Laos invasion. They were used in large-scale attacks in support of tanks at An Loc and in I Corps in 1972, BTR-60Ps predominating. Large numbers of BTR-60s, including BTR-60PBs, were used in the 1975 and later fighting. BTR-60s were also used by Soviet-backed forces in Angola and in the Ogaden War.

Tactical employment

Earlier BTR-60 versions were used as half-platoon APCs

in the same way as BTR-152s and early BTR-50s. The APCs were needed to mechanise the Soviet infantry as quickly as possible – the last "foot" infantry was converted to motorised rifle in 1963 – and the Soviets were willing to tolerate the lack of overhead cover, NBC protection and tactical flexibility just to get the troops on wheels.

The two BTR-60PB-equipped regiments of a motorised rifle division will normally make up its first echelon in both attack and defence.

Vulnerability and countermeasures

To dismount from a BTR-60PB or BTR-60PK, the troops must physically haul themselves out of the two small roof hatches and jump or roll over the side, facing backwards. They will even do this while the vehicle is moving at up to 15km/h, and it is said to be no more hazardous than a parachute landing. To do this requires small, physically tough men and a willingness to accept accidents; the Soviets consider 3% casualties on manoeuvres acceptable.

The petrol carried on the BTR-60 makes it liable to "brew up" if hit. White phosphorus shells can ignite fuel, especially in external tanks. The tyres are vulnerable, though foam-filled, and a small compressor is part of the air-pressure system. But while these measures are adequate defence against small arms, shell fragments will flatten the tyres.

Above BTR-60PU command APC of a FROG-3-equipped missile unit, showing its raised roof and additional antennae. It is followed by a command version of the standard GAZ-69 jeep. These vehicles are crucial to the Soviet command, control and communications effort. *(Chris Foss)*

Below BTR-60PU command APC converted from a BTR-60PA, with additional radio equipment and stowage boxes. *(US Army)*

As are all Soviet APCs, the BTR-60 is constructed of high-quality steel in ballistic areas and lower-quality steel elsewhere. Reports from Afghanistan suggest that the guerrillas have found at least one weak spot through this use of lower-quality steel. A burst of automatic fire into the forward wheel will not only flatten it, but at least one round should penetrate the mild steel wheel well and strike the driver's head.

"BTR-70" armoured personnel carrier

Introduced 1978 **Combat weight** 10.5 tons **Length** 7.8m **Height** 2.43m **Width** 2.9m **Track** 2.4m **Engines** two improved types, possibly diesels. Other data as BTR-60PB. Armour as BTR-60PB, except with greater slope.

Introduced in 1978 and first paraded in November 1980, the "BTR-70" (the Western designation) is an improved BTR-60PB retaining the same armament and basic lay-out of the BTR-60PB while offering enlarged troop compartment hatches, improved engines (although the twin-engine format is apparently retained), improved access to engines for servicing (a weak point of the BTR-60PB) and a new type of radio. It will probably supplant earlier BTR-60 versions.

The BTR-70 APC is apparently an improved version of the BTR-60PB, with improved hatch arrangements and a diesel engine. It retains the 14.5mm machine gun armament of the BTR-60PB. (US Army)

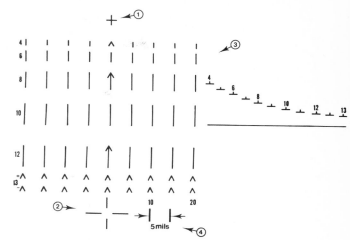

1PN22MI day sight reticle for the BMP gunner, for use with the Sagger, 73mm gun and machine gun. Legend (not present on actual sight): (1) boresight cross (2) Sagger aiming cross (3) rangefinding reticle, graduated for 400–1,300m (4) 5-mils graduated lead lines.(US Army)

BMP infantry combat vehicle

Combat weight 13.9 tons **Length** 6.74m **Height** 1.92m **Width** 2.94m **Track** 2.54m **Clearance** 0.39m **Track width** 0.2m **Ground contact** 3.6m **Ground pressure** 0.57kg/cm² **Max road speed** 70km/h **Max water speed** 7–8km/h **Fuel capacity** 460 litres (all internal) **Oil capacity** 44 litres **Fuel consumption** 0.9litres/km **Fuel consumption (swimming)** 1–1.5litres/km **Oil consumption** 0.05–0.07litres/km **Range** 500km **Vertical obstacle** 0.8m **Trench** 2.0m **Gradient** 30° **Tilt** 35° **Horsepower/weight** 20.1HP/ton **Engine** V-6, 6-cylinder, in-line, water-cooled diesel, 280HP at 2,000rpm **Transmission** Mechanical, constant mesh with synchro-couplings; 5 forward, 1 reverse gears, 2–5 operated hydraulically, rest mechanically **Steering** Planetary, 2-stage clutch & brake, hydraulically operated **Gun** 73mm 2A20 **Calibre length** 19cal **Rate of fire (theoretical)** 7–8rpm **Rate of fire (actual)** 3–4rpm **Effective range** 800m **Max range** 2,200m **Ammunition types** PG-9 HEAT, HE **Muzzle velocity** 400m/sec (HEAT) **Maximum velocity** 665m/sec (HEAT, with rocket) **Ammunition load** 40 rounds **ATGM** Sagger **ATGMs carried (max)** 5 total: 4 internal, 1 on gun tube **Co-axial MG** 7.62mm PKT **AAMG** nil **7.62mm ammunition** 2,000 rounds **Main gun elevation** −4°/+33° **Traverse** 360° **Turret mechanism** Electro-mechanical **Armour** 7mm @ 80° (excluding aluminium engine cover) (upper hull front), 19mm @ 57° (lower hull front), 16mm @ 14° (upper hull side), 18mm @ 0° (lower hull side), 16mm @ 19° (excluding inner armour of door) (hull rear), 6mm (hull top), 5mm (belly front), 7mm

BMP-1 on parade. The additional rocker arms, behind the front road wheels, distinguish it from the basic BMP. The troops standing up in the rear hatches give some indication of how cramped the vehicle is. *(US Army)*

(belly rear), 33–26mm rounded (turret mantlet), 23mm @ 42° (turret front), 19mm @ 36° (turret sides), 13mm (turret rear), 6mm (turret top) **Crew** 3 **Passengers** 8 **Radio** R-123, plus R-107 in company command BMPs

"The BMP has not only given the commander swiftness of manoeuvre; it has increased the firepower of tactical units." – Marshal K. Moskolenko

"The search for new and better ways to use the BMP in battle is one of the most important tasks for Army officers." – Col General V. Merimski

First seen in the November 1967 Red Square parade, and called the M-1967 and BMP-76 by NATO before its correct designation was known, the BMP (*Bronevaya Maschina Piekhota*, armoured vehicle, infantry) is one of today's most significant weapons systems. The first infantry combat vehicle with cannon and ATGMs in addition to a motorised rifle squad, the BMP brings combined-arms integration to the lowest tactical level.

The BMP was designed to an early-1960s specification for an infantry combat vehicle suited to the demands of the high-speed offensive in nuclear war. Mobility was stressed, as it had to keep up with a 70–100km a day advance and cross contaminated ground quickly. Speed of advance was seen as a better defence against enemy nuclear targeting than armour. Secure in their protected compartment, the squad would seldom fight dismounted. Armour protection was to be similar to that of contemporary APCs.

BMP-1 mechanised infantry combat vehicle.

It is misleading to compare the BMP with Western APCs with lighter armament and a higher silhouette. Not only does the infantry combat vehicle have heavier armament, but the squad fights mounted more often than in an APC. The Soviets recognise this distinction between APC and infantry combat vehicle, and use both types.

The BMP's baptism of fire in 1973 was a disaster, with the Valley of Tears on the Golan littered with burnt-out examples. Although the Syrians had been guilty of relying on stereotyped, textbook tactics and failed to use "bold and decisive manoeuvre," such as bypassing strongpoints, these battles were among a number of events that underscored the Soviet understanding that speed, shock and mass were not enough in the face of modern conventional weapons. It required only tactical evolution – hardly a "revolution" – for the Soviets to see the BMP as a superb weapon for working with tanks in exploitation, consolidation, pursuit, and especially forward detach-

ments and *reydy*. Although these concepts antedated the BMP by many years, and the BMP is not the only weapon used for these missions, the Soviets have placed greater importance on these activities since the BMP entered service.

Hull

The hull is divided into three compartments: the engine and power-train compartment, which is mounted forward, the personnel compartment, which includes the driver and commander positions, and the turret. There is no floor escape hatch. The driver's area in the left front of the vehicle contains the controls and instruments, including a T steering bar, clutch pedal, brake pedal, accelerator, idle adjustment screw, master switch and warning lights and indicators. The engine fire-extinguisher system, similar to that used in the T-62, can be activated automatically or from the driver's compartment. Access to the top of the engine and power train is through a hinged, armoured deck. Two towing locks and clevis mounts are at the front and rear of the vehicle. Storage boxes are provided under all seats.

Knocked-out BMP-1 about to be airlifted from Israel to the US, showing the gunports, both the circular AKMS ports (the sighting block is visible over the closed one) and the square PK port. The bulged doors contain extra fuel. *(US Air Force)*

Engine and suspension

The BMP's engine is an improved version of that used in the PT-76 and many other armoured vehicles, and is basically half of a T-54 engine. It has a fuel-injection system, is pressure-lubricated, and has cyclone air filtration units. The BMP's single-stage air filtration system is in contrast to the highly engineered engine, being less efficient than the double-stage, very efficient filters used in most Soviet designs. The manual transmission has five forward gears and one reverse, with standard double clutch shifting. The BMP has the same capability to produce smokescreens from its exhaust as the T-62.

The BMP's suspension embodies many standard components also seen on the PT-76 and several other vehicles. It has six road wheels with an idler at the rear and a drive wheel at the front. The first and sixth road wheels have hydraulic shock-absorbers. There are three track support rollers. The track is wide, dead steel track. Steel grousers reduce traction on paved roads. Double-pin track-block suspension gives a smoother ride cross-country and makes less noise, although weighing more than single-pin systems.

Motorised riflemen armed with AK-74 5.45mm assault rifles advancing with BMPs. The Sagger sight and the squad's periscopes are apparent on the vehicle on the left.

Weapons systems

Five Sagger ATGMs are normally carried, four in internal storage racks and one on its launch rail above the 73mm gun tube. The Sagger launcher cannot be employed dismounted, being permanently fixed above the tube. The missile itself is identical to the standard Sagger, but the gunner requires even greater than usual dexterity and co-ordination. He flies the missile by manipulating the joystick with his right hand, while moving the sight and training the turret with his left hand to keep the Sagger in the sight cross-hairs at all times, a difficult feat. Being under armour, however, the gunner is less vulnerable to suppressive fire. Like any ATGM-armed vehicle, the BMP must fire Saggers from the halt. The Sagger can be loaded on the launcher by the gunner from inside the turret. The gun must be at maximum elevation and not firing while reloading, which takes 45–50sec. According to published reports, the Sagger has been replaced by the Spandrel ATGM on some BMPs.

The 73mm 2A20 smooth-bore gun on the BMP is similar to the SPG-9 anti-tank weapon (the main difference being the propelling cartridge). It fires a PG-9 fin-stabilised rocket projectile much like the PG-7 fired by the RPG-7, and, also like that projectile, the 73mm round is fin-stabilised and vulnerable to crosswinds, which deflect it. Computing deflection against moving targets with the 73mm is a considerable problem, especially in a cross-

wind, despite the vertical lead lines on the gunner's sight. As BMP gunners have only three to six months' training before being considered fit for battle, and must qualify on the Sagger and PKT machine gun as well as the 73mm gun, it is unlikely that this complex aiming method is commonly or easily acquired, especially considering the infrequency of full-calibre firing in training. Moreover, the sub-calibre projectiles used in exercises often do not have the same characteristics as the full-calibre round.

The 73mm gun's sights are graduated to 1,300m, although accuracy deteriorates rapidly above 800m and the Sagger will normally be used against armoured targets at greater ranges. Trajectory is relatively flat to 800m. The shell self-destructs at maximum range.

The BMP carries 40 HEAT and HE rounds in two magazines which feed into the autoloader. The HE round is possibly a recent development, as Syrian BMPs captured in 1973 had only HEAT, and the gunner's sights were calibrated for a single type of ammunition. The autoloader permits a theoretical maximum rate of fire of six to eight rounds per minute. However, the gun automatically goes to 3.5° elevation after each round while the spent brass is ejected and the next round is loaded, possibly blocking vision and making it difficult for the gunner to see the first round's effect on the target, and thus reducing accuracy for the second round. The gun's lack of stabilisation is a significant drawback, preventing accurate firing or even gunlaying while on the move. Attacking BMPs normally fire from the short halt, and the actual rate of fire is three rounds per minute or less.

The 73mm gun is actually less effective than the 20mm cannon on Western infantry combat vehicles. While the 73mm HEAT round has a tank-killing capability that the 20mm lacks, its low rate of fire and low individual accuracy (it is not as accurate as the PT-76's 76mm gun) offset this advantage. An automatic 20mm cannon will be on target against a BMP before the single-shot BMP can get a shot in, and a 20mm round is as capable of knocking out a BMP or APC as a 73mm shell.

The 7.62mm PKT is the standard Soviet co-axial light machine gun, used for suppression and direct support. It is especially important to any BMPs without HE ammunition. It cannot fire, however, while the 73mm gun or a Sagger is being loaded.

The motorised rifle squad is one of the BMP's offensive weapons. They sit, very cramped, back-to-back on adjustable benches in the personnel compartment. To fire, they lock their weapons into airtight firing ports. The forward two firing ports are for PK machine guns and the other seven – three in each side and one in the left rear door – provide overlapping fields of fire for AKMSs. Each firing port is equipped with a periscopic 1×-magnification vision block equipped with a defogger. Soldiers can also sight through a small transparent aperture above the gun barrel, using the weapon's fixed sights. A vacuum exhaust system removes gases which result from firing, but it is inefficient and the compartment often fills with fumes. Small bags are attached to each firing port to collect spent cartridge brass, but these also often do not work properly, leaving the compartment awash with spent brass. The squad can also fire from their four two-man hatches above the troop compartment, also using weapons with back-blasts such as RPG-7s and SA-7s.

The squad dismounts from the BMP through the rear doors or roof hatches while at the short halt or while moving at up to 5km/h. It takes ten seconds for a well trained squad to dismount or remount.

The BMP is hampered by a 55° deadspace on its left front (between 350° and 295°) in which none of its armament can be used. This is created by a bump in the turret ring which pushes the gun tube to full elevation so that it does not strike the commander's infra-red searchlight. The bump also interferes with target tracking, especially when using the Sagger. If the gunner has to track a target through the deadspace, the gun tube will elevate and block the gunner's vision, and the Sagger may miss. The 73mm and the PKT are unable to cover this area, and none of the squad's weapons can reach it either, despite its being the area in which the commander's visibility is best.

As on Soviet tanks, the low silhouette of the BMP has restricted its main gun depression to 4°, limiting its ability to fight "hull-down." The gunner and commander each have only a 120° arc of vision, the gunner from 12 o'clock to 4 o'clock and the commander from 12 o'clock to 8 o'clock. The squad's vision blocks, if all manned, combine to give almost 360° visibility. BMPs, like all Soviet vehicles, will have their hatches open unless in NBC conditions or under artillery or small-arms fire.

Optics

Twenty 1×-power vision blocks are mounted, one for each of the nine firing ports, one in the right rear door, three each in the driver's and commander's hatches and four in the gunner's hatch. The commander has a TKN-3B binocular periscope sight, as on the T-62. The gunner has an IPN-22M1 sight with a stadiametric rangefinder, as used in the T-62's sights, but this is only graduated for distances from 400–1,300m. In its day mode the sight has a 15° field of view and 6× power. At night the passive ambient light intensification has a range of 400–1,000m, depending on conditions. The night field of view is 6° with 6.7× magnification, and there is no ranging scale; the gunner simply estimates unless artificial illumination allows him to use the day sights. The driver has a TVN-2B active/passive infra-red night vision device with a 30° field of view and a 50–60m range using the active infra-red light source, falling to 20m without it.

BMP-I emerging from a river, showing the extended trim vane and the improved nose design that gives it better swimming ability than earlier BMPs. *(US Army)*

NBC protection

The BMP's NBC defence system is based on the maintenance of overpressure and a blower/dust extractor that pulls in contaminated air and extracts the fallout. In an improvement over the T-62 and BTR-60PB systems, the air also passes through a chemical/biological filter. The system does not have a warning device, although there is a radiation indicator. Firing weapons through the gunports is hazardous, as the gas exhaust decreases the overpressure. Any exit, firing the cannon or loading a Sagger will cause contamination. Because of the cramped internal space it is difficult, though possible, to put on NBC suits inside a BMP. The filters are removed from exported BMPs.

Amphibious capability

The BMP is propelled by its tracks in water at a maximum speed of 8km/h. A trim vane on the front gives stability. The BMP is not as good in the water as the BTR-60, and its low silhouette is dangerous in rough water. There is no evidence of swim screens or snorkels being used.

Crew functions

The BMP commander is the squad, platoon or company leader. He normally dismounts when the squad dismounts. He is the only crew member to receive formal cross-training in other tasks, or who knows how to use the radio or read a map. He wears battledress and carries an AKMS.

The driver-mechanic is in charge of the BMP when the squad and the commander dismount. He undergoes six months of specialist training and is normally a PFC, the only person holding rank aboard the BMP apart from the commander. He is responsible for maintenance under the supervision of the company technical officer, and wears overalls and carries a pistol.

The gunner, alone in the one-man turret, has been trained for three to six months in using and maintaining his weapons, and would probably need additional training in his unit to become proficient. When the commander dismounts, the gunner will direct the driver in action, even though the driver outranks him. This is in addition to the gunner's other functions, and combat experience has shown that putting a vehicle commander in a one-man turret is a mistake. The gunner wears overalls and carries a pistol.

BMP-R reconnaissance vehicle.

Other versions

Early BMPs did not have an NBC filtration system. In the BMP-1 the NBC defence system intake was moved from behind the driver's hatch to the left rear of the commander. The BMP-1 version, which is the most common, introduced a larger trim vane and an extra rocker arm behind the front road wheel. The forward gun port on each side is modified to make it easier to use PKT machine guns. The BMP-1 also has a circular snorkel cover behind the turret, a different arrangement of roof hatches, a longer bow and an improved air filtration system. Most BMP-1 improvements have been retrofitted to BMPs as well.

A more important version is what the US Army calls the BMP-80. Introduced to Group Soviet Forces Ger-

many in 1978–79, it reportedly features a 30mm (perhaps 35mm) automatic cannon. It may have a Spandrel ATGM in a tube mounting. The chassis embodies many T-72 components, and the rear door is hinged at the bottom to form a ramp, in place of the two side-hinged doors on the standard BMP. Fuel is carried in the belly. BMPs used by Iran in the 1980 fighting had the rear ramp while retaining the 73mm gun.

The BMP-R is a reconnaissance version of the BMP that is replacing the PT-76. It has a larger (two-man) turret than the standard BMP, although the hull is basically the same. The armament is the same as on the standard BMP. The personnel compartment is smaller to compensate for the larger turret, and there are only two small roof hatches instead of the four two-man hatches on the standard BMP; this vehicle therefore probably contains only a two or three-man scout team.

The BMP-Sh, also referred to as the BMP-U in some sources, is the command version. It mounts a small turret with optical devices and a 7.62mm PKT for self-defence. It features several radio aerials and a modified, raised, rear deck. A canvas extension may be used when halted. It presumably also features a generator and a land navigation system. This version is replacing the BTR-50PU as the main CP vehicle of tank units and is also used in artillery units, reportedly carrying a digital fire-control computer. There are three sub-versions of this type: the M1974, M1977 and M1978, the last having most radio equipment.

The BMP-SON is the artillery reconnaissance version, equipped with a Small Fred radar, the folding rectangular

BMP-SON radar vehicle, showing folded Small Fred radar at the rear of the turret and 7.62mm PKT machine gun at the front. (US Army)

antenna of which is mounted at the rear of a large, two-man turret armed with a 7.62mm PKT for self-defence. This version is used for target acquisition, especially by SP howitzer units.

Weapons effectiveness and combat usage

The effectiveness of the Sagger and PKT on the BMP is approximately the same as that of the standard versions. The probability of a hit by a 73mm gun fired from a stationary BMP against a stationary M60A1 in the open, first round on target, according to US Army figures, is:

sets the gun controls to "ready," then depresses the "load" button on the control handgrip. A loading arm removes a shell from the ready rack. If HE rounds are used, this requires a selective function. The arm moves upwards until the shell is aligned with the breech, the electric rammer automatically seats the round, the automatic horizontal sliding breechblock closes, and the loading arm automatically returns to the ready position. The mangling tendencies of Soviet autoloaders are evident here (as well as the T-64/72), for if the gunner is not careful or does not keep his arm protector up, his left arm is likely to be inserted into the breech instead of the shell.

Range (metres)	50	100	175	250	500	800	1,000	1,300	1,800
Probability	97%	89%	89%	83%	64%	50%	40%	28%	24%(?)

The relatively high accuracy for 1,800m range is unusual, considering that the sight is only calibrated to 1,300m. The shell used against armoured vehicles would be HEAT, capable of penetrating 400mm of armour. If a hit is scored, the US Army estimates that a 73mm HEAT round has a 33% chance of killing an M60A1 and a 50% chance of killing an M113 APC.

In the 1973 War BMPs were the primary equipment in the armoured divisions of Syrian mechanised brigades. The Egyptians also used smaller numbers of BMPs. Syrian BMPs never got the chance to exploit success, suffering heavy losses in the first days that put the units out of action for most of the war.

Tactical employment

All Soviet tank and motorised rifle divisions should have one BMP-equipped motorised rifle regiment, although in lower readiness categories the role is probably still performed by BTR-50s in tank divisions and BTR-60s in motorised rifle divisions. BMP-equipped units are not only used for standard motorised rifle missions, but are assigned a large portion of the forward detachments and *reydy*. As the BMP regiment is normally in the divisional second echelon, they perform much of the pursuit and exploitation. All motorised rifle units organic to tank regiments are BMP-equipped.

Engagement sequence

Because the optics are identical, the target-acquisition and rangefinding segment of the engagement sequence is the same as in a T-62. Aiming is also similar, except that the gunner must take any crosswind into account, using the lateral lead lines. To fire the 73mm gun the gunner pushes the trigger on the gun control handgrip. The spent brass will be ejected into a collecting basket. To reload he

Using a Sagger does not require ranging in. The gunner removes one missile from its ready rack and, opening the loading hatch, slides it with its attached launch rail on to the receptacle on top of the gun tube. He deploys the missile's folding fins by hitting them with a stick. If he forgets to close the loading hatch, the gunner will absorb the force of the Sagger's rocket launch blast. To fire he pulls the control box up from beneath his seat and depresses the activating pedal. The Sagger can then be fired. Cross-hairs at the bottom of the day sight are used for guidance. The Sagger has no night sight.

Vulnerabilities and countermeasures

The BMP's armour is no heavier than that of most APCs. The vehicle is an offensive weapon, and the Soviets apparently were not willing to armour it to an extent that would reduce mobility or make it even more expensive. The BMP's front armour – but not that on its flanks – will stop a 12.7mm round. Considering the heavy losses Syrian T-62s suffered at the hands of Israeli armour, the fact that equally heavy losses of BMPs were considered extraordinary is mysterious. Perhaps the Syrians fell into a common trap when using BMPs: if a vehicle looks like a tank, people tend to use it as such, even though it is not one.

Except for the ribbed engine cover plate of magnesium-aluminium alloy, the BMP is constructed of high-quality steel in ballistic areas, with lower-quality steel elsewhere. In the Middle East brew-ups and secondary explosions were frequent as a result of everything being so close together – including fuel tanks in the rear door. A penetrating shell will almost certainly hit something vital.

MT-LB towing a 100mm T-12 in a November 1977 parade in Moscow. The gunport on each side of the passenger compartment is evident, as are the vision blocks. *(US Army)*

MT-LB (M-1970) armoured personnel carrier and tractor and ACRV-2 (M-1976) vehicle

Weight 9.7 tons **Length** 6.454m **Height** 1.865m **Width** 2.8m **Track width** 0.35m (MT-LB) **Clearance** 0.4m **Ground contact** 4.08m **Max road speed** 61.5km/h **Max water speed** 5–6km/h **Range** 400km **Gradient** 30° **Engine** YaMZ-238 V-8 high-compression, water-cooled diesel, 240HP @ 2,100rpm **Gun** 7.62mm PKT **Traverse** 360° **Armour** 14mm (max) **Crew** 2 **Passengers** 11 **Cargo weight** 2 tons **Towed load** 4 tons

ACRV-2

Weight 11 tonnes **Length** 7.06m **Width** 2.81m **Height** 2.43m **Ground pressure** 19.8kg/cm² **Ground contact** 4.78m **Maximum armour** 14mm **Armament** none or 1 × 12.7mm **Towed load** nil. Remaining data as MT-LB.

The MT-LB is part of a family of vehicles powered by the new YaMZ high-pressure diesel engine originally developed for civilian use. Other vehicles in the series include the MT-L tractor, the ACRV-2 (M-1976) artil- lery command and reconnaissance vehicle, and the SAU-122 self-propelled howitzer.

As these vehicles were developed from the MT-L Arctic tractor, it is not surprising that the MT-LB is designed for use in cold climates, with an engine pre-heating system and a heater and ventilation equipment for the crew com- partment. Its mobility across snow or soft ground is excel- lent, especially when fitted with special wide grouser tracks, vehicles so equipped being designated MT-LBV. The suspension and road gear embody standardised components, similar to PT-76 derivatives. There are six road wheels each side, with the drive sprocket forward and the idler to the rear, and two torsion bars and hy- draulic shock-absorbers on swing arms on the first and last road wheels on each side. There are no support rol- lers. The MT-LB swims, propelled by its tracks, and a folding trim vane is attached to the forward glacis plate. Radios, periscopes and the driver's infra-red driving equipment appear similar to those on the BMP. The crew consists of a commander and driver-mechanic. The com- mander mans the turret-mounted 7.62mm PKT machine gun, its firepower being supplemented by a firing port and vision block in each rear door and on each side of the passenger compartment. The MT-LB has an NBC defence system and can be sealed airtight. Exit is through large roof hatches or two large rear doors.

Variations of the MT-LB include the unarmed MT-L

An early-model ACRV-2. *(US Army Research & Development magazine)*

tractor with a large, unarmoured aluminium body; it is used in the far north of the Soviet Union. The MT-LB-U command version is similar to the BMP-Sh and is fitted with extra radios and a canvas extension for use when halted. The MT-SON mounts a Pork Trough artillery radar.

The ACRV-2 (Artillery Command and Reconnaissance Vehicle, NATO designation) M-1976 is based on the MT-LB and SAU-122 series. It can be used as a mobile command post for all types of units, but is most often associated with self-propelled artillery units. Some early production versions mount a 12.7mm DShKM for anti-aircraft defence, but this is absent from most vehicles. Some versions may be ammunition carriers. The main roles appear to be artillery command, target acquisition and fire control, and it is used in conjunction with the BMP-Sh and radar-equipped BMPs or MT-LBs; one of the group of three vehicles carries a radar, the other a fire-control computer – possibly a digital type – and the ACRV-2 the command post. The ACRV-2 reportedly also mounts a laser artillery rangefinder. It has a small turret to permit the use of optical observation devices, and sports a number of radio aerials and an auxiliary generator.

The ACRV-2's automotive performance is similar to that of the MT-LB and the 122mm SP howitzer.

Weapons effectiveness and combat usage

The MT-LB has apparently never seen action, except in Afghanistan.

Tactical employment

The MT-LB is used mainly as a gun tractor. Along with the URAL-375 truck, it has replaced most of the wide range of Soviet gun tractors. MT-LBs have replaced GAZ-66s for towing the 120mm mortars of BMP-equipped battalions, they are the standard tow vehicle for T-12 100mm anti-tank guns, and are sometimes seen

A later-model ARCV-2, without the 12.7mm anti-aircraft machine gun. The turret may contain a laser rangefinder and associated artillery fire-control equipment. *(AFV G-Z)*

towing larger guns, including the M-30 and D-30 122mm howitzers. They also serve as ammunition carriers and COPs. MT-LBs are used as APCs by some units which will be called upon to operate in snow or marsh. Two divisions stationed near Murmansk and some units in Siberia use the MT-LB as their standard APC, and these vehicles are often seen fitted with unditching timbers.

Foreign usage

The BTR-152 has been supplied to Afghanistan, Albania, Cambodia, Ceylon, China (where it was built as the Type 56 APC), Congo, Cuba, Cyprus (where it saw some action against the Turks in 1974), East Germany, Egypt, Guinea, Hungary, India, Indonesia, Iran, Iraq, Israel, Mongolia, North Korea, North Yemen, Poland, Romania, Somalia, Sudan, Syria, Tanzania, Uganda, Yugoslavia and Ethiopia. The anti-aircraft versions have been used by Warsaw Pact armies, Ethiopia, North Korea and other nations.

The BTR-50 series has been supplied to Afghanistan, Albania, Algeria, Bulgaria, China, Czechoslovakia (before OT-62 production), East Germany, Egypt, Finland, Hungary, India, Iran, Israel, Libya, Vietnam (used at An Loc in 1972), Poland, Romania, Somalia, Sudan, Syria and Yugoslavia. Many of these vehicles are Czech-built OT-62s, and several armies use both Czech and Soviet-built machines. Most of those still in service with the Warsaw Pact are probably Czech-built.

The BTR-60 series has been supplied to Afghanistan, Algeria, the Warsaw Pact armies (except for Czechoslovakia), Uganda, Cuba, Egypt, Iran, Iraq, Israel, Libya, Mongolia, North Korea, North Yemen, Somalia, Ethiopia, Syria, Vietnam and Yugoslavia.

BMPs and BMP-1s have been supplied to Poland, East Germany, Czechoslovakia and probably Hungary in the Warsaw Pact. Syria, Egypt, Iran, Iraq, Algeria and Libya have received exported BMPs. BMP-Rs have probably been exported to East Germany, to be followed by Poland. It is not known whether any BMP-Shs have been exported, but this is unlikely until well into the 1980s.

The US Army has had the opportunity to examine all Soviet APCs and has several OT-62s, BTR-60PBs and BMPs.

MT-LBs and ACRV-2s have been exported to most of the Warsaw Pact nations.

Chapter Nine

Anti-tank Weapons

*"A system of anti-tank defence is built on the basis of all anti-tank
weapons and their co-ordination with nuclear attacks and with each
other, and must envisage their grouping and manoeuvre with due
regard for enemy action and maximum utilisation of the protective
features of the terrain."*

G. BIRUKOV and G. MELINKOV

The importance of anti-tank warfare permeates the Soviet
Army. Every weapon plays a part in the defeat of enemy
armour. Every unit has an anti-tank capability, a legacy of
1941, when Soviet anti-tank weapons, few and
inadequate, proved a weak barrier to the *panzers*. But the
Soviets learned fast, and at Kursk in 1943 a combined-
arms anti-tank defence in depth halted the *blitzkrieg* for-
ever. The success at Kursk still guides Soviet anti-tank
weapons and tactics.

Anti-tank weapons form a mutually supporting system
at each level of organisation, allowing the Soviets to
optimise and integrate their employment. The slow-firing
but accurate anti-tank guided missiles (ATGMs) provide
long-range fire, starting at a range of 3,000m. At 1,500m,
when volume of fire is more important than individual
accuracy, tanks and towed anti-tank guns will open fire.
BMP guns open fire at 800m, being better than the
ATGMs at close range. Close defence is provided by the
many widely deployed RPG-7s, their 300m effective range
being the same as the ATGM's minimum range. In addition, all field and anti-aircraft artillery has an anti-tank
role.

True to its offensive, armoured outlook, the Soviet
Army believes that the best anti-tank weapon is another
tank. But the Soviets have never let their emphasis on
tanks blind them to the importance of other anti-tank
weapons. They are fully aware that the wide range of
modern anti-tank weapons threatens the very basis of
their armoured offensive, and much of their tactical evolution in recent years has been aimed at overcoming this
threat.

The Soviets field a full range of ATGMs, ranging from
the first-generation AT-1 (now obsolete), AT-2 and AT-3,
through the second-generation AT-4 and AT-5, to the
more advanced, possibly third-generation, AT-6. However, they still use towed anti-tank guns, the 100mm T-12

in motorised rifle divisions and the 85mm SD-44 in airborne units. The 82mm and 107mm recoilless anti-tank
guns have been largely replaced by man-portable "suitcase" Sagger ATGMs and the 73mm tripod-mounted
SPG-9 gun, which fires the same rocket projectile as the
BMD and BMP. Masses of the RPG-7 rocket grenade
launchers provide close-range defence. The Soviet anti-
tank defence system is a formidable one.

Anti-tank weapons on the defence

While organic, specialised anti-tank weapons and units
are unnecessary in tank units, every Soviet motorised rifle
and airborne battalion, regiment and division has its own
anti-tank unit. Sub-units below battalion size rely on the
armament of their tanks, APCs and BMPs and the ubi-
quitous RPG-7s. Each motorised rifle battalion's anti-
tank platoon has two suitcase Sagger ATGM launchers
and two SPG-9s. Each motorised rifle regiment has an
anti-tank company with nine BRDM-2 or BRDM-3 scout
cars mounting sextuple Sagger or quintuple Spandrel
launchers. Eighteen T-12 100mm towed anti-tank guns
equip each motorised rifle division's anti-tank battalion,
at least until they are phased out in favour of ATGMs.
Every Soviet commander from sergeant to major-general
can deploy his own anti-tank assets. The different levels of
anti-tank defence create a defence in depth, a defence that
is interlocking in unit size, weapons capability and
deployment.

While the anti-tank defence of the BTR-60PB-
equipped motorised rifle battalion is formidable, that of a
BMP-equipped battalion is much more so. Battalion positions will rarely be without the support of overlapping
fields of fire from battalions on their flanks and behind

INTERLOCKING FIELDS OF FIRE (BTR-60PB-EQUIPPED BATTALION)

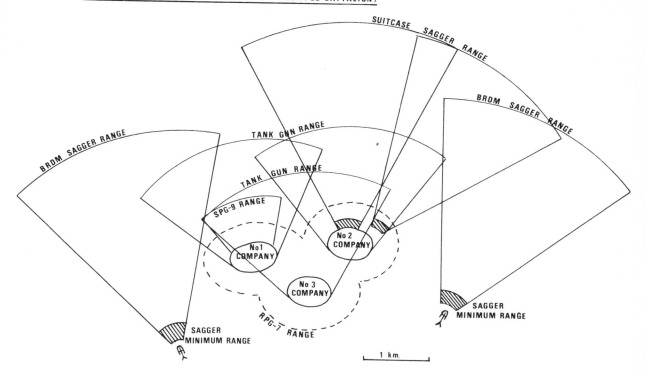

them, and from regimental and divisional anti-tank weapons. The Soviets can mass 25 to 35 tank-killing weapons per kilometre of front. The defence will be aligned so that the heaviest weapon concentrations will cover the most likely avenues of approach. The defensive strongpoints themselves will if possible be on terrain unfavourable to armour, in order to prevent overruns. Whenever possible all Soviet units will plant extensive anti-tank minefields, and engineer equipment will be used to create obstacles and barriers (especially in defiles or wooded tracks) and to dig anti-tank ditches. Minefields and obstacles will channel the enemy into "fire pockets," pre-planned concentrations of anti-tank fire that will hit the targets from all sides and with many weapons. Soviet units will hold their ground even if the enemy breaks through, and their all-round defence will join the second line of defence in creating a fire pocket. Indirect-fire artillery will be the first weapons to engage attacking enemy armour, and will maintain the fire on it through the depths of the defence, forcing them to "button up" and thereby reducing their visibility, or blinding them with smokeshell. The Soviets believe that indirect artillery fire can disorganise an attack before the anti-tank weapons open fire. If necessary, the artillery and anti-aircraft guns will engage tanks with direct fire.

All defending Soviet divisions and regiments, and often battalions, have an anti-tank reserve. This can include tanks, engineers and field artillery, but is usually built around the divisional anti-tank battalion or regimental anti-tank company. Positioned behind the first echelon, they can move to stop any enemy breakthrough, aid counterattacks or beleaguered first-echelon units, or disrupt any attacks on the second echelon. The Soviets attach great importance to this anti-tank reserve, both defensively and as part of the counterattack.

The anti-tank reserve also provides overlapping fields of fire with both first and second-echelon anti-tank weapons. This is especially important in modern warfare. When NBC or conventional fires neutralise a particular sector, the adjacent units will have to cover the gap until the reserves can come up.

Engineers are an important part of Soviet anti-tank defences, laying mines, creating barriers and abatis, digging anti-tank ditches and preparing emplacements for anti-tank weapons.

Anti-tank ambushes are positioned along expected enemy advance or withdrawal routes in conjunction with the rest of the overlapping anti-tank defences. Ambushes are often used by outposts and rearguards, or where there are insufficient anti-tank weapons available to cover the front, after powerful enemy preparatory fire, for example. Ambushes will be set in woods, where the targets cannot manoeuvre and the Soviets can displace under cover to a new position to repeat the process. They are also used offensively to defeat enemy armour, especially when no Soviet tanks are available.

All Soviet anti-tank weapons and tactics have an offensive function. In the meeting engagement they guard against surprise and enemy flank attacks, while also providing a base of fire against enemy armour when the Soviets go into the hasty attack. Anti-tank weapons are distributed throughout the line of march, so that if any unit is forced to assume the hasty defence until the next unit comes up, its crucial anti-tank elements will be at hand and can then join in the Soviet attack. If required, the Soviets will push anti-tank weapons forward even in a mobile, open battle. All of them have a very important offensive role.

In the breakthrough attack anti-tank weapons will join in the preparation. They will also follow immediately behind assaulting troops to consolidate their gains or, if they are halted, reinforce the hasty defence. If they are established in a captured enemy position they can serve as a base of fire to support the second echelon as it moves in to continue the attack.

The future

The impending introduction of a generation of Western battle tanks with compound armour calls into question almost the entire range of Soviet anti-tank weapons. The new armour will reduce the HEAT warheads on which most of these weapons rely from efficient to rather indifferent tank-killers. Live Sagger rounds have been fired at the Chobham-armoured US M-1 tank. Their only effort was reportedly to damage the paint.

One possible course is shown by the AT-6, with a HEAT warhead that may be large enough to defeat even Chobham armour, especially if it strikes the tank's weaker roof armour. The AT-6 may eventually be used in ground mountings, and it has been suggested as a replacement for the T-12. Alternatively, ATGMs may simply become more massive, perhaps based on SAMs such as the SA-8. Another counter to the new armour would be to emphasise kinetic-energy weapons rather than ATGMs with their HEAT warheads. The Soviets have watched Western work on low-pressure guns and long-rod penetrators with great interest, and either of these concepts could be used, perhaps in an offshoot of the SPG-9.

Unit organisation

Divisional anti-tank battalion (motorised rifle and artillery divisions)
Total strength: 23 officers, 259 enlisted men, 18 100mm T-12 AT guns, 6 BRDM scout cars, 18 MT-LB gun

tractors or trucks, 22 trucks (some may be replaced by MT-LB).
One HQ battery (6 officers, 25 enlisted men, 9 trucks, 2 BRDMs or BTR-60PUs)
Three AT gun batteries (each 5 officers and 60 men, organised as a standard artillery battery, guns often towed by MT-LBs)
One service battery (2 officers, 54 men, 11 trucks, 1 BRDM)

Regimental anti-tank guided missile battery (motorised rifle regiments)
Total strength: 4 officers, 53 enlisted men, two/three trucks, nine BRDMs armed with ATGMs. Officers are battery commander and three platoon commanders. Each BRDM also carries an RPG-7 and a light machine gun, used to cover dismounted scouting and to guard against close assault.

Battalion anti-tank platoon (motorised rifle battalion)
Total strength: one officer, 13–17 enlisted men, two suitcase Sagger launchers, two SPG-9s, three RPG-7s, 13–18 AKMSs. Normally mounted in two APCs, this platoon almost certainly is not organic to BMP-equipped battalions.

RPG-7

Calibre of tube 40mm **Calibre of round** 85mm **Length of tube** 95cm **Weight (unloaded)** 8.6kg **Max rate of fire** 4–6rpm **Max range** 920m **Max effective range** 300m **Min range** 5m **Ammunition** PG-7 HEAT **Ammunition weight** 2kg

The RPG-7 (*Reaktivniy Protivotankovyi Granatomet*, rocket anti-tank grenade launcher) is the smallest and most widespread Soviet anti-tank launcher. Every motorised rifle and airborne squad has an RPG-7, which is seen as its single most important weapon. At night or in dense terrain, where other weapons cannot be used at long range, or cannot be used at all, the RPG-7 has increased value. Combat experience throughout the world has shown the effectiveness of the RPG-7.

The RPG-7 is currently issued in two models, the basic RPG-7V and the airborne RPG-7D, which can be broken down into two parts. A development of the earlier RPG-2 (itself developed from the Panzerfaust 150), now replaced in Soviet service, the RPG-7 launches a PG-7 rocket-propelled anti-tank projectile with a HEAT warhead and "fin and spin" stabilisation, or a 7.62mm sub-calibre training round. A replacement, the RPG-9 or RPG-16, is reported to be in service. It has been described as being

RPG-7, showing both optical sights (with protective cap on) and forward "iron" sights. *(US Army)*

73mm calibre and using a new IR sight. Like the RPG-7, it has a two-part airborne version. Reports have also mentioned the development of an improved, two-stage grenade for the RPG-7, extending its effective range by 200 additional metres.

The RPG-7 has two sights, the basic 2½× optical sights with rangefinding stadia, and secondary tangent sights. The optical sights are the most complicated part of the RPG-7, and too complicated for many trainees, according to Soviet publications. The gunner must take many variables into account and make many estimates to sight an RPG-7. The Soviet RPG-7 manual devotes more space to sighting problems than to any other topic. Aiming the RPG-7 is difficult because the PG-7 projectile is seriously affected by crosswinds in flight. The reaction effect of its rocket motor turns it into the wind, and the RPG-7 gunner must estimate the direction and speed of the wind as well as that of the target. The sight picture is gridded off in parallel vertical lines to determine deflection for wind and target motion, while its rangefinder stadia measures the full target height to estimate range. Maximum sight range is 500m; there are horizontal gridded lines on the sight to give proper elevation up to that range, but not beyond. US tests of captured RPG-7s revealed that even well trained gunners are normally 10–15% off in estimating the range, greatly reducing first-round accuracy. Targets which are only partially exposed or are moving are even more difficult to range in on and hit.

Optical sight filters increase vision in glare, smoke and haze, and the sight can be adjusted for temperature extremes. It is internally lit for night use, or it can be replaced with a night sight, either the 6kg, 1956-vintage NSP-2 active infra-red sight or the PGN-1 passive-starlight scope, which amplifies existing light; this 3.5kg unit was introduced in 1969. The PGN-1 was used by the Arabs in the 1973 War. The NSP-2 was used in Vietnam, and can detect targets 150–200m away, while the PGN-1 can do so at twice that range.

When speed of fire is more important than accuracy, the gunner may use the iron tangent sights, which, although they have no wind or deflection adjustment, can be used at 200–500m range. Many foreign users of the RPG-7 rely on the iron sight because the intricacies of the optical sight are beyond them.

Combat usage

Introduced in 1962, the RPG-7 first saw action in the 1967 Middle East war. Each Egyptian infantry platoon had only one RPG-7, which made them extremely vulnerable to armoured attacks, but they still destroyed many Israeli tanks at Rafah and El Arish. Impressed by the RPG-7, the Israelis adopted the captured weapons.

Used in Vietnam in 1967, the RPG-7 was more effective than the widely used RPG-2 (known as the "B40" by the North Vietnamese) and Chinese-built 57mm and 75mm recoilless rifles. As well as serving as an anti-tank weapon, the RPG-7 was used against bunkers and emplacements and in urban combat. Two US Marine battalion commanders stated that the RPG-7 was the most dangerous single weapon in the fierce house-to-house fighting in Hue in 1968.

The Egyptian infantry that crossed the Suez Canal in 1973 were lavishly equipped with RPG-7s, often taken from the units remaining in Egypt (which made those units vulnerable when the Israelis took the offensive). RPG-7s were used in conjunction with Sagger ATGMs to defeat Israeli tank attacks in the first days of the war, and the Syrians also used RPG-7s offensively during the same period. The Israeli tanks that were destroying the Syrian armour at long range were unsupported by infantry, enabling Syrian RPG-7 teams to work their way up close to the Israeli tanks and knock many of them out. On the Syrian front RPG-7s destroyed more Israeli tanks than any other type of weapon.

In addition to the Middle East and Vietnam, RPG-7s have been used in Northern Ireland and in almost every armed conflict in the world since 1967.

Hit probability

Type of target	Range (metres)					
	50	100	200	300	400	500
1st round, exposed, stationary	98%	91%	52%	27%	10%	5%
1st round, hull-down	80%	70%	20%	9%	3%	–
2nd round, exposed, stationary	98%	95%	78%	56%	38%	25%
2nd round, exposed, moving	97%	90%	55%	27%	16%	6%
2nd round, hull-down	80%	68%	35%	18%	10%	–

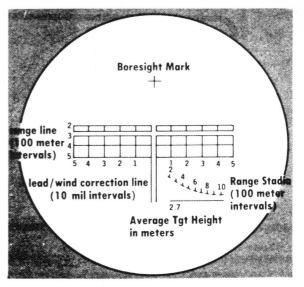

Optical sight picture of an RPG-7 (English-language legends do not appear on the original). *(US Army)*

The target is an M60A1 tank moving at 16km/h at an angle of 30° from the RPG-7, wind at 11km/h. It is apparent that owing to the difficulty in estimating deflection, wind effect and range to hull-down tanks, the RPG-7 gunner must assume a first-round miss at all but the closest ranges and apply corrections to the second round, which takes 14sec to get ready. The RPG-7 requires massed fire for maximum effectiveness.

A PG-7 projectile can punch a 5cm hole through the equivalent of 280mm of armour, pushing hot metal fragments and the jet streaming from the shaped charge into the target, followed by the copper slug produced from the projectile liner, which will ricochet inside a tank and often go through APCs. Armour penetration varies with range and individual grenades. Some have penetrated over 300mm of armour. At under 300m range, however, the PG-7's speed reduces the penetration of its shaped charge.

Tactical employment

The RPG-7 gunner carries a slung AKMS and four PG-7 grenades in a haversack. The assistant gunner is similarly armed. RPG-7s are placed in the centre of each squad strongpoint. Alternative firing positions will be selected and, if time permits, linked by a communication trench or crawlway. The positioning of the RPG-7s gives depth to the defence and creates fire pockets in conjunction with other anti-tank weapons. RPG-7s will hold their fire until the enemy is 300m away.

Range (m)	50	100	150	200	250	300	350	400	450	500
Penetration (mm)	265	220	225	240	265	280	280	280	285	290

If a PG-7 hits an M60A1 it has a 40% chance of knocking it out, but only a 5% chance of completely destroying it.

Although it does not have an anti-personnel round, the RPG-7 is effective against buildings and fortifications. It can penetrate 23cm of sandbags, 45.7cm of reinforced concrete, and 152.4cm of earth and log bunker. The PG-7 can plough through brick and concrete walls, leaving a five-centimetre hole, but it will not knock them down.

In Vietnam and Rhodesia, and against the Soviets in Afghanistan, RPG-7s were often used against helicopters. Probabilities of hitting and killing were both low, but they could be effective if fired from ambush at landing helicopters.

One or more RPG-7 teams may be located in ambush positions to bring flanking fire on tanks attacking the company frontage. Anti-tank ambushes are often positioned to catch tanks in woods (standard North Vietnamese tactics). Using infra-red sights, the North Vietnamese also used the anti-tank ambush offensively in many night attacks on US armour. The Soviets consider the offensive anti-tank ambush particularly effective when used by reconnaissance forces, and it can be used to take prisoners or destroy important weapons.

The RPG-7 is used for close-range defence of Sagger ATGMs. The Egyptians located their RPG-7s 150–200m forward of the Saggers to catch tanks in combined Sagger and RPG-7 fire. The Soviets have three RPG-7 gunners to protect each pair of suitcase Saggers and each platoon of three Sagger-armed BRDMs.

With proper clearance, the RPG-7 can be fired from inside buildings and bunkers. It can also be fired from an open APC or BMP hatch, but this makes the gunner an excellent target and decreases the weapon's accuracy, which is why the RPG-7 gunner normally uses an AKMS when mounted. When a squad dismounts, the RPG-7 gunner advances in the middle of the squad skirmish line, next to the squad leader.

The tactics of the Chinese Army rely heavily on the RPG-7, a version of which, along with the RPG-2, is built in China. The Chinese depend on well dug-in infantry armed with RPGs to halt the Soviet armoured offensive with concentrated fire. They have modified the rangefinding stadia of Chinese-built RPG-7s to allow for the lower height of Soviet-built tanks, although an alternative scale for Western tanks is also provided. The Chinese-built sight is reportedly simpler to use and gives better results.

Engagement sequence

Before a PG-7 projectile is loaded, the gunner or assistant gunner must assemble it, screwing the warhead and sustainer motor together with the booster charge. It is then loaded. The gunner then uses the stadia to estimate range, as on a T-62's sight. He tracks the target until it reaches the 500m maximum sighting range, then switches to the gridded lines on the optical sight, estimating the speed and direction of both the wind and the target and adjusting his aim to compensate for both. When his target reaches the double 300m horizontal line, the gunner will fire. Squeezing the trigger ignites the strip powder charge at the base of the projectile, ejecting it from the RPG-7 at a velocity of 177m/sec. Four stabilising tail fins pop open as the projectile clears the barrel. Its warhead arms after it has travelled five metres, and after 11m the rocket sustainer motor ignites, boosting the speed to 294m/sec. If the projectile has not struck anything after it has been in flight for five seconds, when it will have travelled 900m, it will self-destruct. The gunner will observe where the projectile went, correct, reload and fire again. This takes 14sec. The Soviets believe that 300m is the optimum engagement range for the RPG-7, as it reduces target reaction time for suppressive fire or evasive action while still giving time for more shots if the first does not kill the tank. As the first hit will probably not kill the target tank, the gunner should move after firing whenever possible.

Countermeasures

Suppressive fire is the best countermeasure to the RPG-7. An unguided "fire and forget" weapon, it is less vulnerable to suppression than the Sagger. Although the gunner can move immediately after firing, the backblast will often disclose the firing position. The backblast is a one-metre puff of smoke which remains for up to eight seconds, and the rocket ignition produces a bright flash and a second smoke puff. Most countermeasures effective against the Sagger are also effective against the RPG-7; the exception is evasive action, since the warning time is often too short.

The PG-7's small HEAT warhead can be countered by spaced armour, the first layer of armour detonating the warhead and the second stopping the explosive blast and shaped-charge jet. Many Allied AFVs in Vietnam used appliqué "RPG screens" for armour. If an RPG round hit one of these screens two feet away from the target, its penetration effect would be halved. A screen nine feet away would reduce penetration to 25mm. Almost any type of material can be used to detonate the PG-7. In Vietnam the Americans developed a portable wire mesh screen for the stand-off protection of stationary vehicles. Fifty per cent of the RPG rounds that struck the screen did not detonate at all, thanks to the mesh shorting out the piezo-electric fuse which detonates the warhead. Both the Americans and the Israelis attached lengths of wire mesh RPG screen, which will also "dud out" Saggers, a few feet from the side of their vehicles to increase protection while in combat.

According to some reports from the Lebanon in 1978, Israeli AFVs can generate an electric current the same as that used in the fuze, thereby detonating the warhead in flight. It is uncertain how this current is used – whether passed through wire mesh or transmitted – but US armour officers consider such a countermeasure impractical.

RPG-75

RPG-75 is the provisional designation of the first Soviet single-shot, disposable, hand-held anti-tank weapon. Although the Soviets made use of captured *Panzerfausts* in 1945, they had hitherto avoided the Western practice of providing all riflemen with an anti-tank capability. This was in line with the Soviet belief in "one man, one task" and a realistic response to the limited training time available. However, the appearance of this new weapon indicates a shift away from this policy. The RPG-75 is reportedly of 75mm or 73mm calibre and has an effective range of 300m. According to reports from Afghanistan, where it has been in action, it resembles a flare tube when not deployed for action and there are versions with high-explosive and chemical as well as HEAT warheads.

73mm SPG-9 anti-tank weapon in firing position. *(US Army)*

SPG-9 73mm recoilless anti-tank gun

Calibre 30cal **Weight (firing)** 60kg **Weight (without tripod)** 47.5kg **Length (travelling)** 2.1m **Rate of fire** 6rpm **Effective range** 800m **Max range** 1,960m **Ammunition types** HEAT (rocket assist), possibly HE **Initial muzzle velocity** 435m/sec **Max muzzle velocity (with rocket)** 700m/sec **Shell weight** 1.3kg **Armour penetration (HEAT)** 400mm **Crew** 3 **Carried in** APC

The tripod-mounted, smooth-bore, recoilless SPG-9 replaced the 82mm B-10 and 107mm B-11 recoilless anti-tank guns from 1969. The SPG-9 is similar to the 73mm 2A20 gun mounted in the turret of the BMP and BMD, the main difference being in the propelling cartridge. While it is man-portable, a pair of SPG-9s is normally carried in an APC, though it can only fire from its tripod

and not from an APC hatch. Its rocket-assisted HEAT projectile has a high muzzle velocity, boosted to 700m/sec by the rocket. It can be fitted with both active and passive night sights, including the 800m-range APN-2. The shell self-destructs at maximum range.

Combat usage

The SPG-9 has seen combat in Afghanistan and some may have been supplied to Ethiopia in 1978. Its effectiveness would be approximately the same as that of the 2A20, as would its engagement sequence and the countermeasures effective against it.

Tactical employment

A pair of SPG-9s is organic to each motorised rifle battalion's anti-tank platoon. Like the suitcase Saggers, they are normally positioned in the forward company strongpoint on the defence, while on the attack they follow the attacking APCs or remain in overwatch positions.

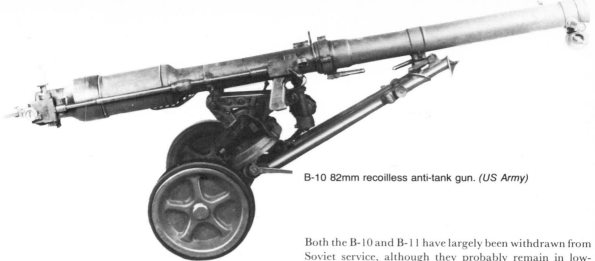

B-10 82mm recoilless anti-tank gun. *(US Army)*

B-10 82mm and B-11 107mm recoilless anti-tank guns

	B-10	**B-11**
Calibre	20cal	28cal
Weight (firing)	72.2kg	305kg
Length (travelling)	1.91m	3.56m
Width	0.71m	1.45m
Rate of fire	5–6rpm	5rpm
Max range (HE)	4,470m	6,650m
Effective AT range	390m	450m
Ammunition types	BK-881 HEAT, OF-881A HE	BK-883 HEAT, OF-883A HE
Muzzle velocity (HEAT)	322m/sec	400m/sec
Muzzle velocity (HE)	320m/sec	375m/sec
Shell weight	3.6kg-HEAT 4.5kg-HE	7.5kg-HEAT 8.5kg-HE
Armour penetration (HEAT)	240mm	380mm

Both the B-10 and B-11 have largely been withdrawn from Soviet service, although they probably remain in low-readiness formations and for training. Both weapons are smooth-bores, introduced in the early 1950s. Both fire fin-stabilised HEAT and HE rounds and are towed by the muzzle on two-wheel carriages that can be broken down into a simple tripod if the weapon has to be carried or emplaced. The B-10's breech opens horizontally, while the B-11's swings down. The B-10 is fitted with a PBO-2 sight, the B-11 with a PBO-4.

Originally intended to equip battalion anti-tank platoons and regimental anti-tank companies respectively, these two guns have been unsuccessful. After the poor performance of Arab B-10s in the 1967 War they were reportedly withdrawn from service in at least some Soviet battalions and replaced with 57mm anti-tank guns from reserve stocks as an interim measure pending arrival of the SPG-9. The B-11 is large and bulky and difficult to traverse. Both weapons were also used in combat by the North Vietnamese Army, and by the Arabs in 1973.

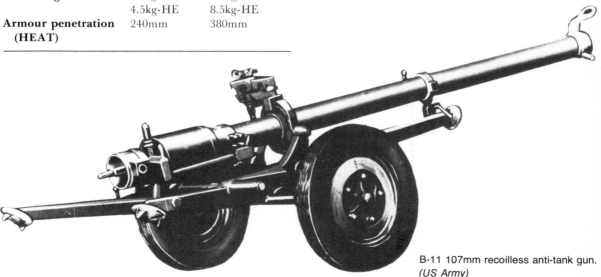

B-11 107mm recoilless anti-tank gun. *(US Army)*

BRDM-I with Swatter mount. *(Department of Defense)*

First-generation ATGMs

NATO designation	AT-1	AT-2	AT-3
	Snapper	Swatter	Sagger
Soviet designation	3M6	PTUR-62	9M14M
	PTUR-61	"Falanga"	PTUR-64
	"Schmel"		"Malatyuka"
Length	1.14m	1.14m	0.815m
Diameter	0.132m	0.132m	0.12m
Weight of missile	24kg	29.5kg	11.3kg
Min range	500m	500m	300m
Max range	2,500m	3,000m	3,000m
		(3,500)	
Velocity	90m/sec	150m/sec	120m/sec
			(150)
Warhead	HEAT, 5.28kg	HEAT	HEAT, 2.7kg
Armour penetration	350mm	480mm (500)	400mm
Control	Wings	Fins	Nozzles
Time to max range	30sec	23.2sec (27)	27sec (21)

Figures for later versions are shown in parentheses where they differ. The Swatter version is the Swatter-B, as used on some helicopters; the Sagger version in parentheses is the improved version mounted on some BRDMs.

The most skilfully aimed tank gun loses accuracy at long range. Dozens of variables, impossible to compensate for in the heat of action, affect the flight of a shell. Even the earliest Soviet ATGMs, however, can attain an 89% hit probability at 2,500m range, much higher than the finest tank gun. The key to this difference is that ATGMs are guided, unlike the shells. The gunner literally flies them to their targets.

The Soviets realised the revolutionary potential of ATGMs when they were introduced in the mid-1950s. This potential first became evident in the first days of the 1973 Middle East war, when the Israeli armour attacked the Sagger ATGM and RPG-7 anti-tank teams screening the Egyptian bridgehead across the Suez Canal. In the words of one Israeli tank commander: "We were advancing, and in the distance I saw specks dotted on the sand dunes. I couldn't make out what they were. As we got closer, I thought they looked like tree stumps. They were motionless and scattered across the terrain ahead of us. I got on the intercom and asked the tanks ahead what they made of it. One of my tank commanders radioed back:

Above Swatter ATGMs on BRDM-1. The Snapper mount is similar, but the Sagger mount has a retractable armoured roof, as on the BRDM-2.

Below Saggers mounted on BMP launch rails. *(US Air Force)*

'My God, they're not tree stumps, they're men.' For a moment, I couldn't understand. What were men doing out there – standing quite still – when we were advancing in our tanks towards them? Suddenly, all hell broke loose. A barrage of missiles was being fired at us. Many of our tanks were hit. We had never come up against anything like this before . . .''

In the first 72 hours of the war all of Mandler's armoured division and a brigade of Adan's armoured division were decimated. The Sagger had shown the potential of the ATGM.

The first Soviet ATGM, the AT-1 Snapper, was large, primitive, heavy and slow. It entered service in the late 1950s and was normally mounted in a rear-facing quadruple mount on a light truck or a triple mount on a BRDM-1. Control was from a remote joystick which could be up to 50m away, although it was normally in the cab of the truck. It has probably been phased out of Soviet service, but is still used in Yugoslavia.

The Snapper was followed into service by the radio-controlled AT-2 Swatter-A and Swatter-B and the wire-guided AT-3 Sagger. The Swatter is mounted on Hind-A helicopter gunships, in triple mounts on BRDM-1 scout cars and in quadruple mounts on BRDM-2 scout cars, although it is apparently being superseded by the Sagger in this role.

The Sagger is the standard Soviet ATGM. It is mounted on BMPs and BMDs, on a sextuple mount on a BRDM-2 or -1 scout car, and is man-portable in an easily carried "suitcase" which contains two rounds and a missile control unit. Since 1973 a slightly improved Sagger has been mounted on BRDMs. It is 25% faster than the standard Sagger, taking 21sec to fly to 3,000m instead of 27sec. The new version is not used in BMPs, BMDs or suitcases. Modified Saggers with semi-automatic guidance reportedly entered service in the late 1970s.

Using first-generation ATGMs

The Snapper, Swatter and Sagger systems require the gunner to "fly" the missile to its target. The gunner tracks the missile visually by a flare in its tail, correcting its course with a miniature joystick. This requires a high level of dexterity, co-ordination and training. Weapons putting such a high premium on gunner skill are perhaps better suited to a professional army's long-serving experienced personnel. The Soviets and other large, conscript armies, like that of Egypt, do not have such soldiers available in sufficient numbers. The Soviets select potential ATGM gunners from those with the best co-ordination in each incoming crop of conscripts, and they undergo extensive training in simulators. A gunner must fire 2,300 simulated Sagger rounds to qualify as proficient. Owing to the expense, each gunner might fire only one Sagger as a graduation exercise, but he must practise with 50–60

BRDM-1 with retractable Sagger mount extended.
(Department of Defense)

simulated rounds a week to stay proficient. Even at the height of the 1973 War, the Egyptians brought truck-mounted simulators up to the front lines so that Sagger gunners could fire 20–30 simulated rounds a day when not actually engaging the Israelis.

Unlike the US TOW, the Sagger can be guided from under armour on the BMP, BMD and BRDM, with the gunner sighting through his vision block. Suitcase and BRDM-2-mounted Saggers can also be controlled remotely. The launch controls are attached to a wire – 15m for the suitcase version, 80m for the BRDM-2 – and the gunner can position himself away from the launcher, at which suppressive fire would be aimed. It also allows the launcher to be put in defilade, or on a reverse slope. All that need be exposed is the missile control box's 8× monocular periscope eyepiece, measuring 10 × 2½cm. However, when the gunner is "flying" the Sagger from a remote location not directly between the launcher and the target, it becomes less accurate, as the gunner must take the lateral offset into account when flying the missile. This

AT-1 Snapper ATGM.
(Missile Intelligence Agency)

BRDM-1s armed with Snapper ATGMs. *(Department of Defense)*

also increases the "capture" range (the minimum range at which the missile can be brought under control). If the gunner is co-located with the launcher the missile can be captured at its 300m minimum range and guided from there to its target. But if the gunner has offset his position away from the launcher he can only capture a Sagger after it has flown at least 500–800m, or 1,000m under combat conditions.

It takes five minutes to deploy a single suitcase Sagger for action and 12 minutes for a full four-missile team to set up. BRDM-2-mounted Saggers can be elevated and ready for action in one minute. A single Sagger control unit can fly only one missile at a time, but a BRDM-2 can fire another missile within five seconds of the first round hitting the target. The suitcase Sagger and those on the BMP and BMD must be reloaded first, which takes about 90sec.

Performance and capabilities

All Soviet first-generation ATGMs are slow in flight. If they were any faster, there would not be enough time for the gunner to correct their flight. This gives targets time for countermeasures and means that many targets will move out of the gunner's field of vision, covered by blocking terrain. While this was not a problem in the sands of Sinai, it would be very important in West Germany, where tanks will move from cover to cover. At 1,500m

range a tank moving at 21km/h would have to be exposed in sight for 150m for a Sagger gunner to acquire the target and fire (which a proficient gunner might do in ten seconds), and fly the missile to the target. Even on the flat North German plain, a tank moving from cover to cover would only be exposed for a 150m interval 30% of the time. At 3,000m range on the North German plain the tank would be able to reach cover before the Sagger reached it 90% of the time. In southern Germany the terrain is denser and Sagger use even more difficult.

On the modern battlefield anything that can be seen can be hit, and anything hit, destroyed. Unlike some ATGMs, such as the US TOW and Dragon, Soviet first-generation ATGMs do not have a backblast or muzzle flash when launched, just a cloud of grey smoke and a loud roar which are difficult to detect under battlefield conditions. In the 1973 War not a single Sagger launch was spotted. But as the Sagger is large and slow-moving, 70% of the Israeli tank commanders could detect the missile or its short smoke trail in flight and take countermeasures.

Both Sagger and Swatter are only effective in the direction in which they are pointing when on their launchers. The effective area for Sagger is a cone 3,000m in length and 2,000m wide at maximum range, narrowing in width to 1,170m at 1,000m range and only directly in front of the launcher at 300m range. Owing to the weapon's radio control, the effective area of the Swatter is broader and resembles a semi-circle. Both missiles can switch targets within their fields of fire during flight. The Sagger is armed from the moment of launch, even though its course

Swatter ATGMs, as mounted on a BRDM-1. *(Department of Defense)*

cannot be corrected until it reaches its minimum range, while the Swatter does not arm until it reaches its minimum range, precluding its use as a "giant RPG-7" in an emergency.

While the primitive Snapper was apparently unreliable – the Egyptians reportedly experienced a 25% malfunction rate – other first-generation Soviet ATGMs are simple and reliable. In US Army tests the Sagger's malfunction rate was negligible. However, its guidance wires will occasionally break, and it has been reported that firing across bodies of water or under power lines will disrupt its guidance system.

The Israelis captured many Saggers in the 1973 War, and in 1979 there were reports that they were considering producing a modified Sagger with a semi-automatic command line-of-sight guidance system, as used on second-generation ATGMs. It has also been reported that the Soviets are modifying both their Saggers and Swatters with the same new guidance system, giving them credibility into the 1980s. Modified Saggers were reportedly being used with BMPs in East Germany in 1979.

In summary, Soviet first-generation ATGMs are simple, reliable, easily used weapons which, when presented with suitable targets in the open, can be accurate at long range. However, accuracy is often reduced in combat conditions because they are susceptible to countermeasures and suppressive fire, and because they lack responsiveness in tracking targets.

Combat usage

Several Egyptian Snapper companies were deployed in Sinai in 1967, and these destroyed at least one Israeli tank on June 7. In 1969, during the Middle East War of Attrition, Saggers destroyed two M-48 tanks during a skirmish at the Port Said causeway. In early 1973 the Syrians knocked out several Centurions with Saggers in border fighting. Although the Israelis knew about Sagger, they did not understand its potential. Thus the surprise effect of massed Saggers greatly increased their effectiveness until the Israelis were able to devise countermeasures.

The Sagger was first used in Vietnam on April 23, 1972, and inflicted considerable losses on the South Vietnamese 20th Tank Regiment. The survivors improvised successful countermeasures, including dodging and suppressive fire, but no one seemed to take notice. North Vietnamese Saggers have been used throughout Indochina.

Egyptian commandos used suitcase Saggers against Libyan armour in 1977. Cuban and Ethiopian forces used Saggers in the Ogaden in 1977, including those mounted on BMDs. The Swatter has possibly never seen action, although Hind-A and Hind-D helicopters have been spotted carrying Saggers and Swatters in Afghanistan.

Sagger-launcher BRDM, showing the sextuple launch rails under the retractable armoured roof. Also evident are the BRDM's two retractable amidships wheels and trim vane for swimming. *(US Army)*

Accuracy of Soviet first-generation ATGMs

	Range (metres)						
	300	500	1,000	1,500	2,000	2,500	3,000
Snapper	0%	54%	73%	82%	87%	89%	0%
Swatter	0%	0%	90%	90%	90%	90%	90%
Sagger	25%	60%	87%	87%	87%	87%	87%

The percentage represents the approximate probability of a hit against a stationary M60A1 tank from a stationary ATGM launcher (ATGMs cannot be fired on the move). Swatter figures are estimates but close. If a Sagger hits an M60A1 it has a 69% chance of knocking it out, while a Snapper or Swatter has a 67% chance. Semi-automatic guidance Saggers would be more accurate.

The Soviets have tested Saggers against helicopters. While helicopters are unlikely to remain stationary long enough to be acquired and hit, the Soviets fear ATGM-firing gunships, and all available weapons, including Saggers, will be fired at them.

Soviet first-generation ATGMs have reduced effectiveness at night and in limited visibility. None have night sights or any type of infra-red device. They must rely on flares or other illumination, which would still make it difficult to track both target and missile. This is a drawback because of the need for 24-hour operations, and fog reduces visibility to under 1,000m one morning out of three during autumn and winter in West Germany. Mirage conditions in the desert also reduce ATGM accuracy and effectiveness.

Tactical employment

In BTR-60PB-equipped battalions the two suitcase Saggers are dug into front-line strongpoints. BRDMs from the regimental anti-tank company will be deployed behind the battalion defensive positions or as part of the regimental anti-tank reserve.

The Soviets do not emphasise positioning ATGMs to achieve flanking fire, due to their superior armour-penetration ability. This allows the ATGMs to engage at longer range but makes them more vulnerable to return fire, although alternative firing positions are provided.

A three-man Egyptian Sagger team would include two gunners with four Sagger rounds. The third man, with an RPG-7, would be 150–200m in front of the Saggers. These teams were supported by light machine guns, Sagger

A man-portable "suitcase" Sagger deployed with its monocular sight and control joystick unit. The warhead is a separate unit, as can be seen from the clips holding it in place. Only two of the four tail fins are attached here; all would have to be attached for launching. *(Tom Woltjer)*

reload carriers and SA-7 SAM gunners. It was easy to site these weapons with overlapping fields of fire in Sinai. Soviet *desants* and other units behind enemy lines will probably use similar Sagger teams against enemy armour heading for the front.

Because Soviet first-generation ATGMs cannot be fired from the move or short halt, regimental BRDM ATGM launchers will fire from overwatch positions in an attack, using the remote missile control unit to reduce exposure. Each BTR-60PB-equipped battalion's anti-tank platoon will either overwatch or advance in two APCs 1,000–2,000m behind the assault companies. It is normally employed as a complete unit in the attack, as an anti-tank reserve or to consolidate positions gained by the battalion. The BMP and BMD have Saggers as their primary anti-tank weapon beyond 800m range. While they will open fire at long range while defending, only overwatching BMPs or BMDs will fire Saggers in the attack, as it would be too dangerous for advancing vehicles to stop and fire within range of the enemy.

Engagement sequence

Saggers are simple to prepare for firing. A suitcase Sagger's launch rail is first removed from the suitcase, where it is stored in collapsed form, and erected. The body of the round is next removed from the suitcase and put on the launcher, the separate warhead being attached. The fins are then extended to the open position. Finally, the missile control box is set up and attached to the launcher. Each box can control two launchers. In a BRDM the retractable roof covering the missiles is elevated. On a BMP or BMD the gunner must seat a round and launch rail over the gun tube, using a stick to deploy the fins.

The gunner next acquires the target in his eight-power sight, which, like the RPG-7 sight, is gridded with lines for range and wind/lead corrections. Once the target is visually spotted, identified as hostile and acquired in the sight, the gunner may fire. The missile then flies straight ahead to its minimum range, a magnesium flare in the rear of the missile igniting to aid the gunner in tracking. When the missile reaches its minimum range he must "capture" it, bringing it into the sight picture. He does this by transmitting commands to the missile through a joystick. The electrical control impulses are carried to the missile by fine wires which unroll as it flies or, in the Swatter, are transmitted by UHF radio commands. Theoretically, all the gunner has to do is ensure that the missile's flare remains superimposed over the target on his sight picture until it hits.

Quadruple Snapper mount on a modified GAZ-69 jeep. *(US Army)*

Nicknamed "the pram" by its Soviet crews, a quadruple Snapper mount on a modified GAZ-69 jeep. The gunner's sight is at the upper right-hand corner of the cab. *(US Army)*

Countermeasures

Soviet first-generation ATGMs are vulnerable to countermeasures. Many of the countermeasures developed by the Israelis during the 1973 War have been adapted and improved by the US, British and other NATO armies.

The Israelis descovered that the best countermeasure against Saggers was to destroy or suppress them by using combined-arms tactics. They increased their use of artillery against the suitcase Sagger gunners, who were without cover. Reorganised to meet the Sagger threat, Israeli armour units now had an even mix of tanks and armoured personnel carriers mounting at least three machine guns. They would advance in checkerboard formation, tanks and APCs alternating. If heavy ATGM or RPG fire was encountered, the APCs would lead the advance, spraying suppressive machine gun fire while the tanks supported them with high explosive or blinded the enemy with smoke or white phosphorus. If the advance was halted, the infantry would dismount and clear the Saggers out.

Advancing Israeli armour in the later stages of the 1973 War also used the "Sagger watch" technique now adopted by NATO. Each tank and APC would search a key point of terrain where a Sagger might be located. When a Sagger was spotted in flight, the watching vehicle would give a warning to whoever appeared to be the target and would immediately fire in the direction of the Sagger launch, hoping to disturb the gunner's concentration, make him lose control of the missile and obscure his vision with the dust raised by firing. Meanwhile, the target would take evasive action. Forces advancing against suspected ATGM positions can also use "bounding overwatch," with half of the force moving while the other half remains in overwatch positions, their weapons trained on likely enemy positions.

The most effective countermeasure against any ATGM is suppressive fire. Joystick-controlled ATGMs are especially vulnerable to gunner distraction, and the threat of powerful return fire will frequently keep a gunner from firing at all. Smoke is the best ammunition for suppressing ATGMs, since the gunner cannot hit what he cannot see. This has greatly increased the importance of smoke shells on the modern battlefield. White phosphorus is also good against ATGMs, as it combines smoke and explosive effect.

Rather than charge an enemy, as the Israelis did in the opening days of the 1973 War, an armoured force today will reduce its vulnerability by limiting exposure, moving from cover to cover, through blocking terrain, or during periods of reduced visibility (although this is impractical in the desert). When moving in the open vehicles stay near cover such as woods, so that they can dodge an incoming ATGM by turning into the woods, where they would be concealed from the gunner. Hull-down tanks can dodge ATGMs spotted in flight by simply reversing down the slope and letting it pass overhead. Even if there is no cover, a tank can still outmanoeuvre a first-generation ATGM. It is difficult for the gunner to correct for sudden, sharp moves by the target, and a turn to the right or left by the target in the last four or five seconds before impact cannot be compensated for, and the missile will go past. Tanks can also dodge these ATGMs by following an erratic, swerving path. None of the first-generation Soviet ATGMs has an autopilot, so the gunner's natural tendency is to overcorrect while trying to keep the missile on target, and thus to lose control. US Army officers estimate that dodging techniques alone can reduce first-generation ATGM effectiveness by at least 50% and possibly by as much as 70%.

The wire-guided Sagger and Snapper are immune to electronic countermeasures, although they use the same vulnerable piezo-electric nose fuze as the RPG-7. The radio-controlled Swatter can be jammed, although the gunner has a choice of three different frequencies on which to transmit radio commands.

Second-generation ATGMs

	AT-4 Spigot	AT-5 Spandrel	AT-6 Spiral
Max range	2,000m	4,000m	5–8,000m
Min range	25m	25+m	unknown
Velocity	175m/sec	135–175m/sec	unknown
Warhead	HEAT (3kg)	HEAT	HEAT (10kg)
Armour penetration	500mm	unknown	unknown

All figures approximate.

AT-5 Spandrel-carrying BRDM, showing its unique rear-deck arrangement. (*Department of Defense*)

Quintuple AT-5 Spandrel mount on a BRDM scout car. The gunner's sight is extended on the right-hand side of the vehicle. The reload hatch is just visible behind the ATGMs, as is the modified rear deck of the BRDM. *(Missile Intelligence Agency)*

Soviet second-generation ATGMs first appeared when the AT-5 Spandrel was seen in a quintuple mount on a BRDM-2 in the November 1977 Red Square parade. Soon after the man-carried the AT-4 Spigot was reported in service. These new ATGMs are used by Soviet units in East Germany and Category I divisions in Russia.

These weapons appear to be comparable to Western ATGMs. They use the same semi-automatic command line-of-sight (SACLOS) system as the US Dragon and TOW and the European Milan and HOT, and share their relatively high speed. A large tracker head is mounted on the BRDM-2 AT-5 carrier, and may include a night sight. The wide-angle periscope, used for target acquisition while "buttoned up," is also mounted on the roof of the BRDM's crew compartment. It is estimated that up to 15 reload missiles could be carried. It has been reported in some publications that the reason these missiles are so similar to Western designs is that they are developed from the Milan. Undoubtedly, the Soviets have had the oppor-

tunity to acquire plans and, more recently, samples from export customers.

The AT-6 Spiral may be a third-generation ATGM, more advanced than any weapon currently in service. The nature of its guidance system is still uncertain, but it is probably guided by a laser designator, or possibly by television. It has been suggested that the laser attachments seen on Soviet tanks can also serve as target designators, perhaps for the Spiral. This would be similar to the

AT-5 Spandrel ATGMs in their launch tubes, as mounted on BRDM scout cars. *(US Army)*

AT-4 Spigot ATGM with periscopic sight. Note resemblance to Milan ATGM. *(Soldat & Technik)*

US Hellfire helicopter-mounted ATGM. The Spiral is currently mounted only on the Mi-24 Hind-D helicopter gunship, replacing the Swatter-B, although a ground version may appear. Hind-A helicopters are not equipped to use the Spiral. The Spiral has been described as a large, powerful missile, more like an air-to-surface missile than an ATGM. The Soviets may believe that only a large warhead would be effective against the revolutionary new armour systems of the latest generation of main battle tanks.

Combat usage

None of the new Soviet ATGMs has seen combat, but their effectiveness would probably be high. The Spigot and Spandrel would probably have about a 70% chance of hitting a stationary tank target between their minimum range and 300m. Between that point and their maximum range their hit probability would almost certainly be 89% to 93%. The Spiral's hit probability would also be close to 90%. Given a hit on an M60A1, probability of a kill would be at least 70%, and probably higher for the large Spiral.

Tactical employment

It appears that second-generation ATGMs will be used in the same way as the weapons they supplant: Spigot and Spandrel being used as suitcase and BRDM-mounted Saggers respectively, while the Spiral is used like the helicopter-mounted Swatter-B. Spandrels mounted on UAZ-469s are used by Soviet and Czech airborne units.

Engagement sequence

The gunner of the Spigot and Spandrel must first sight the target in his telescopic sight, estimated at ten-power. When the target is lined up in the cross-hairs he can fire. The missile is ejected from the launch tube by a piston, and coasts until clear of the gunner, when the sustainer rocket engine starts, creating a small backblast but prob-

ably much less than the US TOW or Dragon. Once it reaches its minimum range, the semi-automatic command line-of-sight guidance system takes control, and all the gunner must do is keep the cross-hairs on the target. If the guidance system is similar to that on the Milan, an infra-red beacon in the missile's tail gives its position to a sensor in the missile guidance unit. If the missile is not heading directly where the cross-hairs indicate, the guidance unit automatically generates corrections, which are passed down the wires to the missile in the form of electrical impulses. This system is much less vulnerable to gunner error than those of first-generation ATGMs. Unlike the US Dragon, the Spigot may be fired while the gunner is prone.

If the Spiral is laser-guided either the launching helicopter, a tank or a soldier with a laser target designator will aim it at the target, and the missile will home in on the reflected laser energy. If it is TV-guided the helicopter gunner will use a low-light television camera to focus on a target. The missile's seeker head would receive the same picture and, when launched, the picture would remain locked-in to its guidance system and it would fly towards whatever was in the centre of the picture.

Countermeasures

The same basic countermeasures used against first-generation ATGMs can be used against the newer weapons, but will be less effective. The gunner is still vulnerable to suppression and distraction, as he must keep the cross-hairs on target. Their high speed makes them hard to spot in flight, there is less time to evade or dodge them, and the target need be exposed for only a short interval. The automatic guidance system prevents overcorrection and reduces the probability of error under battlefield conditions. Because corrections are generated by sensing an infra-red beacon, fires, flares and infra-red emissions can confuse the missile guidance sensors and cause it to miss.

85mm SD-44, showing steering wheel and undercarriage for self-propelled movement. *(US Army)*

D-44 and SD-44 85mm anti-tank guns

Year introduced 1953 (1954) **Calibre** 52cal **Weight (firing)** 1,725kg (2,250) **Length (travelling)** 8.34m (8.22) **Width** 1.78m **Track** 1.43m **Elevation** $-7°/+35°$ **Traverse** 54° **Sights** Telescopic **Night sight** APN-2 **Rate of fire** 15 rpm maximum (10) **Max HE range** 15,650m **Effective APHE range** 950m **Effective HVAP range** 1,150m **Ammunition types** BR-365P, BR-367P HVAP, BR-367 APC-T, BR-365 APHE, BK-2M HEAT, O-365K HE, smoke **Muzzle velocity** 800m/sec (HE, see table for APHE, HVAP) **Shell weight** 9.54kg (HE, see table for APHE, HVAP) **Armour penetration** see table **Crew** 7 (5) **Unit of fire** 140 rounds

---

Figures in parentheses for SD-44 where they differ from D-44. Ballistic projectile error is 0.2m both vertically and in deflection at 1,000m using HVAP-T ammunition, and projectile error range is 37m at 10,500m and 51m at 14,085m using HE ammunition.

The 85mm SD-44 remains in service with at least some airborne regimental anti-tank companies. It is the same as the D-44 anti-tank gun, the anti-aircraft KS-12/12A, and the gun mounted in the ASU-85. Although it is a pre-war design, it uses improved ammunition. A semi-automatic vertical sliding-wedge breech block is used. The recoil system has a hydraulic buffer and a hydropneumatic recuperator behind a steeply raked, wavy-topped shield. A double-baffle muzzle brake and split tubular trails are also recognition features.

The SD-44 version is unique, as it has the ability to move itself over limited distances. A 14HP, two-cylinder M-72 petrol engine is mounted on the left trail, and an ammunition box is mounted on the right trail. Petrol is carried in the hollow tubular trails. A castoring wheel with a conventional steering wheel attached joins the two trails together, the driver sitting behind the engine, and the SD-44 is ready to travel in the opposite direction to that in which the muzzle points. It can travel at 25km/h on roads and 8–10km/h cross-country, and can climb a 25° slope. Its range is believed to be limited, however. The rest of the crew is carried on the breech or trails while moving. When in action or being towed, the third wheel and steering wheel are folded and stowed between the trail legs, and the two-part folded rammer, attached to the front of the gunshield, is removed. The SD-44 retains the ability to be towed, which is its normal mode of transportation.

The self-propulsion equipment weighs an extra 525kg, and its reduced crew and the bulk of the engine cut the rate of fire from 15 to 10 rounds per minute. The 85mm is improved HE and APHE rounds for the 85mm gun.

The SD-44 has probably never seen action. The D-44 was first used in World War Two and later in Korea,

Performance (85mm HVAP ammunition)

Round	Type	Weight (kg)	Muzzle velocity (m/sec)	Armour penetration and velocity (m/sec)		
				500m	1,000m	1,500m
BR-365P	HVAP	4.99	1,050	139mm (895)	108mm (751)	83mm (623)
BR-367	APC-T	9.20	805	135mm (750)	122mm (697)	109mm (646)
BR-367P	HVAP	5.35	1,020	213mm (909)	178mm (803)	148mm (705)

Performance (85mm APHE ammunition)

Round	Weight (kg)	Muzzle velocity (m/sec)	Armour penetration				
			500m	1,000m	1,500m	2,000m	2,500m
BR-365	9.2	792	111mm	102mm	93mm	85mm	78mm

inadequate against modern tanks, but with its HE round it is still useful as a short-range field gun (the standard North Vietnamese usage).

The BK-2M fin-stabilised HEAT round was introduced in 1969, and was the first 85mm HEAT round used by the Soviets. A complete round weighs 13.35kg and the projectile weighs 7.35kg. Armour penetration is unknown, but is probably similar to the 400mm penetration ability of the 73mm PG-9 round.

The standard 85mm HE round is the O-365K with a muzzle velocity of 800m/sec and weight of 9.54kg.

China and Czechoslovakia have developed their own

South-east Asia and the Middle East. Chinese 85mm guns inflicted heavy losses on an attacking Soviet motorised rifle battalion in the Amur River fighting in 1969. The D-44 was replaced as a regimental anti-tank gun by recoilless guns and ATGMs, and as a divisional anti-tank gun by 100mm weapons. However, as late as 1979 some divisions still used 85mm guns as divisional anti-tank artillery and may continue to do so. One low-readiness artillery division in the early 1970s had two regiments of D-44s. The Christian militia in Southern Lebanon uses D-44s supplied by the Israelis. These weapons were originally captured in the Middle East wars.

85mm D-44 in firing position. (*Truppendienst* magazine)

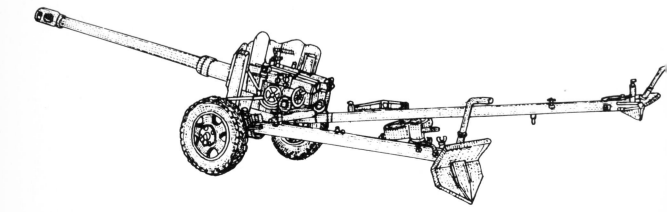

T-12A 100mm smooth-bore, showing angled gunshield and
pepperpot muzzle brake. *(US Army)*

100mm anti-tank guns

	T-12	**BS-3 M-1944 (M-1955)**
Calibre	84.8	56
Weight (firing)	3,000kg	3,460kg (3,000)
Length (travelling)	unknown	9.37m (8.72)
Width	unknown	1.5m (1.58)
Track	unknown	1.8m (1.2)
Elevation	−10°/+20°	−5°/+45°
Traverse	27°	58° (60°)
Sights	Telescopic	Telescopic
Nightsight	Active/passive	None (active)
Rate of fire	10rpm	8–10rpm
Sustained rate of fire	–	1.55rpm
Indirect range	8,500m	21,000m
Effective AP range	1,500m	1,080m
Effective HEAT range	1,150m	900m
Ammunition types	HVAPFSDS, HEAT	As D-10
HVAPFSDS muzzle velocity	1,500m/sec	As D-10
HEAT muzzle velocity	900m/sec	As D-10
Shell weights	HVAPFSDS, 5.5kg	As D-10
	HEAT, 9.5kg	
Armour penetration @ 1km	400mm, HVAPFSDS	As D-10
Crew	6	6
Unit of fire	60 rounds	60 rounds
Tow vehicle	ZIL-131, ZIL-175, AT-P, MT-LB, URAL-375.	As T-12

Figures in parentheses are for the M-1955 where it differs from the M-1944. M-1944 ballistic projectile error in direct fire is 0.15m in
vertical and deflection planes at 1,000m using HEAT, and in indirect fire PER is 52m at 14,500m and 85m at 18,900m using HE.

M-1955 100mm anti-tank gun, showing single tyres
and pepperpot muzzle brake.
(US Army)

The 100mm T-12 smooth-bore anti-tank gun is probably
the last Soviet anti-tank gun, for they are too large, heavy
and vulnerable for the modern battlefield, especially in
comparison with the more accurate ATGM. Despite these
drawbacks, each motorised rifle and artillery division's
anti-tank battalion has 18 T-12s.

Introduced in 1965, the T-12 has replaced many of the
earlier BS-3 M-1944 amd M-1955 100mm rifled anti-tank
and field guns, although some remain, especially in low-
readiness formations. Externally the T-12 is a standard
Soviet artillery design, similar to the M-1955. It is
mounted on a two-wheeled, split-trail carriage, with a
long, thin gun tube ending in a "pepperpot" perforated
muzzle brake. There are two recoil cylinders in place of
the normal one, and castoring wheels at the end of the gun
trails allow for rapid rotation. The T-12 uses the large, flat
gunshield of the earlier 100mm guns, but the T-12A has a
winged shield angled to the rear, although it is otherwise
identical to the T-12.

The T-12 is a smooth-bore, similar to the 115mm
U-5TS tank gun, and is unlike any other Soviet 100mm
gun, including that on the T-54/55 tank. It fires fin-
stabilised, one-piece, non-rotating HVAPFSDS and
HEAT rounds. An APN-3 infra-red sight allows night
firing at up to 900m range. Unlike the rifled 100mm guns,
which were ballistically the same as the D-10 tank gun
and the KS-19A anti-aircraft gun, the T-12 does not have
a field-gun role, as it lacks an HE round and has limited
elevation.

Combat usage

The M-1944 was the biggest towed anti-tank gun in
World War Two, and, along with the M-1955, was used in
Vietnam and the 1967 and 1973 Middle East wars. The
Indian Army has made extensive use of M-1944s and
M-1955s, and used them alongside 25-pounders as stan-
dard divisional field and anti-tank guns in 1971. The T-12
and T-12A have never seen action, except in Afghanistan.

With its high-velocity ammunition, the T-12 is more
accurate than any other 100mm gun, though not as accurate as the U-5TS at ranges over 1,500m. It is estimated
that while rifled 100mm guns could achieve a 50% hit
probability against a tank-sized target at about 1,000m,
the T-12, firing HVAPFSDS, could achieve the same
accuracy at about 1,500m. If an HVAPFSDS round hits a
tank, it would have approximately a 50% chance of
knocking it out. Their high muzzle velocity gives these
rounds excellent armour penetration, but makes it
difficult for the gunner to follow the flight of the shells and
correct his aim.

Ex-Egyptian M-1944 100mm anti-tank gun, showing characteristic dual tyres and double-baffle muzzle brake. *(Tom Woltjer)*

Tactical employment

T-12s form the basis of the motorised rifle division's anti-tank reserve, which may also include field artillery, tanks, ATGMs and engineers. When the division is on the defensive, the T-12s are deployed in battery and platoon positions between the first and second echelon, covering the most likely routes for advancing enemy armour. The T-12s are seldom attached down to regiment; control is retained at division and the battalion is used as a unit. They are too large, too easily spotted and too vulnerable to be deployed in the first echelon, but from their intermediate position the T-12s provide an anti-tank backstop, especially important in an NBC environment when the first echelon may be hit by a nuclear strike. Any enemy armour that penetrates the first echelon will encounter the T-12s, which will delay and channel the enemy advance, weakening and disorganising it before the defences of the second echelon are encountered and giving Soviet forces time to deploy for a counterattack. If a counterattack is launched against enemy forces attacking first-echelon strongpoints, the T-12s will give support or join in the anti-tank fires of the first echelon if the range permits. Minefields are normally placed 1,500–2,000m in front of T-12 positions to force the enemy to turn their flanks to the guns, break up their advance and force them into fire pockets.

T-12 batteries are often deployed on reverse slopes, as they can be depressed to a much greater degree than Soviet tank guns. Depending on the direction of the threat, the guns will be deployed in line, in a two-line "checkerboard" formation, in echelon or in a "U". When all-round defence is important, the guns will be in a rhomboid-shaped formation. Guns are deployed between 200 and 500m apart, often in platoon firing positions. If time permits, one to three alternative firing positions will be designated or prepared for each gun, with concealed routes for changing position.

Like field artillery units, the anti-tank battalion and its component batteries are each commanded by their command and observation post, which is normally co-located with a firing position. Each battery's reconnaissance section deploys forward of the battery position to give warning of enemy tanks.

The T-12 has an offensive role, especially in the break-through attack. The anti-tank battalion deploys in the Soviet forward positions under cover of darkness or an artillery barrage. During the artillery preparation they will repulse any enemy spoiling attacks, cover the deployment of the attacking units along the line of departure, and engage armoured vehicles and anti-tank weapons in the enemy defensive position. During the attack the T-12s will use their fire to prevent enemy armour threatening the flanks of advancing Soviet units and, if the attack is successful, they will cover the deployment of the division's second echelon, and then move forward themselves to consolidate the objective. If the attack fails and the Soviets are forced to adopt a hasty defence, the long-ranged T-12s will support them against enemy counterattacks.

In the pursuit, or in a meeting engagement, the Soviets position T-12s in the open and engage enemy armour at close range. In these situations the Soviets are willing to accept the loss of three or four T-12s for each tank destroyed.

Engagement sequence

The telescopic sight on the T-12 is similar to that on the T-62, so the sighting and aiming procedures are probably the same, although the T-12 lacks any automatic loading or extraction device.

Countermeasures

The usual countermeasures against anti-tank weapons are effective against the T-12: artillery fire (especially airbursts), smoke, close infantry assault, and suppressive fire.

Foreign usage

The RPG-7 is built in China as the Type 69, and it is used by almost every group that employs Soviet- or Chinese-built weapons.

The SPG-9 is used by the Polish, Bulgarian, East German and Hungarian armies, and reportedly by Syria, Iraq, Libya and possibly Ethiopia.

The B-10 remains in service in Poland, East Germany, Hungary and Bulgaria. The Czechs use a similar, indi-genous, weapon, the T-21. The B-10 is also used by most Arab armies, North Korea and Vietnam. A lighter version, the Type 65, is built in China and exported to Pakistan and Tanzania.

The B-11 is still used by the Warsaw Pact armies (with the exception of Czechoslovakia), Arab armies, Vietnam and North Korea. The Chinese received some Soviet-built examples, but never produced their own.

First-generation ATGM users include:
Snapper: Bulgaria (?), China (small number supplied, apparently no longer in service), Cuba, Hungary (?), Romania, Zaïre (supplied, reportedly never operational), Afghanistan.
Swatter: Czechoslovakia, East Germany, Hungary, Poland, Romania.
Sagger: All Warsaw Pact armies, Egypt, Syria, Iraq, Libya, Algeria, Angola, Uganda, Vietnam, North Korea, Peru (?), Afghanistan, Israel.

Second-generation ATGMs are currently used only by the Soviet Union, East Germany, Poland and Czecho-slovakia. Some East German units may have received the AT-4 as early as 1977–78.

The 100mm M-1944 and M-1955 were supplied to Vietnam, Bulgaria, China (no longer in service), Czecho-slovakia, East Germany, Romania, Hungary, Poland, Egypt, Syria, Iraq, Sudan, Vietnam, Somalia, North Korea (still widespread), Mongolia, Yugoslavia and India. The T-12/T-12A is used by the Soviet and East German armies, and may be supplied to other Warsaw Pact armies as well.

The 85mm D-44 and SD-44 are used by Warsaw Pact airborne units. In China it is the Type 56, the standard anti-tank gun. Other nations using the towed version are: Albania (Chinese-built), Algeria, Egypt, Syria, and Iraq (possibly replaced in these nations), Sudan, Morocco (no longer used), Vietnam, Guinea and Cuba. D-44s are in service or reserve stocks in East Germany, Bulgaria, Hungary and Romania.

The Czechs still use recoilless rifles similar to the B-10 and B-11 but of indigenous design. They are still in service in Poland, Hungary and Bulgaria as well as in Egypt, Syria, Iraq, North Korea and Vietnam.

The US has obtained a number of Soviet-built anti-tank weapons, including many RPG-7s and Snappers and some Saggers, but no Swatters.

Chapter Ten

Artillery

"Remember, me lad, though the Irish fight well,
the Rooshian artillery's hotter'n hell."
THE KERRY RECRUIT, FOLK SONG, c. 1855

Stalin called artillery Russia's God of War, and indeed Russia has been strong in artillery since Ivan the Terrible strengthened his peasant levies with massive bombards. Some 15% of today's Soviet Army wears the red piping of the artillery and mans the guns, howitzers, rocket launchers, FROGs and guided missiles that make up the pantheon which the Soviets define as artillery. Yet men and weapons are only the most obvious components of Soviet artillery. Their deployment, organisation, command, control and communications, fire direction, target acquisition, and liaison with tank and motorised rifle units will all determine how Soviet artillery is used on a future battlefield, and what effect it will have. These elements are in turn shaped by the larger concepts of Soviet military thought, which seem particularly applicable to the guns.

Soviet artillery thought, tactics and weapons are currently in a state of evolutionary change. The painstakingly planned massed fires preceding breakthrough attacks are now the exception rather than the rule. While not disputing the effectiveness of such barrages, the Soviets believe that there will usually be no time for mass alone to do the job, no time to stockpile the ammunition, emplace the guns and prepare the detailed barrage plans. Massed artillery is vulnerable to NATO artillery guided by sophisticated target-acquisition equipment, and to aircraft and nuclear weapons. The Soviets believe that their old approach does not meet the requirements of modern war.

The Russian artillery has since recovered from its relative eclipse in the 1950s and early 1960s, when the Soviet belief in the primacy of nuclear warfare led to masses of wartime-vintage weapons using wartime massed-fire tactics. The weapons themselves are greatly improved and include 122mm and 152mm self-propelled howitzers. Numbers have also increased: the Soviet division commander's artillery assets doubled between 1968 and 1978. The 1973 Middle East war and many studies and manoeuvres increased Soviet awareness of the importance of artillery as part of the combined-arms offensive. Artillery is required to suppress the anti-armour weapons that threaten to defeat the Soviet armoured spearheads. Today, in the words of Soviet officers, "the suppression of anti-tank weapons . . . is the most important task of the artillery," and in conventional combat "the task of destroying anti-tank weapons falls almost completely to the artillery." This suppression, to be performed as quickly as possible, is now the primary mission of the Soviet artillery.

Organisation and objectives

Soviet artillery organisation was developed to reconcile two conflicting requirements, those of centralisation and of responsiveness. Centralisation is required for the artillery offensive, and to prepare for the breakthrough attack. However, the mobile battle and the meeting engagement, which the Soviets believe will predominate on the modern battlefield, call for something different. Each regimental – even battalion – commander needs direct artillery support to accomplish his mission. Even in the breakthrough attack this sort of mobile, decentralised battle will predominate once the first attacking units breach the enemy defences.

The Soviets have reconciled the need to supply artillery assets to commanders at all levels with the need to concentrate this same artillery so that it can act with decisive mass and power, and they have done this in a different way from the US and British armies. The British and Americans rely on a flexible system, which can allow a single forward observer to direct all artillery within range, from company mortars to corps-level heavy guns. The forward observer does not have to relay his request through successively higher levels, but speaks directly to the artillery.

Introduced in World War Two and refined in Korea and Vietnam, this system allows centralisation while giving each commander the artillery support he requires. US (and British) artillery can respond to calls from forward observers incredibly quickly. A US forward observer (or any officer with a radio) requesting artillery support can expect the first rounds on target in under 100sec. With batteries dedicated to the support of specific units this can be reduced to as little as 38sec, including 20sec average flight time.

The Soviets know of this system, but have not adopted it themselves. They believe that its almost total reliance on radio communications will cause its collapse in the face of Soviet electronic warfare, which includes the jamming and destruction of radio transmitters located by radio direction-finding (RDF) equipment. The electromagnetic pulse of a nuclear blast will blow out the electronics of many radios and disrupt the use of surviving radios for hours afterwards. It is difficult to use a radio wearing an NBC protective suit or a gas mask. For the Soviets to adopt such a system would run counter to their emphasis on the centralisation of planning at regimental and higher levels, and would probably impose an intolerable strain in terms of numbers of forward observers, radios and technicians to support it. They have neither the tactical nor technical flexibility of the US and British system.

Soviet artillery fights as part of artillery groups (AGs). Organised for a specific operation, AGs are commanded by an artillery regiment or battalion commander from his unit headquarters. An army commander will have at his disposal any army-level artillery and any front-level artillery allocated to his army, which he then either reallocates to divisions or forms into army artillery groups (AAGs), usually of long-range field guns positioned 7–12km behind the front lines. Each division commander then repeats the process, retaining some of his artillery to form a division artillery group(s) (DAGs) (one or more, usually of two to four battalions of D-30s, M-46s and BM-21s for use in general support and counterbattery missions) while usually allocating about two-thirds of his total assets to regimental artillery groups (RAGs). RAGs, deployed 500–4,000m behind the front line, use 122m and 152mm howitzers for direct support and suppression. In addition, each motorised rifle regiment retains its regimental 122mm howitzers. Artillery battalions may also be attached directly to manoeuvre battalions, although they join in RAG fire missions. RAG battalions may also be detailed to support a specific battalion. Unlike an attached battalion, it is subordinate to the RAG commander rather than the manoeuvre battalion commander.

The artillery offensive

The artillery offensive suppresses enemy defences before and during an attack, and precedes manoeuvre units as they advance from one objective to another. The artillery offensive may be combined with air strikes and, if ordered, NBC weapons. Its duration and strength depend upon the time available to prepare the offensive, the type of attack being launched by the manoeuvre units, and many other factors. The recent changes in Soviet artillery are intended to make it more responsive in the mobile battle.

In the attack from the march artillery support will be severely limited, and will often be provided by battalion mortars or whatever howitzers can be used in a direct-fire role. The techniques of the artillery offensive are much more refined in support of the hasty attack, and increase in sophistication, duration and size up to the artillery offensive in conjunction with the breakthrough attack, when the Soviets will mass the fire of 80–100 guns and expend 10,000–20,000 shells per kilometre of frontage.

The essence of manoeuvring fires is that they concentrate the shell impacts, not the guns. Only in the breakthrough attack will the Soviets attempt to re-create the hub-to-hub massing of World War Two, and then only rarely; they know what a good target such concentration of guns would make.

Reconnaissance and target acquisition must precede the artillery offensive. Artillery supporting a hasty attack will often have only the reports of patrols or troops in contact to identify targets and provide information. A breakthrough attack will be preceded by lengthy and thorough reconnaissance and systematic target acquisition. A detailed list of targets will be drawn up, the destruction of nuclear delivery systems having first priority, followed by command posts, observation posts, communication and radar centres, field and air-defence artillery units, combat units in reserve positions, combat support units, and defensive strongpoints. In the hasty attack, target identification and the allocation of guns to each target are carried out orally and on the spot, usually by the artillery regiment or battalion commander.

In the breakthrough attack the artillery offensive will be set out in detailed barrage plans prepared with the aid of extensive formulae and charts to calculate the number of shells each target will require. These plans will be drawn up by the Army's Chief of Rocket Troops and Artillery. If time does not permit, the planning takes place at division or even regiment level. Artillery headquarters at regiment and higher level are normally co-located with the corresponding tank or motorised rifle headquarters. A separate artillery radio network is used to help fit all artillery into the co-ordinated fire plans: the battalion mortars, attached artillery battalions, regimental howitzers, the RAGs, DAGs, and AAGs.

Following target acquisition, the artillery offensive is divided into three phases: the preparation, fires in support of the attack, and fires through the depths of the defence. Attacks from the march are often made with minimal artillery support, while the duration and intensity of the preparation for the hasty attack depend on the tactical situation and how quickly the artillery deployed along the Soviet line of march can go into action. Preparation time for the hasty attack averages ten to twenty minutes while the troops form up for the attack, and includes direct fire. Normally Soviet commanders will not delay such an attack to bring up additional artillery. In a breakthrough attack, preparatory fires last 40–60min. All preparatory fire times are halved if a nuclear strike is planned. The purpose of the preparatory fires is to suppress and "soften up" enemy defences, disorganise command and control, neutralise defending artillery and fire control, and create passages through obstacles, especially by detonating minefields. False preparatory bombardments can be used to disguise the location of an attack.

In the breakthrough attack these fires will be planned and co-ordinated at army level, but the Soviets realise that in modern combat the commanders on the spot may have to make the crucial decisions. It takes three hours to co-ordinate a division's guns for an artillery offensive, which is why the Soviets have put greater emphasis on decentralising their artillery assets for mobile combat. However, when the planning time is available the Soviets will use all possible artillery assets, including tanks in the second echelon of attacking divisions, which will be used for indirect fire if sufficient ammunition can be brought up and dumped for them. Even if planning time is minimal, all Soviet units will join in the preparation with direct fire upon enemy positions. Supplementing tanks and BMPs in this will be artillery, normally SAU-122 SP howitzers and T-12 100mm anti-tank guns, often joined by SAU-152s, D-30 122mm howitzers and other towed guns.

Preparatory fire starts with several minutes' firing at maximum rate, then reverts to a sustained rate of fire for most of the preparation, and ends with another burst of rapid fire. Only enemy batteries which have actually opened fire will be engaged, so that front-line targets can receive the full weight of the preparation.

The preparation ends, and the fires supporting the attack begin, as the tank and motorised rifle units leave the line of departure. Fires supporting the attack are both pre-planned and available on call to engage targets of opportunity, the latter often being hit by direct-fire artillery. The need to provide on-call artillery support requires that those commanding the preparatory fires, which had been centralised at either army, division, or, in the hasty attack, regiment level, now pass control of the artillery assets to the attacking manoeuvre units as they are committed to the attack. As each successively larger unit is committed it assumes control of its artillery assets; as the lead battalions leave the line of departure, their attached artillery and battalion mortars pass from centralised control and revert to battalion control. Similarly, as full regiments attack, the RAGs and regimental howitzers pass to regimental control, and divisions control their DAGs once they too attack. Decentralised Soviet artillery will respond only to its own unit. If one regiment of an attacking division is held up by heavy fighting, it can call on its RAG

and attached or organic artillery, and possibly a DAG. It cannot easily call on the RAG of the adjacent attacking regiment of the same division once command has been decentralised, even if that regiment is encountering only light resistance. While procedures do exist to re-centralise command in such situations, using the artillery radio network, Soviet artillery, like the rest of the Army, apparently tends to regard unit boundaries as inviolable.

The fires supporting the attack will hit enemy front-line positions until the lead attacking tanks are 250m from them; a shorter distance would make the tanks vulnerable to the shells, and a longer distance would give the enemy time to engage the tanks at long range.

Once the lead tanks have reached the enemy position the fires supporting the attack cease, and fires through the depth of the defences begin, preceding the advance of the tank and motorised rifle units after they break through the enemy forward positions and into the depths of the defence. This is not a "rolling barrage" but includes pre-planned shifts to targets in the rear of the enemy to suppress any defences. By this stage the decentralisation of artillery control in the breakthrough attack will have progressed to regimental level. The direct-fire component of the fires through the depths of the defence is provided by the accompanying artillery. These are the regimental howitzers or artillery attached to manoeuvre units that follow close behind the attacking BMPs and APCs. Other indirect-fire artillery will be held in readiness to defeat enemy counterattacks.

Soviet artillery will move forward during this stage of the artillery offensive, a maximum of a third of the batteries moving at any one time. The Soviets believe that effective suppression requires continuous, uninterrupted fire, and their towed artillery, unlike that of NATO, will often not displace after a fire mission if this would disturb the continuity of firing. Soviet SP howitzers will displace more often.

The three-part artillery offensive is a vital part of the Soviet combined-arms offensive. Their increased emphasis on mobility and manoeuvre on the battlefield places a greater onus on the artillery to provide the required firepower. Fire and movement are the two components of tactics. If the tank and motorised rifle units provide the movement, the artillery will provide the fire. Nonetheless the Soviets realise that firepower is not simply a matter of dropping metal on the enemy. "Mobile firepower" is increasingly emphasised in Soviet writings. The on-call, decentralised and often direct-fire use of artillery will be the rule in future combat, not the complete artillery offensive of the breakthrough attack. The increased mobility and reduced vulnerability of the SP howitzers have made these developments possible.

Artillery on the defensive

Soviet artillery organisation and tactics in the defensive are similar to those used in the offensive. The degree of centralisation and planning depends on the time available, and a deliberate defence will have better co-ordinated artillery support than a hasty one.

The Soviets divide defence fires into five phases. They start with long-ranged fires to disorganise attacking units as they make their approach march, followed by massed fires on assembly areas, artillery positions and command posts. When the attack begins, final protective fires will hit pre-arranged locations in front of Soviet first-line positions, called in by radio, wire or flare signal from the defenders. If the enemy breaks through the artillery will continue its fire, including direct anti-tank fire by guns of all sizes. The Soviet artillery has often been called upon to hold the front line, and it will do so again if necessary. They may lose guns but they will not abandon them. Finally, the artillery will support the Soviet counter-attacks, directing prearranged fires against pre-registered targets whenever possible. These missions are performed in the same way as those of the artillery offensive.

The Egyptians used Soviet-style defensive fires against Israeli attacks during the opening days of the 1973 War. Although they did not inflict many casualties on the Israeli armoured forces, the Egyptians disrupted and delayed the attacks and contributed to their defeat by anti-tank weapons.

Target acquisition

The Soviets have an interlocking and complementary network of target-acquisition systems but prefer to rely on the simplest and most direct methods whenever possible. The "Mark I eyeball" of the man aiming the gun has lost none of its importance. "Artillery reconnaissance" includes electronic intercepts, radars, artillery radio direction-finding, and sound and flash ranging. Target data will also be transmitted by aircraft and long-range and troop reconnaissance patrols. Soviet artillery HQs are co-located with tank and motorised rifle unit HQs to allow sharing of reconnaissance information. Each artillery regiment has a target-acquisition battery with radar, sound and flash ranging, and radio direction-finding equipment.

Normally positioned near artillery HQs, Soviet artillery radars, including the new BMP-mounted SON-2 Small Fred which operates with SP howitzers, can detect enemy artillery firing up to ten kilometres behind the front lines. Soviet artillery radars lack the first-round acquisition capability of the latest NATO equipment, and are easily saturated by high volumes of fire.

Radio direction-finding equipment can locate enemy radios and direct artillery fire against them. In the 1973 War Egyptian M-46 130mm field guns, co-located with RDF units, performed effective counterbattery missions which forced the outnumbered Israeli artillery to move frequently. Israeli headquarters using their radios were also targets. Maj Gen Avraham "Albert" Mandler, commanding the 252nd Armoured Division, was killed by artillery fire in this way. The Soviet use of radio direction-finding is even more effective. Truck-mounted radio direction-finding equipment is positioned with BM-21 MRL units. The area in which a Soviet radio direction-finder can pinpoint a radio is smaller than the area covered by a BM-21 battery salvo. Once an accurate fix on the target is obtained the BM-21s will blanket the area. As radio direction-finding data can be obtained in 30sec, even mobile targets are vulnerable, as shells or rockets will be on the way 120sec after the transmission begins.

To survive the Soviet radio direction-finder threat, opposing forces must limit radio use and employ evasive techniques such as frequent movement. However, the US Army depends on its radios to a greater degree than the Soviet Army. Soviet radio direction-finding has a 99% chance of intercepting and locating within 500–700m a US AN/VRC-12 radio operating at high power with a vertical antenna, as is normally done. An AN/PRC-77 FM radio can be detected and localised within 900–1,900m 51% to 74% of the time, depending on power and antenna configuration. If the AN/VRC-12 uses low power, limiting its range, intercept probability is reduced to 75%. The use of a horizontal directional antenna, further limiting range and the direction in which messages can be sent and received, further reduces intercept probability to 15% for the AN/VRC-12 and 8% for the AN/PRC-77. The effect of the radio direction-finder/BM-21 combination lies not only in the destruction caused by the rockets, but in the disruption caused to US command, control and communications by the need for counter-measures.

The simplicity of sound and flash ranging commends it to the Soviets. The standard SChZ-6 sound ranging system was developed soon after World War Two. Its ranging stations are normally positioned 1,000–1,500m apart in a straight line 2,000–4,000m behind the line of contact, and automatically wire the flash/bang times to a central ranging position, where the differences between them are used to calculate range and bearing. Sound and flash ranging can both adjust the fire of Soviet artillery and detect enemy weapons. Sound ranging is effective up to 8–15km for medium guns and 20–25km for heavy artillery, with range accurate to within 1% and bearing to within 0.4%. Flash ranging is effective at five to ten kilometres range and accuracy depends on whether theodolite, stereoscopic or stadiametric equipment is used. Sound ranging is impossible in gusty winds, and flash ranging requires the observation post to have a clear line of sight to the target. Laser rangefinders were introduced into the target-acquisition battalions of artillery divisions in the late 1970s. Their use will probably be extended to regimental target-acquisition batteries in the near future. The ACRV-2 mounts a laser rangefinder. They have a range of 0.25–10km and are often tripod-mounted.

Once a target is located the artillery batteries will register in on it until it is bracketed within 100m. "Shock fire," fire without registration, is used when speed and surprise are more important than accuracy.

Command and control

Each Soviet artillery battery and battalion has a command observation post (COP) that serves simultaneously as headquarters, forward observer, and fire-direction centre. Unlike NATO battery and battalion headquarters, they do not stay with the guns but are positioned forward with the front-line troops, like the Western forward observers to which they are equivalent. This puts the artillery commander on the spot to make decisions about target acquisition, identification and engagement, and centralises command, avoids communications problems and makes the artillery more responsive to the tactical situation. It may well be that the COPs are the most important, and possibly the most vulnerable, element of

the Soviet artillery system, and the best way to defeat the artillery is to defeat the COPs by destroying them, blinding them or cutting off their communications with the guns. An advantage of the use of the COP is that it allows the most experienced officer in each artillery unit to handle target acquisition and fire control. In the US Army this function is in the hands of forward observers who are often less experienced than the officers with the firing battery.

COPs are kept small, containing only the battery commander and his key staff. They are normally mobile in GAZ or UAZ "jeeps," BRDM-2Us or the new ACRV-2. BTR-60PUs are also widely used, and DAG command posts are often deployed in them. COPs are normally co-located with the HQ of the unit being supported, and thus their distances from the front lines vary, although it is normally about 100m for a company, 500–1,000m for a battalion, 1,000–2,000m for a regiment and 2,000–4,000m for a division. If the COP dismounts its position will be kept as small and inconspicuous as possible, making use of abandoned positions, trenches, foxholes and craters. Whenever possible, the Soviets will dig a COP position identical to the one in the diagram, although the location of the personnel varies. COPs are positioned with a good view of enemy positions and well camouflaged, dummy COPs being set up if necessary. If the COP cannot see a target, an advance or lateral COP may be established.

Before a battery displaces, an artillery reconnaissance group is sent to select and prepare firing positions and report on the approach routes. The personnel usually

COMMAND OBSERVATION POST

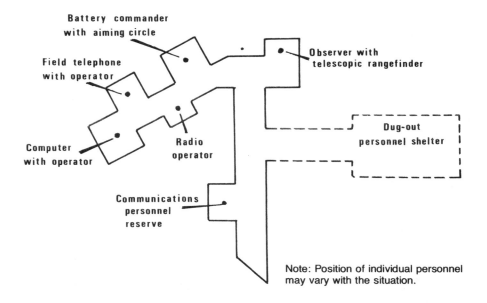

Battery commander with aiming circle

Field telephone with operator

Observer with telescopic rangefinder

Computer with operator

Radio operator

Communications personnel reserve

Dug-out personnel shelter

Note: Position of individual personnel may vary with the situation.

include the reconnaissance squad (of battery headquarters) commander, an operator-surveyor, two radiomen, a driver/mechanic for the vehicle used by the reconnaissance party, and the senior battery ammunition truck driver, all commanded by an officer. A similar party can also be used for topographic reconnaissance.

Battery tactics

Soviet batteries contain six guns organised in two three-gun platoons. As the battery commander is normally away from the firing position in the COP, the battery's most senior lieutenant is in charge of the gun position, assisted by the two platoon commanders.

Battalion command must approve all battery positions. When possible, batteries will be placed on reverse slopes or in woods, with their trucks and tow vehicles under cover nearby. However, the Soviets are willing to deploy batteries in the open, without cover, if the situation requires it. Indeed, ever since Borodino Soviet artillery has usually deployed in a linear formation without depth and without taking advantage of terrain, each battery

occupying a 200m frontage. Because hub-to-hub deployment proved successful in World War Two, and because of limited peacetime tactical training, the linear deployment endured almost as dogma until the 1970s, when it came under intense criticism as being unsuited to modern conditions. Other geometric formations used included the "U" or "V", intended to provide rapid shifts of direct or indirect fire. Alternatively, if tank penetrations are expected, a battery may site two guns in anti-tank ambush positions while the other four continue their missions. Currently the Soviets are adopting a less geometric approach to battery tactics. The guns are dispersed in an area approximately 600 by 300m, making best use of terrain. Alternative firing positions are prepared, as are dummy positions when time permits. SP howitzers are even more flexible in their use.

Weapons effectiveness

Throughout the 20th century artillery has caused the majority of battle casualties. In pure weight of metal and explosive artillery greatly exceeds all the tanks, machine

TYPICAL ARTILLERY BATTALION DEPLOYMENT

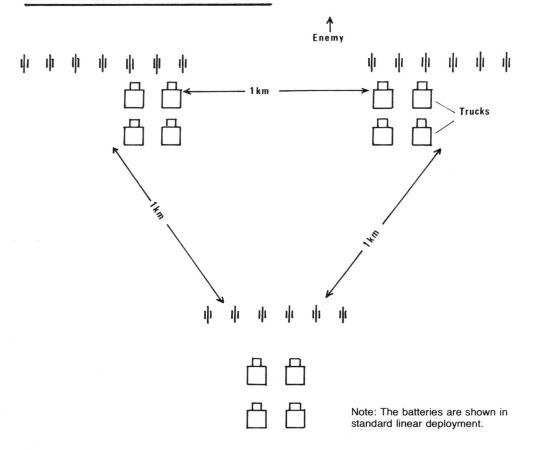

Note: The batteries are shown in standard linear deployment.

STANDARD LINEAR BATTERY DEPLOYMENT

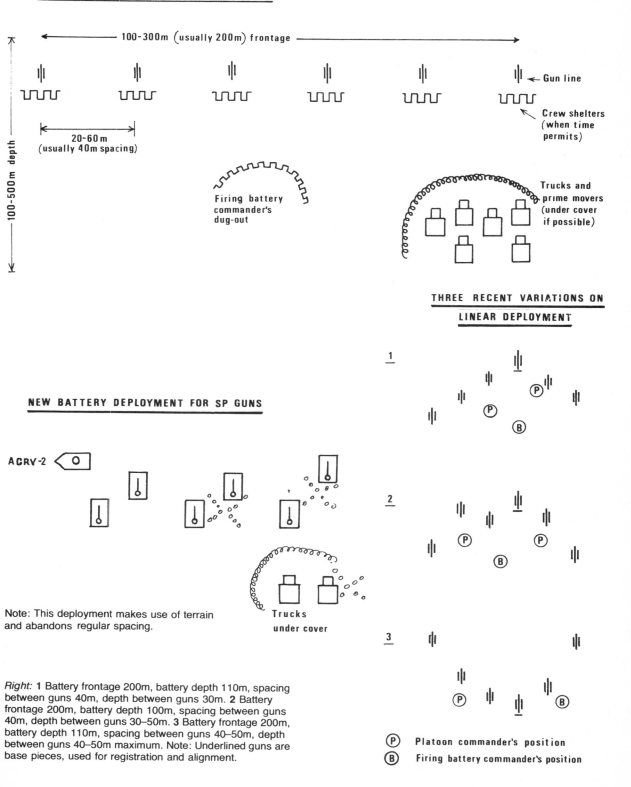

100-300m (usually 200m) frontage

← Gun line

Crew shelters (when time permits)

20-60m (usually 40m spacing)

100-500m depth

Firing battery commander's dug-out

Trucks and prime movers (under cover if possible)

THREE RECENT VARIATIONS ON LINEAR DEPLOYMENT

1

2

3

NEW BATTERY DEPLOYMENT FOR SP GUNS

ACRV-2

Note: This deployment makes use of terrain and abandons regular spacing.

Trucks under cover

Right: **1** Battery frontage 200m, battery depth 110m, spacing between guns 40m, depth between guns 30m. **2** Battery frontage 200m, battery depth 100m, spacing between guns 40m, depth between guns 30–50m. **3** Battery frontage 200m, battery depth 110m, spacing between guns 40–50m, depth between guns 40–50m maximum. Note: Underlined guns are base pieces, used for registration and alignment.

Ⓟ Platoon commander's position
Ⓑ Firing battery commander's position

STANDARD ALTERNATIVES TO LINEAR DEPLOYMENT

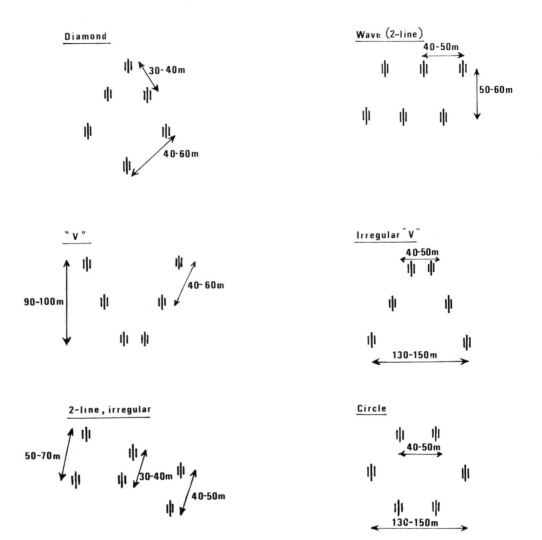

guns and other direct-fire weapons, if only because it is easier to supply a ton of ammunition to an artillery battery than to a motorised rifle company. Soviet artillery will undoubtedly be of crucial importance in any future conflict.

The Soviet perception of war as a science is especially evident in their artillery tactics. The Soviets have developed and perfected their systems of artillery combat since World War Two, and they believe that to be successful a commander need simply achieve a degree of competence in his unit that allows it to follow these systems and procedures. In reality this approach often has the effect of

compelling a commander to choose to act according to either the "scientific" guidelines or the actual tactical situation. Of course, at low levels of command Soviet officers are not trained for any other type of action, but it does not create the initiative that the Soviet military press seems to value so highly.

The Soviets consider the most "complex and creative" element of artillery tactics to be the determination of how many rounds are to be fired at each target. To determine this they have developed a series of projectile expenditure rates (PER), which are based on the assumption that, of a given number of rounds fired, a certain number will impact within the target area and will have a predictable effect – a level of destruction – expressed as a percentage of damage inflicted. Harassing fire requires a 10% level of destruction to be effective. To neutralise and suppress a target is assumed to require a 20–30% level of destruction, and this is the normal goal of Soviet artillery. To destroy a target requires at least a 50–60%, often a 70–85%, level of destruction. All of these assumptions are the result of wartime experience and years of study and tests by the Soviet artillery. Yet the nice, neat charts of PER and weapons effectiveness (not only those put out by the Soviets) appear similar to those prepared before the First World War and which proved to be completely invalid when put to the test of combat. For all the Soviet reliance on performance and armament norms to maintain their command control, it is impossible to say that any view of Soviet artillery effectiveness is correct or accurate. It is only possible to say that these views reflect how the Soviet Army believes its artillery will function in combat.

table is used in US Army Command Post Exercises (CPX) to assess artillery fire effectiveness.

To determine the number of 122mm howitzer rounds required to achieve any required level of destruction at a range of 12km or less, a Soviet commander will use the following norms:

Firing at **troops under cover and weapons in prepared strongpoints**; number of shells required per hectare of target area: 47 rounds using "shock fire" with no preparatory adjustments, 35 rounds if using fire adjustment or shifting fires. VT fuzes would not be used against such targets.

Firing at **troops under cover and weapons and APCs in a hasty strongpoint**; number of shells required per hectare of target area: 35 rounds using shock fire (reduced to 17 rounds if using VT-fuzed rounds), and 26 rounds if using fire adjustment (13 rounds if using VT fuzes in the shells).

Soviet artillery effectiveness (US Army estimate)

Artillery piece	Number of shells	US tank bn		"Chinese" tank bn		Infantry bn (any nation)	
		Attack	Defence	Attack	Defence	Attack	Defence
152mm howitzer	30	3	0	5	1	8	3
	60	4	1	8	2	14	5
	90	5	2	10	3	19	7
	120	6	2	12	4	24	8
	150	7	3	15	5	27	10
	180	8	3	17	5	31	12
122mm or 152mm gun-howitzer or 130mm gun	30	2	1	3	4	7	4
	60	3	2	5	5	12	5
	90	4	3	7	6	17	6
	120	5	4	9	8	22	8
	150	6	5	11	9	26	9
	180	7	5	13	10	29	12
BM-21	32	3	1	6	1	10	4
	64	5	2	9	2	18	6

The table expresses percentages of casualties that would be suffered in a 1,000m-sq attack area by the type of unit indicated, either on the attack or on defence. "Chinese" tank battalions are any that are identical to Soviet tank battalions. The higher effectiveness of the howitzer is due to the plunging trajectory of its shell and the resultant fragment distribution. The chart does not reflect the greater accuracy of field guns, but it does reflect the ability of the BM-21 to deliver its projectiles as a single salvo. The

Firing at **openly deployed ATGMs and anti-tank guns and other individual targets**; number of shells required per target: 33 rounds contact-fuzed or 16 rounds VT-fuzed for shock fire, and 25 rounds contact-fuzed or 12 rounds VT-fuzed for adjusted fire.

Having determined the basic number of shells required, the Soviet commander then multiplies it by two numbers: first, the number of hectares (10,000m²) of target area or the number of targets; second, one of the following,

122mm D-30 firing battery in traditional but highly vulnerable linear deployment in open terrain. *(Marine Corps Gazette)*

depending on the level of destruction required in the target area:

Level of destruction	10%	15%	20%	25%	30%	40%	50%	60%	70%	80%	90%
Multiplier	1.00	1.67	2.43	3.28	4.27	6.67	9.48	14.38	21.1	31.65	53.57

These calculations not only show the anticipated performance of Soviet D-30 howitzers on the battlefield, but also reveal many of the requirements and restraints of artillery tactics. The type of fire used is important. Accuracy is reduced when "shock fire" is used, but if fire is adjusted until the target is bracketed the element of surprise is reduced. In surprise fire the first volley is always the most effective. The type of fuze used is also important. Soviet howitzers did not use VT fuzes until comparatively recently, in contrast to the US and British artillery, which adopted them in 1944. These proximity fuzes are triggered by radar impulses to detonate at a pre-set altitude, and are effective at showering fragments down on troops in foxholes. The number of shells required for the higher levels of destruction, regardless of the type of firing or fuzes, increases exponentially. The Soviets normally consider a 20–30% level of destruction adequate for suppression. A 70% level of destruction is normally considered adequate for destruction, but this requires such large shell expenditures that this effect is normally reserved for weapons with nuclear capability. A 50–60% level is considered acceptable for the destruction of enemy artillery; 10% is for harassment.

PER for counterbattery fire

Target	100mm BS-3	122mm D-74	130mm M-46	122mm D-30	152mm D-1	152mm D-20	120mm mortar	160mm mortar	240mm mortar	122mm BM-21	240mm BM-24
Battery, towed guns	240	220	200	220	180	180	200	120	100	400	170
Platoon, towed mortars	180	165	150	165	135	135	150	90	70	300	130
Battery, armoured SP guns	300	270	260	380	300	285	300	290	175	440	210
Battery, unarmoured SP guns	265	240	230	310	260	240	250	240	130	330	170
Platoon, unarmoured SP guns	230	200	200	270	220	205	210	200	115	350	150
Platoon, SP mortars	360	320	310	430	330	310	320	300	170	540	230
Destruction of a launcher	320	260	240	260	200	200	–	140	110	270	200
Neutralisation of a launcher (rpm)	10	8	7	8	6	6	–	6	5	7	6

The above expenditure rates are based on a target battery frontage of 150m wide by 100m deep. Larger targets will receive proportionally more rounds, so a battery with a 200m frontage would receive 10% more rounds, other considerations being unchanged. If only one or two guns have been located, the frontage of the battery is assumed to be 200m to compensate for target location errors. When the fire is shifted from a registration point and adjusted on target, PER is reduced by 25%. For non-armoured SP gun targets increase the PER by 130%, and increase it by 150% for armoured SP guns. For each kilometre of range over ten, the PER is increased 20% against towed artillery and 40% against SP artillery. Normally only nuclear-capable launchers are destroyed, as shown in the table. However, to achieve destruction against artillery targets at least 200–300% of the PER against batteries in the open and 300–400% against dug-in guns will be required. 5% is added to each PER for ranging-in purposes. These PERs assume a range of approximately ten kilometres, and also assume that the shells will come from three batteries firing for effect. If the range is less than ten kilometres, the PER is reduced. If the target is at eight to ten kilometres range the PER is reduced to 78% of that listed, and if the target is at six to eight kilometres range, the PER is reduced to about 65% of that listed (individual types of guns may be reduced from 62% to 66% of the PER, but most use 65%).

The PER for MRLs will not change appreciably with range. The number of batteries the Soviets consider necessary to produce the PER also varies with range. Against SP artillery they will use three batteries firing together, possibly more at ranges of over 15km. At less than ten kilometres one or two batteries may be used. Against towed artillery or mortars one battery will be used at less than ten kilometres range, one or two at ten to fifteen kilometres range, and three or possibly two at greater ranges. On average, if destruction rather than neutralisation is the goal, the number of batteries firing must be tripled. It is not sufficient to have the same number of batteries fire three times more shells, as this would reduce the overall effect of the fire by stretching it out over time. The fatigue of the gun crews would also become considerable, further increasing the time taken.

The actual level of destruction required to achieve neutralisation of an enemy battery varies with the type of target, the type of gun firing, and the number of batteries firing at it. For D-30 122mm howitzers the level of destruction for neutralisation is 23.5% with one battery firing, 26.1% with two batteries and 28.6% with three batteries. D-20 152mm gun-howitzers achieve a 23.8% level of destruction when firing for neutralisation with one battery, increasing to 27.1% and 30% for two and three batteries respectively. M-46 130mm field guns achieve 22.8%, 25.2% or 27.8% levels of destruction with one, two, or three batteries respectively. These figures reflect the greater destructive power of the howitzer shells and their pattern of fragment distribution.

The PER is also affected by the type of fuzes used in the shells. It is halved when using VT-fuzed shells against towed guns deployed in the open; the fragmentation effect will be deadly without overhead cover, and the fragmentation area of such shells is twice that of impact-fuzed ones. If the target has earth and timber overhead cover, the first shells will be impact-fuzed to blow away the cover, and the remainder will be a mix of VT and impact-fuzed shells. Armoured SP guns will receive impact-fuzed shells, for not only will a rare direct hit destroy them but a near miss may disable them, while fragments from overhead will usually not penetrate their armour. In deep snow impact-fuzed shells will often bury themselves

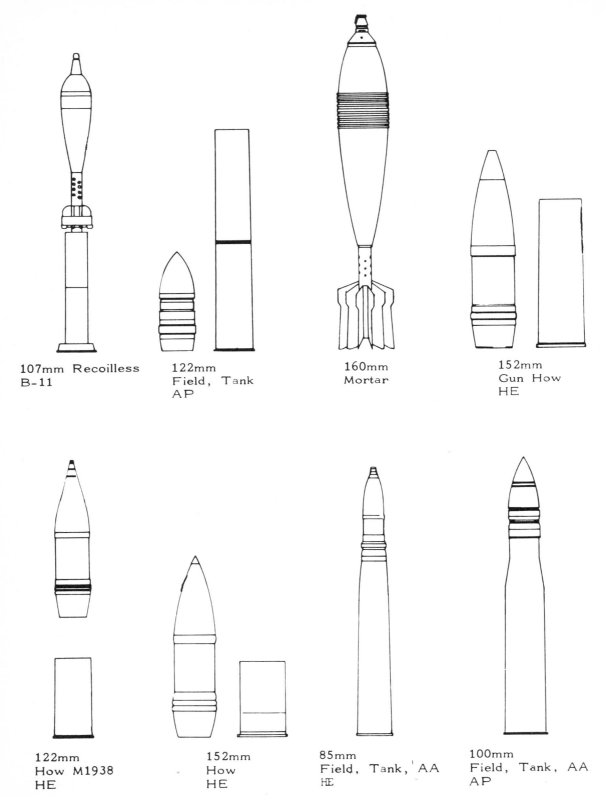

107mm Recoilless
B-11

122mm
Field, Tank
AP

160mm
Mortar

152mm
Gun How
HE

122mm
How M1938
HE

152mm
How
HE

85mm
Field, Tank, AA
HE

100mm
Field, Tank, AA
AP

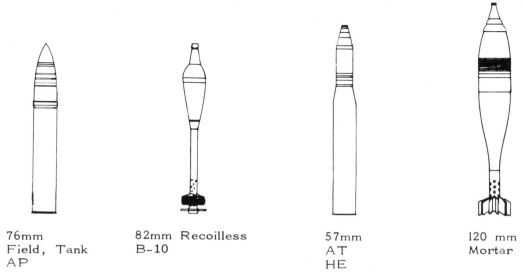

76mm	82mm Recoilless	57mm	120 mm
Field, Tank	B-10	AT	Mortar
AP		HE	

Comparative sizes of selected Soviet artillery ammunition. 122mm gun ammunition is for the A-19 field gun. Scale is 1 = 10. *(US Army)*

before exploding, reducing their blast and fragmentation effects by 50%, so VT fuzes are used whenever possible. If VT fuzes are not available, the PER must be doubled. Towed guns in weapons pits will also attract a mixture of VT and impact-fuzed shells, and the PER is also increased if VT fuzes are not used.

The PERs also assume that a target will be hit by two artillery strikes at an interval of 15–20min or less. It can be longer, as the Soviets state that combat experience has shown that a neutralised enemy battery will usually remain so for 30min. They realise that SP guns are harder to neutralise, and that they may not stay neutralised as long as towed guns.

The PER varies with the type of target acquisition and fire control and correction used, and how current the fire-control solution is. If a relatively inaccurate method of rangefinding is used, such as sound without confirmation from other sources, the PER increases to a point at which the Soviets probably would not fire. But if a helicopter or an aircraft is available to correct fire, or if a target is spotted by the COP directly, then the use of ranging rounds (either smoke or HE) and adjustment of fire will increase accuracy.

The PERs recognise that mass creates effectiveness. To get the equivalent effect of one three-battalion volley (54 shells) against infantry in the open requires ten one-battalion volleys (180 shells) or 43 one-battery volleys (258 shells).

As well as neutralising and destroying specific weapons, the Soviets also have norms for the amount of fire used in the "successive concentrations of fire" employed in support of the attack, and for fire support during the "fires through the depths of the defence" phase of the artillery offensive. Fire is delivered on specific, pre-planned points to suppress enemy defences, and these target points are advanced as the troops advance. These jumps will be relatively small, as transfer of fires is normally limited to 300m in deflection and 200–1,000m in range; otherwise a new aiming point will have to be registered. Successive concentrations require the following expenditures of rounds per hectare of target area per minute and the number of hectares covered by each battery (see table at foot of page).

Thus the Soviets consider that a D-30 battery would fire 12 rounds per minute (two rounds per minute per gun) to suppress a 200m² area.

The massing of artillery is important for effectiveness. For breakthrough attacks against a prepared defence, a minimum of 100 tubes (gun barrels) per kilometre of

	100mm BS-3	122mm D-30	130mm M-46	152mm D-1 & D-20	120mm mortar	160mm mortar
Rpm per hectare covered	3	3	3	2	3	2
Hectares covered per battery	3	4	3	3–6	2	2–3

frontage is required, compared to 80 tubes per kilometre in an attack on a hasty defence and 40 tubes per kilometre for an attack on a minor axis of advance. These norms are achieved by using guns from army and front-level artillery units and second-echelon divisions. The assigned sectors for offensive barrage fires are 20–25m per 100mm or 130mm gun and 150m per battery and 450m per battalion equipped with these weapons. The sectors for all other tubed artillery are 35m, 200m and 600–650m respectively for individual guns, batteries and battalions. Because of the greater intensity of these fires, these sectors are smaller than for other types of fire. When an interdiction barrage is fired, seeking to block enemy movement, coverage is 50m per tube and 900m per battalion. These barrages require great ammunition expenditure and are only fired for short periods on pre-planned lines.

To achieve these firepower concentrations batteries are separated by 400–2,000m with an average 1,000m. Individual weapons in battery positions are separated by 15–40m. These relatively tight concentrations allow for massed fires.

Another measure of artillery effectiveness is the estimated number (not per cent) of losses per ton of shells fired from that weapon at defending targets:

Target	122mm M-30	152mm D-20
Dug-in infantry	3.49	1.58
Infantry in the open	34.9	15.8
SP artillery	0.03	0.01
Artillery crews (in men)	8.6	3.95
Artillery trucks	1.23	0.56
Tanks	0.10	0.04
Tons fired per hour (max)	23.1	34.0

Fatigue reduces artillery effectiveness. A D-30 crew in action for ten minutes can sustain 2.4rpm, falling to an average of 1.6rpm after 30min, 1.2rpm after 60min, 1rpm after 90min, and 0.9rpm after 120min. If the crew is wearing NBC suits or working under adverse conditions the fatigue will be worse.

Soviet artillery uses chemical ammunition as a matter of course. Routine training includes combat under chemical conditions and using chemical shells, making the Soviet artillery competent in the use of chemical weapons once it has been decided to authorise their use. Today, as in 1917, chemical weapons are powerful in both suppression and counterbattery fires. Because chemical weapons affect a large area, targets do not have to be pinpointed, relieving the pressure on Soviet target acquisition. The chemical weapon is perhaps the most effective used by the Soviet artillery, the more so because the US Army, unlike its British and West German allies, is only now beginning to understand the importance of this threat.

At night Soviet artillery is slower in responding to fire requests and target acquisition is less effective. To preserve the element of surprise there will often be no preparatory fires before a night attack. When artillery is used the provision of illumination becomes an important objective. Illumination rounds are also used in conjunction with direct-fire weapons to show the direction of an attack and to dazzle enemy troops. A star shell illuminates a circle 500–1,500m in diameter for 30sec. For continuous illumination the Soviets plan to use one gun and three star shells per square kilometre per minute. Illumination rounds are separate from standard PERs, which are also increased at night. Direct-fire artillery makes heavy use of star shells and infra-red sights.

In the urban combat the Soviets will bring even towed heavy guns to within 200–300m of enemy positions to deliver devastating direct fire. Using direct fire, a single round from any Soviet gun or howitzer can penetrate a building, although structures with thick stone outer walls require five or six hits. A single round will usually create a breach, though eight rounds are needed against stone buildings, five against strong brick, and six against reinforced concrete. Weapons of 152mm and larger can do it in one round less. This is much more effective than indirect fire, which takes eight D-30 battery volleys to reduce even a wooden house to rubble, and 24 volleys to destroy one of reinforced concrete. 152mm and larger guns are more effective but they too find it difficult to level buildings with purely indirect fire.

The US Army calls smoke shell "the thinking man's ammunition." The Soviet Army has apparently been putting increased emphasis on the use of smoke shell in recent

Weapon	Ammunition	Coverage (one round)	Coverage (battery volley)	Time to build screen	Burn time	Height of screen
120mm mortar	WP	80m	160m	30sec	60sec	50m
122mm howitzer	HC	200m	400m	60sec	180sec	50m
130mm gun	HC	200m	400m	60sec	180sec	50m

years, and, as early as 1963, saw it as one of the ways in which the effectiveness of modern direct-fire weapons, especially the ATGM, can be defeated. The effectiveness of smoke is heavily dependent on wind conditions, and it is most effective when the wind is blowing at four to fourteen knots and across the smoke pattern. Soviet smoke shell includes both white phosphorous (WP) and hexa-chloroethane (HC) types. Because WP explodes its smoke builds more quickly, but it does not burn for as long or cover as large an area as HC. The capabilities of different Soviet smoke shells are shown in the table at the foot of page 174.

The areas covered represent the diameter of the area smoked-in given a favourable quartering wind. A quartering wind would increase the area covered by 120–140%, while a head or tail wind would reduce it to 70–80% of its normal diameter using WP and 33% with HC. Burn time is the time the shell actually produces smoke. To maintain a constant smokescreen 122mm and 130mm weapons would fire one HC shell per minute in most conditions, increasing to two or three in adverse conditions, with 152mm weapons firing half these amounts. Some sources report however that Soviet 152mm weapons lack smoke shell. The Soviet use of smoke is likely to be thorough and imaginative. On the basis of exercises the Soviets have concluded that effective smokescreens can reduce the losses of attacking tank and motorised rifle units by 60–80%, and that blinding enemy direct-fire weapons can reduce casualties by 90%.

All Soviet artillery retains a direct-fire anti-tank capability, and 5% of each Soviet artillery unit of fire is anti-tank ammunition. But these weapons are only effective at short range, as shown by these US Army figures assessing the probability of a hit against a stationary vehicle:

tional conditions, and their artillery may often find itself holding the front line.

Engagement sequence

Artillery planning and targeting are performed at as high a level of command as time permits, but the Soviets believe that most artillery action will be directed at battalion or battery level in mobile combat. These artillery commanders decide how to engage targets of opportunity and those spotted by target-acquisition means and supported tanks and motorised rifle units.

Firing data at battery level are prepared by four sources: the battery commander, an officer with the guns at the firing position, the PUO-9 mechanical fire-control computer located in the COP, and the computer positioned with the guns, which the Soviets have found is usually the first to achieve a complete fire-control solution. A PUO-9 can be set up complete in 5½ min, and the time per target from announcement of a target location to the fire order is one minute. This is acceptable in any army, even those using more sophisticated equipment, and the PUO-9 requires only one man to operate it. The data obtained are then passed to the two firing platoons. The battery commander and the COP computer also compute fire-control data as a check on the battery computer, and the battery commander will use whichever solution he believes the most accurate.

Increased use of computers will further reduce response time. The firing battery commander, assisted by the technician operating the computer, applies the latest variable to the firing data; the Soviets place great emphasis on deviations in muzzle velocity in guns. The guns are usually laid on a common grid azimuth. Each gunner elevates

Weapon	Ammunition	Range (metres)					
		50	100	175	250	500	750+
122mm D-30	BK-6M HEAT	97%	94%	89%	72%	50%	31%
152mm D-20	BR-472 APHE	97%	94%	92%	75%	56%	39%

If a hit is scored, a 122mm HEAT round has approximately a 53% chance of killing an M60 and a 93% chance of killing an M113, while a 152mm APHE round, equally approximately, has a 56% and an 83% chance of killing an M60 and M113 respectively. As any gun within 1,000m of a tank will be hit by the tank's machine guns and main armament, Soviet field guns will have to engage tanks from ambush or, more likely, as a self-defence measure. The Soviets realise that there may be no stable front line in modern war, under either nuclear or conven-

his piece using a range drum, simpler than the US (and British) procedure of using an elevation scale or drum. The battery is then ready to fire for effect. In observed fire this starts with firing salvos rapidly to achieve surprise and to let the COP refine range and deflection. After this, fire continues at a sustained rate, possibly ending in a burst of rapid fire. The Soviets believe that this varying of rates of fire increases psychological effect. In unobserved fire the same pattern of rapid volleys, deliberate fire, and then more rapid volleys is followed.

The Soviets follow the same sequence throughout the preparation phase of the artillery offensive. A typical preparation lasting 25min would start with massive surprise concentrations of fire throughout the depth of the defence. After five minutes the fire will shift to priority targets, and after another ten minutes it will change to fire at the sustained rate. After a further ten minutes of this, the last five minutes before the attack will be at rapid fire, repeating the initial strike.

Countermeasures and vulnerabilities

The Soviets realise that their artillery has weaknesses and vulnerabilities, enough for Col V. Ivanov, a leading artillery tactician, to express himself dissatisfied with the overall level of artillery performance. According to the late Marshal A.A. Grechko, former Minister of Defence, the 1973 Middle East war drew attention to the vulnerability of Soviet artillery. It showed that there would seldom be time to dig in guns and that NATO counterbattery fires would be a powerful potential threat.

The linear deployment of Soviet towed artillery batteries, with 80–85% of their personnel without cover, greatly increases vulnerability to counterbattery fire. The effectiveness of Soviet artillery batteries depends heavily on a small number of technicians to direct and control the fire. If counterbattery fire hits any of the officers, senior NCOs or technicians, the battery's effectiveness will suffer disproportionately. Towed batteries are also more vulnerable to NBC weapons. Gun crews suffer from fatigue when wearing NBC suits and gas masks, which also make it hard to give or hear orders.

While Soviet target-acquisition systems form an impressive, complementary, overlapping system, their effectiveness is uncertain because of the time lag inherent in the processing and communicating of data. The combination of new BMP and MT-LB radar vehicles, the ACRV-2 and new command vehicles is an attempt to adapt target-acquisition means to the mobile battlefield. There are few static targets today, and NATO artillery using "shoot and scoot" tactics would be difficult to locate or destroy. The Soviet reliance on the COP for fire control, either on the basis of artillery reconnaissance or, frequently, of targets being spotted by the COP directly, creates direct and responsive target acquisition, as does the use of direct fire, though this is accomplished at the cost of increased vulnerability. The Soviet inability to use their artillery flexibly – a regiment's guns are often unable to support a neighbouring regiment once command has been decentralised – means that the Soviet numerical superiority will often not be brought to bear in mobile combat. The Soviets need their numerical superiority to compensate for their lack of flexibility. Their response time is also much greater than that of NATO artillery, and on-call fires are particularly difficult to use if they have not been pre-arranged. Units smaller than battalion are not netted into artillery COPs. Battalions are only in the artillery net when artillery is attached to the battalion or is in direct support. Regimental HQs cannot talk directly to divisional guns. This creates a ladder up which a request for artillery fire must climb, a time-consuming procedure.

Destroying, suppressing or blinding COPs would greatly reduce Soviet artillery effectiveness and, although the Soviets are less dependent on radio communications than NATO armies and train under simulated electronic warfare conditions, radio jamming could interfere with the crucial link between the COP and its firing battery or battalion. Similarly, breaking the links between artillery group and battalion headquarters will defeat any centralised fire plan. The Soviets will use field phones whenever possible, and will supplement them with couriers, but neither is likely to be practical in the heat of battle.

Counterbattery fire can reduce artillery effectiveness not only through shell damage, but by forcing enemy artillery and target acquisition equipment to move. Today counterbattery fire is more important than ever before. In the 1973 War 60% of the Israeli fire missions were counterbattery. Artillery with HE and smoke ammunition, both greatly improved since World War Two, is so important that no army can afford to allow the enemy to use it unhindered. Counterbattery missions may well receive an even higher priority in the future, especially as the increased effectiveness of air defences limits the use of aircraft against artillery positions (another lesson of the 1973 War).

Unit organisation

Towed artillery battery
Total strength: five officers (battery commander, political officer, firing battery commander, two platoon commanders), one warrant officer (technical officer), 63–75 enlisted men (depending on type of gun), six guns, six artillery tow vehicles (trucks or tracked vehicles), one URAL-375, ZIL-157 or 131 heavy truck, one light truck or BRDM-2U for COP.
One HQ (one officer, two-plus enlisted men, one BRDM-2U or light truck)
One control platoon
One reconnaissance section
Two firing platoons
One firing battery HQ
One support section (one warrant officer, one cargo truck)

Self-propelled artillery battery

Total strength: six SP howitzers, 3 -plus ZIL-157 or URAL-375 trucks, two ACRV-2 (one may be an MT-LB).

BM-21 MRL battery

Total strength: five officers, 56 enlisted men, six BM-21 MRLs, three trucks, one light truck or BRDM-2U.

Towed artillery battalion

Total strength: 20–22 officers, 264 enlisted men (276 in heavy artillery battalions), 18 guns, 18 tow vehicles (trucks or tractors), four COP vehicles, 20 trucks.
One HQ platoon
  HQ section (includes unit commander, with his COP, chief of staff, political officer, operations officer, and intelligence officer)
  Signal section (one truck, one BRDM or light truck, under communications officer)
  Reconnaissance section (under intelligence officer)
Three artillery batteries
One service platoon
  Medical squad
  POL squad (one tank truck)
  Maintenance and supply platoon

BM-21 MRL battalion

Total strength: 23 officers, 234 enlisted men.
One HQ platoon (seven officers, 24 enlisted men, nine trucks, two BRDMs)
Three MRL batteries
One support platoon (one officer, 42 enlisted men, 25 trucks)

SP artillery battalion

One HQ battery
Three artillery batteries
One service and support platoon

Artillery regiment

Total strength: 99 officers, 966 enlisted men (if all three battalions are towed guns), 54 guns, 54 tow vehicles, 182 trucks (if all three battalions towed).
One HQ and service battery (27 officers, 144 enlisted men, 52 trucks, five BRDM-2Us, and BTR-60PUs or ACRV-2s)
Three artillery battalions
One target-acquisition battery (12 officers, 90 enlisted men, one BRDM-2U, seven trucks)
  HQ platoon
  Sound and flash-ranging platoon (one ranging set)
  Counterbattery radar section (one radar)
  Ground surveillance radar (one GS-13 radar)
  Meteorological radar section (one End Tray radar)

The equipment of the regiment varies. Motorised rifle divisions normally have two battalions of D-30 122mm howitzers and one battalion of D-1 152mm howitzers. These are currently being replaced with SAU-122 and SAU-152 SP howitzers respectively. 122mm D-20s can be substituted for the D-30s and 152mm D-74s for the D-1s in some situations. Tank divisions had three 122mm D-30-equipped battalions, but not only have these been replaced by SAU-122s, but one of the three battalions has received SAU-152s in place of the D-30s. Thus, while lower-readiness tank divisions have three D-30 or M-30 battalions, others have one or more SAU-122 battalions, still others have the SAU-152 battalion, while the highest-readiness divisions will probably have two SAU-122 and one SAU-152 battalion. Army-level independent artillery regiments normally have two battalions of M-46 130mm field guns and one of D-20 152mm howitzers. A D-74 battalion may be substituted for one of the M-46 battalions. Artillery divisions usually have two regiments of M-46s and another with a mix of D-20s and 180mm S-23 battalions. Front-level heavy artillery brigades are organised like artillery regiments, but with only two artillery battalions. They primarily use the S-23.

Artillery division

Total strength: 388 officers, 3,859 enlisted men, 655 trucks, 18 AT-P tractors, 108 ATS-59 tractors (or MT-LBs or URAL-375s). Some divisions have 324 tubes, 637 officers, 6,059 enlisted men, 180 tractors and 1,264 trucks.
One divisional HQ (14 officers, 43 enlisted men)
Three artillery regiments (six in some divisions)
One anti-tank battalion (with 100mm guns)
One air-defence battalion (as motorised rifle division)
One target-acquisition battalion (40 officers, 300 enlisted men, 24 trucks, three counterbattery radars, six End Tray meteorological radars, three GS-13 ground surveillance radars, six sound and flash ranging sets, nine laser rangefinding sets)
One motor transport battalion (25 officers, 350 enlisted men, 202 trucks)
One signal company (five officers, 57 enlisted men, 15 trucks)
Division services command (*tyl*) (30 officers, 250 enlisted men, 74 trucks)
  One maintenance battalion
  One ordnance company
  One ammunition-handling company
  One medical unit
  Divisional depots

There is disagreement as to the strength of Soviet artillery divisions. While most sources quote 162 tubes as standard, other sources state that Type "A" artillery divisions have 252 artillery pieces while Type "B" divisions have 72-plus anti-tank guns. The 34th Guards Artillery Division in East Germany is reported to be "three times the strength of a standard artillery division." Organisation apparently differs greatly between divisions; one has been reported with six regiments/brigades.

Divisions apparently standardise on a single type of tow vehicle. The URAL-375 is replacing most of the earlier artillery tractors, although they will doubtless remain in service for some time. MT-LBs are used by some, probably tank, divisions. Other divisions use older types such as the ZIL-151/157.

Artillery units often have a separate set of "training guns" for use while the unit's first-line guns remain in storage, except for a few used for familiarisation and large-scale manoeuvres. It is difficult to determine which guns are for training and which are the first-line equipment. While the Soviets often introduce new equipment into Category I divisions and then let it filter down the readiness categories, this is not always the case, and the future will doubtless see some low-readiness units with new equipment while some Category I formations retain the older weapons.

Mortars

Size	82mm	120mm	160mm	240mm
Designation	M-1937	M-1943	M-1953	M-1952
Calibre length	14.9cal	15.4cal	28.5cal	22.4cal
Weight (firing)	56kg	274.8kg	1,300kg	3,610kg
Length (travelling)	1.22m	3.519m	4.86m	6.51m
Height (travelling)	–	1.63m	1.69m	2.21m
Width (travelling)	–	–	2.03m	2.49m
Elevation limits	+45°/+85°	+45°/+80°	+50°/+80°	+45°/+65°
Bore	smooth	smooth	smooth	smooth
Loading	muzzle	muzzle	breech	breech
Firing	drop	drop & trigger	trigger	trigger
Max rate of fire	15–25rpm	12–15rpm	2–3rpm	1rpm
Sustained (per hour)	–	100 rounds	–	–
Traverse	6°	8°	24°	17°
Max range	3.04km	5.7km	8.04km	9.7km
Min range	100m	460m	750m	1,500m
Ammunition types	F-833 HE, WP	F-843 HE, WP, smoke	F-853A HE, smoke	F-864 HE
Ammunition weight	HE = 3.05kg WP = 3.41kg	HE = 15.4kg	HE = 41.5kg	HE = 100kg
Muzzle velocity	211m/sec	272m/sec	345m/sec	362m/sec
Crew	5	6	7	8
Carriage	truck-carried, bipod	2-wheel towed, bipod	2-wheel towed	2-wheel towed
Tow vehicle	APC or truck	GAZ-66, MTLB	ZIL-157, BTR-152, URAL-375	AT-P, AT-L, AT-S, URAL-375
Unit of fire	120 rounds	50 rounds (42 HE, 8 WP)	60 rounds	–
Battery impact radius	–	150m	–	–

Tactical data (M-1943)

Normal distance behind FEBA: 0.5km offensive, 1.0km defensive.

Time for battery to leave firing position (day/night): 5.5/8min.

Minutes for battery to move one kilometre (day/night): 2.5/3.

Minutes to occupy fire positions (day/night): 12/18.

Mortars superbly suited the needs of the Soviet Army during World War Two. Simple and effective, they gave Soviet infantry commanders their own "jacket-pocket artillery," available when and where they were needed, and could go anywhere an infantryman or pack animal could walk. Mortar shells, with their thin casings, large explosive charges and plunging trajectories, are more

M-1937 82mm mortar, 1942–43 version, captured by US forces in Vietnam in 1967. The bracket for the MP-82US sight is on the left-hand side of the muzzle. *(US Army)*

M-1943 120mm mortar in firing position. *(US Army)*

effective than howitzer shells, even if the mortars lack the range and accuracy of howitzers.

Today's mortars are not very different from those of 1915, and although Western armies have replaced their World War Two mortars with lighter, longer-range weapons, the Soviets continue to rely on the wartime 120mm M-1943. Persistent but unconfirmed reports have mentioned a new mortar replacing the M-1943, and this new weapon may be in action in Afghanistan. An intended replacement, the 120mm M-1965, was apparently not put into service. The 82mm M-1937, M-1941 and M-1942 series of mortars also remain in service with airborne and naval infantry battalions. The large 160mm and 240mm mortars developed in the 1950s are in limited front-line service, if at all.

The standard Soviet mortar is the 120mm M-1943. Six of them, towed behind MT-LB APCs or GAZ-66 or -69 trucks, equip the mortar battery of each motorised rifle battalion, although they were originally regimental weapons. While the Soviets consider mortars to be artillery by definition, their crews are motorised riflemen who receive specialised mortar training at battalion level.

The M-1943 is a conventional, muzzle-loading, smooth-bore mortar. It can be either drop-fired (the shell

instantly firing upon hitting the bottom of the tube) or fired by a lanyard trigger. The muzzle-brake-like device prevents inadvertent double-loading. All Soviet mortars are difficult to traverse rapidly, but the M-1943 can be shifted up to 6° without moving the bipod. The M-1943 is normally folded together with its bipod and towed on a two-wheeled tubular carriage, but can also be broken down into barrel, baseplate and bipod for animal packs or manhandling. It is simple and rugged, and its tolerances were deliberately kept large. Ammunition with either wrought or cast iron casings can be used, the latter giving increased fragmentation effect but less range. The M-1943 is a slightly modified version of the M-1938, the only differences being larger shock-absorber cylinders and more sophisticated elevating and traversing gear. The M-1938 and the M-1943 were interchangeable for many years, but the Soviets no longer use the M-1938, although it is still found in foreign armies.

The large post-war mortars are only in limited first-line Soviet service, if at all. 240mm mortar battalions may still serve in front-level heavy artillery brigades. It has been reported that some howitzer battalions of motorised rifle divisions that may be called upon to operate in difficult terrain, such as the Caucasus, are cross-trained on these weapons, and can use them if the situation requires.

M-1943 120mm mortar in travelling position. (*Charles Yust*)

M-1938 120mm mortar in firing position. It is distinguishable from the M-1943 by its shorter recoil-cylinder shock-absorbers. (*US Army*)

M-1953 160mm mortar in travelling position on a wheeled carriage similar to that used with the 120mm M-1943. *(US Army)*

The 240mm mortar is a particularly large weapon, requiring four men to load the huge mortar bomb into its vertically sliding breech block, which stands over 1.66m above the ground. Both of the large mortars were once reported as being nuclear-capable, and it is possible that a nuclear round was once developed for the 240mm mortar. However, it was either discarded or never deployed, because its blast radius would have exceeded its range.

A new self-propelled 240mm mortar was in first-line service with Soviet units in East Germany and the European USSR in 1980. This weapon is mounted on a tracked vehicle – reported to be the same as an SP howitzer – and incorporates an automatic loading device similar to that fitted to the Israeli 160mm mortar.

Combat usage

The 120mm and 82mm mortars have seen action in World War Two and almost every war of insurgency since then. The effectiveness, ruggedness, simplicity and ease of movement of the M-1943 in particular mean that it will be in service for years to come.

The 160mm mortar (including the earlier M-1943 version, no longer in Soviet service) has seen action with the Indian Army (who thought it a better weapon than the 120mm mortar despite its weight) in 1971 and with Arab armies since the 1967 War, including the Lebanese conflict.

The 240mm has been less widely used, although it has seen combat in Lebanon. Indian and Arab examples may also have seen combat.

Tactical employment

In action M-1943 batteries are normally deployed in a straight line 150–250m in length and 500–1,500m from the line of contact. The battery follows the motorised riflemen in the attack and can go into action in about twelve minutes. It will normally be employed as a single unit, although it can be split into two platoons or attached to companies. During the artillery offensive battalion mortars are included in Soviet centralised artillery command and will receive their fire orders from regimental or higher level if time permits. If not, the battery commander will direct fire from the command observation post. Using a GAZ-69 light truck or APC, he will position himself as

M-1952 240mm mortar in travelling position on its two-wheeled carriage. *(US Army)*

far forward as possible and will be able to provide the battalion with close-in indirect-fire support, including high-explosive, illumination and smoke rounds. In the mobile battle of a meeting engagement, this may be the only indirect-fire support a battalion can employ. If they have to displace while in action, the battery will move by alternate platoons unless covered by howitzer fire, when they would all advance together. On the defensive the mortars are well dug into their battery position, usually on a reverse slope. On the offensive only a small pit for proper setting of the baseplate is dug. For close-in defence each tow vehicle driver has an RPG-7 and the crews have small arms. The 82mm mortar would be used in a similar way, but closer to the front and normally from a covered position, while the 160mm would be used in the same direct-support role as the D-30.

M-1969 76.2mm mountain gun

Calibre	14cal
Weight	815kg (estimated)
Max range	11km
Ammunition types	HE, HEAT, others(?)
Muzzle velocity	HE = 600m/sec
Shell weight	HE = 6.2kg
Crew	6
Tow vehicle	light truck, animal, helicopter

The Soviet M-1969 76.2mm mountain gun replaces the earlier M-1938 model. It is mounted on a split-box trail similar to that of the Italian-made L5 105mm howitzer, and apparently can also be disassembled. The recoil cylinder is located under the barrel. The rest of its construction seems close to standard Soviet practice.

Introduced in 1969 and seen in the 1971 "Yug" exercise, the M-1969 is believed to be used as regimental artillery in place of 122mm howitzers in approximately eight divisions that must operate in mountains or foothill-type terrain.

M-1969 76.2mm mountain guns. (*Soldat & Technik*)

D-30 122mm howitzer with the tow ring on the muzzle brake characteristic of early production versions and showing the unique trail-first travelling position of this weapon. *(US Army)*

D-30 122mm howitzer

Calibre	35.5cal		Ammunition weights	HE = 21.8kg
Weight (firing)	3,150kg			HEAT = 14.1kg (BP-1)
Length (travelling)	5.4m			HEAT = 21.6kg (BK-6M)
Height (travelling)	1.66m			smoke = 22.4kg
Width (travelling)	1.95m			illum = 22.4kg
Track	1.85m		Muzzle velocity	HE = 690m/sec
Elevation limits	−7°/+70°			HEAT = 740m/sec (BP-1)
Traverse	360°			HEAT = 680m/sec (BK-6M)
Max rate of fire	7–8rpm		Armour penetration	HEAT (BK-6M) = 500mm
Sustained rate of fire	4–1.7rpm		Mount	3-trail, 2-wheel carriage
Max range	15.3km		Crew	7
Point-blank range (2m-high target)	800m with HEAT (BK-6M)		Tow vehicles	AT-P, MT-LB, ZIL-157, GAZ-63, URAL-375, KrAZ-214
Ammunition types	OF-462 or OF-462 ZH HE, BP-1 spin-stabilised HEAT, BK-6 or BK-6M HEAT-FS, smoke, chem, illum		Unit of fire	80 (64 HE, 12 smoke, 4 HEAT)

Tactical data

Normal distance behind FEBA: 3km offensive, 4km defensive, but less than a third of that if used as accompanying artillery.

Burst radius (battery pattern): 90–100m.

Minutes for D-30 units to leave firing positions (day/night): (battery) 5–7/9; (battalion) 11/14.

Minutes for D-30 units to move one kilometre (day/night): (battery and battalion) 3/3.5.

Minutes for D-30 units to occupy new fire positions (day/night): (battery) 10–12/18; (battalion) 23/32.

Fragmentation effectiveness radius against armoured vehicles from one shell (against APC/IFV/SP gun): 1.0/0.5/0.75m.

Accuracy: In direct fire at 800m against a 2m-high target, using BK-6M HEAT rounds, projectile error range is 0.4m in both vertical and horizontal components. In indirect fire, using HE shells, projectile error range is 24m at 10,700m range and 23m at 13,800m range.

The D-30 M-1963 122mm howitzer is the standard Soviet divisional and regimental howitzer. Introduced in 1967, it replaced the 122mm M-30 M-1938 and other World War Two-vintage artillery. Since then the D-30 has been produced in large quantities and has apparently proven most successful in service, combining simplicity and ruggedness with effectiveness. While it lacks the range and destructive power of NATO 155mm howitzers, the Soviets believe that deploying the D-30 further forward than comparable enemy guns will negate the range advantage, and that the numbers of these weapons made possible by their simplicity and ease of production will compensate for any individual limitations. Although the D-30 is being replaced by the SAU-122 SP howitzer in many units, it will doubtless continue in service for many years.

The D-30 is often termed a gun-howitzer because of its long barrel. It embodies a semi-automatic, vertical sliding-wedge breech block. Like earlier Soviet 122mm howitzers, the D-30 fires separate, fixed-charge ammuni-

D-30 122mm howitzer (an early production model) giving direct fire in support of attacking tanks. *(Tom Woltjer)*

tion, and only two charges are available. The maximum charge is especially powerful – made possible by the D-30's rugged construction – and also gives a high muzzle velocity. The introduction of the D-30 coincided with that of improved types of 122mm ammunition with a more powerful type of explosive and a design superior to that of earlier, World-War Two-era shells, although D-30s can use the same ammunition as the earlier M-30. Reportedly, a rocket-assisted HE projectile with a range of 21.9km has been developed for the D-30. It also fires a new non-rotating BK-6M HEAT round, showing the continued Soviet emphasis on a secondary anti-tank role for howitzers. A passive infra-red direct-fire night sight can be fitted.

The carriage of the D-30 and the way it is towed are both unusual but apparently efficient. The bulky recoil mechanism is mounted in a characteristic "hump" above the barrel. The D-30 is towed not by the trail but by the muzzle. A towing ring is fitted just behind the multi-baffle muzzle brake, although early production guns had the ring on the brake itself. The carriage is of a unique three-trail, 360°-traverse type. When going into action the crew unhitches the gun and lowers the central firing jack under the breech, which raises the carriage wheels high enough off the ground to clear the trail legs. The three trails, folded beneath the barrel in travelling position, are then unfolded and deployed, allowing the breech 360° rotation around a central pivot, although full elevation is not possible when the breech is directly over a trail. Pads at the end of each trail accept spades which secure the gun. While the arrangement may sound complicated, the Soviets point out that a World War Two howitzer could go from travelling to firing position in one minute, and the D-30 is quicker than that. A small shield between the wheels protects the gun crew.

Combat usage

A small number of D-30s were introduced into combat in the Nigerian civil war in 1969. Larger numbers were used in the 1973 Middle East war. Alongside older guns, the D-30s were one of the mainstays of Arab field artillery strength and proved highly effective. According to some reports, D-30s were also employed as direct-fire anti-tank weapons. In the 1973 War the Syrians used a home-made SP version of the D-30, placing the gun in an open mount on a T-34 chassis. They have also been used by Cuban forces with Soviet "advisers" in Angola and Ethiopia.

Tactical employment

The D-30 equips the regimental howitzer battalions or batteries of motorised rifle regiments, although it is being replaced by the SAU-122 SP howitzer in all BMP and half of all BTR-60-equipped regiments. The divisional artillery regiments of all Soviet divisions have two or three battalions of D-30s, although other guns can be substituted.

Numerically the most important field artillery piece in the Soviet Army, the D-30 is used for most Soviet artillery missions. It is normally used for direct support of regimental and smaller-sized tank and motorised rifle units, forming the regimental artillery groups, organic regimental artillery and divisional guns attached down to regiment, battalion or company command. D-30s are normally deployed close to the front: one to four kilometres back in the offensive and two to seven kilometres in the defensive.

D-74 122mm field gun. This particular gun was captured in Vietnam by the US Marine Corps. *(US Army)*

D-74 122mm gun and D-20 152mm gun-howitzer

Size	122mm	152mm
Designation	D-74	D-20
Calibre	46.3cal	37cal
Weight (firing)	5,568kg	5,650kg
Length (travelling)	9.763m	8.138m
Height (travelling)	2.758m	2.758m
Width (travelling)	2.027m	2.027m
Ground clearance	0.39m	0.25m
Elevation limts	$-5°/+45°$	$-5°/+63°$
Traverse	60°	60°
Max rate of fire	6–7rpm	4–6rpm
Sustained rate of fire	3–1.5rpm	2–1.5rpm
Max range (HE)	24km	18.5km
Point-blank range (2m-high target)	1,060m (APHE)	800m (APHE)
Ammunition types	OF-472 HE, BR-472 APHE, smoke, chem, illum	OF-540 HE, BR-540 APHE, G-545 concrete-piercing, chem, illum, smoke*
Ammunition weight	HE = 27.5kg APHE = 25.0kg Smoke = 21.7kg	HE = 43.6kg APHE = 48.8kg
Muzzle velocity	885m/sec, all ammunition	HE = 655m/sec APHE = 600m/sec
Armour penetration	APHE = 185mm @ 1,000m	APHE = 124mm @ 1,000m
Crew	10	10
Mount	split trail, 2-wheel	split trail, 2-wheel
Tow vehicle	AT-S, AT-L, URAL-375	AT-S, AT-L, URAL-375
Unit of fire	80 (64 HE, 12 smoke, 4 APHE)	60 (48 HE, 9 smoke?, 3 APHE)

* The D-74 probably has a smoke round but this is uncertain.

Tactical data

Normal distance behind FEBA: (D-20) 4km offensive, 5km defensive; (D-74) 5km offensive, 7km defensive.
Burst radius, battery pattern: (D-74) 90–100m; (D-20) 150m.
Time for D-74 or D-20 units to leave firing positions (day/night): (battery) 10/13min; (battalion) 11/14min.
Minutes for D-74 or D-20 units to move one kilometre (day/night): (battery and battalion) 3/3.5.
Minutes for D-74 or D-20 units to occupy fire positions: (battery) 12/18; (battalion) 23/32.
Fragmentation effectiveness of one shell against armoured vehicles (against APC/ICV/SP gun): (D-74) 1.0/0.5/0.75m; (D-20) 1.5/1.0/1.25m.
D-74 accuracy: In direct fire with APHE, projectile error range in both deflection and vertical components is 0.2m at 1,000m range. In indirect fire with HE shells, projectile error range is 55m at 16,010m range and 91m at 21,510m range.
D-20 accuracy: In direct fire with APHE, projectile error range is 0.2m in the vertical and 0.3m in deflection at

1,000m range. Indirect-fire accuracy is believed to produce a projectile error range of 42m at 11,500m range and 63m at 15,500m range, using HE ammunition.

Older and heavier than the D-30, the D-74 M-1955 122mm field howitzer replaced the wartime A-19. D-74-equipped battalions are found in the heavy artillery regiment of lower-readiness artillery divisions in place of M-46-equipped units and may replace D-30-equipped battalions in divisional artillery regiments when long range is more important than mobility.

The D-20 M-1955 152mm gun-howitzer is the Soviet Army's standard heavy howitzer, equipping the howitzer battalions of army-level artillery brigades and artillery divisions, in which it replaced the ML-20. The D-20 never fully replaced the D-1 in motorised rifle divisions, though some may use the D-20 in place of the D-1, either permanently or when the tactical situation requires. Introduced in 1955, the D-20 is now being replaced by the SAU-152 SP howitzer.

The D-74 and the D-20 are similar in most respects.

The D-74's barrel is long (47cal) and low, while the D-20's is shorter (29cal), wider and has a larger double-baffle muzzle brake. Both guns use the same short, split-trailed carriage with castoring wheels at the trail ends, along with spade-like baseplates. A circular firing jack and the castoring wheels allow quick traverse. Both guns have a scalloped, winged shield which is 9mm thick and not highly effective, a two-cylinder recoil mechanism above the prominently stepped tube, and the semi-automatic, vertical sliding-wedge breech used in most rapid-fire Soviet artillery. Both guns fire case-type, variable-charge, separate-loading ammunition. They retain a secondary anti-tank capability, with a low silhouette and APHE rounds, but they are still big weapons and difficult to manoeuvre, deploy or conceal.

Combat usage

Combat usage of the D-20 has been limited, apparently because of its size. India used some in the 1971 War, and they were also used by North Vietnam.

The Egyptians used the D-20 in 1967 and 1973, and a small number were supplied to Nigeria during its civil war. Vietnam and China also have D-74s. The Vietnamese used only a handful of D-74s in action, employing them in the same way as they did the M-46 in I Corps. They were in action in the A Shau campaign.

Tactical employment

The D-20 and D-74 are normally attached down to divisional artillery groups for use in general support missions, although they are also used by army artillery groups. They are sometimes used as division-level weapons, replacing the D-30 and D-1 respectively. The D-20's 18.5km range makes it useful in the counterbattery role, but its large size reduces mobility, even when towed by tracked AT-L vehicles (which is probably why it did not replace the D-1), and it is not deployed as far forward as other similar Soviet artillery, which limits its striking reach. The D-74 is also primarily counterbattery, but, like the D-20, it will also be used in the general support role when long range is needed, hitting targets such as reserve units, assembly areas, headquarters and supply routes.

D-20 152mm gun-howitzer of the East German Army. (US Army)

M-46 130mm field guns being towed by AT-S tractors. *(US Army)*

M-46 130mm field gun

Calibre	55cal
Weight (firing)	8,450kg
Weight (travelling)	7,700kg
Length (travelling)	11.73m
Height (travelling)	2.55m
Width (travelling)	2.45m
Track	2.06m
Ground clearance	0.4m
Elevation limits	$-2\frac{1}{2}°/+45°$
Traverse	50°
Max rate of fire	5–6rpm
Sustained rate of fire	3–1.7rpm
Max range	27.5km
Point-blank range (2m-high target)	·1,170m (APHE)
Ammunition types	OF-482M HE, BR-482B APHE, smoke, SP-46 illum
Ammunition weight	HE = 33.4kg APHE = 33.6kg illum = 25.8kg
Muzzle velocity	HE = 930m/sec APHE = 930m/sec
Armour penetration	APHE = 230mm @ 1,000m
Crew	9
Mount	split trail, 2-wheel
Tow vehicle	AT-S, URAL-375
Unit of fire	70 rounds

Tactical data

Normal distance behind FEBA for M-46 unit: 5km offensive, 9km defensive.

Burst radius, battery pattern: 90–100m.

Minutes for M-46 units to leave firing positions (day/night): (battery) 10/13; (battalion) 11/14.

Minutes for M-46 units to move one kilometre (day/night): (batteries and battalions) 3/3.5.

Minutes for M-46 units to occupy new fire positions (day/night): (battery) 12/18; (battalion) 23/32.

Accuracy: In direct fire with APHE, projectile error range is 0.2m in both vertical and deflection at 1,000m. In indirect fire with HE, projectile error range is 43m at 18,420m and 62m at 24,740m.

Long-ranged and accurate, the 130mm M-46 field gun is excellent for counterbattery work. Developed from the 130mm M-1936 naval gun, it replaced the A-19 in the early 1950s. The M-46 was first seen in the 1954 May Day parade, and an almost identical version is designated the M-1954. The M-46's long, thin tube ends in a pepper-pot perforated muzzle brake. The hydropneumatic recuperator and hydraulic buffer of the recoil system are located above and below the gun tube, as on the D-1. The recuperator has a distinctive front-end collar support in front of the rearward-angled, winged gunshield. The breech block is a manually operated, horizontal sliding-wedge type, and the gun fires case-type, variable-loading ammunition. It is mounted on a standard split-trail,

M-46 130mm field guns of the Egyptian Army being towed by KrAZ-214s. *(Egyptian Army)*

spade-end carriage with two large sponge-filled road wheels. When travelling the barrel is retracted so that the breech is above the trails. Provided with a two-wheel limber, the M-46 can be towed by a truck or armoured tractor at up to 50km/h. A modified 130mm gun with a longer barrel, recuperator and cradle appeared in the mid-1970s.

The M-46's long barrel and high muzzle velocity give it excellent anti-tank capability. It was mounted in the experimental SU-130 assault gun for this role, and the Israelis have reportedly developed a 130mm tank gun based on the M-46. The M-46 is provided with direct-fire sights, including an APN-3 active/passive infra-red sight.

Combat usage

The North Vietnamese fielded no more than a few dozen M-46s during the later stages of the Vietnam War, but used them to great effect. Those who were on the receiving end of 130mm fire in the 1971–72 period consider the gun superior in range, accuracy and shell destructive power to any weapon used by US or ARVN forces, including the big 175mm M-107 SP gun. The M-46 played a major role in the Laos invasion and the fighting in the northern I Corps area of South Vietnam, especially in Quang Tri province.

The M-46s were surprisingly mobile. Towed by tracked vehicles, they could traverse any terrain, even jungle trails, which made them difficult to locate. Their flash was hard to spot in daylight, and North Vietnamese tactics were based on frequent changes of position to avoid counterbattery fire, although their long range protected them from most Allied artillery. Only air strikes could deal with them. On May 7, 1972, the USAF declared open season on M-46s, with combined teams of O-2E forward air controller aircraft and cannon-armed AC-130 gunships assigned to seek out the M-46s. They were not successful, as the M-46s kept moving and were harder to spot once the North Vietnamese protected them with SA-7 SAMs to keep the O-2Es at high altitude. Many airstrikes were devoted to identifying and eliminating individual gun positions, and even B-52s were used against them. Seldom in modern warfare have so few guns been such a problem to so many.

The M-46 was also used in the 1973 Middle East war. The Egyptians put them in army-level artillery brigades and used them, Soviet-style, in the counterbattery role. They were extremely effective, especially in the opening days of the war. The Egyptians co-located M-46 batteries with radio direction-finding equipment, which gave them rapid target acquisition against any Israeli target using its radio. The Israelis currently have battalions of M-46s, and these may have seen combat use.

The Indian Army used M-46s for counterbattery work in its 1971 campaign against West Pakistan, both as a divisional and corps-level gun. They thought highly of the weapon's range and accuracy.

Tactical employment

An M-46-equipped regiment is organic to each Soviet artillery division, and a battalion to each army-level independent artillery brigade. They are frequently assigned down to divisional artillery group level. 130mm batteries on counterbattery missions are often co-located with target-acquisition facilities, especially radars or radio direction-finders.

D-1 152mm howitzers in traditional linear, closely spaced deployment. (Chris Foss)

D-1 (M-1943) 152mm howitzer

Calibre	24.5cal	**Ammunition weight**	HE = 39.9kg
Weight (firing)	3,600kg		SAP = 51.1kg
Length (travelling)	7.040m		concrete-piercing = 40kg
Height (travelling)	1.854m	**Muzzle velocity**	HE = 508m/sec
Width (travelling)	1.86m		SAP = 432m/sec
Track	1.8m		concrete-piercing = 508m/sec
Ground clearance	0.37m	**Armour penetration**	SAP = 82mm @ 1,000m
Elevation limits	−3°/+63.5°	**Crew**	7
Traverse	35°	**Mount**	split trail, 2-wheel
Max rate of fire	3–4rpm	**Tow vehicle**	AT-S, ZIL-151, URAL-375,
Sustained rate of fire	2–1.7rpm	**(current Soviet)**	ZIL-157
Max range	12.4km	**Unit of fire**	60 rounds (48 HE, 9 smoke,
Point-blank range	510m (SAP)		3 SAP)
(2m-high target)		**Design bureau**	Petrov Works
Ammunition types	OF-530/A HE, SAP, chem,		
	smoke*, illun₁,		
	G-530 concrete-piercing		

* The D-1 probably has a smoke round but this is uncertain.

Tactical data

Normal distance behind FEBA: 3km offensive, 4km defensive.

Burst radius, battery pattern: 150m.

Minutes for D-1 units to leave firing positions (day/night): (battery) 5–7/9; (battalion) 11/14.

Minutes for D-1 units to move 1km (day/night): (battery & battalion) 3/3.5.

Minutes for D-1 units to occupy fire positions (day/night): (battery) 10–15/15–20; (battalion) 23/32.

Fragmentation effectiveness of one shell against armoured vehicles (against APC/ICV/SP gun): 1.5/1.0/1.25m.

D-1 152mm howitzer.

Time to emplace single gun: 2min.
Accuracy: in direct fire, using SAP at 510m, projectile error range in the vertical is 0.1m and in deflection is 0.2m.
In indirect fire with HE, projectile error range is 35m at 8,500m and 47m at 11,200m.

One of the last wartime artillery pieces in service, the D-1 equips the heavy howitzer battalion of each motorised rifle division. Replacement by SAU-152 SP howitzers is well under way, but the D-1 will doubtless soldier on in lower-readiness units for years to come. It has the tube of the 152mm ML-20 howitzer fitted with a large double muzzle brake and mounted on a straightened, modified M-30 122mm howitzer carriage. This gives it the capability of the earlier 152mm weapon, but it is lighter and more mobile. Like the pre-war 152mm howitzers, the D-1 has a screw-type breech and a hydraulic recoil system, in this case positioned over and under the tube. The carriage is the standard box split-trail type, and the D-1 is recognisable by its compact size, sharply raked "tombstone" gunshield, and large metal road wheels.

Combat usage

The D-1 was used by the Soviet Army in the Second World War and in considerable numbers by the Arabs in 1967 and 1973. The North Vietnamese used the D-1 in action, and China may have done so.

Tactical employment

The D-1's lightness and mobility were achieved at the expense of range, and it must be positioned close to the front. The D-1 battalion is often used in general support as part of a division artillery group, although it is sometimes used in regimental artillery groups.

D-1 (M-1943) 152mm howitzer. *(Tom Woltjer)*

S-23 180mm gun-howitzer being towed by AT-T tractors. The double tyres and muzzle brake are characteristic of the gun. *(Tom Woltjer)*

Heavy artillery

Size	180mm gun
Designation	S-23
Weight (travelling)	20,400kg
Max range	30.4km (HE)
	43.8km (RAP)
Ammunition types	OF-23 HE, HE/RAP,
	0.2KT nuclear,
	G-572 concrete-piercing
Shell weight	HE = 84.09kg, CP = 97.7kg
Muzzle velocity	790m/sec HE, 850m/sec RAP
Elevation	$-2°/+50°$
Traverse	44°
Max rate of fire	1rpm
Tow vehicle	AT-T, AT-S or KrAZ-255
Crew	15 (estimated)
Unit of fire	40 rounds

Tactical data

Normal distance behind FEBA: 7km offensive, 9km defensive.

The primary Soviet heavy artillery piece, the S-23 180mm gun is the largest towed gun in service anywhere. First seen in the mid-1950s, the S-23, like the M-46, is based on a pre-war naval gun. It embodies a screw-type breech block typical of Soviet heavy artillery, and also features a multi-perforated muzzle brake and a cylindrical jacket around the barrel for much of its length. As with the M-46, the barrel can retract over the trails for towing. Two dual tyres, filled with sponge rubber, support the large box-section, split-trail carriage. A two-wheeled limber can also be used. The buffer recuperator is mounted under the barrel. Conventional ammunition is bag-type, separate-loading, variable-charge, and includes HE and "concrete-piercing" rounds. A rocket-assisted HE round (RAP) has been introduced, apparently during the 1970s. Currently the S-23 can also fire 0.2-kiloton-yield nuclear rounds. Although the S-23 has been thought to be nuclear-capable since its introduction, earlier Soviet artillery-delivered tactical nuclear warhead capability existed mainly on paper. The warheads were big, unreliable and short-ranged enough to imperil the weapon firing them, let alone any troops between them and the enemy. The S-23 apparently received its current nuclear capability during the 1970s (or possible the late 1960s).

Organic to the heavy artillery regiment of artillery divisions and to front-level artillery brigades (if any exist, which is uncertain), the S-23 provides accurate long-range nuclear and conventional fire. It was used by the Egyptian Army in 1973, and at least one example was captured by the Israelis. For many years Western sources referred to this weapon as a 203mm gun, designating it the M-1955. Examination of this captured gun revealed that the S-23 was in fact a 180mm weapon.

Other examples of the earlier, unsuccessful, Soviet artillery nuclear capability were the 310mm and 420mm guns and mortars mounted on IS heavy tank chassis that were paraded through Red Square during the 1950s (they were in fact kept in storage between parades). Firing a winged, rocket-powered nuclear projectile, these weapons were built as an answer to the US 280mm nuclear-capable gun of the 1950s. Nikita Krushchev thought that the building of these useless guns was "pointless imitation . . . showing the smallness of the military mind."

A new Soviet self-propelled heavy artillery piece, reportedly a 203mm weapon, was in first-line service in Russia and East Germany in 1980. Little is known of this weapon except that it has a long barrel, is mounted on a tracked vehicle chassis, and is reportedly also developed from a naval gun, in this case the weapon used on new Soviet cruisers now under construction. Western sources believe that this gun is nuclear-capable.

180mm S-23 captured by Israeli forces. (Marine Corps Gazette)

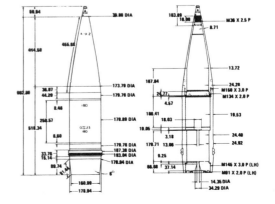

Diagram and cutaway view (right) of 180mm OF-23 high-explosive rocket-assisted projectile (HE/RAP) round. All dimensions in millimetres. (DIA)

Obsolescent artillery: M-30 (M-1938) 122mm howitzer, A-19 (M-1931/37) 122mm field gun, ML-20 (M-1937) 152mm gun-howitzer

Size	122mm	122mm	152mm
Designation	M-30	A-19	ML-20
Model number	M-1938	M-1931/37	M-1937
Calibre	22.7cal	46.3cal	29cal
Weight (firing)	2,500kg	7,117kg	7,128kg
Length (travelling)	5.9m	7.87m	7.21m
Height (travelling)	1.82m	2.27m	2.26m
Width (travelling)	1.975m	2.46m	2.31m
Track	1.6m	1.9m	1.9m
Elevation limits	$-3°/+63.5°$	$-2°/+65°$	$-2°/+65°$
Traverse	49°	58°	58°
Max rate of fire	5–6rpm	5–6rpm	3–4rpm
Max range	11.8km	20.8km	17.265km
Point-blank range (2m-high target)	630m	900m	800m
Ammunition types	OF-462/A HE, BP-460A HEAT, D-462 smoke, S-462 illum, A-462 propaganda, chem	OF-462 HE, OF-471 HE, BR-471 APHE, G-471 concrete-piercing, smoke, chem, illum	OF-530/A HE, BR-540 APHE, SAP, OF-540/B HE, chem, illum, smoke, G-530 concrete-piercing, G-545 concrete-piercing
Ammunition weight	HE = 21.8kg, HEAT = 14.8kg, smoke = 22.4kg, illum = 21.0kg, prop = 21.5kg	HE = 25.5kg (OF-471), APHE = 25kg, smoke = 25.7kg	HE = 43.6kg, APHE = 48.8kg
Muzzle velocity	HE = 515m/sec, HEAT = 570m/sec	HE = 800m/sec, APHE = 800m/sec	HE = 655m/sec, APHE = 600m/sec
Armour penetration	HEAT = 200mm	APHE = 160mm @ 1,000m	APHE = 124mm @ 1,000m
Crew	8	8	9–10
Mount	split trail, 2-wheel	split trail, 2-wheel	split trail, 2-wheel
Tow vehicle (current Soviet)	ZIL-151, MT-LB, GT-T, URAL-375	KrAZ-214, AT-S, AT-T, URAL-375	AT-S, URAL-375
Unit of fire	80 rounds	80 rounds	60 rounds

Tactical data

M-30 accuracy: In direct fire with HEAT, projectile error range at 1,000m range is 0.6m in both vertical and deflection. In indirect fire with HE, projectile error range is 25m at 7,900m range and 35m at 10,600m range.

A-19 accuracy: In direct fire with APHE or HE, projectile error range at 1,000m range is 0.3m in both vertical and deflection. In indirect fire with HE, projectile error range is 70m at 13,200m and 94m at 17,800 range.

ML-20 accuracy: In direct fire with BR-540 APHE, projectile error range at 700m range is 0.2m in both vertical and deflection. Indirect fire with HE yields projectile error ranges of 49m at 11,500 range and 64m at 15,500m.

These weapons were all developed before World War Two and, though obsolescent, linger on as training equipment, in low-readiness units, in storage reserves and in paramilitary organisations such as DOSAAF, which trains secondary school students. All have been exported and have seen much action since 1945.

The 122mm A-19 M-1931/37 was a corps-level long-range counterbattery artillery weapon in World War Two. The wheels, originally solid, are now modern disc tyres. It has a screw breech and hydraulic recoil system mounted beneath the gun tube. The carriage uses the standard box split trail, and the JSU 122 assault gun used the same gun. The A-19 was replaced in Soviet service by

Above M-30 (M-1938) 122mm howitzer captured by Israeli forces in 1973, showing modernised wheels and tyres. *(Tom Woltjer)*

Below M-30 (M-1938) 122mm howitzer with old-style wheels, captured by US forces in Korea in 1950. *(US Army)*

A-19 M-1931/37 122mm field gun, showing the two-wheel limber, captured in Korea. (US Army)

the M-46 and D-74. The Germans and Finns employed captured A-19s, and they were used by the Arabs throughout the Middle East wars. They have been built in China and widely exported to nations such as Cambodia (Chinese version), Cuba, Guinea, North Korea (used by both Chinese and Koreans in 1950–53), Somalia, Tanzania, North Yemen and South Yemen. The Iraqis used A-19s in 1980.

Its ruggedness and simplicity have resulted in the A-19 seeing a great deal of combat in the past. Despite its age and weight, it will probably see more combat in the future.

The 122mm M-30 M-1938 was the standard Soviet howitzer until it was replaced by the D-30, and large numbers remain in Soviet service in first and second-line roles. The M-30 has the same carriage as the D-1. It has a screw-type breech, a hydropneumatic recuperator above the tube and a hydropneumatic buffer below. The Bulgarians and East Germans updated their M-30 carriages

in the early 1960s, adding new wheels and tyres. The M-30's tactical use is identical to that of the D-30. The M-30 saw combat in World War Two, Korea, Southeast Asia and throughout the Middle East. It was the standard Egyptian howitzer in 1967, and many were captured by the Israelis, who incorporated full battalions of them into their order of battle, though in recent years they have been used exclusively for training. The North Vietnamese used many M-30s, especially in the A Shau valley in 1968 and in the Laos invasion. The M-30 is still in Soviet front-line service today. In 1980 artillery units of the 360th Motorised Rifle Division and other units deployed in Afghanistan were equipped with these guns.

Well designed and sturdy, the ML-20 M-1937 152mm gun-howitzer was a major long-range weapon in World War Two. Like most older Soviet artillery pieces it has a screw-type breech, hydraulic buffers and hydropneumatic recuperators, and fires case-type, variable-charge, separate-loading ammunition. Replaced in Soviet service by the D-20, it was used in the same way as that gun. The ML-20 was used in Korea, Vietnam and the Middle East.

ML-20 (M-1937) 152mm gun-howitzer captured by Israeli forces in 1973. *(Tom Woltjer)*

ML-20 (M-1937) 152mm gun-howitzer recaptured from the Germans in 1945. It has the old, solid wheels rather than the pneumatic tyres adopted after the war. *(US Army)*

Self-propelled howitzers: SAU-122 and SAU-152

Designation	SAU-122	SAU-152
NATO model number	M-1974	M-1973
Weight (firing)	16,000kg	23,000kg
Length (travelling)	7.3m	7.8m
Height (travelling)	2.4m	2.7m
Width (travelling)	2.85m	3.2m
Ground clearance	0.46m	0.45m
Max road speed	60km/h	50km/h
Fuel capacity	550lit	500lit
Road range	500km	300km
Fording	amphibious	1.1m
Water speed	4.5km/h	nil
Gradient	35°	30°
Vertical obstacle	1.1m	1.1m
Engine	V-8, 240HP diesel water-cooled, YaMZ-238	500HP diesel water-cooled
Gun	122mm D-30 howitzer	152mm D-20 howitzer
Calibre length	35.5cal	37cal
Rate of fire (max)	4–6rpm	4–6rpm (estimated)
Rate of fire (sustained)	3rpm	2rpm (estimated)
Ammunition types	HE, HEAT, HE/RAP, smoke, chem, illum, leaflet (as D-30)	HE, APHE, HE/RAP (?), smoke, chem, illum, 0.2KT nuclear
Max range (HE)	15.3km	24km
Max range (HE/RAP)	21.9km	37km
Effective range	1.0km (HEAT)	1.2km (APHE)
Muzzle velocity	as D-30	as D-20
Shell weights	as D-30	as D-20
Rounds carried	40 (32 HE, 6 smoke, 2 HEAT)	30 (23 HE, 5 smoke, 2 APHE)
Armour penetration	as D-30	as D-20
Elevation	−3°/+70°	−3°/+65°
Traverse	360°	360°
Armour (glacis plate)	14–20mm (approx)	14–20mm (estimated)
Crew	4	3–5

Tactical data

Distances behind FEBA (direct fire): 0.5–1.0km offensive, 1.0km defensive.

Upon occupying a new firing position SP batteries can be in action in about two minutes, rising to three or four minutes at night. Battalions would take about twice as long.

Burst radii are the same as for the D-30 and D-20 respectively.

The SAU-122 (SAU = *Samochodnaya Artilleriyskiy Ustenovka*, self-propelled artillery mount; designation unconfirmed) self-propelled 122mm howitzer was first seen in 1974. Its chassis is based on the MT-LB series and embodies many standard components of the type first used on the PT-76. It has seven road wheels with a Christie-type torsion-bar suspension having two hy-draulic dampers per side. The drive sprocket is at the front. Unlike earlier types, the dead track has metal-rubber links, and a wider track can be fitted for soft-ground operation. The amphibious hull has a BMP-type boat front, with the driver sitting to the left of the front-mounted YaMZ-238 V-8 240HP diesel, the same engine used by the MT-LB. The manual transmission has the standard five forward and one reverse gears. Swimming is by track propulsion. The SAU-122's hull can have its clearance lowered, making it the first Soviet AFV to have this capability. Intended to facilitate air transportation, this can also decrease battlefield exposure, allow the SAU-122 to pass under low bridges, and possibly lock the suspension against recoil. Battery command SAU-122s have extra radio antennae. An OU-3GK infra-red search-light is carried, and other optics, including the gunner's sight, seem similar to other Soviet designs. There does not

SAU-122 M-1974 122mm SP howitzer of a Guards unit on its way to a parade. *(US Army)*

appear to be a large, artillery-type optical rangefinder. An NBC filter is mounted on the right-hand side of the hull, and NBC protection is probably similar to that on the BMP. Armour protection must be light to achieve such a low weight.

The gun, a development of the D-30 howitzer, is mounted in a long, low turret with a rigidly mounted turret basket and cupolas for commander and gunner. A power rammer and extractor are used, and the semi-automatic sliding-wedge-type breech block automatically extracts the expended cartridge case, which can then be thrown out of the loader's hatch. The muzzle brake is different from that of the D-30, and is similar to that of the D-74. The gun can reportedly fire a rocket-assisted projectile with a range of 21.9km.

The SAU-152 SP 152mm howitzer entered service in 1973–74. Its chassis is based on that used by the SA-4 Ganef SAM launch vehicle, with a modified running gear (only six road wheels, with spaces between the front three only) and different spacing between the four support rollers. The engine, a standard water-cooled diesel, is mounted in the front on the right-hand side. Unlike the SAU-122, the SAU-152 is not amphibious. The turret is big, with slanting sides, and has only one cupola on its roof, though there is another on the side. An OU-3GK infra-red searchlight and an image intensifier are mounted on the commander's cupola. The gun is apparently a modification of the D-20, with a bore evacuator

added behind the muzzle brake. The main difference lies in the ammunition provided. In addition to standard ammunition, the SAU-152 can fire a 37km-range rocket-assisted projectile and a 0.2-kiloton-yield nuclear round. The SAU-152 may have an autoloader.

SP howitzers provide the survivability and mobility needed in a nuclear or conventional war. The increasing importance of surprise, the mobile battle and the meeting engagement meant that all units had to have a substantial artillery capability, able to keep up with the tanks, BMPs and APCs. SP howitzers allow the Soviets to lower the level of combined-arms integration, attaching batteries or even battalions of them to first-echelon manoeuvre battalions or units employed as part of a *reydy* or forward detachment. Instead of relying on complex command, communications and co-ordination systems of US-style "on call" artillery support, the Soviets have achieved the same end by low-level integration of artillery. In mobile combat each battalion or regimental commander will have his artillery when and where he needs it, although, as with all Soviet artillery, another battalion or regiment within range that needs the support of his howitzers may be unable to receive it.

SP howitzers are much less vulnerable to both conventional and NBC counterbattery fire due to their armour and filtration system. They can also move after firing while maintaining continuous fire. A battery of 152mm SP howitzers can displace in about one-fifth the time it would take a towed 152mm battery. When time permits, the Soviets will prepare alternative firing positions in advance, using engineer equipment if available.

Combat usage

The SAU-122 and SAU-152 have seen combat in Afghanistan.

Tactical employment

The SP howitzers are used in the same way as the guns they replaced. The SAU-122 replaces the D-30 and the SAU-152 replaces the D-1, also forming a 152mm battalion in tank divisions, which previously had no tube artillery larger than 122mm. The SP howitzer can be used in general or direct support, as part of divisional or regimental artillery groups or attached directly to manoeuvre units.

An important mission of Soviet SP howitzers is direct fire against enemy positions, unlike Western SP howitzers, which will only use direct fire as an emergency self-defence measure. These tactics are part of the increasing Soviet trend towards "mobile firepower" and "manoeuvre by fire," and away from the massed barrages of the artillery offensive. The Soviets stress that artillery must be able to be where it is needed without delay, or there may be no opportunity for it to come into action at all. One

SAU-122 battalion commander who used standard indirect fire when direct fire was possible was criticised for "overcomplicating" his tactics. Indeed, there may be no stable front lines for artillery to deploy behind in either nuclear or conventional operations.

Unless an attack is being made straight from the march, the SP howitzers will take up overwatch positions and open fire while the tanks, BMPs and APCs deploy for the attack. As these vehicles cross the line of departure, all of the SP howitzers will follow the attacking motorised rifle companies by only 500–1,000m, firing from the short halt. If time is of the essence, the SP howitzers may not fire a preparation at all, but move straight in behind the attack as "accompanying artillery." Alternatively, if there are sufficient SP howitzers available or the situation is favourable, some or all of them may remain in overwatch positions rather than advancing behind the assault. At longer range SAU-152s will perform counterbattery fires, displacing if required but maintaining their position when other defensive means will suffice. SAU-122s will normally conserve their ammunition for direct fire, but will use dumped ammunition if there is time to bring any forward.

These tactics have resulted from the Soviet realisation that unless an attacking force is able to suppress a defence fully and effectively it will suffer tremendous losses, particularly from ATGMs and forward observers. Direct-fire artillery, however, can spot ATGM positions by their

SAU-152 M-1973 152mm SP howitzer of a Guards unit. The asymmetrical arrangement of road wheels is designed to support the enormous turret. *(US Army)*

backblast and immediately open fire on them. Likely positions of forward observers and other priority targets will also be hit. The Soviets consider direct fire ten times as effective as indirect fire for suppression. Direct-fire missions can suppress a defence in less time, with less ammunition expenditure and with higher kill probabilities than indirect fire. The howitzers are much more effective against unarmoured targets than any tank shell, and the SP howitzers give the Soviets decentralised self-sufficiency in firepower.

SP howitzers using direct fire risk heavy losses, but these tactics will form part of a combined-arms assault. There will be many tanks, BMPs and APCs advancing between the howitzers and the enemy, so he will be unable to pick off the SP howitzers at his leisure. Besides, the losses that would be incurred by attacking unsuppressed enemy defences, or by waiting until indirect fire was called down, would far outweigh the loss of a number of SP howitzers.

The Soviets are aware that SP howitzers are not tanks or assault guns. Some Western analysts have overstressed the direct-fire role for SP howitzers. Soviet sourcs warn against needless exposure to counterbattery fire and advise frequent displacement. On the defensive, indirect fire would appear to be the standard method of employment.

In 1978 17% of all Soviet artillery in Group of Soviet Forces, Germany, was self-propelled. This figure will reach 40% by the early 1980s, and soon after that most divisional artillery will probably be self-propelled. Category I formations in the Western USSR are probably being equipped at a similar pace.

Multiple rocket launchers: BM-21 122mm, BM-14 140mm, BM-24 240mm

Size	122mm	140mm	240mm
Designation	BM-21	BM-14 (M-1965)	BM-24
Rockets mounted	40	16 or 17 (16)	12
Rocket length	1.905m (short)	1.092m	1.180m
	3.23m (long)		
Rocket weight	46kg (short)	39.6kg	112.5kg
	77kg (long)		
Warhead weight	19kg	18.8kg	46.9kg
Stabilisation	fin & spin	fin & spin	fin & spin
Rocket range	11km (short)	9.8km	11km
	20.5km (long)		
Max velocity	450m/sec	400m/sec	465m/sec
Reload time	10min	3–4min	3–4min
Rocket fuel	solid	solid	solid
Types of warhead	HE, chem, smoke	HE, chem, smoke	HE, chem (?), smoke (?)
Elevation limits	0°/+50°	0°/+45°	0°/+50°
Traverse	240°	210° (30°)	140°
Mounted on	URAL-375	ZIL-157 or -151	ZIL-151 or -157
		(2-wheel carriage)	
Launcher type	tubes	tubes	open frames
Total weight (firing)	11,500kg	6,432kg (1,200kg)	9,200kg
Length (travelling)	7.35m	6.92m	6.8m
Height (travelling)	2.85m	3.17m	3.0m
Width (travelling)	2.69m	2.3m	2.3m
Engine	175HP V-8 petrol	92HP 6-in-line petrol	92HP 6-in-line petrol
	ZIL-375	ZIL-121	ZIL-121
Speed (max)	75km/h	60km/h	60km/h
Cruising range	405km	600km	600km
Trench	0.875m	0.69m	0.69m
Vertical obstacle	0.65m	0.46m	0.46m
Slope	30°	28°	28°
Ford	1.0m	0.8m	0.8m

Data in parentheses for towed M-1965 version of BM-14 used in airborne units.

BM-21 122mm MRL of a Guards unit in Moscow, November 1977. *(US Army)*

Tactical data (BM-21)

Unit of fire: 80 rounds.

Normal distance behind FEBA: 5km (offensive and defensive).

Time to leave fire position (day/night): (battery) 3–5/6.5min; (battalion) 11/14min.

Minutes to move one kilometre (day/night): (battery and battalion) 3/3.5min.

Minutes to occupy fire positions (day/night): (battery) 10–12/18; (battalion) 23/32.

Effective fragmentation radius, one rocket (against APC/IFV/SP gun): 1.0/0.5/.75m.

BM-14 (16-tube) accuracy: at 2/3 maximum range, projectile error in range is 115m, projectile error in deflection is 36m, and circular error probability is equivalent to 132m. At maximum range the projectile error ranges are 30m and 85m respectively, with a CEP equivalent of 100m.

BM-24 accuracy: at 2/3 maximum range, projectile error range is 61m in range and 46m in deflection, with a CEP equivalent of 93m. At maximum range, projectile error ranges are 40m and 95m respectively, and CEP equivalent is 118m.

The Soviets define multiple rocket launchers (MRLs) as "collective fire systems; they serve to annihilate enemy personnel and fire weapons, combat vehicles and other materiel in concentration areas, as well as to neutralise artillery and mortar batteries. These shells are especially

Individual 122mm rocket as used with the BM-21 in Vietnam. Soviet special forces, like the Vietnamese, use a light single tube. This rocket is the short version. *(US Army)*

M-1965 140mm towed 16-tube MRL. *(US Army)*

effective for repelling massed attacks and for fire assaults on major concentrations of enemy troops and materiel." The MRL fits well with Soviet tactics. It is an offensive weapon, able to create tremendous concentrations of mass firepower in a very short time. An MRL unit can project more firepower in a few seconds than 122mm howitzers could with a longer concentration. In artillery fire the first volley for effect is the most telling, as the enemy has not yet run for cover, so a volley of rockets can make the surprise effect even more deadly. MRLs are also highly mobile. The standard Soviet MRL, the 122mm BM-21, is mounted on a standard URAL-375 truck chassis, possible because it does not need the recoil mechanisms of tube artillery. MRLs are cheap and easy to produce, allowing them to be deployed en masse. A salvo-fire weapon, the MRL is less precise and simpler to use than tube artillery.

Although it falls within the definition of artillery, the Soviets view the MRL as a supplement to tube artillery rather than a substitute for it. The destructive potential of the MRL's massed, surprise concentrations is high, but its rate of fire is low (10min for a full reload) and the rockets are more expensive than shells.

Each tank and motorised rifle division has a BM-21-equipped MRL battalion, although it is not part of the divisional artillery regiment. The BM-21 entered service in 1964 as a replacement for the 140mm BM-14. Although its rockets were smaller, they were longer-ranged and more powerful than the 140mm rockets. The 122mm rocket has a greater punch than the 122mm howitzer shell; without the need for a thick iron casing there can be more explosive. The rockets are single-stage, solid-fuelled

and stabilised by the "fin and spin" method. Spring-loaded fins pop up after launch and the rockets have a low rate of spin imparted by helical grooves in the launch tubes.

Forty launch tubes in four rows of ten are mounted on a single turntable over the URAL-375's rear wheels. A 40-rocket salvo can be fired in a few seconds, or 40 rounds of ripple fire in under 30 seconds. Rockets can also be fired individually. A sight is mounted on a tubular extension on the right of the truck, folding down to the ground for use. This, along with the URAL-375's unprotected cab, limits the arc of fire of the BM-21 to 140° to the left and left rear, and 90° to the right.

To reduce reload time the Czechs have mounted the BM-21 on the large 10-ton TATRA-813 8 × 8 truck, positioning a reload pack of 40 rockets between the launcher and the armoured cab. They can be automatically loaded into the launcher when it is brought to zero elevation after firing, reducing reload time to two minutes. The East German Army also uses this sytem, and it has been reported that the Soviets are using it as well, although it may be difficult to fit a reload pack on a URAL-375.

The 140mm BM-14 MRL series was introduced in 1959 and saw only brief service before being replaced by the BM-21. BM-14s mounted on ZIL-131 trucks were used in Asian military districts in 1980. The RPU-14 airborne version is still in Soviet service. The original 17-tube version of the BM-14 was mounted on a GAZ-63 truck. It was followed by a 16-tube version mounted on a ZIL-151 truck or ATS tractor. One 16-tube version, the RPU-14 M-1965, is still used by the MRL battalions of Soviet

BM-14 140mm MRL, showing blast shields on the cab. *(US Army)*

airborne divisions. It is mounted like a gun on a simple, split-trail carriage and towed by a light truck. Reload time is four minutes. The Polish 6th Airborne Division uses an even lighter version, the eight-tube WP-8. The 240mm BM-24, like the BM-14, has been withdrawn from front-line service, although it also remains in storage and possibly in low-readiness units. The wartime 132mm BM-13 and 1950s-vintage 250mm BM-25 MRLs both probably remain in use for training.

A new 240mm MRL developed in the late 1970s was in first-line service in East Germany in 1980. It is believed to provide an increase in chemical warfare capability over the BM-21.

Combat usage

The BM-24 was the standard Arab MRL in the 1967 War, along with a number of BM-21s, and the Israelis captured most of both types. In 1973 the Arabs used the BM-21 as their standard MRL, and the Israelis also used battalions of Soviet-built MRLs that year. Israeli BM-24s fire an Israeli-designed rocket superior in performance to the Soviet ones. Today the MRLs, along with the M-46, are the only Soviet-built artillery in first-line Israeli units.

The North Vietnamese used single launch tubes taken from BM-14s and BM-21s. The 22kg tube could be mounted on a 28kg tripod, and both were normally man-packed. The "one-two-two rocket" was the most widely used North Vietnamese artillery weapon, and was frequently used against US forces, the attackers firing a few rounds and moving before the defenders could react.

BM-21s were used in Angola and in the Tanzania-Uganda War. In both cases the sound and fury of the BM-21 contributed greatly to its effectiveness. US troops in Vietnam were familiar with the noise of incoming rockets, but the same noise panicked hastily trained UNITA troops in Angola, and Ugandans and Libyans in Uganda. In both Angola and Uganda the BM-21s' area fire was inaccurate, but it was their moral rather than their physical effect that made them crucial.

In the Ogaden fighting Somali BM-14s initially panicked Ethiopian troops. The Soviet airlift, however, provided BM-21s and BMD-20s for the Ethiopians and their allies.

Tactical employment

MRLs are used for massive surprise area HE concentrations and for putting down smoke and chemicals. They are not normally attached to regimental artillery groups or manoeuvre regiments or battalions. They are controlled by a division artillery group and used in the main attack sector. MRL units are frequently co-located with radio direction-finding equipment.

BM-21s are particularly suited to putting down concentrations of smoke and chemical ammunition, which they can deliver almost instantaneously, rather than in a slow-build-up by howitzers. This makes BM-21s especially effective when using deadly blood-agent chemicals, which require high concentrations to be effective and, if delivered quickly, will form a cooling cloud that retards dissipation. One BM-21 battalion salvo can create lethal concentrations of gas over an area greater than two square kilometres.

Although the Soviets see BM-21s primarily as offensive weapons because of their reload time, the rockets will be used in pre-planned final protective fires in the defensive, as well as for counterbattery work or to hit enemy assembly areas and headquarters.

BM-24 240mm MRL. *(US Army)*

Individual 140mm rocket broken down into component parts; fuze is on the right. *(US Air Force)*

Obsolescent MRLs

BM-13 132mm MRL Number of rounds: 16; calibre: 132mm; length of round: 1.473m; weight of round: 42.5kg; max velocity: 350m/sec; max range: 9km; elevation: +15°/+45°; traverse: 20°; time to reload: 5–10min; crew: 6; chassis mounted on: ZIL-151 (postwar). The standard Soviet wartime "Katyusha," the BM-13 was used by units in Asia in 1980.

BMD-20 200mm MRL Number of rounds: 4; calibre: 200mm; length of round: 3.11m; weight of round: 194kg; weight of launch vehicle: 8,700kg; max range: 20km; elevation: +9°/+60°; traverse: 20°; time to reload: 6–10min; crew: 6; chassis mounted on: ZIL-151 or 157. The long, finned, streamlined rockets are launched from an open-frame launcher with a spiral guide to impart spin. These weapons were supplied to Ethiopia in 1978.

BMD-25 250mm MRL Number of rounds: 6; calibre: 250mm; length of round: 5.822m; weight of round: 455kg; weight of launch vehicle: 18,145kg; max range: 30+km; elevation: 0°/+55°; traverse: 6°; chassis mounted on: KrAZ-214. The large frame-type launcher has two banks of three rails with spiral guide rails to impart spin. The rockets are reportedly liquid-fuelled, the only MRL projectiles to be so propelled. The excessive size of the rockets is one of the reasons why this weapon has reportedly left service.

Foreign usage

D-30: Warsaw Pact armies, Cuba, Syria, Egypt, Iraq, Libya, Algeria (?), Finland, Nigeria (possibly no longer in service), Ethiopia, Angola, North Korea, Sudan, Uganda, Tanzania (ex-Ugandan).

M-46: Warsaw Pact armies, Cuba, India, Egypt, Syria, Iraq, Iran, Mongolia, Nigeria (?, probably no longer operational), Vietnam, Yugoslavia, Finland, North Korea, China (Type 59–1, a modified version produced), Pakistan (Chinese versions), Israel.

D-74: Warsaw Pact armies, Cuba, Egypt, Nigeria (?), Vietnam, China (produced as Type 60).

D-20: Czechoslovakia, East Germany, Hungary, Romania, India, Poland, Vietnam, China (produced as Type 66), Afghanistan.

D-1: Warsaw Pact armies (possibly not the Czechs), Egypt, Iraq, Syria, Vietnam, China.

S-23: East Germany, Poland, Egypt, possibly North Korea.

SAU-122 and SAU-152: East Germany, Poland, Czechoslovakia.

BM-21: Warsaw Pact armies, Egypt, Syria, Iraq, Iran, Cuba, Ethiopia, Afghanistan, Vietnam, North Yemen, North Korea.

BM-14: Warsaw Pact armies (second-line use, possibly still first-line in some armies), Israel, Vietnam, Egypt, Syria, Iraq, Algeria, China, North Korea.

Wartime BM-13 132mm MRL mounted on a post-war ZIL-151 truck chassis. *(A. Dupouy)*

BM-20 200mm multiple rocket launchers. *(US Army)*

BM-24: may still be in second-line service in East Germany, North Korea and Poland; was also used by Israel, Egypt, Syria and Algeria.

M-30: All Warsaw Pact armies (mostly second-line, but may be first-line equipment in low-readiness units), Cuba, North Korea, Vietnam, Finland, Libya, Egypt, Syria, Iraq, Algeria, Lebanon, Yugoslavia, China (produced as Type 54 and used on the Chinese 122mm SP gun).

A-19: Warsaw Pact armies (all second-line), Albania, Cuba, Cambodia, Guinea, Indonesia (supplied, no longer used), Egypt, Syria, Iraq, Algeria, North Yemen, South Yemen, China, Yugoslavia, Finland, Germany (WW2), Spain (captured examples), Tanzania, North Korea, Somalia, Zaïre. This weapon was supplied to all these nations but, like the M-30 and the ML-20, it is probably no longer in service with many of them.

ML-20: Warsaw Pact armies (in second-line roles, possibly not in East Germany), Egypt, Syria, Iraq, Algeria, Cuba, Yugoslavia, China, Vietnam, North Korea, Albania.

M-1937: Warsaw Pact armies, Cuba, China, Vietnam and many other nations.

M-1938 and M-1943: Warsaw Pact armies, Austria (designated M-60), Egypt, Syria, Iraq, Algeria, Lebanon, Morocco, North Korea, Yemen, Yugoslavia, Tanzania, Congo, China, Pakistan, Vietnam, Albania and others.

M-1953: India (?), China (designated Type 60), supplied to Egypt and Syria.

M-1952 (240mm): supplied to Hungary, India, Romania, Iraq, Algeria, Syria, Bulgaria, China and others; numbers in service unknown.

BM-25 250mm multiple rocket launchers. *(US Army)*

Chapter Eleven

Nuclear, biological and chemical (NBC) weapons

"Nuclear weapons are the basic means of destruction on the field of battle."

COL V. YE. SAVKIN

Nuclear operations

Soviet warfare is basically nuclear warfare. The great task of post-war Soviet doctrine has been to come to grips with military operations in an environment dominated, if not by actual nuclear weapons, then with the threat of their use at any time. Unlike the US Army, the Soviet Army does not see nuclear-environment tactics as something external and additional to their normal means of operation: they *are* its normal means of operation.

The initial decision to use nuclear weapons must be made at the highest level of the Soviet government. Once the decision to use them is made, their use and delivery will be controlled at front level, even though nuclear-capable weapons are organic to army and division levels. Nuclear weapons control is rarely delegated, although there are signs that this may be changing. Delivery will be either by the tactical aircraft of Frontal Aviation, the FROG-7, Scud-B and Scaleboard missiles, or by the nuclear-capable 180mm gun and 152mm SP howitzer. Long-range targets in theatres of operation will be hit by the SS-4, SS-5 and the new SS-20 IRBMs of the Strategic Rocket Forces or the heavy bombers of the Long Range Aviation.

The Soviets believe that any future war will probably begin with a conventional phase. While open Soviet literature appears to shun the initial use of chemical warfare, their intense chemical warfare effort belies this claim. Reverses in battle or a slowing down of the offensive will probably result in the use of chemical weapons. The nuclear threshold is a more dangerous one. The Soviets are well aware that a theatre-level nuclear exchange could escalate into a strategic conflagration, but it seems possible that the Soviets may use nuclear weapons to restore mobile warfare if they have been halted or fear a battle of attrition. It is almost certain that they would use nuclear weapons if they thought an enemy was likely to use them first. They believe that the "aggressive forces of monopoly capitalism, if desperate, may well carry out their oft-stated threat to initiate nuclear destruction." The Soviets have a great fear of being pre-empted.

Once the Soviets have decided to use nuclear weapons, they will use them in a manner intended to assure full surprise and shock effect. The Soviets view the controlled, limited use of theatre nuclear weapons, once the theatre nuclear threshold has been crossed, as a nonsense. A scenario in which the Soviets might destroy one city with one missile to cross the nuclear threshold is ridiculous.

Just as they are convinced that surprise pays dividends, the Soviets are convinced that restraint is foolhardy, especially when dealing with nuclear weapons, and any idea of limited theatre nuclear operations is seen as a foolish Western concept. As one Soviet military writer has put it, "any delay in the destruction of enemy nuclear attack means will permit the enemy to launch nuclear strikes first, and may lead to heavy losses and even to the defeat of the offensive." The aim of all war and all weapons is victory, a victory which, from a Marxist-Leninist viewpoint, must inevitably mean the collapse of capitalism and the triumph of global socialism.

If the Soviets go nuclear, the first strike will aim at nothing less than the destruction of all nuclear means capable of retaliation. These constitute the highest-priority targets, followed by headquarters and communications facilities, reserves, known defensive positions, and rear-area installations including airfields and ports.

The Soviet initial strike will be large, with up to a third of all available warheads being used if delivery systems are available, and the remainder being used in follow-up strikes over the next several days. Soviet tactical nuclear weapons have traditionally been large and relatively dirty devices, using airburst detonation. They make up in size for lack of accuracy. This inaccuracy determined much of the blanket-like strike planning of previous years. Today there are signs that Soviet theatre nuclear tactics are becoming more flexible and selective, although not limited in scope. This is made possible by more accurate delivery systems: missiles, aircraft and, especially, the new nuclear-capable artillery. Not only can these weapons deliver the warheads where they are needed, but when they are needed, because response time has been lowered. This makes the use of lower-yield devices practical, as up-to-date target intelligence can be used and the large blast radius of earlier weapons is not needed to catch an enemy who may have moved. The Soviets have an interest in minimising collateral damage. They do not wish to advance across a radioactive wasteland if they can avoid it, nor would they wish to control one after the war.

The influence of nuclear weapons can be seen throughout Soviet operations and tactics. There is hardly an element that is not in some way attributable to nuclear weapons. The increased emphasis on surprise, speed and mobility are counters to the potentially devastating effect of even a few nuclear weapons. Target acquisition for nuclear weapons is one of the prime missions of all the forward detachments, *reydy*, long-range reconnaissance patrols and *desants* that have increased in importance in recent years. The build-up of helicopter forces gives a follow-up capability to nuclear strikes. These are just a few of the ways in which Soviet military developments are responses to the requirements of the nuclear battlefield.

In actual use nuclear weapons supplement rather than replace conventional fires. They are not a substitute for normal weapons or tactics. Strikes against enemy frontline troops will be made as close as safety permits, as the Soviets will only rarely withdraw troops to create a safety margin. Usually only one warhead is used against each target.

Soviet nuclear storage sites are separate from the delivery systems and heavily guarded by KGB troops. The warheads are moved to the delivery systems in closed vans as part of small, heavily guarded convoys, often with light aircraft overhead to maintain communications. Alternatively, warheads may be delivered by helicopters with a close escort of gunships and a top cover of fighters.

Rocket and missile launch sites with their attendant radars and support vehicles will be camouflaged. Tube artillery will usually register in against a target using conventional ammunition before firing nuclear rounds. Conventional-warhead FROGs and Scuds may also be used in this manner. While front-line troops will not usually withdraw when a nuclear strike is planned, they may dig in or, if possible, cover their own positions with smoke against the thermal effects of the blast.

Weapons effectiveness

Nuclear weapons effectiveness is created by the many effects of a nuclear explosion. Blast effect creates tremendous overpressure, destroying buildings, trees, vehicles, aircraft and anything else within its radius. Thermal effects follow the blast. The intense heat of the explosion will set fire to anything that can possibly burn, and the debris created by the blast a fraction of an instant before makes good kindling. Thermal effects will also burn exposed skin. Dazzle caused by the blinding effect of a nuclear explosion can put large numbers of troops temporarily out of action, especially at night. Radiation is the

FROG-7 mounted on its ZIL-135 transporter. *(US Army)*

biggest killer, although troops in entrenchments and armoured vehicles or wearing NBC suits have a degree of protection. Radiation also has a residual effect in contaminated areas, and equipment exposed to radioactivity becomes radioactive itself until decontaminated. Electromagnetic pulse (EMP) emanating from a nuclear burst can damage radios, radars and all electronic equipment, although most military electronics are "hardened" against EMP. A communications blackout can endure after the blast, the disturbance in the atmosphere disrupting radio links. Fallout can produce casualties, delay movements and deny terrain.

Unit organisation

FROG battalion (tank and motorised rifle division)
Total strength: 18 officers, 138 enlisted men.
  One HQ battery (eight officers, 66 enlisted men, 34 trucks, one BRDM, one BTR-60, 23 jeeps)

Two FROG batteries (each of five officers, 36 enlisted men, two FROG launchers, two FROG reload carriers [3 missiles each], one truck with an End Tray radar, one truck with a Bread Bin radar).

Scud or Scaleboard brigade (front or army)
Total strength: 178 officers, 1,083 enlisted men.
  One HQ battery (20 officers, 125 enlisted men, 75 jeeps and trucks)
  Three launcher battalions (each of 43 officers, 325 enlisted men, three launch vehicles, three reload vehicles, 10 trucks, possibly including additional reload vehicles)
  One signal company (seven officers, 70 enlisted men, 20 jeeps and trucks)
  One engineer company (seven officers, 78 enlisted men, 15 cranes, 26 trucks, 15 BAT dozers, 5 MDK-2 ditching machines)
  Technical support and services (15 officers, 135 enlisted men, 47 trucks, three End Tray radars)

Surface-to-surface missiles

Missile	FROG-7	Scud-B	Scaleboard
Missile length	9.1m	11.4m	11.25m
Missile weight	2,300kg	6,370kg	8,800kg
Warhead weight	550kg	1,000kg	unknown
Warhead yield	25–40KT	40–100KT	1MT
Missile diameter	0.55m	0.84m	1.05m
Fuel	solid	liquid	liquid
Guidance	none	inertial	inertial
Control	speed brakes	efflux vanes	vanes or fins
Max range	60–70km	280km	700–800km
Min range	11–12km	unknown	unknown
Time to fire	20–30min	1 hour	2–4 hours
Warheads	nuclear, HE, chem	nuclear, HE, chem	nuclear
Stages	1	1	1
Crew	4	4–6	6+
CEP	0.5–0.7km	1km	0.2+km
Level of use	division	army	front
Launch vehicle	ZIL-135	MAZ-543	MAZ-543
Radars	End Tray, Bread Bin	End Tray	End Tray
Year introduced	1965	1965	1967
Launchers in GSFG	80	140	60(?)

The FROG-7, Scud-B and Scaleboard SSMs are the Soviet Army's prime delivery systems for nuclear weapons, supplemented by tactical aircraft and the new nuclear-capable artillery.

The FROG-7 is the latest in a series of unguided tactical nuclear-capable rockets (FROG = Free Rocket Over

Ground). Other earlier FROGs have been exported and still remain in Soviet service for training and in some low-readiness units. The FROG-7 is mounted on an eight-wheeled ZIL-135 truck with its own crane. This vehicle was reportedly selected, like the Scud-B launch vehicle, because it offered much greater reliability over

Scud-B missile. The one in the background is in firing position while the crew prepares the one in the foreground for firing. (*Marine Corps Gazette*)

the tank chassis which it replaced, and its cross-country mobility was good. A similar reload vehicle carries three extra rockets. The FROG-7 is aimed by adjusting elevation and setting speed brakes. The Bread Bin and End Tray radars are used for determining meteorological factors that might affect the FROG's flight. The Soviets use the ZIL-135's good cross-country mobility to move after firing. FROG-7s are kept well forward: 8–18km from the line of contact in the offensive, 25–50% further on the defensive. FROGs are used against tactical targets.

The Scud-B replaces the earlier Scud-A, which was mounted on a IS-III tank chassis. The new missile is carried on an eight-wheel MAZ-543 launch vehicle. Like the larger Scaleboard, the Scud-B uses liquid fuel, apparently of a type that is storable and does not require preheating. Guidance is by an inertial system, although it has been suggested that the End Tray radar is used for

guidance, tracking the missile in flight and shutting down the engine by radio command at a predetermined point in its trajectory. An interim version of the Scud-B retains the fuel tank arrangement of the Scud-A, and its range is also probably closer to that of the earlier missile. The Scud will be used against targets in the enemy rear areas: airfields, headquarters and lines of communication.

The SS-12 Scaleboard is the Soviet Army's largest missile. Like the Scud-B, it is carried on a MAZ-543 and used with the End Tray meteorological radar. Its range gives it the capability to strike targets throughout Western Europe, and its mobility makes target acquisition difficult unless it is spotted as it is being prepared to fire. Some Western sources believe that the Soviets do not normally keep Scaleboards in East Germany.

Although the Scaleboard has never been exported, FROGs and Scuds were used in the 1973 Middle East war. They did not prove effective. Egyptian FROGs were used against Israeli bases and airfields in Sinai, but do not appear to have done much damage. Later they were used against the Israeli bridgehead across the Suez Canal, but again with little effect. The Israelis claim that at least one Egyptian FROG was shot down by air-defence weapons. The Egyptians used modern FROG-7s, as well as earlier versions, but the Syrians apparently had only FROG-2s and FROG-3s. The inaccuracy of these weapons resulted in their impacting throughout Galilee when aimed at Israeli bases. The Israelis, however, interpreted these FROGs as being aimed at *kibbutzim*, and retaliated. The Egyptians fired three Scud-Bs in the last days of the war, two against the Israeli bridgehead and one against a target in Sinai. None hit anything of value. In addition to the Egyptian Scud-B unit, a Soviet nuclear-capable Scud-B brigade was reportedly airlifted into Egypt during the war (without its nuclear warheads, which were sent separately by ship).

The 1973 War emphasised the drawbacks of these weapons. They all suffer from long reaction and preparation times, especially the liquid-fuelled Scud and Scaleboard. Their poor accuracy is compounded by using a primitive manual interface with command control and targeting means, rather than computers and automatic data links. This allows human errors to compound those inherent in the system. Specialised fire-control computer vehicles have not been reported in these units, but their provision is expected in the near future. They are reportedly vulnerable to aircraft and air-defence weapons in flight. Reliability is poor: the US Army estimates a 10–20% dud rate in nuclear-armed rockets.

Some sources use the designation FROG-7B for a version with a 390kg chemical warhead and with its minimum range increased to 14km.

The Soviets have been moving away from the nuclear tactics demanded by the characteristics of these weapons: poor accuracy and large warheads. It is not surprising

SS-12 Scaleboard missile on its transporter. *(US Army)*

that unconfirmed reports in the late 1970s mentioned replacements for these missiles. A missile designated SS-22, with an 800km range and a CEP of 0.3km, has been mentioned as a Scaleboard replacement. The SS-21/FROG-9 (probably the same weapon) has probably entered service, replacing FROG-7s. The new weapon is said to have a 120km range, and is mounted on a three-axle vehicle similar to that used with the SA-8. Approximately 50 were reportedly deployed by late 1979, all in the Soviet Union. The SS-23 may be a 200km-range weapon to replace the Scud-B. The Scud-C, with a 400km range, was reported to be in use in 1978.

While there is no hard evidence that the Soviets have developed or are developing such a capability, the Soviet press has made a number of references to direct-fire nuclear weapons, or to the use of nuclear weapons from helicopters. The material in Soviet sources seems to view this as feasible with sub-kiloton warheads – a 0.02KT warhead would have an effective damage radius of 25m against tanks and 130m against their crews, compared to 120m and 340m respectively for a 0.5KT device and 450m and 800m for a 20KT device. (Other damage radii are: 10KT, 350m/700m; 50KT, 600m/900m; 100KT, 800m/1,100m; 150KT, 1,000m/1,300m; 500KT, 1,700m/1,700m.) With the new capabilities of the 152mm SP howitzer's nuclear round and those of new Soviet missiles, such use of nuclear weapons cannot be ruled out. The small damage radii would allow Soviet forces to use these weapons at comparatively short ranges without running an excessive risk.

Older surface-to-surface missiles

The Soviet Army was still using the FROG-3 in 1979, despite its age, and other Soviet missiles of similar vintage may also be soldiering on. The Scunner, a copy of the V-2, served briefly in the 1950s.

FROG-3, 4 Launch vehicle: modified PT-76 chassis, not amphibious; weight: 2,266kg; length: 1.055m; diameter: 0.4m; warhead weight: 454kg; range: 35km; warhead yield: 25KT. FROG-3, FROG-5 and FROG-4 differ only in the physical appearance of the warheads (the FROG-3 warhead is short and fat, the FROG-4 and FROG-5 warhead longer and thinner). The FROG-6 is a non-operational training version.

Scud-A Launch vehicle: IS-III chassis; length: 10.7m; diameter: 0.85m; launch weight: 4,400kg; range: 130km. Other data similar to Scud-B.

Foreign use

The Soviets have exported NBC defence equipment to their Warsaw Pact allies, Cuba and Vietnam, although many of these nations produce their own equivalents.

Early FROGs were supplied to the Warsaw Pact

nations, Egypt and Syria. FROG-7s were supplied to the Pact nations, Syria, Egypt and Kuwait.

Scud-Bs were supplied to the Warsaw Pact, Egypt, Syria, Iraq and Libya.

Biological weapons

The Soviet Union is a party to international agreements prohibiting the use of toxic chemicals and biological agents and requiring the destruction of stocks of biological (not chemical) weapons. However, the Soviets have renounced only the first use of chemical weapons. Open sources all show adherence to the Biological Warfare Convention of 1972, and the unpredictability of this form of warfare, combined with the effectiveness of their nuclear and chemical capabilities, makes the Soviets less likely to use biological weapons than other types of "weapons of mass destruction."

Despite this, Soviet biological and bacteriological warfare research has apparently been continuing at a rapid pace, and they have reportedly developed a new range of diseases as well as countermeasures to any bacteriological or biological weapons they believe may be used against them. The Soviets have reportedly developed agents that would produce plague, cholera, anthrax, tularemia, lassa fever, ebola fever and marburg fever. There are 40 chemical and biological weapons storage depots in Eastern Europe and the European USSR.

Offensive use of chemical weapons

The Soviet Army is undoubtedly the world's foremost expert in chemical warfare. Chemical offensive capability is present at all levels, and it has reportedly been tested by the Egyptians in the Yemen in 1967, by the Vietnamese in Laos in 1979 and by the Soviets themselves in Afghanistan in 1980, as well as in many manoeuvres and exercises in the Soviet Union which are so realistic that they kill a number of soldiers every year.

The decision to use chemical weapons will apparently be taken at the highest levels of the Soviet national command authority, although in the 1950s and early 1960s the Soviets had reportedly already made the decision to use chemical weapons in any future war. They are more likely to use chemical weapons against an enemy who lacks the ability to retaliate with them or defend against them, a category into which the US Army fell until the late 1970s

at least. Chemical weapons will normally be used in conjunction with nuclear or conventional munitions.

Soviet chemical weapons delivery systems include tactical aircraft (either aerosol spray or bombs), FROG and Scud missiles, multiple rocket launchers of all sizes and all 122mm and larger tube artillery. The missiles and the multiple rocket launchers have the biggest chemical warfare role. There may well be as many chemical warheads for missiles as there are nuclear ones. Multiple rocket ammunition stockpiles also contain considerable amounts of chemical weapons, in excess of the 5% proportion across all types of artillery ammunition.

The extensive Soviet chemical warfare capability allows them to manufacture large quantities of almost any type of gas. It is estimated that the Soviets use sarin (GB) semi-persistent nerve gas, soman (GD) semi-persistent nerve gas, mustard (H) blistering gas, hydrogen cyanide (AC) non-persistent blood agent, and VR-55 thickened nerve gas. They may also use phosgene choking gas, lewisite, adamsite, chloropicrin and other gases not in NATO's small arsenal, which is largely limited to nerve agents and mustard gas. The blood agents require a high concentration to work and therefore are likely to be used with missiles and MRLs, which can achieve the required concentrations.

The Soviets will attempt to use chemical weapons in such a way as to maximise the surprise effect, and introduction in a massive strike is more likely than gradual implementation. They will carefully judge which target requires chemical treatment and which chemicals will be used. Non-persistent agents are seen as excellent weapons of suppression, reducing the defenders' effectiveness without preventing advancing Soviet units, with their excellent NBC defensive equipment and training, from closing with the position. They can also be used where damage to terrain would slow the Soviet advance.

Non-persistent agents are likely to be used against defiles, river crossings and other points on the main axes of attack, to suppress resistance around drop zones or landing zones prior to airborne attacks, or against troops in contact. Persistent gases will be used to interdict supply and movement routes. Key airfields will almost certainly be targets for missile-delivered persistent gas, restricting operations without preventing subsequent Soviet use. Other rear area facilities, ports and headquarters are also potential targets. Well dug-in positions, assembly areas and reserve units may also be hit.

Smoke-generating capability is normally left to the artillery and individual vehicle generators. These may be supplemented by BDSh-5 smokepots. At a wind speed of five metres per second, a pot will generate a screen 500m long and 100m wide for about ten minutes. The TMS-65 can also be used as a smoke generator. Another smoke-generator vehicle, on a KrAZ-214 truck chassis, is believed to use an aircraft turbojet.

Unit organisation

Regimental NBC defence company (tank and motorised rifle regiments)
Total strength: one officer, 34 enlisted men, two BRDM-rkh, two or three decontamination vehicles, two trucks.

Divisional NBC defence battalion (tank and motorised rifle divisions)
Total strength: 12 (18) officers, 138 (142) enlisted men.
One HQ and service company (three [four] officers, 30 enlisted men, one BRDM, three BRDM-rkh, 10 trucks)
Two personnel decontamination companies (each three officers, 36 enlisted men, one BRDM, six ARS-14s, three DDA-53, seven bowsers and trucks)
One equipment decontamination company (three [eight] officers, 36 [40] enlisted men, one BRDM, four [five] ARS-14, three TMS-65, six bowsers and trucks)
Figures in parentheses are for tank divisions where they differ from motorised rifle divisions. ARS-12/14 strength has been reportedly increased to 22 per battalion, and the number of TMS-65s increased as well.

NBC defence battalion (army)
Total strength: 44 officers, 474 enlisted men.
Headquarters and services (three officers, 30 enlisted men, two BRDMs, seven trucks)
Three chemical companies (each of 11 officers, 128 enlisted men, six ARS-14, two DDA-53, one TMS-65, 10 trucks)
One chemical reconnaissance company (eight officers, 60 enlisted men, 15 BRDM-rkh, five trucks)

NBC defence brigade (front level)
Total strength: 71 officers, 668 enlisted men.
Headquarters and services (11 officers, 73 enlisted men, two BRDMs, 12 trucks)
Three chemical battalions (each of 12 officers, 138 enlisted men, 18 ARS-14, six DDA-53, three TMS-65, 20 trucks)
One chemical reconnaissance battalion (24 officers, 181 enlisted men, 45 BRDM-rkh, 15 trucks)

NBC defence

The Soviets realise that for any force to survive in modern warfare it must take steps to defend itself against the NBC weapons that have the potential to dominate the battlefield. NBC defence is designed into all Soviet weapons and vehicles, incorporated into all Soviet strategy, operations and tactics. The technical aspects of NBC defence in the field fall to the Chemical Troops.

BRDM-2rkh vehicles being decontaminated. Some of the soldiers are wearing the dark-coloured heavy protective suits used by decontamination units. These suits are very thick and bulky.

Standard ShM "Shlem" protective mask. Early models lack the
outlet valve mounted on the facepiece. *(US Army)*

The Chemical Troops are a "special troops" branch,
directly responsible to the Ministry of Defence. Its 80,000
– 100,000 men provide NBC defence and training to all
the services of the armed forces. Not only is every soldier
in the Soviet Army thoroughly trained in NBC defence
and personally equipped to enable him to operate under
NBC conditions, but Chemical Troops NBC defence units
are available at all levels of command, from regiment up
to front. NBC reconnaissance vehicles are found throughout the Army, their role being to find contaminated areas
and warn of attacks, aided by radio broadcasts over a
special NBC network. Aided by engineers, NBC defence

units will train troops in NBC defence, decontaminate
areas, personnel and equipment, and detect enemy NBC
activity. This is done by NBC reconnaissance vehicles,
NBC patrols and individual specialists with measuring
equipment.

NBC defence equipment

ShM protective mask   The standard Soviet mask, this
consists of facepiece (without voice transmitter), hose and
canister, which can be changed without taking off the
mask. Like all gas masks, it is fatiguing to wear.
Protective overalls   The Soviets have several NBC
suits, most of rubberised fabric with gloves, hood and
rubber boots. ZFK-58 heavy suits of cloth-lined rubber

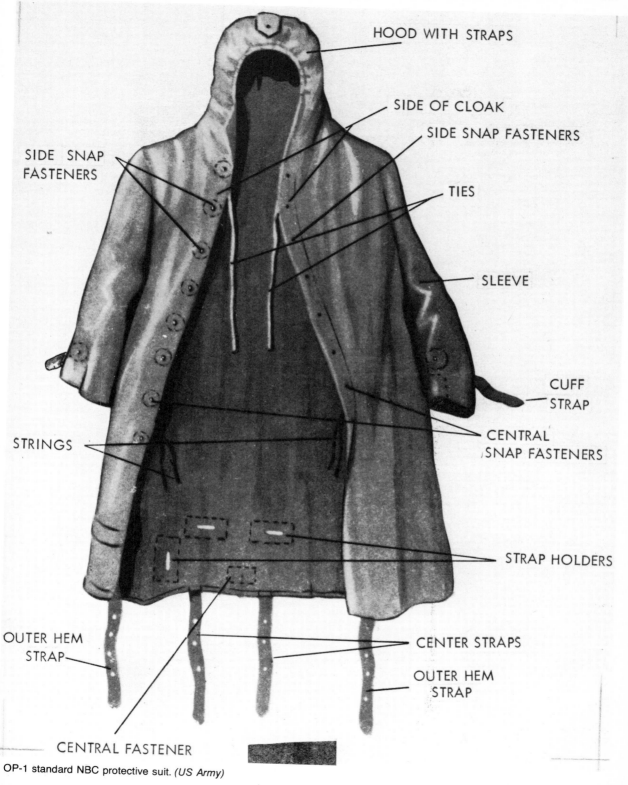

HOOD WITH STRAPS

SIDE OF CLOAK

SIDE SNAP FASTENERS

SIDE SNAP FASTENERS

TIES

SLEEVE

CUFF STRAP

CENTRAL SNAP FASTENERS

STRINGS

STRAP HOLDERS

OUTER HEM STRAP

CENTER STRAPS

OUTER HEM STRAP

CENTRAL FASTENER

OP-1 standard NBC protective suit. *(US Army)*

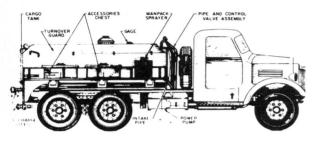

ARS-12U decontamination vehicle. (US Army)

are used by Chemical Troops or others who are liable to work in contaminated areas. Reconnaissance troops use the L-1 butyl rubberised fabric suit.

Individual kits   Each soldier has an MSP-18 treatment kit with antidotes to a variety of chemical weapons, an IDP decontamination kit for weapons, and an IPP individual decontamination kit.

IPDS-69   Squad-level decontamination and degassing kit, normally vehicle-mounted.

DDA-53 decontamination truck.

Weapons decontamination kits   The PM-DK is used on machine guns and mortars; the ADK is used on artillery. Both travel with the weapon and the kits are manually applied by the crew.

DK-4   Decontaminant equipment for trucks; uses exhaust gases for an aerosol spray.

RDP-4W   Portable decontamination device; large tank with sprayer.

ARS-12U/-14   These two vehicles, using ZIL-131/157 truck chassis, are standard decontamination systems. The ARS-12U's 2,500lit tank has enough decontaminant for 12 tanks. The ARS-14 has a larger tank. Both have hoses, brushes and special-purpose nozzles. Steam decontamination and a shower apparatus are also available.

TMS-65   One of the more spectacular NBC defence weapons, the TMS-65 is a modified aircraft turbojet mounted on a URAL-375, using heat and water or decontamination fluid to decontaminate a tank in one to three minutes. It can also be used as a smoke generator.

DDA-53   Two steam chambers and a boiler for clothing and equipment decontamination, mounted on a GAZ-63 chassis.

ADM-48   Mounted in the back of a standard truck, this apparatus has two decontaminant tanks with hoses with brush heads, used to wash equipment manually.

GSP-1 and GSP-1M   Vehicle-mounted radiation and nerve gas detectors, with visual and audible alarms. Used on NBC reconnaissance versions of the BTR-40, BRDM-1, BRDM-2 and UAZ-469.

VPKhR   Standard man-carried chemical detector, used to identify precise agents used.

GSP-11   Automatic version of the VPKhR.

NBC reconnaissance vehicles   "rkh" versions of the GAZ/UAZ-69/469 jeep, BTR-40, BRDM-1 and BRDM-2, with sensor devices and flags for marking contaminated areas and safe lanes.

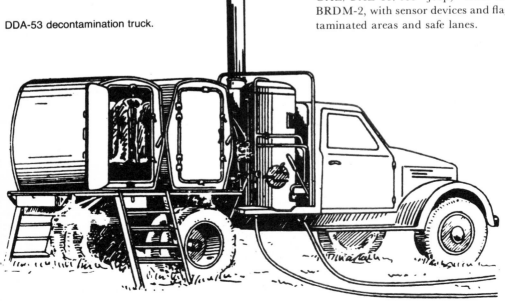

Above TMS-65 in Kabul in 1980, with its jet engine covered. It can also be used for melting snow on runways. *(US Army)*

TMS-65 decontamination vehicle, showing the jet decontamination sprayer and fluid storage tank. *(US Army)*

Chapter Twelve

Air defence

*"The Air Defence troops of the Army are capable of combating
threats at low, medium and high altitude, as well as providing
continuous cover for Army units and rear-area facilities."*
MARSHAL A.A. GRECHKO

The side that controls the air will often control the battle-field beneath it as well. The Soviet Army is determined that its future opponents shall not enjoy this control.

The Soviets recognise that air defence is an essential component of the modern combined-arms force, and have made the Air Defence of the Army a separate branch, on a level with the Tank, Motorised Rifle and Artillery branches. Unlike the defensive belts in Egypt, North Vietnam or even the Soviet homeland, Soviet Army air-defence operations are basically offensive. The mobility, tactical flexibility and combat power of the latest Soviet air-defence weaponry allows the Army's air-defence forces to provide the protection from enemy air strikes that a modern army needs not only to win, but to survive. The Soviets know that NATO tactical air power is very effective and more flexible than their own. Columns of Soviet troops are excellent targets, and the terrain of West Germany abounds in choke points and defiles where air strikes could inflict devastating losses and delay the Soviet advance, an advance that must be relentless to be victorious.

There are four principles to Soviet Army air defence: mass, mix, mobility and integration. Mass has never been a Soviet weakness. Anti-aircraft artillery (AAA) and surface-to-air missiles (SAMs) are provided at all levels of command on a scale greater than in any other army. Mix is created by the complementary nature of the weapons, the differing types that will still provide air cover should countermeasures reduce the effectiveness of any one system. As the air battle in any future war will be largely electronic, this is especially important. Mobility is emphasised in the design of the weapons themselves. Even relatively static systems such as the SA-2 and SA-3 and their radar sites can be packed up and made ready to move to an alternative position in three to four hours. In June 1970 a belt of these SAMs moved forward literally overnight from positions deep in Egypt to the Suez Canal. Finally, air-defence assets are completely integrated throughout the Soviet Army. Every commander can deploy air-defence weapons, from front-level SAM brigades to each platoon's SA-7 launcher.

If the Soviet Army is to carry out its wartime role as the arm of decision, air defence must keep enemy air power from interfering. World War Two taught the Soviets the devastating potential of tactical air power, both in striking combat troops and attacking their supply lines. The air-craft still has the advantage over any enemy on the ground. For all its importance, air defence alone is not, and has never been, a decisive arm. In 1972 Hanoi was defended by 6,000 anti-aircraft guns (three times the number that ringed Berlin), half of them radar-controlled, supplemented by 156 SA-2 launchers with stockpiles big enough to permit the firing of up to 100 missiles simultaneously. However, five days of intensive US air strikes defeated even these powerful forces, and US aircraft roamed the skies of North Vietnam at will. The Egyptian air-defence belt along the Suez Canal in 1973 was as dense as that around Moscow itself, the SAM sites and their attendant radars being fortified by reinforced concrete and ringed by light AAA. The combined expertise of Soviet technicians and Egyptian combat veterans left nothing to chance. In the first three days of the war the Egyptians and Syrians fired off more SAMs than NATO currently possesses, but while the Israelis suffered heavily, the defences destroyed almost as many Arab aircraft as Israeli. Even the modern SA-6 hit a target only about once in every fifty launches, and this was against an air force that was surprised, suffering from overconfidence, and lacking adequate ECM and effective tactics in the first crucial days of the war. In what must have been the best possible case for the air defences, Suez in 1973 demonstrated that no ground air defences – even those of Soviet quality – can ever totally defeat aircraft, although some point targets, especially bridges, can be successfully defended by static air defences. The American defence of the Remagen bridge in 1945, and the effective Egyptian defence of the Suez Canal bridges on October 6–8, 1973, prove this. However, the increasing employment of contemporary precision-guided munitions and stand-off weapons has greatly increased the power of strike aircraft, especially against targets such as bridges.

In modern warfare, if attacking aircraft have the determination to press on, take their losses and attack their targets, all air defence can do is to make it more costly, more difficult, and more time-consuming for them to accomplish their mission. This is all that the Soviet Army's air defences have to do to succeed. They need not destroy NATO aircraft (that can be left to the Air Force); all they need do is reduce the effectiveness of enemy air attacks in the first, crucial days of the war. Their success will be measured not in aircraft destroyed, but rather in the number of bombs or missiles that miss their targets because a pilot has to evade SAMs or AAA, or in the number of air attacks that must be diverted from striking Soviet tanks to suppressing the air-defence forces. Even though the air-defence systems of both North Vietnam in 1972 and the Arab nations in 1973 were defeated, they did accomplish this mission. Over North Vietnam 25–50% of the US sorties on any given day were committed to air-defence suppression, sorties that could otherwise have supported the main bombing effort. US defence analysts termed this "virtual attrition," which, like the "actual attrition" of shooting down aeroplanes, reduced America's ability to defeat North Vietnam. The Israeli air attacks on Arab SAM sites in 1973 also absorbed a large

percentage of their total strike capability, especially at such crucial periods as "the Battle of the Syrian SAMs" on the afternoon of October 7, and during the breaching of the Egyptian SAM belt between October 9 and 14. Every strike at a SAM site was a strike diverted from Arab combat units. The very existence of the Arab air defences prevented the Israeli aircraft from using the long, low, slow passes that allowed them to plant their bombs with such accuracy in 1967. Operations research data from World War Two show that any anti-aircraft fire, no matter how inaccurate, is sufficient to reduce the bombing accuracy of attacking aircraft by at least 50%. The threat of air-defence fire can be as effective as the fire itself.

In the long run, modern aircraft with effective ECM and tactics could probably defeat a typical Soviet air-defence system. The Soviet concept of the short, victorious war is intended to deprive their enemies of that long run.

Weapons and employment

The air-defence weapons of the Soviet Army include both area-defence and point-defence weapons. The big SAMs – SA-2, SA-3 and SA-4 – provide area cover when employed by front and army-level SAM brigades, co-ordinated with massed "Fire Storm" defensive operations

AIR-DEFENCE SYSTEMS

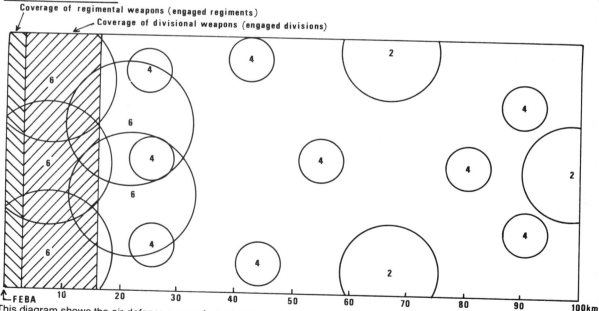

This diagram shows the air-defence cover of a typical Soviet Army sector extending 100km behind the forward edge of the battle area (FEBA) and along 45km of frontage. In addition to the missile and AAA defences shown (each type of SAM is represented by the appropriate numeral), the Soviets position point-defence systems not only on the front lines but throughout the sector. Second-echelon regiments and

divisions will be behind the FEBA, and their ZSU-23-4s, S-60s, SA-8s, SA-9s and SA-7s will fill in any gaps under the area-defence missile systems. The radii shown are the US Air Force's "avoidance radii," which they will not penetrate unless required. If maximum range were used, the whole sector would be covered.

by fighter aircraft of the supporting tactical air army. However, the fighters fly under four kilometres altitude only at their peril, because the Army is primarily responsible for engaging targets below that ceiling. Even without supporting fighters, the SAM units can provide air defence cover throughout the front or army area of operations. Point-defence weapons must be positioned near the targets they defend. The bulk of the Soviet air-defence weapons – the SA-7 and SA-9, and all the AAA – are intended for point defence. The new SA-8 bridges the gap between the point and area-defence weapons. All Soviet air-defence weapons are tied into a comprehensive and efficient early-warning and target-acquisition radar network.

The Soviet Army is only able to have mix, mobility and integration in its air-defence forces because of the individual quality and complementary capabilities of its SAMs, AAA, radars and supporting fighters. The Soviets deploy their air-defence weapons throughout an army sector so that the effective envelopes of each weapon overlap, forming a complete air-defence umbrella. The positioning and coverage of the air-defence assets of a typical Soviet army, illustrated in the diagram, allow the integration of both area and point-defence weapons into an effective, complementary network. In 1973 Israeli aircraft that dived under SA-6s ran into the fire of ZSU-23-4s. Those aircraft attempting to fly above the SA-6's envelope would be driven back into it by having to outmanoeuvre high-altitude SAMs. If a Fan Song radar loses a target in ground clutter (surface reflection of the radar's pulses), a Low Blow, optimised for low-altitude work, will pick it up. Weapons integration is carried down to regimental air-defence batteries with their mixture of SA-9s and ZSU-23-4s. Any pilot will try to adjust his tactics to minimise vulnerability to these weapons and will watch for them on the ground, but in doing so he leaves himself open to enemy fighters. Many US aircraft were lost to MiGs over North Vietnam while their crews were trying to avoid SAMs and AAA. The multiplicity and mass of systems means that even if a particular site is destroyed or an individual type of radar is jammed, the system itself will continue to function, at least until the enemy puts his air effort into a direct and costly assault on the air defences.

Soviet AA and SAM technology has been comparable with that of Western nations since the World War Two era, from guns to the current SA-8, which is similar to the Rapier or Crotale SAM systems being adopted by NATO. It has been widely reported that the Soviets use vacuum tubes in their electronics in place of the transistors used in Western equipment. This increases the fragility and bulk of some electronics, but miniaturisation has seldom been a concern of either the Soviet Army or Soviet society. While they are far behind the West in transistor and microcomputer technology, their increased emphasis on vacuum

tubes has put them 10–15 years ahead in that area. However, they still suffer many of the disadvantages inherent in the use of vacuum tubes. Those of some of the early-warning radars deployed in Egypt developed difficult cooling problems, emitting vast clouds of steam. The temperatures inside the radar vans would reach 70°C, often forcing the crew to evacuate. The latest SAMs and radars are reported to use transistors and printed, integrated circuits.

Command and control

The Soviets aim for close co-ordination of air defence with manoeuvre units from battalion upwards, while retaining flexibility of operation and centralisation of control of all air-defence assets under the Army Air Defence branch, the *Voiska Protivovizdushnoi Oborony Sukhoputiniykh Voisk* (PVO SV).

Air Defence branch officers are attached at all headquarters down to regimental level. They retain centralised control of air-defence assets and deploy them as the situation demands. At front and army level there is a separate Air Defence commander and staff, usually co-located with general headquarters. While the Air Defence commander is subordinate to the unit commander, he is responsible for the co-ordination of air-defence efforts with the manoeuvre units, which, at army and front level, include area-defence SAM brigades and fighter support. The long range and high speed of these weapons necessitate centralised high-level control. The divisional Air Defence commander will be in full charge of the division's air-defence efforts. This will include deploying its AAA, SAMs and radars, setting up co-ordination procedures with the manoeuvre units, and establishing the priority of the points to be defended.

The Soviets normally assign highest priority to protecting their nuclear-capable weapons, followed by headquarters, assembly area, river crossing sites, defiles and other key targets. Tank and motorised rifle regiments are covered by their own anti-aircraft battery.

Early-warning information is passed from front or army-level air-defence headquarters to the divisional air-defence commanders by radio or, if possible, landline. Radio communications are handled by a separate air-defence network which is reserved for warning and target designation. Regimental anti-aircraft batteries are also "netted in," which provides the necessary targeting information for low levels of organisation. The Soviets maintain air-defence command and control at these low levels by having the commander of an air-defence battery or platoon that is attached to a manoeuvre battalion serve as that battalion's staff officer for air defence as long as the unit is attached. The regimental commander must co-ordinate air-defence forces spread throughout the regiment's sector. He receives and relays information not only from higher echelons, but from the units of the battery as well. The SA-8 may also be attached to regiments, especially to those in a breakthrough or exploitation role, though it is basically a division-level weapon.

Tactical framework

The primacy of the offensive dominates Soviet Army air defence as much as any other branch of the Army. Great emphasis is placed on providing protection for advancing units. All AAA and self-propelled SAMs are trained to fire on the move or from short halts on the line of march. If the intensity of the air threat requires it, the Soviets will deploy air-defence units along the axis of advance. Warning radars will move by bounds to provide continuous coverage, supplemented by visual observation from all vehicles.

The actual use of each air-defence weapon depends on its position in the system as a whole. SAMs must always be deployed to minimise the effect of their "dead zones," the spaces below their effective envelope where low-flying aircraft can avoid the SAM's radar, and the cone-shaped zone above the launcher. Because of the reaction time of the SAM launcher – estimated at 16sec with IFF (identification, friend or foe) radar transponder interrogation and eight seconds without it – effectiveness declines against manoeuvring or rapidly closing targets, especially when the flight time of the SAM itself is taken into account. The US Air Force believes that the effectiveness of SAMs will be greatly reduced if its aircraft maintain a certain distance from the launcher – the "avoidance radius". To increase detection range, the Soviets will try to position radars on high ground.

The Soviets place great emphasis on air-defence cover during river-crossing operations, when their manoeuvre units are particularly vulnerable. The basic "leapfrog" technique, whereby units alternate between moving and firing, is retained. One section of a regimental anti-aircraft battery will be deployed on the near bank to cover the attack, and the remainder will cross when enemy direct-fire weapons have been cleared from the crossing area, with radar and resupply vehicles following as closely as possible. The SA-8, with its boat-like hull and integral radar, appears to be designed with the problems of river crossing specifically in mind. If the operation encounters heavy air opposition the spearhead regiment will hold its air-defence assets back to cover the crossing, relying on the second-echelon regiments or the divisional anti-aircraft regiment to cover the troops on the far bank. In

addition, SA-7 launchers may be detached from their units to help guard the crossing site. This is possible because the divisional air-defence commander can use the air-defence radio network to redistribute all the weapons as the situation requires.

"A battery seen is a battery lost" was Napoleon's axiom, and this also forms the basis for much of the Soviet Army's air-defence tactics. To avoid revealing the positions of an entire unit, individual targets will usually be engaged by one or two designated guns or SAM launchers. When concealment is less important or when multiple targets appear, the whole unit will fire, relocating if necessary to avoid being attacked. When possible, alternative positions will be set up, usually within 500m of the original. Failure to provide alternative positions greatly increased the vulnerability of the Egyptians' Soviet-made air-defence weapons in the 1967 War.

The need to change position constantly on the modern battlefield has led to the use of "roving" anti-aircraft units. Able to react in a fluid battlefield situation, these units actively seek to engage enemy aircraft, moving from sector to sector wherever they are needed. This would also serve to confuse enemy estimates of Soviet air-defence strength. The Soviets realise, however, that roving units are vulnerable to attack if caught on the move, especially in daylight. It is also difficult to maintain a flow of information to and from the roving unit and work it into the defence system.

The anti-aircraft ambush relies on concealment for its effectiveness. A defensive tactic, it is used when available assets cannot provide complete cover. Ambushes can also be used to cover any gaps between air-defence systems. An anti-aircraft ambush is usually set up along likely approach routes for low-flying enemy aircraft, especially helicopters. This was the primary North Vietnamese method of using AAA in South Vietnam, and was also used to supplement the belt-type defences in North Vietnam.

The Soviets have great respect for the helicopter gunship, which, armed with anti-tank guided missiles, has the potential to decimate Soviet units. As a result, they have placed great emphasis on defeating the gunship with air-defence weaponry. They will often designate one platoon of an AAA battery to engage helicopters, relying on visual target acquisition rather than radar, which, though more accurate, takes longer to lock on. Guns firing on helicopters do not adjust their fire, as intensity is more important than accuracy. It is only necessary to disturb the ATGM gunner's aim. The Soviets have so inculcated their troops with the need to suppress helicopters that on manoeuvres every infantryman and SA-7 gunner that sees a helicopter will blaze away at it, regardless of whether or not it is in range, wasting much ammunition as a result. Forces operating behind enemy lines will usually hold their fire to avoid being located, however.

National air defence

The Army's Air Defence Forces' mission is to defend the Army's combat and support units and their lines of communication. The air defence of the Soviet Union itself is entrusted to a separate service, the National Air Defence Force (*PVO-Strany*), which ranks third in the Soviet service hierarchy after the Strategic Rocket Forces and the Army itself. Formed in 1948 to meet the threat of Allied strategic bombing, the *PVO-Strany* uses air-defence radars, interceptors, SAMs and, until the 1960s, AAA. While this large and powerful force – with 550,000 men, 7,000 radars, 10,000 SAM launchers and 2,600 interceptors – is outside the scope of this book, it uses the same SA-2 and SA-3 SAMs used by the Army, as well as the obsolescent SA-1 Guild, the high-altitude SA-5 Gammon and the Galosh ABM.

The Soviet distinction between the Army's Air Defence and the National Air Defence Force has been followed by the Warsaw Pact states. In effect, their national air defence forces are extensions of the *PVO-Strany*. North Vietnam and Egypt also formed separate services to control their considerable air-defence forces, although in both cases the Army retained the SA-6 and SA-7 SAMs and much AAA.

Unit organisation

Soviet divisional anti-aircraft regiment (tank and motorised rifle divisions)
Total strength: 32 officers, 392 enlisted men, 24 57mm S-60 AA guns, one Flat Face radar, four Flap Wheel radars, two BRDM or BTR-60PU scout cars, 84 trucks.
One HQ battery (seven officers, 50 men, eight trucks, one Flat Face radar, two BRDM or BTR-60PU scout cars)
Four AA gun batteries (Each of five officers, 66 men, six 57mm S-60 AA guns, and one Flap Wheel radar, 12 trucks. One Fire Can radar and one Ranger PUAZO-6 predictor can be substituted for the Flap Wheel.)
One service battery (five officers, 78 men, 28 trucks)
The large-calibre (130mm, 100mm, 85mm) AAA regiments currently used by some Warsaw Pact nations and previously used by the USSR are organised much the same as above. The anti-aircraft regiments of airborne divisions use the ZU-23 23mm AA gun in place of the S-60, and have one less AA gun battery, no radars except the Flat Face, and fewer and lighter trucks. This organisation is being replaced by SA-6 and SA-8-equipped regiments. Three trucks per gun battery are ammunition and supply carriers and may be with the service battery.

Divisional anti-aircraft regiment (tank and motorised rifle divisions)
One HQ battery
Five firing batteries (each of four SA-8 launch vehicles)
One service battery
SA-6 launch vehicles may replace SA-8s in a regiment, 20 launch vehicles being provided, plus radar and reload vehicles.

Regimental air-defence battery (tank and motorised rifle regiments)
Total strength: six officers, 59 enlisted men, four ZSU-23-4, four SA-9 launchers, several trucks, three BRDM scout cars.
One battery HQ (two BRDM or BTR-60PU, one truck, three officers, 12 enlisted men)
One ZSU-23-4 platoon (two pairs, one BRDM scout car for platoon commander)
One SA-9 launch vehicle platoon (two pairs, one BRDM scout car for platoon commander)
Supply and maintenance platoon (one officer, 23 enlisted men, 10 trucks)
Some Category III motorised rifle regiments may still use ZPU-4s towed by GAZ-66 trucks or ZU-23s towed by GAZ-69s in place of the ZSU-23-4s and SA-9s.

SA-2 regiment (army/front)
Total strength: 51 officers, 466 enlisted men, 18 SAM launchers, 19 generators.
One regimental HQ (eight officers, 60 enlisted men, 1 Spoon Rest radar, one Flat Face radar, one Mercury Grass communications truck, two radar control trucks, three electronics vans, one command trailer, two ambulances, one kitchen truck, eight cargo trucks)
Three SAM battalions
One technical battalion (10 officers, 115 enlisted men, two electronics vans, 12 missile reload trailers, two truck-mounted cranes, two missile checkout trucks, one kitchen truck, six propellant tank trucks, 38 trucks)

SA-2 battalion
One headquarters battery (four officers, 43 enlisted men, one Spoon Rest radar, one radar control truck, one Mercury Grass communications truck, one command trailer, one kitchen truck, three cargo trucks)
One fire-control battery (four officers, 20 enlisted men, one Fan Song radar, four electronics vans, nine trucks)
One firing battery (three officers, 34 enlisted men, six missile launchers, six missile trailers, one generator, nine trucks [six may be replaced by AT-S tractors], organised into an HQ of one officer and two enlisted men and two launch platoons)
SA-3 units are similar, but with four launchers per battery and reload vehicles instead of trailers, as well as their own dedicated radars.

SA-4 brigade (army/front)

Total strength: 145 officers, 1,100 enlisted men, 27 SA-4 launch vehicles, 27 SA-4 reload vehicles, four Long Track radars, 24 ZU-23s or ZSU-23-4s, nine Pat Hand radars, one Thin Skin radar, 135 trucks).

One brigade HQ (eight officers, 51 men, 10 trucks)
Three SAM battalions (each of 40 officers, 285 enlisted men, including one HQ with eight officers, 48 enlisted men, 8 trucks, one Long Track radar, three SAM batteries, and one AAA battery with eight ZU-23s towed by GAZ-66s or ZSU-23-4s)
One signal company (seven officers, 70 enlisted men, 20 trucks)
One technical battalion (10 officers, 124 enlisted men, one Long Track radar, one Thin Skin radar, 20 trucks)

SA-4 battery

Total strength: nine officers, 64 enlisted men, three SA-4 launch vehicles, four SA-4 reload vehicles, one HQ truck, two cargo trucks, one Pat Hand radar.

SA-6 regiment (formerly army/front level, now divisional weapons; organisation possibly obsolete)

Total strength: 84+ officers, 595+ enlisted men, 24 SA-6 launch vehicles, six SA-6 reload vehicles, eight ZSU-23-4s, three Long Track radars, six Straight Flush radar vehicles, one Thin Skin radar, 45+ trucks.

One regimental HQ (nine officers, 60 men, eight trucks)
Three SAM battalions (each of 22 officers, 140 men, eight trucks, one ZSU-23-4 and two SA-6 batteries)
Technical support and services (10 officers, 115 men, three Long Track radars, one Thin Skin height-finding radar, 12 trucks)

SA-6 regiment (divisional)

One regimental HQ (seven officers, 50 enlisted men, two Long Track radars, one Thin Skin-B radar, seven trucks)
Five firing batteries (each of 11 officers, 70 enlisted men, four SA-6 launch vehicles, one Straight Flush radar vehicle, four ZIL-131 SA-6 reload vehicles, 1 truck. One SA-11 launch vehicle can be added to each battery.)
One technical support and services battery (eight officers, 96 enlisted men, 12 trucks)

SA-6 battery

Total strength: four SA-6 launch vehicles, one SA-6 reload vehicle, one Straight Flush radar vehicle. (Batteries in divisional regiments have four launch vehicles.)

SA-8 regiment (divisional)

One regimental HQ (seven officers, 50 enlisted men, one BTR-60PU, two Long Track radars, one Thin Skin radar, seven trucks)
Five firing batteries (each of five officers, 30 enlisted men, 5 SA-8 launch vehicles, 1 BTR-60PU, 5 reload vehicles, 1 truck)
One service battery (eight officers, 96 enlisted men, 12 trucks)

Egyptian SA-6 battery, 1973

Total strength: eight SA-6 launch vehicles, one or more SA-6 reload vehicles, one Straight Flush radar vehicle, one Low Blow radar mounted on a ZIL-157 container truck.

SA-7 organisation

Each Soviet motorised rifle and airborne battalion has nine SA-7 launchers, normally assigned one to each platoon. Each motorised rifle platoon carries four SA-7 rounds, one reload in each BMP or APC. The Soviets can also group all of a battalion's SA-7s together as an air-defence sub-unit, commanded by an NCO.

KS-30 130mm gun. *(Chris Foss)*

Heavy anti-aircraft artillery

Size	130mm	100mm	85mm
Soviet designation	KS-30	KS-19M2	KS-12 (KS-18)*
NATO model number	M-1955	M-1949	M-1939 (M-1944)
Year introduced	1955	1949	1939 (1944)
Calibre	65cal	56cal	55cal (52cal)
Weight (firing)	24,900kg	11,000kg	4,986kg (4,263)
Length (travelling)	11.5m	9.238m	7.049m (8.2)
Height (travelling)	3.048m	2.201m	2.230m (2.25)
Width (travelling)	3.033m	2.286m	2.250m (2.15)
Track	2.388m	2.165m	1.8m
Elevation rate	5°/sec	9°/sec	8°/sec (20°/sec)
Elevation limits	−5°/+80°	−3°/+85°	−5°/+82°
Traverse rate	15°/sec	18°/sec	12°/sec (30°/sec)
Fire control	radar (SON-9A)	radar (SON-9A)	radar (SON-9A)
Rate of fire	10–12rpm	15–20rpm	10–15rpm (15–20)
Max horizontal range	29.0km	21km	12km (16)
Max altitude	22.0km	14.5km	9.6km (12.3)
Effective range	16.5km	11.9km	8.38km
Ammunition types	Frag-HE	Frag-HE, APHE as D-10	Frag-HE, APHE, HVAP, smoke
Muzzle velocity	950m/sec	HE=900m/sec APHE=1,000m/sec	HE=792m/sec (880) APHE=792m/sec (880) HVAP=1,030m/sec (1,000)
Shell weight	22.4kg	HE=15.7kg APHE=15.9kg	HE=9.5kg (9.75kg) APHE=9.3kg HVAP=5.0kg
Armour penetration	unknown	APHE=185mm @ 1,000m	APHE=102mm @ 1,000m HVAP=130mm @ 1,000m
Crew	11	9	7
Mount	4-wheel outrigger	4-wheel cross	4-wheel cross
Tow vehicle	AT-T, URAL-375	AT-S, URAL-375	ZIL-157

* 85mm gun figures in parentheses are for KS-18 where they differ from KS-12.

The now-obsolete Soviet heavy AAA pieces were the result of the development of basic Soviet gun design, which was improved by adapting selected foreign technology. They all featured characteristic Soviet ruggedness and simplicity and were similar to field artillery designs, using hydraulic recoil systems and fixed-charge, separate-loading ammunition.

The 85mm KS-12 was used throughout World War Two in the anti-tank as well as the anti-aircraft role, and was the basis of the T-34/85 tank's successful gun. After the war Soviet AAA benefited from the turning of German operational and technical experience to Russian purposes and the acquisition of new technology from both enemies and allies. Later versions of the 85mm gun (the improved KS-18) and the 100mm and 130mm guns featured radar fire-control equipment copied from that received from the US under Lend-Lease, automatic shell rammers taken from the British 3.7in AAA piece, improved breech designs and higher muzzle velocities. The newer 100mm and 85mm guns retained the KS-12's anti-tank capability. Large numbers of these guns were used by both Army and National Air Defence units until 1960–62, when they were phased out in favour of SAMs. They remain in service with Warsaw Pact and foreign nations, and many are retained in Soviet reserve stocks. The Soviets had 100mm guns in Armenia as recently as 1975.

KS-19M2 100mm anti-aircraft guns in action. A 100mm
projectile in its packing case is in the foreground. *(US Army)*

Combat usage

Soviet heavy AAA has seen much combat. The 85mm
KS-12 was used to good effect by both Soviet and German
forces in World War Two, and 85mm weapons were the
primary Communist heavy AAA in Korea. The Arabs
have used these guns since the mid-1950s, but without
great success. The most intense action for Soviet heavy
AAA was in the defence of North Vietnam.

These are basically medium-altitude weapons. The
100mm KS-19 is most effective at ranges of 925 to 6,150m,
while the 85mm KS-18 is most effective between 1,540
and 3,080m range. Effectiveness is reduced at low
altitudes as a result of the difficulties of acquiring aircraft
with the fire-control radar and of engaging a fast-moving
aircraft with a heavy, cumbersome weapon. High-altitude
effectiveness suffers from increased dispersion of shells.

The 130mm gun, while impressive on paper, seems to
have been a failure in action due to its bulk, much as the
German World War Two 128mm AA gun proved less
efficient than the "88" in many situations. The North
Vietnamese may have used a few 130mm guns. Over
Korea 85mm guns using radar, predictors and
proximity-fuzed shells destroyed between 2% and 3% of
the US aircraft they took under fire, with an average
expenditure of 8,500 rounds per kill. This is similar to the
performance of German 88mm AA guns in World War
Two. It is estimated that the few 100mm guns used in
Korea required 7,000 rounds per kill.

Tactical employment

Intended for point defence of high-priority targets against
medium-altitude air attack, these weapons protected
bridges, factories, transportation bottlenecks and cities in
Korea and Vietnam. The techniques for their use appear
to be similar to those for the 57mm S-60 AA gun.

KS-12 M-1939 85mm anti-aircraft gun emplaced in firing position, with outriggers extended. Three Frag-HE rounds are displayed on the mount. This weapon was captured by US forces near Pyongyang in 1950. *(US Army)*

Radar network and engagement sequence

The Fire Can, Fire Wheel, Flap Wheel, and Whiff fire-control radars used in conjunction with these weapons are all derived from the US-built SCR-584 radar supplied under Lend-Lease. The SON-30 Fire Wheel was used in conjunction with the PUAZO-30 director by 130mm-equipped batteries. The SON-9 Fire Can and PUAZO-6/9 (*Pribor Uprovleneya Artilleriskim Zenitnym Ognyom*, anti-aircraft fire-control device) Ranger predictor were both used with the other guns, although other radars were often substituted.

Early-warning data were provided from radars at regiment level or as part of an air-defence network, as with the 57mm S-60. The engagement sequence for the heavy AAA was similar to that of the S-60.

Countermeasures

The fire-control radars of the Soviet heavy AA guns were consistently jammed by US aircraft over Vietnam. Chaff and the entire series of ECM pods, starting with the ALQ-71/72, were effective against them. The weakness of their radar network in an ECM-heavy environment contributed to these weapons becoming obsolete.

S-60 57mm anti-aircraft gun

Calibre	71cal
Weight (firing)	4,600kg
Length (travelling)	8.5m
Height (travelling)	2.37m
Width (travelling)	2.05m
Elevation limits	−4°/+87°
Fire control	radar
Rate of fire	105–120rpm cyclic, 70rpm practical
Max horizontal range	12.0km
Max altitude	8.8km
Tracer burnout	5.4–6.1km
Effective range	6.0km (radar control) 4.0km (visual control)
Ammunition types	OR-281 HE/HEI, BR-281 APC/API
Muzzle velocity	1,000m/sec
Shell weight	HE/HEI=2.8kg APC/API=3.1kg
Armour penetration	APC/API=106mm @ 1,000m
Feed	automatic, 4-round clips
Unit of fire	200 rounds
Crew	7
Mount	4-wheel outrigger
Tow vehicle	URAL-375
Avoidance radius	5.5km

An excellent basic design still in front-line service with the Soviet Army and throughout the world, the S-60 is thought to have been copied directly from the German 55mm *Flak Gerat 58* prototype captured in 1945.

Combat usage

The S-60 has seen combat in the Middle East and throughout Southeast Asia. In Vietnam it was the keystone of North Vietnamese low-altitude air defence and was most effective between 460m (1,500ft) and 1,540m (5,000ft). Effectiveness has been increased by the introduction of a proximity fuze for the 57mm round in recent years, and it is thought that this is intended for use against missile-firing helicopters. A single direct hit by a 57mm round will destroy most tactical aircraft, but a proximity-fuze detonation will only produce fragmentation damage, although its effects would probably suppress a helicopter's missile-firing capability. When engaging modern jet aircraft an S-60 will have to fire approximately 8,500 rounds for each kill scored.

Tactical employment

Despite increasing reliance on SAMs, the S-60 is still a standard divisional air-defence weapon in the Soviet Army. The S-60s of the divisional anti-aircraft regiment protect regimental and battalion assembly and deployment areas along with headquarters and lines of communication, especially such vulnerable points as truck convoys, bridges and defiles. The S-60s also cover the movement of the division, either from overwatch positions (displacing as required, often by night) or while on the move. They also assist in the Stalingrad-like aerial blockade of surrounded enemy units. The S-60 is relatively large and unprotected. As it is towed by trucks it will seldom be employed closer than 10 kilometres from the forward edge of the battle area.

The S-60s are usually kept under the operational control of the divisional anti-aircraft regiment, and are not attached to tank or motorised rifle regiments. Batteries are normally positioned four to five kilometres apart, providing interlocking coverage. An S-60 battery can cover 13km², while a full regiment defends 30km². A different formation is used when the division is in route column. Each battery may be split into two three-gun platoons, 2–3km apart along the line of march. A battery in this formation protects 7–8km of the column, while the full regiment protects 30km.

The S-60, unlike most towed AAA, can perform air-defence tasks while moving because of the speed at which it comes into action. An S-60 can be in action, firing from its wheels, within five seconds of warning. Within 20sec it can be in action deployed on the ground for greater stability. For a full battery to be in action with its predictor

East German 57mm S-60. *(Marine Corps Gazette)*

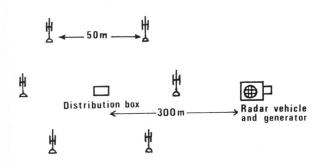

S-60 BATTERY IN ACTION

S-60 BATTERY IN ACTION (ALTERNATIVE FORMATION)

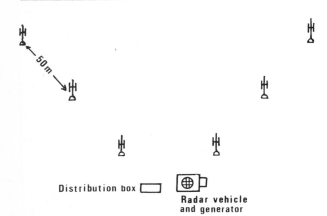

requires 10–14min, and for guns, predictor, generator and radar to be completely emplaced and ready for action takes 25–30min. The Soviets realise that firing without complete preparation degrades accuracy, but that the mobile conditions prevalent on the modern battlefield mean that the S-60 will fire on its wheels most often.

An S-60 battery in action would take up positions in the manner illustrated in the diagram, using engineer support if on the defensive.

In North Vietnam or Arab nations the employment of the S-60 differed from Soviet practice. They were normally used in a static role, frequently with fortified firing positions, and as an integral part of the national air-defence forces. As the primary point-defence AA guns, S-60s ringed any target of value. The Iraqis used S-60s against Iranian air and, especially, ground targets in 1980.

Radar network and engagement sequence

Each S-60 battery has either an SON-9 Fire Can radar which provides fire-control data in conjunction with a PUAZO-6 Ranger predictor, or one Flap Wheel radar which functions as both radar and predictor. Recently Flap Wheels have been retrofitted with a low-light TV camera, for use in ECM conditions, and an IFF interrogator. Each Soviet divisional anti-aircraft regiment has a Flat Face radar for target acquisition and IFF interrogation. Even outside the Warsaw Pact, the Fire Can/Ranger system is being replaced. In North Vietnam and Arab

Right A revetted North Vietnamese eight-gun S-60 57mm battery. The radar is emplaced at the lower left. The absence of trucks or reload vehicles shows this to be a static, air-defence site. *(US Air Force)*

57mm S-60s of the Egyptian Army, towed by URAL-375s, parade on October 6, 1976. *(Defense Intelligence Agency, via Virginia Mulholland)*

nations the national air defence forces' radars would provide early warning.

Once a target has been detected by either the Flat Face or army-level radars, the alert and primary target-acquisition data are passed over the air-defence radio network or landline. The S-60 battery fire-control radar uses this information to acquire the target itself and passes fire-control data to the predictor, whose computer determines the aiming point for each gun. Operation is automatic when the complete radar-directed fire-control system is used. The guns are trained and fired from central fire control, the crews simply loading fresh ammunition clips. Batteries normally fire together in bursts of two or three rounds per gun, shifting targets as required.

Countermeasures

The E-band fire-control radars used with S-60s in Vietnam and the Middle East have been successfully jammed by chaff and US-built ECM equipment. As a result, S-60 batteries were frequently forced to use visual fire control.

Fire Can. *(EW Communications)*

ZSU-57-2s parade through Red Square in November 1959.
Note that they lack the traditional white parade trimmings. *(US Army)*

ZSU-57-2 anti-aircraft gun

Introduced	1957	**Engine**	V-12 diesel, 520HP
Weight	28,100kg	**Armour (glacis)**	13.4mm/58.8°
Length	8.48m	**Armour (rear hull)**	10.6mm/45°
Height	2.75m	**Armour (upper hull)**	13.6mm/0°
Width	3.27m	**Armour (lower hull)**	13.8mm/0°
Ground pressure	0.63kg/cm²	**Armour (turret)**	13.5mm/curved, all-round
Max road speed	48km/h	**Basic load**	316 rounds (264 in clips)
Fuel capacity	812lit + 400lit auxiliary	**Gun elevation**	−5°/+85°
Range	420km, 595km with auxiliary fuel	**Fire control**	optical mechanical computing reflex sight
Fording	1.4m	**Max traverse rate**	30°/sec
Gradient	30°	**Max elevation rate**	20°/sec
Vertical obstacle	0.8m	Other armament data as S-60 (visual fire control)	

The ZSU-57-2 is simply two S-60s in an open-top turret mounted on a lightened T-54 hull and chassis with thin armour and one less road wheel per side than the tank. The S-68 57mm gun mounted on the ZSU-57-2 is identical to the S-60 except that it cannot use radar fire control and the right-hand gun is modified to be loaded from the right (otherwise its feed would be blocked by the other gun).

Combat usage

The ZSU-57-2 has seen combat in the Middle East and Southeast Asia, and it has been considered a failure. While basically as effective as two visually controlled S-60s, the ZSU-57-2 lacks the accuracy and all-weather capability that radar fire control provides. The optical sights are apparently inadequate: crew members have been seen standing on the back of these vehicles using optical heightfinders. The large, open turret of the ZSU-57-2 makes it very vulnerable to artillery fire.

Tactical employment

The ZSU-57-2 was originally intended to perform the role now filled by the ZSU-23-4: close cover for advancing armoured forces. The ZSU-57-2 differed in having a better direct-fire capability against ground targets as a result of its larger guns. Unlike the ZSU-23-4, the ZSU-57-2 served only in the regimental anti-aircraft batteries of tank regiments. It is now relegated to some low-readiness units and reserve storage in the Soviet Army, although some remain in use elsewhere.

ZSU-57-2s of the Egyptian Army parade in 1965.

37mm M38/39 in travelling position with tow vehicle and spare barrel, as captured by the US Army in Korea in 1950. *(US Army)*

M38/39 37mm anti-aircraft gun

Introduced	1938	**Ammunition types**	Frag-HE, AP-T, HVAP
Calibre	70cal	**Fire control**	optical-mechanical AZP-37
Weight (firing)	2,100kg		sights
Length (travelling)	6.16m	**Shell weight**	Frag-HE = 0.74kg
Height (travelling)	2.7m		AP-T = 0.77kg
Width (travelling)	1.7m		HVAP = 0.62kg
Track	1.545m	**Muzzle velocity**	HE = 880m/sec
Elevation rate (max)	22°/sec		AP = 880m/sec
Elevation limits	−5°/+85°		HVAP = 960m/sec
Traverse rate (max)	61°/sec	**Ammunition feed**	5-round clips (2-clip capacity)
Rate of fire	180rpm maximum	**Armour penetration**	AP = 46mm @ 500m, 38mm @
	80rpm practical		1,000m
Max horizontal range	8km	**Crew**	8
Max altitude	6km	**Mount**	4-wheel, 2-axle trailer
Effective range	3km	**Tow vehicle**	light truck

The M38/39 is an old Bofors-type design, widely used in World War Two. With only optical sights and incapable of using the radar fire control needed to engage modern high-speed aircraft, the M38/39 was replaced by the S-60 in Soviet divisional anti-aircraft regiments, though some may remain for training.

Combat usage

Robust and simple, the M38/39 has been widely used. It was the main Soviet light AA piece in World War Two, filled the same role in Korea, and was the Viet Minh's main weapon against French air power at Dien Bien Phu. Arab nations have used the M38/39 since 1956, and the gun has seen combat in small wars and insurgencies throughout the world. Like all Soviet-built AAA, it saw heavy use in Southeast Asia, both in North Vietnam and elsewhere. USAF aircrew in 1972 thought that the M38/39, despite its age, was at least as much a threat as the more modern S-60, especially as ECM had cancelled out much of the advantages of the S-60's radar fire control by then. The M38/39's higher muzzle velocity made evasive action difficult, and its higher rate of fire gave its barrages greater weight. Most effective under 420m (1,400ft) range, it required an average of three hits to destroy an F-4 Phantom or similar aircraft.

Tactical employment

The Soviet and Warsaw Pact armies used the M38/39 in much the same way as the S-60 is used today. Elsewhere, owing to its relatively large size and towing vehicle, it has been used in fixed positions, defending lines of communications and rear areas. The North Vietnamese lost most of those they hand-carried into South Vietnam before 1972. Like the S-60, they are frequently used for close-in defence of airfields, SAM and radar sites, and similar targets. In North Vietnam a battery of M38/39s would be dug in as shown in the diagram, often on a retaining dyke around a paddy field, which the Americans were reluctant to bomb for political reasons.

Engagement sequence

A 37mm battery would be warned of the direction of approaching enemy aircraft by communications from radar sites or lookouts. Each gun would normally be aimed and fired individually, although in World War Two a mechanical predictor was sometimes used. Fire would be massed, the whole battery engaging individual targets.

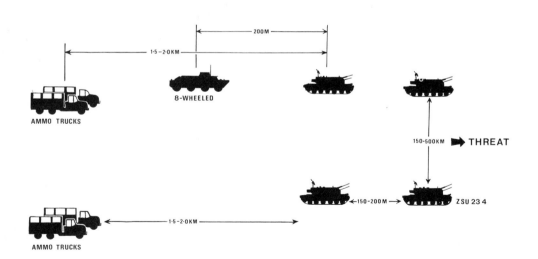

ZSU-23-4 platoon in line of sections formation. Command vehicle is a BTR-60PU. Other ZSU-23-4 unit formations include two pairs in line; convoy escort in two groups of three; line, "vee," diamond and others. 150–250m between ZSUs, 1,000–1,500m between pairs, ammunition trucks 1,500–2,000m behind the ZSUs, command vehicle 200m behind. (*J. W. Loop*)

ZSU-23-4-M, reported to have digital computers and improved radar.

ZSU-23-4 and ZU-23 anti-aircraft guns

	AZP-23
Calibre	81cal
Elevation limit	−7°/+80° (−10°/+90°)
AA fire control	radar (optical reflector; ZAP-23 mechanical computing)
Rate of fire	1,000rpm cyclic,
per barrel	200rpm practical
Max horizontal range	7.0km
Max altitude	5.1km
Effective AA range	3km (2.5km)
Ammunition types	Frag, HEI, API
Muzzle velocity	970m/sec
Shell weight	0.19kg = HEI, 0.189kg = API
Armour penetration	API = 25mm @ 500m, 19.3mm @ 1,000m
Ammunition feed	two box magazines
Magazine capacity	50 belted rounds each
Avoidance radius	2.8km

(Data applicable only to the AZP-23 cannon as mounted on the ZU-23 appear in parentheses.)

	ZU-23
Weight (firing)	893kg
Length (travelling)	4.57m
Height (travelling)	1.83m
Track	1.67m
Crew	5
Mount	2-wheel carriage

Tow vehicle	GAZ-69
Traverse rate	28°/handwheel turn
Elevation rate	19°/handwheel turn

	ZSU-23-4
Introduced	1966
Weight (loaded)	14,000kg
Length	6.3m
Height (travelling)	2.3m
Width	2.95m
Track	2.67m
Ground pressure	0.267kg/cm²
Max road speed	45km/h
Fuel capacity	250lit
Range	260km
Fording	1.07m
Gradient	38°
Vertical obstacle	1.1m
Trench	2.8m
Engine	V-6 diesel, 290HP
Turret rotation	45°/sec
Armour (glacis)	15mm/55°
Armour (hull)	15mm/0°
Armour (mantlet)	10mm/15°
Basic load	2,000 rounds in 40 magazines
Crew	4
Soviet nickname (unofficial)	"Shillka"

The ZSU-23-4 (*Zenitnaia Samokhodnaia Ustanovka*, self-propelled anti-aircraft mount, pronounced "zoo") is the most effective AAA weapons system in large-scale service today. A formidable weapon in the 1973 Middle East war, it has since occupied a crucial place in the Soviet-NATO military balance. The successful use of much of NATO's tactical air power, especially missile-firing helicopters and the USAF's A-10 ground-attack aircraft with its massive tank-killing cannon, requires that the ZSU-23-4s be neutralised or destroyed.

The ZSU-23-4 with its Gun Dish radar is a complete all-weather weapon system and a vital part of Soviet tactics. The chassis is similar to that of the PT-76 light tank, and although it has no amphibious or snorkelling capability it does have an overpressure NBC defence system. For operating "buttoned up" the ZSU-23-4 has a land navigation system and a wide variety of vision equipment. A TPKU-2 daylight observation periscope and two BM-190 lateral viewing instruments are in the turret. At night the TPKU-2 is replaced by a TKN-1T infra-red (IR) electro-optical night vision device with a range of 200–250m. The driver is provided with a BM-130 periscope and lateral viewing instruments. A TVN-2 infra-red device and two FG-125 light elements provide night-driving capability. An R-123 radio is used for communication. The vehicle is not amphibious.

The main armament of the ZSU-23-4 consists of four AZP-23 23mm cannon, separated from the crew compartment in the turret by an armoured bulkhead. The system uses radar and optical sights and an analogue fire-control computer. Ammunition is belted with one round of AP/API for every three rounds of HE/HEI. Both rounds have a tracer base. The Gun Dish radar has a moving-target indicator (MTI) which helps to distinguish moving aircraft from non-moving background, such as chaff, jamming and ground clutter. An azimuth gyro and a kinematic roll gyro are part of the ZSU-23-4's stabilisation circuit. A DG4M-1 turbine auxiliary power unit (APU) can provide power for the Gun Dish. Both the gun and the radar are fully stabilised and can engage targets while the ZSU-23-4 is moving at up to 25km/h, although this reduces gunfire accuracy by at least 50%. ZSU-23-4s will fire from the halt whenever possible. If used in static positions, the ZSU-23-4-M (but not earlier versions) can be linked to off-carriage radar and fire-control equipment.

The ZSU-23-4 and its gun have had a number of problems. Soviet writings have mentioned rapid gun-bore deterioration caused by high rates of fire. Variation in ammunition characteristics has degraded accuracy, possibly to a great degree. A number of electrical system problems associated with the radar-controlled firing of the AZP-23 have also appeared. The most serious of these has been "runaway" firing while traversing after fire has supposedly ceased, which must be a most unpleasant experience for any vehicles or soldiers in the vicinity. To avoid such collateral damage the Soviets always try to maintain adequate spacing between ZSU-23-4s and the units they support. The AZP-23 also apparently suffers from overheating, and it is questionable how long – probably only seconds – it could sustain even its effective rate of fire. As a result of ground clutter, the Gun Dish radar cannot be used against targets at less than 200ft altitude. This means that low-flying targets, including most missile-firing helicopters, would have to be engaged by visual fire control, which greatly reduces accuracy. Gun Dish also cannot pick up small targets, and its range against aircraft with a small radar cross-section is considerably reduced.

No fewer than nine identifiable separate versions of the ZSU-23-4 have been spotted. Most differ only in stowage or cooling vents. Large ammunition panniers, mounted on the turret sides, were introduced in an intermediate production model. The ZSU-23-4-M features these panniers, three access ports on each side of the hull (instead of two), and an armoured cover for the guns. The ZSU-23-4-M's improved electronics probably include a digital fire-control system.

A new Soviet self-propelled anti-aircraft gun, possibly a ZSU-23-4 replacement, was reported under development in 1978. Tentatively designated ZSU-30-6, it is believed to be armed with a 30mm six-barrelled Gatling gun, possibly similar to the weapon used in the Su-25 ground-attack aircraft.

The Soviets believe that the ZSU-23-4 will be an effective weapon system for many years to come. Despite reports of a replacement vehicle being developed, production continues. In 1977–78 the Soviet Army experimented with making one ZSU-23-4 an organic part of every tank platoon in an attempt to drive NATO tactical aircraft from the sky by sheer weight of fire, but it now seems unlikely that this organisation will be adopted. The ZSU-23-4 is highly vulnerable to direct-fire weapons, as it lacks a tank's armour protection. Ammunition resupply in the forward area would also be a problem.

Finally, it appears that the handling of a combined-arms force in action requires more skill than most platoon commanders can offer, especially those of the Soviet Army, whose general lack of training and initiative is recognised by the Soviets themselves.

Combat usage

The ZSU-23-4 first saw action with the North Vietnamese Army in Laos in 1972, and proved itself during the initial fighting of the 1973 Middle East war. Thirty of the 80 Israeli aircraft lost in the first three days of the war fell to ZSU-23-4s when making low-level attacks on Arab armoured columns or when driven into the ZSU's kill zone while evading SA-6s, a perfect example of the complementary and overlapping system of Soviet air defence.

An intermediate-production ZSU-23-4 (identifiable by the antennae and the use of panniers instead of ammunition boxes on the turret sides) ready for shipment from Israel to the USA. (Tom Woltjer)

The ZSU-23-4 underlined the continuing importance of AAA on the modern battlefield. While SAMs have supplemented AAA, they have not replaced it. On average it requires some 16 23mm hits to destroy an aircraft like the F-4 Phantom, so the ZSU-23-4 must rely on weight of fire rather than pinpoint accuracy.

Although the weapon was designed for use against high-performance jet aircraft, US Army figures based on tests of captured ZSU-23-4s show that it is also extremely effective against helicopters. The probability of destroying an AH-1 Cobra helicopter gunship with a 40-round burst (10 rounds per barrel) from a stationary ZSU-23-4 is:

Range (m)	500	1,000	1,500	2,000	2,500	3,000
AH-1 manoeuvring	80%	48%	30%	18%	8%	4%
AH-1 hovering	80%	53%	36%	27%	18%	15%

A single ZSU-23-4 can theoretically fire 20 40-round bursts in a minute, so it has the potential to drive the helicopter from the modern battlefield, or at least make the elimination of its threat a first priority. As the AH-1 is heavily armoured and extremely manoeuvrable, the ZSU-23-4 would be even more effective against transport helicopters.

However, US battlefield helicopters have radar homing and warning equipment that will alert them to a Gun Dish before the ZSU-23-4 is aware of the helicopter, even though the ZSU-23-4 can acquire targets at 20km and track them at 8km range. Other ZSU-23-4 limitations include cooling problems (which is why fire is normally in 40-round bursts), the vacuum-tube technology of the Gun Dish and the crude momentum-wheel gun stabiliser. A drone helicopter reportedly flew five passes at 1,900m range in front of a ZSU-23-4 during US Army tests before being knocked down.

The Soviets are said to be modifying the Gun Dish to allow the radar to operate at different frequencies, and improving the moving target indicator to help pick targets out of ground clutter. Other improvements, first used in the ZSU-23-4-M, allow the radar to swivel and search independently; previously it had been slaved to the gun tubes. Reports also suggest that a 100-round magazine is being introduced to replace the earlier 50-round magazines.

The US Army estimates that a 5–10 rounds per barrel burst from a ZSU-23-4 would have the following chances of hitting a stationary vehicle:

Range (m)	50	100	175	250	500	750	1,000	1,500
Chance of hit	97%	97%	97%	78%	61%	56%	47%	31%

It would be unlikely to knock out a tank, and the chances of knocking out an APC depend on how many rounds actually hit. Any unarmoured vehicle caught by a ZSU-23-4 would almost certainly be destroyed.

Tactical employment

The regimental anti-aircraft battery of a Soviet motorised rifle or tank regiment includes one platoon of four ZSU-23-4s. One pair or platoon is often attached to the regiment's spearhead battalions, and the remaining ZSU-23-4s are normally within one kilometre of each other. To maintain command and control the platoon commander's BTR-60PU APC will be 200m behind the lead ZSU-23-4s. When supporting an attack the ZSU-23-4s will follow the lead elements closely, normally at 400–500m, but less at night or in bad weather. The Soviets believe that this spacing will provide the maximum amount of air-defence cover while limiting the exposure of the ZSU-23-4s to direct-fire weapons. In this linear method of tactical employment the ZSU-23-4s of a pair will be separated by 150–200m. Ammunition trucks will follow the platoon at 1,500–2,000m.

When terrain or the tactical situation does not permit the use of a linear formation, ZSU-23-4s will form a cluster, making best use of terrain and maintaining clear fields of fire. A ZSU-23-4 platoon commander will frequently mass or redeploy his vehicles to meet an air threat, and may form echelon if threatened from the flank, with all guns facing the direction of the potential attack 200–300m from the protected tanks and APCs. During an approach march or pursuit the ZSU-23-4s are deployed along the axis of advance. They are normally near battalion HQ, although one pair is often at the head of the regiment while the other is at the tail. The ZSU-23-4s maintain a 50m minimum separation from other vehicles in the convoy to give themselves a clear arc of fire. In river crossings the ZSU-23-4s normally take up a linear position to support the crossing until they are ferried across one at a time on GSP ferries, ready to fire even while afloat.

The ZSU-23-4 can also engage ground targets. Its AZP-23 would be most effective using direct fire against lightly armoured vehicles, and it is probably capable of indirect fire as well. However, their thin armour makes them vulnerable to 12.7mm machine guns, and Soviet publications repeatedly warn against "needless exposure." It is therefore unlikely that ZSU-23-4s will be much used against ground targets, except in self-defence.

Radar network and engagement sequence

With its Gun Dish radar the ZSU-23-4 is not dependent on outside fire-control radars, although it would receive information from division or army-level air-defence radars over the Air Defence radio network. Gun Dish provides excellent target tracking, and is difficult to detect or evade. It can be used as a search radar.

The ZSU-23-4 has three modes of firing: radar control, electro-optical (when the radar provides range only), and optical. It primarily uses the radar mode of engagement. The Gun Dish will normally be set on surveillance or sector scan for search purposes, the area searched usually being determined by data from early-warning radars. Once an aircraft is spotted by the Gun Dish and identified as hostile by the IFF interrogator the crew switches to automatic tracking. The radar feeds the target co-ordinates directly into the analogue computer to determine the lead angle and elevation necessary to engage the target. The gun itself is automatically trained on the target. When the computer has the correct data and the gun is properly aligned, a green indicator light comes on and either the commander or the gunner can open fire. It takes about two seconds to detect an aircraft and nine seconds to lock on and fire, although some sources believe that these figures are optimistic and should be trebled.

A quicker response is possible when using the electro-optical mode, in which the crew can fire while the target is tracked by angular position, using the optical gunsight. In this mode the radar provides only the range. At one time this feature gave rise to inaccurate reports that the Gun Dish was a range-only radar.

The shortest response time is obtained with purely visually guided engagement, the gun being trained and fired using the optical sights. This is the least accurate method but it is the only one effective against targets at 200ft altitude or less, owing to the effect of surface clutter on the Gun Dish. Optical sights would also be used against ground targets.

Firing is normally by three five or five ten-round per barrel bursts against slow-moving targets such as helicopters, or in 50-round bursts against jet aircraft. In either case all four barrels of the AZP-23 would fire simultaneously.

ZU-23 in travelling position. *(V.M. Martinova)*

Countermeasures

While the ZSU-23-4 and Gun Dish were known to Western military sources before the 1973 War, their precise characteristics remained uncertain. The Gun Dish proved resistant to jamming by Israeli airborne ECM equipment, and its thin pencil beam and high pulse-repetition rate compounded the lack of precise knowledge about the system. By the later stages of the war examination of captured ZSU-23-4s permitted the ALQ-119 and ALQ-101 ECM pods delivered to Israel during the conflict to be modified to jam Gun Dish. Today radar homing and warning equipment, including the AN/APR-39 mounted in US Army helicopters, can detect the Gun Dish's emissions and give a good indication of the ZSU's direction and general location. Airborne jammers are probably still effective against Gun Dish, but the Soviets have doubtless modified it since 1973.

The most effective countermeasure against ZSU-23-4s is to seek them out and destroy them. They are especially vulnerable to artillery fire, and one shell fragment through the Gun Dish's parabolic antenna will put it out of action. A ZSU-23-4 under artillery fire must retract its radar antenna into travelling position and the crew must "button up," making it almost impossible for them to detect an aircraft either visually or with radar.

NATO attack helicopters using TOW wire-guided anti-tank missiles will engage the ZSU-23-4s – surprising them and hitting them from the flanks, it is hoped – before attacking any other targets. The TOW's maximum range of 3,750m is greater than the ZSU-23-4's effective range of 3,000m. The US Army hopes to have its helicopters stand off at maximum range and pick off the ZSU-23-4s, then hit the SA-9 launchers, and only then start dispatching the tanks and APCs. Fixed-wing aircraft would use precision-guided munitions such as the TV-guided AGM-65A Maverick to destroy the ZSU-23-4s and SA-9s at long range, enabling aircraft using free-falling munitions or strafing to attack without having to run the deadly air-defence gauntlet.

Despite the countermeasures available to suppress or destroy the ZSU-23-4, it remains a most effective weapon system. Western armed forces are still seeking an effective counter.

ZU-23 23mm captured by US forces in firing position.

ZU-23

The ZU-23 is a towed twin mount for the 23mm cannon used in a quadruple mount in the ZSU-23-4. Designed primarily for export, the ZU-23 is used in the divisional anti-aircraft regiments of Soviet Army airborne divisions. Its lack of radar fire control limits its effectiveness. It is also used in SA-4 brigades and low-readeness motorised rifle regiments.

The ZU-23 has seen a great deal of combat. The North Vietnamese used it throughout Southeast Asia in the later stages of the war and the Arabs employed large numbers in the 1973 War, their primary role being the close-in defence of SAM sites.

ZPU-4 deployed in firing position, outrigger arms extended.
(US Army)

ZPU-4 14.5mm anti-aircraft gun

Calibre	93cal
Weight (firing)	1,810kg
Length (travelling)	4.48m
Height (travelling)	2.10m
Width (travelling)	1.67m
Elevation limits	−19°/+90°
Fire control	ZAPP-4 mechanical computing, reflex optical (AA); telescopic (ground targets)
Traverse/elevation	24°/handwheel turn
Rate of fire	600rpm (cyclic)
(per barrel)	150rpm (practical)
Max horizontal range	7km
Max altitude	5km
Effective range	1.4km (2km against ground targets)
Ammunition types	AP-I, API-T, I-T, AP-T, HEI
Muzzle velocity	1,000m/sec
Shell weight	0.065kg

Armour penetration	API = 32mm @ 500m, 19mm @ 1,000m
Crew	5
Feed	drum magazine
Magazine capacity	150 rounds, linked belt
Unit of fire	4,800 rounds
Mount	4-wheel, 2-axle trailer
Tow vehicle	GAZ-54, GAZ-63, GAZ-66

The ZPU-4, ZPU-2 and ZPU-1 are respectively the quadruple, twin and single anti-aircraft versions of the basic Soviet 14.5mm KPV heavy machine gun. Dating back to World War Two, the KPV is a most effective weapon for its size. Many US helicopter pilots in Vietnam considered the ZPU to be their most dangerous opposition. Smaller weapons were usually ineffective, and larger ones more cumbersome and easier to spot and destroy – so much so that even today some believe the ZPUs to be more deadly than the ZSU-23-4. On the modern battlefield, what can be seen can be destroyed. The ZPUs, though aged, may still be effective. Some of the ZPU series can be

ZPU-4 in travelling position, being towed by GAZ-66s. Magazines, containing belted ammunition, are loaded on the weapons. *(Defense Intelligence Agency, via Virginia Mulholland)*

dismantled and carried manually where larger weapons cannot go, permitting effective "anti-aircraft ambushes." There is also an obsolescent self-propelled version of the ZPU-2 mounted on the BTR-152 APC, the BTR-152V. A single-barrel mountain version, the ZGU-1, is in service.

Since World War Two the ZPU series has seen action in Korea, in Indochina from the French involvement to the 1979 fighting, in the Middle East since 1956, and in many small wars and insurgencies throughout the world, being used by Iraqi Kurdish guerrillas and ZANU rebels in Rhodesia, for example. The ZPU-1 and ZPU-2 have been used against the Soviets in Afghanistan.

When it was used by the Soviet Army the ZPU-4 equipped the regimental anti-aircraft batteries of motorised rifle regiments, being employed in much the same way as the ZSU-23-4 that has largely replaced it. Many nations continue to use ZPUs, most notably North Korea, which fields a full brigade of ZPU-4s with female crews.

Foreign use

The Warsaw Pact armies, Cuba, Syria, Iraq, Egypt and Vietnam use the full range of Soviet AAA, although the Czechs and the Hungarians often replace the ZSU-23-4 or ZU-23 with SP and towed 30mm guns. Unlike the Soviet Army, these armies also use 100mm and 85mm AAA. In addition, the air-defence forces of many of these nations, unlike the *PVO Strany*, use AAA.

Other users of Soviet AAA include:

Afghanistan: 350+ M38/39, 85mm, 100mm; 20 ZSU-23-4.

Algeria: M38/39 (Chinese model), S-60, 85mm, 100mm.

Angola: ZU-23, M38/39.

China: The largest single user of Soviet AAA, China produces a wide range of copies of older Soviet designs. These are: Type 56 (ZPU-4), Type 58 (ZPU-2), Type 55 (M38/39), Type 59 (S-60), 85mm (KS-18), Type 59 100mm (KS-19).

Congo: 10 ZPU-4, M38/39, S-60 (Chinese-built).

Ethiopia: 37mm, other weapons, ZPU-2.

Finland: ZU-23, ZSU-57-2, S-60, ZSU-23-4.

India: ZSU-23-4.

Iran: 100 ZSU-57-2s and ZSU-23-4s, ZU-23s.

Iraq: S-60, ZU-23.

Kampuchea: 14.5mm, M38/39 (Chinese-built).

North Korea: 14.5mm, ZPU-1, 2, 4, M38/39, S-60, 85mm, 100mm, ZSU-57-2.

Laos: 14.5mm, 37mm.

Libya: ZU-23, ZSU-23-4, S-60.

Mongolia: M38/39, S-60.

Morocco: 50 M38/39, S-60; 100mm delivered, few operational.

Mozambique: ZU-23, M38/39, S-60.

Pakistan: ZU-23, 57mm.

North Yemen: M38/39, S-60.

South Yemen: M38/39, S-60, 85mm, ZSU-23-4.

Somalia: 150 14.5mm, M38/39, S-60, 100mm, ZSU-23-4, few operational.

Sudan: 80 37mm and 85mm (both Soviet and Chinese-built).

Tanzania: 14.5mm, M38/39 (Chinese-built).

Yugoslavia: M38/39, S-60, M-44 85mm, ZSU-57-2.

SA-2 Guideline surface-to-air missile

SA-2 Mk 2 on its trailer, towed by a ZIL-157.

Year introduced	1957/58/60/62/67/68
Length	10.6/10.8/10.8/10.8/11.2/10.8
Diameter	0.5m 1st stage
	0.66m 2nd stage
Launch weight	2,300kg
Mount	single
Guidance	radio command
Control method	movable tail surfaces
Fuel	solid 1st stage, liquid (nitric acid and hydrocarbon) 2nd stage
Max speed	Mach 3/3/3/3.5/3.5/3.5
Max range	35/35/35/50/50/35km
Min range	9.3/9.3/9.3/9.3/7/7km
Max altitude	28km
Min altitude	4.5/4.5/4.5/1.5/1.5/1.5km
Warhead	130kg HE, internally grooved
Burst radius	13.5m, lethal against F-4 at low altitude
Rate of fire (per launcher)	1 missile every 10–12min
Avoidance radius	16.7km
Normal launch angle	80°
Fire-control radar	Fan Song A/B/C/E/E/F

Multiple data refer to: SA-2a V75/SA-2b Mk 1 V75SM/SA-2c Mk 2 V75M/SA-2d Mk 3/SA-2e Mk 4/SA-2f Mk 5 respectively. Soviet system designations are in V750 series.

The SA-2 has had a profound effect on the development of air tactics since an example downed an American U-2 over the Soviet Union on May 1, 1960, proving the ability of the surface-to-air missile to strike even the highest-flying aircraft.

Throughout its long service the SA-2 has been improved and modified. The original "Mk 1" version had rectangular nose fins, while the "Mk 2" version, captured in the 1967 Middle East war, had delta nose fins. The 1967 "Mk 4" version, slightly longer, featured a white-painted, bulged nose cone once thought to contain a nuclear warhead. Despite its age the SA-2 has been upgraded since 1967. There are reports that the SA-2s used in the 1973 Middle East war had a terminal guidance system never previously fitted. The Fan Song F and Mk 5 version can use optical guidance techniques in an ECM-heavy environment.

The whole SA-2 system is very simple and "soldier-proof," built with large plugs and thick switches. In the words of one US soldier familiar with captured SA-2s: "The average 'Joe Arab' could work it with ease". This would contribute to its longevity, and it remains in service with the Soviet Army and National Air Defence Force and with many foreign nations. The SA-2 was being phased out of Soviet Army service in the late 1970s.

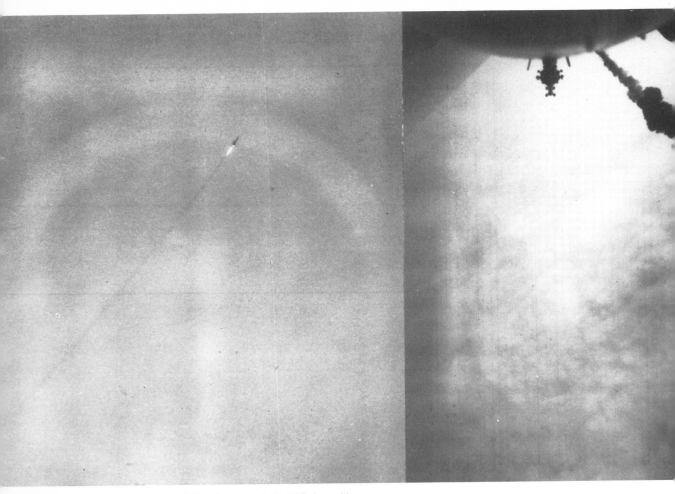

The "Flying Telegraph Pole" as it appears in flight. Taken with a camera mounted on the belly of an F-105D fighter-bomber, this picture shows *(left)* the missile in flight and *(right)* exploding harmlessly. *(US Air Force)*

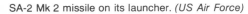

SA-2 Mk 2 missile on its launcher. *(US Air Force)*

Combat usage

The SA-2 has seen more combat than any other SAM. Designed for use against formations of non-manoeuvring heavy bombers at high altitude, its effectiveness was demonstrated by the destruction of six high-flying U-2 reconnaissance aircraft: four over China and one each over the USSR and Cuba. This performance was obtained only at the expense of low-altitude capability and the manoeuvrability needed to engage tactical aircraft. The SA-2 is not effective at less than three kilometres altitude and it accelerates to full speed only at 7.63km (25,000ft). As with most SAMs, the SA-2 has two "dead zones" in which the missile cannot be guided. One zone, a cone above the launcher, is above the missile's performance envelope, while the other, below the performance envelope, demonstrates the difficulty of engaging low-flying aircraft coming in under radar coverage.

Estimated cone dead zone over launcher (km)

Minimum range is:	16	14	12	8	6	10	12
At this altitude:	28.5	25	20	15	10	5	1.5

Estimated low-altitude dead zone (km)

Minimum altitude is:	1.5	2	3	4	7	10	15
At this range:	12	20	30	40	50	55	58

(Assumes dead-flat terrain.)

The Indians fired a number of SA-2s in the 1965 War, but damaged only one Pakistani aircraft. The threat of the SA-2s, however, reduced the accuracy and effectiveness of Pakistani air strikes. The Egyptians fired 22 SA-2s during the 1967 War. All missed, and the Israelis captured at least one SA-2 battery.

The SA-2 was used most intensively in the Vietnam War. Its accuracy rate (percentage of missiles fired yielding kills) was:

1965: 194 SAMs fired, 11 kills = 5.7% accuracy
1966: 1,096 SAMs fired, 31 kills = 2.8% accuracy
1967: 3,202 SAMs fired, 56 kills = 1.75% accuracy
1968 (Jan-Mar): 322 SAMs fired, 3 kills = 0.9% accuracy
1972: 4,244 SAMs fired, 49 kills = 1.15% accuracy
(The 1972 figures may include a number of SA-3 Goas.)

While the SAMs initially achieved a fair deal of accuracy, US countermeasures gradually reduced their effectiveness. But even then they still contributed to the integration of the North Vietnamese defence. They forced the US to divert aircraft to SAM suppression and increased vulnerability to AAA and MiG interceptors. SA-2 batteries would "spoof" aircraft radar homing and warning sets by turning on false launch signals, forcing the supposed target to take evasive action and possibly set itself up for AAA, interceptors or a genuine SA-2. Despite its lack of manoeuvreability and despite its susceptibility to countermeasures, an SA-2 popping out of an overcast can still destroy any aircraft.

Only once did the SA-2 encounter the type of target it was designed to destroy. The B-52s used in the Linebacker II raids against Hanoi in 1972 were ordered to fly unmanoeuvring, direct bomb runs to avoid hitting civilian targets. Many of them were early models and their ECM had not been modernised. Even when faced with these almost ideal targets the SA-2 achieved less than 2% accuracy. Much of this inaccuracy was due to the heavy use of ECM support aircraft and large-scale defence suppression. Although this divered aircraft away from the main bombing effort, the North Vietnamese were soon reduced to firing off huge salvos of SA-2s completely unguided, "like huge bottle rockets," in the words of one

US Air Force officer. Were it not for the ECM of the B-52s and the intensive defence suppression, the USAF estimates that the SA-2s would have achieved 10% accuracy against the B-52s. This is still in marked contrast to the optimistic estimates of SAM accuracy made before the missiles ever saw combat; the Yugoslavs, for example, believed that their SA-2s were capable of attaining 80% accuracy.

The SA-2s used by the Arabs since the 1967 War have been less effective than those used over Vietnam. Israeli aircraft flew at lower altitude than US aircraft, which was possible because Arab AAA was numerically inferior to that of North Vietnam. The Israelis soon developed effective evasive manoeuvres and bought US ECM equipment to minimise vulnerability to the missile they called "the flying telegraph pole."

Tactical employment

The SA-2s of the Soviet National Air Defence Forces and those of most foreign nations are normally deployed in static positions. Those which remain in service with the Soviet Army have a more mobile role, and so lack permanent installations. The Soviets lay out all their SA-2 firing positions to set patterns which are also used by North Vietnam, Egypt and, presumably, most of the other nations using the weapon.

North Vietnam left many of its SA-2 sites unhardened, relying on camouflage. The launchers were simply dug into pits or left at ground level. The Fan Song radar and fire-control equipment normally remained in their vans, increasing the vulnerability of these sites to US aircraft.

In the years preceding the 1973 War the Egyptian air-defence force hardened their SAM sites. The Fan Song radar, command posts and fire-control equipment were all in deep concrete bunkers, and the launchers were dug in and surrounded by concrete revetments. Communications were provided by well protected landlines. Most sites were ringed with light AAA against low-level attack. After a series of Israeli commando raids on SAM sites during the 1967-70 "War of Attrition" many sites were

SA-2 BATTERY

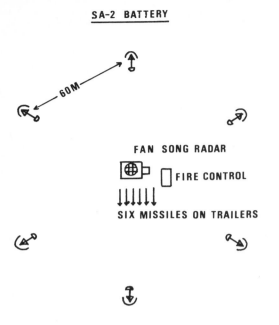

FAN SONG RADAR

FIRE CONTROL

SIX MISSILES ON TRAILERS

reinforced with a company of infantry for ground defence. These sites proved very difficult for the Israeli Air Force to destroy in 1973.

Radar network and engagement sequence

An SA-2 battery would normally be linked to a Spoon Rest early-warning radar (the North Vietnamese often used the earlier Knife Rest) and a regiment-level Side Net height-finding radar. Once these radars have acquired and identified a target, the contact is passed by radio or landline (*not* modern automatic data link) to the SA-2 battery's Fan Song radar, which tracks and acquires the target, feeding information to the battery's fire-control computer. Each Fan Song can track up to six targets and engage one with one or more missiles. All Fan Song versions can track-while-scan (tracking some targets and passing their range, speed and rate of closure to the fire-control computer while scanning and trying to acquire others), using the flapping fan-shaped radar beams from which the radar gets it name. Once the fire-control computer has sufficient data, an SA-2 can be launched,

North Vietnamese SA-2 site, showing typical early war period shallow revetments and unhardened command post and radar, but with trucks at hand for mobility. A Fan Song B or C radar is at the right, in the centre of what appears to be a standard hexagonal battery deployment. An insert of a single launcher is at upper left. (*US Air Force*)

RADA

NG

Fan Song C radar array at maximum elevation. *(Defense Intelligence Agency)*

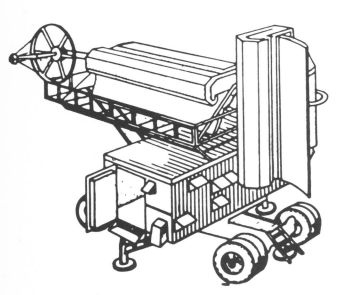

Fan Song B. *(EW Communications)*

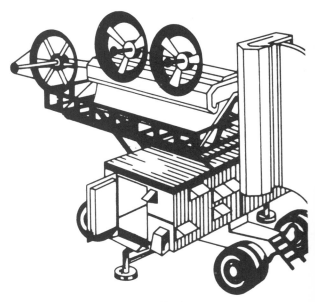

Fan Song E. *(EW Communications)*

P-12 Spoon Rest. *(EW Communications)*

powered by its solid-fuel booster. When it is clear of the battery the booster drops away and the liquid-fuel second-stage sustainer cuts in. Once the missile is launched, the computer receives the inputs of the target's movement from the Fan Song, which is also tracking the missile's flight. The computer generates commands to steer the missile towards the target, and these are transmitted over a UHF radio beam link to four strip antennae mounted forward and aft of the missile's wings. The missile's guidance system will then adjust its course by moving the wings. An SA-2 must pick up the narrow, line-of-sight UHF beam within six seconds of launch or it will go ballistic and miss the target.

In this manner the SA-2 can be steered close enough to its target to activate its proximity fuze. The North Vietnamese overestimated the effectiveness of the SA-2's warhead against B-52s in 1972. Apparently only after American TV had shown pictures of damaged B-52s was it realised that the SA-2 must be set to explode very close to one of the big bombers to bring it down. As its circular error probability (CEP, the radius of the circle in which 50% of all missiles fired will hit) is at least 76.3m (250ft) and its burst radius is considerably less, the reason for the low accuracy of the SA-2 against even non-manoeuvring targets becomes apparent.

Countermeasures

The US and Israel have both developed a wide range of countermeasures to the SA-2. US passive countermeasures included strike aircraft "rolling in" at 3,664m (12,000ft) to 5,496m (18,000ft) altitude, below the

Side Net

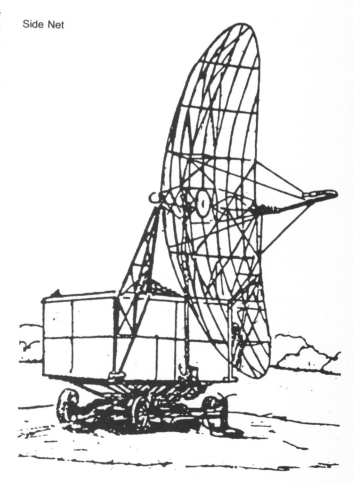

optimum height for the SA-2 and above the most deadly altitude for AAA, although the latter was more effective than it had been when the aircraft could fly at higher altitude. US aircraft were also obliged to spread out their formations in order to avoid the possibility of an SA-2 hitting more than one. This in turn increased their vulnerability to being "bounced" by MiGs.

Starting in 1967, a whole range of electronic countermeasures reduced the effectiveness of the SA-2. These included the USAF's ECM pods, the US Navy's internal deception jammers, and new radar homing and warming equipment such as the "Samsong." These systems were refined many times during the war. The original ALQ-71 pods, which required the aircraft using them to fly a rigid jamming formation, were supplanted by the ALQ-87 and, by 1972, the ALQ-101 and ALQ-119. Chaff also proved an effective countermeasure against SA-2s, and was dropped in quantity by flights of chaff bombers or carried in the airbrakes of US aircraft as a self-defence measure.

The Israelis relied on outmanoeuvring the SA-2 rather than using ECM against it. Once a pilot was aware of an SA-2 launch, either by radar homing and warning or visual sighting, it could almost always be evaded. The large size and the exhaust of the SA-2 make it easy to spot, especially in the clear skies and open spaces of the Middle East. But it was deadly when fired from camouflaged sites or through clouds. To evade an SA-2 Israeli pilots would normally turn into the missile and dive under it, a manoeuvre the missile could not follow. The Israeli success in countering the SA-2 without sophisticated ECM led to the overconfident belief that later Soviet SAMs could be defeated in the same way. The 1973 War showed that they were badly mistaken.

The most effective US countermeasures in Vietnam were the Wild Weasel electronic warfare aircraft and the Iron Hand SAM suppression flights. US aircraft were, for political reasons, prevented from attacking SAM sites for many months, even though their missiles were destroying US aircraft daily. But when the US finally did hit the unhardened North Vietnamese SAM sites they were often highly successful. For example, on August 11, 1967, a single flight of four Wild Weasel aircraft destroyed six SAM sites and damaged four others. In 1968 the Shrike anti-radiation missile (ARM, a missile that homes in on radiating radars) came into service. A Shrike would home on an SA-2 site in action, and the only way to avoid it was for the North Vietnamese to shut down their radars, provided they saw the Shrike coming. If they did shut down in time, any SA-2s then in flight would lose control and crash, and no more could be fired until the Wild Weasels had departed. This led to the Fan Song F of 1968, which permits optical target tracking, retaining the UHF command link.

SA-3 Goa surface-to-air missile

Year introduced	1961 (1964)
Length	6.1m
Diameter	0.6m 1st stage
	0.45m 2nd stage
Launch weight	946kg (950)
Mount	double (double or quad)
Guidance	radio command
Terminal homing	semi-active (in later versions only)
Control method	movable foreplane surfaces
Fuel	2-stage solid fuel
Maximum speed	Mach 3.5
Max range	29km (18.3)
Min range	6km (2.4)
Max altitude	12.2km (18.3)
Min altitude	1.5km
Warhead	60kg HE
Burst radius	12.5m, lethal against F-4 at low altitude
Rate of fire (per launch rail)	1 per min
Avoidance radius	16.7km

Data in parentheses are for SA-3b where it differs from the SA-3a.

Above SA-3s on their ZIL-157 transporters.

Below Quadruple SA-3 launcher. *(V.M. Martinova)*

The SA-3 was a necessary complement to the SA-2. Designed to hit aircraft at low and medium altitudes, the SA-3 is more manoeuvrable than the SA-2 but shares its vulnerability to countermeasures. Unlike the SA-2, the SA-3 is currently in production, and new SA-3 sites are still appearing in the Soviet Union.

SA-3 missiles are normally transported in pairs on a modified ZIL-157 or ZIL-131 truck and fired from a double, ground-mounted launcher. A more recent quad launcher is also used by the *PVO Strany*.

Combat usage

First introduced in the War of Attrition in the Middle East, the SA-3 scored some initial successes, but the Israelis soon found that countermeasures effective against the SA-2 also defeated the SA-3. The North Vietnamese first used the SA-3 in 1972, and their first kill was an F-4 Phantom that used up too much fuel evading a barrage of missiles. The SA-3 was the most numerous Arab SAM in the 1973 War but was overshadowed by the much more effective SA-6. Overall, it is more effective than the SA-2, and can engage targets below the SA-2's high minimum ceiling. The Soviets normally use SA-3s for airfield defence.

Estimated cone dead zone above launcher (km)

Minimum range is:	8.5	7.5	3	5	6
At this altitude:	12	10	5	3.75	1.5

Estimated low-altitude dead zone (km)

Minimum altitude is:	1.5	1.75	2.5	3.5	5
At this range:	6	10	20	30	32

Minimum arming distance is 50m.

Tactical employment

Basically a static, area-defence weapon, the SA-3 is used in a way similar to that of the SA-2. The future may see SA-3s being transferred from the Army to the Air Defence forces, as the system's launchers lack sufficient mobility.

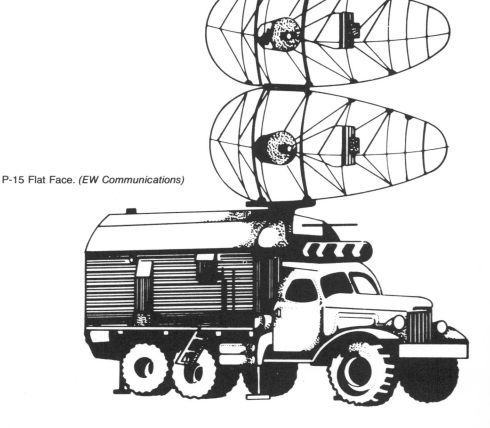

P-15 Flat Face. *(EW Communications)*

Squat Eye. *(EW Communications)*

Radar network and engagement sequence

Both the radar network and engagement sequence of the SA-3 are similar to those of the SA-2. The long-range early warning and target acquisition are handled by a P-15 Flat Face. In Egypt and other Arab nations Squat Eye radars are co-located with the Flat Face to provide low-altitude coverage. Both radars are usually hardened under ten feet of concrete. The Side Net radar provides height-finding information, as it does for the SA-2. The Low Blow radar organic to each SA-3 battery and its fire-control computer functions in the same way as the SA-2's Fan Song. Unlike Fan Song, however, Low Blow is optimised for low and medium-altitude targets, and is reported to be effective in picking targets out of ground clutter. A Low Blow can track six aircraft simultaneously and guide one or two missiles to each. For operating in an ECM-intense environment, late-model Low Blow radars are coupled with a 30km-range TV camera that is said to provide the fire-control system with the same data as the radar, enabling the SA-3 to remain in action even if the Low Blow is jammed or forced to shut down by the threat of anti-radiation missiles. Fire control is still in the command bunkers; SAMs never fire under "local control."

Engagement sequence begins with searching at ranges of 83–28km, alternating five seconds of radiating with ten seconds of dummy load. Tracking of a target is performed the same way until the target is less than 28km away, when it is engaged or tracked continuously. The SA-3 cannot fire if the target is closer than 5.5km.

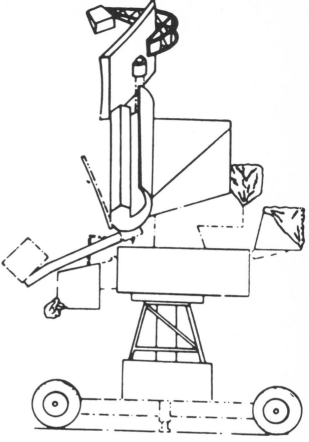

Low Blow. *(EW Communications)*

Countermeasures

Although the early USAF jamming pods and radar homing and warning equipment was not designed to counter the SA-3, the missile can be defeated by methods the same as those which defeat the SA-2.

SA-4 Ganef surface-to-air missile

Year introduced	1964 (1974)
Length	8.8m (8.3)
Diameter	0.9m
Wing span	2.3m
Tail span	2.6m
Launch weight	2,500kg
Mount	double, self-propelled
Guidance	radio command
Control method	movable forward wings
Fuel	four solid-fuel external boosters, ramjet sustaining engine
Max speed	Mach 2.5
Max range	70km
Min range	9.3km
Max altitude	27.4km (25)
Min altitude	1.1km
Warhead	HE
Rate of fire	1–2 launched simultaneously
Avoidance radius	7.4km

Data in parentheses are for the Ganef Mod 1 where it differs from the initial version.

SA-4 reload vehicle of the East German Army, using URAL-375 truck chassis. The SA-6 reload vehicle, using a ZIL-131 chassis, is similar. Unlike the SA-3 reload vehicle, these load alongside the launcher.

SA-4 launch vehicle

Weight	25,000kg
Length	7.8m
Width	3.2m
Max road speed	50km/h
Gradient	30°
Vertical obstacle	1m
Engine	500HP diesel, water-cooled
Track	2.66m
Track width	0.54m
Ground contact	5m
Road range	300km
Fuel capacity	500lit

The SA-4 is the only self-propelled high-altitude SAM system in service with any army, and the Soviet Army relies on it for high-altitude protection of its forward elements. The mobility of the SA-4 system comes from its tracked chassis (which is similar to that used with the SAU-152 and GMZ), the use of self-propelled Pat Hand radars for fire control on the AT-T tracked chassis, and the large-scale provision of URAL-375 reloading vehicles. An improved version, the Ganef Mod 1, was first seen in 1974. With a continous-taper nose section and a smaller (0.6m) diameter, this version is reported to have improved low-altitude capability. The SA-4 may have terminal radar homing.

Left Late-model SA-4 Ganefs in firing position.

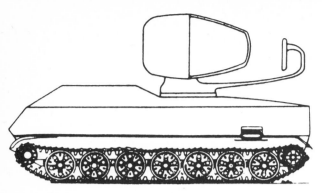

Long Track. *(EW Communications)*

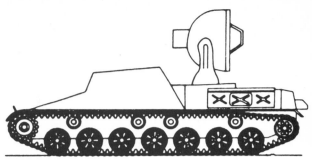

Pat Hand *(EW Communications)*

Thin Skin-B.
(EW Communications)

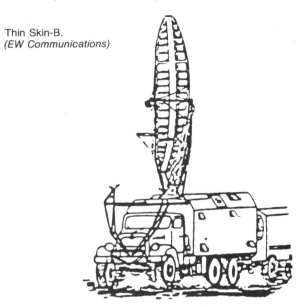

Combat usage

The SA-4 has apparently never seen action, although some were deployed to Egypt in 1970–72. From its size, it would appear to be unmanoeuvrable and it is likely to be vulnerable to jamming, as are most Soviet SAMs and fire-control radars of similar vintage.

Some sources credit the SA-4 with a secondary surface-to-surface role. The similar US-built Nike Hercules can be used against ground targets by computing the correct trajectory and then guiding the Nike to a predetermined point in the sky. Guidance is then stopped and the missile goes ballistic on to the target. The accuracy of this method is relatively high.

Estimated cone dead zone above launcher (km)

Minimum range is:	18.5	15	12	9.3	10	11	12
At this altitude:		18	15	10	7	5	2.5	1.1

Estimated low-altitude dead zone (km)

Minimum altitude is:	1.1	1.25	2.35	2.55	3	6
At this range:	12	20	30	40	50	60

Arming distance is 300m.

Tactical employment

The SA-4 is a mobile area-defence weapon used by army/front-level SAM brigades. The SA-4 batteries are positioned forward of the more static high-altitude SAM systems and provide continuous high-level coverage. The lead SA-4 battery would be 30km behind the forward edge of the battle area.

Radar network and engagement sequence

Long-range early warning is performed by a Long Track radar and an H-band Thin Skin height-finder. Pat Hand is used for battery target acquisition and fire control. Contrary to published reports, Pat Hand and Long Track are not mounted on the same chassis as the SA-4 launcher, but on AT-T tractors.

As the SA-4 uses a command guidance method similar to that of the SA-2, it is believed that the engagement sequence is generally similar.

Countermeasures

Opportunities to study the SA-4 and its radar net have been limited. It has not been used in combat, and there is no evidence that the US has acquired a specimen. However, the SA-4 Pat Hand system has been in service for a number of years and Western electronic intelligence has probably collected enough information about it for late-model ECM to be effective against it.

SA-6s on launch vehicle of the Egyptian Army. In travelling position the launcher is trained to the rear.

SA-6 Gainful surface-to-air missile

Year introduced	1967
Length	6.2m
Diameter	0.335m
Tail span	0.124m
Launch weight	550kg
Mount	triple, SP
Guidance	radio command
Terminal homing	semi-active radar
Control method	control surfaces
Fuel	integral 2-stage rocket/ramjet
Max speed	Mach 2.8
Max range	30m+
Min range	4km
Max altitude	18km
Effective altitude	11km
Min altitude	30m
Warhead	80kg (40kg of which is HE)
Burst radius	5m, lethal against F-4 at low altitude
Rate of fire	1–3 missiles, ripple-fired
Avoidance radius	24km or under 152m altitude

SA-6 launch vehicle

Length	6.8m
Height (travelling)	3.45m
Width	2.95m
Crew	3

Other data identical to those of ZSU-23-4 vehicle

The SA-6 weapon system consists, like the SA-4, of two vehicles: a missile launcher (with three launch rails) and a radar vehicle. Both are extremely mobile. Along with the ZSU-23-4, the SA-6 was the strongest part of the Arab air defences in the 1973 War. Today it gives the Soviet Army the ability to deploy an all-weather, all-target, highly mobile SAM system close to the front lines.

The SA-6 was the first Soviet SAM system designed to defeat low-flying fighter-bombers, filling a crucial gap in the Soviet SAM umbrella, which was previously directed against bombers at high and medium altitude. This was made possible by improvements in Soviet electronics that allowed the missile's radar to detect targets in spite of surface clutter and increased manoeuvrability; this was

SA-6s in travelling position on their launch vehicle, showing the prominent ramjet air intakes on the missiles.

the result of using transistors and printed circuits rather than the bulky vacuum tubes of earlier SAMs. The introduction of the SA-2 meant that aircraft could no longer fly over Soviet air defences. The introduction of the SA-6 meant they could no longer fly under them.

The chassis of both the SA-6 launch vehicle and the Straight Flush radar vehicle is similar to that of the ZSU-23-4, and shares its NBC protection, night vision equipment and lack of amphibious capability.

Combat usage

The SA-6 destroyed large numbers of Israeli aircraft during the first two hours of the 1973 War. To a large extent this was due to technological surprise. The Israelis, having developed effective countermeasures against the SA-2 and SA-3, were little worried by the SA-6 before the war. As a result they were surprised by the SA-6's manoeuvra-

bility, low-altitude capability and especially its continuous-wave (CW) terminal radar guidance. Once the surprise wore off, the effectiveness of the SA-6 declined. By the end of the war the SA-6 had proven to be hardly more accurate than earlier SAMs. The accuracy rate was about 1.8%, with 55 missiles fired for each kill scored. Although other sources have reported that SA-6 accuracy was somewhat above the 2% average for all Arab SAMs excluding SA-7s (a 2.3% figure – 840 SA-6s fired for 20 kills – has been proposed), the SA-6 is not a wonder weapon. The Soviet introduction of the SA-8 shows that they perceive limitations to the SA-6. A large measure of the SA-6's effectiveness in 1973 was not in the aircraft it shot down but in those it forced to fly lower, into the teeth of intense Arab AAA, especially the ZSU-23-4s. The mere threat of the SA-6s prevented the Israelis from striking targets that they would otherwise have hit hard.

The tactics the Israelis evolved to defeat the SA-6 Guideline were similar to those used against earlier SAMs. When an Israeli aircraft was alerted of an SA-6 launch, it turned towards the missile in a steep diving turn. The pilot opened his airbrakes, releasing two clouds of chaff that the SA-6's terminal semi-active radar homing guidance would usually lock on to. The Israeli aircraft then dived under the SA-6 launch. The SA-6 could not manoeuvre to intercept the steeply diving Israeli aircraft, which then either proceeded to its target or hit the SA-6 launcher from its steep dive, coming in from the launcher's cone blind spot.

Estimated cone dead zone over launcher (km)

Minimum range is:	17	15	11	7.5	5	(1–6)
At this altitude:	12	10	7.5	5	2.5	minimum

Estimated low-altitude dead zone (km)

Minimum altitude is:	minimum		1.75	2.5
At this range:	(1–6)		20	30

The close-in capabilities of the SA-6 are difficult to ascertain. While the minimum effective range may be as much as four to six kilometres, it has also been reported that the SA-6 can engage targets as close as one kilometre. It arms itself after flying as little as 30–50m, which would contribute to a short minimum range.

Tactical employment

Soviet Army SA-6s in divisional units provide low and medium-altitude area defence throughout the area of operations, relying on their mobility to keep pace with advancing units. By 1978 50% of the Soviet divisions in East Germany had received SA-6s (or SA-8s) as replacements for the S-60 57mm guns in the divisional anti-aircraft regiment. All Category I Soviet divisions will probably receive SA-6s or SA-8s in place of S-60s. How the SA-6s will be used by these units is not certain, but their mission will probably remain the same as when equipped with the S-60. By 1980 the SA-6 was almost exclusively an army-level weapon.

In Syrian service the SA-6s seem to have been used in a basically static role, positioned either in the forward air-defence belt that covered the Syrian advance into the Golan or held back around Damascus. The Egyptians seemed more aware of the missile's mobility, but only two batteries advanced into Sinai because the Egyptians lacked a mobile early-warning radar. Moreover, since the SA-6s were tied into the overall national air-defence plan, it would have taken eight hours to re-integrate them in their new positions. The majority of the SA-6s held their positions in the Egyptian air-defence belt along the Suez Canal.

SA-6s of the Egyptian Army in firing position.

Radar network and engagement sequence

In the Soviet Army SA-6 batteries receive their long-range search, early-warning, target-acquisition and altitude-discrimination data from the Long Track radar and their associated Thin Skin height-finders. The Arabs were not equipped with the Long Track in 1973. To compensate, the Egyptians assigned one Flat Face radar mounted on a ZIL-157 truck chassis – as used by SA-3 units – to each SA-6 battery. However, Flat Face is not a mobile radar system, and this hindered the advance of Egyptian SA-6s to cover the troops in Sinai.

The rest of the SA-6 system's radar network is self-contained in the self-propelled Straight Flush radar, which gets its name from the fact that it operates on five different radar bands. It can perform limited search, low-altitude detection and acquisition, target tracking and illumination, and missile radar command with secondary radar response for missile tracking. The same vehicle also contains the fire-control computers for the battery. Some Straight Flush vehicles have been observed with a TV camera similar to that used with the SA-3. The

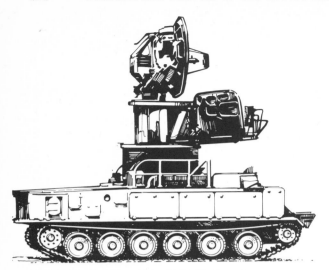

Straight Flush radar vehicle. *(V.M. Martinova)*

Straight Flush can also be linked to the SA-6 launch vehicle directly by a 10m-long cable.

When a target is detected by the Long Track/Thin Skin combination (or Flat Face in Egyptian service), target data such as range, bearing, altitude, speed and rate of change are passed by radio data link to the SA-6 battery's Straight Flush radar vehicle. The Straight Flush acquisition radar, operating in the 5–6GHz band, then takes over, locating the target more accurately and confirming that it is an enemy through IFF interrogation. This is done by the pulse-Doppler method (individual pulses of radar energy) rather than continuous-wave. The fire-control system computer processes this data. The Straight Flush's G/H-band target-tracking and illumination radar, operating in the 8–10GHz band, now illuminates the target with continuous-wave radar. Israeli aircraft radar homing and warning systems, which could tell when their aircraft were illuminated by pulse-Doppler radar (as used with the SA-2 and SA-3), could not detect illumination by continuous-wave radar. This contributed to the SA-6's technological surprise effect.

Once the Straight Flush is locked on the target aircraft it will follow its movements unless the aircraft's manoeuvres or ECM throw off the radar beam. As soon as the fire-control data are complete – about nine seconds from IFF interrogation – the missiles may be fired. Any number of missiles may be launched against a single target.

When launched, an SA-6 performs a characteristic "snake dance," weaving back and forth until the command receiver on the lower left tail fin picks up the continuous-wave command signals from the Straight Flush, while the seeker head in the missile's nose picks up reflected radar energy from the illuminated target. The missile then moves on a lead-pursuit course to intercept.

All this occurs while the missile is accelerating at 20 times the force of gravity. Its integral solid-fuel rocket engine pushes it through Mach 1.5 in the boost phase of its flight, at which point the tail cone drops off and the rocket propellant chamber, now empty, becomes the combustion chamber for the ramjet engine, which brings the speed up to a maximum of Mach 2.8. While in flight the missile transmits G/H-band beacon signals which report its position to the Straight Flush. The fire-control computer uses these signals to generate course corrections which are transmitted up by the Straight Flush. Once the SA-6 gets close to the illuminated target it will go into semi-active terminal homing, homing in on the radar reflection from the target, and the seeker head will continue its lead-pursuit course until the proximity fuze detonates.

Countermeasures

The initial effectiveness of the SA-6 was largely due to the inadequacy of Israeli countermeasures. Jamming and radar homing and warning equipment that was effective against the SA-2 and SA-3 did not work against the SA-6. According to some reports the SA-6 possessed a "home on jamming" function that actually made it *more* accurate against Israeli aircraft using older ECM equipment. Israeli radar homing and warning equipment did not pick up SA-6 launches or alert the pilot when the aircraft was illuminated. The Israelis were forced to rely on spotting the SA-6 launches visually, aided, according to some sources, by observation helicopters hovering over Israeli positions. Once an SA-6 was spotted, the target aircraft would turn sharply towards it and dive, passing under the climbing missile.

This manoeuvre was normally effective, but it often put the evading aircraft within range of light AAA, used up a great deal of fuel, and required the aircraft to be lightly loaded with bombs to perform such aerobatics. The Israelis also adopted the US tactic of putting chaff in their airbrakes. After the first week of the war the Israelis had learned enough about the SA-6 to modify their ECM equipment to jam it. With large numbers of ECM pods being airlifted from the US, SA-6 effectiveness plummeted. However, Soviet technicians in Egypt and Syria worked feverishly to modify the SA-6's engagement procedures; they may have had a least a partial answer to the new Israeli ECM equipment by the end of the war. Even pod-equipped aircraft started to suffer losses. Since then, as the US has had several SA-6s, launchers and Straight Flush radars to study, it is thought that effective countermeasures have been developed. Of course, the Soviets, knowing that the US has been working on these countermeasures, have probably modified their SA-6s to counter them. The "wizard war" continues, with both sides searching for countermeasures and ways to counter the countermeasures.

SA-7 Grail surface-to-air missile

SA-7 gunners of the East German Army.

Year introduced	1966 (1972)*
Length	1.3m
Diameter	0.07m
Launch weight	9.2kg
Mount	man-carried
Guidance	infra-red homing
Control method	canard fins
Fuel	2-stage solid-fuel
Max speed	Mach 1.5 (Mach 1.95)
Max range	3.5km (5.6km)
Min range	45m
Max altitude	1.5km (4.3km)
Min altitude	150m (23m)
Warhead	1.8kg, inc 0.37kg HE ("increased")
Soviet nickname	"Strella"
Soviet designation	9M32 (9M32M)

* Data in parentheses relate to later "Mod 1" version where it differs from earlier versions.

SA-7 launcher

Length	1.346m
Width	0.1m
Weight	9.2kg
Soviet designation	9P54 (9P54M)

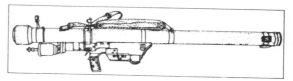

Drawing of SA-7 missile tube (with sights flipped up and carrying strap attached) on its gripstock launcher. The projecting assembly at the front of the gripstock is the thermal battery. The audible alarm which gives the launch tone is at the rear of the gripstock. (*Truppendienst*)

Early-model SA-7 round, removed from its launch tube. (*US Army*)

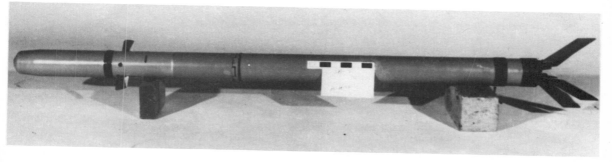

SA-9s mounted on a BRDM of the East German Army.

SA-9 Gaskin surface-to-air missile

Year introduced	1974
Length	1.37m
Diameter	0.11m
Span	0.34m
Launch weight	40–50kg
Mount	BRDM-2 scout car
Guidance	infra-red homing
Control method	cruciform canard fins
Fuel	solid fuel
Max speed	Mach 2
Max range	7km
Min range	0.56km
Effective range	3–8km
Max altitude	5km
Min altitude	20m
Effective altitude	0.9km
Warhead	5kg HE
Rate of fire	1 round every 5sec
Reloads on BRDM	4

The two models of the SA-7 and the larger SA-9 allow the smallest Soviet tactical units to have SAMs for self-defence. They differ from other Soviet SAMs in having infra-red homing; they home in on heat, normally that of the target aircraft's engine exhaust. Consequently, early SA-7s are usually only fired directly behind the target aircraft's tail, in its 6 o'clock "slot," which means that the aircraft must be going *away* from the gunner. Later versions of the SA-7 and the SA-9 are thought to have a larger angle of fire; they can be up to 30° off the aircraft's tail and still find their target. Sometimes the sunlight glinting off a helicopter's canopy may create enough of an infra-red heat signature for a SAM to home in on.

Because these missiles can only fire at aircraft heading away from them, they must overtake their targets. Thus only aircraft moving at less than 500kt are vulnerable to the early model of the SA-7, and it is most effective against those moving at 250kt or less. The SA-7's lead sulphide seeker head, unlike those of more sophisticated heat-seeking missiles, is uncooled and thus easily saturated, especially as it does not attempt to filter out spurious heat sources. Its primitive seeker head means that if the SA-7 is pointed within at least 20° of the sun, it will home in on that rather than its target. Reportedly, if the missile is fired at less than a 20–30° elevation, the seeker head will pick up geothermal heat and home in on that, which makes it almost impossible to hit low-flying aircraft, especially helicopters flying nap-of-the-earth. This seeker head also makes the SA-7 vulnerable to countermeasures.

The "Mod 1" vesion of the SA-7, first seen in the mid-1970s, has a more sophisticated guidance system, including a filter for the seeker head. It also has longer range and a higher maximum altitude: a Hawker Hunter fighter-bomber of the Oman Air Force was hit while flying at 3,422.5m (11,500ft). Its minimum range is still 45m, as with the earlier version. The Polish Army has displayed an IFF interrogator for use with this model of the SA-7; it is mounted on the gunner's helmet. An SA-7 replacement is reportedly under development. This new weapon has laser guidance and will enter service soon.

The small size and lack of sophistication of the SA-7,

SA-9 in flight after launch from a BRDM mount. The missile appears similar to the AA-8 Aphid air-to-air missile.

while making it man-portable, meant that only salvo firing gave worthwhile results. The quad-mounted SA-9 system was an answer to this. Mounted on top of a BRDM-2 scout car, the SA-9 is a relatively large, single-stage missile that appears similar to the AA-8 Aphid air-to-air missile.

The SA-9 has greater range and a larger warhead, and is more manoeuvrable than the SA-7.

Combat usage

The SA-7 was used in the 1967 Middle East war, and was deployed into Southeast Asia in 1969, being introduced into action in April 1972. Initially its accuracy was very high, a 33% accuracy rate being achieved against US gunship and transport helicopters. The SA-7 also shot down several slow-moving aircraft such as O-2Es, A-1s and C-130s, which were then forced to operate above 1,830m (6,000ft). After this step was taken and the surprise wore off, SA-7 effectiveness was reduced. The low overall accuracy of the SA-7 is thought to have been due to its instability; most of those launched were observed to porpoise and miss.

In the 1973 Middle East war the Arabs made extensive use of SA-7s; US Department of Defence officials have stated that 5,000 were launched. Other sources estimate 4,356 launched from 1,468 launchers. The results were surely disappointing: two Israeli aircraft were definitely destroyed, four were "possibles," 28 suffered tailplane damage and were out of action for a few hours, and a few suffered engine damage and were grounded for a few days. These poor results were due to the SA-7's inadequate warhead, susceptibility to countermeasures, tail-chase operation and, undoubtedly, the low level of training of the men who used it.

In 1975 the SA-7 was used widely by the North Vietnamese in their conquest of South Vietnam. According to a CIA operative on the scene, "the effect on the South Vietnamese Air Force's morale was devastating, which in turn lowered the morale of the ground troops and contributed to the rapid collapse of resistance." South Vietnamese strike aircraft were forced to stay above 3,053m (10,000ft), and as the South Vietnamese were trained in the low and slow attacks the US had used before the introduction of the SA-7, they found themselves performing medium-altitude missions for which they were not trained in aircraft that were not designed for such operations. Their effectiveness plummeted. Thus the SA-7 successfully performed the deterrent role that is the key to ground-based air defence. Even a poor air defence can be effective when it minimises the accuracy of air strikes on the advancing columns. The number of aircraft shot down did not matter – they were all eventually captured on the ground.

The SA-7's simplicity makes it very attractive to guerillas and insurgents throughout the world. Palestinians in Lebanon and Jordan, Polisario rebels in Morocco and Mauritania, and groups in Iraq, Angola, Mozambique,

Rhodesia, the Philippines and Oman have used it. Americans who have used captured SA-7s say that one day's training can produce an effective gunner. Whatever its failings, the SA-7 has rendered the whole class of low-technology, low-performance, low-cost, high-payload counter-insurgency (COIN) aircraft almost obsolete. The SA-7 has given the guerilla an effective plane-killing capability for the first time.

The SA-9 has never seen action, but it is believed that its greater sophistication would make it more accurate than the SA-7. Iraqi SA-9s may have been used in 1980.

SA-7 tactical employment

The SA-7 is used as a self-defence weapon by each Soviet motorised rifle platoon. In motorised rifle platoons the gunner stands up in his APC hatch, prepared to engage enemy aircraft. When attacking dismounted, the SA-7 gunners advance 20–30m behind the company skirmish line with 15–20m between launchers. On the defensive an SA-7 is emplaced in each platoon strongpoint. Egyptian SA-7 tactics in the 1973 War were more centralised, employing groups of three gunners who normally fired in a salvo. Both the Soviets and Egyptians use triple and quadruple SA-7 launchers mounted on vehicles.

SA-9 tactical employment

A platoon of four quadruple SA-9 launchers complements the four ZSU-23-4s of each regimental anti-aircraft battery. During the advance to contact or the exploitation phase of a battle the SA-9s stay near regimental HQ. When the regiment moves into the attack, SA-9s take up overwatch positions one to three kilometres behind the line of contact, behind the close-support ZSU-23-4s. They will be positioned either in a "linear" or "cluster" formation, similar to the ZSU-23-4s. Special emphasis is placed on protecting the SA-9 launchers from missile-firing helicopters. When the regiment is on the defensive the SA-9s will be sited around regimental HQ or second-echelon battalions.

Radar network and engagement sequence

The SA-9 can be connected with divisional air-defence radars through radio, and is often connected by radio with the Gun Dish radars of ZSU-23-4s when on the defensive.

The SA-7 gunner must identify and acquire his target visually, although his platoon will receive air-defence alerts over the radio. The gunner first loads the SA-7 missile in its disposable fibreglass tube onto the launcher gripstock. He then pulls the trigger to energise the uncooled seeker head, a sealed optical tracker containing a folded reflective optical system sensitive to heat. It also supposedly functions as a space-stabilised gyroscope,

which may be the reason for the SA-7's reported lack of stability. When the seeker head is energised and uncaged, ready to seek out a target, a red light on the launcher lights up. The gunner then points the launcher at the target. When the infra-red detector cells in the seeker head detect heat energy reflecting off them, a green light comes on and the gunner will fire. The first stage fires in the launch tube, forcing the second stage out, and then falls away at a safe distance from the gunner. The tail fins and canards then unfold, and the missile coasts until it is a safe distance from the gunner. At this point the second-stage sustainer engine cuts in and accelerates the SA-7 to its maximum speed. The seeker head determines the angle of the heat it is reflecting and its guidance system tries to resolve the difference between the direction the seeker head is pointing and the missile's line of flight by moving the missile's variable-incidence wings. Throughout its flight the missile is spinning anti-clockwise for stability. The SA-7 then follows the target in a lag-pursuit course. If it has not hit its target in 15sec it will self-destruct.

The SA-9's engagement sequence is believed to be similar.

Countermeasures

The early SA-7 was very susceptible to countermeasures, and could easily be decoyed on to flares ejected by the target aircraft. Later versions are reported to have a filter in the seeker head to reduce spurious emissions, and it can be set to home in on the second hottest heat source it acquires, rather than the hottest. To defeat this counter-countermeasure, however, aircraft drop flares in salvos of different heat intensities so that, regardless of how the SA-7's seeker head is set, it will still have a flare to home on to. This can be countered to an extent by salvo firing of missiles set for different intensities, and it is believed that this method is usually used with the SA-9.

Flares are not the only countermeasure effective against these missiles. US Army helicopters have had heat suppressors installed around their exhausts, and A-4 Skyhawks of the Israeli Air Force now sport long, heat-hiding tail pipes. These make it more difficult for the SA-7 to acquire a target. Infra-red decoy pods, such as the US ALQ-123 caesium lamp, can also defeat heat-seeking missiles by letting them lock on to their heat source and then jamming the missile's seeker head. The SA-7 is reportedly easy to outmanoeuvre and, like many heat-seekers, it can be decoyed by a climb into the sun followed by a quick turn away, which causes the missile to aim for the sun.

SA-8 Gecko surface-to-air missile

SA-8 launch vehicles on parade in Moscow, November 1977. The Land Roll's search radar and TV tracker are folded back behind the turret, but the tracking radar and the two command-link horns are visible on the turret front.

Year introduced	1974
Length	3.2m
Diameter	0.21m
Tail span	0.6m
Launch weight	180–200kg
Mount	quad, self-propelled
Guidance	radio command
Terminal homing	semi-active radar or infra-red.
Control method	canard fins and tail surfaces
Fuel	dual-thrust solid fuel
Max speed	Mach 2
Max range	12–15km
Min range	1.6–3km
Max altitude	12km
Min altitude	45m
Warhead	30–40kg HE
Burst radius	5m, lethal against F-4 at low altitude
Rate of fire	two missiles simultaneously
Missiles on mount	4
Avoidance radius	11.1km or under 152m altitude

A quadruple SA-8 launcher and its multi-purpose Land Roll radar mounted on a unique six-wheeled amphibious vehicle form a complete and independent integral SAM system, designated a ZRK (*Zentniy Raketniy Komplex*, missile system) by the Soviets. The chassis features full NBC protection, a central tyre pressure regulation system and a rear-mounted engine. It carries four SA-8s.

Combat usage

The SA-8 has never seen action. It appears to be a highly manoeuvrable missile, and possesses the acceleration needed to engage manoeuvring high-performance fighter-bombers at low altitude. An SA-8 ZRK can engage two separate targets with two missiles each.

SA-8 missiles on their launch vehicle, with the Land Roll scanner folded in travelling position. *(US Army)*

SA-8 launch vehicle on its way to a parade, showing the folded Land Roll Scanner and the water jets in the stern. Recently SA-8 vehicles have been seen with six missiles in launch boxes, rather than four on rails as in the vehicles illustrated.

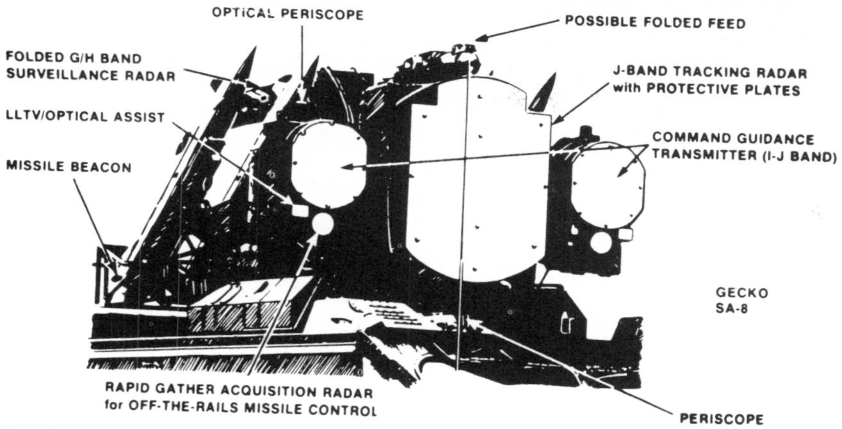

The elements of the Land Roll radar. *(EW Communications)*

Labels on diagram:
OPTICAL PERISCOPE
POSSIBLE FOLDED FEED
FOLDED G/H BAND SURVEILLANCE RADAR
J-BAND TRACKING RADAR with PROTECTIVE PLATES
LLTV/OPTICAL ASSIST
COMMAND GUIDANCE TRANSMITTER (I-J BAND)
MISSILE BEACON
GECKO SA-8
RAPID GATHER ACQUISITION RADAR for OFF-THE-RAILS MISSILE CONTROL
PERISCOPE

Tactical employment

The SA-8, along with the SA-6, is replacing the S-60 in many Soviet divisional anti-aircraft regiments, and it may even be attached down to regimental level. It is believed that BMP-equipped motorised rifle regiments operating in the exploitation role have an SA-8 battery, but it is not known whether this is organic to the regiment or attached down from division. The boat-like hull of the SA-8 launch vehicle shows that it is designed to support river crossings and can swim rivers with advancing BMPs, rather than having to wait to be ferried across. The characteristics of missile, radar and launcher indicate that the SA-8 system is intended to fill the gap between point and area-defence weapons in the fluid situations which the Soviets expect in modern combat.

SA-8 launch vehicle

Type ZIL-167E4 **Length** 9.1m **Width** 2.9m **Height** 4.1m (scanner retracted) **Maximum speed** 80km/h **Maximum water speed** 10–12km/h **Range** 650km **Engine** Diesel **Crew** 4 **Night vision** TVN-2 system **Water propulsion** twin hydrojets

Radar network and engagement sequence

Early warning and long-range target acquisition is passed from division-level radars. The SA-8's Land Roll radar comprises a single turret mount including a mast-mounted search radar which operates in the 4–8GHz band with a 30km range. In front of the turret is the tracking radar with a 20–25km range, operating in the 13–15GHz band. On the turret sides are the twin antennae of the I-band command-link horns which transmit instructions to the missile in flight. An improved, low-light version of the TV tracker used with the SA-3 is mounted on top of the turret. The Land Roll radar is conical-scan rather than continuous-wave, making it

more efficient (and cheaper) and enhancing its low-altitude performance.

When the Land Roll's surveillance radar acquires the target and IFF interrogation shows it to be hostile, the vehicle commander selects the target to be attacked on a panoramic display of radar information and automatically or manually designates the target to the weapons controller or the tracking radar. The whole turret assembly then tracks the target and, when the fire-control system has data, two missiles are usually launched. Command guidance is then similar to that used by the SA-2 and SA-3. The SA-8 probably has terminal homing, either semi-active radar (like the SA-6) or infra-red (like the SA-7/9).

The SA-8/Land Roll system is believed to be similar to the SA-N-4/Pop Group naval SAM system and may have been developed from it.

SA-10 surface-to-air missile

Year introduced	1978
Length	7m
Diameter	0.45m
Launch weight	1,500kg
Mount	static
Guidance	active radar homing
Terminal homing	radar
Fuel	1-stage solid fuel
Max speed	Mach 6
Max range	64km
Max altitude	30km
Min altitude	0.3km
(All figures approximate)	

The SA-10 presages a new generation of Soviet SAMs. Very fast, long-ranged, capable of extremely high acceleration (100g) and manoeuvrable, the SA-10 is a threat to cruise missiles and low-flying strike aircraft such as the F-111, Tornado and B-52. It uses continuous-wave pulse-Doppler radar guidance. Deployment with the National Air Defence Forces started along the Baltic Coast in 1978 and will be complete by 1986. It is believed that the Army will receive the SA-10 in the near future. When it does, the missile may be on a self-propelled mount. It is possible that the SA-10 may also be able to intercept surface-to-surface missiles such as the Lance.

SA-11 surface-to-air missile

Mount	tracked vehicle
Guidance	radar
Max speed	Mach 3
Max range	25km
Max altitude	15km
Min altitude	25m

Little is known of the SA-11. Reportedly similar to the SA-6, it is carried in a triple or quadruple launcher on a tracked vehicle and is used alongside SA-6s, one SA-11 operating with each SA-6 battery. The SA-11 is said to have radar guidance – the precise type is unknown – and is capable of 23g acceleration. It was reported to be in service in 1978. One SA-11 launcher is part of many divisional SA-6 batteries, usually as the fifth launcher. The SA-11 has on-launch-vehicle radar.

Another and quite different weapon has also been referred to as the SA-X-11. This is a high-altitude SA-2 type that may be intended to replace the earlier missile.

Foreign use of Soviet SAMs

Bulgaria: Air Defence uses two battalions of SA-2, eight battalions of SA-3. The Army uses the SA-6 and SA-7.

China: Produces and employs the SA-2 in large numbers; designated CSS-1.

Cuba: Air Defence has 24 "battalions," including 144 SA-2 launchers, the remainder being equipped with SA-3s. The Army uses SA-7s and may have received SA-6s and SA-9s in 1978–79.

Czechoslovakia: Air Defence has 28 battalions of SA-2 and SA-3, including 20 SA-2 sites. The Army uses SA-4, SA-6, SA-7 and SA-9.

Egypt: The Egyptian SAM defence is no longer as dense or effective as it was in 1973. Currently it consists of 25–30 six-launcher SA-2 batteries and at least 14 four- or six-launcher SA-3 batteries. The Army has a minimum of 48–60 and a maximum of about 140 SA-6 launchers, plus SA-7s.

East Germany: Air Defence has two brigades with a total of 22 SA-2 and four SA-3 batteries. The Army employs SA-4, SA-6, SA-7 and SA-9 SAMs.

Hungary: Air Defence uses 18 SA-2 batteries. The Army has two SA-2 battalions plus SA-6s, SA-7s and SA-9s.

India: Has 120 SA-2 launchers at 20 sites, and also uses SA-3s.

Iraq: Uses SA-2, SA-3, SA-6 (25 launchers) and SA-7 SAMs. SA-9s were reportedly supplied in 1978.

North Korea: 250 SA-2s in 20 battalions, plus some SA-3s. SA-7s used by the Army. The North Koreans have an air-defence belt along the DMZ that can cover an advance into the south. It is orientated to provide offensive cover of advancing troops rather than to act as a defensive barrier.

Libya: 62 SA-2, SA-3 and SA-6 launchers organised in eight batteries are emplaced at the Oka Ben Nafi air base. SA-7s and SA-9s are also used by the Army. Libya has been the source of many of the SA-7s used by guerillas.

Peru: Has received a number of SA-3s, but is reported to be dissatisfied with them.

Poland: Air Defence includes 40 SA-2 batteries and 12 battalions of SA-3s. Army has SA-6, SA-7 and SA-9.

Romania: Air Defence has 108 SA-2 launchers at 18 sites. The Army uses the SA-7.

Syria: It is believed that the Soviets have replaced the severe losses of 1973. SA-2 and SA-3 strength is at approximately 1973 levels: eight SA-2 batteries with six launchers each and 17 SA-3 batteries with four or six launchers each. SA-6 battery strength has increased from ten in 1973 to 14 today. They are organised on the Soviet rather than the Egyptian model. The Army uses SA-7s and SA-9s.

Vietnam: It is unknown how much of Vietnam's dense air-defence umbrella was rebuilt after the 1972 US raids, but it is believed that it is now at least as strong as it was then. 20 SA-2 regiments with 18 launchers each are deployed, along with substantial numbers of SA-3, SA-6 and SA-7.

Afghanistan: Has two SA-2 battalions.

Albania: Has the CSS-1.

Mongolia: Fields one SA-2 battery and some SA-7s.

Ethiopia: Received SA-3s and SA-7s.

Mozambique: Received 24 SA-6s, plus SA-7s.

Somalia: Used SA-2s, SA-3s and SA-7s during its friendship with the USSR. Probably few if any are operational.

Algeria: Uses SA-2, SA-9 and SA-7.

Yugoslavia: Has eight SA-2 batteries plus large numbers of SA-3 and SA-7, SA-6 and SA-9.

Angola, **Uganda**, **Yemen PDR** and **Kuwait** all use the SA-7, as do rebels in Morocco, Mauretania, Chad, Oman, the Philippines and Iraq, plus the PLO.

US use of Soviet air-defence weapons

The US armed forces are among the lesser known but most significant users of Soviet air-defence weaponry. While the US inventory of these weapons is small, they are studied and used in training, especially in the "Red Flag" exercises at Nellis Air Force Base, Nevada; this contributes to the development of weapons and tactics to defeat them. The protection of the A-10 ground-attack aircraft was tested by firing a Soviet 23mm cannon at a full-size mock-up. The shells bounced off the titanium armour.

It is an open secret that most of these weapons have been acquired from Israel, although many of the older systems were captured in Southeast Asia. Indonesia has quietly disposed of some of its Soviet-built arsenal, and US military personnel in Iran are known to have examined the ZSU-23-4s in use there.

Among the types of Soviet air-defence weapons possessed by the US are the ZPU-4, the ZU-23 (captured in Southeast Asia and treated mainly as trophies or museum pieces), ZSU-57-2 (one was seen at Nellis AFB in 1978), the S-60 (believed to be from Southeast Asia, possibly from Israel), and a number of ZSU-23-4s, also probably from Israel. According to reliable sources, the US Air Force has purchased no fewer than 60 ZSU-23-4s at the bargain price of $5,000 each. The seller was not named, but is believed to have been Iran or Egypt. It is probable that the US has other Soviet air-defence weapons as well.

The US obtained SA-2s from Israel as early as the late 1960s, and this may have contributed to the increasing effectiveness of countermeasures against them in the later stages of the Vietnam War. These may have been supplemented by later acquisitions. At least one working SA-3 launcher is reported at Nellis AFB, where it has been used in the testing of the cruise missile. SA-7s are also used for training.

Less is known about Soviet air-defence radars in US hands. The most spectacular acquisition was a P-12 Spoon Rest early-warning radar, heli-lifted from the Egyptian island of Ras Gahrib after being captured by Israeli commandos on December 26, 1969. After thorough examination by the Israelis it went to the US. The US SA-2 and SA-3 sites doubtless have their Fan Song and Low Blow radars.

Soviet Army air-defence radars

Early-warning and target-acquisition radars

P-15 Flat Face

Power: 400–500kW; frequency: C-band; maximum range: 250km; emplacement time: 10min; vertical beamwidth: 5°; horizontal beamwidth: 2°; accuracy: 90–100m in range, 0.5° in angle; antenna: two elliptical parabolic reflectors. Van-mounted; two allocated per tank or motorised rifle division, four to each early-warning battalion of each air-defence brigade. Also used by National Air Defence Forces.

P-15M Squint Eye

Performance: as **Flat Face**, but with improved low-altitude capability. Antenna mounted on 30m mast.

P-12 Spoon Rest

Power: 350kW; frequency: A-band, 147–167MHz; maximum range: 270km; vertical beamwidth: 2.5°; horizontal beamwidth: 1°. Mounted in two vans; used by the early-warning battalions of air-defence brigades and by the National Air Defence Forces.

Long Track

Frequency: E-band, 2,600MHz: maximum range: over 100km. AT-T-mounted; one used by each SA-4, SA-6 or SA-8 brigade/regiment; one per SA-4 battalion.

Thin Skin A and B

Frequency: H-band. Truck or trailer-mounted. Height-finding radar with low-altitude capabilities, used in conjunction with Long Track. One used by each SA-4 or SA-6 brigade/regiment headquarters.

Side Net

Frequency: 2,560–2,710MHz; maximum range: 176km. Height-finding radar used with Spoon Rest and Flat Face. Mounted on the side of a van.

AAA fire-control radars

Gun Dish

Power: 100–135kW; frequency: J-band; maximum range: 20km. Mounted on each ZSU-23-4.

SON-9A Fire Can

Power: 300kW; frequency: E-band, 2,700–2,900MHz; maximum range: 90km for search, 80km for target acquisition, 35km for tracking; accuracy: 12–15m in range, 2m in elevation; pulsewidth: 0.3–0.8 microsec; PRF: 1,840–1,900pps. Uses parabolic dish antenna. Trailer-mounted; one is organic to each S-60 battery. Being replaced by Flap Wheel.

Flap Wheel

Frequency: I/J-band, 9,130–9,850MHz. Truck-mounted, it also acts as a predictor. Organic to S-60 batteries, also used by the 130mm AA gun.

SAM fire-control and command-guidance radars

Fan Song A/B

Power: 600kW; frequency: E/F-band, 2,965–2,990MHz for the A model, 3,025–3,050MHz for the B model; maximum range: 60–120km; vertical beamwidth: approx 10°;

horizontal beamwidth: approx 2°. Two orthogonal antennae. Mounted on a trailer or in a bunker. Has a track-while-scan function and uses two flapping beams, one from each antenna. One used per SA-2 battery.

Fan Song D/F

Power: 1.5MW; frequency: C-band, 4,910–4,990, 5,010–5,090MHz; vertical beamwidth: approx 7.5°; horizontal beamwidth: approx 1.5°. Has lobe-on-receive-only function to minimise vulnerability to sidelobe jamming. F model has a visual observer's position on top of the mount, but is otherwise the same as earlier versions. E version has tract-while-scan function.

Low Blow

Power: 250kW; frequency: I-band, 9,000–9,460MHz; vertical beamwidth: 12°; horizontal beamwidth: 1.5°; maximum range: 45–80km, depending upon conditions, target size and altitude; pulse repetition rate: 1,750–3,500 pps; pulsewidth: 0.25–0.5 microsec. Effective in surface clutter. Allocated one per SA-3 battery. Has a pair of antennae mounted orthogonally on a trailer, with control in van or bunker.

Pat Hand

Frequency: H-band, 6–8GHz. Mounted on AT-T tractor. One per SA-4 battery.

Straight Flush

Frequency: uses D-band for illumination, and G, H, and I/J bands for acquisition and missile guidance; maximum range: 60–90km, depending on conditions, target altitude and size. Mounted on chassis of SA-6 launch vehicle; one allocated per SA-6 battery.

Land Roll

Frequency: G/H, I/J-bands, 14,200–14,800MHz; maximum range: 30km surveillance, 20–25km target tracking; vertical beamwidth: 1°; horizontal beamwidth: 3°. One mounted on each SA-8 launch vehicle.

Soviet Army air-defence radar jamming

Ground-based radar jammers are the least known Soviet air-defence weapons. They include the Brick-series jammers, the trailer-mounted Mound Brick, Box Brick and Tub Brick, and the truck-mounted Cheese Brick, High Brick and Long Brick.

Other ground-based jammers, probably of the same type, are used by the National Air Defence Forces. While Soviet jammers are also used against ground radars and radios, in the air-defence role they supplement AAA and

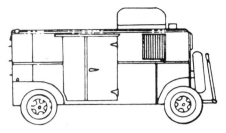

Tub Brick. *(EW Communications)*

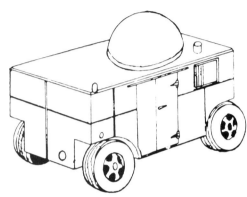

Mound Brick. *(EW Communications)*

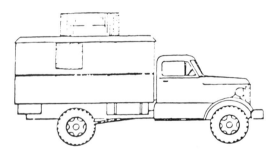

Cheese Brick. *(EW Communications)*

SAMs. The Soviets can jam the sophisticated bombing and navigation radar system of the A-7 Corsair II strike aircraft. Parts of the F-111's bombing and navigation system are also vulnerable to jamming, and the Soviets undoubtedly intend to force the F-111s to fly higher by jamming their terrain-following radar. The North Vietnamese, lacking jammers, picked off several F-111s penetrating down valleys by firing chaff in mortar shells. This jammed the F-111s' terrain-following radar, forcing the aircraft into a 3g pull-up and into a waiting anti-aircraft ambush. It is likely that the Soviets will use their jammers in a similar way. Presumably other Western tactical aircraft are also vulnerable to these jammers. Air-defence jammers are organic to front and army-level radio-electronic combat battalions.

Chapter Thirteen

Reconnaissance vehicles

"Under modern conditions the importance of reconnaissance continues to increase. At the present time each unit commander is obliged always to have at his disposal complete and reliable data on the enemy, with such data being obtained not only from higher headquarters, but through the use of his own resources."

COL M. TRUSHCHENKO

The Soviet concept of reconnaissance and intelligence – *razvodka* – is broad, including all information-gathering activities. Military intelligence work, espionage, naval reconnaissance, strategic and tactical air reconnaissance, electronic reconnaissance and intelligence, army long-range reconnaissance patrols, troop reconnaissance and combat reconnaissance patrols are complementary and interlocking ways of providing the information needed by Soviet commanders at all levels, especially in a mobile battle. Reconnaissance – of the enemy, the terrain and other conditions – is required for successful combat operations.

Military intelligence work and espionage have information inputs throughout the chain of command, from prisoner interrogation at company level to the KGB and GRU reporting to the highest levels of the Soviet national command authority. Naval reconnaissance will only indirectly affect army operations, unlike air reconnaissance. High-speed, high-altitude reconnaissance aircraft will be used on the directions of a front commander. The MiG-25 Foxbat (the latest model of which, the Foxbat-D, mounts a Sidekick side-looking airborne radar as well as electronic intelligence equipment, cameras and sensors) can overfly any point in Europe from bases in East Germany and the European USSR. A Foxbat unit is part of each front's tactical air army, as is a reconnaissance air regiment, whose aircraft – normally MiG-21 Fishbeds and Su-7, Su-17 and Su-22 Fitter types, but now increasingly MiG-23 and MiG-27 Floggers – can operate up to 450km behind the front. Using cameras, infra-red sensors and ELINT equipment, these aircraft normally operate in pairs at low altitude. Unlike most Western tactical reconnaissance aircraft, they are usually armed or escorted by fighter-bombers to attack any targets of opportunity, especially nuclear weapons or their delivery systems. Front headquarters can have the information obtained from a priority air reconnaissance mission within two hours. Helicopter reconnaissance is not stressed.

Electronic reconnaissance can ascertain unit locations and identity by the type of electronic activity monitored. Detection of a cluster of AFV radios, for example, may indicate an armoured unit HQ. The wide range of Soviet electronic equipment can detect artillery radars within 25km of the front line, VHF radio transmissions at up to 40km and HF transmissions at even greater ranges. Electronic intelligence aircraft give a more complete picture of the enemy electronic order of battle while standing off at long range, allowing the Soviets to destroy or avoid the emitters or prepare their countermeasures against them. Acoustic, disturbance, electromagnetic and seismic sensors are reportedly also used, but are seldom mentioned in Soviet sources.

Operating together, the different Soviet information-gathering means can in theory provide a flow of accurate, timely information. The use of complementary and overlapping reconnaissance systems reduces the possibility of enemy deception and provides a back-up in case one reconnaissance means overlooks something of importance. However, the emphasis on anti-deception measures and redundant information may lead to an unwillingness to act on information without confirmation. For all the sophistication of information-gathering means, much is accessible only to the eyes of a soldier on the ground. Because of this, the Soviet Army puts its emphasis on trained ground-based reconnaissance units.

Long-range reconnaissance patrols

Long-range reconnaissance patrols (LRRPs) operate 50–350km forward of the main body. Motorised LRRPs are normally drawn from the long-range reconnaissance companies of divisional reconnaissance battalions, often from second-echelon divisions. Using BRDM and

BRDM-rkh scout cars, these LRRPs penetrate into the enemy rear by infiltration. The furthest-ranging LRRPs are composed of paratroops or of personnel from divisional, army or front long-range reconnaissance companies, and are often inserted by helicopter or parachute.

LRRPs range from company strength to a five-man airborne team. Lightly armed, they seek to avoid action unless in furtherance of their information-gathering mission or to destroy a high-priority target. Patrols may evade combat by dispersing and regrouping or concealment. LRRP long-range radios transmit reports in speeded-up "bursts" at predesignated times to avoid enemy ELINT.

Target acquisition of enemy nuclear weapons and delivery systems is the highest-priority LRRP mission, since well-camouflaged firing sites are difficult to locate from the air. Soviet aircraft, rockets or artillery will then be used to destroy them, though in some cases the LRRP may attack the target themselves, relying on the element of surprise. LRRPs may also attack headquarters or communications facilities, or stage raids and ambushes to capture prisoners or equipment. They may also link up with airborne *desants*, secret agents or GRU intelligence troops to increase their striking power and report back information. Unlike a *reydy*, however, reconnaissance remains their primary mission.

Long-range reconnaissance companies are élite units, requiring great flexibility from their commanders. The enlisted men receive much better and more thorough training and conditioning than the average soldier; unarmed combat, wilderness survival and resistance to interrogation are all taught. LRRP assault rifles and pistols are often equipped with silencers and flash-suppressors, and they carry additional camouflage equipment and engineering tools for constructing patrol hiding places.

Troop reconnaissance

Troop reconnaissance is tactical, combat reconnaissance. An army commander will occasionally form a "reconnaissance detachment" of a reinforced battalion to operate forward of the advance combat elements of a first-echelon division but behind the patrols of the division's reconnaissance battalion. These patrols are up to a day's march – 35–50km – in front of the division. Each reconnaissance battalion will send out six to eight patrols of two to four scout cars (often two pairs) and motorcyclists, often supported by one or two BMP-Rs or PT-76s. Patrols are spread throughout the divisional sector, along the main axes of advance, on parallel routes and along the flanks, especially if a meeting engagement is expected to develop, as the Soviets depend on receiving current information

from their patrols to enable them to outmanoeuvre the enemy.

Patrols will often move in pairs of vehicles, alternating rapid movement between cover with overwatching and reporting on enemy forces, terrain, road conditions and NBC contamination. Engineer squads are often attached to reconnoitre specialised objectives and remove hastily prepared obstacles along the patrol's route. BRDM-rkhs discover and mark contaminated areas. The divisional reconnaissance battalion is often reinforced by a motorised rifle company with attached tanks.

Each regiment's reconnaissance company operates in a similar way in the regimental sector, half a day's march ahead of the regiment's main body. In addition, a patrol is often the point detachment for the regiment's leading battalion(s).

On the defensive, reconnaissance patrols stay forward of the defensive zone to report the main enemy axes of advance, but they do not attempt to engage the enemy and will withdraw instead. Screening and security duties are performed by motorised rifle or tank units.

The distances between Soviet troop reconnaissance patrols and their main bodies give commanders a cushion of reaction time, enabling the Soviets to react to reports while continuing the advance. Nor will troop reconnaissance be allowed to preclude surprise when other information-gathering means can be used, especially in the opening hours of an offensive.

Reconnaissance tactics

Unlike their Western counterparts, Soviet reconnaissance units are purely for scouting. They do not have a primary screening and security mission. NATO reconnaissance units tend to follow late-World War Two patterns: strong, often combined-arms forces, able to fight on their own for information. This is a completely different concept from Soviet reconnaissance tactics, which are reflected in their reconnaissance vehicles: light and mobile, designed to cover the long distances of their far-ranging patrols quickly and to depend on speed and concealment for protection.

When a Soviet troop reconnaissance patrol encounters the enemy it will return fire and then attempt to break contact, aided by the fire of overwatching vehicles. It will retire to the nearest cover and report the encounter by visual signal (small patrols will try and maintain visual contact with their parent units), radio or courier. The patrol will then seek to infiltrate around the enemy forces and resume its mission. It will only engage the enemy if they also appear to be a reconnaissance patrol, or if the Soviets have the advantage. If required, ambushes and "silent" or "combat" raids will be made to take prisoners.

Soviet troop reconnaissance patrol tactics are aggressive, even if they do not normally accomplish their mission by battle. Once the enemy is encountered, the Soviets will not simply observe from cover, but press on to their objectives or, if required, maintain observation of an enemy unit. Observation posts will be established during reconnaissance missions to provide early warning of enemy movement, direct supporting fires and monitor NBC effects. However, most Soviet reconnaissance is performed from the scout vehicles, although vehicle crews and the light machine gun and RPG-7-armed scout teams carried by most scout cars will dismount when necessary.

Combat reconnaissance patrols are troop reconnaissance patrols sent out by a tank or motorised rifle unit, often as a point detachment. They are used when action is expected, or when contact with the enemy must be maintained, as in a pursuit. Any patrol will however use reconnaissance by battle or probing attacks if necessary to accomplish its mission, usually covered by overwatching vehicles, or a patrol or a single vehicle or motorcyclist can be ordered to engage or approach the enemy in a probing attack to determine weapon strengths and locations; the inevitable losses are high even by Soviet standards. Soviet patrols will also use reconnaissance by fire, to force the enemy either to withdraw or return the fire. Reconnaissance in force is conducted by tank and motorised rifle units, and the Soviets distinguish it from the probing attacks and reconnaissance by battle that all units perform. While the reconnaissance in force was widely used in World War Two, it is less emphasised today. It involves collecting information by launching an attack that the enemy believes is a full-scale offensive, a costly process and one which may make it impossible to achieve surprise in later attacks. Reconnaissance in force is most often used in urban or wooded terrain.

Command and reconnaissance

The whole spectrum of Soviet reconnaissance is valueless if it cannot be acted upon by the field commanders. The use of forward command posts and command observation posts allows the commanders to be on the spot at crucial moments, though the Soviets do not rely so much on the personal action of the commander as on his detailed plans and instructions to his subordinates. Soviet command tends to "push" more than "pull." Nonetheless the Soviets realise that there is no substitute for direct front-line leadership. A command reconnaissance is almost always made before a breakthrough attack or any attack in dense terrain. Often a commander will not commit his second echelon or reserve until he has examined the battlefield personally. Defensive weapons siting is often determined by a command reconnaissance.

Reconnaissance effectiveness

Soviet army troop reconnaissance is relatively straightforward. Compared with the activities of Western units, it depends less on radar and sensors and more on direct visual observation. While this makes Soviet troop reconnaissance less susceptible to countermeasures, it does give patrols less flexibility and may well result in more exposure and higher losses than would be the case if they had a greater radar/sensor capability in individual patrols. Unless reconnaissance units have avoided the widespread Soviet problems with maps and map-reading, they will find their capabilities undermined. Similarly, the junior officers and NCOs who will lead the reconnaissance patrols will be called upon to demonstrate flexibility and initiative well above the average, yet these are qualities that have often been in short supply amongst such people. Unless the Soviets deliberately put their better men in reconnaissance units, they may not be able to use their mobility to the best advantage. The absence of organic scout helicopters may also prove a drawback. Despite these limitations the Soviets realise the importance of reconnaissance, and have attempted to adapt their tactics to reflect this and to reduce the effect of any limitations.

Unit organisation

Regimental reconnaissance company (tank and motorised rifle regiment)
Total strength: four or five officers, 43–57 enlisted men, three BMP-Rs or PT-76s, four to nine BRDMs, three to five motorcycles, one GS-12 radar, 1 URAL-375. (BRDMs can include up to three BRDM-rkhs.)

Divisional reconnaissance battalion (tank and motorised rifle division)
Total strength: 39 officers, 261 enlisted men, 18–21 BRDM, four BRDM-rkh, four to eight SA-7, 15+ jeeps, 36 trucks, seven PT-76s or BMP-Rs.
  One headquartes and support company (nine officers, 40 enlisted men, two BRDM, 16 trucks, 1 motorcycle)
  One tank company (four officers, 31 enlisted men, seven BMP-Rs or PT-76s in two platoons of three, and one HQ tank)
  One reconnaissance company (five officers, 63 enlisted men, four to eight SA-7)
    HQ section (one BRDM)
    Two or three scout car platoons (six BRDM each)
    NBC reconnaissance platoon (four BRDM-rkh)
    Motorcyle platoon (32 motorcycles)
  One long-range reconnaissance company (six officers, 27 enlisted men)

HQ section (one officer, two enlisted men)

Five reconnaissance teams (each of one officer, five enlisted men)

One radio interception company (15 officers, 110 enlisted men)

Three RDF platoons

One intercept platoon

One sigint (signals intelligence) shop section

Standard BMPs were used as interim PT-76 replacements pending introduction of the BMP-R in at least some units. Some reconnaissance units are reportedly receiving main battle tanks and standard BMPs.

Scout cars

Introduced in 1951, the BTR-40 is a four-wheel-drive scout car built on the chassis of the GAZ-63 truck, the hull design being an up-armoured improvement of that on the US-built White scout car. Throughout the 1950s the BTR-40 design was refined in a number of versions. The basic open-topped BTR-40 was armed with a pedestal-mounted 7.62mm SGMT machine gun. The BTR-40B featured overhead armour and two gun ports on each side of the passenger compartment. The BTR-40A was an anti-aircraft version with twin 14.5mm guns, mainly used for export. The East Germans have retrofitted some of their BTR-40s with a Sagger launcher under a retractable roof, similar to that on BRDMs. The BTR-40rkh was the NBC reconnaissance version of the BTR-40B, with monitoring equipment and an automatic flag-planting

Vehicle	BTR-40	BRDM-1	BRDM-2
Combat weight	5.3 tons	5.6 tons	7.0 tons
Length	5.0m	5.7m	5.75m
Width	1.9m	2.225m	2.35m
Height	1.75m	1.9m	2.31m
Wheelbase	2.7m	2.8m	3.1m
Track	1.6m	1.6m	1.84m
Clearance	0.275m	0.315m	0.335m
Tyre size	9.75 × 18	12.00 × 18	13.00 × 18
Max road speed	80km/h	80km/h	100km/h
Max water speed	nil	9km/h	10km/h
Fuel capacity	120 litres	150 litres	290 litres
Fuel consumption	0.42 litres/km	0.3 litres/km	0.35–0.45 litres/km
Range (paved road)	285km	500km	750km
Fording	0.9m	swims	swims
Gradient	30°	30°	30°
Vertical obstacle	0.47m	0.4m	0.4m
Trench	0.7m	1.22m	1.25m
Engine	GAZ-40 6-cylinder in-line, 80HP, petrol, water-cooled	GAZ-40P 6-cylinder in-line, 90HP, petrol, water-cooled	GAZ-41 V-8, 140HP, petrol, water-cooled
Horsepower/weight	15.09HP/ton	16.07HP/ton	20.0HP/ton
Main gun	7.62mm SGMT	12.7mm DShKM	14.5mm KPV
Secondary gun	nil	7.62mm SGMT/PKT	7.62mm PKT
Main gun ammunition	1,250 rounds	1,250 rounds	500 rounds
Secondary gun ammunition	nil	1,250 rounds	2,000 rounds
Main gun elevation	−6°/+23.5°	−6°/+23.5°	−5°/+30°
Main gun traverse	90°	90°	360°
Armour (overall)	8mm	10mm*	10mm*
Crew	2	2	2
Max passengers	8	3	6

* Detailed armour for BRDM-1 is: upper hull front 5mm @ 80°, lower hull front 7mm @ 45°, hull rear and sides 7mm @ 0°, hull top 7mm, belly 3mm; superstructure: front 10mm @ 50°, sides 10mm @ 30°, rear 7mm @ 60°, top 4mm; MG mantlet 4mm @ 90° where fitted, nose plate 14mm @ 40°.

BRDM-2 is as BRDM-1, with the addition of turret with 7mm of armour @ 40° all around and 7mm top.

BTR-40 with open top captured by the Israelis. Soviet Army vehicles usually carry their spare tyre in the rear. *(Tom Woltjer)*

BTR-40A scout cars of the Hungarian Army. *(Tom Woltjer)*

BRDM-1 armed with a 12.7mm DShKM and 7.62mm SGMB. *(US Army)*

device to designate clear lanes. Like all BTR-40s, it had no NBC defence system; the crew had to rely on their protective suits. The BTR-40 lacked the cross-country mobility required by a scout car, it was not amphibious and lacked a tyre pressure regulation system. Despite its age, the BTR-40 was still in service in the Group of Soviet Forces Germany in 1979. They are also widely used by the Commandant's Service (military police) and paramilitary organisations.

The BRDM-1 (*Bronevaya Rasvedyvateinaya Dosornaya Maschina*, armoured reconnaissance vehicle) was introduced in the spring of 1959 and rectified many of the failings of the BTR-40. Engine horsepower was increased, although the new vehicle retained the front-mounted petrol engine of the BTR-40. The BRDM incorporated many components of the GAZ-63 truck. The boat-like hull and alligator nose of the BRDM-1, similar to those of the MAV amphibious trucks, are designed for swimming, the vehicle being propelled by a single-water jet and using a bow vane for stability. Cross-country mobility was increased by the provision of the standard Soviet internal tyre pressure regulation system, and by two pairs of small-diameter belly wheels. Normally kept retracted in the chassis, these can be lowered from inside the vehicle to aid in traversing rough terrain without impeding high

speeds on roads. They also aid flotation. The BRDM-1 is fully enclosed, although the main armament – a pintle-mounted 12.7mm DShKM (omitted on many BRDM-1s) and 7.62mm SGMB or PKT machine guns – cannot be fired from under armour. Six firing ports – two in each side and two in the rear – allow passengers to use small arms.

A retractable triple Snapper or quadruple Swatter-A or Sagger mount was fitted into the passenger compartment of some BRDM-1s used by regimental anti-tank companies. The armoured roof could be raised and the ATGMs made ready for action within one minute. The BRDM-1U headquarters version is recognisable by its four antennae and additional generator. The BRDM-1rkh NBC reconnaissance version has an NBC protection system and an improved range of sensors. Soil samples can be automatically gathered and brought into a shielded compartment for analysis. Crews of NBC reconnaissance BRDMs are also trained in dismounted analysis of NBC effects and to use sensor devices. Marking flags are dispensed from two box-like devices on the rear deck.

The BRDM-1 may remain in Soviet service for some years to come, but the primary scout car is the BRDM-2. Sharing the all-welded steel construction of its predecessors, the BRDM-2 is a much more conventional design than the BRDM-1. An improved V-8 petrol engine (two small petrol engines, like the BTR-60's, in early examples) is mounted in the rear of the vehicle, eliminating the

BRDM-2s at the edge of a burning river. The extended trim vanes and the open propeller housings show that they are about to enter the water. The black canvas bags on the rear decking are for equipment storage. The whip-type aerials indicate that these vehicles have long-range radios, as used in reconnaissance BRDMs. *(US Army)*

BRDM-1's "snout" and reducing vulnerability. The BRDM-2 retains the central tyre pressure system and the retractable belly wheels. It mounts the same turret as the BTR-60PB, with 14.5mm KPV and 7.62mm PKT machine guns, and there is a firing port and vision block on each side of the passenger compartment. The commander sits in the turret and acts as gunner, while the driver is in front; in the BRDM-1 the two sat side by side.

The BRDM/2rkh is an improved NBC reconnaissance version with the same flag-planting, soil-sampling and environment-monitoring capabilities as its predecessors. The command version, the BRDM-2U, has its turret removed to provide more room for a commander and staff. Additional radios and a generator are carried. In widespread use throughout the Soviet Army, this version is the standard command observation post or forward command post for Soviet units, although standard BRDM-2s are also used in these roles. Some BRDM-2s used by long-range reconnaissance companies have high-power, long-range radios equipped for "burst" transmission or radio direction-finding equipment; all of these units' BRDMs carry external petrol tanks and jerrycans stowed internally. Because of its widespread use and large internal space, the BRDM-2 is an excellent choice as a weapons platform. Those of regimental anti-tank companies are armed with a retractable sextuple Sagger launcher or five retractable Spandrel launch tubes in place of its turret, the latter vehicle reportedly being designated BRDM-3. The Sagger launch vehicle carries eight reload rounds, and the Spandrel carrier is believed to carry at least as many, possibly as many as 15. The SA-9 Gaskin quadruple SAM mount is on a BRDM-2 chassis and hull. BRDM-2s also mount radars, jammers, communications systems, target designators and other weapons.

In addition to their two-man crews, BRDM-2s in reconnaissance units often carry a two-man scout team armed with a light machine gun and RPG-7. In winter these teams can operate on skis which are stowed externally on the BRDM. A two-man team with an RPG-7 rides shotgun in each Sagger-equipped BRDM, providing close-range defence against armour or, using their rifles, protecting the BRDM commander when he is firing the Saggers while dismounted.

The radios fitted to a BRDM depend upon its function. Each will have at least a basic R-123 set. In addition a

BRDM-2U command vehicle, showing extra radio antennae.

battalion command BRDM-U will have an R-107 set to communicate with company commanders and specialist or combat support units, an R-131 set for air and NBC threat warnings, and an R-112 to communicate with tank battalion and company commanders. An R-126 radio for dismounted use will also be carried on board. A BRDM used as an artillery command observation post would have an R-104M set to contact the parent battalion, and an R-108M set to keep in contact with the battery and gun positions if it is not co-located with them.

Optics have improved throughout the development of Soviet scout cars. Although it is absent from the BTR-40, all BRDM-2s and some BRDM-1s feature the TVN-2 intra-red night driving system. As in the BTR-60PB, the 14.5mm KPV machine gun can be fitted with a PPN-2 400m-range night sight. Both BRDMs use the same vision block system as the BTR-60PB. All BRDM-2s apparently use the same land navigation system as the T-62 command tank.

Egypt used BTR-40s in 1965. In 1967 both the Egyptians and Syrians had numbers of BTR-40s, BRDM-1s and a few BRDM-2s, but no ATGM-armed versions of any of these. Many were captured by the Israelis, the BRDM-1s being used by Israeli raiding forces and the BTR-40s being rearmed with Israeli weapons and radios and used by the Border Police. Both the BRDM-1 and BRDM-2, including Sagger-armed BRDM-2s, were used in the 1973 War. Some captured vehicles went to the US. All three Soviet scout car designs were used in Angola, and BRDM-1s of the Ugandan Army attempted to defend Kampala in 1979. BRDM-2s have also been used in Ethiopia and in Afghanistan.

PT-76 amphibious reconnaissance tank with later-production D-56TM gun, identifiable by its double-baffle muzzle brake. Extra fuel tanks are mounted on either side of the rear decking. Up to two extra tanks can be carried on each side. *(US Army)*

PT-76 amphibious tank

Combat weight	14.0 tons	Maximum range	12.1km (indirect fire, on incline)
Length (gun forward)	7.63m		
Length (gun rear)	6.91m	Point-blank range (2m-high target)	APHE = 820m
Width	3.14m		HVAP = 1,000m
Height	2.26m (2.195)*		HEAT = 500m (BP-353)
Width	3.14m	Ammunition types	OF-350 Frag-HE, BR-350B
Track	2.74m		APHE, BR-354P HVAP,
Clearance	0.37m		BP-353/UBP-350M
Track width	0.36m		spin-stabilised HEAT,
Ground contact	4.080m		BK-354R fin-stabilised HEAT
Ground pressure	0.479kg/cm²	Muzzle velocity	HE = 680m/sec
Max road speed	44km/h		APHE = 655m/sec
Max water speed	10km/h		HVAP = 965m/sec
Fuel capacity	250 litres		HEAT = 325m/sec (BP-353)
Fuel consumption	0.96 litres/km	Shell weight	HE = 6.2kg
Gradient	30°		APHE = 6.5kg
Range (road)	260km		HVAP = 3.1kg (BR-354P)
Range (water)	100km		HEAT = 4.0kg (BP-353/
Vertical obstacle	1.1m		UBP-350M)
Trench	2.8m	Ammunition load	40 rounds
Engine	V-6, 6-cylinder in-line water-cooled diesel, 240HP @ 1,800rpm	Co-axial MG	7.62mm SGMT
		MG ammunition	1,000 rounds
		Main gun elevation	−4°/+30°
Transmission	mechanical synchromesh, 5 forward, 1 reverse gears	Traverse	360°
		Armour (glacis)	11mm @ 80°
Horsepower/weight	17.14HP/ton	Armour (hull side)	14mm @ 0°
Main gun	76.2mm D-56TM (D-56T)	Armour (mantlet)	11mm @ 30°
Calibre length	42cal	Crew	3
Rate of fire (claimed)	15rpm	Radio	R-123, plus R-112 in company command tanks
Rate of fire (actual)	4–6rpm		

* Figures in parentheses are for PT-76 Model 1, otherwise as Model 2. Detailed armour is: lower hull front 14mm @ 45°, hull rear upper 7mm @ 0°, hull rear lower 7mm @ 45°, top 7mm, belly 5mm, turret front 17mm @ 35°, turret sides 16mm @ 35°, turret rear 11mm @ 35°, turret top 8mm.

An early-production PT-76 with a D-56T gun (recognisable by its multi-baffle muzzle brake) in Prague in 1968. The white cross is a standard Warsaw Pact manoeuvre marking. *(US Army)*

Although it is being replaced by the BMP-R, the PT-76 (*plavuchii tank*, amphibious tank) is still used as a reconnaissance tank in regimental and divisional reconnaissance units. It is also used as a main battle tank by the tank battalions of Naval Infantry regiments.

The PT-76 did not follow the usual Soviet evolutionary process. Light tank development had reached a dead end during the war, and the PT-76 was essentially a new design. Prototypes started trials in 1952, and large-scale deliveries began in 1955. The design emphasised amphibious capability, and armament and mobility were adequate by early-1950s standards but armour protection was light. The PT-76 is of conventional all-welded steel construction, having torsion-bar suspension and six road wheels with the drive sprocket at the rear and the idler at the front. The rear-mounted straight-six water-cooled diesel is half of the V-12 engine of the T-54. The front-mounted transmission has suffered a number of problems, leading to poor acceleration.

Internally the PT-76 is less cramped than most Soviet tanks, although almost half its space is taken by the engine compartment, which is separated from the crew compartment by an armoured bulkhead. As in the T-34 (and unlike most Western tanks), no bulkhead separates the driver from the rest of the crew compartment. The PT-76 has a turret cage and basket. Communication is by an R-123 radio, and company command tanks also carry an R-112. The PT-76 lacks a navigation system, NBC protection system and NBC monitoring equipment, important omissions in a reconnaissance vehicle. It has an infra-red driving light and a standard white-light searchlight (retrofitted to earlier models), and can make smoke by injecting diesel fuel into the exhaust.

The Soviets felt the lack of amphibious armour throughout the Second World War, and so the PT-76 was intended to be able to provide mobility in the reconnaissance role and armour support during river crossings and amphibious landings. Water propulsion is by two stern-mounted hydrojets. Two intake ports, covered by clam-shell covers when not in use, are opened in the bottom of the hull. Pumps driven by the engine pull water into these openings, and it is expelled under pressure from the hydrojets. Steering is achieved by varying the amount of water taken into each intake. A deflector vane on the front of the tank is raised for stability while swimming. The PT-76's swimming ability leaves much to be desired, its surf and rough-water capabilities being inferior even to those of the BTR-60PB. Early PT-76s could be left dead in the water by waves drowning the engine, but most now use a snorkel while swimming. However, they can still lose power or sink. It is hard to keep a PT-76 on course while swimming. The raised trim vane, waves and spray block most of the driver's view, and he must rely on the commander's directions. It is also difficult to fire the gun while swimming. If the gunner's view is obscured the commander must determine the range (although he lacks a rangefinder on his binocular viewing device, which is similar to that on the T-54), aim the gun while allowing for the roll of the waves, and give the order to fire from the turret. It is often hard to observe the burst of shell because spray and oil film fog the vision devices. To minimise this a protective shield, electrically connected to the gun-firing mechanism, covers the vision and optical devices at the moment of firing, uncovering them in time to observe the fall of shot.

The PT-76 has appeared in four versions. The Model 1's D-56T gun has a slotted muzzle brake and no bore evacuator. The most common type, the Model 2, has an unstabilised D-56TM gun with a double-baffle muzzle brake and a bore evacuator, which the Model 3 lacks. The PT-76B has the same gun as the Model 2, though in this version the weapon is fully stabilised. The PT-76 chassis has been used as the basis of a wide family of Soviet vehicles: the ASU-85, ZSU-23-4, SA-6 missile and radar vehicles, BTR-50, BMP, early FROG missile transporters, GSP heavy amphibious ferry and many others. Many of the components first used in the PT-76 were adopted as standard for other Soviet vehicles.

The D-56T and the slightly improved D-56TM are ballistically identical and can fire all Soviet 76.2mm ammunition. Based on the wartime 76.2mm tank gun, the D-56 series has a vertical sliding-wedge breech block and a hydropneumatic recoil system. Elevation is manual. A rate of fire of 15 rounds per minute has been claimed, but there is no loader – the gunner must load and fire – and four to six rounds per minute is a more probable maximum figure. The optics, both the commander's binocular sight and the gunner's TSh-66 telescopic sight, are similar to those on the T-54. The PT-76 does not normally mount a night sight. The sight has reticles only for machine gun, Frag-HE and APHE ammunition. Use of HEAT and HVAP ammunition must rely on firing tables or estimation.

Late-model PT-76s of the Soviet Naval Infantry swimming in calm waters, trim vanes extended. They have the short snorkel used to help prevent engine flooding and are marked with the white cross used for air recognition on manoeuvres. *(Chris Foss)*

Weapons effectiveness and combat usage

Despite its age, the D-56T is reportedly an accurate weapon, especially at short ranges. The following table gives the probability of a first-round hit from a standing PT-76 against a standing AFV:

Ammunition	Range (metres)									
	50	100	175	250	500	750	1,000	1,500	2,000	2,500
HVAP BR-354P	97%	89%	89%	89%	86%	83%	68%	39%	17%	0%
HEAT	97%	83%	83%	83%	83%	75%	61%	33%	3%	0%

These figures are from the US Army, which has had a number of PT-76s for many years.

Penetration against flat, vertical steel armour

Ammunition	Range (metres)			
	500	1,000	1,500	2,000
APHE	69mm	61mm	54mm	48mm
HVAP BR-354P	92mm	58mm	?	?

The older, spin-stabilised BP-353 or UBP-350M HEAT rounds could penetrate 120mm of oblique, homogeneous armour at any range; the newer fin-stabilised BK-354R can penetrate 280mm.

The HEAT or HVAP round has approximately a 33% chance of killing an M60A1 tank and a 50% chance of killing a lightly armoured vehicle such as an M113 or M109.

At close range the 76mm gun can breach the walls of all but the most impregnable buildings in four (for light buildings) to nine hits.

Polish-made PT-76s have a 12.7mm anti-aircraft machine gun.

The PT-76 saw action in Kashmir in the 1965 India-Pakistan War. Egypt used PT-76s in 1967 without much success. The Israelis used captured PT-76s in a number of raids against Egypt during the War of Attrition. In 1973 Egyptian and Syrian patrols with PT-76s made the deepest penetration of the war. PT-76s also equipped part of the Egyptian 130th Mechanised Infantry Brigade which swam the Great Bitter Lake on the first day of the war and advanced into Sinai, only to be overrun by Israeli tank reserves hurrying to the front. There are reports that the Israelis also used PT-76s in special operations.

The PT-76 entered combat in Vietnam in the pre-dawn darkness of February 7, 1968. Eleven PT-76s of the 68th Armoured Regiment, supported by two battalions of North Vietnamese regulars, surprised and overran the Special Forces camp at Lang Vei. The US LAW anti-tank weapon was found to have reduced effectiveness against the PT-76, the flotation spaces of which apparently functioned as spaced armour. Losses were however still heavy, as they have been whenever the PT-76 has been used as a main battle tank. PT-76s of the 68th and 203rd Armoured Regiments fought throughout I Corps area in 1968–69, and were reinforced with other tank units for the 1972 offensive. Other North Vietnamese PT-76s were used in the Laos invasion and served as main battle tanks – without infantry support – in the Battle of An Loc in 1972, when they were defeated.

Also used in Vietnam was the Chinese Type 63 light tank, an upgunned version of the PT-76 which weighs 18 tons and mounts an 85mm gun. Along with standard PT-76s, it is used as a reconnaissance vehicle by the Chinese Army.

The Indian Army used PT-76s successfully in the 1971 war with Pakistan. In the waterlogged country of Bangladesh PT-76s were used for many cross-river operations, some swimming long distances to outflank Pakistani resistance. The Indians like the PT-76's amphibious capability, simplicity and light weight, which allow it to go where other Indian armour cannot reach.

Tactical employment

The PT-76's main role is support of troop reconnaissance patrols, often supporting BRDMs from overwatch positions. If strong positions are to be scouted or the terrain is not suitable for scout cars, PT-76s will make the first troop reconnaissance. They will also be the first elements to cross rivers. The BMP-R is now assuming these roles.

Each Naval Infantry regiment includes a tank battalion with 31 PT-76s and ten T-55s. East German and Polish amphibious units also use PT-76s. They swim ashore from landing ships 3,000m off the beach, firing on the way in if possible. Once ashore they support the BTR-60PBs of the Naval Infantry regiment's three battalions in the same way that main battle tanks support the battalions of a motorised rifle regiment. The Soviets do not intend to keep Naval Infantry units in sustained combat.

Late-production PT-76s swimming. They do not have snorkels extended – standard PT-76 swimming procedure – and their guns are locked directly forward. Each carries two unusual large fuel drums and a periscopic sight to enable the commander to see over the spray. *(US Army)*

Engagement sequence and countermeasures

The PT-76 engages a target in much the same manner as any other Soviet tank, and it is vulnerable to the same countermeasures. In addition, 0.50-calibre machine guns and 20mm cannon can penetrate its thin armour.

Foreign use

The BTR-40 has been in service with the Warsaw Pact armies, Angola, Cuba, Albania, Yugoslavia, China (built as the Type 55), Afghanistan, Algeria, Egypt, Guinea, Indonesia, Iran, Libya, Mali, Israeli Border Police, North Yemen, Somalia, Ethiopia, Sudan, Syria, Tanzania and a number of insurgent groups.

BRDM scout cars have seen service with the Warsaw Pact armies, Cuba, Egypt, Syria, Israel, Afghanistan, Angola, the Congo (one only), Uganda (one only), Mali (two only) and Yugoslavia (two only).

Sagger-armed BRDMs are in service with the Warsaw Pact armies, Egypt, Syria, Iraq, Libya and Algeria. Spandrel-armed BRDMs are expected to enter service with the East German and Polish armies in the near future.

PT-76s have been supplied to the Warsaw Pact nations, Afghanistan, China, the Congo, Cuba, Egypt, Finland, Hungary, India, Indonesia, Iraq, Israel, Laos, North Korea, North Vietnam, Pakistan, Syria and Yugoslavia.

The US Army has seven PT-76s and at least one Sagger-armed BRDM-2.

Chapter Fourteen

Airborne combat vehicles

"Our airborne troops have been provided with the most up-to-date combat equipment and are capable of tackling a wide variety of complex missions."

GENERAL OF THE ARMY V.F. MARGELOV,
COMMANDER OF AIRBORNE FORCES

Airborne forces were a Soviet creation, but the men who conceived the idea in the 1930s perished in the purges. Soviet airborne assault operations in World War Two were mostly small in scale, haphazard in execution and almost invariably disastrous in outcome. However, the Soviet Union today musters the world's largest jump-trained force – eight divisions wearing the blue beret and striped sailor's shirt of the paratroopers – though the Soviet Air Force can transport only two divisions at once.

Soviet airborne operations

Soviet airborne operations can be strategic, operational or tactical in scope and objective.

Strategic operations use airborne divisions as the long arm of Soviet power, projecting them great distances to establish a new theatre of operations or to seize bases of strategic importance. They have not yet been used in any postwar operation, though during the 1973 Middle East war the crack 103rd Guards Airborne Division was reportedly flown to a camp outside Belgrade Airport, where it remained poised to intervene if required. Other airborne divisions went on the alert in the Soviet Union. The increased importance that the Soviets attach to the potential for conflicts outside the Eurasian land mass in recent years has led to a corresponding increase in the importance of the airborne divisions. Their value as a rapid-reaction, strategic force is shown by the fact that all airborne divisions (except possibly the division at Tula-Ryazan, which has a training role) are kept at Category I readiness in peacetime. They are under the direct command of the Ministry of Defence, and so are highly responsive to the national command authorities. In wartime, however, airborne divisions will be assigned to theatres of operations or fronts.

The usual employment of Soviet airborne units will be on operational missions. Operational airborne assaults are similar to Operation Market Garden (the Arnhem landings) in World War Two. Regiments, and possibly division-sized units, will drop up to 300km behind the front lines to take key objectives – airfields, bridges, logistics centres, weapons storage, nuclear weapons and delivery systems, headquarters, transportation centres, key terrain features – and "hold until relieved," which may take up to a week or, optimistically, two or three days. The most important operational mission is the *desants*. The Soviet concept of the *desants* is based on inserting forces in the enemy rear or flank. *Desants* can be transported by any means, but they will most frequently be air-dropped. Such missions will involve units as large as a regiment or as small as a sabotage squad, dropped beyond the Soviet main forces to destroy nuclear-capable weapons and installations, attack headquarters and the lines of communication, spread confusion and demoralisation, gather reconnaissance information in co-operation with long-range patrols and, along with forward detachments, seize routes for the Soviet advance. Operation airborne assaults and *desants* are not intended to operate independently of the main ground forces. The Soviets realise that their airborne units are too small to do that. But they have the capability to cause great disruption in NATO rear areas. There are so many vulnerable areas that it would be necessary to divert troops away from the main battle to serve them. The actions of the 103rd Guards Airborne Division in seizing Prague Airport in 1968 and the 105th Guards Airborne in securing much of Kabul in 1979 are examples of the operational use of airborne divisions in conjunction with a larger force.

Tactical airborne operations are normally carried out in conjunction with land attacks. They never occur more than 100km in advance of the front, and the units that drop are seldom bigger than battalion size, intended to hold a position for up to 48h until the tanks arrive. Such air drops will be used especially in support of break-through attacks, river crossings and amphibious inva-

Soviet paratroopers in action, showing the characteristic camouflage suit, blue beret and striped sailor's jumper. They are using the new AKS-74 5.45mm assault rifle.
(V.M. Martinova)

sions, sealing off the battlefield from enemy reinforcements and blocking retreat routes. Heliborne troops, usually drawn from motorised rifle units, will supplement the paratroopers in tactical air assaults.

Desants can also be used tactically as well as operationally, as shown by the Egyptian commando battalions on the first day of the 1973 War. Although none were airdropped, some were inserted by helicopter deep inside Israeli positions, while most moved past suppressed Israeli strongpoints and created an anti-armour screen to prevent their relief and to cover the infantry moving across the Canal. The deep-penetration groups had some successes: one Israeli battalion lost several tanks in an ambush while still on their transporter trucks. The advancing Egyptians soon linked up with most of the *desants* and used them to reinforce their own defences. But other groups were never relieved, and helicopters attempting to insert more *desants* on the second day of the war were virtually wiped out by Israeli aircraft – all hazards inherent in the *desants* concept.

Operationally and tactically, the importance of airborne forces increases in a nuclear conflict. The airborne unit's BMD's and ASU-85s can move quickly through contaminated areas and, combined with the BMD's airdrop capability, they can take advantage of any gaps in enemy positions created by nuclear weapons. The high rates of advance the Soviets envisage in nuclear war would allow link-ups with units dropped far behind the lines. Small *desants* would also be highly effective on the dispersed nuclear battlefield.

Soviet airborne tactics

The Soviets believe that a purely airborne attack cannot succeed against an alerted enemy without either intense preparatory fires or high losses. Air drops will be made where enemy defences are weak or have been neutralised by air strikes, artillery or NBC weapons, and where enemy air defences cannot inflict losses on transport aircraft.

An initial air drop could rely purely on surprise, but the Soviets would have to secure air superiority for the widespread use and resupply of airborne units, especially those of regiment or division size. Resupply will be difficult at any time, owing to the shortage of transport aircraft.

Air drops are normally made at night. The transport aircraft will approach the drop zones along routes clear of enemy air-defence forces, and will be escorted by fighters.

Displaying the pride and *esprit de corps* found in paratroopers worldwide, Soviet airborne forces are highly effective. This trooper carries an AKS-74. *(V.M. Martinova)*

Drop zones can be on the objective or 5,000+m from it. The zones – four to six for a division, one or two for a regiment – are marked by pathfinders from the divisional reconnaissance company, who are trained in precision jumping and have steerable canopies. They use visual and electronic beacons to guide the transports. Pathfinders may also be dropped on dummy zones as a diversion. The first wave drops with all its heavy equipment and secures the zone for subsequent waves and resupply. In division or regiment-sized operations an airhead for An-12 transport aircraft will also be secured as soon as possible. The paratroopers start with patrols from the drop zones, and follow these with rapid attacks, possibly supported by pre-arranged air strikes or artillery fires, though they will have to rely largely on their own weapons.

The weapons the paratroopers can bring to bear are considerable, and Soviet airborne units are heavily mechanised. While other paratroopers must march when they land, the Soviets will also drop BMDs, ASU-57s, and light trucks. Their degree of mechanisation depends on airlift capacity. Theoretically a completely mechanised airborne division could be created by providing each squad with a BMD, as each motorised rifle squad has a BMP or APC. But while this would create a formidable force, especially in an NBC environment, it would be a tremendous burden on the already stretched Soviet airlift capability. The number of BMDs in Soviet airborne units

can apparently be adjusted to suit the type of mission and airlift capability available. The introduction of the BMD has definitely increased the power of the Soviet paratroopers.

Soviet airborne units will defend against enemy counterattacks with the standard strongpoints with interlocking fields of fire. Their AFVs will be used as self-propelled anti-tank weapons, although all except the BMD's Saggers lack stopping power against modern tanks.

Airborne units are not intended to fight long or intense battles. They have too few men and heavy weapons. The Soviets will try and relieve them with motorised rifle units if that sort of fighting is called for. Airborne units are expendable – as is any Soviet unit – if the objective is of sufficient priority. The airborne will infiltrate and bypass enemy positions, and only when this is impractical will they attack. The assault is similar to that of a motorised rifle unit, although artillery support will be less and the attacking troops will ride in or on ASU-57s, ASU-85s or BMDs to a dismounting point, probably further away from the enemy position than in a motorised rifle unit's attack. The airborne armoured vehicles will then lead the attack, although the Soviets are aware that they are not tanks and cannot be successfully used as such. They do however give mobility, which the Soviets consider important in the sort of missions to which the airborne will be assigned. Airborne battalions may form forward detachments. Their march formation is similar to that of a motorised rifle battalion, with ASUs forward. If the enemy is encountered the ASUs will engage with direct fire to screen the battalion's deployment. Trucks, both dropped and captured, can supplement the BMDs.

Soviet airborne forces receive high priority in manpower. All of their personnel have complete pre-induction military training, a distinction shared only by the Strategic Rocket Forces, which shows the strategic importance the Soviets attach to the airborne forces. Half of the airborne inductees undergo pre-induction parachute training. They also realise that it is difficult to make a man both a soldier and a paratrooper in two years and, because the airborne divisions must be kept ready, they cannot afford to have 25% of their strength as raw recruits. Once a Soviet paratrooper is jump-trained at Tula-Ryazan he must make at least ten jumps a year to remain qualified. The "airborne mystique," the strong pride and cohesion of airborne units worldwide, seems to exist in the Soviet Army as well. The men in the blue berets are an elite, and they know it.

Soviet special forces

Soviet special forces and commando units include the long-range reconnaissance patrol units of army reconnaissance companies and battalions, airborne reconnaissance troops, the Naval Infantry commandos, the *Raydoviki*, the *Vysotniki* and the GRU Military Intelligence Troops.

A non-divisional Soviet airborne regiment is stationed in Neurippem, East Germany. Intended for a commando or *desants* role, each of its battalions will probably be attached to an army.

The Naval Infantry commandos – one platoon in each fleet – are equivalent to the US Navy SEALS. They will be used in support of invasions or to make amphibious raids. Personnel are trained as paratroopers and as frogmen.

The *Raydoviki* correspond to US Ranger units. Their mission includes training partisans in the Soviet Union in case of invasion. There are between three and six *Raydoviki* brigades, designated *Brigada Osobovo Naznachaniya* (special operations brigades), each organised into three or four battalions and an air transport support unit. *Raydoviki* companies are 40–50 strong and divided into six commando squads, and are supported by stronger ATGM and mortar companies and 122mm rockets in individual man-carried tubes, as used in Vietnam. Wheeled transport includes GAZ-66 and -69 light trucks. *Raydoviki* will probably operate in company-sized forces. According to press reports, *Raydoviki* units began arriving in Afghanistan in the spring of 1980.

The *Vysotniki* correspond to the US Special Forces. They normally operate in squad-sized units for deep airborne sabotage, reconnaissance and intelligence penetrations behind enemy lines using HALO (high-altitude, low-opening) parachute techniques. They do not have the partisan training role of the *Raydoviki*. There are several administrative special operations brigades of these units, equivalent to US Special Forces groups. Unlike the *Raydoviki*, however, they would not be deployed in company or battalion-sized formations, but only as special teams.

There is no US equivalent to the GRU Military Intelligence Troops. GRU military intelligence agents work with KGB agents, simultaneously keeping a watchful eye on them. In addition to its agents, the GRU has several "diversionary battalions" which include both male and female soldiers who often work in civilian clothes, infiltrating an objective in time of peace. One GRU diversionary battalion using both uniformed and disguised troops helped to seize Prague Airport in 1968, allowing an airborne division to fly in unhindered. GRU troops would work in conjunction with paratroopers, using deception to achieve surprise. GRU units positioned in West Germany prior to a Soviet attack could seize vital installations, attack headquarters or eliminate key personnel. The potential effectiveness of these battalions is far greater than their small numbers suggest.

A number of Soviet special forces units are known to be trained in impersonating NATO troops, wearing US, British, Danish and West German uniforms. But it is the East Germans who specialise in this field. They have two commando battalions at Prora, on the island of Rugen in the Baltic: the 40th and 5th "Willi Sanger" battalions. One or both of these will drop behind NATO lines wearing West German uniforms. Another East German force, estimated at two companies, has M-48 tanks and M-113 APCs. These vehicles, obtained from Vietnam, are stationed in southern East Germany and are painted in West German markings. Other Warsaw Pact states also maintain special forces units, including the Czech 7th Airborne Battalion at Hoelleschau and several Polish units.

Unit organisations

Airborne division
Total strength: 800 officers, 7,673 enlisted men, 128 BMDs, 18 ASU-85s, 18 MRLs, 18 D-30s, 27 "suitcase" Saggers, 18 SD-44s, 18 M-1943 120mm mortars, 27 M-1937 82mm mortars, 18 BRDMs, 200 SA-7s, 445 GAZ-69 trucks, 764 GAZ-66 trucks, 1,082+ trailers, 36 ZU-23s, 27 ASU-57s (being removed), one radar, 96 motorcycles, 12 ATGM BRDMs.

One divisional HQ (76 officers, 122 men, two BMDs, three SA-7, 10 GAZ-69, 29 GAZ-66, 15 motorcycles)
Three airborne regiments
One artillery regiment
One anti-aircraft battalion
One engineer battalion (28 officers, 344 men, one bridge set, 13 mine planters, two mine trailers, one-plus armoured recovery vehicles, 11 GAZ-69, 25 GAZ-66, three SA-7)
One signal battalion (22 officers, 221 men, 30 GAZ-69, three SA-7, 23 GAZ-66, 11 motorcycles)
One reconnaissance company (four officers, 76 men, can be issued with nine GAZ-69, nine BRDM, nine RPG-7D, nine motorcycles, nine SA-7)
One NBC defence company (eight officers, 90 enlisted men, nine GAZ-69, 19 GAZ-66, three SA-7)
One transport battalion (24 officers, 237 men, 165 GAZ-66, two GAZ-69, two motorcycles, three SA-7)
One services and supply company (three officers, 40 enlisted men, six GAZ-66, three SA-7)
One maintenance battalion (eight officers, 108 enlisted men, nine GAZ-69, 11 GAZ-66, two armoured recovery vehicles, three SA-7)
One parachute rigging company (seven officers, 94 enlisted men, three SA-7)
One medical battalion (35 officers, 123 enlisted men)

Artillery regiment

Total strength: 120 officers, 732 enlisted men, 39 SA-7, 54 GAZ-69, 72 GAZ-66.

One HQ battery (five officers, 59 enlisted men, 12 GAZ-69, two GAZ-66, four motorcycles)

One target-acquisition battery (with GS-12 radar set)

One howitzer battalion (22 officers, 299 enlisted men, 18 122mm D-30 howitzers, trucks)

One multiple rocket launcher battalion (27 officers, 240 enlisted men, 18 140mm M-1965 MRLs, trucks)

One assault gun battalion (six officers, 99 enlisted men, 18 ASU-85 assault guns, 7 GAZ-69, 14 GAZ-66)

One ATGM battalion (six officers, 60 enlisted men, 12 Sagger BRDM, two GAZ-69, four GAZ-66, two motorcycles)

Airborne regiment

Total strength: 164 officers, 1,401 enlisted men, approx 102 GAZ-69 and 115 GAZ-66 light trucks, 191 trailers, nine ASU-57(?), 15 motorcycles, six SD-44, nine ATGM BRDMs or suitcase Saggers, six ZU-23, 42+ BMDs, depending on mission.

One regimental HQ (28 officers, 41 enlisted men, 14 GAZ-69 with trailers, three motorcycles, three SA-7, two RPG-7D)

Three airborne battalions

One assault gun battery (five officers, 55 enlisted men, nine ASU-57, two GAZ-69, four GAZ-66; ASU-57 currently being replaced with BMDs or deleted completely)

One ATGM battery (four officers, 30 enlisted men, nine suitcase Saggers or ATGM-armed BRDMs, organised as mechanised rifle regiment)

One mortar battery (four officers, 44 enlisted men, six M-1943 120mm mortars, six RPG-7D, three GAZ-69, six GAZ-66)

One air-defence battery (three officers, 45 enlisted men, six ZU-23, one GAZ-69, six GAZ-66)

One anti-tank battery (four officers, 43 enlisted men, six RPG-7D, three GAZ-69, six GAZ-66, six SD-44 85mm auxiliary-propelled anti-tank guns)

One engineer company (three officers, 50 enlisted men, six GAZ-66)

One signal company (four officers, 47 enlisted men, eight GAZ-69, four motorcycles)

One NBC defence platoon (one officer, 17 enlisted men, three GAZ-69)

One medical company (eight officers, 24 enlisted men, two GAZ-66, five GAZ-69)

One reconnaissance platoon (believed to have a pathfinder role, two officers, 25 enlisted men, three BRDMs, three GAZ-69)

One transport company (five officers, 38 enlisted men, 25 GAZ-66 with trailers)

One maintenance company (four officers, 30 enlisted men, five GAZ-69, five GAZ-66, one armoured recovery vehicle)

One supply platoon (one officer, 26 enlisted men, four GAZ-69, four GAZ-66)

Airborne battalion

Total strength: 29 officers, 306 enlisted men, 14 BMDs, three M-1937 82mm mortars, 17 GAZ-69, seven GAZ-66.

One battalion HQ (five officers, five enlisted men, one SA-7, three GAZ-69, one GAZ-66)

Three airborne companies

One mortar platoon (one officer, 19 enlisted men, three 82mm mortars, four GAZ-69)

One signal platoon (one officer, 14 enlisted men, three motorcycles, three GAZ-69)

One support squad (10 enlisted men, five GAZ-66)

One maintenance section (seven enlisted men, two GAZ-66)

One medical section (one *feldsherr*, two aid men, one GAZ-69)

One assault engineer platoon (It is uncertain whether this unit is organic to the battalion. Strength is unknown)

One BMD company (14 BMDs and crews. It is unknown whether crews are drawn from rifle squads or are organic to the BMD company, which may be a "paper" organisation)

Airborne company

Total strength: seven officers, 83 enlisted men, 12 RPG-7s, three SA-7s, nine PK LMGs, three SVD rifles (probably); all other personnel have AKMS.

Company headquarters (three officers, seven enlisted men, three SA-7, two GAZ-69)

Three rifle platoons (each of one officer, 21 enlisted men, with three PK LMG, one SVD and three RPG-7s, each platoon having three squads)

One anti-tank platoon (one officer, 12 enlisted men, three SPG-9, three RPG-7D, three GAZ-66)

All numbers are approximate, especially those of BMDs and personnel. BMD numbers and organisation depend on the unit's mission. Division-level assets are normally attached to regiments on operational missions, and regimental assets are attached down to battalion, forming regimental and battalion combat teams (reinforced). ASU-85 platoons are often attached to first-echelon battalions. It is estimated that each battalion can mount one company in BMDs. BMDs can also be centralised to mechanise one battalion per regiment or one regiment per division. Reportedly, three such BMD-mounted regiments were lifted into Afghanistan in 1979.

Independent, non-divisional airborne units also exist, apparently. These include large weapons such as FROGs.

UAZ-469s frequently replace GAZ-69s.

An-12 Cub, standard Soviet tactical transport. *(Department of Defense)*

Airlift capability

All Soviet military airlift capability is provided by the Military Transport Aviation (VTA) of the Air Force, supplemented by the resources of Aeroflot, the state airline. The airlift capability of the VTA is sufficient to carry two airborne divisions 480km simultaneously or one airborne division 1,610km. Recent Soviet airlift exercises, including some to Ethiopia, have apparently been aimed at improving long-range airlift capability. Reinforced by Aeroflot, VTA can sustain impressive airlifts, as it did during the 1973 Middle East war, the 1978 Ogaden fighting and in the invasion of Afghanistan in 1979.

The usual aircraft used by the airborne forces are the turboprop An-12 Cub, which can drop 80 paratroops or two BMDs, and the turbofan Il-76 Candid, which can drop 150 men or three BMDs. Other aircraft – notably the huge An-22 Cock – are used for airlifts, but normally do not drop paratroopers. The Cock can drop four BMDs or 300 troops.

A total of 157 An-12 sorties would be required to airlift one BMD-equipped airborne regiment. When supplies and spare aircraft are counted, this total will be close to 200 sorties. To air-drop a regiment would require even more sorties.

Parachutes

All paratroopers have main and reserve parachutes. The main D-1 parachute can be used above 150m altitude from aircraft flying at a maximum speed of 189kt. Opening is by static line (four seconds delay) or manually. Rate of descent is 5m/sec. The chest reserve parachute is the Pz-41a, which can be used at speeds of up to 216kt and has a descent rate of 8m/sec. Special training parachutes are also used, as is a wide range of cargo parachutes.

VTA airlift aircraft

Type	Troops (max)	Payload (max, kg)	Range (km) (max payload/empty)
An-12 Cub turboprop	105	20,000	550/5,000
An-22 Cock turboprop	350	80,000	5,000/10,950
An-26 Curl turboprop	38	5,500	980/2,930
Il-14 Crate piston	32	3,300	1,750*/3,200
Il-18 Coot turboprop	90	13,500	3,700/6,500
Il-76 Candid jet	200	40,000	5,000/?

* Range with 50% maximum payload.

ASU-57 and ASU-85 airborne assault guns

Vehicle	ASU-57	ASU-85
Introduced	1957	1962
Weight	3,350kg	14,000kg
Length	4.995m	8.49m
Height	1.180m	2.1m
Width	2.086m	2.8m
Ground pressure	0.35kg/cm²	0.49kg/cm²
Max road speed	45km/h	44km/h
Fuel capacity	140 litres	250 litres
Fuel consumption	0.56 litres/km	0.96 litres/km
Road range	250km	260km
Fording	0.7m	0.9m
Gradient	30°	29°
Vertical obstacle	0.5m	1.1m
Trench	1.4m	2.8m
Track	3.0m	2.66m
Ground clearance	0.2m	0.4m
Engine	4-cylinder petrol, 55HP, water-cooled	6-cylinder diesel, 290HP, water-cooled
Gun	57mm Ch-51 or Ch-51M	85mm M-44
Calibre length	73cal	53cal
Rate of fire (max)	12rpm	3–4rpm
Rate of fire (sustained)	6rpm	2rpm
Max range (HE)	6,000m	15,300m (requires 29° gradient)
Max effective range (APHE)	1,100m	950m
Max effective range (HVAP)	1,250m	1,150m
Ammunition types	BR-271SP APHE-T, BZR-27 APHEI-T, BR-271P HVAP-T, O-271 Frag-HE, Shch-271 canister	see SD-44
Muzzle velocity (HE)	706m/sec	792m/sec
Muzzle velocity (APHE)	990m/sec	792m/sec
Muzzle velocity (HVAP)	1,255m/sec	1,030m/sec
Shell weight (HE)	3.7kg	9.5kg
Shell weight (APHE)	3.1kg	9.3kg
Shell weight (HVAP)	1.8kg	5.0kg
Rounds carried	30	40
Armour penetration @ 500m	APHE = 106mm HVAP = 140mm	see SD-44
Armour penetration @ 1,000m	APHE = 85mm HVAP = 100mm	see SD-44
Co-axial MG	can be attached	7.62mm PKT
Elevation	−5°/+12°	−4°/+15°
Traverse	22°	12°
Armour (glacis plate)	6mm @ 60°	40mm @ 60°
Armour (hull side)	6mm @ 0°	15mm @ 30°
Crew	3	4

An ASU-57 with the standard-production double-baffle muzzle brake for its Ch-51M 57mm gun. Its light construction is evident. *(US Army)*

The ASU-57 and ASU-85 (*Aviadesantnaya Samakhodnaia Ustanovka*, airborne self-propelled mount) airborne assault guns provide armour support for Soviet paratroopers. Both vehicles are old designs, and their guns do not pose a threat to modern tanks except at short range. An An-12 tactical transport can carry two ASU-57s or one ASU-85. Each ASU-57 is dropped on a pallet with four main and four stabilising parachutes. Retro-rockets fitted to the pallet slow its descent immediately before landing. Once on the ground, the crew, parachuted separately, run to the vehicle, collapse the parachute, unfasten it from its pallet, and can be ready for action in minutes. While the ASU-85 is capable of being air-dropped, it is normally flown to an airhead instead. The ASU-85 can also be lifted by Mi-6 Hook and Mi-10 Harke helicopters, and the ASU-57 by the Mi-8 Hip as well.

This airborne capability has been achieved by reducing weight. The ASU-57's protection will not even keep out the rain. The ASU-85 has thicker armour, but it is still vulnerable to 50cal rounds in the side and rear.

The first production ASU-57s were of steel and more heavily armoured than the service model, which uses both steel and duralumin alloy and has a 55HP four-cylinder passenger car petrol engine. Unlike the ASU-85, it lacks an NBC defence system. Its large, open top, frequently covered by a tarpaulin, makes it vulnerable to artillery. The engine and transmission are front-mounted, as is the drive sprocket. The running gear consists of four road wheels and two return rollers per side. Three paratroopers can be carried in the open rear compartment, and they can mount a machine gun to fire alongside the 57mm. It lacks amphibious capability, and the entire vehicle is comparatively primitive.

The ASU-85 is a much more useful vehicle than the ASU-57. Its box-shaped, low-silhouette hull with a sharply sloping glacis is mounted on a chassis which has the same rear-mounted engine, gearbox, suspension and track arrangement as the PT-76, lacking its amphibious capability. Optics are apparently similar to those used on the T-62, and include the same night vision devices. To compensate for the lack of visibility from the non-rotating fighting compartment, there is a vision block on each side of it, plus three for the driver and one for the commander.

An ASU-85 provides mobility for paratroopers in Prague, 1968. Like all invading armour in 1968, it is marked with a white cross for aerial recognition. *(US Army)*

Large external fuel tanks are usually hung on the rear. Smoke is generated by two drum-like BDSh smoke generators at the rear of the vehicle.

The main weakness of these vehicles is their armament. The 57mm gun is basically the M-1943 ZIS-2, which proved quite effective against the *panzers*, achieving a 3–1 kill ratio in its towed form. Today, however, its armour penetration is inadequate, and outdated sights reduce accuracy except at close range. The original 57mm Ch-51 gun mounted on the ASU-57 had an unusual large, 34-slotted muzzle brake, while the later and more standard Ch-51M had a double-baffle type. The 85mm gun on the ASU-85 is the standard Soviet design, as used in the T-34/85 and in the anti-tank and anti-aircraft role. It features a double-baffle muzzle brake and a bore evacuator. Even with its HEAT and HVAP rounds it has only a limited capability to defeat modern tanks. As with the 57mm, its traverse and elevation are limited and hand-operated. The sights are basic, telescopic equipment.

Combat usage and weapons effectiveness

The ASU-57 saw limited service with the Egyptian Army in 1967, and was used in the Ogaden in 1978. ASU-57s were used by the North Vietnamese Army in Southeast Asia. ASU-57s and -85s were flown into Prague in 1968, and ASU-85s were airlifted to Kabul in 1979. The accuracy of the 57mm and 85mm guns with modern ammunition is probably superior to that of the PT-76's 76mm gun.

Tactical employment

Both vehicles provide paratroopers with mobile armoured striking power, either as assault guns, supporting attacks with AP or HE fire, or acting as self-propelled anti-tank guns in the defence. Both vehicles will also enhance the mobility of paratroopers riding in or on them.

BMD on parade in Moscow in 1977. Six paratroopers are crammed into the rear compartment for parades only. (US Army)

BMD airborne infantry combat vehicle

Introduced	1970
Weight	8,900kg
Length	5.3m
Height	1.85m
Width	2.65m
Track width	0.23m
Clearance	variable
Ground contact	2.84m
Ground pressure	0.61kg/cm²
Fuel capacity	300 litres
Max road speed	80km/h
Water speed	10km/h
Road range	320km
Gradient	30°
Vertical obstacle	0.8m
Trench	1.6m
Engine	V-6 diesel, 280HP water-cooled
Transmission	mechanical, 5 forward 1 reverse gears
Weapons	as BMP
73mm rounds carried	30
Sagger rounds carried	4 or 5
Elevation	−4°/+33°
Armour (frontal)	15mm (hull), 25mm (turret)
Crew	2
Passengers	6

"The introduction of the BMD to Soviet airborne forces has provided Soviet military planners with a force which is capable of the projection of meaningful military power beyond the borders of the Soviet Union." Lt-Col Joseph Dye, US Army.

The BMD (*Bronevaya Maschina Desantnaya*, airborne combat vehicle) is a lightened, smaller version of the BMP, with the same main armament, basic suspension and hull. The BMD's hull front is shaped differently, and the shorter bow gives it a distinctive snub-nosed, boat-like appearance. Although the BMD has one less road wheel per side than the BMP, it has 10km/h more road speed. The BMD is almost six tons lighter than the BMP. It has a rear-mounted engine and a hydropneumatic suspension with variable-height capability for air transport use. Six men can fit in the BMD's cramped passenger compartment, but two of these – the squad leader and one rifleman – normally sit forward, firing the two side-mounted 7.62mm PKT machine guns. Most BMDs have no firing ports and only one vision block in the passenger compartment, but a few late-production versions (seen from 1976 onwards) have two BMP-style firing ports and vision blocks each side. The paratroopers in the rear compartment must dismount by climbing through the large roof hatch. There is no rear exit. Early BMD models had a visible air filtration intake similar to that of the BMP, but a later version appeared without the intake and the latest has a modified exhaust port, the rectangular shape of which was changed for a circular design. Later models may be designated BMD-1s. The two PKT machine guns may be capable of being fired by the gunner when the squad dismounts. The BMD's optics are apparently similar to those on the BMP, although it lacks the comman-

Turretless BMD-U command vehicle in Afghanistan, 1980. Supports for a canvas roof appear to be stowed on the side of the vehicle. *(US Army)*

der's infra-red searchlight. Late-production BMDs have a tow hook. Other characteristics are similar to those of the BMP. The BMD is fully air-droppable, both with and without a pallet. Special versions include the BMD-U command vehicle, without a turret but with a longer hull, one extra road wheel per side, several radios and a generator. Used in Afghanistan, the BMD-U, like all late-production BMDs, features additional rear fuel cells. BMDs have been seen in Afghanistan with what appears to be a 30mm grenade launcher in place of the 73mm gun.

BMD production is less than 250 machines annually.

Combat usage and weapons effectiveness

BMDs were used in the 1977–78 Ogaden war between Ethiopia and Somalia. Crewed by Cubans, with Soviet and East German "advisers," the BMDs were reportedly used as light tanks in the Ethiopian attack that finally forced the Somalis back across the border. The BMDs and ASU-57s were airlifted over terrain impassable to armour and dropped by parachute. Once an airhead was established they were delivered by transport aircraft. The BMD was apparently only able to operate as a tank because of the lack of Somali anti-tank weapons. The technical capability and characteristics of the BMD allowed the Cubans to achieve the surprise that the Soviet way of war emphasises, and this helped to bring victory.

BMDs have been used extensively in Afghanistan.

With its identical main armament, the BMD has the same effectiveness and limitations as the BMP. However, the BMD lacks the BMP's infamous "bump" in the turret ring.

Tactical employment

The BMD can be used as an infantry combat vehicle, the way the BMP is used in the attack, defence and *reydy taktik*. In the attack, when the paratroopers are not supported by tanks, the BMDs will probably precede the dismounted men, rather than following them like the BMP. Alternatively, in an assault when anti-tank resistance is slight, the BMD may function as a light tank. As much of the mission of the airborne involves raiding, ambushes and attacks on rear areas, the BMD is well suited for these operations, with its cross-country mobility, firepower and ability to carry an airborne squad. It is in these missions, rather than in breakthrough attacks, that the BMD is intended to be used. On the defensive BMDs will engage attacking armour from defending strongpoints, and will probably be used as a counterattack force.

Foreign usage

The ASU-57 is used by the Soviet Union and Yugoslavia, although a number were supplied to Vietnam, Egypt and Ethiopia. The ASU-85 is used by the Poles as well as the Soviets. The BMD is used by the Soviets, but it is unclear what happened to those used by the Cubans in Ogaden; they may have been returned to the USSR. Poland is expected to receive the BMD soon. The US Army has at least one ASU-57, Canada at least two.

Chapter Fifteen

Infantry weapons

"There is no place in war for delicate machinery."
A.P. WAVELL

Bullets from Soviet rifles and machine guns killed half of the two million German soldiers who fell on the Eastern Front. Almost half of the US casualties in Vietnam were from bullets, most of them fired from Soviet-built infantry weapons. Throughout the world it is unshaven men brandishing Kalashnikovs – their banana-shaped magazine silhouette already a universal symbol of revolution – rather than masses of tanks that topple governments and shape world events. These weapons are simple, reliable, rugged and highly effective.

Soviet infantry weapons are intended for suppressive fire. The Kalashnikov assault rifles are basically improved submachine guns using a medium-power cartridge. Neither the submachine gun nor the assault rifle is

Soviet paratroopers armed with the folding-stock AKS 5.45mm assault rifle. (*US Army*)

accurate or long-ranged, but few of today's soldiers have the skill or training to take advantage of long-range accuracy. However, even if a rifleman cannot hit anything, he can at least point his weapon at the enemy and spray – which is all the Soviet Army requires him to do. Only snipers need individual accuracy. In the attack, suppressive fire delivered on foot or from vehicles keeps enemy heads down until they can be defeated by close assault. The over-the-shoulder straps of all Soviet infantry weapons allow the use of "marching fire" – suppressive fire from the hip. In defence, infantry weapons pin down attacking infantry and separate them from their armour, which can be destroyed by anti-tank weapons no longer threatened with suppression by the enemy infantry. These simple tactics are demanded by the Soviet emphasis on speed in the offensive, the degree of training that can be

expected from their conscript riflemen and their equally green squad leaders, and the design of their infantry weapons. They are also a response to a command and control problem. Studies have shown that most riflemen do not fire their weapons in combat: in the US Army during World War Two only 10–15% usually did so. However, soldiers armed with automatic weapons tended to blaze an entire clip away rather than remain silent. The Soviets, aware that their command and control at low level is limited, optimised their weapons and tactics so that all a soldier has to do is blaze away, suppressing the enemy with weight of fire. Some of the bullets fired have to hit.

The Soviet concept of complementary mix of weaponry extends to the lowest levels. The main anti-infantry power of a Soviet squad is its one or two machine guns, while the RPG-7 is the anti-armour punch. The remaining AKMS-armed squad members provide suppression, guard the machine guns and RPG, and make close assaults. For the rare occasions when aimed, long-range single shots are required, each platoon has a sniper.

Soviet motorised rifle units are largely self-sufficient on the battlefield, as they will probably not be able to call on heavy weapons to supplement their firepower in many situations. However, they are almost always used in a combined-arms force. There is no Soviet "foot" infantry. Every Soviet motorised rifle squad will have its APC or BMP in direct support, usually 300–400m away. In addition, tank support is normally provided. As is the case with all Soviet units, motorised rifle squads and platoons fight as part of a combined-arms team.

Assault rifles

Weapon	AK-47	AKM(AKMS)
Calibre	7.62mm	7.62mm
Barrel length	41.5cm	41.5cm
Weight (loaded)	4.81kg	3.76kg (2.96*)
Weight (empty)	4.31kg	3.26kg (3.46)
Length	86.9cm (64.5)	88.8cm (65.3)
Cyclic RoF	600rpm	600rpm
Practical RoF (auto)	100rpm	100rpm
Practical RoF (semi-auto)	40rpm	40rpm
Max range	800m	1,000m
Max effective range (auto)	200m	200m
Max effective range (semi-auto)	300m	300m
Ammunition types	ball, tracer, blank, API, grenade launch	as AK-47
Muzzle velocity	710m/sec	715m/sec
Cartridge	7.62 × 39 intermediate	as AK-47
Unit of fire	300 rounds	300 rounds
Carried by soldier	120 rounds	120 rounds
Magazine	30 rounds	30 rounds

* Figures in parentheses for folding-stock AK-47 and AKMS respectively; length is with stock folded.

The Kalashnikov assault rifles have been the most widely used and most successful of post-war small arms. The three 7.62mm versions all share the same basic characteristics: the Kalashnikov action, automatic fire, 30-round "banana" magazine, and the intermediate cartridge. The original AK-47 has been replaced in the Soviet Army by the AKM and AKMS, which are lighter, easier to produce and maintain, have their rear sights set for ranges up to 1,000m rather than 800, and have straighter stocks.

The new weapons can employ an NSP-2 night sight and a knife-bayonet that, unlike the AK-47's straight bayonet, can function as a wire-cutter. The AKMS is the folding-stock version of the AKM, and is the standard weapon of motorised rifle and airborne units. The intermediate round used with all of these weapons is lighter and less powerful but faster in operation than full-sized rifle ammunition. In addition, it has much greater range, destructive power and accuracy than the pistol rounds used

Soviet-built AK-47 7.62mm assault rifle. *(US Army)*

7.62mm AKM assault rifle. *(US Army)*

7.62mm AKMS assault rifle with folding stock, shown extended in firing position. *(US Army)*

in most submachine guns. The AK-47, first of the series, was introduced in 1949 to replace wartime submachine guns. Designed by Mikhail Kalashnikov, it was an adaptation of the German MP43 and MP44 assault rifles. It proved so successful in Soviet service that it also replaced the SKS carbine, the post-war replacement for the Moisin-Nugant bolt-action rifle. The AKM and AKMS are simply upgraded versions of the basic design.

The ruggedness, simplicity and ease of construction of these weapons has led to their almost universal acceptance. The North Vietnamese and Arabs, and guerrilla and insurgent forces, have even less time than the Soviet Army for sophisticated training and individual marksmanship. Their logistical support is often tenuous; a weapon with a high maintenance requirement is worse than no weapon at all. Simplicity and serviceability, while hard to quantify, are frequently more important than high performance in combat, when a jammed or ammunition-less rifle often results in a casualty. AKMs have functioned normally even after total immersion in mud or water. They have only a few weaknesses. The exposed gas tube is easily dented, which can cause malfunctions due to uneven gas pressure distribution. Sustained firing causes overheating, making them hard to handle, and rounds sometimes "cook off" in the chamber.

Despite their simplicity, Soviet-built Kalashnikovs exhibit a high degree of workmanship. The interior of the barrel is chromium-plated, which reduces wear and fouling and makes it easier to clean. The receiver (the main body of the gun) of the AK-47 was originally milled from solid steel. In the AKM this was replaced by a simpler press-formed sheet-steel receiver, but the bolt and bolt carrier were now rust-proofed, rather than being left bright steel as in the AK-47.

The latest Kalashnikov assault rifle, the AKS or AK-74, was first seen in the November 1977 Red Square parade. It uses a new 5.45mm-calibre round, the first break from 7.62mm weapons since the nineteenth century. Ball and tracer 5.45mm rounds are known to exist. The new round is doubtlessly lighter, although the plastic magazine apparently holds the standard 30 rounds. The new round weighs 53.5 grains and is fast (900m/sec), giving a flat trajectory to 400 or even 500m. The round's design gives it a hollow-point effect. The potentially considerable recoil of such a round is countered by a muzzle brake, which would also reduce the tendency of the weapon to "climb" when fired on automatic. Recoil and muzzle climb are minimal, increasing accuracy. Both the wood and folding-stock versions appear externally similar to the AKM and AKMS. Many of these weapons are possibly rebuilt 7.62mm rifles. The folding-stock version also has a different trigger-guard assembly and plastic magazine. Its muzzle brake/flash suppressor is modified, and it has been reported that it can fire rifle grenades. The designation AKD-74 (*Automat Kalashnikov Desantiia*, air-borne automatic Kalashnikov) has been suggested for the folding-stock version, although its correct designation is probably AKS-74. The muzzle brake on all 5.45mm Soviet weapons is removable, as it makes a considerable flash at night, reducing night vision. By 1981 most Category I motorised rifle units were using 5.45mm weapons.

Combat usage

Kalashnikovs have proved highly effective in almost every war, insurrection and rebellion in the last 25 years, though accuracy in any weapon using the M43 intermediate cartridge is less than that of comparabe NATO weapons. The Soviet round has a trajectory higher than almost any modern service round and is not effective beyond 400m, and its accuracy falls off greatly even before that range. The short distance between sight blades makes fine aiming difficult at short range. Loose tolerances compound the problem. However, the lack of long-range accuracy is not as serious as might be thought. Few soldiers can hit anything over 200m away, and most firefights are at much closer range.

Combat veteran US paratroopers in Vietnam, recipients of much more realistic and longer training than the average Soviet rifleman, scored an average of four to six hits per 1,800 M-16 rounds fired at man-sized targets at 50m – and this was on a target range, without return fire. This can be taken to show that the Soviets are right in emphasising mass over accuracy. It also leads to a suspicion that individual AKMS are very inaccurate indeed. Soviet writings admit that "only one soldier in six" can hit anything through a vehicle gunport. While an AKMS has a 50% probability on paper of hitting a stationary, man-sized target at 300m on a target range, combat experience has shown that while the weapons are deadly up to 100m, effectiveness falls off rapidly over this range. Over 250m their effect is minimal.

Engagement sequence

To fire any Kalshnikov-action weapon the soldier first pulls the charging handle to the rear, ensuring that the chamber is clear. He then lets the bolt slam forward and, putting the selector level on "safe," inserts a magazine into the receiver well. He then pulls the charging handle back and lets it slam forward, drawing the bolt back and chambering a round. He now sets the weapon for either automatic or semi-automatic fire. Then, taking aim through the extremely simple "vee" tangent rear sight and a hooded front-post adjustable sight, he fires. Unlike US Army service rifles, which are supposed to be used for semi-automatic fire, these weapons are normally fired in short bursts.

All Kalashnikov weapons are gas-operated. The gases produced when a round is fired are channelled from the firing chamber into the gas cylinder above the barrel, and the piston in the cylinder is pushed backwards by the expanding gas. The piston is attached to the bolt, which it pulls back, ejecting the spent brass through the ejector and cocking the firing hammer. As the bolt travels, it compresses a return spring which then pushes it forward, stripping off a new round from the magazine and feeding it into the chamber as it goes. The bolt then locks itself in firing position with two rotating-block lugs which give a strong, rigid action and good extraction. All these moving parts are solidly machined and their number kept to a minimum. The weapon can be easily stripped. The recoil system and strong ejection allow the use of ammunition with differing characteristics and reduce jamming. The position of the gas cylinder above the barrel keeps the recoil thrust line low and reduces – but does not eliminate – muzzle climb when firing on automatic. Muzzle climb and recoil – the result of using inferior non-Soviet ammunition – caused some North Vietnamese soldiers to discard their AK-47s in favour of M-16s, which were easier on the small soldiers. Many of their US Marine Corps opponents, however, scorned the M-16 and used the AK-47.

Foreign production

Kalashnikovs are also produced throughout the Warsaw Pact countries, in China, Yugoslavia, Finland and many workshops and factories in the Middle East. Many of these weapons are inferior to the Soviet original.

Light and general-purpose machine guns

Weapon	RPK	PK	SGMT/SGMB
Calibre	7.62mm	7.62mm	7.62mm
Barrel length	61cm	65.8cm	72cm
Weight (bipod)	5.6kg	9kg	13.5kg (AFV)
Weight (tripod)	–	16.5kg	–
Length	104cm (82)*	108cm	115cm
Cyclic RoF	600rpm	650rpm	600rpm
Practical RoF	150rpm	250rpm	250rpm
Ammunition types	ball, tracer blank, API	ball, steel ball, tracer, API, AP, ranging	as PK
Muzzle velocity	745m/sec	825m/sec	800m/sec
Cartridge	7.62 × 39 M43 intermediate	7.62 × 54R full power	7.62 × 54R full power
Effective range	800m	1,000m	1,000m
Armour penetration (AP round) @ 500m	6mm	8mm	8mm
Feed	magazine	belt	belt
Magazine/belt size	30/40/70 rounds	50/250 rounds	250 rounds
Unit of fire	1,000 rounds	2,500 rounds	2,500 rounds
Carried by squad (per gun)	1,000 rounds	1,000 rounds	–

* Figures in parentheses are for folding-stock, airborne version of RPK.

From 1926 to the 1950s the Soviets used developments of the basic DP-series light machine guns: the DP, DTM, DPM and RP-46, plus the heavier SGM series, firing the standard full-sized 7.62mm rifle cartridge. The post-war RPD was the DP design using the intermediate M1943 cartridge. Despite its bulk, the RPD was the standard North Vietnamese light machine gun duirng the Vietnam War, and is still standard issue in China and North Korea. However, like all the previous machine guns, it has been replaced over the last 20 years by two Kalashnikov-action weapons, the RPK light machine gun and the PK general-purpose machine gun series, which remain in front-line Soviet service.

The RPK was introduced in 1960. Basically an

RPK 7.62mm light machine gun with 30-round magazine. *(US Army)*

PK 7.62mm general-purpose machine gun with bipod mount. *(US Army)*

enlarged, bipod-mounted AKM, with many interchange-able parts, it used the M1943 intermediate cartridge and could fire standard AK magazines as well as its 40-round box and 75-round snail drum magazines. It retains the usual Kalashnikov ruggedness and simplicity. As with all Soviet machine guns, the gunner does not have to set head space or timing, making them simpler than Western models. The RPK, however, lacks an easily detachable barrel – a great drawback, as it overheats rapidly and wear is considerable at high rates of fire. Combined with the poor long-range characteristics of its ammunition, this makes the RPK inadequate. Nonetheless, it still remains in front-line Soviet service, and each BTR-60-mounted squad normally has one, plus a PKM.

The PK series has much greater capability than the RPK. It is a general-purpose machine gun capable of sustained fire from a variety of mounts. Weighing almost

twice as much as the RPK, it uses full-power 7.62mm cartridges, which means that squads using the PK must carry two different, non-interchangeable types of 7.62mm ammunition. This was probably unavoidable as a result of the different roles of rifle and machine gun rounds: machine guns must sustain fire at 1,000m and do not have to be as light as rifles. The PK series employs the basic Kalashnikov action, with a gas cylinder under the easily changed barrel. The modified feed system – based on that of the SGM – uses the strong ejection pull to handle the belted, full-size ammunition. All versions of the PK have little recoil and no tendency to climb when fired. Its construction is simple and robust, consisting of riveted stampings. When fitted on vehicles or tripod mounts, its belts are kept in 250-round boxes; otherwise 50-round magazines are used. The non-disintegrating belt can get in the way if the PK must be moved during firing. Lighter

PKMB 7.62mm tripod-mounted GPMG. *(US Army)*

and easier to use and maintain than the US M-60, the PK has 100m less effective range than the American weapon. Extensive tests of PKMs by the US Army at Fort Benning found the Soviet gun much better received than the M60. The PKM's reliability was especially praised, its stoppage rate being negligible.

Each motorised rifle squad in a BMP has two bipod-mounted PKs or PKMs, improved models which are slightly lighter and easier to produce. The PKB and the improved PKMB are the respective tripod-mounted versions. The PKT is the standard vehicle-mounted light machine gun, and is the basic Soviet coaxial AFV weapon, replacing the 7.62mm SGMT/SGMB Gorunov machine gun still used on some older vehicles.

A new 5.45mm light machine gun, the RPK-74, is in service, replacing RPKs in airborne units using 5.45mm assault rifles. Similar to the RPK (possibly even built from the earlier gun), the RPK-74 weighs 5.35kg with a full 40-round metal and plastic magazine and measures 1.06m in length. Its maximum automatic rate of fire is 600rpm and its maximum effective range is 800m. All the examples currently in the possession of the US Army are new production weapons rather than rebuilds. The RPK-74 fires the same PS 5.45mm round as the AKS-74 and can take an NSP night sight.

Combat usage

Soviet light machine guns have seen almost as much combat as the assault rifles, and have proved to be effective weapons in action. Unlike riflemen, machine gunners almost always fire in combat, and most casualty-causing bullets have come from machine guns. The Soviets know that the machine gun is the key to dismounted firepower.

A 6-9-round burst with a PKB has a 50% chance of hitting a stationary, fire-team-sized target at 1,000m under firing range conditions (800m in the case of the PKM). The PKM has the same chance of hitting a standing man at 550m. The number of targets it can hit depends upon terrain and deployment. In Vietnam light machine guns seldom hit more than one target per burst. However, wartime German light machine guns proved capable of decimating whole battalions when firing from enfilading positions. Today's Soviet weapons are no less capable.

A PKM's chances of hitting a moving, man-sized target in the open with a 6-9-round burst (range and accuracy approximate to ±10%) are:

Range (m)	50	100	175	250	500	750	1,000
Chance of hit	97%	83%	69%	56%	42%	31%	3%

SGMB 7.62mm machine gun as mounted on BTR-60P APCs, including collecting bag for spent brass. *(US Army)*

Light machine guns can be effective against unarmoured vehicles. With a six-nine-round burst a light machine gun has the following chances of damaging an unarmoured, stationary vehicle:

Range (m)	100	200	300	500	800	1,000
Chance (%)	95	70	60	45	35	15

If hits are scored, the target will be destroyed approximately 65% of the time.

The PK's full-size cartridge gives superior penetration. At close range it can penetrate 37mm of mild steel, 127mm of concrete, 178mm of sand and 280mm of earth, compared to 25mm, 100mm, 150mm and 229mm respectively for the intermediate round.

Tactical employment

While mounted, light machine guns are fired from the foremost gun port of BTR-60PBs, BMPs and BMDs. Whether fired from a gun port or mounted coaxially, the accuracy of a machine gun fired from a moving vehicle is

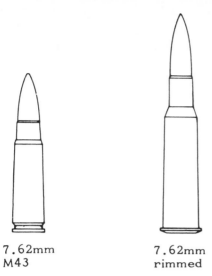

7.62mm
M43

7.62mm
rimmed

Comparative sizes of Soviet intermediate and full-power cartridges.

The "51 calibre" of the Vietnam War: a 12.7mm DshK with a simple leaf sight on a tripod mount, the standard Communist air-defence weapon in South Vietnam for much of the war. (*US Army*)

extremely low, even if moving over a paved surface, as the US Army found out in Vietnam. The main function of these weapons is suppression. When a squad dismounts, the light machine gunners stay in the centre of the squad skirmish line, close to the squad leader, with one AKMS-armed soldier acting as assistant gunner for each light machine gun. Light machine guns will be fired from the assault position, giving marching fire while advancing, which degrades accuracy but adds to the weight of fire.

On the defensive, machine guns are positioned on likely avenues of approach for dismounted attack, using inter-locking, co-ordinated fields of fire. They will protect the RPG-7 against enemy small-arms fire. At night machine guns will be readied to fire on fixed lines.

Foreign manufacture

The RPK was built in Yugoslavia and East Germany.

Heavy machine guns

Weapon	DShKM	KPV
Calibre	12.7mm	14.5mm
Barrel length	96.7cm	135cm
Weight (on AFV)	34kg	51kg
Length	158.8cm	200.7cm
Cyclic RoF	540–600	600
Practical RoF	80	150
Max range	7,000m	8,000m
Effective range (AA)	1,000m	1,400m
Effective range (ground)	1,500m	2,000m
Ammunition types	ball, tracer, others	API, AP, HE
Muzzle velocity	830–850m/sec	1,000m/sec
Cartridge	12.7 × 108	14.5 × 114
Operation	gas	gas
Cooled	air	air
Armour penetration (AP round) @ 500m	20mm	32mm
Feed	belt	belt

Heavy machine guns are used either as the armament of scout cars and APCs or as anti-aircraft defence for tanks. The latter practice was abandoned by the US Army, but has recently been re-emphasised by the Soviets, probably as a result of the threat posed by ATGM-firing helicopters. T-62 tanks that were produced without anti-aircraft machine guns have been retrofitted with them. All new T-64 and T-72 tanks also have them.

The 12.7mm DShK and the similar DShKM (which differs only in having a simpler ammunition feed system)

DShKM 12.7mm machine gun and sight on the standard tank turret anti-aircraft mount. *(US Army)*

are pre-war designs. Originally used in a variety of ground mounts, they are now used exclusively in the Soviet Army as the standard tank anti-aircraft machine guns, although a new design of 12.7mm machine gun has been seen mounted on T-72s.

This Kalashnikov-action weapon is designated the NSVT. It is basically a scaled-up PKM and is much lighter and more reliable than earlier 12.7mm designs. It has a quick-change barrel and a flash-hider. It uses 50-round belts, probably made up of new-model ammunition. Performance is similar to that of the DShKM, although practical rate of fire is increased to 100rpm.

The 14.5mm KPVT is used as dual-purpose main armament on BTR-60PB APCs and BRDM-2 scout cars. It is a simple weapon, without adjustable head space or timing. Well sealed against dirt and dust, the body is basically a steel cylinder to which components are riveted or welded. The same basic gun as the KPV is used in the ZPU-4, its heavy ammunition, originally used by anti-

tank rifles, giving superior armour penetration. It has a chromed barrel.

Both guns are old, and too heavy for their limited effectiveness. Light machine guns can be more effective against troops, and heavy machine guns lack the armour penetration of automatic cannon. Fitted with reflector sights, they retain a deterrent anti-aircraft role, disrupting attacks with streams of spectacular green tracer rather than shooting aircraft down.

Combat usage

Soviet heavy machine guns have seen extensive combat. The DShK was a standard weapon in World War Two and Soviet, Czech and Chinese-built versions have been used worldwide since then. In South Vietnam the DShK and DShKM, named "51 calibre" by the Americans, were the primary anti-aircraft weapons. The Soviets have been on the receiving end of both weapons in Afghanistan.

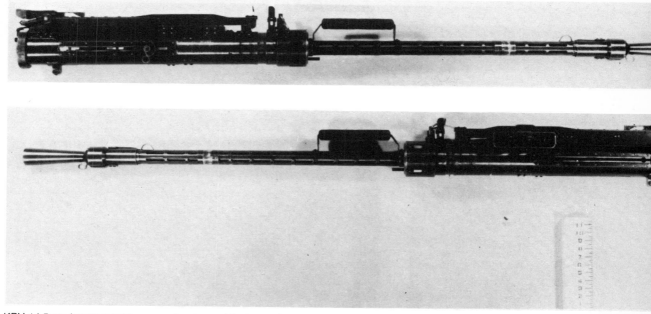

KPV 14.5mm heavy machine gun, showing quick-change handle on barrel. *(US Army)*

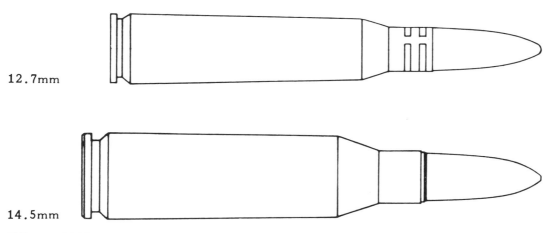

12.7mm

14.5mm

12.7mm and 14.5mm machine-gun ammunition (full size). *(US Army)*

US Army simulator tests indicate that a pintle-mounted DShKM on top of a tank has the following chances of shooting down an AH-1 Cobra helicopter gun-ship, based on a 6-8sec burst at a crossing helicopter exposed for 20sec:

US Army estimates give a DShKM the following chances of scoring a "hit" (which could entail more than one round striking the target) with a 9-15-round burst on a vehicle standing in the open:

Range (m)	500	1,000	1,500
Chance of kill (%)	10	10	5

Range (m)	100	200	300	500	800	1,000
Chance (%)	95	80	70	50	40	20

65% of the unarmoured vehicles hit will be killed, as will 30% of the armoured vehicles hit, if their armour can be penetrated.

If stationary, a DShKM engages ground targets with several short bursts. When firing on the move, long bursts are walked on to the target. Aircraft receive one continuous burst.

Foreign manufacture

The DShK was produced in Czechoslovakia and in China as the Type 54.

Dragunov SVD 7.62mm sniper rifle. *(US Army)*

SVD Dragunov 7.62mm sniper's rifle

Barrel length	62cm
Weight (loaded)	4.52kg
Weight (empty)	3.72kg
Length	122.5cm
Maximum RoF	30rpm
Aimed RoF	4rpm
Max range	2,500m
Effective range	1,300m
Muzzle velocity	830m/sec
Cartridge	7.62 × 54R full power
Unit of fire	800 rounds
Carried by sniper	140 rounds
Magazine	10 rounds

The Soviets have emphasised the importance of sniping since World War One and developed it into a fine art in World War Two. The SVD Dragunov, however, is the first Soviet rifle designed especially for sniping. Introduced in the 1960s to replace the bolt-action Moisin-Nugant M1891/30, the Dragunov uses a single-shot or semi-automatic version of the basic Kalashnikov action and a full-size, long-range 7.62mm × 54R rimmed cartridge. Its PSO-1 sight is basically a four-power telescope with a 6° field of vision and an integral rangefinder that is lit at night. It has an infra-red viewing metascope that can detect infra-red light sources and can itself be used passively or in conjunction with an infra-red light source. A combination flash-suppressor and compensator reduces muzzle jump and flash. The skeleton stock with cheekpad improves balance. The pull of the trigger mechanism has been made more sensitive than that of other Kalashnikov-action weapons, and the trigger guard is large enough for the sniper to use mittens. The Dragunov can use the AKM's wirecutting bayonet. The standard of workmanship in the Dragunov is higher than that of other Soviet infantry weapons.

Combat usage

The effectiveness of the Dragunov depends heavily on the skill of the sniper. Snipers are trained in 45–60 days by their units, at least some of which have special sniper schools. They are normally selected from those who did well in pre-conscription DOSAAF target shooting, and receive much more intensive marksmanship training and target practice than the average Soviet soldier.

A Dragunov-armed sniper has the following chances of striking a standing, man-sized target:

Range (m)	50	200	300	500	700	800	1,000	1,600
Chance of hit (%)	95+	95	90	80	60	50	20	5

A sniper could not engage more than two targets in 30sec if he wanted to obtain this level of accuracy.

Accuracy varies with the type of ammunition used. The Dragunov can fire light ball, heavy ball, steel core, tracer and anti-tank incendiary ammunition, but only the ball rounds are accurate. The tracer, in particular, makes precise shooting difficult.

Tactical employment

Each Soviet motorised rifle platoon has one Dragunov-armed sniper, who aids the suppressive fire by picking off high-priority individual targets at long range. Prime targets are officers, tank commanders, scouts, weapons crews (especially those of ATGMs) and messengers. The Soviets believe that harrassing fire at long range, even if it does not cause casualties, will keep enemy heads down, and that knowing a Soviet sniper is watching their every move will reduce enemy morale.

In the defence the sniper takes up a position within the platoon strongpoint. He will engage individual enemy scouts either on foot or in vehicles at long range, so that the platoon does not have to fire its light machine guns. The sniper will move if necessary to avoid return fire. Concealment is stressed. Bushes and treetops often provide cover for snipers, and they use an effective, light camouflage screen. Snipers are also used in dismounted patrolling and raids. The Soviets believe that much sniping will take place at night as the enemy attempts to move under cover of darkness, and snipers may be aided by mortar flares and similar illumination.

Engagement sequence

The Dragunov is loaded and readied in much the same way as other Kalashnikov-action weapons. Fire is always by aimed single shots.

PM Makarov 9mm automatic pistol, with the characteric star on the butt. *(US Army)*

Pistols are not significant weapons, and the Soviets minimise their use. Nevertheless, officers above platoon commanders and many AFV and weapons crews carry the Makarov PM 9mm pistol. A very compact piece, the PM has an eight-round magazine. Its design is based upon the German Walther PP pistol, with the same double-action hammer and slide-mounted safety catch. Light and handy, it is adequate for self-defence but does not measure up to heavier pistols for combat shooting. Its numerous small components make disassembly difficult.

AGS-17 automatic grenade launcher

The Soviet automatic grenade launcher, introduced in the late 1970s, is believed to fire 30mm grenades from a belt or from a large, 30-round drum. Mounted on a tripod,

AGS-17 grenade launcher. *(Soldat & Technik)*

Makarov PM 9mm pistol

Barrel length	9.6cm
Weight (loaded)	0.81kg
Weight (empty)	0.75kg
Length	16cm
Rate of fire	30rpm
Max effective range	50m
Cartridge	9mm × 18 pistol
Operation	gas blow-back
Unit of fire	16 rounds
Carried by soldier	16 rounds
Magazine	8 rounds

AGS-17 grenade launcher in action while a motorised rifle platoon advances past in textbook echelon formation, their BTR-60PBs providing close support. *(Soldat & Technik)*

this weapon, designated the AGS-17 (*Automatichesky Granatomat Stankovy*, automatic grenade launcher), is reportedly in service with Soviet forces in East Germany. Two are reportedly issued to each motorised rifle company. Each 30mm grenade weighs 300–400g.

Little is known of the AGS-17's performance. The grenade's effectiveness is probably similar to that of the US 40mm grenade, which has a five-metre burst radius and can penetrate 50mm of armour at close range. The AGS may use beehive rounds in addition to HE, HEAT or HE-Frag types. The US weapon has a maximum range of 400m, but the AGS may well have a longer range; up to 1,500m has been suggested. Effective range is 800m. There are reports that a Soviet grenade-launching system – possibly the AGS-17 – is being adapted for helicopter use. Its area-fire capabilities would make it an effective helicopter weapon.

The AGS-17 is currently in action in Afghanistan.

The scale of AGS-17 issue is now reported to be two per BTR-60PB-equipped company. It can be fired from on-vehicle mountings as well as from its tripod.

Grenades

Grenade	F-1	RG-42	RGD-5	RKG-3M	RDG-1
Type	HE	HE	HE	AT	smoke
Diameter	55mm	54mm	57mm	55mm	46mm
Length	124mm	127mm	114mm	362mm	250mm
Type charge	HE	HE	HE	HEAT	smoke
Charge weight	60gm	118gm	110gm	567gm	–
Fuze (delay)	3–4sec	3–4sec	3–4sec	contact	5sec
Range	34m	40m	45m	15–20m	–
Burst radius	15–20m	15–20m	15–20m	impact	20 × 8m
Armour penetration	–	–	–	125mm	–

Soviet riflemen carry both fragmentation and anti-tank grenades. The fragmentation grenades include the wartime F-1 and RG-42 types and the modern, more compact RGD-5. The standard anti-tank grenade is the RKG-3M. This uses a stabilising drogue to ensure the proper angle of impact for its HEAT warhead, and although it is relatively ineffective and short-ranged (it must be tossed underhand or dropped from a window), it apparently remains in service. The RDG-1 and -2 smoke grenades emit a dense white smoke. The RDG-2 can cover an area 20m long and 8m wide, burning for 90sec.

The Soviet Army does not use rifle grenades, although unconfirmed reports suggest that one may be introduced for use with the AKS-74.

RG-42 offensive HE grenade. *(US Marine Corps)*

RKG-3 anti-tank grenades, showing the parachute used for stabilisation. A cigarette lighter provides scale. *(US Marine Corps)*

Chapter Sixteen

Helicopters

"Helicopters, equipped with diverse types of modern weapons and capable of destroying ground targets, have become an indispensable part of modern combat."

COL M. KIRYUKHIN

Soviet interest in helicopters and their military use began in the early 1950s, but it was only in the mid and late 1970s that the Soviets began to place an increasing emphasis on helicopters as a key element of army operations.

There is no Soviet Army Aviation on the Anglo-American model. All helicopters are part of the Air Force's Frontal Aviation and, like the rest of the air armies of which helicopter regiments are a part, will be placed under the operational control of front commanders. Helicopter regiments, either in whole or in part, may be further subordinated to army or division level – the lowest level to have direct interface with Air Force command – or even lower levels for special missions.

The roles of Soviet helicopters are attack and transport, although there is no distinct line between the two tasks. While all Soviet units have a reconnaissance mission to a greater or lesser degree, the absence of specialised scout helicopters on the Anglo-American model probably means that this is not considered a priority function of helicopter units. For many years attack missions were performed by armed versions of standard transport helicopters – Mi-2s, Mi-4s and especially Mi-8s – but starting in 1972 these have been supplanted by the purpose-built Mi-24 Hind series, which are now the main Soviet attack helicopters.

Their major role is the destruction or suppression of enemy tanks, anti-tank weapons (especially ATGMs) and helicopters, the weapons which the Soviets believe pose the greatest threat to their attacks. Attack helicopters support heliborne assaults, *desants* and other special operations, providing a flexible tactical air power capability that is especially important to units that lack heavy weapons. In addition to providing close air support, attack helicopters can attack ground targets in the same way as fighter-bombers and aid in target acquisition for other weapons systems. Transport helicopters move both supplies and troops. Although the Soviet supply requirement is very much greater than the helicopter resupply capability, transport helicopters allow the Soviets to transport high-priority items quickly and to resupply

forces beyond the reach of wheeled transport, especially heliborne units and *desants*.

Although demonstrations were carried out as early as 1956, the transportation of units by helicopter for heliborne assaults was first seen in the 1967 "Dnepr" manoeuvres, and since then the practice has played an increasingly important role in Soviet operations. Heliborne assaults are used to seize key operational and tactical objectives in the offensive and to act as operational mobile reserves on the defensive. In addition to heliborne assaults, helicopters can bring units into secured areas to consolidate objectives or bypass obstacles on the ground. The extensive use of transport helicopters in Ethiopia and Afghanistan shows the importance that the Soviets attach to this new aid to the mobility of firepower, troops and supplies.

The Soviets do not recognise any great distinction between helicopters used by Aeroflot and the Air Force. As Aeroflot helicopters are owned by the state and their crews are invariably reservists, they can be counted as practically a part of the Air Force helicopter strength. Some civilian Mi-6s are even camouflaged in peacetime.

Total Soviet Air Force helicopter strength is about 3,700–4,000 aircraft. Aeroflot helicopter strength is unknown, but probably numbers 1,200 machines or more. Production is reported to be 1,200 helicopters a year, although estimates vary.

Heliborne assault operations

The Soviets do not maintain specialised airmobile units with their own helicopters for heliborne assault operations. They believe that any well trained motorised rifle battalion should be capable of use in the heliborne assault role with a minimum (one day or less) of special training. This is similar to the practice of the US Marine Corps and the British Army, both of which believe heliborne operations to be within the competence of normal infantry

Mi-2 Hoplite. *(US Army)*

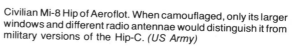

Civilian Mi-8 Hip of Aeroflot. When camouflaged, only its larger windows and different radio antennae would distinguish it from military versions of the Hip-C. *(US Army)*

Afghan Hip-C brought down by National Islamic Movement forces in 1979.

units. When there are no motorised rifle battalions available for these missions the Soviets may employ airborne battalions in heliborne assaults, as they did in "Dnepr." The motorised rifle battalion appears to be the standard force used in a heliborne attack, and may be reinforced by engineers, NBC reconnaissance teams, air and artillery liaison parties and, if sufficient heavy-lift helicopters are available, a 122mm artillery battery. The battalion will of course be lifted without its APCs or BMPs, although light trucks may also be lifted in. Such a force could be lifted by 30 Mi-4s and five Mi-6s (more Mi-6s would be required for heavy equipment), or 20+ Mi-8s, depending on attachments. Mi-8s can lift light trucks and BRDMs. Such a force is intended to be able to hold until relieved for 24 or possibly 48h, despite its lack of mobility and heavy weapons.

Seizing river crossing sites and isolating them from enemy reserve units by emplacing blocking forces is one of the most important tasks of heliborne units, and is usually performed by heliborne forward detachments. The Soviets believe that the helicopter's mobility greatly enhances the capabilities of forward detachments in both conventional and nuclear environments. Helicopters allow units to exploit the results of nuclear strikes: troops can land 15–20min after detonation, before the enemy has had time to react. Other objectives of heliborne assaults include seizing key terrain or crossroads, acting as a blocking force during a pursuit, interfering with enemy troop movements, locating and destroying nuclear weapons, headquarters, communications facilities and other priority targets, and target acquisition for other weapons. Heliborne assaults are often mounted in co-operation with airborne *desants*, *reydy*, forward detachments and amphibious operations; in the last-named case heliborne forces will often be used to isolate beach heads from the enemy.

Heliborne assault tactics

The planning of a heliborne assault is initiated at division or higher level. How far the assaulting units will be placed behind the enemy front lines depends on the situation and mission. In a tactical heliborne assault, such as one carried out in conjunction with a breakthrough attack against a river line, the assault may be made one to ten kilometres ahead, within range of supporting artillery. In conventional operations a battalion may be inserted 35–50km or more ahead of the advancing forces, while in nuclear operations this distance can be as much as 100km.

Soviet troops move out of the landing zone, while their Mi-8 transport helicopters withdraw. The Mi-8s are each armed with four 57mm rocket pods for LZ preparation. *(V.M. Martinova)*

Because the Soviets realise that heliborne battalions will either have to be linked up with the main force or withdrawn in a relatively short time, they are most likely to be used in mobile battle conditions.

Heliborne operations are mounted from a pickup zone, 20km or more behind the front line, often at night. The assault force will be assigned a fly-through route that minimises exposure to enemy air-defence weapons. Defence suppression will be provided by artillery, fixed-wing aircraft or nuclear weapons. The transport helicopters will fly at 50–100m altitude, taking advantage of terrain, and will be escorted by Hinds and a top cover of fighters. The landing zone (LZ) should be clear of enemy units as a result of the pre-assault suppression, but the Hinds and the armament fitted to the transport helicopters will also be used to clear the LZ – although taking transport helicopters into a "hot" LZ is likely to result in heavy losses. The Soviets hope to unload (or load) a battalion in 10–15min. Alternative or dummy LZs will be designated and used as required. Once the battalion forms up on the ground, it moves out for the objective. Hinds or Hip-Es will remain in the area as long as possible to provide close air support.

Transport helicopters are vital to military operations in difficult terrain. In Ethiopia helicopters flew supplies and transported Cuban and Ethiopian troops over otherwise impassable terrain. In Afghanistan the Soviets have emphasised the use of helicopters from the start of their involvement, employing helicopters to secure the roads snaking through mountain valleys and passes for the passage of motor convoys by detecting and attacking any enemy forces in ambush position on the overlooking heights. Outpost detachments are landed by helicopter to secure these heights until the column passes and are then lifted out. If these outposts are attacked, the firepower of hovering Hinds will prevent them from being overrun.

Attack helicopter operations

While the Hind is the first specialised Soviet attack helicopter, attack missions have also been carried out by armed Mi-2, Mi-4 and especially Mi-8 transport helicopters, using rocket and machine gun pods and Sagger ATGMs on outrigger mounts. Today transport helicopters are often armed for defence suppression when landing troops or for self-defence against enemy helicopters. Even the big Mi-6 Hook sometimes carries a 12.7mm machine gun in the nose.

In recent years Soviet writings have shown an awareness of both the effectiveness and limitations of the attack helicopter. Like anything else on the modern battlefield, an attack helicopter that is seen can be killed, but the Soviets know that less than 40% of the battlefield exposures of attack helicopters are detected by enemy troops, and less than 33% are detected by fixed-wing aircraft. Additionally, the lethality of the attack helicopter's weaponry has increased, making judiciously timed and placed exposure highly effective.

As well as killing ATGM-armed helicopters and acquiring targets for other weapons systems, the Hind can conduct its own air-mobile operations, as it can carry a number of troops in its large cabin. Thus it can also perform transport helicopter missions, although it is more likely to be used in small-scale operations, such as anti-tank *desants*, while the Mi-8s carry the bulk of the battalion-sized assaults. The Hind could also fill the Soviet gap in dedicated close air-support aircraft. As fixed-wing air strikes are normally pre-planned at high levels of command, Hinds may be able to provide Soviet tactical units with an on-call air capability. Maj-Gen M. Belov, the Soviets' leading theorist on helicopter warfare, has stated that the success of offensives is doubtful "unless mass use is made of helicopters." It is obvious that the strong emphasis on the attack helicopter has been one of the Soviet responses to the challenge posed to their tactical system by improving technology.

Attack helicopter tactics

Soviet attack helicopters normally fly in flights of four, with pairs in mutual support. Normally two or more flights will operate in mutual support against a target, making co-ordinated attacks from different directions or, if "stepped up" like flights of fighter aircraft, a high flight may act as a diversion and draw fire while the low flights go in to the attack. Pairs of attack helicopters may use similar tactics, one hovering at 100m to spot targets and draw fire, while the other stays at low altitude to attack. The Soviets will attempt to co-ordinate the use of attack helicopters with artillery (especially against enemy air-defence weapons) and fixed-wing aircraft, which also guard against enemy fighters.

Like their US counterparts, Soviet attack helicopters will use woods and ridges for pop-up attacks, popping up from five or ten metres altitude to 20–100m and firing at targets 2,000–3,000m away, a procedure that should take 20–30sec. If terrain permits, they will also use ground-level concealed firing positions. Although even the latest models of the Hind are not as manoeuvrable as the US AH-1, and they cannot use the extreme forms of nap-of-the-earth flying upon which US helicopters rely, there is little doubt that Hinds are capable of effective operations at low altitude. When the target requires, or when opposition is light, Hinds will make diving attacks from about 1,000m altitude, using machine guns, rockets and even bombs in an attack pattern similar to that used by US gunships in Vietnam, but breaking away at the end of the firing pass into a sharp evasive turn or terrain-hugging flight. Hinds have been observed using these tactics when bombing rebel villages in Afghanistan. Although Hind-A crews seem to lack night sights for their Swatter-B ATGMs, they train for night action with rockets and machine guns. The Spiral ATGM reportedly fitted to the Hind-D and subsequent models may have all-weather capability. Heavy use is made of simulators, especially for weapons training.

These tactics place a heavy burden on the helicopter crews. Each flight commander is responsible for guiding his formation through complex tactical manoeuvres, and it would appear that Soviet attack helicopter tactics are not as flexible as those used by Western armies, just as Soviet fighter tactics in air combat are more rigid than those used in the West. Because of its recent rapid expansion the Soviet helicopter force may well have experienced growing pains, and it is doubtful whether it can match the US tactical expertise gained in Southeast Asia, or the skill of US helicopter pilots. This would help to give the US the edge in helicopter-to-helicopter combat.

The integration of attack helicopters with ground forces may present a problem. In Afghanistan Soviet sub-units have apparently co-operated closely with attack helicopters, although the scale of operations there would allow ground forces to use Air Force liaison teams on a scale that would not be possible in a general war. The Soviets have mentioned that there are co-ordination problems between ground troops and helicopters, resulting in helicopters destroying a target already knocked out by ground units or not engaging the proper target, for instance. It must also be noted that helicopter crews are "blue-suiters," Air Force personnel. In the US Army, by contrast, all the helicopters are equipped with Army radios and their officers are all trained as ground unit – usually armour – officers as well. The Soviets are not likely to achieve a comparable degree of co-operation.

Because helicopters belong to the Air Force, Soviet co-ordination of their use with the Army is not the same as in Western armies. The Air Force representative at division and army headquarters has a four to six-man staff that assists in preparing air support for the unit and in relaying this request – which, at division, means going through the army-level Air Force representative – to the supporting air units. In special circumstances a member of the Air Force representative's staff may be assigned to work with an Army commander at his forward command post. This is not a continuing assignment, and lacks the broad co-ordinating powers of a US-style forward air controller. It has been reported that Soviet mobile forces in Afghanistan make extensive use of Air Force "guides" for co-ordination with helicopters.

The Soviets may well hope to make up with weaponry what they lack in tactics or experience. While it is never expressly stated, many Soviet articles imply that the best anti-helicopter weapon may be another helicopter. US tests have shown that jet fighters have a difficult time killing helicopters. US helicopters using tactics of minimal exposure and stand-off ATGM use, made possible by close co-ordination between attack helicopters and light observation helicopters (Hinds must perform both roles), were shown in the Ansbach tests of the 1970s to be capable of inflicting an 18:1 kill ratio on Soviet-type tank units despite dense air defences. Each US Army division in Germany will soon have a full battalion of anti-tank helicopters, and the thought of what such a battalion could do to a second-echelon tank division caught moving to the front cannot be reassuring to Soviet planners. Because of this, the Soviets may be adding another element to their complementary weapons systems: the world's first anti-helicopter helicopter. Unofficially called the Hind-F, it is reported to be similar to the Hind-D but armed with either AA-8 air-to-air or suitably modified SA-9 surface-to-air heat-seeking missiles and an air-combat gunsight. US intelligence sources cannot confirm or deny the existence of an air-to-air Hind, but the Soviets undoubtedly have the capability to produce such an aircraft if they consider it necessary.

Helicopter technology

The first, piston-engined, Soviet helicopters were crude and unreliable; Krushchev stated that he was advised not to fly in them. The Chairman himself was able to help to rectify this by personally asking President Eisenhower for two Sikorsky VH-34s, from which the Soviets reportedly copied extruded aluminium spar rotor blade construction, still used in Soviet helicopters today.

Soviet rotor-head components (much of the head is steel) and shafting are of cast (not forged) titanium. Their turboshaft helicopter engines also make extensive use of titanium to withstand the increased turbine inlet temperatures (rather than an increased compression ratio) that, Western engineers believe, account for the increased power of the more recent turboshafts. Despite this, Soviet helicopter engines are still based on 1950s technology, and the power:weight ratio of these engines (without transmission) is over 40% less than that of comparable Western engines. Despite the increased inlet temperatures, it is estimated that inefficient cooling makes them approximately 150°C cooler than Western designs. Fuel consumption is approximately 25% higher than that of Western powerplants. However, the engines are rugged and simple, requiring minimum maintenance between overhauls. Time between overhauls is 500h for the turboshaft and gears, with an operating life of 1,500h, the same as for the rotor blades. The US Army foresees a maximum 12h-per-day usage for each helicopter, so the Soviets should be able to sustain a short war with their present equipment. But the inability of the holding unit to perform overhauls on many items of equipment (in line with Soviet policies of centralisation) could reduce operating capabilities over the long term.

All Soviet helicopters are structurally strong and stressed to at least three times the force of gravity. Hinds, Hooks and Hips all have strong multiple-plate structures, at least around the engine transmission area, shown by the flat inner surface to the access panels on which ground crew stand during engine maintenance. The Hind may use high-quality steel behind the aluminium skin to form spaced armour around vulnerable points. In addition to the armour that is known to be fitted in the cockpit front and around the cabin fuel tank (but not the belly tank) and engine on the Hind-A, some Western analysts believe that the Hind-D has titanium structural belly armour, supposedly proof against machine gun fire (Afghans have apparently downed Hinds with small arms by firing from high ground). All Hinds have a retractable landing gear.

Transport helicopters

Type	Mi-2 Hoplite	Mi-4 Hound	Mi-8 Hip
First flown	1961	1952	1961
Production	1963–	1953–64	1964–
Empty weight	2,372kg	5,200kg	6,816kg
Normal take-off	3,550kg	7,150kg	11,100kg
Max take-off weight	3,700kg	7,550kg	12,000kg
Payload (max)	800kg	1,740kg	4,000kg
Payload (slung)	800kg	–	3,000kg
Fuel (max)	500kg	700kg	1,450kg
Fuselage length	11.4m	16.79m	18.31m
Main rotor diameter	14.5m (3 blades)	21.0m (4 blades)	21.29m (5 blades)
Height	3.45m	5.18m	5.6m
Engine	2 × 1,400HP Isotov GTD-350 turboshafts	1 × 1,700HP Shvetsov ASh-82V piston	2 × 1,500HP Isotov TB-2-117A turboshafts
Max speed	210km/h	210km/h	260km/h
Cruising speed	160km/h	180km/h	225km/h
Range (max load)	170km	200km	460km
Ferry range	580km	410km	950km
Initial climb rate	4.5m/sec	5.0m/sec	6.5m/sec
Service ceiling	4,000m	5,000m	4,500m
Hover ceiling*	2,000m	1,700m	1,800m
Cargo hold†	2.27 × 1.2 × 1.4m	4.2 × 1.86 × 1.6m	6.3 × 2.34 × 1.82m
Cargo door‡	1.12 × 1.07m	1.86 × 1.60m (ramp)	2.34 × 1.82m (ramp)
Troops	8	14	32
Stretchers	4	8	12
Crew	1	2–3	2–3
Saggers or pods	4	4	4
MGs	–	1 × 12.7mm	–

* In ground effect. † Length × width × height. ‡ Width × height.

Mi-4 Hound helicopter, as used by East Germany. Note the gunports in forward cabin windows. *(US Army Research & Development magazine)*

Mi-4 Hound-A. *(US Air Force)*

Heavy-lift helicopters

Type	Mi-6 Hook	Mi-10 Harke (Mi-10K)*
First flown	1957	1960 (1965)
Production	1959–	1960– (1969–)
Empty weight	27,240kg	27,300kg (24,680)
Normal take-off weight	40,500kg	38,000kg (32,000)
Max take-off weight	42,500kg	43,450kg (38,000)
Payload (max)	12,000kg	15,000kg (11–14,000)
Payload (slung)	9,000kg	8,000kg (11–14,000)
Fuel (max)	9,804kg	6,340kg
Fuselage length	33.16m	32.86m
Main rotor diameter	35m (5 blades)	35m (5 blades)
Height	9.86m	9.9m (7.8)
Engines	2 × 5,500HP Soloviev D-25V turboshafts	2 × 5,500HP Soloviev C-25V turboshafts
Max speed	300km/h	200km/h
Cruising speed	250km/h	200km/h
Range (max load)	620km	220km (240)
Ferry range	1,450km	630km (795)
Service ceiling	4,500m	3,000m
Cargo hold†	12 × 2.65 × 2.01m	20 × 10 × 3.1m
Cargo door‡	2.65 × 2.5m	nil
Troops	70	28
Stretchers	41	–
Crew	5	2–3
MGs	1 × 12.7mm	nil

* Figures in parentheses are for the Mi-10K flying crane where they differ from the standard Mi-10. Cargo-hold figures indicate external platform with the Mi-10.
† Length × width × height.
‡ Width × height.

Aeroflot Mi-6 Hook. In peacetime many Aeroflot helicopters are already camouflaged. *(US Army)*

Mi-10 Harke of Aeroflot, with bus on the cargo platform. *(US Army)*

Mi-1 Hares, demonstrating the use of a flexible ladder to lower a messenger to ground units. *(US Air Force)*

Obsolescent helicopters

Mi-1 and Mi-3 Hare Weights: 1,863kg empty, 2,358kg normal, 2,550kg maximum; maximum speed 170km/h; cruising speed 135km/h; ferry range 580km; initial rate of climb 6.5m/sec; service ceiling 4,500m; hovering ceiling in ground effect 3,300m; main rotor diameter 14.34m (four blades); fuselage length 12.11m; engine one 575HP Ivchenko AI-26V piston. One or two-man crew, three troops or two stretchers or 180kg payload. First flown 1948, produced in USSR until 1956, when production shifted to Poland. Mi-3 is improved version. May still be used in training role.

The Mi-1 Hare first flew in 1948 and was produced for many years, the Poles taking over its construction as the SM-1 in 1956. Used for a long time for liaison, casualty evacuation and other light helicopter duties, the Mi-1 is now probably gone from front-line Soviet service.

The Soviets have never produced a light observation helicopter. The turbine-powered Mi-2 Hoplite is a transport helicopter comparable with the US UH-1 series. Also produced in Poland, this helicopter can be used in heliborne assaults (especially by Polish units) and can also be armed. A new enlarged and more powerful version, the Mi-2M, entered production in 1975.

The first Soviet medium transport helicopter was the piston-engined Mi-4 Hound, designed in 1951. It could be armed with a 12.7mm gun, and Mi-4s were the first Soviet helicopters to use ATGMs, testing air-fired Saggers in 1967. The standard transport Hound-A has been largely replaced by the Mi-8 Hip. The Hound-C, a communications jamming version with a large serrated aerial on each side of the fuselage, was first identified in 1977 and probably remains in service. Hound-B is an anti-submarine version. Hounds are also still used for border patrol and aerial minelaying, although they are being replaced by the Mi-8 in the latter role (Aeroflot Mi-8s have been seen with minelaying equipment in Afghanistan).

The Mi-8 Hip is the standard Soviet transport helicopter. A large, unarmoured, turbine-powered aircraft, the Mi-8 is less manoeuvrable than the UH-1 or UH-60 helicopters used by the US Army, and less capable of nap-of-the-earth flying. Despite this, Soviet heliborne assaults will normally be carried out by Hips, and their substantial lifting ability allows them to carry heavy armament on outrigger mounts. Bombs, TKB-481 12.7mm machine gun pods, up to eight 57mm rocket pods, up to four Sagger ATGMs and an airborne version of the AGS-17 grenade launcher have been reported as being among the range of armaments. There are gun ports in the fuselage sides for the passengers. In addition to using this armament to support their own transport missions, Hips can be used as attack helicopters, especially when Hinds are not available.

The Soviet Army uses a number of military and civilian versions of the Hip. The Hip-A prototype had one large turboshaft and a four-bladed main rotor, later changed to a five-bladed rotor in the prototype Hip-B. The Hip-C, the standard model, was the first to enter production, in 1962. Three civilian Hip models include a 28-seat passenger version, a 24-seat passenger/cargo version and a VIP transport. As with all Soviet civil aircraft, the Air Force has first claim on them in peace or war.

The Hip is likely to be in use for years to come, as new versions, the Hip-E and Hip-F with improved engines and increased lifting capability, were reportedly under development in the late 1970s. A specialised attack version of the Hip-E has also been developed, reportedly with armour protection and heavily armed with a wide variety of weapons, including four Spiral ATGMs, six 57mm rocket pods, and a nose-mounted cannon or machine gun. Testimony before the US Congress has referred to the Hip-E as the most heavily armed helicopter in the world. It has been predicted that Soviet attack helicopters will evolve into armoured "weapons platforms," and an up-engined Hip would have the size and power required. The US Army has used large attack helicopters in Vietnam – the ACH-47 "Guns-A-Go-Go" Chinooks – although none are currently in the inventory.

The Mi-6 Hook, Mi-10 Harke and the huge Mi-12 Homer (which was not apparently produced except in prototype form) are the Soviet heavy-lift helicopters. The Hook is recognisable by its stub wings, which are removable when the aircraft is used as a flying crane. Its rear clamshell doors allow vehicles and artillery pieces to be carried internally. Other loads can be slung externally, and reportedly include BMD airborne combat vehicles. Hooks provide much of the Soviet helicopter resupply capability. When the Mi-4 Hound was used, Hooks were required in a battalion-sized heliborne assault, many being fitted with single 12.7mm machine guns for these missions.

The Mi-10 Harke is the flying-crane derivative of the Mi-6, designed to lift large items of equipment, either slung or on an external platform. The Mi-10 gives the Soviets the capability of flying large weapons into otherwise inaccessible areas. It can also be used to recover downed helicopters and aircraft, as US flying cranes were in Vietnam. The Mi-10K is a pure "crane" version with a small cabin and no platform.

The Halo, the Mi-6 replacement, was identified in 1978. Little is known of this helicopter, and it is uncertain whether it will enter production.

Attack helicopters

Type	Mi-24 Hind-A (Hind-D)*
First flown	1969 (1974)
Production	1972–75 (1975–)
Normal weight	10,000kg (similar)
Weapons load	1,275kg
Max fuel load	1,500kg
Fuselage length	17.0m
Main rotor diameter	17.0m (5 blades)
Height	4.25m
Engines	2 × 1,500HP Isotov turboshafts
Max speed	295km/h
Cruising speed	225km/h
Combat radius	277km
Range (loaded)	475km
Initial climb rate	8–18m/sec
Service ceiling	5,500m
Troops	8–16
Crew	4 (2)
Pods	4
ATGMs	4
MGs	1 × 12.7mm (1 × 12.7mm [?] 4-barrel Gatling gun)

* Figures in parentheses are for known differences of Hind-D.

The Mi-24 Hind series is currently the only purpose-designed Soviet attack helicopter in service. The Hind-A was designed in the late 1960s and probably first flew in 1969. Trials were completed and production began in 1972, the first Hinds reaching East Germany in 1973. By 1974 there were two squadrons of Hinds in East Germany; total Hind strength was 150–360 in 1977 and over 650 in 1979, the majority being Hind-Ds. In 1980 there were at least 72, possibly 108 or even 180 Hinds in East Germany, and probably a similar number in Afghanistan. Hind production reportedly exceeds 180 aircraft a year.

Mi-24 Hind-A showing racks for Swatter ATGMs and rocket pod armament. The passenger windows show the size of the troop compartment. *(US Army)*

The Hind-A is recognisable by its large flat glass canopy, tail rotor on the right-hand side, and two-by-two seating for the crew of pilot, co-pilot, gunner/navigator and forward observer or crew chief. A large passenger cabin and access door are fitted. Depending on equipment carried a Hind can lift eight to sixteen troops or a full reload of weapons for re-arming in the combat zone.

Weapons are carried on the Hind's stub wings, which display a large degree of anhedral and have three large weapons pylons and twin wingtip launch rails for ATGMs. (The Hind-B, apparently only built as a prototype, had no anhedral or ATGM rails and only two pylons on its stub wings.) The usual weapons load for the Hind-A and D consists of four UB-32 rocket pods, each containing 32 57mm S-5 rockets. With a range of 1,200m and an armour penetration capability of 220mm (in its HEAT version), the S-5 makes an excellent suppressive weapon, and each Hind or Hip can carry 128 of them in four pods. One pod of the comparable US 2.75in FFAR can inflict considerable damage over a 10m radius, destroying 30% of the light armoured vehicles, 15% of the medium tanks, 40% of the trucks, 35% of the standing troops and 25% of the semi-protected troops caught in the area. The rocket pods may be replaced by 250kg bombs. The 12.7mm machine gun is in a flexible chin mount.

Other armament options include chaff-dispensing rockets (five per 57mm pod), a wide variety of rockets and machine guns or 23mm cannon pods.

Avionics in the Hind-A include a radar gunsight for the 12.7mm machine gun, radio-control equipment for the Swatter-B, VHF and UHF radios, and a short-range navigation system which, along with a radar altimeter and gyro compass, gives it a limited night capability.

All Hinds have some armour protection. In addition to the reports of spaced armour on all Hinds and titanium belly armour on Hind-Ds, the Hind-A has armour to guard against frontal fire striking the cockpit and around the fuel tank in the aft cabin. The forward glass surfaces are apparently bulletproof; the Hind-D's glass is reportedly all bulletproof. The glass also increases crew protection by being constructed so as to avoid sun glint, which would give away the helicopter's location or provide a possible target for infra-red SAMs. There are no armoured bulkheads in the cockpit.

Hinds also feature main and tail rotor blade deicing. The main rotor has five blades with flapping hinges, drag hinges, swivel dampers and an automatically adjustable flapping-angle regulator, which is believed to increase stability and reduce sensitivity to turbulence.

The ADF navigation system gives continuous co-ordinate readout and a map display. The control system includes stability augmentation, and the Hind, like most Soviet helicopters, has three generators and two electrical systems.

Hind-D in flight, with what appears to be two Swatter-B ATGMs and two 57mm rocket pods on each of its stub wings.

The Hind-C did not appear in large numbers, and some have been reported with ATGM launch rails and the machine gun removed, apparently being used for crew training. The Hind-C has the tail rotor switched from starboard to port, a change also seen on some late-production or converted Hind-As and on standard production Hind-Ds.

The Hind-D shows many improvements over the Hind-A. Introduced in 1976-77, it surprised US intelligence agencies both by its sophistication and by the speed with which it appeared. A new front fuselage has tandem seating with individual canopies for the gunner in the forward position and the pilot, whose seat is raised for forward visibility, in the rear position. While the wing armament stations remain the same, the under-nose machine gun has been upgraded to a four-barrel Gatling-type weapon in a turret mount, allowing it a wide field of rotation and elevation. This weapon is believed also to be a 12.7mm machine gun, although some sources report it as a 23mm cannon. However, it is the improvements in avionics and fire-control equipment that make the Hind-D so effective. what appears to be a laser range-finder is mounted either on the inboard pylons or, in most cases, on the tip of the port wing. What seems to be a low-light television is mounted along with the rangefinding radar. It has been suggested that there is a forward-looking infra-red (FLIR) sensor mounted along with these items, but this is probably not likely to be used, at least for a few years. Either the laser or the television may be used in conjunction with the Spiral ATGM. While Hind-Ds have been photographed with the same Swatter-Bs and Saggers used with Hind-As, they reportedly also have the electronics to use the new missile (which the Hind-A lacks). The AS-7 Kerry air-to-surface missile carried on MiG-27 Flogger-Ds uses a laser designator for guidance, and it is possible that the Hind-D may carry AS-7s. Other sources believe that the Hind-D cannot use any ATGMs more advanced than the Swatter and that any advanced missiles would be carried by the Hind-E and Hind-F versions, about which little is known. A large, pitot tube-like projection in the nose of the Hind-D is thought to be a precision low-speed airspeed sensor for accuracy in using these weapons. Some of these devices have been retrofitted to Hind-As, which have been seen with a pylon-mounted television and an under-nose ball mount which is probably connected with Swatter guidance. Any Hind version can use Saggers on its four ATGM rails. A helicopter version of the AGS-17 grenade launcher may also be fitted, although no helicopters with such a weapon visible have been observed.

One apparently significant failing on all Hinds is the lack of any radar homing and warning device. The US

Army believes such equipment necessary for helicopters to survive. It also allows them to locate and destroy enemy radars. Hinds also lack any infra-red suppressors or countermeasures or electronic countermeasures (except for the chaff-filled 57mm rockets). Hinds do however have intakes for air-cooling the gearbox and exhaust to reduce infra-red emissions.

The Hind-F (which may be designated Mi-28), may be the world's first helicopter to carry air-to-air missiles. Similar to the Hind-D, it has its pylons modified to provide extra hardpoints for these weapons. The Hind-E and

Hind-F may also have improved engines and may possibly be configured to use advanced air-to-ground missiles. Some of these late-model Hinds reportedly have a 30mm cannon, possibly a Gatling type. Hind-Es were in Afghanistan in 1980. As of January 1981, the designation Hind-F had not been officially assigned; it is a shadowy aircraft, built of rumours.

Combat usage

Soviet-built helicopters have seen a great deal of combat. In the 1967 Middle East war the substantial Arab helicopter fleets were practically wiped out. Israeli photographs show the Egyptian Mi-6 squadron burning in its revetments. In 1973, however, Mi-8s inserted Egyptian and Syrian commandos in successful attacks on the first day of the war, the Syrian assault on Mt Hermon being

Hind-D being prepared for a mission, showing the four-barrel Gatling gun in the nose turret and the various sensors. The dividing line between the aircraft's armoured belly and the rest of the fuselage is also apparent. The thickness of the Hind-D's skin is apparent from the open engine panels.

especially spectacular. However, starting on the second day, the Arabs discovered the vulnerability of Soviet helicopters. Formations of Egyptian Mi-8s, flying into Sinai at 1,000m altitude, were intercepted by Israeli fighter-bombers and SAMs and suffered heavy losses. On October 18 five Mi-8s were used as level bombers in an attack on Israeli bridges over the Sweetwater Canal. All were shot down by ground fire.

The North Vietnamese used Soviet helicopters for moving high-priority supplies into Laos and for moving artillery and SAMs into otherwise inaccessible locations.

Both sides used Soviet-built helicopters in the 1971 India-Pakistan War. Casualty evacuation appears to have been a major role, but Indian helicopters were used to ferry troops across the many rivers in Bengal and assisted in the capture of Dacca.

Soviet helicopters were used heavily in Ethiopia, flown by Russian crews. The Cuban offensive that defeated the Somali Army used helicopters both for resupply and for mobility, allowing the Cuban forces to cover ground they could not traverse otherwise. In 1978 and 1979 helicopters were the mainstay of the Soviet effort in Afghanistan before regular divisions were committed. The Soviets have learned from the US experience that the helicopter often spells the difference between victory or defeat in a limited war in Asia. It gives them tactical and logistical mobility, and reduces their dependence on road-bound troop and supply columns that might otherwise doom the mechanised Soviet Army to impotence among the barren hills. Recent reports from Afghanistan have emphasised the continued importance of helicopters, especially Hinds, and without doubt new Soviet helicopters tactics are being forged daily in the crucible of combat.

Unit organisation

Helicopter transport regiment
Regimental HQ
Aviation service unit
  Signal flight
  Ground control flight
  Aviation flight (utility section of two Hips, two Hoplites; spares section of eight Hips, two Hooks)
Two or three transport squadrons (four flights of four Hips each)
One transport squadron (three or four flights of four Hooks each)
One aviation technical battalion

Assault helicopter regiment
Regimental HQ

Aviation service unit
  Signal flight
  Ground control flight
  Aviation flight (utility section of four Hind-Ds, two Hind-Cs; spares section of 16 Hind-Ds)
Four assault helicopter squadrons (four flights of four Hind-Ds each)
One aviation technical battalion

Independent assault helicopter regiment
Regimental HQ
Aviation service unit
  Signal flight
  Ground control flight
  Aviation flight (utility section of two Hips, two Hind-Cs; two Hoplites; spares section of 12 Hind-Ds, four Hips)
Three assault helicopter regiments (four flights of four Hind-Ds each)
One transport helicopter regiment (four flights of four Hips each)
One aviation technical unit
One aviation technical battalion

Foreign usage

The Mi-1 was produced in Poland, starting in 1969, and designated the SM-1. Soviet and Polish-built versions were exported to the Warsaw Pact nations, Cuba, China, Albania, Egypt, Finland, Guinea, Iraq, Syria and South Yemen.

The Mi-2 was also built in Poland, as the SM-2. It was also exported to Bulgaria, Hungary and Romania.

The Mi-4 was exported to Afghanistan, Algeria, Austria, Cambodia, China, Cuba, Czechoslovakia, East Germany, Finland, Hungary, India, Indonesia, Nepal, North Vietnam, Pakistan, Poland, Romania, Somalia, Syria, Yemen, Yugoslavia, Egypt and Ghana.

Mi-6s were exported to Indonesia, North Vietnam and Egypt.

Mi-8s have been exported to Afghanistan, Cuba, Czechoslovakia, Egypt, Ethiopia, Hungary, India, Iraq, Peru, Pakistan, Poland, Romania, Bulgaria, Sudan, Syria, Libya and Finland.

The Mi-10 has not been exported.

Hinds were not exported until the late 1970s. All Warsaw Pact air forces except that of Romania have received at least small numbers of Hind-Ds. Libya has received 26 Hind-Ds. Other Hind deliveries include 17 to Afghanistan (where they have seen much action against the rebels), 41 to Iraq and six to South Yemen.

Chapter Seventeen

Engineer equipment

The Soviet Army demands a high rate of advance throughout its operations. Soviet engineers help to achieve this goal by clearing mines and obstacles, crossing and bridging water barriers, building and maintaining roads, and keeping the lines of communication open. Engineers aid combat as well as movement, digging field fortifications and creating minefields and obstacles. The Soviets field a wide variety of engineer equipment which is generally simple and rugged but often technically excellent: the PMP pontoon bridge system is acknowledged to be the finest in the world, and the US Army could only slightly improve on it as the Ribbon Bridge. Supplementing the engineer equipment are "strap-on" items such as mine rollers, mine detectors and dozer blades that give combat vehicles the ability to perform some engineer tasks. Engineer equipment is provided in large quantities throughout the Soviet Army and engineer units are provided at all units from regiment up to front, usually being attached downwards to the units that will most need their support. Command of engineers is centralised as much as possible, allowing an efficient allocation of resources and concentration when needed. All units of regiment and larger strength have a Chief of Engineers (who in regiments is also the engineer company commander) to control engineer activities in his unit.

Tactical employment of engineer detachments

Soviet engineer units, unlike most Soviet combat units, are tactically employed in ad hoc mission-tailored detachments attached to manoeuvre units. Only pontoon bridge and assault crossing units are not used in these types of detachment. The major types of Soviet engineer detachments include the movement-support detachment, OOD (*otriad obespecheniia dvizheniia*); engineer reconnaissance patrol, IRD (*inzhenernoe ravedyvatel'nyi dozor*); reconnaissance/obstacle-clearing detachment, OR (*otriad razvedki i razgrahdeniia*); and the mobile obstacle detachment, POZ (*posvizhnoi otriad zagrazhdenii*).

The movement-support detachment is highly mobile, normally built around a road engineer sub-unit. In a march formation the movement-support detachment is well to the front, one to two hours ahead of the main body. The composition of a movement-support detachment varies with its mission. It often includes tank and motorised rifle units for security, BRDM-rkhs for NBC monitoring and marking contaminated zones, and sapper engineer units. In some cases a sapper engineer sub-unit rather than a road engineer unit may be used as the basis of a movement-support detachment. A movement-support detachment has many missions, including reconnaissance of the route of march and the removal of any obstacles or mines along it, bridging water obstacles, and marking the route to avoid contaminated areas. Sub-groups may be formed to handle these tasks. If the movement-support detachment encounters the enemy it will retire and let the following tank or motorised rifle unit's advance guard engage, and then proceed behind them. If the enemy is strong the movement-support detachment may have to follow the unit's first echelon. Each separate axis of advance will have its own movement-support detachment.

Engineer reconnaissance patrols advance along each axis of advance. They can form part of the patrols of reconnaissance units, or whole engineer sub-units can perform the reconnaissance mission, using their expertise to report back on conditions – the state of roads and bridges, for example – and assess the engineer tasks that will have to be performed by following units. Helicopters are also used as vehicles for engineer reconnaissance patrols.

Reconnaissance/obstacle-clearing detachments are sometimes part of a movement-support detachment, but they frequently operate independently. Their main function is the clearing of minefields and obstacles, and they will often immediately precede the combined-arms assault. In the outflanking and enveloping attacks that the Soviets emphasise, these detachments are required both to locate and remove anything that would inhibit mobility.

The mobile obstacle detachment is also used to create

BAT/M in travelling position. *(A. Dupouy)*

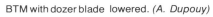

BTM with dozer blade lowered. *(A. Dupouy)*

obstacles and lay minefields whenever they are needed, on the attack or defence, whether it is to protect the flank of an advancing unit from counterattacks, consolidate a captured position or force an enemy armoured breakthrough into the "fire pockets" of the defenders. The Soviets place a great deal of emphasis on these mobile obstacle detachments. They are the catalyst of their overlapping anti-tank defence system. On the march, mobile obstacle detachments are positioned on the flanks of the column. On the defensive they are part of the anti-tank reserve.

Engineer support in the offensive

All Soviet engineer weapons contribute to offensive capability. The field fortification diggers will be employed to create hasty positions for towed artillery and especially FROG and Scud units. If time permits, engineer subunits will aid in creating camouflaged and secure assembly areas. In any case, movement-support detachments may lead the Soviet units as they leave the assembly areas for the line of departure. When time does not permit this, tanks with dozer blades will be relied upon for cross-country mobility. The Soviets realise the importance of such vehicles for mobility, as demonstrated by the Israelis when they created their own desert tracks with dozer blades in 1967. T-64/72s, with their retractable dozer blades, will not require support.

The most important offensive task is the breaching of minefields. The number of lanes to be cleared through enemy minefields depends upon the formation adopted by an attacking unit when crossing it. This in turn depends upon the opposition expected, and can range from one lane per company to one per platoon. The normal method of clearing is by tanks mounting the KMT-4 and KMT-5 mine ploughs and roller-ploughs. Because of the narrowness of paths created by the tanks, explosives, especially rocket-propelled line charges fired from modified tanks or BTR-50PK APCs, will project an explosive hose across the minefield, detonating it to clear a lane. Bangalore torpedoes and explosive charges, emplaced by sappers on foot, can also be used to clear minefields and obstacles. A battalion that has to attack through minefields will normally have at least one or two sapper platoons, up to nine mine rollers and three dozer blades for attachment to tanks, one or more MTU bridges and 300–600kg of explosives. The combination of rollers and ploughs, line charges (both rocket-propelled and winched forward), bangalore and explosive charges, and, if required, manual clearing (only performed when there is no alternative or when silence is required) gives the Soviets the redundant, overlapping mine-clearing capability that they believe will result in battlefield effectiveness. Nor is mine-clearing solely an engineer's task. The Soviets stress that any unit should be able to lift or plant mines if required.

Mobile obstacle detachments are also used in the offensive, as part of the anti-tank reserve. They create obstacles and emplace minefields to protect the flanks of advancing units and consolidate positions, as well as aiding the hasty defence if the attack is halted.

Engineer support in the defence

Soviet engineers both prepare defensive positions and participate in the action. The preparation for the defence includes constructing and camouflaging field fortifications, preparing demolitions, emplacing minefields and preparing routes for the Soviet counter-attack and resumption of the offensive. Whenever possible, the Soviets will take full advantage of engineer equipment to improve their defensive strongpoints. Engineer observation posts are established throughout the defences to aid in these tasks. Engineer reconnaissance detachments can also be used to help select defensive positions, but it is the mobile obstacle detachments that have the largest defensive role, operating as part of the unit's anti-tank reserve.

Engineer support in river crossings

Facilitating the river crossing is seen as one of the most important missions of Soviet engineers. While every effort has been made to give Soviet tank and motorised rifle units their own river-crossing capability, engineers are still most important in allowing the Soviets to achieve the high rates of advance they demand across Western Europe, where rivers are close and often wide. They have evolved a wide range of amphibious vehicles, ferries and bridging that will help them to maintain their momentum.

Engineer reconnaissance detachments will investigate and report on all water obstacles along the line of march. Using specialised equipment to determine depth, current and width and, if necessary, scuba divers to check on bottom conditions for fording or snorkelling, these detachments will mark appropriate crossing sites. They will be supplemented by other reconnaissance means such as troop reconnaissance patrols, aerial photographs and prisoner of war interrogation. The information will be passed to the unit's Chief of Engineers, who, along with the unit commander, will plan the river crossing in such a way that the advancing Soviet units can continue without having to stop and consolidate bridgeheads. Engineer bridging units will either be brought up to the front of the column if time and road conditions permit, or will be kept back and will "leapfrog" forward when the river is

TMM bridge (on KrAZ-214) in travelling position. *(A. Dupouy)*

reached. Helicopters will often be used to lift troops or engineers to the far bank. MTU tank-mounted bridges will probably be the first engineering equipment on the scene, either with a forward detachment or *reydy* or attached to the advance-guard battalion of the leading regiment. If the MTU is not adequate to bridge the river, regimental TMMs will be used, but no bridges will be erected until the crossing site is secured from enemy direct-fire weapons. This may require the BMP and APCs to swim across. Tanks will normally not cross in the first echelon because of the extensive preparations required for snorkelling. Tanks will either be ferried across by GSP ferries or PMP bridge sections used as ferries, wait for a bridge to be constructed, or will snorkel or be winched across underwater. K-61 ferries will also set up a crossing site until a bridge can be established. The ferrying and rafting operations will continue until the area is secure, and then the bridge, usually a PMP from the divisional engineer battalion, will be built.

Opposed river crossings are very difficult operations that require large numerical superiority and careful preparation, especially by engineers. The river banks and bottom are likely to be mined, and will have to be dealt with by underwater equipment or line charges. While the first echelon will swim across in APCs or BMPs, ferries will bring across tanks and heavy equipment as soon as possible. The Egyptian crossing of the Suez Canal on October 6, 1973, was an example of such a crossing.

Effectiveness and capability

Soviet engineers appear to be a relatively effective force. Their equipment meets the Soviet standards of simplicity and ruggedness, and its effectiveness in the hands of the Egyptians in 1973 suggests that it will be at least as good in the hands of the Soviet Army. While the limited training time available to Soviet enlisted personnel may reduce the multi-purpose capability which the Soviets seek, it would appear that they are at least effective in their primary tasks. Any individual weaknesses can be made up by the relatively lavish scale on which the equipment is provided. This was also seen in the 1973 War. The Egyptians had large enough stockpiles of PMP sections to ensure that any bridge damaged by Israeli bombs could be back in service within minutes. Already the Soviets have stockpiled prefabricated line-of-communication bridges throughout Eastern Europe, and similar measures will doubtless be taken with tactical bridges. While it is uncertain whether Soviet mine-clearing methods and tactics will be adequate to deal with the new generation of artillery-delivered minelets, it remains true that Soviet mine warfare capability is the equal of any in the world.

Unit organisation

Regimental engineer sapper company (tank and motorised rifle regiments)

Total strength: 90–100 officers and men.

Headquarters and services (16–22 officers and men, one to three KMT-5, nine KMT-4, one to three BTU, six to nine trucks, one BRDM command scout car)

One road-bridge platoon (29–33 officers and men)

One road section (one DIM, two BAT/PKT, trucks with wooden bridge parts)

One bridge section (four TMM, one to three MTU)

One field fortification section (one BTM/PZM, one MDK-2, one IMR)

One sapper-minelayer platoon (12–15 officers and men)

Three sections

Total equipment: three PMR-3/PMZ-4, three APC or trucks, *or* three GMZ (M-1977); plus three pioneer kits, one demolition kit, three KR clearing kits

Two sapper platoons (each of 27 officers and men)

Three sections

Total equipment per platoon: two APC or truck, nine mine detectors, three pioneer kits, three KR clearing kits, three demolition kits, three chain saws, mines, explosives, and bridge elements when required.

Divisional engineer battalion (tank and motorised rifle divisions)

Total strength: 30 officers, 378 enlisted men in motorised rifle divisions; 31 officers, 401 enlisted men in tank divisions.

Headquarters company

Total strength: nine officers, 59 enlisted men.

One headquarters platoon (two APC, one BRDM, one signal van)

One reconnaissance platoon (three BRDM scout cars carrying six mine detectors, three pioneer kits, three KR clearance kits, three scuba kits)

One service platoon (one APRIM-M, one TRM-A/B, 10 trucks)

Engineer sapper company

Total strength: five officers, 89 enlisted men.

One headquarters and service platoon (one to three trucks with KMT-5, one truck with KMT-4 or -9, one to three trucks with BTU, three cargo trucks)

One minelaying platoon (600 anti-tank mines, three PMR-3/PMZ-4, three APC or trucks *or* three GMZ; three pioneer kits, three KR clearance kits, one demolition kit)

Two sapper platoons (with a total of six APCs/trucks, six mine detectors, six pioneer kits, six KR clearance kits, two demolition kits, UZ mines, bridge elements when required)

Engineer road company

Total strength: nine officers, 113–117 enlisted men.

One headquarters platoon (one K-61 or PTS, one MAV or BRDM)

Two engineer road platoons (with a total of four to six BAT or PKT, two TMM sets, two DIM, two IMR, three MTU)

One engineer bridge construction platoon (one KMS set, one LRV with ESB-4-ID, one K-61 crane, one ESD-20, three-plus trucks with bridge elements)

One field fortification platoon (two or three BTM or PZM, one or two MDK-2, one truck with ESB-4-IG, three-plus trucks with prefabricated shelters, UZ mines, shaped charges)

Pontoon bridge company

Total strength: four officers, 82 enlisted men.

One headquarters platoon (one-plus trucks, roadway matting)

Two pontoon bridge platoons (with a total of two PMP shore link "square" sections and 16 PMP river link "boat" sections carried on 18 KrAZ-214/155)

One boat platoon (six BMK-150 or BMK-T motorboats on KrAZ or ZIL trucks)

Assault crossing company

Total strength: five or six officers, 39–54 enlisted men (tank division battalions use greater strength).

One headquarters platoon

Two transporter platoons (with a total of 12 K-61/PTS or 12 PKP with PTS)

One (two in tank division battalions) ferry platoon (with three GSP ferries)

Assault crossing battalion (one or two per army, up to three per front)

One headquarters company (including a reconnaissance platoon)

Two transporter companies (each with 18 K-61 with PTS or PKP with PTS)

One or two ferry companies (12 GSP ferries per company in units with two companies, 9–10 GSP ferries in units with one company)

Pontoon bridge regiment (one per army, two per front)

One headquarters company (eight K-61/PTS, ? GSP ferries)

Two pontoon bridge battalions (each of three pontoon bridge companies identical to those in the divisional battalions)

Engineer regiment/brigade (army or front level)

One headquarters and services element

One construction battalion

Three engineer battalions

IMR combat engineer vehicle, showing both its dozer blade
and lifting arm, here clearing away debris after a simulated
nuclear strike. *(Chris Foss)*

Combat engineer vehicles, ditchers, diggers and dozers

IMR combat engineer vehicle Weight 34,000kg; length
10.6m; height 2.48m to crane operator's cupola, 3.37m to
top of crane in travel position; ground clearance 0.42m;
speed 48km/h; crew 2. The IMR (*inzhenernaia maschina
ragrazhdeniia*, engineer obstacle-clearing machine) is
based on a T-54/55 chassis with a T-54 engine. It has
NBC protection, an infra-red searchlight and vision
equipment, and mounts an extendable hydraulic
"manipulator," much like a "cherry-picker." It also has
an adjustable, hydraulic dozer blade and earth bucket
and grab for digging. An unditching beam is mounted at
the rear. Although it lacks the demolition gun of Western
combat engineer vehicles, the IMR can clear obstacles
under fire as well as dig emplacements and perform road
repair. The crew of two – driver-mechanic and
commander-operator – have a high degree of armour
protection.

BTM and BTM-TMG digger and ditcher Weight
26,500kg (30,000kg for BTM-TMG); length 7.35m (7.6m
for BTM-TMG) travelling, 10.85m working; width 3.2m;

height 4.3m travelling, 3.5m working; ground clearance
0.425m; road speed 35km/h; range 400km; ground pressure 0.71kg/cm²; track 2.64m; track width 0.50m; engine
V-401 V-12 water-cooled 415HP diesel; trench crossing
2.1m; crew 2; trench-digging capability 1,120m of
0.8m-deep trench per hour, 500m of 1.6m-deep trench per
hour. The BTM-TMG can dig 100m of 0.6m trench per
hour in frozen ground. Digging is by a wheel of ten buck-
ets. Maximum trench or ditch size: 1.5m deep, 1m wide.
Able to move 240m³ of unfrozen or, in the BTM-TMG,
90m³ of frozen earth per hour. Based on the AT-T artillery
tractor chassis, this bizarre-looking vehicle is reported to
be unreliable in use.

PZM digging and ditching machine This regimental-
level digging machine digs trenches up to 1.1m deep and
weapon or vehicle pits up to 3m deep at a rate of 100m³ per
hour, using ladder bucket entrenching.

MDK-2M rotary excavator Weight 27,000kg; length 8m
travelling, 10.23m working; width 4.0m; height 3.95m
travelling, 3.9m working; ground clearance 0.425m; road
speed 35km/h; track 2.64m; track width 0.5m; engine
V-401 V-12 415HP water-cooled diesel; range 400km;
ground pressure 0.71kg/cm²; trench 2.1m; vertical obstacle 1.0m; slope 20°; ford 0.75m. Using its rotary cutter,
the MDK-2M can excavate 300m³ of earth per hour to a

BTM ditching machine in travelling position, with digger up; it is lowered from the rear of the vehicle in operation. *(US Army)*

maximum depth and width of 3.5m. It also mounts an OTT hydraulic dozer blade.

E-305V universal single-bucket crane shovel Built on a KrAZ-214 chassis, the E-305V can be used either for digging or as a crane with a 5,000kg lift capacity. It can use its 0.3m³-capacity shovel to dig 50–60m³ per hour to a maximum depth of 4.1m.

BAT dozer Weight 25,300kg (26,000 for BAT/M); length 10m; height 2.845m working, 3.5m travelling; width 4.78m; ground clearance 0.425m; road speed 35km/h; cross-country speed 20km/h; range 400km; max slope 30°; vertical obstacle 1m; trench 1.575m; track width 0.5m; track 2.64m; ground pressure 0.65kg/cm²; ford 0.75m; crew 4. Based on the AT-T artillery tractor, the BAT/M version also mounts a 2,000kg-capacity jib crane. Both have a dozer blade, lifted mechanically in the BAT, hydraulically in the BAT/M. A winch has a 20,000kg pull. Work speed is 4–8km/h, and it can move 120–400m³ of earth in an hour. The width of blade sweep is 4.15–4.78m,

depending on configuration. It is often used to lay out cross-country tracks, working at a rate of 4–6km/h in bush or light forest and 4–10km/h in snow-covered terrain.

PKT dozer Length 7.9m; height 3.1m; width 3.2m; road speed 45km/h; cross-country speed 20–25km/h; engine 375HP diesel; weight 21,000kg. Based on the MAZ-538 and mounting a dozer blade, the PKT can move 80–100m³ of earth an hour in either two-bladed or dozer configuration. It can lay tracks across bush or light forest at a rate of 2–3km/h, and across snow-covered territory at a rate of 6–10km/h. It has four-wheel drive.

BTU-55 tank-mounted dozer blade A T-54, 55 or 62 main battle tank fitted with this blade can move 250m³ of earth in an hour and dig three or four tank pits an hour. The STU and STU-2M tank snowploughs are similar.

New-model combat engineer vehicle Little is known of this vehicle except that its chassis is similar to that of the SAU-122 and the ACRV-2. Its main mission is mine clearance, and it reportedly can fire rocket-propelled line charges and is fitted with a dozer blade or mine roller or plough of unspecified design.

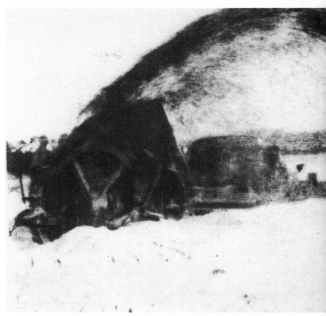

Above Sequence of MDK-2 operations: travelling position, lowering the digger, and digging. *(US Army)*

Left BAT/M dozer, moving its dozer blade from travelling position at the rear of the cab to digging position. *(US Army)*

Mines

Type	Construction	Role	Weight (kg)	Dimensions (cm)	Charge	Force (kg)	Blast radius
YaM-5	wood	AT	7.7	47.5 l × 18.5 w × 9.5 h*	3.6–5kg	136	–
TM-57	steel	AT	9.5	29.9 d × 7.4 h	7kg	200–700	–
TM-46	steel	AT	8.7	31 d × 7.4 h	5.3kg	180	–
KhF-2	wood	gas	15	18.5 d × 28 h	4.5l	–	–
OZM-3	metal	AP (bounding)	3	6 d × 13.5 h	75gr	–	25m
POMZ-2	metal	AP (frag)	2	6 d × 13.5 h	75gr	0.5–1.3	4m
PDM-6	–	river bottom	47.5	100 d × 55 h	28kg	–	
PMD-6	wood	AP (blast)	0.4	20 l × 9 w × 6.5 h	0.2kg	6–28	–
YaM-10	wood	AT	11.8	62 l × 21.6 w × 19.6 h	10kg	130	–
TMD-B	wood	AT	7.7	32 l × 28 w × 14 h	5–6.8kg	200	–
PDM-1M	–	river bottom	29	100 h	10kg	40–50	–
PDM-2	–	river bottom	100+	140 h	15kg	40–50	–
TM-60	plastic	AT	11.3	32 d × 11.7 h	7.5kg	200–500	–
TMB-2	cardboard	AT	7	27.4 d × 155 h	5kg	200	–
PMD-7	wood	AP (blast)	0.3	15 l × 17.5 w × 6.5 h	75gr	–	–
PM & PFM-1	plastic	blast	0.6	11.2 d × 5.6 h	0.24kg	0.227	–

All mines are normally pressure-activated, but can also be command or pull-activated. The gas mine normally uses mustard gas. Force shows the pressure in kilogrammes that must be exerted to detonate the mine. * l = long, w = wide, h = high, d = diameter.

YaM-5. *(Jane's)*

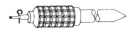

POMZ-2 anti-personnel stake mine. *(Jane's)*

TM-46. *(Jane's)*

PM mine. The PFM-1, though of similar weight and charge, is butterfly-shaped, surface-scattered from aircraft, and filled with a liquid explosive. *(Jane's)*

Rear view of a GMZ (M-1977) tracked minelaying vehicle, its mine planter covered by a tarpaulin. *(Chris Foss)*

Minelayers

GMZ armoured minelaying vehicle Length 10.3m with plough lowered, 9.1m with plough raised; width 3.1m; height 2.5m to top of plough; weight 25,000kg; track 2.66m; track width 0.54m; ground contact 5m; road speed 50km/h; gradient 30°; vertical obstacle 1m; engine 500HP water-cooled diesel; armament 14.5mm KPVT; work speed 4–10km/h laying mines on surface, 2–3km/h burying mines; crew 4; minelaying rate 8 surface or 4 buried mines per minute; space between mines 4–5.5m; mine capacity 208 mines (estimated); reload time 12–15min. Has full night vision equipment.

PMR-3 (2) towed mechanical minelayer trailer Usual tow vehicle BTR-152; length 3m; width 2m; height 2.5m;

mine spacing 4–5.5m; mine burial depth 30–40cm in soft soil (surface only); capacity 120 mines; reload time 12–15min (15–20); planting chutes 1 (2); crew 4–5 (7); mines laid per minute 10–12; work speed 4–10km/h (3–5km/h) surface, 2–3km/h buried (furrows). Figures in parentheses are for earlier PMR-2 where it differs from the PMR-3. For both systems the capacity varies as follows if the tow vehicle is other than the standard BTR-152: ZIL-157 200, BTR-60 100–130, URAL-375 350, GMZ 180-200. The PMR-3 can plant a 500m buried mine belt in five minutes. The PMZ-4 towed minelayer is the same as the PMR-3 but with a 200-mine capacity.

Helicopter minelaying equipment Length 4.8m; width 0.4m; height 0.13m; surface only; mines carried 200+; laying rate 4 per min. Mines are dropped from a chute projecting from the helicopter fuselage. It is used on Mi-4 and Mi-8 helicopters of both the Soviet Air Force and Aeroflot.

GAZ-69 jeep with DIM mine detector in travelling position. *(US Army)*

Mine detectors
DIM/DIM-3 vehicle-mounted detecting equipment

Vehicle operating speed 10km/h, less cross-country; max detection depth 25cm; sweep width 2.2m; crew 2. Usually mounted on a GAZ/UAZ-69/469 jeep, this detector gives an audio alarm and automatically brakes the vehicle when a mine is detected. This system is mounted on T-62s in Afghanistan.

DIM vehicle-mounted mine detector on a GAZ-69.

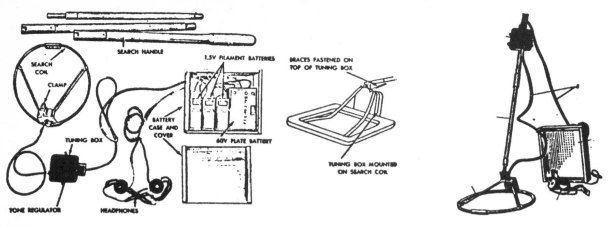

VIM-203M mine detector.

VIM-625 mine detector.

VIM-203M/VIM-612 mine detectors Wartime-vintage, can detect metallic mines only at up to 20–30cm depth. Weight 13–14 kg, mounted on a pole or rifle stock. VIM-625 and VIM-695 are similar.

UMIV/UMIN portable mine detector Post-war man-portable mine detector. Weighs 6.6kg, 45cm detection depth, examines 3m path.

IMP portable mine detector An improved, recent, transistorised design, capable of detecting metallic fuzes in plastic mines. Weighs 7.2kg, detection range of 0.3–0.46m, like others is battery-powered and mounted on a pole with a detector head. Audio alarm.

Helicopter mine detector A detector head can be lowered from a low-flying helicopter as part of an engineer reconnaissance mission.

KMT-5 roller-plough set. *(US Army)*

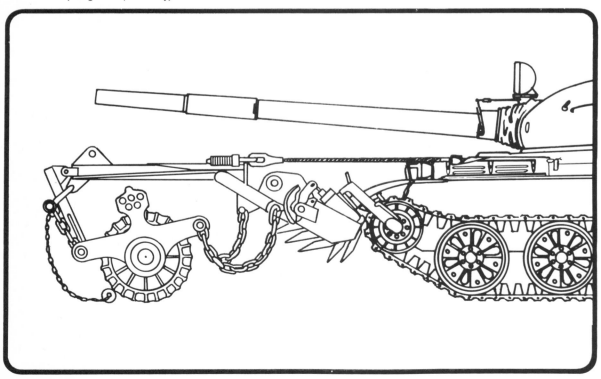

PT-54M mineclearing tank, now largely replaced by KMT-4 and KMT-5 equipment. *(US Army)*

Mineclearing equipment

KMT tank-mounted mine roller and plough Weight 7,500kg; width of swept lane 0.73–0.81m per roller; operating speed 8–12km/h; attachment time 10–15min; assembly length 3.18m; assembly width 4m; width of unswept lane 2.1m; plough and roller depth effectiveness 0.35m. The KMT-4/5 combination roller and plough can be mounted on any Soviet main battle tank. With three roller sections and a lane-marking plough, it can survive eight to ten 5–6kg explosions. At night it can be fitted to mark the cleared lanes with luminous tape. When not in use it is carried in a 7.5-tonne cargo truck with a KM-61 crane, such as the KrAZ-214. The KMT-4 element is the plough, lowered by a hydraulic ram, which pushes the mines out of the tank's way rather than detonating them.

The rollers are improved, lighter versions of those used in the PT-54/55 system.

PT-54/55 mine-clearing rollers Tank-mounted mine-clearing rollers, each of two independent roller sets mounted on arms in front of each tread, clearing a path ahead of each one. The gap between the treads remains uncleared. It can survive ten anti-tank mines, takes 10–15min to attach and 3–5min to detach. It is used at speeds of 8–12km/h, and the swept lane for each tread is 0.8–1.3m wide.

SPZ-2 and SPZ-4 mine-clearance charges The metal-framed SPZ-2 is connected to a cable with an anchor attached to one end. The anchor is fired across a minefield and the charges are winched across at a rate of 200m/h, then detonated. The SPZ-4 is pushed into a minefield by a tank at a rate of 100m/h, or it is laid behind a tank in the gap between the cleared path left by the mine rollers and then detonated.

BDT mine-clearing charge A light metal tube, 50mm in diameter, maximum length 500m (which takes 90min

T-55A(M) of the Polish Army fitted with mineclearing rocket charges and mine rollers and plough. The installation on the BTR-50 is similar. *(Chris Foss)*

to assemble). It can contain either a single, double or triple charge. It is pushed into a minefield and detonated. A triple charge will clear a 6m path.

ITB-2 A rocket-launched cable-and-anchor system that uses a winch or other motive power to draw the charge towards the anchor and into the minefield, where it is detonated.

UZ-1 bangalore torpedo A standard weapon. Each section is 2.1m long and clears a 2.5–3m passage. Double or triple charges can also be used.

UZ-2 A double-charge line explosive used in 500m lengths.

UZR-3 A triple-charge bangalore torpedo with propulsive rockets attached, used in 500m lengths.

Rocket-propelled tube charges Mounted on the left and right rear of tanks or BTR-50PK engineer APCs. Rockets (similar to Swatter ATGMs) carry flexible tubes (in 170m lengths) forward into a minefield, where they can be detonated. The rockets are reported to be unreliable.

Tank-mounted bridges

MTU A cantilever-type bridge on a T-54 chassis. Carrying capacity 50 tonnes; span length 12.3m, able to span an 11m gap; emplacement time 3–5min; bridge width 3.274m; crew 2; total weight 34,000kg. Bridge hydraulically launched and recovered.

MTU-20 A cantilever-type bridge on a T-55 chassis. Carrying capacity 50 tonnes, possibly 60 tonnes; span length 20m, able to bridge an 18m gap; emplacement time 5min; total weight 37,000kg; crew 2; bridge width 3.5m.

MTU-55 A Czech-designed scissors bridge on a T-55 chassis. Emplacement time 2–3min; span 18m, good for 16m gap; time to recover bridge 5–6min; carrying capacity 50 tonnes; crew 2; bridge weight 6,500kg; total weight 36,000kg. Equipped with a gap-measuring device, inclinometer, snorkel, full night vision and NBC equipment. One of the few items of Warsaw Pact-designed equipment adopted by the Soviet Army.

MTU-20 armoured vehicle-launched bridge. *(Chris Foss)*

MT-55 raises its bridge for deployment.

TMM truck-mounted scissors bridge being lowered into position.

Engineer bridges

TMM (*tiazhelyi mekhanizirovanny most*, heavy truck-mounted bridge) Truck-launched tactical fixed bridge. Carrying capacity 60 tonnes; length: a set consists of four 10.2m sections with 3m adjustable trestles, a total length of 40m; construction time: assembling a single section takes three men 8–15min, while with the full 12-man crew a 40m bridge takes 45–60min by day, 60–80min by night; maximum water depth bridged 3m; launch vehicle KrAZ-214 or KrAZ-255B; roadway width 3.8m; removal time: = erection time; weight 7,000kg/segment. Trestles are integral with spans. May also be erected underwater.

KMM (*koleino-mekhanizirovannyi most*, truck-mounted treadway bridge) Obsolescent, largely replaced by the TMM. Carrying capacity 15 tonnes; length 5 × 7m spans, a total of 35m; construction time 30–60min during the day, 60–80 min at night, with full crew of 15 men; launch vehicle ZIL-157 (hydraulically launched); maximum river depth 3m; max vehicle speed while crossing: wheeled 12–20km/h, tracked 1km/h, must have at least 15m spacing; width of roadway 2.95m; weight of segment 1,420kg. The four trestle legs are adjustable in height. The KMM may be recovered in the same way as it was constructed and may also be built underwater.

PMP pontoon bridge (*pontonno-mostovoi park*, pontoon bridge set) The standard Soviet tactical bridge. The basic PMP pontoon link section, which can be used as a ferry or inserted in a bridge, consists of four hinged accordion-folded pontoon sections with an integral roadway. These automatically unfold as soon as they hit the water, and the crews have only to join the sections together. The full 36-link (32 river links, 4 shore links) set may be set up as bridges or rafts. Divisions usually have half a PMP set with 16 river and two shore links, and 6 boats. This allows them to construct 118m of 60-tonne bridge, 225m of 20-tonne bridge, or two 170-tonne, three 110-tonne, four 80-tonne or five or six 60-tonne rafts. Maximum current 3m/sec with bow shields, 2m/sec without; assembly rates 7m/min, a total of 50min for a whole set and 30min for a half (divisional) set with a working party of 70–80 men. The split-pontoon bridge with a 20-tonne capacity takes the same amount of time. Construction time for rafts: 40-tonne (2 pontoons) 8min, 60-tonne (3 pontoons) 10min, 80-tonne (4 pontoons) 12min, 110-tonne (5 pontoons + 1 shore section) 15 min, 170-tonne (8 pontoons + 1 shore section) 20min. Ferry passage width 6.5m; roadway width 6.5m; maximum speed of armour on bridge 30km/h; recovery time: double the construction time.

TPP (*tiazhelyi pontonno-mostovoi park*, heavy pontoon bridge set) Largely replaced by the PMP, the TPP system consists of bow and centre sections of rigid metal pontoons with an integral roadway superstructure, transported on

(continued on page 346)

PMP bridge being crossed by T-55 tanks. *(US Army)*

PMP bridge sections on KrAZ-255B trucks of the Finnish Army. *(A. Dupouy)*

BMK-T powerboat mounted on a KrAZ-255B of the East German Army. The BMK-T works with PMP bridging equipment, using its broad, flat bow to push the sections into place. The BMK-T is also used to power PMP sections when they are employed as ferries. *(V.M. Martinova)*

TPP heavy bridge pontoon on ZIL-151. *(A. Dupouy)*

TPP pontoon bow section on a ZIL-151 truck. *(US Army)*

(continued from page 343)

ZIL-151/157 trucks. A full TPP set includes 48 bow sections, 48 centre sections, 12 BMK-150 powerboats and auxiliary equipment. It may also be configured as ferries rather than a bridge. Capacity: up to 70 tonnes, depending on length; maximum current 4m/sec; length of assemblies 6m bow, 4.9m centre section; length: using an entire set, a 16-tonne-capacity bridge can be 335m (333) long, a 50-tonne-capacity bridge can be up to 265m long, and a 70-tonne-capacity bridge can be up to 205m (185) long. For a half set, the lengths are 163m (148), 135m (133) and 103m (93) respectively, and 77m, 73m and 58m (52) for a quarter set. 16-tonne-capacity bridges can have their length extended by use of local materials to 506m (404), 258m (203) and 133m (108) for full, half and quarter sets. The 16-tonne bridge requires 2½h (4), the 50-tonne bridge requires 2h (2½), the 70-tonne bridge requires 3h working time with 384 men in daylight. Night building takes 50–100% longer. Figures in parentheses are used when current is over 1.5m/sec. Roadway width 3.2m for 16-tonne version, 4.0m for others. There are two pontoon sections per support. When used as a ferry, capacity is 50 tonnes.

LPP light pontoon bridge Carrying capacity 12/24/40 tonnes, depending on length (160/88/64m respectively); building time 50–60min with 105 men. Similar to a lightened TPP, carried on GAZ-63s. It can be used in 24-tonne and 40-tonne-capacity rafts. No longer in extensive frontline Soviet service, it is used where weight makes the use of PMP impractical.

PVD-20 airborne pontoon bridge This is used by the engineer battalions of airborne divisions, and can be air-dropped or heli-lifted. Total weight 13 tonnes; ground transport 10 GAZ-66 or 6 ZIL-157; length 64m for 8-tonne capacity, 88.2m for 4-6-tonne capacity; time to build 50min. Uses pneumatic boats as pontoons. Can also be built as 4, 6 or 8-tonne-capacity rafts.

MARM sectional bridge Used on lines of communication. 50-tonne capacity, built at a rate of 20m per hour. 6m length per span. Can also be used as overpass at busy roads.

SARM sectional bridge Used on lines of communication. Truss bridge, usually 158m long, but can be longer. Construction speed 20m per hour. Panel-type crib piers provide support. Truss sections 6m long, 1.5m wide, 2m high are carried in semitrailers behind MAZ-504s or ZIL-130Vs. If the bridge is constructed low to the water, panel-type crib piers can also be used.

NZh-56 floating railway bridge Used on lines of communication. 150-tonne capacity. Pontoons are transported on KrAZ-214. Railway can be either Soviet or European gauge. Used by Railway Troops, not by Engineers. Other types of line of communications bridges are also used by Road and Railway troops.

Metal roadlaying equipment Normally mounted on KrAZ-214 trucks, this flexible steel matting is laid out with the truck in reverse. Each truck carries 38m of road.

Suspension bridges There are three types of suspension bridge for use in mountainous country: the 120m PVM

LPP light pontoon bridge deployed. *(US Army)*

LPP pontoon section carried on GAZ-63 truck. *(A. Dupouy)*

footbridge, the 2,000kg-capacity, 80m LVM and the 10,000kg-capacity, 60m TVM.

Underwater pontoon bridge Many Soviet bridges can be erected underwater, but there is one specific underwater type. This is similar to a scaled-down PMP carried on ZIL-131s.

Prefabricated wooden bridges With 12, 40 and 60-tonne capacities, the bridges are used to replace destroyed spans in wartime. The steel RMM-4 is similar.

REM-500 railway and road bridge Used on lines of communication. Can carry both rail and road traffic. REMs come in both Soviet and standard gauge. Maxi-

mum depth 7m, maximum current 1.2m/sec. A flatcar-mounted gantry is used for assembly.

SP-19 self-propelled pontoon bridge Rail and road sections mounted on standard motorised barges, with a maximum capacity of 180 tonnes as a bridge and 100 tonnes as a five-pontoon raft; the latter is the most probable mode of employment. Used on lines of communication and held in reserve.

Heavy barge bridges The Soviets have many methods of using standard Eastern European river barges as pontoons for road and railway bridges. Most bridges built in this manner would require 12–30 hours to construct.

GSP amphibious ferry – with two sections joined together –
carrying a T-55. (*US Army*)

Left-hand GSP ferry section of the East German Army, with its
pontoon in travelling position. The right-hand unit of each pair
would be hinged on the opposite side. This GSP is a
later-production version with improved suspension, cab and
hull. (*A. Dupouy*)

Amphibious vehicles and ferries

GSP amphibious ferry Carrying capacity 50 tonnes;
maximum current in which it can be used 2m/sec; time to
ready for operation 3–5min with six-man assembly crew;
length 12m; width 3.24m (per half unit); height 3.2m;
track width 0.36m; engine: 135HP 4-cylinder in-line
water-cooled YaMz-M204VKR diesel; water propulsion
4 propellers (in complete ferry); maximum road speed
40km/h; maximum water speed 7.7km/h; minimum
draught 1.2m; maximum height of river bank 0.5m; crew
3. The GSP (*gusenichnii samokhodnii parom*, tracked self-
propelled ferry) consists of two non-interchangeable left
and right half units with large foam-filled outer pontoons.
Carried on top of the vehicle, the pontoons are rotated
outwards when the two ferry halves are connected in the
water. The GSP is capable of ferrying tanks, which can
fire their guns while afloat.

PTS/PTS-M tracked amphibious transporter
Weight (empty) 17,000kg; length 11.6m; width 3.5m;
height 2.9m cab, 3.4m bows; crew 2; track 2.9m; clearance
0.5m; track width 0.5m; cruise range 300km land,

PTS-M amphibian carrying a URAL-375. *(US Army)*

100–110km water; ground pressure 0.32kg/cm² empty, 0.41kg/cm² loaded; trench crossing 3.6m; gradient 30°, exit gradient from water, loaded 25°; suspension: torsion bar, six road wheels; load area 7.9 × 2.6m; track on ground 5.63m; trailer used: PKP; payload 5,000kg land, 10,000kg water; passengers 70; engine: 250HP A-712P V-12 water-cooled diesel in PTS, 350HP V-54P V-12 water-cooled diesel in PTS-M. Speed 40km/h land, 10km/h water (15km/h for PTS-M). PTS-M has infra-red searchlight and driving lights and a fully sealable cab. Designated medium amphibious transporter (*plavaiuschii transportr srednii*, PTS).

K-61 tracked amphibious transporter Weight 9,550kg empty; length 9.15m; width 3.15m; height 2.15m; track 2.6m; crew 3; clearance 0.36m loaded, 0.4m unloaded; track width 0.3m; length of track on ground 4.56m; ground pressure 0.36kg/cm² empty, 0.45kg/cm² loaded; trench 3.0m; vertical obstacle 0.65m; gradient 42° empty, 25° loaded, 20° river bank exit gradient; fuel capacity 260 litres; fuel consumption 0.95 litres/km; payload 3,000kg land, 5,000kg water; passengers 50; speed 36km/h land, 10km/h water; water propulsion: two propellers; range 260km land, 64km water; engine: 135HP YaAZ-M204 VKR 2-stroke 4-cylinder in-line diesel. The K-61 can carry all but the largest towed artillery with their tow vehicles. Also referred to as the GPT (*gusenichnii plavaiushchii transportr*, tracked amphibious transporter), it is being supplanted by the PTS/PTS-M.

ZIL-485 BAV Weight 7,150kg; length 9.54m; width 2.485m; height 2.66m; crew 2; engine: 110HP ZIL-123 or ZIL-157K 6-cylinder water-cooled petrol; water propulsion: one 3-bladed propeller; range 460km land, 48km water; wheelbase 3.668 × 1.120m; track 1.62m; clearance 0.28m; tyre size 11 × 18 (12 × 18 in BAV-A); trench crossing 0.6m; vertical obstacle 0.4m; gradient 30°; fuel capacity 240 litres; maximum load 2,500kg; passengers 28; armament 12.7mm DshKM. The central tyre pressure regulation system has internal air lines in the BAV-A, external air lines in the later version. The BAV (*bol'shoi plavaiushchii avtomobili*, large amphibious truck) is an improved version of the US wartime DUKW. It has been almost completely replaced by the K-61.

K-61 amphibian of the East German Army. *(US Army)*

BAV amphibian carrying a 76.2mm field gun. *(US Army)*

TPO-50 cart-mounted flamethrower.

LPO-50 manpack flamethrower. *(US Army)*

Flamethrowers

Soviet sapper sub-units are trained in flamethrower use. Soviet assault engineer regiments – formations about which little is known – are believed to use many flame-throwers.

LPO-50 light flamethrower Standard Soviet man-carried flamethrower, heavily used in urban combat. Used in Vietnam. Range 50–70m; compound capacity: enough for six blasts; tanks: three; chances of hitting vehicle or building with LPO-50 blasts: 97% at 25m, 81% at 50m.

TPO-50 heavy flamethrower Cart-mounted with three fuel tanks. Capable of firing thickened fuel to 180m and unthickened fuel to 65m. Ignition, like the LPO-50, is by battery. Weight is 170kg.

Tank-mounted flamethrowers Still in service in the Soviet Army, unlike those of Britain or the US. Found in tank units, rather than engineer units, and used mainly for direct support of motorised rifle units in urban combat and when attacking fortifications. A platoon of flame-thrower tanks is used with a motorised rifle battalion. Flamethrowers are usually mounted in T-55 tanks, in place of the co-axial machine gun. Performance is prob-ably similar to that of the TPO-50.

Inflatable boats

	NL-5	NL-8	NDL-10	NL-15	NDL-20	NL-30
Weight	50kg	55kg	80kg	95kg	150kg	200kg
Length	3.2m	—	5m	—	6m	—
Capacity (men)	5	8	15	15	27	30
Capacity (cargo)	700kg	650kg	1,500kg	1,500kg	2,510kg	3,400kg

Folding assault boats

	MSL	DSL	DL-10 (half size)	DL-10 (full size)
Weight	65kg	180kg	170kg	420kg
Length	3.2m	5.5m	4.2m	8.6m
Capacity (men)	4	14	15	25
Capacity (cargo)	400kg	1,500kg	1,500kg	3,000kg

Chapter Eighteen

Signals, intelligence and electronic warfare

Signals

Although the Soviets still make much use of messengers and employ reliable wire communications systems whenever possible, they realise that any army must rely on radio communications in modern war. Soviet radios are rugged, moisture-proof, simple and effective, and frequency coverage and overlap are adequate. While they lack the technological refinement of their Western counterparts, they have a generally low failure rate and are easy to use and maintain. Most, however, use vacuum tubes and are large and bulky, and so are confined to vehicle mounts. The exception is the R-126, a small, lightweight FM transceiver with limited range and frequency.

The way Soviet radios are used is as important as their technical characteristics. As in all armies, the radios function in networks, and only radios on the same network can communicate with each other. Special networks exist for NBC warnings, air defence, artillery and communication with the Air Force. The Soviet insistence on strict radio discipline allows a battalion to use one network for all three companies if required, although separate company networks are also used. The R-123M set found in almost all Soviet AFVs is normally set to the "receive only" mode in all except company and higher-level command vehicles, although this can be altered if the situation requires it.

The strict Soviet network structure does have some disadvantages. A motorised rifle company commander could not normally communicate with his own battalion's mortar platoon, anti-tank platoon or maintenance section, or with an artillery battery if one were attached to the battalion. He would only be "netted in" to the other company commanders, his nine subordinate vehicles, and the battalion commander and chief of staff. A message to the anti-tank platoon requesting help or reporting a target would have to be relayed through the battalion commander or chief of staff. If company networks are used, a separate fire-support network would allow direct communication. In some cases, however, the Soviets have procedures which make it possible to skip echelons in communications. Passing the word is time-consuming. Using NATO double-callsign procedures, the standard time for the passage of a short message is three minutes per radio network. Minimising the number of different networks a message must pass over reduces the time lag.

The four manoeuvre companies of a motorised rifle battalion will usually be netted in together on a single radio network with battalion HQ, using the R-123 set. Thus anything broadcast in any one of 30 APCs or 13 tanks will be heard by every other one, requiring strict radio discipline. Alternatively, the battalion commander can give orders to just the four company commanders by using the R-107 set, which is also netted in to the tank company command tank's R-112 set. If the companies are not operating as part of a complete battalion, each company will have its own radio network and will only receive or send within their own company, except, of course, for the company commander. By comparison, a US tank company operates no fewer than four internal radio networks, plus a fifth connecting it with battalion. Soviet platoon and even company commanders will use hand and flare signals whenever possible, this being made easier by the tight Soviet tactical formations. Individual tanks broadcast only in an emergency. Tactical messages are in clear voice. Reduced radio traffic increases security, reduces vulnerability to RDF and jamming, reduces the total number of frequencies required, and reduces interference. But it also contributes to tactical inflexibility.

Electronic warfare

Electronic-warfare capability is found throughout the Soviet Army, not just in specialised units. It includes intercepting and analysing enemy radio and radar signals, jamming them and defeating enemy countermeasures. It also aids in reconnaissance by compiling electronic order of battle and location data and providing target acquisition for artillery by the use of RDF units. Soviet electronic-warfare capability is extremely effective, according to many Western observers. Some NATO officers believe that Soviet jamming would reduce any future battlefield communications to the level of 1916, and that the US Army, heavily dependent upon radio communications for both its tactical and operational effectiveness, would suffer heavily. US Army exercises conducted under electronic warfare conditions tend to confirm this view.

Soviet electronic interception and direction-finding systems are linked to a variety of automatic data-processing equipment. Older models were large and had long processing times, but more modern, digital, versions are reportedly entering service.

Radioelectronic combat is the Soviet term for offensive electronic warfare. The strength and number of the front and army-level radioelectronic combat units show the emphasis the Soviets place on this type of warfare. Radioelectronic combat includes the use of RDF equipment to locate and identify enemy units, providing both intelligence and targeting data. It also includes signal intercept and intelligence work, studying and if possible decoding enemy messages. Jamming is used to put out of action any enemy radios or radars that cannot be destroyed. Specially trained personnel will be used for "spoofing": broadcasting to enemy units over their own networks to give spurious or confusing orders. The Soviet radioelectronic combat threat is a powerful one.

Intelligence

Soviet specialised intelligence units perform the same basic functions as comparable NATO units, collecting and analysing data. These are often data collected by reconnaissance means, but they can also be obtained by the unit itself through PoW interrogations, observation or any number of other means. Airborne and special-forces companies are often attached to these units, giving them the ability to mount raids to collect vital information. Soviet Army intelligence troops should not be confused with the GRU army intelligence agency. The difference between the two is akin to that between US Army Intelligence and the Counter-Intelligence Corps, the former handling battlefield intelligence and the latter the longer-range and strategic considerations.

Unit organisation

Signal battalion (motorised rifle division)
Total strength: 27 officers, 253 enlisted men, four BRDMs, 13 motorcycles, 52 trucks.
   HQ and service company (nine officers, 45 enlisted men, one BRDM, 13 motorcycles, 13 trucks)
   CP company (six officers, 48 enlisted men, one BRDM, 16 trucks)

   Radio communications company (six officers, 80 enlisted men, one BRDM, 10 trucks)
   Wire communications and radio relay company (of one line-construction and two radio relay platoons) (six officers, 80 enlisted men, one BRDM, 13 trucks, six R-401, six R-405)
Tank division signal batteries are identical, except that the radio and wire companies each have two more trucks and five more enlisted men.

Signal regiment (army)
   Headquarters and services
   Radio battalion
   Wire communications battalion
   Radio relay battalion

Signal brigade (front)
   Headquarters and services
   Command post
   Radio relay battalion
   Wire communications battalion
   Messenger unit

Signal interception battalion (army)
Total strength: 38 officers, 395 enlisted men, 114 trucks.
   HQ and services (15 officers, 80 enlisted men, 18 trucks)
   Radio interception company (seven officers, 90 enlisted men, 31 trucks, 28 SR-50-M radio interception sets)
   Radio direction-finding company (eight officers, 110 enlisted men, 39 trucks, 16 RDF units of various types)
   Radar interception and locating company (eight officers, 115 enlisted men, 26 trucks, 15 radar interception systems)
   Area support element (ad hoc unit formed for specific mission)

Signal interception regiment (front)
Total strength: 111 officers, 1,170 enlisted men, 334 trucks.
   HQ and service elements (20 officers, 100 enlisted men, 18 trucks)
   Radio interception battalion (31 officers, 350 enlisted men, 111 trucks, 72 radio interception sets)
   Radio direction-finding battalion (34 officers, 410 enlisted men, 135 trucks, 48 RDF sets)
   Radar interception and location battalion (26 officers, 310 enlisted men, 70 trucks, 30 radar interception systems)
   Area support element (composition dependent upon mission)

Radioelectronic combat battalion (army and front)
Total strength: 38 officers, 454 enlisted men, 175 trucks.

HQ and services (11 officers, 73 enlisted men, 12 trucks)

Three radio jamming companies (each of seven officers, 98 enlisted men, four radio interception sets, four RDF sets, 12 radio jammers, three multi-channel jammers, 38 trucks)

One radar jamming company (six officers, 87 enlisted men, 49 trucks, 10 radar interception and location sets, 11 radar jammers)

One area support element (composition depends on mission)

Intelligence battalion (army-level)

Headquarters and service elements

Command post support element

Intelligence collection company

Interrogation company

Special operations company (attached)

A wide range of special-forces units can be attached.

Intelligence regiment (front-level)

Headquarters and service elements

Command post support element

Intelligence-collection battalion

Intelligence analysis and production company

Two interrogation companies

One special operations company (attached)

A wide range of special-forces units can be attached.

TYPICAL MOTORISED RIFLE RADIO NETWORK

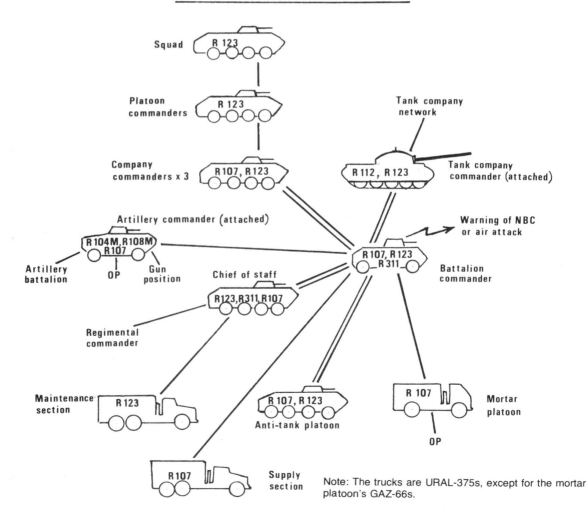

Note: The trucks are URAL-375s, except for the mortar platoon's GAZ-66s.

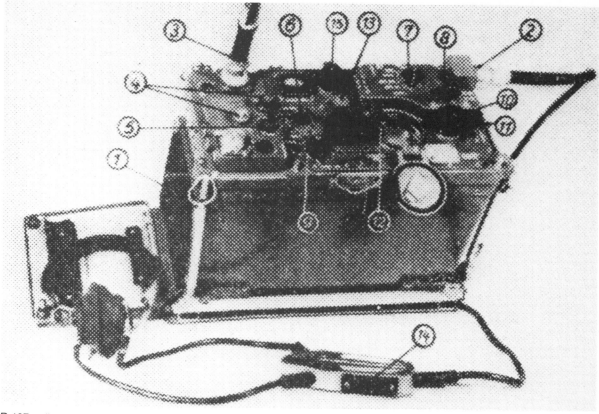

R-107 radio.

Radios

Designation	Frequency (MHZ) & Mode	Range (km)	Antenna	Use
R-105D & M	36–46.1 FM	4–6	whip/wire	Old, vehicle or pack
R-107	1–15 FM	4–6	whip/wire	Vehicle or pack, company and above level. Replaced R-105, R-109, R-114
R-108D & M	28–36.5 FM	4–6	whip/wire	Artillery use, vehicle or pack
R-109D & M	21.5–28.5 FM	4–6	whip/wire	Air-defence use, vehicle or pack
R-112	2.8–4.99 AM	40–200	whip	Tanks, company commander and higher
R-113	20–23.375 FM	20	whip	Tanks & AFVs
R-114D & M	20–26 FM	4–6	whip/wire	Company & above, pack or vehicle
R-123 & 123M	20–51.5 FM	20	whip	Standard tank, APC, BMP, AFVs
R-126	48.5–51.5 FM	1–2	whip	Standard pack, MR platoon level
R-311	1–15 AM, CW or MCW	–	any	Receives only, monitors fire-control and other networks
R-401	60–70 FM	40–50	twin yagi	Division and higher level
R-405	320–420 FM	40–50	corner reflector	Division and higher level

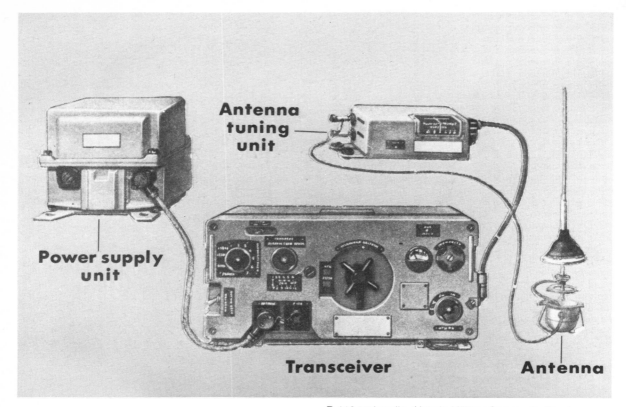

R-113 tank radio. *(Jane's Military Communications)*

R-105D man-pack radio. *(Jane's Military Communications)*

Tactical radio networks

Units communicating	Radios used	Distance
Company-platoon	R-105, 107, 108, 123, 126	0.5km
Company-company	as above	3km
Battalion-company	R-105, 107, 123	5km
Regiment-battalion	as above	6km
Regiment-company	as above	8km
Regiment-regiment	as above	9km
Division-regiment	as above	7km
Division-division	as above	9km
Division-battalion	as above	12km

This shows the possible tactical networks in Soviet units. In two instances, regiment-to-company and division-to-battalion, it is possible to communicate directly and skip an echelon in transmitting signals, but otherwise a message must go through several hands to reach its ultimate recipient.

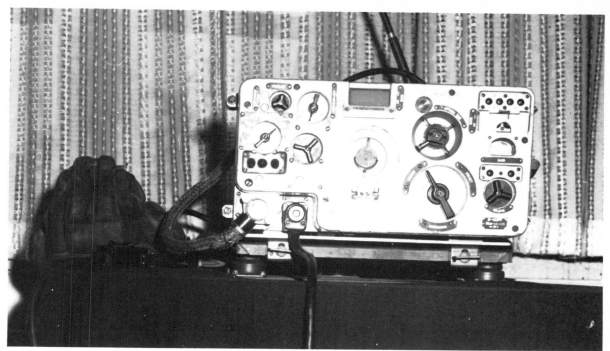

R-123M AFV radio with tankman's helmet and microphone. *(US Army)*

R-126 radio, used at motorised rifle platoon level. *(Jane's Military Communications)*

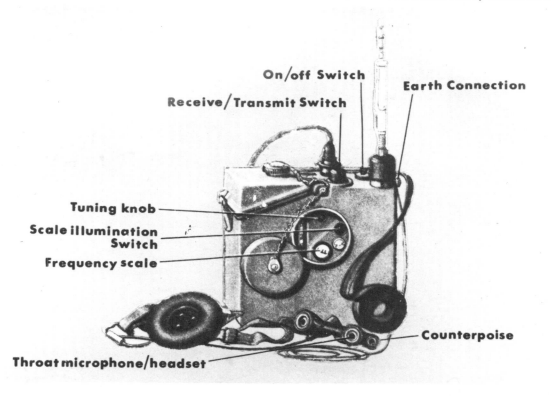

Electronic interception and location systems

Designation	Mission	Frequency range	Modes	Antenna	Receiver sensitivity	Power	Required time	Gain
SR-53-V (System A)	HF intercept	3–30MHz	AM, voice, CW, MCW	Rhombic	−105dBm	15kW	3h	15dBm
SR-52-V (System B)	VHF/UHF intercept	30–300MHz	FM, voice	LP	−110dBm	15kW	2h	10dBm
SR-51-V (System B-1)	VHF/UHF intercept	30–300MHz	FM, voice	Whip	−110dBm	5kW	15min	1dBm
SR-50-M (System C)	VHF/UHF intercept	30–450MHz	FM, voice	Whip	−110dBm	Battery	2min	1dBm
SR-54-V (System D)	relay intercept	30–300MHz	Voice, TTY	Dish or LP	−110dBm	10kW	1h	40 or 15dBm
SR-20-V (System 1)	HF/DF	3–25MHz	AM	Adcock	−90dBm	15kW	5h	10dBm
SR-19-V (System 2)	VHF/DF	30–300MHz	FM, voice	Loop or Adcock	−90dBm	10kW	2h	0 or 10dBm
SR-25-V (System 3)	VHF/DF	30–300MHz	FM, voice	Loop	−90Bm	5kW	10min	0dBm
SB-20-V (System I)	Artillery and surveillance radar	50MHz–11GHz	–	Dish	−110dBm	15kW	1h	40dBm
SM-21-V (System II)	Surveillance radar, intercept and DF	50MHz–10GHz	–	Dish	−110dBm	10kW	30min	40dBm

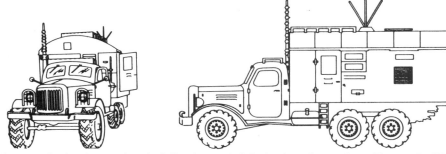

Soviet VHF tactical communications jammer is typical of truck-mounted electronic warfare systems. The standard RDF station has an Adcock antenna in place of the three-pole type and the air communications jammer has a basket-type antenna. *(US Army)*

End Tray.
(EW Communications)

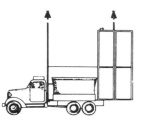

Home Talk long-range communications system.
(EW Communications)

Loop Three HF DF system.
(EW Communications)

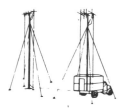

Mercury Grass VHF communications system, frequently seen on SA-2 sites.
(EW Communications)

Soviet Army radars

Ground surveillance radars

GS-11 Use: company-level, short-range surveillance; power 10kW; frequency 9,700MHz; max range 1.2km to detect personnel, 4.5km to detect vehicles; emplacement time 10min; mount: tripod; carried: manpack, two loads. Used by reconnaissance units.

GS-12 Use: regimental-level surveillance; power 12kW; frequency 9,000MHz; range 3.5km to detect personnel, 12.0km to detect vehicles; emplacement time 15min; carried: three manpack loads or light truck. One per manoeuvre regiment.

GS-13 Use: division-level surveillance; power 50kW; frequency 9,500MHz; range 12.0km to detect personnel, 25.0km to detect vehicles; emplacement time 15min. Truck-mounted, one per target-acquisition battery.

Meteorological radar

RMS-1 End Tray Trailer-mounted, used by all artillery and missile units. Parabolic dish antenna.

Counterbattery radars

Small Yawn I-band; mounted on a tracked vehicle; dish antenna; used for mortar location or counterbattery.

Pork Trough J-band; mounted on AT-L; parabolic cylinder antenna; used for counterbattery role.

Long Trough E-band; mounted on MT-LB SON and AT-L; parabolic cylinder antenna; used for counter-mortar role. Reportedly also mounted on a new halftrack vehicle.

SNAR-6 J-band; counter-mortar radar.

SNAR-2 I-band; mounted on AT-L; "orange peel" antenna; surveillance range 40km; artillery detection range 9km; oldest Soviet counterbattery radar.

Small Fred Believed J-band; power 200–300MHz; approximate detection range 39km; tracking range 7km; mounted on BMP-SON vehicle.

In addition to these radars the Soviets have a full range of unattended sensors which include acoustic, disturbance, electromagnetic and seismic types. Their design may be based on US-built types captured in Vietnam.

Soviet electronic-warfare battalions use a variety of jammers. These include the trailer-mounted Box Brick, truck-mounted Cheese Brick, truck-mounted High Brick with its power source in a trailer, truck-mounted Long Brick, trailer-mounted Mesh Brick, trailer-mounted Mound Brick used against aircraft radars, and Tub Brick, also used against aircraft.

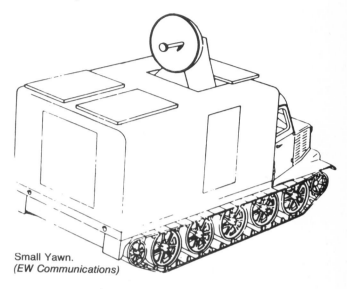

Small Yawn.
(EW Communications)

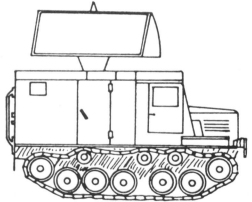

Pork Trough. *(EW Communications)*

Long Trough. Nothing is known of the halftrack vehicle on which this radar is mounted.

Chapter Nineteen

Combat support vehicles

Mechanised warfare requires mechanised support. The Soviet Army has provided itself with a degree of logistic support that, while not as elaborate or effective as its US counterpart, is considered adequate for a short, victorious, mobile war.

The Soviet Army has access to over 350,000 trucks of all types, including those with their units and those loaned to other state agencies in peacetime under the *autokolomka* system. Annual production of trucks and buses exceeds 700,000 vehicles, and a large proportion of these could have military applications. The increasing production of trucks has enabled the Soviets to remedy many of the logistic shortcomings seen in the 1968 invasion of Czechoslovakia, and to decrease their reliance on railways for troop movement and supply.

The Soviet Army emerged from World War Two still relying on horse transport and marching infantrymen. Only in the 1950s, after post-war reconstruction, did the Soviet Army receive a new generation of trucks and tractors to replace its wartime equipment and provide complete mechanisation. They were the GAZ-69, GAZ-63, ZIL-164, ZIL-151, ZIL-157, BAV, MAV, AT-P, AT-S, AT-L and AT-T. These vehicles established the basic characteristics of Soviet combat support vehicles: ruggedness, simplicity, a high degree of standardisation and interchangeability of parts, and good cross-country performance. Soviet engine technology lagged behind that of the vehicles, however, and many of them suffered from unreliable or underpowered engines. The ZIL-151 was particularly deficient, and was soon supplanted by the ZIL-157.

Reorganisation and rationalisation in the Soviet automotive industry in the early 1960s, along with the increasing production of the Warsaw Pact nations, allowed the Soviets to field a new generation of combat support vehicles including the UAZ-469, GAZ-66, URAL-375, ZIL-130, ZIL-131, KrAZ-255B, ZIL-135, MAZ-543, ATS-59, K-61, PTS-M and other improved vehicles. These featured improved engines and performance. Some, such as the GAZ-66 and URAL-375, were particularly successful, the latter's cross-country load-towing performance being so good that it was able to replace most

UAZ-469. (v/o *Autoexport*)

of the artillery tractors in service. Other vehicles, such as the ZIL-130 and ZIL-131, were less successful. Engine, axle and transmission problems persisted, while vehicles such as the KrAZ-255B and MAZ-543 were criticised as being too heavy and technically complex.

Vehicles introduced in the late 1960s were intended to fill any gaps and remedy limitations in the preceding generation. The big MAZ-500–537 series of tank transporters gave the Soviet Army a powerful new operational capability in the late 1960s. Transmissions and axles improved, and high-horsepower diesel engines were introduced; the big MAZ-537 received a tank engine, for instance. Specialist vehicles such as fuel tankers were also emphasised. The GT-T and GT-SM are the latest gun tractors. Today Soviet automotive technology has solved many of its problems, although it is still not at the level of Western nations or even that of some of its Warsaw Pact allies. Soviet trucks in service abroad show continuing limitations, including poor-quality components resulting in high breakdown rates and frequent overheating in warm climates. Nevertheless, the results of 60 years' emphasis on mechanising both Soviet society and its military arm have borne fruit.

Specialised vehicles

The Soviet Army still uses large numbers of M-72 motor-cycles, primarily for courier duties, both with and without sidecars. Based on the German BMW R-75, the M-72 has a maximum speed of 85km/h and a range of 300km, weighs 350kg and has a 22HP engine.

Other specialised vehicles use the chassis of standard trucks or artillery tractors whenever possible. These include rocket-launcher, radar, RDF, ATGM simulator, and other combat-support trucks. The ATZ-3-157K fuel-dispensing bowser carries 3,500 litres on a ZIL-157 chassis, and can deliver 300 litres/min through four hoses. The ATs-8-200 bulk fuel transport uses an MAZ-200 chassis to carry 8,000 litres. Three versions of the standard URAL-375 are the ATMZ-4.5-375, which can carry 4,500 litres of fuel or lubricant; the TZ-5, which carries 5,000 litres and five fuelling hoses; and the ATs-5-575 tank truck, which also carries 5,000 litres. These replace the ATZ-34-131, a 3,400-litre fuel truck on a ZIL-131 chassis, the ATsM-4-157K tank truck carrying 4,040 litres of fuel or water, and the ATZ-2-157K fuel service truck, the last two being on ZIL-157 chassis. Light fuel haulage is carried out by the MZ-66 oil supply truck (820 litres) and the ATs-PT-1.7 1,700-litre tank trucks, both on the GAZ-66 chassis.

While there are liquid transport and POL versions of most modern Soviet trucks, dump trucks are normally only found at army and front-level engineer construction brigades. There are dump truck versions of the GAZ-53, ZIL-130, MAZ-200 and MAZ-500. The last-named is apparently the closest to a standard military model, although the other types will also be used.

There are tractor versions of a great many Soviet trucks: ZIL-164, ZIL-130, ZIL-157, ZIL-131, URAL-375, URAL-377, MAZ-200, MAZ-500, KrAZ-219, KrAZ-258, KAMAZ-5410 and KrAZ-255. Other trucks, such as the MAZ-537, are intended primarily for use as tractors. Most tractor trucks can also be configured to carry bulk cargo.

The Pipeline Troops use a variety of modified trucks, the most significant reportedly being a modified ZIL-135 used for laying flexible pipelines while moving.

The Soviet Army does not emphasise special ambulance vehicles. In prolonged action, the URAL-452 light ambulances would be overwhelmed by the numbers of wounded. For such cases the Soviets appear to rely on standard trucks, with their uncomfortable suspension.

The KAMAZ trucks, from the Kama River plant, are a substantial addition to the Soviet's Army's combat support strength and contributed to the great improvement in Soviet logistics capability that occurred in the 1970s. The Kama River plant, built with imported Western technology, is capable of producing 150,000 trucks and 250,000 diesel engines a year. While KAMAZ trucks are delivered almost exclusively to civilian users in the Soviet Union, they can be easily added to the armed forces, as indeed can any Soviet vehicle. KAMAZ trucks were used in the 1979 invasion of Afghanistan.

M-72 motorcycle with sidecar. *(Leon Conjour)*

Trucks

Type	Weight (tonnes)	Max payload (tonnes)	Towed load (tonnes)	Cruise range (km)	Personnel	Engine type	HP	Length (m)
GAZ-69A, 0.5t*, 4 × 4	1.5	0.8	0.8	280	2 + 6	petrol	55	3.85
UAZ-469, 0.5t, 4 × 4	1.38	0.6	0.85	475	2 + 5	petrol	75	4.03
GAZ-66, 2t, 4 × 4	3.64	2.0	2.0	720	2 + 16	petrol	130	5.66
GAZ-63A, 2t, 4 × 4	3.28	2.0	1.6	350	2 + 12	petrol	70	5.53
ZIL-164, 4.5t, 4 × 4	4.1	4.5	4.5	410	3 + 14	petrol	100	6.7
ZIL-151, 4.5t, 4 × 4	5.58	4.5	3.6	600	3 + 16	petrol	95	6.93
ZIL-157, 4.5t, 6 × 6	5.45	4.5	3.6	580	3 + 14	petrol	104	6.68
ZIL-131, 3.5t, 6 × 6	6.7	5.0	4.5	425	3 + 24	petrol	150	6.9
URAL-375D, 4.5t, 6 × 6	8.4	5.0	10	600	3 + 24	petrol	175	7.35
ZIL-164, 4.5t, 4 × 2	4.1	4.5	4.5	410	3 + 14	petrol	100	6.7
KrAZ-214, 7t, 6 × 6	12.3	7	10	530	3 + 14	diesel	205	8.53
KrAZ-255B, 7.5t, 6 × 6	12.18	8	10	650	3 + 14	diesel	265	8.65
MAZ-500, 7.5t, 6 × 6	6.4	7.5	10	698	3	diesel	180	7.31
ZIL-135, 10t, 8 × 8	10	12	18	650	4	petrol	180 × 2	9.27
MAZ-535, 16t, 8 × 8	19.25	7	15	650	4	diesel	375	8.78
MAZ-537, 16t, 8 × 8	22.5	15	75	650	4	diesel	525	9.13
MAV, 4 × 4 (amphibious)	1.98	0.5	0.5	320	5	petrol	55	5.06
BAV, 6 × 6 (amphibious)	7.4	2.5	–	530	2 + 25	petrol	110	9.54
KAMAZ-5320, 12.5t, 6 × 6	16	12.5	13.5	650	2 + 30	diesel	205	7.82
KAMAZ-5410, 13.5t, 6 × 4	14.2	13.5	13.5	650	2 + 30	diesel	205	8.1

* t = tonnes standard capacity.

GAZ-69 light truck. *(US Army)*

Trucks and vehicles of secondary importance

Type	Weight (tonnes)	Max payload (tonnes)	Towed load (tonnes)	Cruise range (km)	Personnel	Engine type	HP	Length (m)
GAZ-51, 1.5t, 4 + 2	2.7	2.5	3.5	450	2 + 10	petrol	70	5.71
GAZ-53, 3t, 4 + 2	3.25	4.0	4.0	375	2 + 10	petrol	115	6.4
URAL-355M, 3.5t, 4 × 2	3.4	3.5	5.0	450	2 + 12	petrol	95	6.3
ZIL-150, 3.5t, 4 × 2	3.9	4.0	4.5	405	2 + 14	petrol	90	6.7
ZIL-130, 4.0t, 4 × 2	4.2	5.5	6.4	475	2 + 14	petrol	170	6.67
MAZ-502, 4.0t, 4 × 4	4.48	4.0	9.5	590	3 + 16	petrol	135	7.15
MAZ-200, 5.0t, 4 × 2	6.75	7.0	9.5	500	3 + 16	diesel	120	7.62
MAZ-500, 7.5t, 4 × 2	6.5	7.5	12.0	900	3 + 14	diesel	180	7.33
URAL-377, 7.5t, 6 × 4	6.64	8.0	10.5	500	3 + 16	petrol	175	7.86
ZIL-133, 8.0t, 6 × 4	6.2	8.0	9.5	520	3 + 24	petrol	220	9.0
KrAZ-219, 10.0t, 6 × 4	11.3	12.0	15.0	750	3 + 28	diesel	180	9.66
YaAZ-210, 10.0t, 6 × 4	11.3	12.0	15.0	820	3 + 28	diesel	165	9.66
KrAZ-257, 12.0t, 6 × 4	11.13	12.0	16.6	1000	3 + 28	diesel	240	9.66
LuAZ-967M, 0.5t, 4 × 4	0.93	0.42	0.3	411	2 + 1	petrol	37	3.682
LuAZ-969, 0.5t, 4 × 4	0.82	0.40	0.35	400	2 + 1	petrol	27	3.2
URAL-452, 0.8t, 4 × 4	1.67	0.80	0.85	430	2 + 4	petrol	72	4.46
KAMAZ-53202, 8.0t, 6 × 4	7.24	8.0	11.5	650	2 + 24	diesel	180	8.3
KAMAZ-4310, 6.0t, 6× 6	8.0	6.0	12.0	650	2 + 18	diesel	210	7.6

Production dates

Soviet equipment policies ensure that their armed forces will field a variety of motor transport that is as bewildering as it is fascinating. The Soviets rely on mobilised civilian motor transport for units throughout the Soviet Union, and a full-scale call-up will probably result in vehicles of considerable antiquity entering military service. When new models of trucks appear, they do not totally replace older models. The requirements of both the Soviet military and the Soviet economy for trucks is almost insatiable. On the other hand, the poor mechanical reliability of many Soviet motor vehicles, particularly the earlier models, and the poor maintenance many civilian-operated trucks are known to receive mean that the attrition rate of vehicles, especially those in civilian hands in peacetime, is likely to be considerable.

GAZ-66 truck of the Czech Army. *(Department of Defense, via Virginia Mulholland)*

GAZ-63A captured by the 101st Airborne Division in the A Shau Valley, South Vietnam, in 1969. *(US Marine Corps)*

ZIL-151. *(Department of Defense, via Virginia Mulholland)*

Above ZIL-157K. (v/o Autoexport)   *Below ZIL-131. (v/o Autoexport)*

PAZS-3152, based on a ZIL-130 chassis, has a capacity of 4,500 litres of fuel and 200 litres of oil. Fuel is dispensed at a rate of 40 litres/min.

ATsMM-4-157K is a ZIL-157K chassis carrying 4,000 litres of fuel and 250 litres of oil. It can top up two T-62s in 15min.

The TZ-5, ATs-5-375 and ATsG-375, three 5,000-litre capacity tank versions of the URAL-375, are standard POL movers.

URAL-375 *(v/o Autoexport)*

KrAZ-214 towing 130mm M-46s. *(Egyptian Army)*

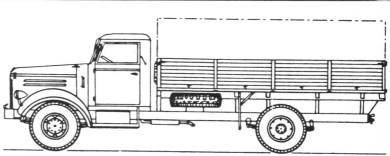

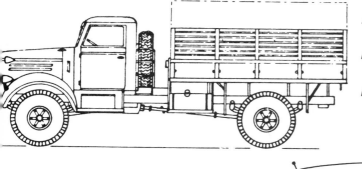

Above MAZ-200 5,000kg truck. *(Jane's)*

Left MAZ-502 4,000kg truck. *(Jane's)*

Below URAL-377 7,500kg truck. *(Jane's)*

KrAZ-255B truck carrying a PMP pontoon section. There is one such bow section in each half-set of PMP bridging, in addition to the normal boat-shaped folding centre sections. *(Defense Intelligence Agency, via Virginia Mulholland)*

ZIL-135 truck. *(Department of Defense, via Virginia Mulholland)*

MAZ-535. *(US Army)*

MAZ-543 configured for carrying bulk cargo. *(Defense Intelligence Agency, via Virginia Mulholland)*

MAZ-537. *(US Army)*

MAV (GAZ-46) amphibious light truck of the Polish Army. The suspension is similar to that of the GAZ-69. (US Army)

Combat support vehicles and the supply base

The effectiveness of Soviet combat support vehicles must be evaluated in the context of their logistic system (as outlined on page 61–63). Whenever rail transport is impractical – which will be most of the time in an armoured offensive into enemy territory – it will fall on the combat support vehicles to carry supplies forward. If the combat support vehicles fail in this task, all the tanks and BMPs might as well have stayed at home. The size of the task can be judged from a breakdown of a Soviet army supply base. Commanded by the army-level deputy commander for rear services ("chief of the rear"), it includes the following installations, with their distance behind the line of departure in offensive operations shown in parentheses:

One mobile advanced army base per division in army (25–35km)
One or two ammunition depots (50–100km)
One rocket and missile ammunition depot (50–100km)
One chemical depot and repair shop (75–150km)
One engineer depot and repair shop (75–150km)
One signal depot and repair shop (75–150km)
One mobile artillery repair shop (75–150km)
Two ration depots (75–150km)
Two field bakeries and flour mills (75–150km)
Two or three POL depots (50–100km)
One artillery and small arms depot/repair shop (50–100km)
Two tank depot and repair shops (75–150km)
Two vehicle depot and repair shops (75–150km)
Four to six bath and laundry units (75–150km)
One recovery and salvage depot (75–150)
One clothing and equipment depot/repair shop (75–150km).

Also depending on the army's combat support vehicle resources are:

One medical depot (75–150km)
One mobile therapeutic hospital (75–150km) (from front level)
One to four mobile army surgical hospitals (10–14km) (from front level)
One KGB nuclear weapons depot (75–150km).

The front-level supply base is even more elaborate and further from the line of departure. Similar to that found at army level, it includes:

One front supply base section per army in the front (60–100km)
One chemical depot/repair shop
One signal depot/repair shop
Two replacement centres
One to three motor transport regiments
One or two rocket and missile depots
Two or three ration depots
Two material recovery battalions
One to four ammunition depots
One artillery and small arms depot/repair shop
Two tank depot/repair shops
Four mobile tank repair battalions
Two vehicle depot/repair shops
Two equipment depot/repair shops
Two to five bath and laundry units
Two or three bakeries and flour mills

Also drawing on front vehicle resources are:

Two or three aviation supply stations
One general hospital
One convalescent hospital
One medical replacement company
Two medical depots (all the above under the front medical directorate)
One to three KGB nuclear weapons depots.

Even a logistically "lean" force puts a tremendous strain on its combat support vehicles.

KAMAZ-5320. *(Department of Defense)*

Above KAMAZ-5410. *(Department of Defense)*   Below KAMAZ-5320. *(Department of Defense)*

KAMAZ-5510 *(Department of Defense, via Virginia Mulholland)*

KAMAZ-5410. *(Department of Defense)*

Artillery tractors, tracked prime movers, and amphibious ferries

Type	Weight (tonnes)	Max payload (tonnes)	Towed load (tonnes)	Cruise range (km)	Personnel	Engine type	HP	Length (m)
AT-P	5	2	3.7	360	3 + 6	petrol	110	4.05
AT-S	12	3	16	380	3 + 12	diesel	250	5.87
AT-L	8	2.7	5	320	2 + 12	diesel	130	5.12
ATS-59	13	3	14	350	2 + 14	diesel	375	6.3
ATS-59G (M-1972)	13.8	4	18	500	2 + 14	diesel	415	6.1
AT-T	20	5	25	700	2 + 14	diesel	415	6.99
MT-L	8.5	4.2	7	500	2 + 17	diesel	240	6.36
GT-S (amphibious)	4.65	1	2	725	2 + 9	petrol	85	4.9
GT-T (amphibious)	8.2	2	4	500	3 + 10	diesel	200	6.5
GT-SM (amphibious)	4.8	1	2	300	2 + 10	petrol	115	5.36
K-61 (amphibious)	9.55	3/5	8	530	3 + 32	diesel	135	9.15
PTS-M (amphibious)	17.7	5/10	8	300	3 + 70	diesel	350	11.5

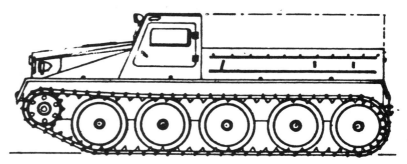

GT-S tractor. *(Jane's)*

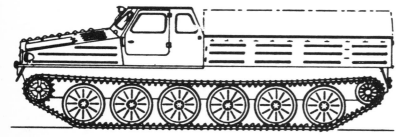

GT-T tractor. *(Jane's)*

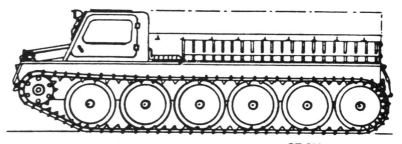

GT-SM tractor. *(Jane's)*

Soviet trucks are designated by the plant from which they originated: GAZ = *Gorki Auto Zavod* (factory), MAZ = Minsk, ZIL = *Zavod Imeni Likatshov* (factory named for Likatshov), YaAZ = Yaroslavl, KrAZ = Kremenyschug, URAL = Shodino ("Tankograd" in the Urals). Amphibious means that the vehicle can swim by jets or tracks. The MAV and BAV have water speeds of 9 and 10km/h respectively, propeller-powered. The tracked K-61 and PTS-M ferries use twin propellers to attain speeds of 10 and 15km/h respectively. The GT-S and GT-T use hydrostatic propulsion. The more modern Soviet trucks all have centralised air pressure control for their tyres. The URAL-375D series is currently the standard Soviet Army truck, although the ZIL-157, which it replaced, still continues in service, as does the earlier ZIL-151. Heavy hauling is done by the MAZ series and the new ZIL-135, with its excellent cross-country load-carrying capability. The GAZ-66 is the standard light truck, while the GAZ-69 and the newer UAZ-469 are the Soviet equivalents of the jeep. All weights are given in tonnes, and are for hard surface. They may be reduced by up to 50% for cross-country travel. Cruise range is also on hard surface roads. "Personnel" indicates crew in cab *plus* passengers, if any. Trucks may be overloaded with both personnel and payload. While this will burn them out in the long run, it gives the Soviets a significant logistic "surge" capability. Standard chassis are also used for almost all specialised combat support roles, from tank transporting to engineer work.

Soviet trucks are equipped with a wide variety of trailers, from the small, two-wheeled versions used by the GAZ-69 to the massive tank and missile carriers pulled by the MAZ series.

GT-T tractor being used as an APC by KGB Border Troops. *(Chris Foss)*

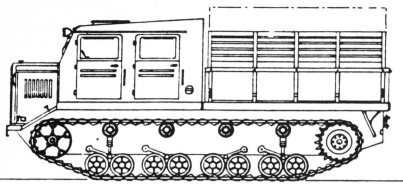

AT-S medium artillery tractor. *(Jane's)*

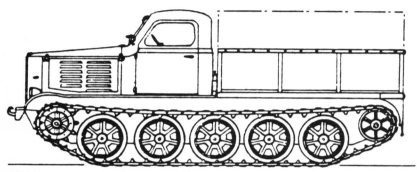

AT-LM light tracked artillery tractor. *(Jane's)*

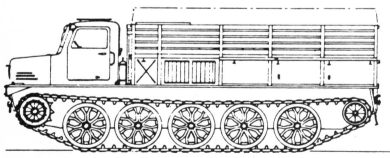

ATS-59 medium artillery tractor. *(Jane's)*

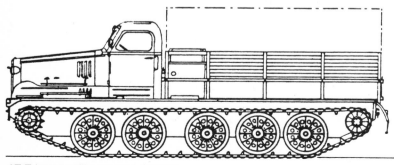

AT-T heavy artillery tractor. *(Jane's)*

AT-P tractor. *(US Army)*

AT-L light tractor. *(US Army)*

Above AT-T heavy tracked artillery tractor.

Below AT-S tractor. *(D. Isby)*

MT-L tractor.

Soviet trucks are also frequently used as tractors. This version of the ZIL-157 is towing a Scud-A reload SSM on a trailer. *(A. Dupouy)*

Index